1976

A HISTORY *of* AMERICAN
POLITICAL THOUGHT

A HISTORY *of* AMERICAN POLITICAL THOUGHT

FROM THE CIVIL WAR
TO THE WORLD WAR

BY

EDWARD R. LEWIS

1969

OCTAGON BOOKS

New York

Reprinted 1969

by special arrangement with The Macmillan Company

OCTAGON BOOKS

A DIVISION OF FARRAR, STRAUS & GIROUX, INC.

19 Union Square West

New York, N. Y. 10003

LIBRARY OF CONGRESS CATALOG CARD NUMBER: 75-96185

Printed in U.S.A. by

NOBLE OFFSET PRINTERS, INC.

NEW YORK 3, N. Y.

To My Wife and Children

PREFACE

I PROPOSE, in this book, to study the history of political thought in the United States from the Civil War to the World War. In the course of it, I shall draw largely on the ideas of our political leaders, expressed sometimes in the turmoil of political contests. The contributions of our public men have been, in certain periods, at least, fecund and stimulating. Out of them has flowed, to a large extent, the political philosophy of the period. To some extent, the formal studies of specialists have merely codified the thought of our men of affairs, who have struck off our political theory as they have blazed the trail.

Men like Lincoln, Bryan, Roosevelt, and Wilson have been our political philosophers, as much as in a different time, Locke and Milton were in England; Jefferson, Hamilton and Madison were during our formative period; and Calhoun and Webster were in the middle period. The development of the theories of the separation of powers, of the separation between State and Federal powers, of the extent and limits of political action, has been as much the work of our public men as of specialists in the theory of political science.

By broadening the field of our study, we shall see, moreover, how persistent are political ideas. Students may say that natural rights and the separation of powers are rejected ideas, but they persist in the daily reasoning of the people long after the students have discarded them. The political thought at any moment is made up of many and recurrent strands.

Broadly speaking, our political thought in this period did not flow from the contributions of a few great leaders of thought, but has been made by the contributions of many persons and influences, and I have drawn from a great variety of contributors to show the course of the growth and change of our political opinion.

It has been suggested by one of the persons who has read the manuscript that the book might better have started with a consideration of the nature of the state and of sovereignty, and that the order of the chapters should be (following the numbers used in the Table of Contents) IV, V, VI, I, II and III, instead of the order adopted. But as the book is an attempt at a consideration of the entire stream of our political thought and not merely the classical and somewhat technical subjects of the theory of the state and of sovereignty, I felt it better to begin with a consideration of what the country was actually absorbed in when the Civil War ended, namely the adoption of the War Amendments.

It has also been suggested that I include a chapter on our political thought on what may be called international or external politics, such as the Monroe Doctrine, the Imperialism debate after the Spanish War, and our policy of national isolation. However, I felt that the book was already long enough. Moreover, those subjects are somewhat outside the course of what we ordinarily mean by a country's political thought; and finally, the Monroe Doctrine and national isolation have so many ramifications, and are in so great a state of flux, that it seemed to me better to leave them for treatment at other hands.

I am greatly indebted to Mr. Bliss Perry, Professor of English, Emeritus at Harvard, who read several chapters in the inception of the writing of the book and has given me valuable suggestions and much encouragement; to Mr. Franklyn Bliss Snyder, Professor of English and Dean of the Graduate School of Northwestern University, who has also read several chapters; and to Mr. Arthur N. Holcombe, Professor of Government at Harvard; Mr. Arthur M. Schlesinger, Professor of American History at Harvard; Mr. Andrew C. McLaughlin, Professor of American History, Emeritus at the University of Chicago; to Mr. Joseph S. Davis, Director of the Food Research Institute of Stanford University; to Mr. William R. Odell, Jr. of Lake Forest, Illinois; and Mr. Joseph J. Daniels of the Indianapolis Bar; all of whom have read the manuscript in various stages of its development and have given me much help with their criticisms and suggestions. I also wish to acknowledge my indebtedness to Miss Barbara Shaffner, who copied the final draft of the manuscript and who has been of much help in her advice. Needless to say, none of the above persons is in any way responsible for any of the errors or opinions in the book. I wish to thank the attendants in the Chicago Public Library and the Northwestern University Library for the many courtesies extended to me.

CONTENTS

A HISTORY *of* AMERICAN
POLITICAL THOUGHT

CHAPTER I

THE WAR AMENDMENTS AND THE NATIONALIZATION OF CIVIL RIGHTS

THE five years following the Civil War saw tremendous developments in both our legislative and our constitutional theories, which have profoundly influenced our thought and action ever since. The whole relation between State and Nation, the control of the Nation over State action, the relation of the government to individual rights—all had a development during the war and the five years next succeeding which has placed its mark on almost every question which has arisen in the past fifty years. There is not an act of a State legislature which deals with labor or corporations or which regulates conduct that is not a possible subject of national control through the provisions of the Fourteenth Amendment— that no State can deprive any person of life, liberty, or property without due process of law, nor deny the equal protection of the laws. The result has been not only to increase national control over State legislation, but to limit the very possibility of State legislation.

The war had been won by a tremendous assertion of national power. Inevitably in any war, the full powers of government are brought into play. A war is a test of the utmost strength, and the utmost strength is brought to bear. But after the war, the muscles and sinews which have been strengthened and tested by the great effort, which in fact have been called into being by that test, remain ready and eager for new uses. Seldom are these new powers allowed to atrophy: there are too many people who want them used, and the old resistance against their employment is weakened. This was true after the Civil War. We have just found it to be true after the World War. In the Civil War, national powers which until then had been unused, and which in ordinary times would have been bitterly opposed, were used to the full to win the victory. A draft law was passed. A confiscation act was passed. A presidential proclamation had declared free all slaves within the limits of the Confederate armies. A high tariff and an income tax act had been passed.

With tremendous effort and immense emotion, the war had been fought and at last won. Nothing can reclaim for us of two generations later that deep emotion. We can get some sense of it from the songs of the period and from the poems of Whitman and Lowell.

Now the war was over. The triumphant majority had to arrange the details of ensuring its victory by law. The relations of the seceding States to the Union had to be determined. The question of the status of the former slaves had to be settled. All these were to involve not only profound extensions of the theory of the relation of the Nation to the States, but of the relation of the national government to the individual, and of all government to the individual.

There was little doubt that slavery was at an end. No institution could survive that conflict, the emotions aroused by four years of struggle, and the increasing conviction of its essential wastefulness and evil character. James Russell Lowell, in an essay published in 1865, declared, "We take it for granted at the outset, that the mind of the country is made up as to making no terms with slavery in any way, large or limited, open or covert." [1]

The Republican majority in Congress had moved to this end before the war was over. What became the Thirteenth Amendment came up for the first time in April, 1864. The end of the war was more than a year away, although no one knew then how near the end was. The amendment passed the Senate but failed in the House. But the speeches in the Senate are an admirable statement of the political theory on which the amendment was finally passed after the war was over.

THE THIRTEENTH AMENDMENT—NATIONAL PROTECTION OF FREEDOM

It was introduced in the Senate by Lyman Trumbull of Illinois.[2] He was a descendant of the famous family which from

---

[1] James Russell Lowell, "Reconstruction, 1865," in *Political Essays*, p. 224.
[2] The Thirteenth Amendment as adopted, reads as follows:

"Section 1. Neither slavery nor involuntary servitude, except as a punishment for crime whereof the party shall have been duly convicted, shall exist within the United States, or any place subject to their jurisdiction.

"Section 2. Congress shall have power to enforce this article by appropriate legislation."

colonial times had been prominent in the affairs of Connecticut. He had emigrated in his youth to Illinois, had studied law in the traditional way, and for a generation had been one of the leading lawyers of his State. He was tall and angular, shrewd and forceful, with strong emotions and unusual moral courage. A few years later, he distinguished himself as one of the Republican senators who voted against the conviction of Andrew Johnson, on his impeachment trial, despite the intense pressure and vehement demands of his party associates. In later life he was one of the counsel for Eugene V. Debs, in his contest against punishment for violation of a Federal injunction issued in the great railroad strike of 1894.

Trumbull based his argument on the simple ground that the war had been fought to end slavery. "Without stopping to inquire into all the causes of our troubles, and of the distress, desolation and death which have grown out of this atrocious rebellion," he said that, "it will be generally admitted that they sprung from slavery. If a large political party in the North attribute these troubles to the impertinent interference of Northern philanthropists and fanatics with an institution in the Southern States, with which they had no right to interfere, I reply: if there had been no such institution, there could have been no such alleged impertinent interference; if there had been no slavery in the South, there could have been no abolitionists in the North to interfere with it."

If there had been no slavery, he continued, there would have been no attempt to perpetuate the slave-holding power in the Union, and failing that, to set up an empire founded on slavery. If the freedom of speech and of the press, he cried, "has been denied us all our lives in one-half of the states of the Union," it was due to slavery. "If these Halls have resounded from our earliest recollection with the strifes and contests of sections, ending sometimes in blood, it was slavery which almost always occasioned them." [3]

He recalled that in the beginning of the war, we did not interfere with slavery. Then the Federal government ordered that all slaves who came within the Northern lines should be freed. Lincoln followed this step with the Emancipation Proclamation. But he made that proclamation a war policy only. It was limited in its scope to those slaves within the lines of the Confederate armies,

[3] *Congressional Globe,* March 29, 1864, p. 1313.

and who belonged to "rebel masters." There was no war power which gave the national government the right to free the slaves in that part of the South which was already conquered, and above all, no right to interfere with slavery in the States which had remained in the Union—Maryland, Kentucky, Delaware and Missouri.

Henry Wilson of Massachusetts had been a cobbler, had risen by slow degrees to political prominence in Massachusetts, and was noted for his political intuition, his uncanny ability to divine the feelings of the people of his commonwealth, rather than for original or incisive political thought. His opinion is therefore undoubtedly indicative of public opinion in Massachusetts at the time. He declared that "this gigantic crime against the peace, the unity, and the life of the nation, is to make eternal the hateful dominion of man over the souls and bodies of his fellow-men. . . . Yes, slavery is the conspirator that conceived and organized this mighty conspiracy against the unity and existence of the Republic. Slavery is the traitor that madly plunged the nation into the fire and blood and darkness of civil war. Slavery is the criminal whose hands are dripping with the blood of our murdered sons." Slavery, "defying the Government, its Constitution, and its laws, has openly pronounced itself the mortal and unappeasable enemy of the Republic. Slavery stands today the only clearly pronounced foe our country has on the globe." [4]

But there was still a determined and able opposition. It may seem surprising that after three years of a terrible Civil War, which had resulted in tragic loss of life, there should have been any opposition to the abolition of slavery. But in 1864 the war was not yet won. Moreover, Lincoln's course from the beginning had been that the war was to preserve the Union, for he well knew that in States like Indiana, Ohio, and Illinois, to say nothing of the border States, there was much deep-seated opposition to freedom for the slaves, and if not that, at least a complete lack of enthusiasm for the proposal. We must realize also, in any history of human thought, that the progress of thought as evidenced by the leaders of opinion, does not represent all the opinion of the community—sometimes not even the opinion of the majority. The old opinion remains stubbornly cherished by large portions of the

[4] *Congressional Globe*, March 29, 1864, p. 1320.

public. Sometimes it is not articulate; it remains dormant, only to express itself on some different question which, however, arouses the same emotions and the same prejudices. The Tory remains a Tory. He may not have an opportunity to express his Toryism on the issue or set of issues just decided, but when a new one arises, he will express the same fundamental philosophy. We have seen in the last few years what an immense strength of fundamental religious belief there is in this country, after all these years of scientific thought.

So there remained a strong opinion in favor both of slavery itself and of its control by State as opposed to Federal authority. Senator Saulsbury, of Delaware, asserted that he did not regard slavery as "unconstitutional, illegal, immoral, impious, or sinful, in any aspect of the case, but in perfect accordance with the ways of Providence to man." But his main point was that the Constitution could not be amended to abolish slavery. Slavery was property; property was a corner-stone of the Constitution; and no amendment could be made which would destroy any kind of property. He admitted that the popular theory was that three-fourths of the States were sovereign, and could make any amendment they chose; that absolute sovereignty was in them "in respect to every right which the people of the States have. . . . If that be so," he said, "then I ask you, could three-fourths of the States say that you should have no manufactories; that you should plant no corn; that you should not have property in anything else which is the subject of property?" [5]

He held that if so, they could blot out a State. "Sir," he declared, "if you can go into the States and attempt to regulate the relation of master and slave, you can go into a State and attempt to regulate the relation between parent and child, or husband and wife." If so, you could "say that any other subject of property heretofore shall not be property in the future," or that "there shall be no such thing as property at all," or make an equal distribution of property. If the amendment were based on the sinfulness of slavery, he could not agree. He thought that argument "a sickly sentiment," and the utterers of it professed to be "wiser than the Almighty"—wiser "than the Savior of the world." [6]

Garrett Davis of Kentucky, an able constitutional lawyer, ex-

[5] *Congressional Globe*, March 31, 1864, p. 1366.   [6] *Ibid.*, p. 1366.

claimed that if slavery were the cause of the war, so had religion been the cause of war, and yet no one had ever proposed to abolish religion in order to stop war. He, too, declared that there was a difference between the power of amendment and the power of revolution. If the Federal government, he said, could take cognizance of slavery, "it may of every other local and domestic concern of the States."[7] The amendment struck at "one of the most essential principles of our commingled system of national and of State governments."[8] An amendment that Representatives be chosen for life, that the Senate be hereditary, that the President should be a king, "would be revolutionary, and out of the power of the pale of amendment." The proposed change also was revolutionary and beyond the power of amendment.[9]

S. S. Cox, a witty, brilliant, and high-minded Congressman from Ohio, later from New York, made it very clear that he did not doubt the power of amendment. "I will not," he said, "deny a power so essential to peace, safety, and sovereignty." With fine philosophy, he said that no "ingenious refinement or dazzling eloquence shall lead me to deny a power which may yet prove our salvation, when wisely used." The power might now threaten to destroy, but the power to save "is forever bound up with it." All power, he added, was dangerous. "This is no argument against its existence; only against its exercise." The power over slavery of the States themselves was a dangerous power. He asked why "should the dead forever rule the living?" and if a law were immutable "because made by the fathers?"[10] He said he had always been against slavery. It was to him "the most repugnant of all human institutions."[11] But he made his argument against the amendment solely on its expediency, on "the perennial beauty, exquisite symmetry, and enduring perfection of that system which reserves to the local communities their local interests and the very genius of all permanency, the very element which secures us against that homogeneity so dreaded by the gentleman from New York, the happy concord of diverse interests. . . ."[12]

Reverdy Johnson of Maryland, a distinguished lawyer from a loyal slave State, made a trenchant argument against the theory that the Constitution could not be amended to prohibit slavery.

---

[7] *Congressional Globe*, March 30, 1864, Appendix p. 106.   [8] *Ibid.*, p. 104.
[9] *Ibid.*, p. 106.   [10] *Ibid.*, Jan. 12, 1865, pp. 238–39.   [11] *Ibid.*, p. 242.
[12] *Ibid.*, p. 239.

His argument for national sovereignty will be considered in the chapter on "The Nature of the Union." It was the standard Union argument. It is enough to say here that he declared there never was a greater political heresy than Calhoun's conclusion that "the only sovereignty was that which belonged to the States." [13] The people had won their independence unitedly, and they had invested the national government with a portion of that sovereignty. A portion of that sovereignty was the amending power. He asked if the original Constitution could not have prohibited slavery, and answered that it could. The preamble, itself, with its ideal of securing justice, tranquillity, and liberty, declared a purpose consistent with the prohibition of slavery. Then, if slavery could have been prohibited in the beginning, why could it not be prohibited later by amendment? [14]

The present situation, or something like it, he went on, was bound to come. "I never doubted," he affirmed, "that the day must come when slavery would be exterminated by a convulsive effort on the part of the bondsmen, unless that other and better reason and influence which might bring it about should be successful." There could be no prosperous peace without it.[15]

The result, he continued, could be effected only by a constitutional amendment. The President could go no further than the war power allowed him. His Emancipation Proclamation covered only the slaves who came within "our power." Congress likewise could act only under its war power and was similarly limited. The power of the government went only as far as its troops went. There was no power to touch a slave in Maryland or Delaware.

The debate may so far be summarized as consisting of a demand, on the part of the advocates of the amendment, that slavery should be abolished because it had been the cause, or at least a great cause, of all the dissension of a generation and a half between North and South; and, on the part of the opposition, the contention that, even assuming that slavery was evil, it was a local and domestic problem which the States should still be allowed to handle.

But Charles Sumner, with all the passion of his nature, argued the essential wickedness of slavery, and its violation of the inherent

[13] *Congressional Globe*, April 5, 1864, p. 1422.   [14] *Ibid.*, p. 1423.
[15] *Ibid.*, April 5, 1864, p. 1420.

rights of man. Sumner was a graduate of Harvard, a Boston lawyer who never distinguished himself in practise, of wide but diffuse reading, handsome, eloquent, vain. But he had an immense moral earnestness and fire. There is no doubting his deep sincerity and the influence he exercised on his time. It is the fashion now to condemn him and Stevens for all the evils of the Reconstruction era. That he made many errors of judgment, and failed to show the charity and generosity which history finds so easy, but which at the time is difficult for all but the greatest, may well be admitted. But his effort later to restore the Confederate flags indicates that his spirit was, after all, not vindictive, and that he deeply felt that the measures he advocated were necessary to insure the success of the cause in which he devoutly believed.

It is impossible, I believe, for a fair-minded person to read his eloquent speeches in behalf of the Thirteenth Amendment, and his two speeches on the Fourteenth Amendment, without agreeing that he had a passionate belief in that Equality of Man which became almost a religious tenet to him. Like others of the abolitionists, he became so filled with deep indignation at the existence of slavery, and so determined to do justice to the negro, that he exaggerated the capacity of the negro and over-estimated the effect which mere legal freedom would have on his status. He assumed that freedom was the answer to all of our troubles. At that time, indeed, there had been none of the later scientific studies, which have made us less confident of the immediate power of environment and freedom to raise the standard of living of millions of people. There was apparently little or no conception that the negro was uneducated and untrained, that economic power and intelligent experience are necessary precursors to the successful use of political power.

Sumner began his speech on the Thirteenth Amendment on April 8, 1864, by asserting that "There is nothing in the Constitution on which Slavery can rest, or find any the least support. Even on the face of that instrument it is an *outlaw;* but if we look further into its provisions, we find at least four distinct sources of power, which, if executed, must render Slavery impossible . . ." [16]

Yet, he said, slavery exists, in defiance of reason and justice, "the perpetual spoiler of human rights, and disturber of the public peace, degrading master as well as slave, corrupting society, weak-

[16] Charles Sumner, *Works,* Vol. VIII, p. 370.

ening government, impoverishing the very soil itself, and impairing the natural resources of the country. Such an outrage, so
offensive in every respect, not only to the Constitution, but also
to the whole system of order by which the universe is governed,
can be nothing but a *national nuisance* . . ." [17]

He utterly refused to consider compensating the owners for
their slaves. "Ay, sir," he added, "millions of dollars—with millions
of strong arms also—for defense against Slave-Masters; but not a
cent for tribute to Slave-Masters." [18] If money were paid, he went
on, it clearly could not be paid to the slave-masters. If any were
paid, it must be to the slaves. Compensation, he argued, is founded
on the idea of property in man. But there could be no property in
man. "No man," he asserted, "can make black white or wrong
right; nor can any Congress or any multitude overcome the everlasting law of justice." [19] Hisses, he said, should break forth at
every mention of compensation. [20]

The four sources of power under which Sumner held that Congress could act to destroy slavery without the aid of a Constitutional
Amendment were: the general power granted by the Constitution
to provide for the general welfare; the war power; the power to
guarantee each State a republican form of government; and the
power to secure liberty against all restraint without due process of
law, namely, the Fifth Amendment. Under these powers, he said,
the government could make slavery impossible. In the face of
these powers, he asked, "how can any 'person' be held as slave?"
These powers, he said, were duties, as well as powers. They commanded the government to destroy slavery. "And yet," he said, "we
are constantly and painfully reminded that pending measures
against Slavery are unconstitutional. Sir, this is an immense mistake. *Nothing against Slavery can be unconstitutional*. It is hesita-
tion that is unconstitutional." [21]

The way to enforce these provisions, he continued, was, first, to
appeal to the courts. The courts alone could destroy slavery.
"Every law and every judgment of Court," he cried, "to be binding,
must have at its back the everlasting, irrepealable law of God." [22]
If the courts would do their duty, no judgment could be made
which was based on the premise that property in man was lawful.
All, apparently, a negro need do was to bring a writ of habeas

[17] *Ibid.*, p. 371.   [18] *Ibid.*, p. 373.   [19] *Ibid.*, p. 375.   [20] *Ibid.*, p. 374.
[21] *Ibid.*, pp. 369, 371.   [22] *Ibid.*, p. 381.

corpus, and show that he was held to labor without his consent.

Here was natural law with a vengeance. Since slavery was wrong, it must be declared to be unlawful, despite all the protections which the law and Constitution in two centuries had given it.

But Sumner admitted that the courts would not do their duty. The judges who would follow his law of nature against the law of the land were too few, and the courts therefore were hopeless.

Secondly, he held that Congress could destroy slavery by statute. Congress could do so directly, or indirectly, by repeal of the Fugitive Slave Law, by stopping the coastwise slave-trade, by forbidding interstate commerce in slaves, by allowing negroes to testify in the Federal Courts.

But this also, he said, was not enough. What Congress did might be undone by a later Congress, and of course there was the possibility that some of the above measures would be held unconstitutional. It was necessary to amend the Constitution. We must make all equal before the law. Clearly, where all are equal, "there can be no Slavery. Equality makes Slavery impossible, while it broadens Liberty into that community of right which is the essence of Republican Government." [23]

As a constitutional lawyer, Sumner, of course, was far from sound. The power to promote the general welfare—a power which has been invoked by every party or group which has demanded an assertion of national power for which it could find no specific warrant—could, of course, give no foundation for a denial of property in slaves. While the Constitution did not specifically protect slavery, it did—as was frequently emphasized, indeed as had been bitterly objected by abolitionists—impliedly recognize and sanction it by recognizing it in one of the great compromises of the Constitutional Convention: that which gave the small States equal representation with the populous States in the Senate, while granting in the House representation on the basis of population, in which five negroes counted as three whites. Under the general welfare clause, Congress could not destroy a right in property which was fully protected by the Fifth Amendment.[24] Indeed, the general

---

[23] Sumner, *Works*, Vol. VIII, p. 397.

[24] Under the principle of the Dred Scott case, I think the Supreme Court, even in 1865, would have held that to have freed the negroes by statute without compensation, would have taken property without due process of law. While the Dred Scott case was still intensely unpopular, I believe that its theory of due process would have been maintained.

welfare clause has never been allowed to sanction a power not found in some other part of the Constitution.

The war power, as Trumbull had admitted, gave neither Congress nor the President power to deal with slavery in the border States nor in the States already occupied by Federal troops.

The power to guarantee a republican form of government was much relied on in the Reconstruction debates, as we shall see in the discussion of the status of the seceded States. In the discussion on the Fourteenth Amendment, Sumner took the position that if a State permitted slavery, it was unrepublican in form. If he was correct, every State in which slavery existed, including Maryland, Kentucky, Delaware and Missouri, did not have a republican form of government. Moreover, Sumner's argument went so far as to say that every State which denied the negro the suffrage was unrepublican.

As for the Fifth Amendment, Sumner simply turned the argument around. The Fifth Amendment, as decided by Chief Justice Marshall in *Barron* vs. *Baltimore*,[25] gave the Federal government no power over the States. It did not say that no State could pass a law depriving any person of property without due process of law, but simply that Congress could pass no such law. And to say that Congress could pass no such law, did not mean that Congress could enact legislation positively granting due process of law, or abrogate any State legislation which took property without due process of law.

Sumner was not unaware of this distinction, which he said he, himself, had avowed; but, characteristically, he exclaimed that the prohibition was as "broad and general as the Constitution itself; and since this provision is in support of human rights, it can not be restricted by any limitation."[26]

As a constitutional argument, therefore, Sumner's argument had serious flaws. But it was none the less a powerful presentation of the emotions and the ideas which dominated abolition sentiment at the end of the war.

The result, then, was that the Thirteenth Amendment was adopted, and freedom was thenceforth guaranteed by the national government.

[25] 7 Peters 243 (1833).   [26] Sumner, *Works*, Vol. VIII, p. 369.

The Fourteenth Amendment—National Protection of Civil Rights

But the leaders of the so-called radical group, indeed the leaders of the Republican Party, felt that it was necessary that the national power protect the freedman in the exercise of his Civil Rights. Accordingly, in 1866, Congress passed the Civil Rights Bill of 1866. It provided that all persons born or naturalized in the United States were citizens of the United States, and "shall have the same rights in every State and Territory in the United States, to make and enforce contracts, to sue, be parties, and give evidence, to inherit, purchase, lease, sell, hold, and convey real and personal property, and to full and equal benefit of all laws and proceedings for the security of person and property, as is enjoyed by white citizens, and shall be subject to like punishment, pains, and penalties and to none other; any law, statute, ordinance, regulation, or custom to the contrary notwithstanding." A penalty of $1,000 fine or one year's imprisonment, or both, was provided.[27]

Trumbull introduced this bill into the Senate. He regarded it as fully warranted by the Thirteenth Amendment, that is, that it was proper to enforce an amendment declaring freedom for the slaves by giving them Civil Rights. "That amendment," he began, "declared that all persons in the United States should be free. This measure is intended to give effect to that declaration, and to secure to all persons practical freedom." Of what avail is the Thirteenth Amendment, he asked, "if, in the late slave-holding States, laws are to be enacted and enforced depriving persons of African descent of privileges which are essential to freemen?"[28] He detailed the laws of the Southern States which discriminated against the negro, and charged that although "they do not make a man an absolute slave, yet deprive him of the rights of a freeman; and it is perhaps difficult to draw the precise line, to say where freedom ceases and slavery begins; but a law that does not allow a colored person to go from one county to another is certainly a law in derogation of the rights of a freeman. A law that does not allow a colored person to hold property, does not allow him to teach, does not allow him to preach, is certainly a law in violation of the rights of a freeman, and being so, may properly be declared void."

---

[27] Fleming, *Documentary History of Reconstruction,* Vol. I, p. 197.
[28] *Congressional Globe,* Jan. 29, 1866, p. 474.

He concluded that the power granted by the Thirteenth Amendment authorized Congress to enact any law which would secure freedom to all the people of the country.[29]

This was the first attempt to make personal rights a matter of national legislation. Saulsbury exclaimed that he regarded the bill "as one of the most dangerous that was ever introduced in the Senate of the United States," and that he had never seen one so "fraught with danger." He did not want the States subject to the "omnipotent will of the Federal Congress." The bill took away the State police power, and it exercised control over local matters, such as rights of property, voting, inheritance, and contracts.[30]

Davis, of Kentucky, said that if the bill were not centralizing with a vengeance, and by wholesale, he did not know what was. It "would produce a perfect and despotic central and consolidated government." It breaks down in one short bill "all the penal laws that inflict punishment or penalty upon all the people of the States, except so far as those laws shall be entirely uniform in their application." [31]

Reverdy Johnson declared that if "Congress can legislate in relation to these rights in behalf of the black, why can not they legislate in relation to these same rights in behalf of the white? And if they can legislate in relation to both, the States are abolished . . ." The proponents of the bill seemed, he said, to want all power vested in the government of the United States.[32]

The Civil Rights Bill of 1866 became a law over President Johnson's veto. But it never came before the Supreme Court. Two Federal Courts, on each of which sat a justice of the Supreme Court, sustained it. But the opposition to it was so pronounced, the feeling that once the Southern States were able to vote they would combine with the Northern Democrats to repeal it was so strong, that the dominant majority proceeded to formulate the amendment which became the Fourteenth Amendment.

The Adoption of the Fourteenth Amendment

The amendment was first introduced on January 22, 1866 by Thaddeus Stevens, of Pennsylvania. As first introduced, it simply provided that,

[29] *Ibid.*, p. 475. [30] *Ibid.*, Jan. 29, 1866, pp. 476–77.
[31] *Ibid.*, Feb. 2, 1866, p. 598. [32] *Ibid.*, April 5, 1866, p. 1777.

"Representatives and direct taxes shall be apportioned among the several States which may be included within this Union according to their respective numbers, counting the whole number of persons in each State, excluding Indians not taxed: Provided that whenever the elective franchise shall be denied or abridged in any State on account of race or color, all persons of such race or color shall be excluded from the basis of representation." [33]

In short, this did not give suffrage to the negro, but simply provided that if the suffrage were denied him on account of race or color, the representation of the state should be correspondingly reduced. It gave no protection to the negro in his other political rights, nor to white men in any political rights. Stevens himself declared that it could not be claimed that the amendment "either grants a privilege or takes away a privilege from any State on that subject. It does, however, punish the abuse of that privilege if it exists." The States, he said, had always had the right to fix their elective franchise. "And I hold that this does not take it away from them. Ought it to take it from them? Ought the domestic affairs of the States to be infringed upon by Congress so far as to regulate the restrictions and qualifications of their voters? How many States would adopt such a proposition? How many would allow Congress to come within their jurisdictions to fix the qualifications of their voters? Would New York? Would Pennsylvania? Would the northwestern States? I am sure not one of them would."

Instead of granting the negro suffrage, he would penalize the Southern States if they excluded the negro on account of race or color. And he much preferred that result. He said that the Southern States would lose thirty-five seats in Congress. "Now, I prefer that," he observed, "to an immediate declaration that all shall be represented; for if you make them all voters and let them enter this Hall, not one beneficial act for the benefit of the freedmen or for the benefit of the country could ever be passed." Their eighty-three votes would be enough to give the South control. If the negro were excluded, however, the South would lose thirty-five seats and the North would retain control.

It was better, he said, to let the negroes wait. We should teach them their duties as citizens, and then, "when they shall have be-

[33] *Congressional Globe,* Jan. 22, 1866, p. 351.

come intelligent enough, and there are sufficient loyal men there to control the representation from those States, I shall be glad to see them admitted here." He did not want to grant the suffrage to the negro until the "great work of regenerating the Constitution" in accordance with the principles of the Declaration of Independence, was done. He believed passionately in equal rights, but he did not look on suffrage as a right. In this he differed profoundly with Sumner and those of his school.[34]

Conkling insisted that if the South disfranchised the negro, there should be a diminution of Southern representation. He said that the South would have twenty-eight votes representing her negro population, which was "held not fit to sit as jurors, not fit to testify in court, not fit to be plaintiff in a suit, not fit to approach the ballot box. Twenty-eight votes, to be more or less controlled by those who once betrayed the Government, and for those so destitute, we are assured, of intelligent instinct as not to be fit for free agency.

"Shall all this be? Shall four million human beings count four millions, in arranging the affairs of the nation, who are pronounced by their fellow beings unfit to participate in administering government in the States where they live, or in their counties, towns or precincts; who are pronounced unworthy of the least and most paltry part in local political affairs?" [35]

Congressman Rogers, of New Jersey, protested that the amendment, by providing that Southern representation should be diminished if the negro were denied the ballot on account of race, violated the fundamental principles of democratic government. "What is there," he asked, "more democratic and representative in the institutions of this country than that the people of all classes, without regard to whether they are voters or not, white or black, who make up the intelligence, wealth, and patriotism of the country, shall be represented in the councils of the nation?" If one negro were denied the suffrage on account of race, because he could not meet a property or educational qualification, then the State would lose all its representation based on its entire negro population. The amendment would drive every State in the Union, except

[34] *Congressional Globe*, Jan. 31, 1866, p. 536.
[35] *Congressional Globe*, Jan. 22, 1866, p. 357.

where the negro was in the majority, to grant the negro unqualified
negro suffrage. Indeed, that was its only purpose.[36]

Sumner, however, attacked the proposed amendment with all the
fervor and strength of his nature. He was shocked that Congress
did not directly grant the suffrage by statute. Suffrage, he said,
was the corner-stone of equality of rights. He called the amendment "another compromise of Human Rights," as if "the country
had not already paid enough in costly treasure, and more costly
blood, for such compromises in the past. I had hoped," he
went on, "the day of compromise with wrong had gone forever.
Ample experience shows that it is the least practical mode of
settling questions involving moral principle. A moral principle can
not be compromised." [37]

His argument for negro suffrage we shall treat more at length
when we come to consider the Fifteenth Amendment.

Fessenden was much annoyed at Sumner's speech. He had advocated an amendment which would protect all civil and political
rights from discrimination on account of race or color. The committee had rejected it. He still favored that proposal. He reiterated
that Congress should protect all free men in all their rights. But
failing that, he favored Stevens' amendment. He said that an
amendment was necessary; Congress did not have the power without it.[38]

This proposal for the Fourteenth Amendment failed of adoption.
Undoubtedly, Sumner's speech had much to do with its defeat.
Stevens bitterly laid the defeat to Sumner. Fessenden and Bout-
well blamed him too.

But meanwhile the Joint Committee on Reconstruction had
been at work. It is not necessary to detail all the steps the amendment took in the deliberations of that committee. Its journal for
many years disappeared, until finally it was presented to the
United States Supreme Court by Senator Conkling in the San
Mateo case in 1882. We shall see later what construction Conkling
put on it. The committee started off with a proposal by Stevens,
providing for basing representation on voters. The committee did
not agree to it.

A few days later, Bingham, who was a leader in the demand for

[36] *Ibid.*, p. 353.   [37] Sumner, *Works*, Vol. X, p. 119. Feb. 5, 1866.
[38] Francis Fessenden, *Life and Public Services of William Pitt Fessenden*, Vol.
II, p. 38–43. Speech of Feb. 7, 1866.

an equal rights amendment, for the first time made a proposal which struck at the question of equal rights. His wording was:

"The Congress shall have power to make all laws necessary and proper to secure to all persons in every state within this Union equal protection in their rights of life, liberty, and property."

This was agreed to, tentatively.

On the same day Stevens proposed that,

"All laws, state or national, shall operate impartially and equally on all persons, without regard to race or color."

This was also agreed to.[39]

Then, on the same day, January 12, 1866, it was decided to appoint a sub-committee, consisting of Fessenden, Stevens, Howard, Conkling and Bingham.

On January 16, 1866, the sub-committee reported to the full committee, two alternative amendments; containing prohibitions of discrimination in civil rights, and a third which provided that whenever the "elective franchise shall be denied or abridged on account of race, creed, or color, all persons of such race, creed, or color shall be excluded from the basis of representation." [40]

The full committee quickly agreed on the amendment providing for reduction of representation when the suffrage was denied, and referred the question of an equal rights amendment to a new sub-committee of three. There was further consideration of various proposals for equal rights amendments. Finally, on February 3, Bingham submitted the following resolution:

"The Congress shall have power to make all laws which shall be necessary and proper to secure to all citizens of each State all privileges and immunities of citizens of the several States (Art. 4, Sec. 2), and to all persons in the several States, equal protection in the rights of life, liberty, and property (5th Amendment)."

This proposal was agreed to, and the amendment to the Constitution was then accepted as amended and ordered reported to the Senate.[41]

Bingham spoke in the House in favor of this amendment, but it did not meet with great favor. He said that the amendment "stands in the very words of the Constitution of the United States,

---

[39] Benjamin B. Kendrick, *The Journal of the Joint Committee of Fifteen on Reconstruction*, p. 46.
[40] *Ibid.*, pp. 50, 51.   [41] *Ibid.*, pp. 60–61.

as it came from the hands of its illustrious framers," and that if the amendment had been in the Constitution from the beginning, no rebellion would have occurred.[42] Immunity, he said, meant exemption from "unequal burdens."[43] There never was even "colorable excuse, much less apology, for any man, North or South, claiming that any State Legislature, or State Court, or State Executive, has any right to deny free protection to any free citizen of the United States within its limits in the rights of life, liberty, and property."[44]

But the amendment was attacked bitterly. Thomas T. Davis, of New York, argued that an amendment which gave Congress power to make all laws to secure "to every citizen in the several States, equal protection to life, liberty, and property, is a grant for original legislation by Congress." Its legislation, he added, "may be universal."[45] Rogers, of New Jersey, asserted that it was but another attempt to "consolidate the power of the States in the Federal government. It is but another step to an imperial despotism." He was out of sympathy with the whole demand for equal rights. He seemed to consider it an unanswerable point that under the amendment, Congress could compel the abrogation of State laws which punished a negro more severely than a white man for the same crime.[46]

Even the Republicans were doubtful. The resolution was finally postponed on motion of Conkling, of New York.

Meanwhile the situation was rapidly changing on account of the struggle over the admission of Tennessee, and because of the President's veto of the Civil Rights Bill. The sentiment for an amendment which would place civil rights under the protection of a national amendment, steadily grew.

Robert Dale Owen wrote that he had watched the winter's work with much misgiving. The resolution proposed by Stevens on January 8, 1866, did not satisfy him at all. He felt that it "touched not the substance of the great problem."[47] It did not protect equality of rights. As chairman of a governmental commission, he had come in contact with the negro, and had found him genial, emotional, and cheerful, but of extreme ignorance, lack of self-

---

[42] *Congressional Globe*, Feb. 26, 1866, p. 1034.   [43] *Ibid.*, Feb. 28, 1866, p. 1089.
[44] *Ibid.*, p. 1090.   [45] *Ibid.*, p. 1087.   [46] *Ibid.*, Feb. 26, 1866, App., p. 134.
[47] Robert Dale Owen, "Political Results from the Varioloid," *Atlantic Monthly*. Vol. XXXV, pp. 660, 661. (June, 1875).

reliance, and easily misled. He was convinced that the negro was at that time unfit for suffrage. He went to Stevens near the end of March, and presented him with the draft of an amendment. He began by saying that the negro was "for the present, unprepared wisely to use the right of suffrage, and still more incapable of legislating with prudence." As we made minors wait until they were twenty-one before they could vote, and immigrants five years, we could properly ask the negro to wait until he was ready. Stevens answered that he hated to deny full justice so long. Owen replied that it was for the welfare of the negro that he be required to wait. Then he presented his proposed amendment.

The first section provided that "No discrimination shall be made by any State, nor by the United States, as to the civil rights of persons, because of race, color, or previous condition of servitude." [48]

The second section provided that after July 4, 1876, no discrimination should be made by any State, or the United States, on account of race, color, or previous condition of servitude, in the enjoyment of the right of suffrage.

The third section provided that until July 4, 1876, no class of persons, excluded from the suffrage on account of race, color, or previous condition of servitude, should be included in the basis of representation.

The fourth provided that debts incurred in aid of the rebellion, should not be paid by any State, or the United States.

The fifth gave power to enforce the amendment.

It will be seen that there was no protection of the civil rights of all citizens: they were protected only against discrimination on account of race or color.

Stevens, however, told Owen that "nothing . . . anywhere near being as good as this, or as complete" had come before the committee. It would be likely to pass, too, he added. There was not then in the House a majority for negro suffrage. Fessenden, Conkling, Washburne, Howard and Boutwell—all approved the Owen proposal. Sumner disapproved. He said that it tacitly recognized the right to withhold suffrage for ten years. "It is a question" he added, "of abstract principle; not of expediency." [49]

[48] *Ibid.*, p. 662. But as we have seen, Bingham had already proposed an amendment for the protection of civil and equal rights. *Supra*, p. 24.
[49] *Ibid.*, pp. 663–65.

But the amendment was adopted by the committee and ordered reported. Fessenden, however, became ill of the varioloid, and it was suggested that the report be delayed until he was well. According to Stevens, the delay was fatal. Stevens later told Owen that the report became known; that the New York, Illinois and Indiana members held caucuses, and because of their antagonism to negro suffrage, the committee gave way. A new amendment was patched together "in the next three hours." Stevens called it a "shilly-shally, bungling thing.[50] . . . Damn the varioloid," he exclaimed. "It changed the whole policy of the country." [51]

It was on April 28 that the Committee recast the amendment. Stevens reported it on April 30. It was debated and passed in the House in the form reported. But after it passed the House, it was recast in Republican caucuses into the form it stands today. Hendricks in the Senate charged that the Committee draft was so unsatisfactory that the Republicans realized that it must be re-moulded. He declared that "we witnessed the astounding spectacle of the withdrawal, for the time, of a great legislative measure, touching the Constitution itself, from the Senate, that it might be decided in the secret councils of a party." [52]

Owen felt that the amendment, even in its final form, was very unsatisfactory. He called it "crude and verbose." He felt that the specification of rights was inappropriate in a constitutional amendment; that a census would be necessary to reduce representation under the second section; that the second section would penalize a State even under an educational test; and that the punitive Section three was a great mistake.[53]

I have given in some detail the history of the wording of the amendment, in the endeavor to show the process by which a simple amendment for the reduction of southern representation, if the southern States did not grant the ballot to the negro, grew into an amendment which has profoundly affected our whole theory of the limits of governmental action.

Stevens, in presenting the amendment,[54] admitted that it fell far

---

[50] *Ibid.*, p. 665.   [51] *Ibid.*, p. 666.   [52] *Congressional Globe*, June 4, 1866, p. 2938.
[53] *Atlantic Monthly*, Vol. XXXV, pp. 666–67.
[54] The Fourteenth Amendment, as introduced in the Senate and adopted, reads as follows:

"Section 1. All persons born or naturalized in the United States, and subject to the jurisdiction thereof, are citizens of the United States and of the State wherein

short of his wishes, but added that it fulfilled his hopes. But he went on to say that on a careful survey of the whole question, the committee did not believe that nineteen of the loyal States could be induced to ratify any more stringent proposal than the one presented. He then dwelt at length on the evidence taken by the committee on the condition of the negroes in the South, the vagrancy laws which bore heavily on the negro, the limitations in the southern black codes. This had been the burden of many a northern speech and article in the past year and a half.

Then he came to the provisions of Section one. "I can hardly believe," he said, "that any person can be found who will not admit that every one of these provisions is just." They are "all asserted, in some form or other, in our Declaration or organic law. But the Constitution limits only the action of Congress, and is not a limitation on the States. This amendment supplies that defect, and allows Congress to correct the unjust legislation of the States, so far that the law which operates upon one man shall operate *equally* upon all. Whatever law punishes a white man for a crime,

they reside. No State shall make or enforce any law which shall abridge the privileges or immunities of citizens of the United States; nor shall any State deprive any person of life, liberty, or property, without due process of law; nor deny to any person within its jurisdiction the equal protection of the laws.

"Section 2. Representatives shall be apportioned among the several States according to their respective numbers, counting the whole number of persons in each State, excluding Indians not taxed. But when the right to vote at any election for the choice of electors for President and Vice President of the United States, Representatives in Congress, the Executive and Judicial officers of a State, or the members of the Legislature thereof, is denied to any of the male inhabitants of such State, being twenty-one years of age, and citizens of the United States, or in any way abridged, except for participation in rebellion, or other crime, the basis of representation therein shall be reduced in the proportion which the number of such male citizens shall bear to the whole number of male citizens twenty-one years of age in such State.

"Section 3. No person shall be a Senator or Representative in Congress, or elector of President and Vice President, or hold any office, civil or military, under the United States, or under any State, who, having previously taken an oath, as a member of Congress, or as an officer of the United States, or as a member of any State legislature, or as an executive or judicial officer of any State, to support the Constitution of the United States, shall have engaged in insurrection or rebellion against the same, or given aid or comfort to the enemies thereof. But Congress may by a vote of two-thirds of each House, remove such disability.

"Section 4. The validity of the public debt of the United States, authorized by law, including debts incurred for payment of pensions and bounties for services in suppressing insurrection or rebellion, shall not be questioned. But neither the United States nor any State shall assume or pay any debt or obligation incurred in aid of insurrection or rebellion against the United States, or any claim for the loss or emancipation of any slave; but all such debts, obligations and claims shall be held illegal and void.

"Section 5. The Congress shall have power to enforce, by appropriate legislation, the provisions of this article."

shall punish the black man precisely in the same way and to the same degree. Whatever law protects the white man, shall afford 'equal' protection to the black man. Whatever means of redress is afforded to one, shall be afforded to all. Whatever law allows the white man to testify in Court, shall allow the man of color to do the same. These are great advances over their present codes. Now different degrees of punishment are inflicted, not on account of the magnitude of the crime, but according to the color of the skin. Now color disqualifies a man from testifying in courts, or being tried in the same way as white men. I need not enumerate these partial and oppressive laws."

To the suggestion that equality could be achieved by a Civil Rights law, he replied that a mere law could be repealed by a majority. "And I need hardly say," he added, "that the first time that the South with their copperhead allies obtain the command of Congress, it will be repealed. . . . This amendment, once adopted, can not be annulled without two-thirds of Congress. That they will hardly get. And yet certain of our distinguished friends propose to admit State after State before this amendment becomes a part of the Constitution. What madness! Is their judgment misled by their kindness; or are they unconsciously drifting into the haven of power at the other end of the avenue? I do not suspect it, but others will."

He said that the effect of Section two, which provided that if the suffrage were denied to any portion of the male citizens twenty-one years of age, except for participation in the rebellion or "other crime," representation should be reduced, would be either to compel the States to grant universal suffrage or so to "shear them of their power as to keep them forever in a hopeless minority in the national Government, both legislative and executive. If they do not enfranchise the freedmen, it would give to the rebel States but thirty-seven Representatives." The South would be restive under such a loss and would grant the suffrage; but before that could be done, the Constitution would have been amended "to secure the rights of every human being and render disunion impossible." [55]

This seems inconsistent with his reluctance expressed to Owen to keep the negro waiting "so long." It was quite in accord, however, with his public statement in January that he was indifferent

[55] *Congressional Globe,* May 8, 1866, p. 2459.

as to negro suffrage. But he was evidently deeply concerned that the Southern States should not obtain the controlling power.

James A. Garfield, after expressing his deep regret that the amendment did not grant the suffrage, concluded nevertheless that "I am glad to see this first section here, which proposes to hold over every American citizen, without regard to color, the protecting shield of law." He contended that the Civil Rights Act was constitutional, but said that a constitutional amendment would lift that law "above the reach of political strife" and the plots of any party.[56]

The discussion of Section one—the section which gave national protection to equality of rights—was brief. Most of the debate was on Section two, which provided for cutting down the representation of Southern States that did not grant negro suffrage; and on Section three, which temporarily disqualified for office the leaders of the Confederacy. It has been said that the Supreme Court, which later held that the section protected the rights of all citizens, as well as negroes, went farther than Congress intended. But, as we shall see later on, the words of the amendment were all-inclusive. Moreover, while the references are brief, it is clear that Congress realized that the scope of the amendment was universal. Raymond, of New York, for example, referred to the "principle of the first [section], which secures an equality of rights among all the citizens" of the country; and said that he had always favored "equality of rights to all citizens of the United States, and to all persons within their jurisdiction. . . ."[57]

Bingham made the most extended argument for the famous first section. He said that the necessity for the first section was one of the lessons that had been taught to all the people of the country "by the history of the past four years of terrific conflict,—that history in which God is, and in which He teaches the profoundest lessons to men and nations. There was a want hitherto, and there remains a want now, in the Constitution of our Country, which the proposed amendment will supply. What is that? It is the power in the people, the whole people of the United States, by express authority of the Constitution to do that by Congressional enactment which hitherto they have not had the power to do, and have never even attempted to do; that is, to protect by national law the

---

[56] *Ibid.*, p. 2462.   [57] *Ibid.*, May 10, 1866, p. 2502.

privileges and immunities of all the citizens of the Republic, and the inborn rights of every person within its jurisdiction, whenever the same shall be abridged or denied by the unconstitutional acts of any state."

He expressed the general feeling at the time, that the amendment would give Congress power by positive legislation to secure equality of rights in the Nation. As we shall see, the Supreme Court later held that the amendment gave no power to Congress to legislate on local matters, but merely to pass corrective legislation which would prevent the injustice of local laws. But the advocates of the amendment were full of the idea that under the amendment Congress could bring into its scope all local matters which affected equality of rights.

Bingham went on to say that the amendment took no right from a State which it ever had. "No State," he added, "ever had the right, under the forms of law or otherwise, to deny to any freeman the equal protection of the laws, or to abridge the privileges and immunities of any citizen of the Republic, although many of them have assumed and exercised the power and that without remedy." [58]

In the Senate, Howard argued that the last two clauses of Section one "disabled a State from depriving not merely a citizen of the United States, but any person, whoever he may be, of life, liberty, or property without due process of law; or from denying him the equal protection of the laws of the State. This abolishes all class legislation in the States, and does away with the injustice of subjecting one caste of persons to a code not applicable to another." The great need was to be protected by national law from unconstitutional State enactments. He quoted from Corfield vs. Coryell, defining the privileges of a State of which a citizen of another State could not be deprived of under the Fourth Article; and said that such rights, together with those protected from Federal interference by the first eight amendments, were now protected against State interference by the Fourteenth Amendment. The great object of the first section, he concluded, was to "restrain the power of the States, and compel them at all times to respect these fundamental guaranties." Congress formerly had no power to enforce them; now, by the fifth section of the amendment, Congress was given power to pass laws to attain the equality of all citizens before the

[58] *Congressional Globe*, May 10, 1866, p. 2542.

law. Here again, was expressed the dominant idea that the amendment gave power to enact positive Federal legislation to ensure equal rights.[59]

Senator Poland, of Vermont, said that the clauses providing for due process and the equal protection of the laws, in Section one embodied "the very spirit and inspiration of our system of government, the absolute foundation upon which it is established. It is essentially declared in the Declaration of Independence and in all the provisions of the Constitution. Notwithstanding this, we know that State laws exist, and some of them of very recent enactment, in direct violation of these principles." [60]

The members of the opposition did not attack the famous clauses providing that no State should deprive any person of life, liberty, or property without due process of law nor deny the equal protection of the laws, which have so profoundly influenced our political thought and legislation for forty-six[61] years. They attacked the clause which disqualified the Southern leaders; they objected to Section two, which provided for reduced representation if the Southern States excluded the negro from the ballot; but they said practically nothing on the due process clause, and little on the equal protection of the laws. They were most concerned—as the Republicans were most concerned—with the questions of disqualification of the leading Southerners and the reduction of Southern representation.

The opposition was based on the traditional anti-national belief that the States should settle questions of citizenship and the rights of citizens. Randall of Pennsylvania, later Speaker of the House, said that "there is no occasion whatever for the Federal power to be exercised between the two races at variance with the wishes of the people of the State. . . ." He said: "I would leave all this to the States themselves. . . ." [62]

Senator Hendricks, of Indiana, was a Democrat of the strict party school, and a lawyer of ability. "The Constitution," he asserted, "is to be changed; the foundations of the Government are to be disturbed; some of the old oak timbers are to be removed,

---

[59] *Ibid.*, May 23, 1866, p. 2766.
[60] *Ibid.*, June 5, 1866, p. 2961. *Corfield* vs. *Coryell*, 4 Wash. C.C. 371 (1825).
[61] It is really only since 1890 that the Amendment has had an effect on State legislation.
[62] *Ibid.*, May 10, 1866, p. 2530.

and timber of recent growth is to be substituted. Upon the foundations fixed by the fathers, our institutions have rested firmly and
securely for three-quarters of a century. They have stood unmoved
by the contests of ambitious leaders, the angry strife of parties,
and the rolling waves of war." He charged that the amendment
was the work of partisan desires.[63]

Hendricks was not reconciled to making negroes citizens. He
objected that it would diminish the worth of our citizenship to make
it open to all. "How our citizenship will be esteemed at home and
abroad should this amendment be adopted, we may judge by con-
sulting the sentiments with which we regard Mexican citizenship." [64]

The second section, that reducing representation in proportion to
the number disfranchised, except for participation in crime or rebellion, he asserted, was an attempt to coerce the Southern States
to grant negro suffrage. "Our institutions," he said, "rest for their
support upon the intelligence and virtue of the people, and who may
say that the untaught negroes, so lately manumitted, are qualified
to exercise the privileges and discharge the duties of an American
citizen?" It were better, he contended, to grant the suffrage openly.
If the States wanted to grant the suffrage to negroes, he said, "I
am content," although, he added, "I am not for it directly, nor will
I coerce the States to its allowance." [65]

Blaine summarized the purpose of the Fourteenth Amendment
as the imposition of certain conditions before granting the Southern
States representation again. These were, first, "to make citizenship
National." The Fourteenth Amendment, he said, was for the white
man as well as the negro. It made citizenship national for all.[66]
Secondly, the Republican leaders desired to change the basis of
representation; thirdly, to prevent disloyal Southern officers from
holding Federal office; and fourthly, to provide that the war debts
could not be repudiated.[67]

The great ideal of Sumner, Bingham and Julian was equal rights
for negroes. Sumner, as we have seen, thought that the Fourteenth
Amendment was not necessary to attain that end; but to the end
he was passionately devoted. Equal rights was the central purpose
of the amendment. The framers of the amendment wanted to make

[63] *Ibid.*, p. 2938.   [64] *Ibid.*, p. 2939.   [65] *Ibid.*, p. 2939.
[66] James G. Blaine, *Political Discussions*, p. 64. Speech at Skowhegan, Maine,
Aug. 29, 1866.
[67] *Ibid.*, p. 66.

citizenship and freedom national. They wanted to protect the rights of men in the enjoyment of their liberty and property, and they wanted to do it by Federal legislation. Civil Rights were to be protected in the Federal courts and by Federal laws.

The Congressional leaders apparently believed that when they provided that no State could abridge the privileges and immunities of citizens of the United States, they had provided that no State could deny to any citizen of the United States the same rights which were protected from Federal interference by the first eight amendments.[68]

They believed, too, that the privileges and immunities which no State could deny to citizens of another State, were secured to all citizens of the United States by the Fourteenth Amendment. We have seen also that Congress did consider—although very briefly— that all rights were to be protected; that all persons were to be safeguarded in the enjoyment of life, liberty, and property.

Roscoe Conkling argued, however, before the Supreme Court in the San Mateo case (to which I have already referred), that the amendment extended to the prevention of all unequal or oppressive laws, to the protection not only of whites but of corporations. In this argument he set himself to overcome Miller's dictum in the Slaughter House cases, that the amendment applied only to negroes. He quoted from the journal of the Joint Committee on Re-

[68] These were:

(1) Protection of freedom of speech, the press, and religion; the right of assembly and petition.

(2) The right to a militia and to bear arms.

(3) That no soldier shall be quartered in the time of peace in any house, without the consent of the owner; nor in time of war, save as prescribed by law.

(4) Freedom from unreasonable searches and seizures; and that warrants shall be issued only on probable cause, stating the place, person or things to be searched.

(5) That no person shall be held for a capital or other infamous crime except on indictment by a grand jury, except in cases arising in the land or naval forces, or in the militia, when in actual service in time of war or public danger; that no one shall be put twice in jeopardy, nor be a witness in a criminal case against himself, nor be deprived of life, liberty, or property without due process of law; nor shall property be taken for public use without just compensation.

(6) The right to a speedy and public trial in all criminal cases by an impartial jury in the State and district where the crime was committed; to be informed of the nature and causes of the accusation; to be confronted by witnesses; to have compulsory process of witnesses in his own favor; and to have counsel for his defense.

(7) That in suits at common law, where the value in controversy exceeds twenty dollars, to have a jury trial; and that no fact tried by a jury shall be otherwise re-examined in any Court of the United States, save according to the rules of common law.

(8) That excessive bail shall not be required; nor excessive fines, nor cruel and unusual punishments, imposed.

construction, which until then had been unknown. He sought to show that the committee first drafted an amendment to protect the suffrage of the negroes, and then proceeded to draft a distinct amendment for the protection of the rights of all persons. The amendment did not, he said, have a "single inspiration and design." Its parts were separately conceived and reported on.[69]

Conkling admitted that the "rights and wrongs of freedmen were the chief spur and incentive of the occasion," that, "no doubt, regard for the rights of the freedman was uppermost in public thought." [70] But he insisted that "the men who framed, the Congress which proposed, and the people who through their Legislatures ratified the Fourteenth Amendment, must have known the meaning and force of the term "persons." [71] They did not think that the word

[69] Roscoe Conkling, Oral Argument in *San Mateo County* vs. *Southern Pacific R.R.*, 116 U.S. 138 (1885). File Copies of Briefs, U.S. Supreme Court, Vol. 6, 106–11, p. 15.

Conkling read extracts from the Journal showing that, first, an amendment was agreed to providing that "whenever the elective franchise shall be denied or abridged in any State on account of race or color, all persons of that race or color shall be excluded from the basis of representation." Conkling concluded that when the joint committee had adopted the resolution for reduction of representation if the suffrage were denied on account of race or color, it had "not only acquitted itself of the whole matter of the proposed amendment, to wit, the right to suffrage of the freedmen of the South, connected with representation, but quoad the subject the committee was functus officio. A special committee falls when it reports the subject committed to it, as an insect dies when it stings." (Oral Argument, p. 19.) He added: "You will perceive also that before what now constitutes the first section, was perfected or even considered, the committee had reported and lost all jurisdiction and power over, the portion of the amendment which did in truth directly relate to the freedmen of the South. The subject of suffrage, the ballot, and representation in Congress, was disposed of before the committee reached the language on which today's argument proceeds." (*Ibid.*, p. 15.)

After the report was made, the committee continued with other matters "with which it was charged." (*Ibid.*, p. 19.) It proceeded to consider an amendment for equal rights. This, he went on, did not concern negroes particularly. "The elective franchise," he argued, "citizenship, and the privileges and immunities of citizens, were all undoubtedly associated with the emancipated race, and the two former with that race exclusively. This can not be said of any other subject of the Fourteenth Amendment." (*Ibid.*, p. 28.)

He went into the history of the independent amendment,—the amendment for equal rights. He noted that it was referred to a new subcommittee. He reminded the Court that he had moved to amend the resolution by changing the word "citizens" to "persons," so that all persons would be protected in equal rights. (*Ibid.*, p. 18.) He noted that Bingham, in his draft of the amendment, had inserted "(Art. 4, Sec. 2)" after the words "all privileges and immunities of citizens in the several States," and "(5th Amendment)" after the words "equal protection in the rights of life, liberty, and property," as indicating that Bingham intended to protect by the amendment the same rights as were protected from Federal interference by Article 4, Section 2, and the Fifth Amendment. He concluded in the words of Justice Bradley in a case long afterwards, that the American people "understood what they were doing, and meant to decree what has, in fact, been decreed." (*Ibid.*, p. 24.)

Article IV, Section 2, (1) provides: "The Citizens of each State shall be entitled to all Privileges and Immunities of Citizens in the Several States."

[70] *Ibid.*, pp. 25, 27.   [71] *Ibid.*, p. 31.

"person" and the word "citizen" were synonymous. Corporations, he argued, were constantly called "persons." The word "persons," as used "in the Constitutions and in other solemn and exact instruments was, as it is now, familiar as a term embracing artificial as well as natural beings." [72]

Then he intimated that the Committee actually intended to protect corporations. "At the time the Fourteenth Amendment was ratified," he argued, "as the records of the two Houses will show, individuals and joint stock companies were appealing for Congressional and administrative protection against the invidious and discriminating state and local taxes. One instance was that of an express company whose stock was largely owned by citizens of the State of New York, who came with petitions and bills seeking acts of Congress to aid them in resisting what they deemed oppressive taxation in two States and oppressive and ruinous rules of damage applied under State laws.

"That complaints," he went on, "in respect of property and other rights, made by citizens of Northern States who took up residence in the South, were rife, in and out of Congress, none of us can forget; that complaints of oppression in various forms, of white men in the South—of 'Union men,'—were heard on every side, I need not remind the Court.

"The war and its results, the conditions of the freedman, and the manifest duty owed to them, no doubt brought on the occasion for constitutional amendment; but when the occasion came and men set themselves to the task, the accumulated evils falling within the purview of the work were the surrounding circumstances, in the light of which they strove to increase and strengthen the safeguards of the Constitution and laws." [73]

Even Conkling did not go beyond the equal protection clause. He did not refer to due process. Nor was anything specific said in the debates about due process, or the power to annul laws under the police power, or control rates, or taxation.

Conkling himself, later in his argument, spoke as if he realized that the interests of corporations were not in the mind of the Committee. "The true question," he said, "in exploring the meanings of the Fourteenth Amendment, is not, in a given case, whether the framers foresaw the particular case and acted in reference to

[72] *Ibid.*, Brief, p. 20.　　　　　　[73] *Ibid.*, Oral Argument, p. 25.

it,—the inquiry is, does the case fall within the expressed intention of the amendment?" [74]

He thought it did, and that the framers of the amendment "builded better than they knew." [75]

There is no doubt that the Committee and Congress intended to protect the rights of all men. I have already quoted several statements to the effect that the amendment was intended to prevent all unequal laws, and to protect the same rights from State interference as were protected from Federal interference by the Fifth Amendment, and the same privileges and immunities which the States could not deny to citizens of other States under Article 4, Section 2. But it seems stretching things to say that the Committee had lost jurisdiction over the provisions of the amendment as to the rights of the freedmen, before it took up what became the famous Section 1. The Committee was certainly primarily concerned with the rights of the freedmen when it considered the equal rights provisions of the amendment. It was primarily concerned with the condition of the freedmen from first to last. Moreover, the entire amendment was really recast by the Committee on April 28, and was again remolded by the Republicans in their caucuses after it passed the House.

But there is not a line in the Journal, nor in the debates in Congress on the amendment, which gives any support to Conkling's intimation that unequal taxation or the protection of business was in the mind of the Committee or of Congress. There was much talk of unequal laws, but none of unequal laws respecting business or taxation. It was inequality of personal rights which the Committee and Congress had in mind. Moreover, Conkling himself voted four times against an amendment for equal rights and the protection of political rights, when it came up in the Committee. [76] It is evident that if there was any such intention as Conkling asserted, he did not have that intention himself in 1866.

Finally, it is clear that the public at large had no conception of the range of the amendment which was in process, and in view of the slowness with which the Supreme Court took jurisdiction, few could have contemplated the scope of the section which Conkling referred to. But we shall consider the development of the amendment in the following chapter.

[74] *Ibid.*, p. 31.   [75] *Ibid.*, p. 34.   [76] Kendrick, *Journal,* pp. 61, 62, 98, 99.

Two of the great war amendments had been passed: the first, to make freedom national; and the second, to make citizenship national, and to prevent any State from taking life, liberty, or property without due process of law, or denying any person the equal protection of the laws.

THE FIFTEENTH AMENDMENT—NATIONAL PROTECTION OF THE SUFFRAGE

But the end was not yet. The so-called radicals had pressed from the beginning for negro suffrage. We have seen that Stevens, in introducing the Fourteenth Amendment, declared that it was not then believed that any proposition more stringent could be adopted by the loyal States; and, of course, he meant by anything "more stringent," negro suffrage. I have noted that the southern parts of such States as Indiana, Illinois and Ohio had been settled by people from the Carolinas, Kentucky, Virginia and Tennessee, who were vigorously opposed to negro suffrage. Indeed, it was the reluctance of Northern sentiment to favor emancipation that had made Lincoln insist for months that the war was to save the Union, and not to free the slaves. But the abolitionists, generally called the humanitarians or the radicals, had pressed from the beginning for the final consummation,—negro suffrage itself.

James Russell Lowell, in his essay entitled "Reconstruction," published in 1865, asked what should be done about the negro. He answered that we must do more than emancipate him. We must, he said, render the slave-holder powerless, we must take land from the slave-holding aristocracy and give it to the negroes; and then he asked, "Must we not make them voters also, that they may have that power of self-protection which no interference of government can so safely, cheaply, and surely exercise in their behalf?" Both expediency and justice called for the grant of the suffrage.

"As a matter of expediency," he said, "it is always wisest to shape a system of policy with a view to permanence, much more than to immediate convenience. . . . Both the late master and the late slave should begin on the new order of things, with a sense of its permanence on the one hand and its rightfulness on the other. They will soon learn that neither intelligence can do without labor, nor labor without intelligence; and that wealth will result only from a clearly understood and reciprocally beneficial dependence of each upon the other." Unless we make the black man a citizen, he said, we take away the strongest inducement for the white man to educate him; for the ignorance of the negro voter becomes a danger which it would be to the interest of the white man to remove.[77] Neither he nor any of the advocates of negro suffrage ever seemed to consider the result which happened; namely, that the negro—although given the vote—would not be allowed to vote.

But he also asked the suffrage on the ground of justice. We must get rid, he asserted, of the delusion that right is in any way dependent upon skin, and not on an inward virtue. The war had been carried on for the principles of democracy, and "a cardinal point of those principles is that the only way in which to fit men for freedom is to make them free; the only way to teach them how to use their political power is to give it to them." [78] He was aware that equality could not be conferred by law or the Constitution. But he asked for the suffrage because it is the only "effectual warranty of freedom; and accordingly we are in favor of distinctly settling beforehand" the grant of the suffrage as a "conditional right of admission" of the Southern States to the Union.[79]

Again, in his article, "Scotch the Snake or Kill It," also published in 1865, he argued that a contest begun for such ends and maintained by such expedients as the Civil War, was not to be "concluded by merely crying quits and shaking hands." The slave-holding States "chose to make themselves a foreign people to us, and they must take the consequences." We must safeguard the principles for which we had sacrificed so much. "The war," he went on, "has established the unity of the government; but no peace will be anything more than a pretence unless it rest upon the unity of the nation, and that can only be secured by making everywhere supreme the national idea that freedom is a right inherent in man himself, and not a creature of the law, to be granted to one class of men or withheld from it at the option of another." He asked what we had conquered; and said it was not the Southern States or the Southern people merely, but that the fruit of our victory, "as it was always the object of our warfare, is the everlasting validity of the theory of the Declaration of Independence in these United States, and the obligation before God and man to make it the rule of our practice." [80]

[77] Lowell, *Political Essays*, p. 228. [78] *Ibid.*, p. 230. [79] *Ibid.*, p. 237. [80] *Ibid.*, p. 256.

The question for us was not whether we had a right to interfere, but rather whether we had "the right to let them alone." If we could stipulate "for the abolition of slavery, what is there to prevent our exacting further conditions no less essential to our safety and the prosperity of the South?" He said that our institutions must be homogeneous.[81] "We could not live together half slave and half free. Shall we succeed better in trying a second left-handed marriage between democracy and another form of aristocracy, less gross, but not less congenial? . . . We can have no permanent peace with the South but by Americanizing it, by compelling it— if need be—to accept the idea, and with it, the safety of democracy." He would therefore make the law "equal for all men." Democracy, he concluded, is safe because it is just, and "safe only when it is just to all." [82]

Even Godkin favored the granting of suffrage to the negro, although he would grant it only to negroes who were fit. However, in a letter to Charles Eliot Norton in 1865, he criticized Lowell, for arguing that suffrage was a natural right. He declared that there was "no natural right to share in the government, and that the precise form of government in any given country is purely a question of expediency." The state, he said, has a right to say who shall vote and who shall not vote, and has in all ages and countries exercised this right. The natural right to suffrage had been so inculcated in our people as to be a "powerful obstacle to the establishment even of that educational test which you acknowledge to be necessary to the security of a government resting on the intelligence of the people." He hated logic in politics: the practical effects of policies should be the test. But he admitted that the suffrage basis should be as broad as possible and agreed that it should be granted, with an educational test which should be applied to both whites and blacks, and the further requirement for negroes, for a period of ten years, that they show evidence of a willingness to support themselves.[83]

Probably the most eloquent—certainly the most powerful—of the advocates of suffrage for the negroes was Sumner. We have already alluded to his speech against the first draft of the Fourteenth Amendment, which he opposed with all his force because

[81] *Ibid.*, p. 259.   [82] *Ibid.*, pp. 260–62.
[83] Rollo Ogden, *Life and Letters of Edwin Lawrence Godkin*, Vol. II, pp. 45–7.

it did not grant the suffrage. In that speech, he said that the time had come when all compromise with human rights should cease. He submitted an amendment providing that there should be "no denial of rights, civil or political, on account of race or color; but all persons shall be equal before the law, whether in the court room or at the ballot box." [84] It was vain to expect, he began, full fellowship in the Union until we had obtained that security for the future which is found only in the Equal Rights of all, at the ballot box, as in the court room. This is "the Great Guaranty, without which all other guaranties will fail."

As in arguing for the abolition of slavery, he said that there were four great powers under which Congress could act to grant equality of rights: necessity, the war power, the guaranty clause of the Constitution, and lastly, the Thirteenth Amendment.

First, he argued necessity, overwhelming compulsion called for enfranchisement. The argument for enfranchisement was the same as that for emancipation. By enfranchisement, he meant "Equal Rights of All, so that there shall be no exclusion of any kind, civil or political, founded on color, and the promises of the Fathers shall be fulfilled." [85] No individual and no people could afford to be unjust. The Freedman was exploited; the Master dominates; the Freedman will resist; and, therefore, to "avoid insurrection and servile war," we must "perform the promises of the Republic. . . ." He argued that our business and credit depended on enfranchisement. The Southern whites would refuse to pay the national debt.[86]

Sumner was thoroughly convinced that the guaranty clause gave full power to Congress to act. With characteristic energy, he had collected the opinions of political students from Aristotle down, on the meaning of the phrase, "a republican form of government," but he found them all unsatisfactory. He concluded that we would have to find the true meaning of the words in the declarations of the Fathers, in "solemn declarations" of public policy, in our declared opinions, and in public acts.[87]

Our Fathers, he said, plainly intended, by a republican form of government, one representing the principles for which they had struggled. James Otis had "planted himself on the Rights of Man which he insisted were, by the everlasting Law of Nature, inherent

---

[84] Sumner, *Works*, Vol. X, p. 114.
[85] Sumner, *Works*, Feb. 5, 1866, Vol. X, pp. 124, 131.
[86] *Ibid.*, pp. 133–34.   [87] *Ibid.*, p. 154.

and inalienable; and these rights, he nobly proclaimed, were common to all, without distinction of color." [88]

There was no such thing, he asserted, as virtual representation. Otis had declared that representation of the colonies by Parliament was no representation at all. Representation, to be in accord with the inherent rights of man, must be actual, and taxation without representation was tyranny.

The primal truth was that Equality is "the Alpha and the Omega, wherein all other rights are embraced. Men may not have a natural right to certain things; but most clearly they have a natural right to *impartial laws,* without which, justice, being the end and aim of government, must fail. Equality in rights is the first of rights." [89]

Then he argued that the Southern States were not republican in form. The 1860 census showed 5,447,220 white persons and 3,656,-112 negroes in the Southern States. When they excluded three-eighths of their population from the suffrage, they were not republican in form. If the Southern States could exclude three million negroes, they could exclude others. The Southern States, therefore, were not republican. One-half of Louisiana, more than half of Mississippi, were disfranchised. Such States were oligarchies. "A representative government is a government by the people, not less than a democracy, provided all the people are represented." [90]

So he said the guaranty clause should be enforced. As in arguing for the Thirteenth Amendment, he insisted that the guaranty is made by the United States, and that Congress is the sole judge of how it shall be enforced.

He was not embarrassed by the fact that certain Northern States had also "done a mean and a wrong thing," namely, denied the suffrage to the negro. "Pray, Sir," he exclaimed, "how can the failure of these States affect the power of Congress in a great exigency under the national Constitution?" [91]

Finally, he found the power under the Thirteenth Amendment. To effect the full freedom of the slaves, it was necessary to give them equal rights. He said that the Civil Rights bill had been passed under the theory that it was a fulfillment of the Thirteenth Amendment, and that equal rights were likewise such a fulfillment. Political rights, he said, were as essential as civil rights.

So Sumner argued that suffrage and equal rights could be en-

[88] *Ibid.,* p. 159. [89] *Ibid.,* p. 174. [90] *Ibid.,* p. 207. [91] *Ibid.,* p. 215.

acted by statute without a new amendment. He was insistent that suffrage was a natural right. He admitted that there might be educational tests. Still the right was an inherent right.

But, while his whole basis was natural rights, he went on to show the practical effects of granting suffrage. The ballot, he said, was a peacemaker, a reconciler, a schoolmaster, and a protector. "How godlike in transforming power alike on master and slave!" The ballot would bring mutual self-respect, peace between former master and slave. It would give the negro "the strength and glory of manhood."

The ballot was a reconciler: it teaches men to work together in harmony. It is a teacher: it teaches manhood. Above all, it is a protector: the only sufficient guaranty. "Let the freedman vote, and he will have in himself under the law a constant, ever-present, self-protecting power. . . . When the master knows that he may be voted down, he will know that he must be just, and everything is contained in justice." The ballot was the one thing needful. "To him who has the ballot, all other things shall be given,—protection, opportunity, education, a homestead. The ballot is the Horn of Abundance, out of which overflow rights of every kind, with corn, cotton, rice, and all the fruits of the earth." [92]

In a letter to John Bright on May 27, 1867, he admitted, "Without the colored vote, the white Unionists would have been left in the hands of the rebels; loyal governments could not be organized. The colored vote was a necessity: this I saw at the beginning, and insisted pertinaciously that it should be secured. It was on this ground, rather than on principle, that I relied most; but the argument of principle was like a reinforcement." [93]

I think, however, that with Sumner the principle was all-powerful. Natural rights were eternal truths to him, and they inspired him with a passionate fervor. Lamar, later Justice of the Supreme Court, then in the House, declared, "Charles Sumner was born with an instinctive love of freedom, and was educated from the earliest infancy to the belief that freedom is the natural and indefeasible right of every intelligent being having the outward form of man. In him, in fact, this creed seems to have been something more than a doctrine imbibed from teachers, or a result

[92] *Ibid.*, pp. 221, 223, 224.
[93] Pierce, *Memoirs and Letters of Charles Sumner*, Vol. IV. p. 319.

of education. To him it was grand intuitive truth, inscribed in blazing letters upon the tablet of his inner consciousness, to deny which would have been for him to deny that he himself existed." [94]

No ideologue of France could have believed more passionately than he in the divine truth of the phrases of the Declaration of Independence. Freedom and equality of rights were natural rights to him—as real as Plato's ideas, to Plato. Expediency, the test of experience, the practical application of ideas,—could never stand against the glowing principles of the Declaration. Nothing in the Constitution could be declared inimical to human rights.

George W. Julian of Indianapolis, an old and valiant abolitionist, held the same ardent belief. In a speech in the House in January, 1866, on suffrage in the District of Columbia, he demanded the ballot for colored men of the District, "on the broad ground of absolute right." To the objection that natural rights were those of a state of nature, he replied that there was no state of nature; that he meant natural social rights; and that he did not care what the rights were called, but he was certain they were natural. Without the ballot, no man was really free. This view of the suffrage as a natural right he said rather naively, "greatly simplifies the whole subject." [95]

In the same vein he asked, in June of the same year, if we still doubted the truths of the Declaration, "thus named self-evident, after having seen them written down in fire and blood, during the past four years?" If all men are equal, he said, "in their inborn rights, every man has the right to a voice in the governing power; and that right is as natural as the right to the breath of his nostrils. It is not a privilege, but a *right;* and you insult republicanism and brand the great Declaration as a lie, when you dispute it." [96]

The belief in natural rights, therefore—given power by the great emotions of the anti-slavery struggle and the war—was, with him, as with Sumner, the prime moving force. But even Julian added that practical considerations called, too, for the gift of the suffrage. He dwelt on Southern action against the rights of the negro. If the negroes were given their rights, he argued, "a stake in society, an equal chance with the white man in the battle of life, instead of becoming an element of weakness and a source of danger, they

[94] Hoar, *Autobiography,* Vol. II, p. 178.
[95] *Congressional Globe,* Jan. 16, 1866, pp. 255–56.
[96] *Ibid.,* June 16, 1866, p. 3209.

will be found our allies and friends, and thus lend unity and strength to the Government. If we shall continue to disfranchise and degrade them, we shall make them aliens, domestic foes in our midst, a perpetual source of danger and discord, from which we shall suffer quite as much as the party thus wronged by our cruel folly." [97] Both whites and blacks should have the ballot, "because they are men and citizens, and require it for their protection." Universal suffrage, he believed, was one "of the surest means of securing a higher level of intelligence for the whole people." If you wish to teach a man to swim, "you must first put him in the water." [98]

The burden of his argument was that an excluded class is a dangerous class,—surely a statesmanlike belief, which sixty-six years of bitter experience has amply substantiated.

Senator Henderson, of Missouri, never wavered in his conviction that suffrage must be granted the negro. He was willing that the negro be excluded by educational tests, but not on the ground of race. He would "as soon think of giving treasure to the idiot" as the "ballot to an uneducated negro." But if exclusion were made by an educational test, whites would be excluded as well as blacks; and the excluded classes, "combining in the course of a few years, will compel the suffrage to be extended to whites and blacks alike." The ballot could not be denied. "You can not," he predicted, "get along without it." [99]

So likewise Garfield, in speaking on the Fourteenth Amendment, regretted that it did not provide for negro suffrage. He believed that "the right to vote, if it be not indeed one of the natural rights of all men, is so necessary to the protection of their natural rights as to be indispensable, and therefore equal to natural rights." He felt that the "golden sentence of John Stuart Mill, in one of his greatest works, ought to be written on the Constitution of every State, and on the Constitution of the United States, as the greatest and most precious of truth, 'That the ballot is put into the hand of men, not so much to enable them to govern others—as that he (sic.) may not be misgoverned by others." Suffrage, he continued, "is the shield, the sword, the spear, and all the panoply that best

[97] *Ibid.*, Jan. 16, 1866, p. 256.   [98] *Ibid.*, Jan. 16, 1866, p. 257–58.
[99] *Ibid.*, March 9, 1866, p. 1283. His inconsistency is manifest. He would as soon give the ballot to the negro as treasure to the idiot, but evidently rejoiced that the ballot could be denied neither to the uneducated negro nor to the uneducated white.

befits a man for his own defense in the great social organism to which he belongs. And I profoundly regret that we have not been enabled to write it and engrave it upon our institutions, and imbed it in the imperishable bulwarks of the Constitution as a part of the fundamental law of the land." [100]

It is easy for us now to take a detached view, and calmly insist that all politics must be based on the test of results, on the empirical consequences of laws. But when, for a score of years, a man has put all of his energy and purpose into a conflict with a very real and terrible evil, which had caused great misery, had denied liberty and progress to millions of men and women, kept our government in turmoil ever since 1820, and all but destroyed our national unity, it is natural that he should assert his beliefs in terms of absolute right and wrong. As has been often said, always in great emotional conflicts, it is natural for men to revert to those great expressions of human aspiration, which in ages past in similar conflicts have comforted the minds of men.

But Sumner and Julian and the so-called humanitarians were in 1865, indeed even in 1866, still in a distinct minority. But events moved swiftly to bring their wishes to pass. Partly it was the old story of the power of a few men of ability, who believe intensely in their cause and are willing to fight for their beliefs, to overcome a mass which is indifferent. Partly it was the force of more or less extraneous events which aided them.

It is probable that if the South had ratified the Fourteenth Amendment, negro suffrage would not have been granted by the Federal Constitution at that time. But in the fall of 1866, the Southern States uniformly rejected it. Congress met that fall in a temper which gave the radicals their chance. There is no need here to detail the bitter and sad history of the reconstruction legislation. I think that the verdict of Rhodes is just, that the program of the majority up to the end of 1866 was reasonable and statesmanlike. It included the adoption of the Congressional program, with the added requirement that the Southern States adopt the Thirteenth and Fourteenth Amendments. It involved no confiscation; no death penalties. The Thirteenth Amendment was the minimum that could be expected of victory. Though the penalty of Section three of the Fourteenth Amendment—that no person who had taken the oath as

[100] *Congressional Globe,* May 8, 1866, p. 2462.

a member of Congress, or of a legislature, or of any State or Federal office, to support the Constitution of the United States, and had taken part in the rebellion, should be admitted to the House or Senate, but providing that Congress by a two-thirds vote of each House could remove the disability, was a grievous mistake, it was not harsh, in view of the history of rebellions. The disability was actually removed in 1872. No one can say that the provision of Section two of the Fourteenth Amendment—to reduce representation if voters were disqualified except for crime or participation in rebellion, was any mere bitter reprisal. To base representation on the population represented by voters, was consistent with principles of representative government. This still remains true, although the provision has never been executed.

Kendrick, however, in his "The Journal of the Joint Committee of Fifteen on Reconstruction," makes a strong case for the Southern States. He claims, in the first place, that there was no offer to the Southern States that if they ratified the Thirteenth and Fourteenth Amendments, they would be admitted to representation. The Committee recommended such an offer, but Congress did not make it. And he believes that it was too much to ask the South to adopt the Fourteenth Amendment. To ask them to disqualify their own leaders, was to ask them to stultify themselves. As to Section two, providing for reduced representation if the negro were disqualified, he answers that the South believed that representation should be according to population; and that it "seems hardly *generous* to have asked the Southern people to act the lie by ratifying the Fourteenth Amendment, and virtually saying that they believed in the principle of Section two, when as a matter of fact, they could, not have done so, since that section was meant to reduce their power in the National Government by thirty or forty per cent." [101]

Reasonable as the Fourteenth Amendment was in the light of all the circumstances, perhaps it is too much to ask of human nature for the South to accept it. At any rate, the South rejected it, and from that day, reprisal was the dominant note.

The fiercely punitive Reconstruction legislation was put through. It provided that the ten unreconstructed Southern States should be divided into five military districts, to be governed by Northern

[101] Kendrick, *The Journal of the Joint Committee of Fifteen on Reconstruction,* pp. 348-49.

troops until such time as the people should organize governments under the Congressional plan, and adopt constitutions ratifying the Thirteenth and Fourteenth Amendments and providing for unqualified male suffrage. The Northern senators were met by the objection that the Northern States themselves did not grant the suffrage. The Republican national platform of 1868 approved the Reconstruction act, but opposed national negro suffrage.

But events moved with great swiftness. Senator Henderson of Missouri, who was the prime mover in the struggle for negro suffrage, declared in the Senate in 1866 when his amendment to the Fourteenth Amendment, providing for negro suffrage, was defeated, "Let them vote it down. It will not be five years from to-day before this body will vote for it. You can not get along without it." [102] He was correct. Men came to feel more and more strongly the inconsistency of forcing negro suffrage on the South, while the North was left free to act on its own motion. And again, the same feeling which prompted the Fourteenth Amendment operated to force the Fifteenth, namely, that the rights of the negro should not be protected by mere statutes, subject to repeal by any Congress. So the movement for the Fifteenth Amendment gathered power swiftly.

Stevens, who in 1866 had expressed indifference on the question, said in 1867 as to negro suffrage, "In the first place, it is just. Have not loyal blacks quite as good a right to choose rulers and make laws as rebel whites? In the second place, it is a necessity in order to protect the loyal white men in the seceded States. . . . Another good reason is, it would ensure the ascendancy of the Union party." Otherwise, he said, "you will be the perpetual vassals of the free trade, irritated, revengeful South." [103]

The question came before Congress in January, 1869, and was soon disposed of.[104] In the House, Boutwell of Massachusetts presented at the same time a bill enfranchising the negro for Federal elections, and a resolution for the Fifteenth Amendment. He said that under the Fourteenth Amendment, under the guaranty clause,

[102] *Congressional Globe*, March 29, 1866, p. 1283.
[103] Fleming. *Documentary History of Reconstruction*, Vol. I, p. 150.
[104] The Fifteenth Amendment as adopted, reads as follows:

"Section 1. The right of citizens of the United States to vote shall not be denied or abridged by the United States or by any State on account of race, color, or previous condition of servitude.
"Section 2. The Congress shall have power to enforce this article by appropriate legislation."

under the power to determine the election of its own members, Congress had power to grant the ballot to whomever it chose for Federal elections.[105] The bill provided that no State should deprive any person of the right to vote for President, Vice President, Representative in Congress or the State legislature, on account of race, color, or previous condition of servitude.

But in addition, he wanted a constitutional amendment for negro suffrage, because it would secure "the people against any abridgment of their electoral power, either by the United States or by the States." Only a constitutional amendment would give power to prevent discrimination in local elections, and a constitutional amendment would protect against changes in political majorities. And he wanted the negroes enfranchised first, so that they could be counted on the very question of the ratification of the amendment.[106]

Senator Wilson, of Massachusetts, as always, well represented the opinion of his State. He admitted that negro suffrage was unpopular. He said that the program of the Republican Party had cost it a quarter of a million votes. There was not a square mile in the United States, he said, "where the advocacy of equal rights and privileges of those colored men has not been in the past, and is not now, unpopular. Yes, sir, the cause of the poor, wronged, oppressed negroes has been, now is, and for some years will continue to be, an unpopular cause." But, he went on that no matter how unpopular the cause was, it was their duty to struggle on, "until we make the humblest citizen of the United States, the peer and the equal in rights and privileges of every other citizen of the United States. . . . Let us give to all citizens equal rights, and then protect everybody in the United States in the exercise of those rights." Then, he said, we "shall have carried out logically the ideals that lie at the foundation of our institutions. . . ."[107]

Sumner had opposed the Fourteenth Amendment because he in-

---

[105] This was too broad a statement. The Federal government had, indeed, always had the power to punish fraud and violence at elections at which Congressmen were elected, *Ex parte Siebold,* 100 U.S. 371 (1879), and *Ex parte Yarbrough,* 110 U.S. 651 (1883), holding that under Art. 1, Sec. 4(1), and under the inherent power of the national government, Congress could punish fraud and violence at elections for Congressmen. But the States still fixed the qualifications of voters at such elections; Art. 1, Sec. 2. But this power was now subject to the Fourteenth Amendment. As we shall see (*infra,* p. 46), discrimination on account of race in the right to vote, could be prevented under the Fourteenth Amendment. The Fifteenth Amendment was not necessary for that purpose.

[106] *Congressional Globe,* Jan. 23, 1868, pp. 560–61.   [107] *Ibid.,* p. 672.

sisted that it was not necessary. The Federal government had power under the Thirteenth Amendment, under the guaranty clause, on the basis of natural rights to grant the suffrage and to ensure equal rights. So, likewise, he now opposed the Fifteenth Amendment for the same reasons and almost by the same argument. He repeated, as he did again and again, "No learning in books, no skill acquired in courts, no sharpness of forensic dialectics, no cunning in splitting hairs," could impair that constitutional principle. "Whatever you enact for Human Rights is Constitutional," he exclaimed. The State is local in its character, not universal. Whatever was local belonged to the State; whatever was universal in its scope, belonged to the Nation. There could be no State Rights against Human Rights.[108]

Concluding our survey of this debate, we may note that Davis, of Kentucky, admitted that the people, and not the States, were sovereign. The people had delegated some powers to the National government and some to the States. But suffrage belonged, by its nature, to the States, and it would be revolutionary to take it away.[109] So likewise, Hendricks, of Indiana, granted that the States are not sovereign in the sense that they "have control of every subject"; but he insisted that they were sovereign within the sphere of their jurisdiction or reserved powers, and the general government in its sphere, and that suffrage control was essential to the independence of the States,—"essential to the very nature of the Government itself." He did not believe that the two races "can mingle successfully in the management of government. I believe that it will bring strife and trouble to the country."[110]

So the amendment passed. What, then, were the influences that brought it about? Blaine, in an article in the North American Review in March, 1880, declared that the Fourteenth Amendment was wholly caused by the anti-negro legislation of the Southern states. "It is impossible," he said, "to quote all the hideous provisions of these statutes, under whose operation the negro would have relapsed gradually and surely into actual and admitted slavery." The Fourteenth Amendment was the inevitable result. The Southern States could have been readily admitted to all their powers and privileges in the Union by accepting the Fourteenth

[108] Sumner, *Works*, Feb. 5, 1869, Vol. XIII, pp. 38–39.
[109] *Congressional Globe*, Feb. 8, 1869, pp. 994–95. [110] *Ibid.*, pp. 988–89.

Amendment, and negro suffrage would not have been forced on them. "The gradual and conservative method of training the negroes for franchise, as suggested and approved by Governor Hampton, had many advocates among Republicans in the North; and though, in my judgment, it would have proved delusive and impracticable, it was quite within the power of the South to secure its adoption or at least its trial." [111]

The rejection of the Fourteenth Amendment, he asserted, was "the origin of negro suffrage." The Southern whites "knowingly and wilfully brought it upon themselves." [112] In his "Twenty Years in Congress," he admitted that, "The truth was that the Republicans of the North, constituting, as was shown by the elections of 1865, a majority in every State, were deeply concerned as to the fate and fortune of the colored population of the South. Only a minority of Republicans were ready to demand suffrage for those who had been recently emancipated, and who, from the ignorance peculiar to servitude, were presumably unfit to be intrusted with the elective franchise." [113]

But the rejection of the Fourteenth Amendment probably only hastened the process, for it is evident that a mixture of motives were at work and all were potent. There was the belief in natural rights which animated Sumner and Julian, Wilson and Garfield. There was the great humanitarian sentiment—the desire to protect the negro. The belief that the ballot was an educator and a protector—that an excluded class was a dangerous class—was widely held. The Republican leaders would not forego the opportunity of forcing negro suffrage on the South, while some Northern States still restricted suffrage to the whites; and this inconsistency was finally too much even for the masterful authors of the policy of Thorough to defend. Lastly, there was the desire to maintain political power through the negro vote, which even Sumner admitted was predominant with him.

There is a modern school which would explain negro suffrage by the materialistic motive alone. The creed is that, where several motives operate, one of which is materialistic, the materialistic one alone is important. But history is not so simple. No psychologist, even at the time of events, can safely allocate the proportions of

---

[111] James G. Blaine, *Political Discussions*, pp. 292–23.   [112] *Ibid.*, p. 294.
[113] James G. Blaine, *Twenty Years of Congress*, Vol. II, p. 92.

the strength of different emotions which bring about an ultimate result. No one can possibly do so later. We can only take the reasons which were actually given. On this basis there was a mixture of motives: the selfish or desire for power, the ideological, the humanitarian, and the feeling that the ballot was an educator and a protection to the negro. No one can read the quotations I have given from the speeches of Sumner, without realizing the depth of his passion for equal rights. It is mere modern cynicism to doubt it. The materialistic motive alone, is far too simple an explanation. Men's motives are mixed: they advocate policies because they think they are right; because they think they will benefit by them; because they think the public will benefit; because they are essential to their own protection; because they merely want them. No one can safely say which motive controls. They all contribute to the final result.

The triumph of negro suffrage was, after all, a triumph for the few who believed in it passionately, and prevailed over the majority which was either indifferent, or less determined or frankly hostile. History, after all, is made by those who believe hard enough to fight for their beliefs.

What, then, shall we say of the wisdom of granting negro suffrage, and of adopting the Fifteenth Amendment in 1870? These acts have been severely criticized. We are told that the advocates of negro suffrage had no clear understanding of the ignorance of the negro race, its backwardness, and of the desirability of making the suffrage a reward of merit, rather than a grant of right. The whole history of the grandfather clauses, it is argued, the generation, and more suppression of negro suffrage in the South, the results of negro suffrage in the cities of the North, prove the folly of the Fifteenth Amendment. The negro has not yet attained the suffrage. The Fifteenth Amendment is a dead letter in the South. When the States are ready to permit the exercise of the suffrage, they will do so, as the Northern States have long since done and as the States of the South are beginning to do. The attempt to make suffrage national has been, we are told, a terrible failure: suffrage is a State problem, and should be left to the States.

But it is necessary to keep two questions separate: one is the granting of suffrage to the negro; the other is the Fifteenth Amendment.

The confident predictions of Sumner have not been verified. The grant of the ballot did not make the master respect the negro. It did not reconcile, nor bring peace. Sumner never seemed to have considered the possibility that the master would not let the negro vote. He never considered that the law would not operate as intended. The warping effects of the forces of a democracy were not in his contemplation. The legal structure was all he saw.

An excluded class is a dangerous class, but likewise an included class of four million people—ignorant, unused to political action—is a dangerous class. A class excluded temporarily until it arrives at a minimum of qualifications, is not a dangerous class.

It would, of course, have been far better if, as Blaine said was at first hoped, the negro had been required to wait until he could have fitted himself for his new duties. A flat waiting period of ten years before any negroes exercised the suffrage could, and should, have been required. Then educational tests could have been adopted, and both illiterate whites and negroes forced to wait still longer until they could qualify. But an educational test would have had to be equal for all races and classes. It would have involved a loss of representation in the States that had considerable numbers of illiterates. Something of the same result could have been achieved without an educational test by providing ballots without party insignia, under the Massachusetts system. But the North was unwilling to apply an educational test or the Massachusetts ballot either to the negro or to the illiterate immigrant, and the South to the "poor white." Educational tests run against all the selfish interests of practical politics and the stubborn belief in natural rights.

But the argument on the wisdom of adopting the Fifteenth Amendment is altogether different. Once the Fourteenth Amendment was adopted, the question was settled: the Fifteenth Amendment really added nothing to it. The Fourteenth Amendment stated a great national ideal—that all men should be equal before the law. It placed in the Constitution the great ideal of Magna Charta —that all should be entitled to a day in court, and added the requirement of the equal protection of the laws. Once that was adopted, no negro could be legally denied the suffrage on account of his race or color. In a case in 1927, Holmes bluntly said, in considering a statute barring negroes from all Democratic primaries in Texas, that "we find it unnecessary to consider the Fifteenth Amendment, because it seems to us hard to imagine a more direct and obvious infringement of the Fourteenth." [114]

Even in the South, it is difficult to say that the amendment has not, in a real measure, brought results. The negro generally has not voted, but the Southern States have adopted methods of restriction which could not be permanent. The grandfather clauses have been held void. The very fact that unlawful methods have been used, has aroused the more intelligent elements of the South to opposition, and has resulted not only in progress for the negro, but for the illiterate whites. Now the negro has begun to vote in small numbers, and in a few places where party lines are close, his vote is being sought after precisely as it long has been in certain cities of the North.

REFERENCES

BLAINE, JAMES G., *Political Discussions: 1856–1886*. Norwich, Conn.: Henry Bill Pub. Co., 1887.

————*Twenty Years of Congress* (2 vols.). Norwich, Conn.: Henry Bill Pub. Co., 1884–86.

BOUTWELL, GEORGE S., *Reminiscences of Sixty Years in Public Affairs*. New York: McClure, Phillips & Co., 1902.

BRADFORD, GAMALIEL, *Union Portraits*. Chapter on Charles Sumner. Boston: Houghton Mifflin Co., 1916.

COLLINS, CHARLES WALLACE, *The Fourteenth Amendment and the States*. Boston: Little, Brown & Co., 1912.

DUNNING, WILLIAM A., *Essays on the Civil War and Reconstruction*. New York: The Macmillan Co., 1898.

FESSENDEN, FRANCIS, *Life and Public Services of William Pitt Fessenden* (2 vols.). Boston: Houghton Mifflin Co., 1907.

FLACK, HORACE E., *The Adoption of the Fourteenth Amendment*. Baltimore: John Hopkins Press, 1908.

FLEMING, WALTER L., *Documentary History of Reconstruction* (2 vols.). Cleveland: Arthur H. Clarke Co., 1906.

GUTHRIE, WILLIAM D., *Lectures on the Fourteenth Article of Amendment to the Constitution of the United States*. Boston: Little, Brown & Co., 1898.

HOAR, GEORGE F., *Autobiography of Seventy Years* (2 vols.). New York: Charles Scribner's Sons, 1903.

KENDRICK, BENJAMIN B., *The Journal of the Joint Committee of Fifteen on Reconstruction*. New York: Columbia University, Longmans, Green & Co., agents 1914.

LOWELL, JAMES RUSSELL, *Political Essays*. Boston: Houghton Mifflin Co., 1913.

[114] *Nixon* vs. *Herndon*, 273 U.S. 536, 540 (1927).

OGDEN, ROLLO, *Life and Letters of Edwin Lawrence Godkin* (2 vols.). New York: The Macmillan Co., 1907.

OWEN, ROBERT DALE, "Political Results from the Varioloid." *Atlantic Monthly*, Vol. XXXV, p. 660 (June, 1875).

PIERCE, EDWARD L., *Memoirs and Letters of Charles Sumner*, Vol. IV. Boston: Roberts Bros., 1893.

SUMNER, CHARLES, *Works*, Vols. VIII, X. Boston: Lee & Shepard, 1873–1883.

WHITE, HORACE, *The Life of Lyman Trumbull*. Boston: Houghton Mifflin Co., 1913.

WOODBURN, JAMES ALBERT, *The Life of Thaddeus Stevens*. Indianapolis: Bobbs-Merrill Co., 1913.

CHAPTER II

THE POWER OF THE COURTS OVER LEGISLATION

THE Thirteenth, Fourteenth and Fifteenth Amendments may be truly described as revolutionary. They resulted from and they induced an entirely different concept of the nation, of the nature of the Federal government, of the control of the Federal government over the States, of the control of the courts over legislation, of the protection of the individual by the national government, than had existed before. There had been control by the Federal courts before, through the commerce clause and the prohibition of the impairment of contracts, but the increase now was such as to be in effect a new power. Now, we had the Thirteenth Amendment, prohibiting slavery by national act; we had the Fifteenth Amendment, declaring that the right to vote should not be denied on account of race, color, or previous condition of servitude; and, above all, we had the Fourteenth Amendment, forbidding any State to abridge the privileges and immunities of citizens of the United States, or to take life, liberty, or property without due process of law, or deny the equal protection of the laws.

By the end of the period, we were to see the courts holding unconstitutional statutes regulating labor and business conditions, fixing rates, levying taxes, because they held that these new burdens took property without due process of law.

It is one of the anomalies of history that our whole conception of political action, and the trend of our political thinking, have been changed by an amendment largely caused by the vagrancy legislation of the South. As a result of the extension of Federal power over the States, and of the power of the courts over all legislation, through the operation of the Fourteenth Amendment, there has been a necessary limit to the very consideration of proposals for political action. And, perforce, the arguments of the courts in cases on the Fourteenth Amendment are, as I shall show, political arguments based on political theories. The arguments of counsel before the Supreme Court, the decisions on questions of due process, have become political arguments on the philosophy of government and the limits of political action. The theory of our political science, for a generation, has been argued out before the Supreme Court.

This development of the fifty years following the Civil War is still going on. It would seem to be an opportune time to consider that development, now that we have finished the consideration of the war amendments themselves.

Development of the Thirteenth and Fifteenth Amendments

The Thirteenth and the Fifteenth Amendments, broadly speaking, resulted not in a greater but in a lesser degree of Federal control over the States, and of court control over legislation, than was anticipated when they were adopted. They decreed that henceforth freedom was nationally protected. They decreed, moreover, that the courts would hold void any State act which created a condition of slavery, or interfered with the right to vote on account of race or previous condition of servitude. But those two extensions had been contemplated surely with fair prevision when they were adopted. They were first tested under the Civil Rights acts.

The Civil Rights Acts

The Civil Rights Act of 1866 we have already noted. It declared that all persons, without regard to race or color or previous condition of servitude, should have the same right to make contracts, sue and be sued, inherit property, and be entitled to the same protections of persons and property as were enjoyed by white persons. It made the violation of the act a Federal offense.

The Civil Rights Act of 1870 became law on May 31, 1870,—only two months after the Fifteenth Amendment had been proclaimed fully adopted. It declared that all should be entitled to vote at all elections, without distinction of race; provided for the punishment of any person who should deny equal rights to all to become qualified for voting; that, if any person should apply to vote who had been wrongfully refused the right to become qualified, he should be entitled to vote, and that the election officer who should refuse his vote should be guilty of an offense; and, lastly, for the punishment of anyone who, by force or bribery, prevented anyone from voting. This applied to all elections,—city, State, and Federal. It was an attempt to subject all elections to Federal control.

Section Six struck at the Kuklux Klan which, in secret hooded bands, rode the roads and terrorized negroes, and prevented them from voting. Section Six made it an offense for two or more persons to go in disguise on the highways or on the premises of another, to violate any provision of the act, or to oppress or intimidate any person with intent to prevent him from exercising any right granted by the Constitution or the laws of the United States. It applied to acts of any individual hindering anyone voting at all elections.

Then the Kuklux act of 1871 was passed. It was similar, in general, to the provisions of Section Six of the Act of 1870.

Finally, came the Civil Rights Act of 1875, which embodied Sumner's ideas but which was passed after his death. It declared that all persons, without regard to race or color, should have the same rights in inns, theaters, and public conveyances.

Here was a great code of Federal law, extending to voting at all elections, to interference with the ordinary rights of individuals, to freedom from assault and molestation, and to the enjoyment of equal privileges in inns, theaters, and public conveyances.

These acts were advocated on the broadest grounds of national power. Sumner, in favoring the Kuklux bill of 1871, declared, "The evidence is cumulative. Ruffians in paint and in disguise seize the innocent, insult them, rob them, murder them. Communities are kept under the terrible shadow." He demanded action—and action by the Nation—to suppress the Kuklux.[1]

"What makes us a Nation?" he asked. The national life, he answered, "is found in the principle of Unity, and in the Equal Rights of all our people,—all of which, being national in character, are necessarily placed under the great safeguard of the Nation. Let the National Unity be assailed, and the Nation will spring to its defense. Let the humblest citizen in the remotest village be assailed in the enjoyment of Equal Rights, and the Nation must do for that humblest citizen what it would do for itself." He declared that, "Equality implies universality; and what is universal must be na-

[1] Sumner, *Works*, Vol. XIV, p. 277 (April 13, 1871).

tional. If each State is left to determine the protection of Equal Rights, then will protection vary according to the State, and Equal Rights will prevail only according to the accident of local law. There will be as many equalities as States. Therefore in obedience to reason, as well as solemn mandate, is this power in the Nation." [2]

He said that he was not "deterred from this conclusion by any cry of Centralism, or it may be Imperialism." He declared that no "interference of any kind with matters local in character," was proposed. "The Nation will not enter the State, except for the safeguard of rights national in character; and then only as the sunshine, with beneficent power, and like the sunshine, for the equal good of all. . . . Give me," he cried, "the Centralism of Liberty. Give me the Imperialism of Equal Rights." [3]

Equal Rights was Sumner's God. Equal Rights were essential to freedom. The Thirteenth Amendment alone was enough to sustain any law granting equal rights. Indeed, as we have seen from his argument on the Thirteenth Amendment, he believed equal rights could be obtained without any further amendment.

He argued in a similar vein for the bill which, after his death, became the Civil Rights Act of 1875. It granted equal rights in inns, theaters, and public conveyances.

"Ceasing to be a slave," he said, the negro "became a man whose foremost right is Equality of Rights." All of the rights granted by the bill were rights, he declared, without which a free man could not exist. [4] "Equality of Rights is not only the first of rights: it is an axiom of political truth. But an axiom, whether of science or philosophy, is universal, and without exception or limitation; and this is according to the very law of its nature." [5] The belief in natural rights and an a priori, mathematically determined politics, could hardly be more strongly stated.

He declared that the war had been fought for equality of rights, and then proceeded to take up in turn, hotels, schools, public conveyances, and theaters, in each of which, on pain of Federal punishment, the negro was to be granted equal rights. Without them, he could not be free.

All of these acts were attacked as unconstitutional by some of the ablest lawyers in Congress. They held that the Thirteenth

[2] *Ibid.*, Vol. XIV, p. 279.   [3] *Ibid.*, Vol. XIV, p. 280.
[4] *Ibid.*, Vol. XIV, p. 370 (Jan. 15, 1872).   [5] *Ibid.*, p. 375.

Amendment gave no power of Federal legislation, save on the one subject of slavery; and that slavery was not involved in the denial of equal rights. The Fourteenth and Fifteenth Amendments, they said, gave no power to act against individuals but only against States, to correct unequal State laws.

Thurman of Ohio, a rugged and high-minded Senator, said that the Civil Rights bill of 1870 sought to protect the right to vote against all interference by individuals. But the Fifteenth Amendment, he answered, gave no power to Congress to punish a breach of local law by an individual nor a combination of individuals. Its prohibitions were directed solely against States.[6] Likewise, in opposing the Civil Rights bill of 1871,—the Kuklux Klan bill,—he said that the Fourteenth Amendment provided that "the State shall not deny the equal protection of the laws; but that does not give you the right to punish three or more men who shall combine together to make a riot, or three men who shall combine together to whip another." The Federal government could not punish men for violating a law of a State.[7]

Senator T. F. Bayard, of Delaware, argued in much the same vein. The Act of 1871, he objected, would "completely destroy all police powers of the States themselves. An assault and battery, a riot, an invasion of any right, any privilege, any immunity, is now sought to be punished by Act of Congress.[8] What then is left to the State?"

Again, when the Civil Rights bill of 1875 was before Congress, Senator Bayard asserted that granting equal rights in inns, public conveyances, and theaters had nothing to do with life, liberty, or property. If the United States government had power to enter a State, and take "control of the vast domain of rights under the State regulation which a citizen acquires by virtue of the State laws which are regulated by the State, which are conferred by the State . . . and the State alone,—if the United States can assume guardianship of all those, then the State laws and the State governments are absolutely worse than useless. . . ."

He cited the Slaughter House and Bartemeyer vs. Iowa cases, already decided, and said—quite in the line of the later decisions—that the Fourteenth Amendment protected only against action by

[6] *Congressional Globe*, May 20, 1870, p. 3661.
[7] *Ibid.*, April 13, 1871, p. 218. App. Vol. CI.
[8] *Ibid.*, April 12, 1871, p. 243. App. Vol. CI.

the States, and gave no power to control individual action. He quoted the first words of the statute, which referred to "the great fundamental principles" of equal rights; and remarked that "then we find such a terrible fall from so great a height of argument to daily hotel life, to every-day carriage in railways, to visits to theaters and concert halls, and these are gravely and sonorously proclaimed 'fundamental principles,' and full and equal enjoyment is enjoined." [9]

THE DEVELOPMENT OF THE THIRTEENTH AMENDMENT

The Thirteenth Amendment was first tested. The Act of 1866, giving equal rights to sue and be sued, testify, make contracts, buy and sell property, came before a Federal Circuit Court in 1878. The decision was given by Justice Swayne, then a Justice of the Supreme Court. He held that the act was constitutional under the Thirteenth Amendment. He argued that the mere abolition of slavery without more, would have been "a phantom of delusion . . . Blot out this act," he went on, "and deny the constitutional power to pass it, and the worst effects of slavery might speedily follow." [10]

This case did not go to the United States Supreme Court. But it has been quoted with approval in a number of decisions by the Supreme Court. In the Civil Rights Cases argued in 1883, involving the Civil Rights Act of 1875, which forbade anyone to deny equal rights in inns, public conveyances, and theaters on account of race, Bradley distinguished the Civil Rights act of 1866 from that of 1875 by declaring that, so far as the Thirteenth Amendment was concerned, there was no badge of servitude in the denial of an equal place in inns, theaters or public conveyances; while there was a badge of servitude in denial of the right to sue and to testify. [11] We shall see later how he distinguished the two acts, so far as the Fourteenth Amendment was concerned.

Harlan, it is true, dissented vigorously. He said that the right to enter an inn or a public conveyance was a right essential to freedom. But he did not prevail. It was settled that the prohibition of slavery did not cover such acts as the denial of privileges

---

[9] *Congressional Record,* Feb. 26, 1875, App., pp. 103–04.
[10] *U.S.* vs. *Rhodes,* 27 Fed. Cases No. 16151 p. 785; 1 Abbott, U.S. 28. (1866.)
[11] 109 U.S. 3 (1883).

enjoyed by the white race. Slavery meant more than the denial of the ordinary enjoyments of life. While the Thirteenth Amendment bore directly on individuals,—while, that is, the Federal Government could directly punish individuals for acts denying freedom,— it meant the prohibition of acts which directly denied the liberty of action of the individual.

In the famous Slaughter House cases, the Supreme Court held that, by prohibiting slavery, the Amendment meant personal slavery, applicable only to human beings; and that a perpetual grant by a city of a slaughter house privilege, did not create a servitude.[12]

So, likewise, it held that it was too clear for argument that a statute which required railroads to provide separate accommodations for whites and negroes, did not create a condition of slavery, and did not violate the Thirteenth Amendment. A statute, it said, which implies merely a legal distinction between the two races,— a distinction founded on color,—had no tendency to "destroy the legal equality of the two races, or re-establish a state of involuntary servitude." [13]

The Court has sustained legislation forbidding peonage. The law involved was direct legislation,—a Federal law forbidding peonage, —not legislation merely correcting discriminatory legislation by the States. The Court said that there was little doubt that the attempt to bring two negroes from Florida to Georgia, on a warrant for larceny, was merely "an excuse for securing the custody" of the two negroes, "and taking them back to Georgia to work out a debt." It was not open to doubt, it said, that Congress could "enforce the Thirteenth Amendment by direct legislation, punishing the holding of a person in slavery or in involuntary servitude, except as a punishment for crime." [14]

In a later case, it reversed the conviction of a negro in Alabama, who had contracted to work for one year at $12.00 per month, and had received $15.00 in advance. After working for a few days, he refused to work further. The statute punished anyone who made a contract to work, obtained money from his employer, and refused to do the work or return the money. The sentence was that the negro pay the fine of $30.00; or, in default thereof, per-

---

[12] 16 Wallace, 36 (1873).   [13] *Plessy* vs. *Ferguson,* 163 U.S. 537, 543 (1896).
[14] *Clyatt* vs. *U.S.,* 197 U.S. 207, 218, 222 (1905).

form labor for his employer for thirty days in lieu of the fine, and one hundred and sixteen days on account of the costs.

Hughes, writing the opinion, said that the Alabama law was void under the Thirteenth Amendment, and under a Federal statute which declared that any State law which imposed an involuntary servitude was void. "The State," he said, "may impose involuntary servitude as a punishment for crime; but it may not compel one man to work for another in payment of a debt by punishing him as a criminal, if he does not perform the service or pay the debt." The employer could not directly force the employee to perform the service, and he could not do so indirectly, by punishing him if he did not do the service.[15]

Holmes and Lurton dissented. Holmes argued that, in the first place, the Thirteenth Amendment did not prohibit contracts of labor, and that punishment for breaking a contract was not peonage. But the case was narrower than that, for the Alabama law made the breach of the contract prima facie evidence of an intent to obtain money under false pretenses, and he said that fraud could certainly be punished by imprisonment.

But the Court refused to declare that peonage was involved in a mere breach of personal rights. In one case it appeared that certain men had threatened negroes and forced them to quit work, which they were under contract to do. The Court said that interference with the right of a person to work, did not reduce him to slavery. A freeman had a right to be "protected in his person from an assault and battery. He is entitled to hold his property safe from trespass or appropriation, but no mere personal assault or trespass or appropriation operates to reduce the individual to a condition of slavery."[16]

Although, then, the amendment (as the Court has distinctly admitted) gives power to Congress to legislate directly to prevent slavery, the Court has limited the amendment to the prevention of slavery itself. It has allowed imprisonment for crime. It has allowed the enforcement of the discipline of the army and navy, and of the merchant marine. It has upheld the punishment of peonage by the Federal government. In dictum, it has said that to deprive a negro of the right to sue in the courts and to enforce contracts

[15] *Bailey* vs. *Alabama*, 219 U.S. 219, 244 (1911).
[16] *Hodges* vs. *U.S.*, 203 U.S. 1, 17 (1906).

was to deprive a man of the essentials of freedom, but it has refused to agree that equal rights in inns and railroad cars are an incident of freedom; and later it upheld a statute requiring separation of facilities,—in common parlance, Jim Crow cars,—provided the facilities were equal.

Whether a denial of equal rights to sue and make contracts is a deprivation of freedom, has never been settled. Swayne's opinion that it was, has been cited with approval by the Supreme Court several times on other points. But, of course, it is a denial of the equal protection of the laws under the Fourteenth Amendment.

We have come a long way, then, since the eloquent and moving appeals of Charles Sumner, who argued that, to make the negro truly free, he must have equal rights in inns, theaters, places of amusement, and public conveyances; and that the Federal government should take over the whole field of the protection of the negro. We have come to believe that separation of the races is not incompatible with freedom; that, in fact, it is essential to the maintenance of peace between the races. A generation has grown up which fully acknowledges the deep and inherent differences in race, which is ready to admit the presence of fundamental prejudices, and believes that society must see that justice is done and equal opportunity afforded, but does not believe that common enjoyment of the protection and advantages of society is either desirable or necessary.

THE SCOPE OF THE FIFTEENTH AMENDMENT

Likewise, there have been few cases under the Fifteenth Amendment. The early tendency of the Court was severely to limit the power of Congress over State elections.

First, in U.S. vs. Reese,[17] the Supreme Court held unconstitutional the Act of 1870, giving equal rights to vote at all elections. Waite, the chief justice, had been a Whig and was a Republican, but he was strongly opposed to the nationalistic trend of the past ten years. Two election officials in Kentucky, were indicted for refusing to receive and count the vote of a negro in a municipal election. As this is not a study of constitutional law, but rather of the course of political thought, it is not necessary to go into the reasoning of the decision save as it indicates the political theory of the

[17] 92 U.S. 214 (1875).

Court. It should be noted that the case was decided after the Slaughter House cases, in which the Court held that the rights, privileges, and immunities protected by the Fourteenth Amendment were not the fundamental rights of the citizen protected under State laws. That decision did not necessarily affect the decision in the Reese case, since the Reese case involved the Fifteenth Amendment and not the Fourteenth, and since the right to vote without discrimination because of race was directly granted by the Fifteenth Amendment. But, as Boudin says in his "Government by Judiciary," the narrowness of the Slaughter House decision did pave the way for the narrow construction of the Reese case.[18] The Court was evidently determined to restrict the amendments, and to safeguard the rights of the States as much as possible. Waite said that the right to vote was not a Federal right. The right to vote without discrimination because of race was a Federal right, but the statute tried to punish all interference with the right to vote. The third and fourth sections of the act—the ones on which the indictments were based—did not confine themselves to discriminations on account of race. They extended generally to all unlawful denials of the right to vote. To limit the statute to those who were discriminated against because of race, would be to make a new statute.

Hunt dissented vigorously. He said that sections three and four made it unlawful to prevent anyone from exercising his right to vote "as aforesaid," namely, because of race or color as provided in sections one and two, and therefore it was clear that only racial discriminations were aimed at. It is enough to say that the Court construed the statute narrowly, in the evident desire to restrain the power of the Federal government over local elections. There is little doubt that, under any reasonable construction, the statute aimed only at discrimination on account of race. Certainly it could easily have been so construed, if the Court had desired to give effect to it.

It is true that the Court held that the Fifteenth Amendment was self-executing, and that all laws which prevented a negro as a negro from voting were at once of no force. So it held that a provision in Delaware, prohibiting negroes from voting, at once became void; a negro could vote with the same rights which a white

---

[18] Louis B. Boudin, *Government by Judiciary*, Vol. II, p. 127.

man enjoyed; and accordingly, a negro could not be convicted by a jury from which negroes were excluded because the State Constitution limited jurors to voters.[19]

This protection was of little avail unless a negro could prove that in practice negroes were denied the vote by the connivance of the State; and if the State law were, on its face, equal in terms, the difficulty of proving discrimination in practice was all but insuperable.

In James vs. Bowman,[20] the Court held that a Federal statute forbidding the denial of the right of suffrage at all elections by bribery, was unconstitutional. The Fifteenth Amendment, it declared, prohibited only State action infringing the right to vote, and bribery was the act of individuals. Moreover, bribery did not discriminate against the negro on account of race or color.

Beginning about 1895, the Southern States attempted to avoid the force of the Fifteenth Amendment by enacting the so-called grandfather clauses. Generally speaking, they provided that anyone who was entitled to vote on January 1, 1866, or the descendant of any such person, could vote at all elections; but that all others, namely, negroes (and the same would apply, of course, to immigrants), must prove that they could read and write and explain a section of the Constitution selected for them.

One can easily imagine the discrimination which the grandfather clauses rendered possible. A white man who could not qualify as a descendant of a voter or a voter himself on January 1, 1866, could qualify by explaining that a President must be thirty-five years of age; while a negro could be asked the meaning of an ex post facto law. A son of a veteran in the Civil War could qualify without more ado, but a negro would have to prove that he could read and write and explain a section of the Constitution. The grandfather clauses were purely and simply devices to nullify both the Fourteenth and the Fifteenth Amendments. Yet they continued in effect for two decades.[21]

Several times the Supreme Court refused to pass on the validity of grandfather clauses, on the ground either that the question was political or that no property right was involved. At last, however, in 1915, a grandfather clause was held void. In Guinn vs. United

---

[19] *Neal* vs. *Delaware*, 103 U.S. 370 (1880).   [20] 190 U.S. 127 (1903).

[21] Of course, laws requiring the voter to interpret a clause of the Constitution, which lend themselves to great discrimination, are still in effect.

States,[22] the Court held that the Oklahoma grandfather's clause was void. White said that the Fifteenth Amendment was self-executing; that it operated directly to render void any statute which denied the suffrage on account of race, color, or previous condition of servitude; and that therefore the right of suffrage could be enjoyed by striking out the discrimination against the right. The clause was void, the negro had the right to vote, and anyone who denied him the right to vote could be punished.

But long before this decision was handed down, the Republicans had abandoned the attempt to regulate elections. They concluded that Federal control of elections could not be enforced. Senator Hoar, in his autobiography, notes that for sixteen years, from 1873 to 1889, the Republican Party had never been in control of both houses and the Presidency, and therefore legislative action had been impossible.

In 1889, an attempt (it proved to be the last attempt) was made to pass a Federal elections law. Hoar said that there was general belief among his party that the will of the people had been defeated in large sections of the country. He quoted Senator Tillman as saying, "We took the Government away. We stuffed ballot boxes. . . . With that system—force, tissue ballots, etc.—we got tired ourselves." [23] So he said they called a constitutional convention and adopted the grandfather clauses.

Hoar declared that in 1889 the Republicans wanted to right "this great wrong." A bill was introduced, providing that on application officers appointed by the Federal court should be present and watch the count. In case of dispute, the Federal court should hear the case, and issue a certificate entitling the person named to be placed on

---

[22] 238 U.S. 347 (1915).

In the same year the Court held that an election judge could be punished for refusing to receive a negro's ballot for a member of Congress, because he was not entitled to vote under the State's grandfather clause. The Court considered the old Kuklux section. It said that the old Kuklux section as now written, where it punishes all conspiracies to deny the protection of any law of the United States, and whereby the provision as to going on the highway was put in a subordinate place, was now applicable to punish an election officer who denied a negro the right to vote under a grandfather clause. A State election judge, therefore, could be punished for denying a negro the right to vote under a grandfather clause. *U.S.* vs. *Mosley,* 238 U.S. 383. Also, in the same year, the Court held that a judge was liable in damages for denying a negro the right to vote under a grandfather clause in a municipal election. *Myers* vs. *Anderson,* 238 U.S. 368. It is probable that it would be held that a criminal liability also exists for denial of the right to vote in a State or city election on the ground of race.

[23] George F. Hoar, *Autobiography of Seventy Years,* Vol. II, p. 150.

the Clerk's roll, subject to the action of the House. Hoar stated that much excitement and great criticism of the bill, which was called the Force Bill, ensued. Finally, it was decided to drop the bill. With great reluctance, Hoar came to believe that the legislation could not be permanent, and that it could be maintained only so long as his party remained in power. He sadly recalled that no Southern representative, save Reverdy Johnson, had ever protested against the Southern methods, and concluded that it was a matter of deep regret that the principles of the Declaration of Independence could not be carried out.[24]

The Republican majority was still for the bill, but a powerful minority felt as did Senator Cameron, who did not want to disturb the relations between the North and the South. The bill was sidetracked. In 1894 most of the election provisions in the Civil Rights Act of 1870 were repealed.

Nine years later, Elihu Root stated the general conclusion of the North,—that the experiment of giving the negro the suffrage had failed.[25]

But of course, the Fourteenth and Fifteenth Amendments still remained. While the Federal government might give up the attempt to regulate elections through Federal tribunals, no government could ever afford to say that it would give up the ideal of equal rights at the polls. Moreover, the sections of the Civil Rights Act still remained, which punished any officer of a State, who under color of any State law deprived any person of a right under a law or constitutional provision of the United States. If a negro were denied the right to vote on account of race, he had a remedy in the courts. As a practical matter, the right was of little avail. Congress, of course, always had the right to regulate elections at which Federal officers are nominated or elected. So in 1911, Congress passed a statute providing for the punishment of fraud at such elections. But the remedy was left to the courts,—no Federal officers were entrusted with its enforcement.

The fervent desire of the early post-war period for the enforcement by the Federal government of the right to vote at all elections, has passed completely away. The remedy is limited to a resort to the courts, on proof that the right has been denied on account of

---

[24] *Ibid.*, pp. 150–65.
[25] Quoted in Rhodes, *History of the United States*, Vol. VIII, p. 363, from *Boston Herald* of Feb. 8, 1903.

race. Broadly speaking, the right is denied, or at least not exercised. It is a stigma on our political system that this is so, but we have merely found that the enforcement of such rights depends absolutely on the political desires of the local community: it can not be forced by the central government.

The whole experiment began under the most unfavorable auspices,—under tragic auspices. Instead of returning the governments of the Southern States to their own peoples, they were turned over to negroes, "scalawags," and carpet-baggers, and the Confederate whites were excluded. Instead of making the negroes wait, say for ten years, before assuming the suffrage, they were entrusted with the great responsibility at once and almost alone. The result was such a tragic mess that it has injured the cause of negro suffrage to this day.

Moreover, the negroes have been almost wholly Republican. It was inevitable that the white race would use every means to prevent domination by another race. If the negroes had been split between both parties, the vote would have come much sooner. It is to be hoped that, with time, more and more negroes will vote; that some of them will finally align themselves with the Democratic party, and eventually competition for their votes arise, just as it has arisen in certain cities of the North.

THE DEVELOPMENT OF THE FOURTEENTH AMENDMENT. DUE PROCESS OF LAW, AND EQUAL LAWS UNDER NATIONAL PROTECTION

So we come to a consideration of the revolutionary Fourteenth Amendment. I have already tried to show what Congress had in mind when it adopted that amendment. What, then, did its words mean at the time they were adopted?

Naturally, there had been no decisions on the equal protection of the laws. The phrase was a new one. There had, however, been sporadic decisions that special and unequal laws were not due process of law or were opposed to common and natural right.

Privileges and Immunities

The first part of Section one provided that no State should deprive any citizen of the United States of the privileges and immunities of a citizen of the United States. Article IV, Section two, of the Constitution, provides that citizens of each State shall be entitled to all the privileges and immunities of citizens in the several States. As we have seen, Congress undoubtedly thought that it was providing that the same kind of privileges and immunities which a State government could not deny to the citizens of other States, were being put under Federal protection, so that they would be protected in the citizens of that State itself. There have been few decisions under Article IV, Section two, and the courts have been loath to go farther than the cases have required, in defining what is a privilege and immunity of a citizen of a State.

Clearly, whatever is a privilege of a citizen of New York must be accorded by New York to a citizen of Pennsylvania. The right to carry on business in New York can not be denied to a citizen of Pennsylvania, nor can a tax law of New York discriminate against a citizen of Pennsylvania. But it has been held that New York, for example, can allow its citizens the exclusive right to hunt and fish in New York, and of course can accord to New York citizens political rights not accorded to citizens of Pennsylvania. Justice Washington, in the well-known case of Corfield vs. Coryell, expressed the opinion that protection by the government of the enjoyment of life and liberty, the right to possess property, to pass through the State and trade in it, the right to equal taxation with the citizens of the State, were privileges and immunities which could not be denied to citizens of other States.[26]

It was such rights that the leaders of Congress thought they were putting under Federal protection, so that no State could deny their enjoyment to any citizen of the United States within its borders.

The Meaning of Due Process in 1866

We have seen that little was said of due process of law in the debates. What, then, did the clause mean in 1866? It is well known

---

[26] *Corfield* vs. *Coryell*, 4 Wash. C.C. 371, 6 Fed. Cases No. 3230 p. 546 (1823). Article IV, Sec. 2, of the Constitution prevented New York, for example, from denying to citizens of Pennsylvania the privileges and immunities of citizens of New York. Such men as Bingham felt that under the Fourteenth Amendment, New York must protect all citizens of the United States within its borders, thus including New York citizens, in the enjoyment of the privileges and immunities of citizens of the United States; namely, such rights as the enjoyment of life, liberty, and property, and equal taxation. The point was that hitherto, New York need only grant to citizens of other States the same privileges and immunities it granted its own citizens; whereas it was believed that after the Fourteenth Amendment, no State could deny its own citizens the privileges of citizens of the United States, which in turn were the same as the States had hitherto granted but had not been required to grant to their own citizens.

that it came in a direct line from Magna Charta,—from the famous Thirty-ninth Article, which declared that no freeman "shall be taken or imprisoned or disseized or exiled, or in any way destroyed; nor will we go upon him, nor send upon him, except by the lawful judgment of his peers and by the law of the land."

This clause has had a long history in England and in the United States. In the Federal Constitution, the Fifth Amendment declared that Congress could not take life, liberty, or property without due process of law. The States sometimes used the words, "law of the land," and sometimes, "due process of law." In some, the words, "law of the land," were used in a section relating to criminal procedure; in some, in a separate section; in some, the words, "due process of law," were used in a section dealing with criminal procedure; and in some, in a separate section.[27]

Broadly speaking, the phrases, "law of the land" and "due process of law," were understood to apply to procedure only, to guarantee a day in court, an orderly hearing, according to accepted forms. But what the legislature enacted, was the law of the land.

Up to the Puritan Rebellion, as McIlwain has shown in his *The High Court of Parliament and its Supremacy,* Parliament had not been supreme as a legislature in England. Parliament had exercised the powers both of a court and of a legislature. There was a fusion of powers, and for long, the legislative powers were distinctly secondary. Law was the common law, the ancient custom of the realm. Parliament, as a court, declared what the common law was, rather than consciously made or changed it; and what was not law according to the ancient custom, was not enforced.

Coke, he said, was not merely "captious" or "petulant," [28] when he declared in Dr. Bonham's case that "in many cases the common law will control Acts of Parliament, and sometimes adjudge them to be utterly void; for when an act of Parliament is against common right and reason, or repugnant or impossible to be performed, the common law will control it and adjudge it to be void." [29] He was merely stating what was then the common belief of English lawyers, who did not realize that Parliament could change the law: they then thought it could only declare the law.

---

[27] Mott, *Due Process of Law,* Chapter II. See p. 29.
[28] Charles Howard McIlwain, *The High Court of Parliament and Its Supremacy,* p. 327.
[29] Thayer, *Cases on Constitutional Law,* Vol. I, p. 48.

With the Puritan Rebellion, a change was necessitated. If the Parliamentary party were to maintain itself, it must have the power of making statutes to change the law. The theory of Parliamentary supremacy was then developed. By Blackstone's time, the theory of the supremacy—indeed, of the omnipotence—of Parliament was established. But in the United States, the older view has retained great influence. In our early days the belief in natural rights was widespread; and it reinforced the conception that legislation against the natural rights of man and common right and justice, was of no force and could be abrogated by the courts. Otis, during the Revolution, used all his eloquence against the idea of Parliamentary omnipotence. The Declaration of Independence as McLaughlin has often emphasized, was ardently animated by the ideal of natural rights, which no legislature could infringe.

From the time of the Revolution to the Civil War, there were a few scattered decisions that statutes against the natural rights of man or common right and justice, particularly special and unequal laws, were not the law of the land.

In Calder vs. Bull, the United States Supreme Court held that a special act of the legislature of Connecticut, setting aside a decree disapproving a will and granting a new trial, was not an ex post facto law, because the ex post facto clause related only to criminal procedure and was not "inserted to secure the citizen in his private rights, of either property or contracts."

But Justice Chase took occasion to add that an act of the legislature, "contrary to the great first principles of the social compact," which should take away the security for personal liberty or private property, could not be "considered a rightful exercise of legislative authority." Justice Iredell, however, in his concurring opinion, warned emphatically that the courts could not declare an act void on the ground that it was against natural justice; and that if Congress or a State legislature should pass an act "within the general scope of their constitutional power, the court can not pronounce it to be void, merely because it is, in their judgment, contrary to the principles of natural justice." [30]

The Court did not adopt Chase's view. But in North Carolina the Court held that a statute which divested the State university of escheated property formerly granted to it, was a denial of due

[30] *Calder* vs. *Bull*, 3 Dallas 386, 388 (1798).

process of law.[31] It flatly said that the legislature could not make the law of the land. In Massachusetts the Court held that a suspension of the statute of limitations in suits against administrators was void, since it was contrary "to the first principles of civil liberty and natural justice, and to the spirit of our constitution and laws, that any one citizen should enjoy privileges and advantages which are denied to all others under like circumstances. . . ."[32] Tennessee held that an unequal law denied due process, "Simply because," it said, "the law of the land is a rule alike embracing and equally affecting all persons in general, or all persons who exist or may come into the like state and circumstances."[33]

In Taylor vs. Porter,[34] a case later famous because of its citation by Cooley in his "Constitutional Limitations," the New York Court had held that a statute permitting an applicant to obtain a private road over another person's land, subject to payment of compensation, was not due process of law. The statute did not require that the damages be paid in advance of the taking. But the Court said that the difficulty lay deeper. The law attempted to compel one man to sell his land to another, "when the property is not to be applied to public use." Then it said, in the words later quoted by Cooley and a host of decisions: "The words 'by the law of the land' as here used, do not mean a statute passed for the purpose of working the wrong. That would render the restriction absolutely nugatory, and turn this part of the constitution into mere nonsense. The people would be made to say to the two houses: 'You shall be vested with the "legislative power of the State," but no one "shall be disfranchised, or deprived of any of the rights and privileges" of a citizen, unless you pass a statute for that purpose;' in other words, 'You shall not do the wrong unless you choose to do it.' "

New York also held that a woman's property law denied due process in so far as it applied to the property of women already married.[35]

Shaw, in Massachusetts, while upholding a statute establishing wharf lines, had said that the power of the legislature was not un-

---

[31] *Trustees, etc.* vs. *Foy*, 1 Murphy 58, 3 Am. Dec. 672 (1805).
[32] *Holden* vs. *James*, 11 Mass. 396, 6 Am. Dec. 174, 178 (1814).
[33] *Budd* vs. *State*, 22 Tenn. 483, 39 Am. Dec. 189, 193 (1842); *Wally's Heirs* vs. *Kennedy*, 10 Tenn. 554, 24 Am. Dec. 511 (1831).
[34] *Taylor* vs. *Porter*, 4 Hill (N. Y.) 140, 40 Am. Dec. 274, 278 (1843).
[35] *White* vs. *White*, 5 Barb. 474 (1849).

limited.[36] The Vermont court, while upholding a statute requiring a railroad to maintain cattle guards, also remarked that the power was not unlimited.[37]

Shortly before the Civil War, two striking decisions were made that the legislative power was limited by the due process clause: In New York it was held, in Wynehamer vs. People, that a prohibition statute was void as taking property without due process of law.[38] In Dred Scott vs. Sandford, Chief Justice Taney, after holding that the lower court had no jurisdiction since Scott was not a citizen of Missouri entitled to sue in the United States courts on the ground of diversity of citizenship, went on to say that the Missouri Compromise Act was unconstitutional; and that an "act of Congress which deprives a citizen of the United States of his liberty or property, merely because he came himself or brought his property into a particular Territory of the United States, and who had committed no offense against the laws, could hardly be dignified with the name of due process of law." [39]

But the Wynehamer decision was alone in the field of prohibition decisions, and the Dred Scott decision was anathema to the whole North. A storm of abuse, cries of conspiracy and judicial usurpation, burst forth against it.

When the Fourteenth Amendment was adopted, therefore, it may fairly be said that the prevailing opinion was that due process applied only to procedure; that it was not a restraint on the legislature; and that what the legislature enacted was the law of the land.

Yet, as we have seen, there were dissentient forces. Professor

---

[36] *Com.* vs. *Alger,* 7 Cush. 53 (1853).
[37] *Thorpe* vs. *Rutland, etc., Ry. Co.,* 27 Vermont 140 (1855).
[38] *Wynehamer* vs. *Peo.,* 13 N. Y. 78 (1856).
[39] 19 Howard 393, 450. The declaration that the Missouri Compromise Act was unconstitutional, was unnecessary to the decision. The court had already said that the lower court had no jurisdiction because Scott was not a citizen, and that ended the case. Moreover, it was not necessary to say that the Missouri Compromise Act was unconstitutional as forbidding slavery in the territory of Minnesota, because Scott had also been in Illinois, which forbade slavery, and there was no question of the power of Illinois to forbid slavery. However, public opinion in the North, and even able lawyers, generally misconceived the effect of the Missouri Compromise Act. A State could prohibit slavery within its borders, or the United States in a territory; but that did not mean that if a slave were brought into free territory, he became free. It merely meant that the master could not enforce his rights against the slave while in the free territory. But if he were taken back to slave territory, he was still a slave. I think Taney was correct in saying that a law which would divest a slave owner of his right merely because a slave was temporarily in free territory, would take property without due process of law.

Corwin, of Princeton, in two articles on "The Doctrine of Due Process of Law before the Civil War," concluded that, while the general theory was that the legislature was sovereign, "there were a number of restrictive principles, one of which was due process, now in a state of suspended animation, so to speak, but easily susceptible of resuscitation." [40]

He instanced the language in Murray vs. Hoboken, Lessee, which held that all arbitrary and summary procedure was forbidden; the extension of due process and the law of the land to cases of special legislation; the Wynehamer case in New York; the Dred Scott case; the fact that Massachusetts had always held that the police power was a power of reasonable legislation; that New York had never surrendered the idea that the legislative power is inherently limited; that the vested rights theory had never been given up;— as indicating, among other forces, that the ground was ready for an extension of judicial power under the Fourteenth Amendment.[41] To these should be added the belief in natural rights, and the persistence of the tradition of the power of the courts.

In 1868, Cooley published the first edition of his "Constitutional Limitations." Mott, in his "Due Process of Law," asserts that Cooley was the first commentator "to state clearly that due process was a limitation upon all branches of government." [42] Almost single-handed, he believes, Cooley caused a "shift of emphasis from personal to private rights." [43] It is true that Cooley declared that every reasonable doubt must be resolved in favor of the constitutionality of statutes; that the courts were not legislators, and could not overthrow statutes merely because they thought them unwise, or even unjust or oppressive, but only if they violated "rights guaranteed or protected by the Constitution." [44]

But his test of what violated such rights was open to great expansion by those who followed him. He bluntly said that a legislative enactment is not necessarily the law of the land. He quoted from Taylor vs. Porter: "The words 'by the law of the land' as used in the Constitution, do not mean a statute passed for the purpose of working the wrong." The design, Cooley went on, was

---

[40] 24 *Harvard Law Review*, 366, 460, p. 477, March and April, 1911.
[41] *Ibid.*, p. 478.   [42] Mott, *Due Process of Law*, p. 184.
[43] *Ibid.*, p. 185.   [44] Cooley, *Constitutional Limitations*, 1871 ed., p. 164.

"to exclude arbitrary power from every branch of the government." [45]

And it was not merely special legislation that was condemned: a general rule could be as obnoxious as a special one. A statute must be tested "by those principles of civil liberty and constitutional protection which have become established in our system of laws, and not generally by rules that pertain to forms of procedure only." [46] In short, each statute must stand or fall on the opinion of the judges as to whether it was consistent with our system of government. Here was a basis for the later tendency of courts to declare lacking in due process any law which laid a new or heavy burden on business, or a new restriction on individual activity.

We now have the background for a consideration of the decisions of the courts under the Fourteenth Amendment. We could take up the cases arising under the Fourteenth Amendment strictly in their sequence in time, but it seems preferable to consider them in the various divisions into which they fall.

Cases under the Civil Rights Acts

The amendment was primarily designed, as we have seen, to protect the negro in his civil rights. The Civil Rights Acts of 1870, 1871 and 1875, which we have outlined, show the kinds of rights which it was designed to secure. In U.S. vs. Cruikshank, Section six of the Civil Rights Act of 1870 was involved—the anti-Kuklux section.[47] It was charged that the defendants had prevented negroes from holding a public meeting, and thereby deprived them of their rights under the Constitution and laws of the United States. It was contended that the negroes had been denied the privileges and immunities of citizens of the United States, and that they had been denied due process of law and the equal protection of the laws. But Miller held that they had been denied no privileges and immunities as citizens of the United States.

In the Slaughter House cases, which we shall consider later under the question of the power of the courts to regulate business and the activities of citizens, Miller had said that the Federal government had no power over the privileges and immunities of citizens, save as expressly granted by the Federal constitution. The funda-

[45] *Ibid.,* p. 354.   [46] *Ibid.,* p. 356.   [47] 92 U.S. 542 (1875).

mental privileges of the citizen were under the protection of the States, where they had always been. Only such privileges and immunities as had been expressly granted by the Federal government, such as the right to deal in foreign commerce, to petition the Federal government, the right to peaceable assembly, the right of habeas corpus, and now the suffrage without discrimination because of race, were Federal privileges.

He utterly rejected the theory that the privileges and immunities protected by the first part of Section one of the Fourteenth Amendment, were the same as those which the States could not deny to citizens of other States under Article IV, Section two, or the same as the Federal government was forbidden from infringing by the first eight amendments.

There was vigorous dissent by Bradley and Field. They said that to limit the privileges and immunities to the few granted by the Federal government, was to strip the clause of all force. It was intended to give the Federal government the power to protect the same privileges as the States were prevented from denying to citizens of other States. Bradley, moreover, said that it was not difficult to tell what rights were protected: they were the same as those protected from Federal interference by the first eight amendments. And he said that to limit the privileges to those of a national character, was to take all the strength from the provision.[48]

The decision caused great criticism. Boutwell and Howe declared that the Court had denied the amendment the scope that was intended for it.[49] Years later, Justice Moody said that criticism of the case had never entirely ceased.[50]

The Supreme Court in the Cruikshank case followed the lead of the Slaughter House cases. It said that no rights under the Constitution or laws of the United States were involved. If the negroes had attempted to hold a meeting to petition Congress the defendants could have been punished. But the right to peaceful assembly; the right to bear arms; the right of freedom from violence—these were rights protected by the States. No Federal right was involved. With the States lay the right and duty to protect the most sacred rights of men. The Fourteenth Amendment did not protect against violence by individuals. It protected only

[48] Slaughter House Cases, 16 Wall. 36, 118 (1872).
[49] Charles Warren, *History of the Supreme Court*, Vol. II, pp. 540–41.
[50] *Twining* vs. *New Jersey*, 211 U.S. 78, 96 (1908).

against interference with such rights by the State. Lastly, it was not charged that the threatened denial was made on the ground of race. The Court added: "We may suspect that race was the cause of the hostility; but it is not so averred." [51]

Again in U.S. vs. Harris,[52] it refused to permit the national government to take over the enforcement of the ordinary protection of citizens. It considered an indictment of twenty men, who beat some negroes while in the custody of the sheriff. The indictment was under Section two of the Kuklux Act of 1871, which made punishable a conspiracy to deprive any person of the equal protection of the laws. The Court held the statute void. It could not be sanctioned under the Fourteenth Amendment, because that amendment allowed Congress to act only against unequal State action; whereas the section in question punished individuals. It was not good under the Thirteenth Amendment, because the statute did not try to protect only negroes from violence, but all persons, white and black. Besides, for a man to be subjected to violence and assault did not make him a slave.

Again, the Court made clear that the enforcement of the peace and order of the community belonged to the States.

Finally, the Court held that equal rights in inns and public conveyances could not be enforced by the Federal government. We have already seen that the Supreme Court held that the Civil Right's Act of 1875, which granted equal rights in inns and public conveyances, could not be sustained under the Thirteenth Amendment. The rights were not essential to freedom. But it also held that it could not be sustained under the Fourteenth. It said that the Fourteenth Amendment prohibited only State action. "It nullifies and makes void all State legislation and State action of every kind, which impair the privileges and immunities of citizens of the United States, or which injures them in life, liberty or property without due process of law, or which denies to them the equal protection of the laws." [53] It was State action which was prohibited, and the power to enforce the article was the power to prevent State action of a discriminating character. It granted that Congress could pass legislation to enforce the article; but that it was not general legislation upon the rights of the citizen but corrective legislation,

[51] 92 U.S. 542, 556 (1875). [52] 106 U.S. 629 (1882).
[53] Civil Rights Cases, 109 U.S. 3, 11 (1883).

counteracting the effect of State laws. But in the case at hand, the State had not, by law or custom sanctioned by the State, denied equal rights in inns or public conveyances. The rights granted by the Fourteenth Amendment could not be impaired by wrongful acts of individuals. The State had no primary right to legislate under the Fourteenth Amendment, as it had under the Thirteenth.

In conclusion, the Court questioned whether equal rights in inns and railroad coaches were rights which could be protected under the Fourteenth Amendment. The law was an attempt to enact a code of Federal law for the protection of equal rights, but the Court declared that if this were appropriate under the Fourteenth Amendment, "it is difficult to see where it is to stop. Why may not Congress, with equal show of authority, enact a code of laws for the enforcement and vindication of all rights of life, liberty, and property?" Why, it continued, could not "Congress proceed at once to prescribe due process of law for the protection of every one of these fundamental rights [namely, life, liberty, and property], in every possible case, as well as to prescribe equal privileges in inns, public conveyances, and theaters?" [54]

Harlan was a vigorous, ardent Union man from Kentucky. He had warm emotions and a deep belief in the ideal of equal rights. He wrote a spirited dissenting opinion, declaring that equal rights in inns and public conveyances were not only essential to freedom under the Thirteenth Amendment, but that the Fourteenth Amendment gave the Federal government positive rights of direct action; not to make a code of municipal law for the States, but to create a code for the enjoyment of citizenship which had now become a National right. Citizenship, he said, required, not—it is true— equality of social rights, but of civil rights, and among these were equal rights in inns and public conveyances. Exemption from discrimination in civil rights was a new constitutional right; and the Nation, by direct primary legislation, could protect that right. His argument was long and able, but it did not prevail. It was settled that the Fourteenth Amendment gave no right of direct action. The Federal government could prevent only State action. The mere acquiescence of the State in action of individuals, gave the Federal government no power to act.

[54] *Ibid.*, p. 14.

Years later, in Plessy vs. Ferguson,[55] the Court held that a State law, providing for separate railroad cars for whites and blacks,—in common language, Jim Crow cars,—was not violative of the Fourteenth Amendment. It noted that separate schools had been "held to be a valid exercise of the legislative power even by courts of States where the political rights of the colored race have been longest and most earnestly enforced," such as Massachusetts and Ohio. It said that there was no badge of inferiority in the separation. If there were, it could only be "because the colored race chooses to put that construction upon it. . . . Legislation," it said, "is powerless to eradicate racial instincts or to abolish distinctions based upon physical differences, and the attempt to do so can only result in accentuating the difficulties of the present situation." Here was a real consideration of realities. But it was in 1896 when that consideration was given.

In the Civil Rights cases, therefore, the Court laid down the rule which has been followed ever since,—that the Fourteenth Amendment prohibited State action, and that it did not act against individuals. The Federal government could not legislate directly, as it could under the Thirteenth Amendment.

The Court proceeded to extend the principle of the Slaughter House cases that the amendment did not create a new code of Federal law of privileges and immunities. There was no new citizenship of the United States as distinguished from citizenship of the States. The only privilege and immunity granted by the amendment was freedom from the taking of life, liberty or property without due process of law and the equal protection of the laws. So the Court held, in Bradwell vs. The State,[56] that a citizen of Vermont was not entitled to practise law in Illinois, if the laws of Illinois did not allow women to practise law. The right to practise law was a privilege granted by the laws of the State,—not of the United States. In Minor vs. Happerset,[57] it decided that the right to vote was not a privilege of women granted by the amendment. "The amendment," said Miller, "did not add to the privileges and immunities of a citizen. It simply furnished an additional guaranty for the protection of such as he already had." If

---

[55] 163 U.S. 537, 544, 551 (1896).   [56] 16 Wall. 130 (1872).
[57] 21 Wallace 162, 171 (1874).

women could not vote in the States before the amendment, they could not vote after it.

The tendency was strong to leave to the States the determination of the rights and privileges of citizens, save those specifically protected by the Federal constitution.

Unequal Laws

But the Court showed, despite its tendency to cut down the power of the national government, that it could speak vigorously against discriminatory action by the State authorities. In Strauder vs. West Virginia,[58] it reversed the conviction of a negro, because in that State no negro could serve on a grand or a petit jury. A Federal statute provided that whenever a negro was deprived of any right granted him by the Constitution, he could remove the case to a Federal court. The Court said that race prejudice existed; that the negro had a right to be protected against it; and that consequently he had a right to a jury, not of negroes or partly of negroes, but to one from which negroes were not excluded by law. The Court asked, "Is not protection of life and liberty against race or color prejudice, a right, a legal right, under the constitutional amendment? And how can it be maintained that compelling a colored man to submit to a trial for his life by a jury—drawn from a panel from which the State has expressly excluded every man of his race, because of color alone, however well qualified in other respects, is not a denial to him of equal legal protection?" [59]

It repeated the words of the first clause of the amendment, and asked, "What is this but declaring that the law in the States shall be the same for the black as for the white; that all persons, whether colored or white, shall stand equal before the laws of the States; and, in regard to the colored race, for whose protection the amendment was primarily designed, that no discrimination shall be made against them because of their color?" It admitted that the amendment merely prohibited State action, but it said that it gave the right to positive action to protect against unfriendly legislation. The West Virginia law, excluding negroes from juries, was such unfriendly legislation, and Congress could protect against it.[60]

In Ex Parte Virginia,[61] the Court held that a trial judge who

[58] 100 U.S. 303 (1879).   [59] *Ibid.*, p. 309.   [60] *Ibid.*, p. 307.
[61] 100 U.S. 339 (1879).

had excluded negroes from juries on the ground of race, could be tried under a Federal statute which made it an offense to exclude a person from a jury on the ground of race.

So the negro is protected under the Fourteenth Amendment from discriminatory legislation, just as we all are; but he has no right to positive legislation for his protection, save to protect from the operation of discriminatory state legislation. The States are recognized as the local legislators: the Federal government can act only to prevent discriminatory state action.

But, of course, the protection extends to all persons,—not negroes only. In a famous case, the Court held that arbitrary and discriminatory legislation, or legislation which gave the local authorities an opportunity to be arbitrary or discriminatory, was unconstitutional. In Yick Wo vs. Hopkins,[62] the Court overthrew an ordinance of San Francisco, which provided that there should be no laundries in wooden buildings unless the owner secured a permit from the city authorities. When the ordinance was passed, there were about three hundred and twenty laundries, of which two hundred and forty were conducted by Chinese. About three hundred and ten were made of wood. It appeared that one hundred and fifty Chinese had been arrested for violation of the ordinance, and that the eighty laundries in wooden buildings, owned by other than Chinese, had not been disturbed.

The Court said that the Fourteenth Amendment was not confined to citizens. It extended to all persons: to unnaturalized Chinese, as well as to citizens. It was universal in its application, "without regard to any differences of race, color, or of nationality; and the equal protection of the laws is a pledge of the protection of equal laws." [63] It said that it clearly appeared that the ordinance, as administered, was so "unequal and oppressive as to amount to a practical denial by the State of that equal protection of the laws" secured to all persons by the "benign provisions of the Fourteenth Amendment. . . ." [64]

It was a wholesome and fine decision. It upheld the best traditions of the Fourteenth Amendment, and the desire for equal laws and rights, which was the great demand of Sumner.

The Court then refused to allow positive legislation to secure equal rights, but it announced that unequal State laws would be

[62] 118 U.S. 356 (1886).   [63] *Ibid.*, p. 369.   [64] *Ibid.*, p. 373.

overthrown. The victory was a great one for State rights—for leaving with the States the protection of the fundamental rights of man. Fundamentally, the position is consistent with the principles of government. And yet the difficulty of proving discrimination in a State law, particularly in proving discrimination in the administration of a law equal on its face, is so great that the protection of equal laws has been of little avail to negroes. While it is true that the protection of the rights of man should, generally speaking, be left to the local communities, nevertheless a strong central government does owe a duty to see that some of the dearest rights are protected. The right of the negro to vote, to serve on juries, to have a jury chosen without discrimination from men of all races, the right to a fair trial—have all been subject to the partial action of local prejudices. It is one of the penalties that we pay for a race problem. But that the feeling has never died out that the Federal government owes a duty beyond the mere setting aside of a law when it comes before its courts, or of declaring that administration is in fact discriminatory, is shown by the attempt even today to provide that a State official who does not protect a prisoner from a mob, is guilty of a Federal offense in denying the prisoner due process of law.

Procedure

The early cases were strong in defending the right of the States to control procedure. So long as the procedure was of ancient force, so long as it gave a day in court and a hearing, it would be sustained. No radical new principles were established by the Fourteenth Amendment. Following its principle that the amendment did not guarantee the same rights as were protected from Federal interference by the first eight amendments, the Supreme Court held that the Fourteenth Amendment did not guarantee a trial by jury in the State Courts. In this it clearly denied the dearest intention of the framers of the amendment. In Walker vs. Sauvinet, the Court held that a statute of Louisiana which provided that if a jury disagreed, the court should decide the case, did not violate the Fourteenth Amendment. Due process was accorded "if the trial is had according to the settled course of judicial proceedings." [65] The States could settle what the procedure should be.

[65] 92 U.S. 90, 93 (1875).

The Court proceeded to decide that a judge appointed to fill a vacancy, was given due process on the question of his right to hold his office, if he were given a hearing before a court of competent jurisdiction.[66]

In *Missouri* vs. *Lewis,* the Court held that a statute of Missouri, allowing appeals to the Supreme Court only in cases involving more than $2500 and questions under the Constitution of the State, was valid. If the State did not have this power, it said, "the Fourteenth Amendment has a much more far-reaching effect than has been supposed." Each State had a right to impose such restrictions as it deemed fit. There is nothing "in the Constitution to prevent any State from adopting any system of laws or judicature it sees fit, for all or any part of its territory." The Fourteenth Amendment does not "profess to secure to all persons in the United States the benefit of the same laws and the same remedies. Great diversities may exist in two States, separated only by an imaginary line. On one side there may be a right of trial by jury, and on the other side no such right." [67] There might, then, be diversities between States and between different parts of the same State.

The Court also decided that a trial for murder on information, and not on indictment by the grand jury, was due process of law. It declared that "flexibility and capacity for growth and adaptation is the peculiar boast and excellence of the common law." Instead of stagnation, "we should expect that the new and various experiences of our own situation and system will mould and shape it into new and not less useful forms." Due process, it said, quoting the famous words of Webster, was not a special rule for a special case, but the "general law, a law which hears before it condemns, which proceeds upon inquiry, and renders judgment only after trial," so that "every citizen shall hold his life, liberty and property and immunities under the protection of the general rules which govern society. . . ." So Bills of Attainder, pains and penalties, acts of confiscation, acts reversing judgments, legislative judgments and decrees, are not due process. But trial by information was an ancient process: it gave the accused right of counsel and right to be heard, and it was due process.[68]

Justice Harlan, who had a deep faith in the old liberties and

---

[66] *Kennard* vs. *Morgan*, 92 U.S. 480 (1875).   [67] 101 U.S. 22, 29, 31 (1879).
[68] *Hurtado* vs. *California*, 110 U.S. 516, 530, 531, 535, 554 (1884).

was a staunch defender of them, protested that "Anglo-Saxon liberty would, perhaps, have perished long before the adoption of our Constitution, had it been in the power of the government to put the subject on trial for his life whenever a justice of the peace, holding his office at the will of the crown, should certify that he had committed a capital crime."

In the case of a man charged with robbery, the Court upheld a Utah statute which allowed a jury of eight in criminal cases. In this case, the Court considered the objection that jury trial was a privilege and immunity of a citizen of the United States, and a fundamental right protected by the first ten amendments from Federal interference, and now protected by the Fourteenth Amendment from action by the States. The same answer was given: jury trial was not protected from State action.[69]

Again Justice Harlan dissented with strong emotion. He said that a trial by a jury of twelve was necessary for due process. The result of the opinion, he said, would be that "the Constitution of the United States does not stand in the way of any State striking down guarantees of life and liberty that English-speaking people have for centuries regarded as vital to personal security, and which the men of the Revolutionary period universally claimed as the birthright of freemen." [70]

Again, in Twining vs. New Jersey, the Court ruled that it was no violation of the due process clause for the Court to comment on the fact that the defendants had not testified in their own defense. The right not to testify was, if anything, a right under State laws. The States had sometimes denied the right and sometimes granted it. But, above all, it said that the exemption from testifying was not essential to due process. It declared that in a free government nothing is more "fundamental than the right of the people, through their appointed servants, to govern themselves in accordance with their own will, except in so far as they have restrained themselves by constitutional limits specifically established; and that in our peculiar dual form of government, nothing is more fundamental than the full power of the State to order its own affairs and govern its own people, except in so far as the Federal Constitution, expressly or by fair implication, has withdrawn that power." [71]

[69] *Maxwell* vs. *Dow,* 176 U.S. 581 (1900).   [70] *Ibid.,* p. 617.
[71] 211 U.S. 78, 106 (1908).

Here are a long line of cases upholding the right of the States to determine for themselves the general methods of procedure. So long as the procedure applied equally to all, so long as it gave a hearing and a day in Court, it may be said broadly that it did not deny due process and would be upheld. The Supreme Court steadily refused to interfere, and it asserted time and again the right of the States to change, to adapt themselves to new conditions, to experiment. The Fourteenth Amendment did not remove the great field of procedure from the States.

So far as ordinary procedure is concerned, the result is a desirable one. But the framers of the amendment undoubtedly intended to preserve the right of trial by jury in the States, especially in criminal trials, and the Court has denied that desire. Moreover, as trial by jury is inviolate in the Federal Courts, it would seem that it should be in the State Courts. The most precious rights of men should not be at the mercy of State constitutions. The Supreme Court has allowed change and experiment, then, in the protection of historic personal rights: it has not been so liberal with economic change.

The Fourteenth Amendment and the Regulation of Rates, Taxation, and Legislation Under the Police Power

So far, as we have seen, the Supreme Court steadily encouraged the independence and freedom of action of the States. But a development slowly made its way, which no one foresaw in 1866, in which the Court extended its power over the regulation of the rates of public utilities, taxation, and the whole police power of the States; the broad power to regulate labor conditions, business, and generally to provide for the health and welfare of the community.

I have already referred to the Slaughter House cases. The carpet-bag legislature of Louisiana—ostensibly as a health measure—had granted a monopoly in 1869 to one company to conduct slaughter houses in the city of New Orleans. The monopoly, which threw out of business twelve hundred slaughter houses, was bitterly resisted. It was attacked in the Slaughter House cases on the ground that it violated the Thirteenth and the Fourteenth Amendments. It was the first great case involving the application of the new amendments to other than cases involving negroes.

We have already seen that Miller said that the slavery which was prohibited by the Thirteenth Amendment, was personal servitude. The Fourteenth Amendment, he said, was adopted to secure the negro from the force of unequal laws—such laws as the "black" codes of 1865 and 1866. The Fourteenth Amendment made citizenship national, but it did not make citizenship in the State the same as citizenship in the nation. As we have seen, he held that the only privileges and immunities which were protected, were those of citizens of the United States. The fundamental rights of citizens were under the protection of the States, where they had always been.

Then he came to due process of law, and remarked that such a clause was in the Fifth Amendment and had long been in most State constitutions. No one had thought that it prevented such a monopoly as Louisiana had granted.

As to the equal protection clause, he stated that it was intended to protect the negro, and he doubted "very much" whether any action of a State not directed by way of discrimination against the negroes as a class, or on account of their race, "will ever be held to come within the purview of this provision. It is so clearly a provision for that race and that emergency, that a strong case would be necessary for its application to any other." On this point he reversed himself in thirteen years.[72]

He ended by observing that our sentiment from the beginning had been in favor of the preservation of the States; that under pressure of the war, the great amendments had been adopted; but that still there was in the war amendments no "purpose to destroy the main features of the general system. Under the pressure of all the excited feeling growing out of the war, our statesmen have still believed that the existence of the States with powers for domestic and local government, including the regulation of civil rights— the rights of person and of property—was essential to the perfect working of our complex form of government, though they have thought proper to impose additional limitations on the States, and to confer additional power on that of the Nation."[73]

It is strikingly evident that he did not conceive that the slaughter

[72] 16 Wall. 36, 81 (1872).   [73] *Ibid.*, p. 82.

house monopoly denied due process of law. Thirty years later, the whole case would have turned on that point.

In the dissenting opinions, however, by four justices, the view that later was to have great vogue in State courts and some influence in the Supreme Court, was vigorously presented. Bradley said that the amendment deprived people of liberty and property, and that the right of choice in lawful employments "is a portion of their liberty; their occupation is their property." [74] Here is the freedom of contract argument that later was to have such sway.

Field, of California, also declared that the monopoly denied the people of Louisiana fundamental rights belonging to the people of all free governments. He admitted that the police power "undoubtedly extends to all regulations affecting the health, good order, morals, peace, and safety of society, and is exercised on a great variety of subjects and in almost numberless ways. All sorts of restrictions and burdens are imposed under it, and when these are not in conflict with any constitutional prohibitions, or fundamental principles, they can not be successfully assailed in a judicial tribunal. With this power of the State and its legitimate exercise, I shall not differ from the majority of the Court. But under the pretense of prescribing a police regulation the State can not be permitted to encroach upon any of the just rights of the citizen, which the Constitution intended to secure against abridgment." [75]

Here was the first assertion that the Fourteenth Amendment stated a political purpose for all citizens; that it was intended to prevent changes in the ordinary rights of men. Here was an assertion that an exercise of the police power, which restrained the individual in the exercise of his accustomed rights, was prohibited by the Constitution.

But the Court did not follow him. Its early decisions strongly upheld the police power over those matters on which the States had anciently exercised jurisdiction. In Bartemeyer vs. Iowa, a prohibition law was attacked on the ground that it violated a privilege and immunity of a citizen of the United States, and took property without due process of law. Miller answered that, up to the Fourteenth Amendment, such a law had been regarded as falling within the police power of the State, and that

[74] *Ibid.,* p. 122.　[75] *Ibid.,* p. 87.

the amendment could not protect any right which did not exist before the amendment. As to taking property without due process of law, he said that the defendant must show that the glass of liquor he sold had been in existence before the Iowa prohibition law took effect, and that he had not shown this.[76]

Even Field saw no reason to protect the right to carry on the business of selling liquor. "No one has ever pretended, that I am aware of," he observed, "that the fourteenth amendment interferes in any respect with the police power of the State." He reverted to the Slaughter House cases, and declared that that monopoly transcended a police regulation. The Fourteenth Amendment, he added, was intended to "justify legislation extending the protection of the National government over the common rights of *all* citizens of the United States, and thus obviate objections to the legislation adopted for the protection of the emancipated race." It erected a national citizenship. It protected the "pursuit of happiness." [77]

Bradley, in his concurring opinion, asserted that the Slaughter House monopoly was an "unconscionable monopoly, of which the police regulation was a mere pretext." But "police regulations intended for the preservation of the public health and the public order are of an entirely different character." [78]

In Butchers' Union Co. vs. Crescent City Company,[79] Field once more vigorously asserted this belief in the right of the people under the police power; but it was based not on the rights of the legislature, but on his inherent belief in the rights of the individual. In this case his dominant theory prevailed. Louisiana had changed its constitution to prohibit monopolies. New Orleans then granted a license to a slaughter company, in contravention of the monopoly held valid in the Slaughter House cases. The Court said (Miller writing the opinion) that the monopoly could be nullified. The police power could not be granted or bargained away. "It can not be permitted," he said, "that, when the Constitution of a State, the fundamental law of the land, has imposed upon its legislature the duty of guarding, by suitable laws, the health of its citizens, especially in crowded cities, and the protection of their person and property by suppressing and preventing crime, that the

---

[76] *Ibid.*, 18 Wall., 129, 133-34 (1873).   [77] *Ibid.*, p. 138, 140.   [78] *Ibid.*, p. 137.
[79] 111 U.S. 746 (1884).

power which enables it to perform this duty can be sold, bargained away, under any circumstances, as if it were a mere privilege which the legislator could dispose of at his pleasure." [80]

Field, in his concurring opinion, asserted that "certain inherent rights lie at the foundation of all action, and upon a recognition of them alone can free institutions be maintained." Among the rights referred to in the Declaration of Independence, he said, "is the right of men to pursue their happiness, by which is meant the right to pursue any lawful business or vocation, in any manner not inconsistent with the equal rights of others, which may increase their prosperity or develop their faculties, so as to give them their highest enjoyment." [81]

The right to pursue these rights, without let or hindrance save as applied to all, he said, is "a distinguishing privilege of citizens of the United States, and an essential element of that freedom which they claim as their birthright." [82] He quoted the laissez faire ideals of Adam Smith, and said that the Fourteenth Amendment did not limit "the subjects upon which the States can legislate" but did no more than inhibit "discriminating and partial enactments, favoring some to the impairment of the rights of others." [83]

These words were to be quoted again and again by State and Federal courts, in the next twenty years. They were the starting point, I think, of all the cases denying the power of the legislature to regulate the conditions of labor and business.

Generally, the Court continued to uphold the police power and the authority of legislatures. In Barbier vs. Connolly,[84] and in Soon Hing vs. Crowley,[85] the Court upheld ordinances of San Francisco forbidding the operation of laundries at night in certain sections of the city. In the former case, Field observed that "it would be an extraordinary usurpation of the authority of the municipality, if a federal tribunal should undertake to supervise such regulations." [84]

It upheld a New Hampshire statute which allowed manufacturing companies to build dams and overflow lands above the dams, on paying damages therefor, as a reasonable regulation of the rights of owners along the streams for the purpose of developing the resources of the State.[86]

[80] *Ibid.*, p. 751.   [81] *Ibid.*, pp. 756–57.   [82] *Ibid.*, p. 757.   [83] *Ibid.*, p. 759.
[84] 113 U.S. 27, 30 (1885).   [85] 113 U.S. 703 (1885).
[86] *Head* vs. *Amoskeag*, 113 U.S. 9 (1885).

In Mugler vs. Kansas,[87] it again upheld a prohibition law. It said that it was difficult to "perceive any ground for the judiciary to declare that the prohibition by Kansas of the manufacture or sale within her limits, of intoxicating liquors for general use there as a beverage, is not fairly adapted to the end of protecting the community against the evils which confessedly result from the excessive use of ardent spirits."[88] Harlan asserted stoutly that the power to regulate must be somewhere, and that the legislature must primarily decide. Every possible presumption was in favor of the statute. If, however, the law were a mere pretense, if it had "no real or substantial relation" to the objects of protecting the public health, morals, or safety, or if it "were a palpable invasion of rights secured by the fundamental law," the courts could interfere.[89] "Palpable invasion of rights secured by the fundamental law," might mean anything, but it is clear that Harlan felt that the courts should interfere only as a last resort. He adopted, in effect, the reasonable rule,—that if a reasonable man could say that the statute was adapted to the end of regulating the public health and morals, the courts should not interfere.

In Powell vs. Pennsylvania, the Court upheld a statute making it a misdemeanor to sell butterine as food. Harlan, writing the opinion, held sturdily to the theory that the wisdom of the law was solely for the legislature to determine. It must be assumed, he argued, that there were injurious substances in butterine, and that it was not the function of the Court to enter into the consideration of questions of public policy. If the legislation were unwise or unnecessarily oppressive, appeal must be made to the legislature, not to the judiciary. "The latter can not interfere without usurping powers committed to another department of government."[90]

But the regulation shocked Justice Field's strong sense of individualism. It denied the right of men to pursue their own callings. He declared that "The right to pursue one's happiness is placed by the Declaration of Independence among the inalienable rights of man, with which all men are endowed, not by the grace of emperors or kings, or by force of legislative or constitutional enactments, but by their Creator; and to secure them, not to grant

[87] 123 U.S. 623 (1887). [88] *Ibid.*, p. 661. [89] *Ibid.*, p. 661.
[90] 127 U.S. 678, 686 (1888).

them, governments are instituted among men. The right to procure healthy and nutritious food, by which life may be prolonged and enjoyed, and to manufacture it, is among these inalienable rights, which in my judgment no State can give, and no State can take away except in punishment for crime. It is involved in the right to pursue one's happiness." [91]

But Field's views did not yet prevail.

The Court proceeded to uphold a statute making a railroad liable for killing cattle along its right of way where there was no fence,[92] and a statute confiscating fish nets.[93]

Without entering then into the subject of the desirability of any particular law, the Court held consistently that the States had the right to determine for themselves what experiments they would make in the government of their communities. It gave no encouragement yet to the idea that there were certain inherent rights of man, which the legislature under the police power could not restrict.

So far we have seen a steady refusal by the Court to hamper the legislatures of the States. The amendment was to be used to prevent unequal laws, and to prevent legislation denying the individual a day in Court. But so far it had not been allowed to hamper the police power.

The Regulation of Public Utilities

But there grew up three great classes of cases where the Court began to restrict the legislative power of the States. The first was legislation regulating rates of railroads and public utilities. After the Civil War, there arose a demand for action by the legislatures fixing railroad rates and grain elevator charges. We shall consider that demand more at length, when we come to the Grange movement in Chapter VII. Suffice it to say now that the farmers felt bitterly aggrieved by the charges of the elevator owners and the railroad companies, and the result was the Granger legislation of the seventies. This legislation fixed rates by legislative act: there was no judicial finding by a commission of what was a reasonable rate.

The question came before the court in the famous case of Munn

[91] *Ibid.*, p. 692.
[92] *Minneapolis etc. Co.* vs. *Beckwith*, 129 U.S. 26 (1889). Field wrote this opinion.
[93] *Lawton* vs. *Steele*, 152 U.S. 133 (1894).

vs. Illinois. Chief Justice Waite held that, from time immemorial, the state had had the right to fix the rates at which those engaged in public callings sold their services to the public. The rates charged by inn keepers, ferrymen, and common carriers had long been so fixed. When private property "is devoted to a public use, it is subject to public regulation." [94] He said that the warehousemen conducted a business impressed with a public use. It mattered not that there was no precedent for the law. The business was of recent growth, had come to have public importance, and it could be regulated. The law did not make a new declaration of principle, because the principle had always been in effect. The reasonableness of the rates fixed by the law was not considered. The legislature had the power, and the legislature could determine what was reasonable.

Field and Strong dissented. Field exclaimed that if the public could regulate rates, it could destroy all rights of property, and the legislature could intermeddle with the "business of every man in the community." [95] The warehouseman's calling was not a public nuisance. The decision gave "unrestrained license to legislative will." [96]

At the same time, the Court upheld statutes of three other middle western States, fixing maximum rates for railroads.

A few years later, a momentous decision was made. The Court held, in the case of Santa Clara County vs. The Southern Pacific Railroad,[97] that the equal protection of the laws applied to corporations, as well as natural persons. We have already alluded to the argument of Conkling in the San Mateo case in December, 1882, in which he set himself to overcome the statement of Miller in the Slaughter House cases that the amendment was limited to negroes, and to prove that it protected the rights of corporations. Kendrick, the historian of the report of the Reconstruction Committee, believes Conkling's argument—that Section one of the amendment was intended to prevent oppressive legislation against corporations and business—made a deep impression on the Court, and

[94] 94 U.S. 113, 130 (1876).

[95] *Ibid.*, p. 154. The Supreme Court has recently repudiated the doctrine of public use, and declared that "affected with a public interest" means merely "subject to control for the public good." *Nebbia* vs. *New York*, 291 U.S. 502, 533, the statute fixing milk prices in New York.

[96] *Ibid.*, p. 148.   [97] 118 U.S. 394 (1886).

that the San Mateo case marks a change in the whole attitude of the Court towards the Fourteenth Amendment.

Miller, repudiating his dictum in the Slaughter House cases, declared during the San Mateo argument that he had "never heard it said in this Court, or by any judge of it, that these articles [namely, the Fourteenth Amendment] were supposed to be limited to the negro race." [98]

The Santa Clara case was argued a few weeks after the San Mateo argument. Chief Justice Waite stated at the outset of the argument on the Santa Clara case that the Court did not wish "to hear arguments on the question whether the provision in the Fourteenth Amendment to the Constitution, which forbids a State to deny to any person within its jurisdiction the equal protection of the laws, applies to these corporations." He added, "We are all of opinion that it does." [99]

In the same year, as we have seen, the Court decided, in Yick Wo vs. Hopkins, that an ordinance discriminating against Chinese laundrymen was void.

A few years later, it held that the due process clause applied to corporations.[100]

The way was opened for all persons, and for corporations as well as individuals, to invoke the amendment for the protection of their property rights.

After the Granger legislation, the railroads suffered losses, and investors were reluctant to aid railroad financing. The States began to repeal their Granger laws; they began to establish commissions with power to fix rates. The first law for such a purpose which came before the Court was that of Mississippi, in 1886, ten years after the Granger cases. The Court upheld the statute; but it took pains to say that the power "to regulate is not a power to destroy, and limitation is not the equivalent of confiscation. Under pretense of regulating fares and freights, the State can not require a railroad corporation to carry persons or property without reward; neither can it do that which in law amounts to a taking of property for public use without just compensation, or without due process of law." [101]

---

[98] Kendrick, p. 35.   [99] 118 U. S. 396.
[100] *Minneapolis Ry. Co.* vs. *Beckwith*, 129 U.S. 26 (1889).
[101] *Stone* vs. *Farmers' Loan & Trust Co.*, 116 U.S. 307, 331 (1886). Field and Harlan dissented.

Finally, in 1890, in Chicago etc., Railway Company vs. Minnesota, the Court held that whether a rate fixed by a commission was a fair rate, was a judicial question. Minnesota had created a commission which fixed milk rates between certain points. No hearing was provided for; no determination by the commission that the rates were reasonable. The Court said that such a statute deprived the railroad of property without due process of law.[102]

A warm dissent was filed by three justices. They said truly that it reversed the case of Munn vs. Illinois. Justice Bradley, writing the dissenting opinion, said that the governing principle of that case, and the cases following it, was that "the regulation and settlement of the fares of railroads and other public accommodations is a legislative prerogative and not a judicial one." [103] The determination of what is a reasonable charge, he declared, "is preeminently a legislative one, involving considerations of policy as well as remuneration; . . ." He said that the majority say "in effect, if not in terms, that the final tribunal of arbitrament is the judiciary; I say it is the legislature. I hold that it is a legislative question, not a judicial one, unless the legislature or the law (which is the same thing) has made it judicial, by prescribing the rule that the charges shall be reasonable, and leaving it there." [104]

He said that the Court had made an assumption of authority which "it has no right to make." [105] If the legislature had acted directly, there would have been due process. It was a method of rate fixing sanctioned by the common law. And if the legislature could act directly, he saw no reason why it could not act through a commission. He admitted that the legislature or the courts might err, but he replied that all human tribunals were imperfect— courts as well as legislatures and commissions. If the legislatures became arbitrary, the remedy was in the people to elect better legislatures.[106] It was the theory of a self-reliant democracy. But the majority opinion prevailed. The courts have ever since acted to prevent confiscatory rates.

We can not say to what the change from the Munn case to the Minnesota case was due. As we have seen, the change was gradual. It was twenty-four years after the amendment was adopted before the power was definitely asserted. Conkling's argument may

[102] 134 U.S. 418 (1890).   [103] *Ibid.*, p. 461.   [104] *Ibid.*, p. 462.   [105] *Ibid.*, p. 463.
[106] *Ibid.*, p. 465, 466.

have had its effect. Cooley's argument that the due process clause restrained the legislature, undoubtedly had its influence: it was cited time and again. Field's dominant individualism, which held that the freedom of the individual to pursue his calling should not be restrained, also played its part. The pressure of forces on the Court, and the natural desire of the Court for power—all worked to the same end.

It will be noted that the Court stressed the fact in the Minnesota case that the rates were fixed by a commission, and the minority assumed that if the rates had been fixed directly by the legislature, the courts could not have interfered. But finally, in Smyth vs. Ames, it was settled that an act of the legislature of Nebraska could be enjoined, because the rates fixed would not allow a fair return on the investment. It was settled that whether a rate was confiscatory or not, whether it allowed a fair return on the investment—were questions for the courts.[107]

And now we find that every ordinance fixing rates for local utilities, every statute, every order of a commission, is subject to review in the courts under the authority granted by the Fourteenth Amendment.

The general result of rate regulation, however, has been a victory for the legislative power. In an able dissenting opinion, in the case of Southwestern Bell Telephone Company vs. Public Service Commission,[108] Brandeis, in attacking the cost of reproduction method of fixing rates, declared that the efforts of courts to control commission findings of value had largely failed. The Supreme Court had decided in Smyth vs. Ames that no one test was final for the Court in determining whether a rate was confiscatory, but that original cost, additional investments, cost of reproduction, the value of bonds and stock outstanding, the revenue to be expected from the rate proposed and the operating expenses under it, all must be taken into account. Well advised commissions, accordingly, in their findings state that they have taken all these elements into account, have fixed the rates "not so low as to be confiscatory," and thus, as Brandeis noted, "effective judicial review is very often rendered impossible." The Supreme Court has held that a rate order will not be set aside, "unless the evidence compels conviction" that a fair-minded board could not

[107] 169 U.S. 466 (1898). [108] 262 U.S. 276, 296 (1923).

have reached the conclusion that the rate would prove inadequate.

The control of the courts has been a real restraint against confiscation, but in the end the legislative power has remained with the commissions.

Due Process and Taxation

The second great group of cases in which the Court has taken jurisdiction under the Fourteenth Amendment, has been taxation. Here again, the Court was slow to take power, but its authority has gradually but greatly widened.

In 1877, in Davidson vs. New Orleans,[109] an assessment under a Louisiana statute providing for the draining of swamp lands, was upheld. Justice Miller noted that the due process clause had been in the United States Constitution for nearly a century; and that while, during all that time, the powers of the government had been jealously watched, "this special limitation upon its powers has rarely been invoked in the judicial forum or the more enlarged theatre of public discussion. But, while it has been a part of the Constitution as a restraint upon the power of the States only a very few years, the docket of this court is crowded with cases in which we are asked to hold that State courts and State legislatures have deprived their own citizens of life, liberty, or property, without due process of law." [110]

He felt that there was some misconception of the scope of the amendment; and that it was looked upon as a means for every unsuccessful litigant in the State courts to test "the merits of the legislation" on which the decision against him was founded. He then said that whenever, by the laws of a State, a tax or burden or assessment on property was laid, and a hearing was provided for, to contest the charge imposed, the judgment could not be said to lack due process. It might violate some provision of the State constitution, but so long as there was notice and a fair hearing, there was due process.[111]

But finally the Court held in 1898 in Norwood vs. Baker,[112] that the power of the legislature or the legislative body "in these matters is not unlimited." [113] An Ohio village had fixed an assessment of benefits for opening a street, assessing a Mrs. Baker a

---

[109] 96 U.S. 97 (1877).   [110] *Ibid.*, pp. 103–04.   [111] *Ibid.*, p. 104.
[112] 172 U.S. 269 (1898).   [113] *Ibid.*, p. 278.

fixed amount of benefits according to her front foot ownership, irrespective of whether her lot had benefited that much or not. The Court said that it could not be done. The ordinance did not allow the owner to prove that he had not been benefited. The theory of such assessments was that they did not really cost the owner anything, since he was benefited by the amount he paid. But he had a right to show that he was not benefited. If he were required to pay more than his property was really benefited, his property was taken without due process of law. Consequently, it has since been necessary for provision to be made to give property owners a chance to show that their property actually has not been benefited by the amount of the assessment.

It was only slowly that the Court extended its power over taxation statutes. Of course, there was already power to annul a State tax statute, because it burdened interstate commerce or impaired the obligation of contracts, or because the subject taxed was an instrumentality of the Federal government.[114]

But the Fourteenth Amendment was to afford a great new source of power over taxation,—the due process clause. It was long, however, before it was realized that the Fourteenth Amendment could be used. In Loan Association vs. Topeka, in 1874, the Court held void a Kansas statute which authorized cities to issue bonds to pay for grants to manufacturing establishments. It was a time when government aid to industry was very popular. But the Court said that it could not be done under the general taxing power.

Miller decided the case on very general principles. He did not refer to the Fourteenth Amendment; but, on general theory, said that it was simply not taxation to raise money to give it to a particular industry. Taxation could be laid only for a public purpose, and aid to a particular industry was not a public purpose. If the object of tax was a purely private or personal one, it was simply not taxation. Miller said that there are certain rights in every free government "beyond the control of the State." The theory of our government, he said, is opposed to "the deposit of unlimited power anywhere." To tax in order to give to a few

---

[114] As to interstate commerce, see *Hays* vs. *Pac. Mail S.S. Co.*, 17 How. 596 (1854).

As to the obligation of contracts, see *Wilson* vs. *New Jersey*, 7 Cranch 164 (1812).

As to Federal instrumentalities, see *McCulloch* vs. *Maryland*, 4 Wheat. 316 (1819); *Weston* vs. *City of Charleston*, 2 Peters 449 (1829).

favored individuals, was "not legislation. It is a decree under legislative forms." His political theory completely dominated his legal argument.[115]

But the great advance was the theory that to tax property outside the jurisdiction was to take property without due process of law. It is true that, as early as McCulloch vs. Maryland, Marshall had asserted that it was "self-evident" that the taxing power extends only to "subjects over which the sovereign power extends." [116] In 1870, the Court, without referring to the Fourteenth Amendment, held that a tax on property outside of the jurisdiction was as much "a nullity as if in conflict with the most explicit constitutional inhibition." [117]

Again, in Louisville etc. Ferry Company vs. Kentucky, the Court said that the principle that a State could not tax property outside the jurisdiction, inhered "in the very nature of constitutional Government." [118]

Finally, in 1905, in a striking case, the Court flatly said that to tax property not in the jurisdiction, was to take property without due process of law, in violation of the Fourteenth Amendment. A Kentucky corporation owned two thousand refrigerator cars. Kentucky attempted to tax all of them as belonging to a Kentucky corporation. The company contended that the State could tax only the actual average in the State, which was from twenty-eight to sixty-seven in the years in question. The Supreme Court upheld the company. It said that the power to tax came from the benefits and protection given by the State. The State could not tax land in another State because it did not protect the land. So it could not tax cars in another State.

Holmes dissented in a decision of five lines. He thought the result reached was probably a desirable one, "but I hardly understand how it can be deduced from the Fourteenth Amendment." [119]

This principle has had momentous consequences. From that day to this, the Court has steadily extended the rule that to tax property outside the jurisdiction, or to measure a tax by property outside the jurisdiction, is to take property without due process of law, and will not be permitted. Formerly, it had held that a

[115] 20 Wall. 655, 662, 663 (1875).   [116] 4 Wheat. 316, 429 (1819).
[117] *St. Louis* vs. *The Ferry Co.*, 11 Wall. 423, 430 (1870).
[118] *Louisville etc. Co.* vs. *Kentucky*, 188 U.S. 385, 396 (1903).
[119] *Union Ref. Transit Co.* vs. *Kentucky*, 199 U.S. 194, 211 (1905).

foreign corporation could be taxed on its entire capital. The State had unlimited power of taxation. But in 1910, the Supreme Court held that a State franchise tax could be laid only on the proportion of the capital stock in the State.[120] So also, a State can tax only the proportion of income of a foreign corporation earned in the State. The process is still going on. The Court's power over State taxation has been a mighty force for well-ordered legislation by the States,—an immense source of unification. Holmes recently declared, "The power to tax is not the power to destroy while this Court sits." [121]

The Control of the Police Power

The third great field in which the Court has restrained the legislatures has been in cases under the police power. With the discussion of cases under the police power, it is necessary to broaden the discussion to include the State cases. It is true that they do not affect the subject of the extension of Federal power over the States, with which we began this study of the War amendments. But the consideration of the War amendments inevitably overlaps into several fields; and it is much more feasible to consider the effects of the War amendments and their application in one place, than to separate them into several compartments.

The War amendments involve not only the extension of Federal power over the States, but of the protection of individual rights, and, above all, of the exercise of political power by the courts.[122]

Beginning about 1886, the State courts began to hand down a series of decisions on labor questions, which showed a very re-

---

[120] *Western Union* vs. *Kansas,* 216 U.S. 1 (1910).

[121] *Panhandle Oil Co.* vs. *Mississippi, etc.,* 277 U.S. 218, 223 (1928).

[122] The decisions of the State courts, holding State statutes unconstitutional as violating the Federal Constitution, were not reviewable by the United States Supreme Court until 1914. In that year the United States Supreme Court was given the right to call such cases up on certiorari. 38 U.S. Statutes at Large, 790. Prior to that time, the State court's judgment or decree was final when it held a State statute unconstitutional, and there was review by the United States Supreme Court only when the State court held that the State statute did not violate the Federal Constitution. Therefore, up to 1914, the State decisions, holding State statutes unconstitutional as violative of the Federal Constitution, were not direct exercises of Federal power. They were rather declaratory of what the State courts thought the Federal courts would do. But they were, of course, decisions involving the Fourteenth Amendment. Moreover, these State cases as well as State cases based on State constitutional provisions bear directly on the philosophy of the courts as to individual rights and the limits of governmental action, and they bear directly on the question of the exercise of political power by the courts. Therefore, we shall briefly consider some of the State decisions here.

actionary sense of the limits of political action, and a strong sense of the power of the courts over legislation. They based their decisions on the ground that these labor laws violated the liberty of contract of the individual. This was the theory, as we have seen, that Field had expressed in his dissenting opinion in the Slaughter House cases, and again in the Butchers' Union and later decisions.

In Godcharles vs. Wigeman,[123] the Pennsylvania court held that a statute forbidding token money was void, because it prevented people "who are sui juris from making their own contracts. The act is an infringement alike of the rights of employer and employe." It was an "insulting attempt to put the laborer under a legislative tutelage, which is not only degrading to his manhood, but subversive of his rights as a citizen of the United States." [124] The court did not cite a single case or constitutional provision.

In State vs. Goodwill,[125] the West Virginia court, noting that the State constitution provided that men had certain inherent rights, among which were the "enjoyment of life and liberty, with the means of acquiring and possessing property, and of pursuing and obtaining happiness and safety," held void a statute forbidding token money void, because denying the liberty of contract. It referred to Field's theory in the Butchers' Union case, and cited Cooley to the effect that the police power is subject to the power of the courts. It noted Marshall's words in Brown vs. Maryland [126] that, "Questions of power do not depend on the degree to which it may be exercised. If it may be exercised at all, it must be exercised at the will of those in whose hands it is placed."

Therefore, the court concluded, if "the legislature, without any public necessity, has the power to prohibit or restrict the right of contract between private persons in respect to one lawful trade or business, then it may prevent the prosecution of all trades, and regulate all contracts." [127] So it held that it could regulate none: it had no power. It turned Marshall's argument completely around. If the question were purely one of power, with no question of degree, the legislature could act as the police power gave it the power. But the West Virginia court said that the question was one of power,—and there was no power.

---

[123] 113 Pa. St. 434; 6 Atl. 354 (1886).   [124] *Ibid.,* 6 Atl. 356.
[125] 10 S.E. 285 (1889).   [126] *Ibid.,* p. 287.
[127] *Ibid.,* p. 287. See *Brown* vs. *Maryland.* 12 Wheat. 419 (1827).

In Frorer vs. People [128] and Ramsey vs. People,[129] the Illinois court held void statutes forbidding payment of wages in token money and providing that miners' wages should be based on the weight of coal before it was screened. In the Frorer case, it said, with a sublime disregard of actuality, "Theoretically, there is no inferior class, other than that of those degraded by crime or other vicious indulgences of the passions, among our citizens." It quoted Cooley, that due process does "not mean a law passed for the purpose of working the wrong." [130] In the Ramsey case, in which it cited merely the Frorer case, it said that the statute took away from both the employer and the employee a property right, namely, the power to fix by contract "the mode in which such wages are to be ascertained and computed." [131]

In State vs. Loomis,[132] the Missouri court held void a statute forbidding token money in payment of wages by manufacturers or mine operators. It cited Cooley, and declared that everything is not law which the legislature enacts: due process required equal laws. It declared that the statute said to the employee: "Though of full age and competent to contract, still you shall not have the power to sell your labor for meat and clothing alone, as others may." These "sections of the statute," it said, "are utterly void. They attempt to strike down one of the fundamental principles of constitutional government. If they can stand, it is difficult to see an end to such legislation, and the government becomes one of special privileges, instead of a 'compact to promote the general welfare of the people.' " [133]

In State vs. Haun,[134] the Kansas court overthrew a token money statute, declaring that "Freedom of action—liberty—is the cornerstone of our governmental fabric." The law, it said, classified the workman "with the idiot, the lunatic, or the felon in the penitentiary." As between persons sui juris, it asked, "what right has the legislature to assume that one class has the need of protection against another?" It is "our boast," the court went on, "that no class distinctions exist in this country." The statute constituted "a suppression of individual effort, a denial of inalienable rights." [135] It, too, quoted Cooley on equal laws.

Here are five cases forbidding statutes against token money.

[128] 31 N.E. 395 (1892).   [129] 142 Ill. 380; 32 N.E. 364 (1892).
[130] 31 N.E. 395, 398, 399.   [131] 32 N.E. 365.   [132] 22 S.W. 350 (1893).
[133] *Ibid.*, p. 352.   [134] 59 Pac. 340, 346 (1899).   [135] *Ibid.*, p. 346.

The statutes attempted to prevent the practise of mine owners and similar employers of paying their men in scrip instead of in currency. The scrip was payable, save by consent of other merchants, only at company stores, and there was a widespread belief among employees that companies charged extortionate prices for goods at their stores, knowing that the men could not buy elsewhere. For years the unions struggled to obtain laws forbidding the practise, and when they succeeded, in State after State the laws were held to forbid the free right of contract of the employees.

The same theory was applied in other labor cases. In In re Jacobs,[136] the New York Court of Appeals overthrew a statute prohibiting cigar-making in tenements, because it denied the worker the right to work in his own home, if he wanted to. It, too, cited Marshall's words on power in Brown vs. Maryland, the Wynehamer case, and Field's words in the Butchers' Union case.

In Commonwealth vs. Perry, the Massachusetts court held void a statute prohibiting fines for imperfect weaving. The court said that the Declaration of Rights of the Massachusetts Constitution declared that "among the natural, inalienable rights of men," was the right "of acquiring, possessing, and protecting property." The right to possess property included the right to make reasonable contracts. If the employer could not fine his employees, his right to make contracts of employment was of no avail.[137]

Holmes dissented. He asserted (in words which, in the forty years following, he was to repeat in substance many times) that if, speaking as a political economist, he thought the law wrong, he would not overturn it on that ground, "unless I thought that an honest difference of opinion was impossible, or pretty nearly so." He felt that the law was passed because the employees thought they were being cheated "under a false pretense that the work done by them was imperfect"; and added that the employers had still the right under the law to sue for the wages paid for the poor work, and if that right was thought to be illusory, it was no more so than the right of the workman to sue for wages lost through fines for work which he claimed was well done.[138]

In Braceville Coal Company vs. The People, the Illinois court held that a statute providing for weekly payment of wages in mining was unconstitutional, because it denied the employee the

---

[136] 98 N.Y. 98 (1885).   [137] 155 Mass. 117, 121 (1891).   [138] *Ibid.*, pp. 124–25.

right to contract for payment at different intervals, thus treating the employees practically as if they were "under guardianship" and as if they were "minors." [139]

In Low vs. Rees Printing Co., the Nebraska court, citing almost all of the foregoing cases, held a statute unconstitutional, which provided an eight hour day except for farm and domestic labor. It said that under the police power, "the legislature can not prohibit harmless acts which do not concern the health, safety, and welfare of society." [140]

The Illinois court, which was one of the most stubborn in its denial of the right of the legislature to deal with modern conditions, continued its course in Ritchie vs. People.[141] It overthrew a statute limiting hours for women in manufacturing establishments to eight a day and forty-eight a week. "In this country," it said, "the legislature has no power to prevent persons who are sui juris from making their own contracts, nor can it interfere with the freedom of contract between the workman and the employer." It referred to the bill of rights. There was nothing in the employment contemplated which was, "in itself, unhealthy or unlawful or injurious to the public morals or welfare." For the State to act, the injury must be to the public and not to those employed; and "it is questionable whether it [the police power] can be invoked" to "prevent injury to the individuals engaged in a particular calling."

The same doctrine of the right to contract was applied in other cases dealing with the regulation of working conditions. In State vs. Kreutzberg,[142] the Wisconsin court held unconstitutional a statute forbidding employers to discharge union men on the ground of union membership, because "All men are born equally free and independent, and have certain inherent rights; among these are life, liberty, and the pursuit of happiness . . ." [143]

In People vs. Williams, the New York court held invalid a statute forbidding night work for women in factories. "I find nothing in the language of the section," said the opinion (with a complete disregard of actual conditions), "which suggests the purpose of promoting health, except as it might be inferred that for a woman to work the forbidden hours would be unhealthful." [144] Justice Brandeis was later to prove, by a mass of evidence, that there was

[139] 35 N.E. 62, 64 (1893).
[141] 40 N.E. 454, 455, 458, 459 (1895).
[143] *Ibid.*, p. 1099.
[140] 59 N.W. 362, 368 (1894).
[142] 90 N.W. 1098 (1902).
[144] 81 N.E. 778, 779 (1907) (N.Y.).

a difference in the physical constitution of women which made long hours of work harmful to health; and there was enough evidence, when the above case was decided that night work was also deleterious, to make the court's statement appear hopelessly ignorant to anyone who was well-informed. But, as we shall observe later, perhaps all the fault was not with the courts. Much must be laid to the lawyers, who failed to bring the mass of modern evidence to bear in their presentations to the courts.

The court, in the Williams case, went on to say that the law "arbitrarily deprives citizens of their right to contract with each other. The tendency of Legislatures, in the form of regulatory measures, to interfere with the lawful pursuits of citizens, is becoming a marked one in this country, and it behooves the courts, firmly and fearlessly, to interpose the barriers of their judgments, when invoked to protect against legislative acts plainly transcending the powers conferred by the Constitution upon the legislative body." [145]

Then came the important series of cases dealing with workmen compensation statutes and employers' liability laws. These were enacted after many years of discussion, as the result of a grievous sense of injustice among working-men in the rules of the common law known as assumption of risk, the fellow servant rule, and contributory negligence.

First was assumption of risk. It was said the employee assumed the ordinary risks of the employment. He was held to assume even the risk of dangerous and unsafe conditions, if he stayed on and did not exact a promise from his employer to remedy the conditions. Then there was the fellow servant rule. The workman could not recover if the injury were caused by the negligence of a fellow workman. Lastly was contributory negligence. The workman could not recover if he were himself negligent, and if his negligence were partly the cause of the accident. Finally, of course, there was no relief for the employee if the injury were due to a mere accident and no one was actually at fault. Working-men had felt for years that they had been deprived of recovery and their families impoverished and thrown on charity, when the accident was only partly the fault of the employee, or not his fault at all, but that of another employee.

[145] *Ibid.*, p. 780.

The fellow servant rule was, in a sense, an accident of our law. It had been started by Justice Shaw in a famous case before the Civil War, when the court could as well have gone the other way.[146] Moreover, employers were liable for injuries to third persons caused by the negligence of their employees, although the employers were without fault. These rules were not fundamental rules of property; they were not known when the original constitutions were adopted. Yet courts had come to regard them as sacred rights of life, liberty, and property; they could not conceive that a legislature had the right to change them.[147]

About the end of the first decade of the new century, a movement began to place new obligations on employers. Some were known as employers' liability laws, which merely removed the common law defenses of the fellow servant rule, assumption of risk, and contributory negligence. More advanced were the workmen's compensation statutes, which made the employer liable for all injuries received in the course of the employment, whether due to negligence or not, on the theory that the industry should bear the burdens of its accidents. Employers were required to insure in a State fund, and fixed amounts of compensation for various injuries were provided for.

These laws caused great discussion and a long legal struggle. In Hoxie vs. New York, New Haven and Hartford R.R.,[148] the Connecticut court held unconstitutional the Second Federal Employers' Liability Law, which denied the defenses of assumption of risk and the fellow servant rule, and made contributory negligence only mitigation of damages in injuries arising in interstate commerce. It said the statute "denied them, one and all, that liberty of contract which the Constitution of the United States secures to every person within their jurisdiction." [149]

---

[146] *Farwell* vs. *Boston etc. R.R.*, 4 Met. 49 (1842) (Mass.).

[147] It is only fair to observe that the courts had materially modified these bald rules, by requiring that the employer must provide a reasonably safe place to work, and safe tools and appliances, and must employ a competent vice-principal, namely, a superintendent, to carry on the work. Statutes requiring safe appliances and methods sometimes provided that the employee could not assume the risk resulting from their violation. Yet in the absence of such provisions, some courts actually held that an employee, by remaining at work without protest, assumed the risk caused by the violation of a safety appliances statute. In some States, if the negligent fellow employee worked in another department, the injured employee could still recover for his injury. Even as modified, assumption of risk, the fellow servant rule, and contributory negligence were harsh doctrines.

[148] 73 Atl. 754 (1909). [149] *Ibid.*, p. 761.

In Ives vs. South Buffalo Railway,[150] the New York Court of Appeals found it utterly impossible to approve the New York Workmen's Compensation statute. It gave the case the most thorough and sincere study, but it utterly failed to comprehend how the legislature could change these rules of defense which the courts had made. It called the statute "revolutionary," judged by "our common law standards." [151] It quoted from the Jacobs case to the effect that a man's liberty was "the right to use his faculties in all lawful ways, to live and work where he will, to earn his livelihood in any lawful calling, and to pursue any lawful trade or avocation." The right to hold "and enjoy his property until it is taken away from him by due process of law," was an inalienable right of man.

Then came this striking sentence: "When our Constitutions were adopted, it was the law of the land that no man who was without fault or negligence could be held liable in damages for injuries sustained by another." [152] Yet, at that time, a master was liable for injuries sustained by a third person through the fault of an employee, although the master was without fault. The Court went on: "It is conceded that this is a liability unknown to the common law, and we think it plainly constitutes a deprivation of property under the federal and state Constitutions, unless its imposition can be justified under the police power, which will be discussed under a separate head."

The Court said that the police power could not justify the change, and that a right of property could be changed only by the people and "not by the legislature." [153]

Yet there was no justification for the statement that a rule of common law when the Constitution was adopted, could be changed only by constitutional amendment. The decision simply meant that in a wide field of action, the legislature was helpless. The whole trend of these State decisions had been lamentable. On a large field of legislation, the Courts wholly denied the power of the legislatures.[154]

---

[150] 94 N.E. 431 (1911).   [151] *Ibid.*, p. 436.   [152] *Ibid.*, p. 439.   [153] *Ibid.*, pp. 439–40.
[154] A prominent group of law professors protested against the theory that what was due process in 1789 was due process in 1914, and declared that the court "should not read into the fundamental law of the State any limitations that stand in the way of the progress of the law toward better social justice within the limits of established institutions." No principle, they added, that "we should be willing to see introduced by Constitutional amendment, should be held contrary to due process." Boudin. *Government by Judiciary*, Vol. II, pp. 457–58.

The United States Supreme Court, from the beginning, showed a far more liberal tendency. In Holden vs. Hardy,[155] it upheld a statute for an eight hour day in underground mines, stating that it had not failed to recognize that the law is a progressive science; and that, while restriction for certain classes had become no longer necessary, "certain other classes of persons, particularly those engaged in dangerous or unhealthful employments, have been found to be in need of additional protection." Law, it said, must "adapt itself to new conditions of society." The police power could not be limited nor bargained away.[156] It noted that safety appliance laws, laws for fire escapes in hotels and theaters, and sanitary laws had been repeatedly approved.[157]

But the Court took pains to say that the police power was not unlimited. It noted that, while it had never defined with precision the words, "due process of law," it would be a denial of due process to deprive any class of persons of the general right to make contracts or to acquire property.[158] And it emphasized that it was deciding only that in underground mines, the hours of labor could be limited.[159]

With little argument, the Court disposed of a token money statute, holding constitutional a law similar to those the State courts had rejected in case after case of dreary and unreal argument.[160]

Four years later came a famous case, Lochner vs. New York.[161] It was one of the great cases which Roosevelt used in his argument for the recall of judicial decisions. New York had enacted a law limiting the hours of labor in bakeries to sixty per week. The Court held that it violated the due process clause. It denied the right of liberty of contract of employees to work more than sixty hours, if they wished to do so. "There is no reasonable ground for interfering with the liberty of person or the right of free contract, by determining the hours of labor in the occupation of a baker. There is no contention that bakers, as a class, are not equal in intelligence and capacity to men in other trades or manual occupations, or that they are not able to assert their rights and care for themselves without the protecting arm of the State interfering with their in-

---

[155] 169 U.S. 366 (1898).   [156] Ibid., pp. 385–87, 392.   [157] Ibid., pp. 392–93.
[158] Ibid., p. 391.   [159] Ibid., p. 395.
[160] Knoxville Iron Co. vs. Harbison, 183 U.S. 13 (1901).
[161] 198 U.S. 45 (1905).

dependence of judgment and of action. They are in no sense wards of the State." [162]

The Court added that it thought that "the limit of the police power has been reached and passed in this case. There is, in our judgment, no reasonable foundation for holding this to be necessary or appropriate as a health law to safeguard the public health, or the health of the individuals who are following the trade of a baker." If the statute were valid, the Court felt "there would be no length to which legislation of this nature might not go." [163] It and similar statutes were "mere meddlesome interference with the rights of the individual. . . ." [164]

No more striking case of basing a legal argument on a general political theory, could be found. Justice Peckham did not base his decision on the reasonable rule. He admitted that if the act were in the power of the legislature, it would be valid, although "the judgment of the court might be totally opposed to the enactment of such a law." But the question would remain, he said, whether it was within the power of the legislature. That question, he insisted, was for the Court; and he held that the law was unreasonable and arbitrary, not because there was no demand by reasonable men for the law, not because there was no evil proposed to be met by the law, but simply because, in his opinion, there was no power to regulate hours.

Holmes gave a short and memorable dissent. It brilliantly expressed the theory of the opposition to the tendency to declare State laws unconstitutional under the due process clause. As in all of his decisions, he did not state his own economic theory, but simply (as he rigidly insisted until the day of his retirement) that the Supreme Court had no right to impose its theory of economics under the guise of the due process clause. The States had the right to experiment. The opinion is so notable that it should be quoted at length:

"This case is decided upon an economic theory which a large part of the country does not entertain. If it were a question whether I agreed with that theory, I should desire to study it further and long before making up my mind. But I do not conceive that to be my duty, because I strongly believe that my agreement or disagreement has nothing to do with the right of a majority to embody their opinions in law. It is settled

[162] *Ibid.*, p. 57.　　[163] *Ibid.*, p. 58.　　[164] *Ibid.*, p. 61.

by various opinions of this Court that State constitutions and State laws may regulate life in many ways which we, as legislators, might think as injudicious or if you like as tyrannical as this, and which equally interfere with the liberty to contract. Sunday laws and usury laws are ancient examples. A more modern one is the prohibition of lotteries. The liberty of the citizen to do as he likes so long as he does not interfere with the liberty of others to do the same, which has been a shibboleth for some well-known writers, is interfered with by school laws, by the Post-office, by every state or municipal institution which takes his money for purposes thought desirable, whether he likes it or not. The Fourteenth Amendment does not enact Mr. Herbert Spencer's 'Social Statics.' "

He noted that the Court had sustained the Massachusetts vaccination law, the prohibition of margin dealings in the California constitution, and the eight hour law for miners (Holden vs. Hardy). "Some of these laws," he said, "embody convictions or prejudices which judges are likely to share. Some may not. But a constitution is not intended to embody a particular economic theory, whether of paternalism and the organic relation of the citizen to the State or of laissez faire. It is made for people of fundamentally differing views, and the accident of our finding certain opinions natural and familiar or novel and even shocking, ought not to conclude our judgment upon the question whether statutes embodying them conflict with the Constitution of the United States.

"General propositions do not decide concrete cases. The decision will depend on a judgment or intuition more subtle than any articulate major premise. But I think that the proposition just stated, if it is accepted, will carry us far toward the end. Every opinion tends to become a law. I think that the word liberty in the Fourteenth Amendment is perverted when it is held to prevent the natural outcome of a dominant opinion, unless it can be said that a rational and fair man necessarily would admit that the statute proposed would infringe fundamental principles, as they have been understood by the traditions of our people and our law. It does not need research to show that no such sweeping condemnation can be passed upon the statute before us. A reasonable man might think it a proper measure on the score of health. Men whom I certainly could not pronounce unreasonable, would uphold it as a first instalment of a general regulation of the hours of work." [165]

No more brilliant exposition of the theory that the Fourteenth

[165] *Ibid.*, pp. 75–76.

Amendment did not limit the police power, save where legislation shocks the conscience and sense of fairness of reasonable men, has been written. The Fourteenth Amendment, Holmes deeply felt, did not intend to make the Supreme Court a sort of House of Lords, which could pass on the desirability of legislation according to the economic and political views of its members. The States should be left free to experiment, so long as their experimentation did not shock the sense of fairness. The diversity and the essential freedom of the State jurisdictions should be allowed to remain.

Again, in Adair vs. U. S.,[166] the Court overthrew a statute of Congress forbidding a railroad to make it a condition of employment that an employee should not join a union. It followed this up in Coppage vs. Kansas,[167] by holding void a Kansas statute forbidding an employer to require employees to agree not to join a union as a condition of obtaining or keeping employment.

Pitney said that, included in "the right of personal liberty and the right of private property—partaking of the nature of each—is the right to make contracts for the acquisition of property. Chief among such contracts is that of personal employment, by which labor and other personal services are exchanged for money or other forms of property." [168] This right was as essential to the poor as to the rich. He answered the argument, that the employee did not have equality in bargaining, by saying that inequalities in fortunes could not be avoided, and that therefore freedom of contract could not be maintained without inequality in wealth.[169] Holmes (for the minority) again asserted that, if the belief which many held,—that, to have liberty of contract, it was necessary to have "equality of position,"—was reasonable, the Fourteenth Amendment should not prevent the State from permitting the equality to be attained.[170]

But these labor union cases were the only striking exceptions to the liberality of the Supreme Court's attitude on labor cases in the years in question. The Lochner case was, in effect, overruled in Muller vs. Oregon.[171] That case considered a ten hour law for women in factories and laundries in the State of Oregon. It was made memorable by the fact that Brandeis, then a practising lawyer, submitted a remarkable brief. Only a few pages were given to a consideration of the cases. Four hundred pages were devoted

---

[166] 208 U.S. 161 (1908).   [167] 236 U.S. 1 (1914).   [168] *Ibid.*, p. 14.
[169] *Ibid.*, p. 17.   [170] *Ibid.*, p. 27.   [171] 208 U.S. 412 (1908).

to a mass of statistics and quotations from medical authorities on the evil effects of long hours of labor on women. It was a great massing of actual experience. And it carried the day. The Supreme Court noted in its opinion that the testimony of those with actual experience was overwhelming to the effect that long hours of work for women were attended by injurious consequences. The law was held to be a reasonable exercise of the police power.

The result convinced lawyers that the bar had failed in its duty to the Court in confining its attention too much to the precedents of similar cases, and had not brought the Court abreast of the experience of the times.

Again, some years later, the Court upheld the Oregon law requiring payment for all employes of time and a half for overtime in a day's work of over ten hours.[172]

In a series of cases, the Court upheld the principle of employers' liability acts removing the defenses of assumption of risk, contributory negligence, and the fellow servant rule, and workmen's compensation acts fixing definite rates of compensation for all injuries, whether caused by negligence or not.

It reversed Judge Baldwin in the Hoxie case, shortly declaring that there was no property right in a rule of defense allowed by the common law.[173]

After the Ives case, New York adopted a constitutional amendment, and a workmen's compensation act was passed which provided that, if an employer did not insure, he could be sued at common law, but would be deprived of all the old defenses of assumption of risk, contributory negligence, and the fellow servant rule. The law was then attacked as violative of the Fourteenth Amendment. The Court said that "The close relation of the rules governing responsibility as between employer and employee to the fundamental rights of liberty and property, is of course recognized. But those rules, as guides of conduct, are not beyond alteration by legislation in the public interest. No person has a vested interest in any rule of law, entitling him to insist that it shall remain unchanged for his benefit."[174] In a Washington statute, the employer was compelled to insure in the State fund. That law was also upheld.[175]

[172] *Bunting* vs. *Oregon*, 243 U.S. 426 (1917).
[173] *Mondou* vs. *New York etc. R.R.*, 223 U.S. 1.
[174] *New York Cen. R.R.* vs. *White*, 243 U.S. 188, 197 (1917).
[175] *Mountain Timber Co.* vs. *Washington*, 243 U.S. 219 (1917).

Up to 1917, then, the Court had refused to apply the Fourteenth Amendment to negroes, except to protect them against unequal laws—a protection which in practice was of slight effect. It had denied the right of Congress to enact legislation directly enforcing the amendment. It had steadfastly refused to limit the procedure of the States. In three great fields it had asserted its power: the regulation of rates; the prohibition of taxing property outside the jurisdiction; and generally, under the police power, it had insisted that the regulation must be reasonable. Just what the implications of that requirement are, we shall examine soon. But up to 1917, while there had been lapses from liberality,—such as the cases holding invalid the statutes forbidding the discharge of men because they belonged to unions, and the Lochner case,—the record had been, on the whole, one of breadth of vision and recognition of the social needs of the times, but in its theory lay the seeds of great extensions.

The opinion of the Court at the end of this liberal era may be summarized in the much quoted words of Justice Holmes (not in a labor case, but in a case involving an Oklahoma statute, providing that all banks must contribute to a fund to reimburse depositors in failed banks), that, "It may be said in a general way that the police power extends to all the great public needs. . . . It may be put forth in aid of what is sanctioned by usage, or held by the prevailing morality or strong and preponderant opinion, to be greatly and immediately necessary to the public welfare." [176] He added that the state could take the whole business of banking under its control, could go from "regulation to prohibition, except upon such conditions as it may prescribe." Rights, Holmes said again about this time, "tend to declare themselves absolute to their

---

[176] *Noble State Bank* vs. *Haskell*, 219 U.S. 104, 111, 112 (1911).

Since 1917 the Court has shown an unfortunate tendency away from the liberal trend up to 1917, in which it has clearly decided cases on a political bias, as Justice Stone said in the New York Minimum Wage Case, on the basis of the "personal, economic predilections" of the members of the Court. In *Adkins* vs. *Children's Hospital*, 261 U.S. 525 (1923), it overthrew a minimum wage statute for women and children for the District of Columbia; in *Tyson* vs. *Banton*, 273 U.S. 418 (1926), it held void a New York law regulating re-sale theater prices; in *New State Ice Co.* vs. *Liebmann*, 285 U.S. 262, it disapproved an Oklahoma statute licensing the manufacture and sale of ice; and in 1936 it overthrew the New York Minimum Wage law, *Morehead* vs. *New York, ex rel. Tipaldo*, 80 Law Ed., 921. Vigorous dissents were filed in all these cases. The course of the decisions emphasizes their political nature, for they vary according to the inherent political prejudices of a majority of the Court. The question of the limit and nature of Court control is clearly not a settled one.

logical extreme," but they are all limited by principles of policy and other public interests.[177]

However much the public, some of the bar, and even at times the Court, might think of the Constitution as a fixed document speaking revealed truth and of its provisions as axioms, the Supreme Court actually has treated it as a changing, developing, growing thing. In a remarkable dissenting opinion in 1932, Justice Brandeis argued that the Supreme Court had recognized that the rule of *stare decisis* (namely, the rule that the precedents control) did not apply to constitutional questions, because constitutional decisions can be modified or reversed only by the Court or by constitutional amendment. Correction "through legislative action," he said, "is practically impossible." So the Court must make the necessary changes. He listed a large number of cases in which the Supreme Court had reversed, qualified, or modified its previous opinions on constitutional questions. There were no less than thirty-one of these cases,—twenty-one of them before 1917.[178]

We have seen that Justice Miller said in 1882 that it was very doubtful if the Fourteenth Amendment would ever be applied to other than negroes. Now it is applied to a host of questions: tax, rate, corporation, and labor legislation. Formerly the Court held that a State could tax a foreign corporation on its entire capital. Now it holds that it can tax it only on the portion employed in the State. It reversed itself on the legal tender cases. It held an hours of labor law unconstitutional, and later upheld a similar law. The Constitution is a growing, living thing.

REFERENCES

Boudin, Louis B., *Government by Judiciary* (2 vols.). New York: William Godwin, Jr., 1932.

Conkling, Roscoe, Oral Argument in *San Mateo County* vs. *Southern Pacific R.R. Co.*, 116 U.S. 138. In File Copies of Briefs, U.S. Supreme Court, Vol. 6, 106–11 (Oct. Term, 1885).

Cooley, Thomas M., *Constitutional Limitations*. Boston: Little, Brown & Co., 1871 (2d ed.).

Corwin, Edward S., The Doctrine of Due Process of Law Before the Civil War. 24 *Harvard Law Review*, 366, 460 (March, April, 1911).

[177] *Hudson County Water Co.* vs. *McCarter*, 209 U.S. 349, 355 (1908).
[178] *Burnet* vs. *Coronado Oil & Gas Co.*, 285 U.S. 393, 406–8 (1932). Brandeis also argued that constitutional questions involving the reasonableness of statutes, are essentially questions of fact. I shall consider this point in Chapter III.

HOAR, GEORGE F., *Autobiography of Seventy Years* (2 vols.). New York: Charles Scribner's Sons, 1903.

KENDRICK, BENJAMIN B., *The Journal of the Joint Committee of Fifteen on Reconstruction.* New York: Longmans, Green & Co., 1914.

MCILWAIN, CHARLES HOWARD, *The High Court of Parliament and Its Supremacy.* New Haven: Yale University Press, 1910.

MOTT, RODNEY L., *Due Process of Law.* Indianapolis: The Bobbs-Merrill Co., 1926.

RHODES, JAMES FORD, *History of the United States,* Vol. VIII. New York: The Macmillan Co., 1919.

SUMNER, CHARLES, *Works,* Vol. XIV. Boston: Lee & Shepard, 1875–1883.

THAYER, JAMES BRADLEY, *Cases on Constitutional Law* (2 vols.). Cambridge: George H. Kent, 1895.

——"The Origin and Scope of the American Doctrine of Constitutional Law (1893)" in *Legal Essays.* Boston: Boston Book Co., 1908.

WARREN, CHARLES, *The Supreme Court in United States History.* Boston: Little, Brown & Co., 1926 (revised edition).

CHAPTER III

THE OPPOSITION TO THE POLITICAL POWER
OF THE COURTS

THE TESTS OF DUE PROCESS OF LAW

To THE lay reader, this long summary of the decisions of the Courts over fifty years on questions of due process, may seem dull and inappropriate in a discussion of the course of political thought. But the summary must have shown that these cases do actually delineate the process of political thought. In the first place, the decisions of the Courts on due process and the equal protection of the laws are, after all, discussions of political questions. They are discussions of the limits of political action.

The general power of the legislature is clear. The courts have said, time and again, that the police power extends to all the needs of society, and that it can not be bargained away. The power, therefore, is there.

But we have found the courts overthrowing statutes on the ground that they violated the due process clause, although they were not special, although there was no question of violation of any specific provision of the Constitution. They have held that they denied due process on the ground that they were unreasonable exercises of the police power.

But if the question is one of reasonableness, it is one of fact. Whether statutes regulating the hours of labor, forbidding token money, changing the common law defenses, forbidding night work for women, establishing a minimum wage, forbidding discharges of employees for joining a union, are reasonable, are, after all, questions of fact which depend on the economic and political experience of the time. They are questions of whether there is an evil to be met, and whether the statute is reasonably desired to cure or alleviate the evil. They involve the whole question of the limits of political action; in short, they are political questions.

Moreover, the method of discussion has been political. The

standard test is that the court must never declare a statute void, unless the invalidity is established beyond a reasonable doubt. Professor Thayer likened this test to that applied by courts in negligence and criminal cases. The courts must decide, not whether the man was guilty, or whether they as jurors would have returned a verdict that he was guilty, or whether the defendant was negligent, or as jurors they would have held him negligent; but simply whether a reasonable man could say that he was guilty, or that he was negligent. The court therefore, he said, must not determine what was desirable legislation, but simply fix "the outside border of reasonable legislative action. . . ."[1] The test was what a legislature might reasonably do in the circumstances. Thayer admitted that the function of the courts was political; and therefore he urged that the courts, in exercising this "great and stately jurisdiction," must not imperil it by stepping into the shoes of the lawmaker.[2]

Holmes accepted this test. He repeated time and again that the wisdom of the statute was not for him to decide. In the Lochner case, he said, "A reasonable man might think it a proper measure on the score of health. Men whom I certainly could not pronounce unreasonable, would uphold it as a first instalment of a general regulation of the hours of work."[3] If a reasonable man could uphold it, there was no denial of due process.

It is needless to say that the Supreme Court has not adhered to the reasonable rule. It repeats that the test is whether the legislation is arbitrary and unreasonable; but the test has become whether it is arbitrary and unreasonable in the mind of the Court, and not whether a reasonable man could believe the statute desirable. In the Lochner case, Peckham actually insisted that the presumption was against any interference by the state with liberty of contract. He admitted that if the act were within the legislative power, it was valid, although the Court might disagree as to the desirability of the law. But he said the legislature had no power, for there was no reasonable ground for interfering with the hours of work.[4] Day declared in another case that, if "such action was arbitrary interference with the right to contract or carry on business, and having no just relation to the protection of the public within the scope of the legislative power, the act must fail."[5]

[1] J. B. Thayer, *Legal Essays*, "Constitutional Law," p. 27.   [2] *Ibid.*, p. 32, 33.
[3] *Lochner* vs. *New York*, 198 New York 45, 76.   [4] *Ibid.*, p. 57.
[5] *McLean* vs. *Arkansas*, 211 U.S. 539, 548 (1909).

It is evident that the decision of what is arbitrary interference is that of the court: the decision is not that of a supposed reasonable man. If the court, acting on the basis of its conceptions of the limits of political action, thinks that the law is arbitrary, it is arbitrary, whether or not a reasonable man could think it desirable. The test in a number of crucial cases has been Justice Field's test, —that an interference with the right to contract and carry on business, is a denial of due process.

Boudin, in his *Government by Judiciary*, argues that the reasonable test gives the "progressive" case away.[6] If you really mean to abide by the unreasonable rule, you foreclose discussion; for a court could hardly say that reasonable men did not think a statute desirable which a legislature had enacted.[7] If you concede that there is still a question of reasonableness after the legislature has acted, you give the court the opportunity to say that the legislature was unreasonable.

Thus, Holmes, in the Lochner case, said that he thought the word, "liberty," in the Fourteenth Amendment, was "perverted, when it is held to prevent the natural outcome of a dominant opinion, unless it can be said that a rational and fair man necessarily would admit that the statute proposed would infringe fundamental principles, as they have been understood by the traditions of our people and our law."[8] This, indeed, gives to the courts the chance to say that the statute does infringe fundamental principles, as they have been understood by the traditions of our people and our law. It is sounder, Boudin argues, to say, with Marshall, that the question is one of power; and that if the power exists, there is no question as to the degree of its exercise.

Holmes, indeed (in a case decided later than the period covered by this book), seems to adopt this standard. In Tyson vs. Banton,[9]

---

[6] Boudin, *Government by Judiciary*, Vol. II, p. 490. [7] *Ibid.*, p. 495.
[8] *Lochner* vs. *New York*, 198 U.S. 45, 76.
In the years after the end of our period, Brandeis has attacked the question of reasonableness in an entirely different way from Holmes. Holmes said that if a reasonable man could hold the statute desirable, it was not for him to vote that it was arbitrary. He saw no reason to examine into the necessity of the proposed reform. Brandeis—whether from belief, or because he conceives that the best way to convince the other members of the Court is to show that there is an evil, and that the statute is well calculated to meet that evil—goes thoroughly into the whole question. With astonishing labor, he marshals evidence of the conditions that brought the statute into being; and argues that it is designed to meet a real evil, and that therefore the burden laid is due process of law.
[9] *Tyson* vs. *Banton*, 273 U.S. 418, 446 (1926).

he said that he thought "the proper course is to recognize that a State legislature can do whatever it sees fit to do unless it is restrained by some express prohibition in the Constitution of the United States or of the State. . . ."

I believe that this is the proper rule in due process cases, though it would seem too late now for it to be adopted. I think, however, that a strict adherence to the rule of unreasonableness would have resulted in but few statutes being held lacking in due process, and would have avoided most of the controversy.

The context of Holmes' dissenting opinion in the Lochner case, and many other expressions by him, clearly show that he did not mean that what was reasonable was to be determined by the Court's own idea of what is reasonable or politically desirable. His test of reasonableness was, like Thayer's, the test of what reasonable men might desire or believe.

Courts constantly affirm negligence cases, where, as jurors, they would have decided differently; and there is no reason why, in constitutional cases, they should not as steadily sustain statutes of which they disapprove. They could overthrow any statute which was special, which denied a hearing, which was ex post facto, or which violated an express prohibition; but they could not deny that due process was allowed, unless a reasonable man could not say that he thought it desirable. Nor would this rule prevent action in all cases on the theory that a legislature must be reasonable. It is perfectly possible for a legislature, composed entirely of reasonable men, to pass a statute which, once it had had time for reconsideration, it would agree is wholly unreasonable.

But the courts have not followed the rule of reasonableness. As in negligence cases they have often usurped the province of the jury, so in constitutional cases they have often usurped the province of the legislature. They have held statutes unconstitutional because they were opposed to the fundamental political theories of the courts. It is true that they have decided the cases by reference to the authorities, and apparently by the deductive method familiar in the decision of legal cases. But the method, after all, is illusory: the cases are often decided, as the decisions I have quoted from show, on general political theories.

This is strikingly exemplified in the decisions of Justice Field. He was shocked at the granting of the Slaughter House monopoly in Louisiana. But he insisted that the Fourteenth Amendment did not infringe upon the police power of the States. He was in favor of permitting prohibition legislation, an ordinance restricting laundries in California, and laws changing the ordinary procedure of the States. But an oleomargarine law outraged his sense of the right to pursue one's calling. He was strenuously opposed to the Granger laws; but, on the other hand, when Missouri enacted a law providing for double liability for injuries to cattle when railroads failed to fence in their rights of way, he answered, "This court is not a harbor where refuge can be found for every act of ill-advised and oppressive State legislation." The remedy, he said, "for evils of that character [i.e., hardship or injustice] is to be sought from State legislatures." [10] But he would have none of that remedy when the Granger cases or the Slaughter House monopoly were involved.

The personal element is involved in all law cases, but the pressure of precedents reduces its play in old branches of the law until it becomes comparatively negligible. But in cases under the due process clause, the element of personal judgment is much greater than in any other field of the law. This tendency has decreased with time; for a body of precedents has been built up. But, after all, the difference will always remain, for the simple reason that the questions are truly more political than legal.

There is a famous story of Professor John Chipman Gray, who had long taught the law of perpetuities and restraints on alienation, with their almost mathematical tests for decision, and then was asked to teach constitutional law. He threw up the course, with the remark that it was not law at all, but politics. The contrast between the exactitude of the law of perpetuities and the empiricism of constitutional law was too great.

Lawyers have become so accustomed to consider constitutional law as of the same piece with other branches of the law, that this conception that it is not law at all, is disconcerting to them. They attempt to argue constitutional cases as they argue other cases; they cite precedents; they attempt to bring the case in hand under the precedents of other cases.

But, after all, the cases are decided frequently on the basis of political preconceptions, on the political theories of the justices, by

[10] *Missouri Pacific R.R.* vs. *Humes,* 115, U.S. 512, 520. (1885).

deduction from a political major premise. Holmes, in the Lochner case, referred to an articulate major premise. In a brilliant article, Albert M. Kales of the Chicago Bar, argued that the premise was inarticulate, but should be made articulate. The Supreme Court, he said, had never defined the criteria by which it tested the limits of due process. He quoted the statement of Day given above, and a similar one from Hughes, and said that they revealed nothing. He likewise discarded the reasonable rule. He declared it would not work; because if the premise is inarticulate, and each side proceeds on a different premise, neither can be said to be unreasonable. As the premise is inarticulate, and intuition supplies the place of the application of a rule to the facts, "the judicial aspect of the Court's function diminishes to the vanishing point, and the function itself becomes suspiciously like an ideal legislator."

The Supreme Court, he went on, refuses to make the major premise articulate, because it wants to leave itself with a wide discretion "to do what it thinks best." But counsel appearing before the Court should endeavor to break the formula down, and make it more explicit.

Kales, therefore, proposed that the premise be made articulate. He said that there were three paramount evils which legislation should control: the selfishness and stupidity of managers, and the fact that the rewards of the managers were more than necessary. So far as legislation was exerted to correct these evils, it should be sustained. But if it attempted to substitute a legislative fiat for the judgment of the managers, if it acted to impair the competitive system, or interfere with the ownership and distribution of private property, or undermine the managers' chances and motives for successful management, it was invalid.

He thought that the Court's decisions sustained his test, and on that basis he approved the Lochner, Coppage and Adair cases.[11]

In seeking to make the premise articulate, he merely made three

---

[11] Albert M. Kales, " 'Due Process,' the Inarticulate Major Premise and the Adamson Act." 26 *Yale Law Journal* (May, 1917), pp. 519, 530, 538, 543.

In this discussion of inarticulate and articulate major premises in the decision of constitutional questions, it is interesting to recall that Justice Iredell warned us in 1798 that abstract rules like considerations of "natural justice" are too subjective to be the basis of court decisions. He wisely observed: "The ideas of natural justice are regulated by no fixed standard; the ablest and the purest men have differed upon the subject. . . ." Calder vs. Bull, 3 Dall. 386, 399 (1798). The Supreme Court's decisions amply justify his belief. A friend of mine observed that the decisions are apparently often based on "cosmic hunches."

sub-formulas. The main formula has been avowed ever since the days of Field, that an arbitrary interference with the right of contract is void. Kales would simply add that legislation restricting the cupidity or stupidity of managers, or to prevent the rewards of managers being too great, is not arbitrary interference; and that legislation interfering with the judgment of managers, is arbitrary interference.

But to break down the test by these three sub-tests, leaves it almost as vague and general as before. The difference of opinion on what is a restraint on selfishness and stupidity, and what is a restraint on judgment, would be as great as the differences on what is an arbitrary interference with the right to contract. The regulation of hours, Kales felt, was a restriction on the judgment of managers; and yet it has been generally approved. The Lochner case was over-ruled when he wrote. Zoning laws, laws against billboards, are not restraints on cupidity or stupidity; and yet they have been generally approved. Assuming that the management must not be interfered with, does not tell us when restraints on definite evils may be imposed. Nor do I know any reason in the Fourteenth Amendment why any aspect of private property is sacrosanct. There are conservative lawyers who assert that it does not prevent socialism, if the people want it.

But Kales' article shows vividly how political the test has been, and how much its application depends on the political beliefs of the judges. Indeed, while he admitted that, in operation, the judicial aspect of the Court's function has diminished to the vanishing point, he proposed that the premise be made articulate in order to limit the political discretion of the Court. Yet he rejoiced that the Court has acted as "our substitute for a second legislative chamber for the United States and the states." [12]

Actually, the vagaries of the decisions show that, as Holmes said, the decisions have often depended on intuitions rather than deduction from an articulate major premise. But in the expressed reasoning of the Courts, the premise has, I think, become pretty articulate. The reasoning has been simple, and in case after case, has been somewhat as follows:

Freedom of contract is a natural right of man, or is a foundation of our bill of rights. Token money statutes, limitation of hours,

[12] *Ibid.*, p. 537.

minimum wage and workmen's compensation statutes, theater price regulation,—one and all, deny freedom of contract. Therefore, they deny due process of law.

It is no exaggeration to say that some such process has been at work in many constitutional cases. The economic and political precepts imbedded in the minds of judges, who have not been specialists in economics or political science, have controlled in most of the cases where courts have denied the right of the legislature under the police power. The great mass of experience, the pressing evils to be met, have been brushed aside, and a universal formula has had the victory. The courts of last resort have been, to an appreciable extent, legislative bodies. They have acted as brakes on legislation. The fact that the legislatures have in the end had their way, in no way disproves the point. The courts have not prevented legislation; but they have, indeed, measurably delayed it.

A great body of conservative opinion looks on this process with equanimity, if not with strong approval. In fact, it would be happy if the power of the courts were oftener and more strongly exercised. It rejoices in the courage of the courts in opposing the will of majorities, and that the United States is the only country in the world where the courts exercise a control over legislation. It considers the power an essential protection to the rights of the individual, and looks upon any restriction on it as dangerous to the rights of minorities.

THE McCARDLE CASE

But, manifestly, no such power could exist in a democracy without being called in question. There have been several great occasions in the period of our study, when the power has been attacked. The first came with the Reconstruction legislation after the Civil War. The Supreme Court realized that opinion ran high. The Republican majority, then in control, was perhaps more determined than any majority in our history. Twice, when direct attacks were made on the Reconstruction legislation, the Supreme Court definitely refused to take jurisdiction. In Mississippi vs. Johnson,[13] and following that, in Georgia vs. Stanton,[14] the Court said that it had no jurisdiction: the question was political. There was no sufficient showing that any property rights were involved.

[13] 4 Wall. 475 (1866).   [14] 6 Wall. 50 (1867).

These were attempts by injunction to restrain, in the first case, the President; in the second case, the Secretary of War, from carrying out the Reconstruction acts.

But in 1867 a new attack was made. An editor named McCardle was arrested in Tennessee for some violent attacks on the military government. He sued out a writ of habeas corpus before the United States District Court. The court remanded him over to the military authorities. He appealed to the Supreme Court. The attorney general moved to dismiss the appeal on the ground that the Court had no jurisdiction. The Court denied the motion, and therefore held that it did have jurisdiction.

Then the determined Republican majority in Congress took decisive action. It was keenly aware of the danger, and determined that its power should not be curtailed. In the House of Representatives, Schenck proposed an amendment to the Judiciary Act which was adopted, which took away the appellate jurisdiction of the Supreme Court. The Constitution grants the Supreme Court original jurisdiction only in cases affecting ambassadors, consuls, ministers, and those in which a State is a party. In all other cases, the jurisdiction of the Court is appellate only, and is subject to the control of Congress. Congress, in all probability, can not say that some court shall not decide a judicial question; but it can say what court shall be the court of last resort. The lower court had decided in favor of the Reconstruction legislation. The majority in Congress was afraid that the Supreme Court would overthrow the legislation. Therefore, it determined to take the Supreme Court's power away.

Schenck was charged with abusing the confidence of the House by proposing an amendment with such consequences, without making its effect clear. He replied bluntly: "Sir, I have lost confidence in the Supreme Court of the United States. Is not that plain enough? I believe that they usurp power whenever they dare to undertake to settle questions purely political in regard to the States, and the manner in which those States are to be held subject to the lawmaking power. And if I find them abusing that power by attempting to arrogate to themselves jurisdiction under any statute that happens to be upon the record from which they claim to derive that jurisdiction, and I can take it away from them by a repeal of that statute, I will do it. . . . Now I hold that the

Supreme Court of the United States, arrogating to themselves the pretension to settle not merely judicial but political questions, and trampling upon the principle of the decision made in the case of the Dorr Rebellion, and upon every other decision of that kind, are, the majority of them, proceeding step by step to the usurpation of jurisdiction which does not belong to them. And I hold it to be not only my right but my duty, as a Representative of the people, to clip the wings of that Court wherever I can, in any attempt to take such flights." [15]

The bill went to the President. Meanwhile the public and the opposition, which had been taken by surprise, began to wake up. *The New York Times* protested against the denial of the test of the Reconstruction Act, by "forcing out of court a case rightfully there, awaiting argument and judgment, and forbidding the recognition of cases affecting the constitutionality of statutes under which the States are to be brought into the union. . . ." [16]

The President vetoed the bill. When it came up again in the Senate, Senator Hendricks attacked it in a long speech. He asked, "Why is it that you are not willing that the Supreme Court shall pass upon the legislation of last year? . . . Then, sir, you say you are right, but you will not let it be tested." [17] Senator Saulsbury called it an act of despotism, and said that if the legislative power is to be absolute, "then will freedom not only be denied to McCardle but to every American citizen." [18]

But the opposition was not daunted. *The New York Times* was not a Republican paper, anyway, said Congressman Wilson of Iowa, who added, "Most assuredly it was my intention to take away the jurisdiction given by the act of 1867, reaching the McCardle case or any other case depending on the provisions of that act affected by the amendment." [19]

The recurring note in all the Republican speeches was the charge that the Court had been doing political work, and holding back a political majority. The McCardle case, said Senator Maynard, "was brought up for no purpose in this world except to test and settle political questions. It is a political suit; that and nothing else, and brought for that purpose alone. And decency and propriety,

[15] *Congressional Globe,* March 14, 1868, p. 1883.
[16] *Ibid.,* March 21, 1868, p. 2064.   [17] *Ibid.,* March 26, 1868 p. 2117.
[18] *Ibid.,* March 26, 1868, p. 2122.   [19] *Ibid.,* March 21, 1868, p. 2061.

according to my ideas, require that we should, by our legislation, put an end to that suit and save the Court from further annoyance or further occasion to engage in any discussion, or to make any decision of that kind." [20]

Again, Wilson exclaimed, "Why, sir, we could not shut our eyes or close our ears to the information which come to us from all quarters, particularly in the press representing the party to which the gentleman belongs, that it was a thing certain that the McCardle case was to be made use of to enable a majority of that court to determine the invalidity and unconstitutionality of the reconstruction laws of Congress." [21]

Again, Senator Stewart said that "we are not afraid of the Supreme Court. The Supreme Court has no power to interfere with the question of reconstruction." [22] The Supreme Court could decide cases, but "it has no will, no policy; it must follow the lawmaking power of the Government." If that Court wanted to interfere with political matters, he asked, why did it start so late? "Why did it not issue an injunction and stop the firing upon Fort Sumter?" [23]

And so the bill was passed óver the veto. The Supreme Court, when the case came before it, decided that it had no jurisdiction.[24] Here was a bold, and even passionate, partisan determination to hold power and maintain a course of political action. It would brook no opposition, and went so far as to take a case from the docket of the Supreme Court which that Court had already refused to dismiss. Surely, a bolder defiance was never made!

THE LEGAL TENDER CASES

Another serious issue arose when the Legal Tender cases came before the Court, although there was then no suggestion that the Court be deprived of its power.

During the war Congress had authorized the issuance of greenbacks. The question of the constitutionality of the legal tender provision did not come up before the Supreme Court until almost eight years later. A number of State and lower Federal courts had upheld the law. In 1870, the Supreme Court held in Hepburn vs. Griswold [25] that the act was unconstitutional as to contracts made before its passage. When it was realized that the reasoning of the

---

[20] *Ibid.*, March 21, 1868, p. 2064.
[22] *Ibid.*, March 26, 1868, p. 2118.
[24] *Ex parte McCardle*, 7 Wall. 506.

[21] *Ibid.*, March 21, 1868, p. 2062.
[23] *Ibid.*, March 26, 1868, p. 2119.
[25] 8 Wall. 603.

Court would also result in holding it unconstitutional as to contracts made after its passage, a strong demand came for a re-hearing. The re-hearing was finally allowed, and the Court, with two new members on it, upheld the act both as to contracts made before and as to those made after the passage of the law.

The whole transaction was most unfortunate. It was heatedly charged that the Court was packed to get a favorable decision. The charge was unjust but both the granting of the re-hearing and the changed decision resulted in weakening the prestige of the Court for many years to come.

In the campaign of 1892, James B. Weaver, the Populist candidate for President, in his campaign book, "A Call to Action," attacked the political power of the Supreme Court. He declared that those who exercise power "should always be under the restraint of those from whom it was derived. Elective control is the only safeguard of liberty." [26] He charged that the Supreme Court had aided the slave power. He criticized the decision in the case of the Chicago, St. Paul and Milwaukee Railroad, where the Court first intimated that the regulation of railroad rates were subject to court review. He concluded that a "Century of experience shows that new safeguards should be provided, and the great Tribunal must be brought back to a sense of its accountability to the people." [27] But he did not specify what steps should be taken.

THE INCOME TAX CASE

The Wilson Tariff Act of 1894 imposed an income tax on all incomes from whatever source derived. The Supreme Court held the tax unconstitutional. The case was decided by a five to four decision, and that result was caused by one justice changing his mind in the last month. Here again there was a re-argument, but the re-argument did not change the first decision. The Supreme Court had held that the Civil War income tax on business and personal income was constitutional. [28] Now it held that a tax on income from land was a tax on land, and therefore a direct tax, and that as a direct tax it must be apportioned among the States according to population.

It is strange now to read the words of Choate, who made the chief

---

[26] James B. Weaver, *A Call to Action*, p. 70.   [27] *Ibid.*, p. 135.
[28] *Springer* vs. *U.S.*, 102 U.S. 586 (1880).

argument against the law. He declared, "I do not believe that any member of this Court ever has sat or ever will sit to hear and decide a case, the consequences of which will be so far-reaching as this,—not even the venerable member who survives from the early days of the Civil War, and has sat upon every question of reconstruction, of national destiny, of state destiny that has come up during the last thirty years. No member of this Court will live long enough to hear a case which will involve a question of more importance than this, the preservation of the fundamental rights of private property, and equality before the law, and ability of the people of these United States to rely upon the guaranties of the Constitution." [29]

Choate's biographer, Edward S. Martin, quotes a newspaper correspondent of the time as saying that Choate felt that, for the Court to affirm the law, "would be the most dangerous influence in its results which this country has met with, since the pro-slavery men of the South determined upon secession. It seemed to him if the Supreme Court should find itself impelled to declare this law constitutional, that we should have the most startling illustration of the influence of Populism; and he felt as though such a decision would, in the impulses which would follow it, simply accelerate the purposes of the Populists, so that the next legislative attempt of theirs would be greatly to increase the amount of taxes taken from the wealthy, and also greatly increase the discrimination in favor of those who have not great possessions." [30] He objected both because the law would tax the rich States for the benefit of the poor, and because it was an attempt, in his opinion, to take from those with great possessions for the benefit of those with small possessions.

But it is not the place here to dwell on the arguments of the case. We are concerned only with the question of the desirability of declaring the law unconstitutional. In his argument in behalf of the tax, James Coolidge Carter spoke of the danger that the Court would be shorn of its power if it declared the law unconstitutional. Choate called this "stage thunder;" and added that it would never have occurred to him "to present either as an opening or closing argument, to this great and learned Court, that if, in their wisdom,

[29] *Pollock* vs. *Farmers'* etc. Co., 157 U.S. 429, 553 (1895).
[30] Edward S. Martin, *The Life of Joseph Hodges Choate*, Vol. II, p. 4.

they found it necessary to protect a suitor who sought here to cling to the Ark of the Covenant and invoke the protection of the Constitution which was created for us all, against your furnishing that relief and protection, that possibly the popular wrath might sweep the Court away. It is the first time I have ever heard the argument presented to this or any other court, and I trust it will be the last." [31]

It is interesting to recall that, fourteen years later, President Taft (surely a conservative, if there ever were one) recommended an income tax amendment as necessary to the national power. It was passed unanimously by the Senate, and with only a few votes in opposition in the House. The World War financing leaned heavily on it.

The income tax case brought strong disapproval, both on the ground that it was far too technical in holding an income tax to be a tax on land because a burden on land (although any excise tax levied on a business is also a burden on the real estate of the business), and because of the closeness of the vote, and the shift of one justice from one side to the other in the last month.

The question of the right of the Court to pass on the constitutionality of such a law as the income tax is very different from all questions of due process; for it mainly involves the distribution of powers between the State and the Federal governments, and such questions there is no other body but the Supreme Court to decide. No one questioned the power of a State to pass an income tax. But, nevertheless, the opinion caused deep dissatisfaction; and the result furnished another proof that Carter, after all, was right in declaring that an adverse decision would imperil the power of the Court.

The Democratic platform of 1896 took notice of the decision in the Income Tax case. It said that, but for the failure of that law, there would be no deficit; and called attention that the law was passed in "strict pursuance of the uniform decisions of that court for nearly one hundred years, that court having in that decision sustained Constitutional objections to its enactment which had previously been overruled by the ablest judges who have ever sat on that bench." [32]

---

[31] E. S. Martin, *The Life of Joseph Hodges Choate*, Vol. II, p. 6.
[32] A. K. McClure, *History of the Presidency*, p. 375.

In the heated campaign, this statement was denounced as anarchistic. It is customary for political opponents to stigmatize thus anyone who disagrees with any decision. Of course, it would be proper for anyone to dissent from a decision on a question of substantive law in such mild terms as the Democratic platform used, let alone a decision on a great political question.

Bryan, in his speeches, noted the criticism and defended the platform statement. There was "no suggestion," he said, "of an attempt to dispute the authority of the Supreme Court." The party "was simply pledged to use 'all the constitutional power which remains after that decision, or which may come from its reversal by the Court as it may hereafter be constituted.' "[33]

The discussion died down, but the memory of the case remained and had its effect in the great discussion of the Court's power in 1912.

In the great railroad rate debate of 1906, the conflict between the courts and the legislative power sprang up anew. Those who favored rate control wished to make the power of the commission as broad as possible. They distrusted the courts as a clog on the rate making power. Their opponents wished to make the court review as broad as possible.

Senator Knox expressed the old fundamental insistence on protection by the courts. Men "of our inheritance," he said, "repel summary and arbitrary methods, and none the less if these methods proceed from acknowledged power, accompanied by the mere empty phrases and forms of law. Judicial review of every substantial controversy affecting persons and property is a right." It was a right won from tyranny, and must be held against tyranny even "if masquerading in the name of the people." It is the sober truth, he said, "that the courts are the guardians of our rights and liberties."[34]

In the end, court review, of course, won; but, after all, it was a narrow review. The courts finally were limited to preventing arbitrary and confiscatory rates.

THE RECALL OF JUDICIAL DECISIONS

The impetus to the next discussion was given by Theodore Roosevelt in the campaign of 1912. It was a period of great re-

---

[33] Bryan, *The First Battle*, p. 319.
[34] Nathaniel W. Stephenson, *Nelson W. Aldrich*, p. 301.

surgence of the democratic ideal. The initiative, referendum, and recall were in the air. The long line of State cases, denying the right of the legislature to enact industrial legislation, had just culminated in the Ives case in New York holding the workmen's compensation statute unconstitutional, and the Hoxie case holding the second Federal employers' liability act unconstitutional. The Lochner case was only eight years old. We can see now that the crest of State court negation of social legislation had been reached, and that the courts were slowly becoming more liberal in the construction of legislation.

But at that time, Roosevelt, with many others, was deeply stirred by the denial of the New York Court of the right of a legislature to take away the old common law defenses of assumption of risk, the fellow servant rule, and contributory negligence. In the course of his address before the Ohio Constitutional Convention in February, 1912, after treating the recall of judges, he said that we should be very cautious about the recall "of a good judge who has rendered an unwise and improper decision." [35] Every public servant at times makes mistakes. "But when," he went on, "a judge decides a Constitutional question, when he decides what the people as a whole can or can not do, the people should have the right to recall that decision if they think it wrong." [36] He argued by analogy from the position taken by Lincoln on the Dred Scott decision. He said that the remedy, in case of a decision by the United States Supreme Court, was difficult; but that in the case of a State court decision, it was not difficult. "If any considerable number of the people feel that the decision is in defiance of justice, they should be given the right by petition to bring before the voters at some subsequent election, special or otherwise, as might be decided, and after the fullest opportunity for deliberation and debate, the question whether or not the judges' interpretation of the Constitution is to be sustained." [37] If it were not sustained, the construction of the Constitution would be "definitely decided,—subject only to action by the Supreme Court of the United States." [38]

The cases he referred to were the famous bakeshop case in New York—the Lochner case,—the Hoxie case decided by Judge Bald-

---

[35] Theodore Roosevelt, *Progressive Principles*, p. 71. February 21, 1912.
[36] *Ibid.*, p. 71.   [37] *Ibid.*, p. 73.   [38] *Ibid.*, p. 74.

win, and the Ives case in New York. He said, with truth, that the Ives case had been, in effect, reversed (that is, not followed) by the Supreme Courts of Washington and Iowa, and the United States Supreme Court which had already upheld compensation statutes. In fact, as we have seen, the United States Supreme Court later reversed Judge Baldwin in the Hoxie case.

He repeated that the judges who rendered these decisions were able and upright men, and he would not favor their recall; but "most emphatically," he added, "I do wish that the people should have the right to recall the decision itself, and authoritatively to stamp with disapproval what can not but seem to the ordinary citizen a monstrous misconstruction of the Constitution, a monstrous perversion of the Constitution, into an instrument for the perpetuation of social and industrial wrong and for the oppression of the weak and helpless." [39] No ordinary amendment of the Constitution would fit the case, he went on; for the trouble was not with the Constitution, but with its construction, and what was needed was a different construction on the very point involved.

The proposal met with a storm of abuse. Opinion in that election was hot and vehement. It was charged that Roosevelt was in favor of overthrowing the courts,—that he advocated appeal from the decision of a court to the decision of the mob.

Roosevelt had unfortunately used the words: "recall of judicial decisions." Years later he was asked by a friend who gave it that name. He answered: "I did, for my sins." [40] The title, he admitted, "was inaccurate and unlucky." What he really advocated was the amendment of the constitution of a State by statutory referendum, piecemeal. Instead of adopting a general clause, the people would merely vote that a particular statute was constitutional. As we shall see, the proposal had much merit, and was as far as possible from being inimical in motive to the courts. But Roosevelt had given an opportunity to the opposition to charge that he was an enemy of orderly judicial procedure.

But his unfortunate phrase was no excuse for the misrepresentation that followed. Any lawyer who read his proposal carefully could not fail to understand that he proposed no change with reference to the Supreme Court of the United States; that he did not propose to recall any particular decision, but merely to give the

[39] *Ibid.*, p. 79.   [40] Owen Wister, *Roosevelt: The Story of a Friendship*, p. 292.

people the right to decide—after a State court had held that a statute was unconstitutional—that they wished to amend the constitution to make it constitutional.

Roosevelt and his friends tried to make this clear. In his speech at Carnegie Hall one month later, he said that he felt that the Ives case was "intolerable" and was "based on a wrong political philosophy." [41] In cases involving the police power, he asked that the people should have the right to determine, after "sober deliberation," whether the "law which the court set aside shall be valid or not." [42] He explained that he was proposing nothing with regard to the United States Supreme Court, which he admitted to have been generally liberal in its interpretation of the due process clause. He was proposing nothing with respect to the recall of decisions in actual controversies. He was not proposing the recall of judges. He was advocating only that, in cases involving the police power, the people of a State should have the right to vote constitutional a statute which the courts had held unconstitutional.

Lawyers who saw merit in Roosevelt's proposal showed that it involved in reality no recall of a decision, in the sense of the recall of a judgment or a decree in a particular case, but rather only an amendment of the constitution to the effect that a particular statute was within the police power.

Thus William Draper Lewis, Dean of the Law School of the University of Pennsylvania, explained that what was proposed, was to give the people the right to "re-enact legislation which a court decision has declared is contrary to some clause in the existing State Constitution." [43] He said that anyone who has been asked to draft specific amendments to a constitution, would hesitate to condemn the suggestion. A specific statute, like the New York Workmen's compensation statute, had been declared unconstitutional. New York did not really want—and it did not need—a general constitutional amendment. It is very difficult to frame an amendment which will permit a workmen's compensation statute, and not permit a further extension of power. If the people wanted a compensation statute, they were entitled to get it, and they should not be forced to amend the constitution generally in order to get it. The Roosevelt method would make "explosions unnecessary." [44]

[41] Theodore Roosevelt, *Progressive Principles*, p. 25. March 20, 1912.
[42] *Ibid.*, p. 25.   [43] *Ibid.*, p. 40.   [44] *Ibid.*, p. 42.

William L. Ransom, a New York lawyer, President of the American Bar Association in 1935–1936, presented the same argument more elaborately in his "Majority Rule and the Judiciary." He pointed out that, when a committee of lawyers came to draft the amendment to the New York Constitution, which would make possible a workmen's compensation law which the ablest legal opinion believed was constitutional anyway, they felt it necessary to provide that nothing in the Constitution, namely, the due process clause, should "limit the power of the legislature to enact laws for the protection of the lives, health, or safety of employees"; as though, he said, "the decisions of the court had left some doubt about this, and as though this was the desired 'definition' of the 'police power' . . ."

Then the amendment added that neither did the constitution limit the power of the legislature "to enact laws . . . for the payment of compensation for injuries to employees, or for death to employees resulting from such injuries"; as though, he said, they did not feel sure that a law for compensation for injuries was a law to protect the health, lives, and safety of employees.[45]

Ransom felt as Lewis felt, that the Federal Supreme Court had been consistently liberal in its attitude,—on the whole, treating the question as one of fact, whether the legislation was reasonably adapted, in the minds of a dominant majority, to meet a real evil; and that many State courts had followed its example.

To this view, he said, was opposed the view that the question of the exercise of the police power is a narrow question of law, to be determined by "purely legal precedents that antedate both our constitutions and our courts."[46] Quoting Charles F. Mathewson, a prominent New York lawyer, as declaring that a ten hour law was tyranny of the majority over the minority, and asking "What right has anyone to say that a man working ten hours for three dollars a day, may not work twelve hours and receive four dollars?", Ransom remarked that evidently Mathewson did not believe "in *any* method which would enable the people to regulate the hours of labor, and that *he* did not believe in correcting the Ives decision, even by the constitutional amendment proposed by his brethren of the bar and passed by the New York legislature at its session of 1912."[47]

[45] Ransom, *Majority Rule and the Judiciary*, p. 58.   [46] *Ibid.*, p. 64.
[47] *Ibid.*, p. 72.

He then declared that there were only three ways to meet the situation: one was to take the court's power away entirely; one was by constitutional amendment; one was the method proposed by Roosevelt.

He agreed that it was too radical and dangerous a step to take the power away.

As to the method of amendment, he declared that in many States it was so difficult and cumbrous a process as to be practically unworkable. Many States require that an amendment be proposed by two successive legislatures, and adopted by a majority of all those voting at the election. As amendments are usually voted on at a general election, and as many voters ignore constitutional amendments, it is difficult, if not impossible, in many States to amend the constitution.[48]

But he went further, and argued that when a court has held that a specific law is not due process, what is needed is not a constitutional amendment, but simply a declaration by the people that they do consider it due process.

He then reasoned that, if what is due process depends on the prevailing opinion and morality, the best test of what that opinion was, was to put the matter to a vote. Public opinion, and not precedents, should decide whether a bake-shop law or a workmen's compensation law was desirable.

Like Dean Lewis, he argued that, if an amendment must be resorted to, the people might adopt an amendment which would permit not only the law in question, but a score more, many of which were not in mind at the time and possibly far more radical. The New York amendment would permit not only a workmen's compensation act, but also laws as to wages and hours. Yet, in the opinion of good lawyers, reasonable laws on those subjects were already permitted. The result would make a patchwork of the due process provision. How much better simply to vote a specific statute constitutional!

The opposition to the recall of judicial decisions was bitter and, in the beginning, very ill-informed. It was declared that Roosevelt proposed to substitute the decision of the mob for the decision of a court. There was much said of the passions and the caprices of the mob. It was charged that the recall of decisions would destroy

[48] *Ibid.*, p. 101.

our form of government, that it was socialistic, that it would enthrone the tyranny of the majority,—a temporary majority. It is probably a sober statement that nine-tenths of the lawyers who discussed it had no clear conception of just what the proposal or the issue was.

Roosevelt said that he was more concerned with the tyranny of the minority than that of the majority. It is, indeed, a striking fact that on all the questions at issue twenty-five years ago,—limitation of hours, workmen's compensation, and before that, token money,—public opinion has merely become more settled in favor of the legislation rather than less so. It was no caprice of the moment. Those who talk of the caprices and passions of the mob, have never explained why an old, stubborn, and mischievous prejudice is any more desirable than the caprice of the moment, even if it be a caprice. Surely, moreover, there was much of passion in the talk of those who spoke of the passions of the mob.

Constantly, the opponents of the recall of decisions and, as we shall see, of the initiative and referendum, spoke of the passions of the mob, although the vote of the people, however mistaken it may be, has no psychological similarity to the action of a mob or a popular assembly. Even after the proposal and the issue had been explained, the opponents of the recall of judicial decisions denounced it as an extremely dangerous form of innovation. A prominent Minnesota lawyer, Rome G. Brown, could hardly contain himself in his denunciation. He said it was based on a fallacy, on the socialistic doctrine "that the judiciary has 'usurped' the function to pass final judgment upon the question as to whether a statute is repugnant to the Federal Constitution." [49] He declared that "This charge of 'usurpation' is a mere pretext for striking at the very keystone of our system of government." [50] The question was, "Shall we replace our present constitutional democracy with a democracy which has no enforceable bill of rights; which has no stable, sure, consistent, or equally administered constitutional protection for the individual as to his life, liberty, or property?" [51] Again, he declared that, "The primary function of the courts is to stand between temporary demands of a majority and the oppression and injustice which must, or at least may, follow unrestrained

[49] Rome G. Brown, "The Judicial Recall." Sen. Doc. 617, 62d Cong., 2d Sess., p. 17, 1914.
[50] *Ibid.*, p. 19.   [51] *Ibid.*, p. 21.

power." [52] And he added that, "Any measure by which there is given to the people of a locality the direct power of adjudication upon a constitutional question, means the elimination of constitutional limitations and safeguards established for the security of liberty of person and of property. In place of methods of careful and deliberate amendment of constitutions, it substitutes the spasmodic, vacillating, and inconsistent expressions made from time to time of the arbitrary will of a majority temporarily in power. It substitutes for decree of (sic "or") judgment under the law, the spasmodic will or caprice of the mob." [53]

Brown overlooked the fact that the proposal did not apply to all constitutional limitations, but only to the due process clause. He overlooked the fact that what was proposed was, in effect, simply an easier and specific power of amendment of the constitution. To declare that the people are a mob, and that they are moved by caprice and passion at all times, is hardly sober argument in a country whose officers are elected by that same "mob." Nothing could better illustrate the fundamental clash in philosophy which the controversy aroused. It was a clash of temperaments between those who instinctively distrust democracy and those who instinctively trust it.

Ezra Ripley Thayer, then Dean of the Harvard Law School, made a much more temperate and sober criticism of the proposal. He admitted that it was limited to the due process clause, but he feared that it would be extended to other constitutional limitations. He objected that, "A judicial decision on a point of private right is made the starting point of the referendum, and the court's reward for putting principle above popularity is a popular nullification of its decree. Such a measure is aptly contrived to strike at the dignity and independence of the judiciary." [54] Rather than adopt the recall of decisions, he preferred to take away the power of the courts altogether.

Elihu Root felt that the Recall of Judicial Decisions struck straight at the separation of powers, at the "very foundation of our system of government." It would be a reversion to the system of the ancient republics, where the state was everything and the

---

[52] Rome G. Brown, *"The Judicial Recall, A Fallacy Repugnant to Constitutional Government."* Sen. Doc. 892, 62d Cong., 2d Sess., p. 18, 1912.

[53] *Ibid.*, p. 25.   [54] Sen. Doc. 28, 63d Congress, 1st Sess., p. 8, 1913.

individual nothing except as a part of the state, and where liberty perished; "a repudiation of the fundamental principle of Anglo-Saxon liberty, which we inherit and maintain, for it is the very soul of our political institutions that they protect the individual against the majority." He demanded that we jealously preserve, "at all times and under all circumstances, the rule of principle which is eternal, over the will of majorities which shift and pass away." We could amend the Constitution if we desired, but the difference between amendment and the recall of judicial decisions was vital. It was the difference between making a rule and breaking a rule.[55]

Meanwhile, scholars had been examining the nature of the power of the courts over legislation. In 1907, J. Allen Smith had published his "The Spirit of American Government." It was one of the first of a series of studies of the social and economic bases of the Constitution, and had much influence on the Progressive movement. He argued that the Federal Convention of 1787 deliberately adopted Hamilton's suggestion of giving the Supreme Court the power to determine all controversies concerning the interpretation of the Constitution. He showed that in the colonies the courts had already begun to declare legislation void, and that the leading members of the convention believed that the power could be exercised without an actual grant. The judiciary was definitely intended to be a curb on the legislature which they feared.

The result of the power of the courts over legislation, Smith felt, was to give an aristocratic control to an appointive body, which actually had molded the Constitution to its will. In no other country have the courts this power. "It is the exclusive possession of this most important prerogative of a sovereign legislative body, which makes our Supreme Court the most august and powerful tribunal in the world." [56] It had become the controlling branch of the government.

Smith claimed that in the first hundred years of its life, the Court had decided two hundred and one cases in which either a law of Congress, a provision of a State constitution, or a State statute had been held unconstitutional; and he felt that these decisions had been almost uniformly advantageous to the capital

[55] Elihu Root, *Addresses on Citizenship and Government*, pp. 112–14.
[56] Smith, p. 102.

owning class "in preserving property rights and corporate privileges." [57] He added that the effect of the Court's exercise of power had been not only to overthrow certain laws, but to prevent others being enacted. Finally, he said that the fact that the Court acted only when a case is brought before it,—perhaps, several years after the law had been enacted,—results frequently in a law being annulled several years after its passage; so that, in effect, the Court possesses ex post facto legislative power, and the country does not know whether a law is the law until the test has been made.

Like others who later treated the subject, he argued that the Supreme Court was perpetuating an eighteenth century concept of liberty,—the concept in effect at the time of the adoption of the Constitution; and he said that our economic conditions required a new definition of liberty and individual rights. The old laissez faire doctrine could not control modern industry. The courts were the last refuge of our minorities. And he concluded, "If the will of the majority is to prevail, the courts must be deprived of the power which they now have to declare laws null and void. Popular government can not really exist, so long as judges who are politically irresponsible have power to override the will of the majority." [58]

Smith's exposition was the most thorough the subject had then received. His was the first treatment of the economic and social basis of the Constitution, which Beard later was to make more elaborately. I shall treat Smith's proposals for political change later in this book. But on the question of judicial control, I think it may be said that he overemphasized the reactionary tendencies of the courts. The State courts had, indeed, up to 1907 when he wrote, shown often a stubborn blindness to modern conditions in labor legislation, but the United States Supreme Court had been generally liberal. The number of cases in which it had then shown a reactionary tendency was extremely small. Smith, moreover, would have abolished the power of the courts entirely. But on all questions involving the separation of powers between Nation and the States, there is no body but the Supreme Court to decide the issues of conflict. The question of judicial power is too complicated to be settled by such sweeping changes as he proposed.

[57] *Ibid.*, p. 111.   [58] *Ibid.*, p. 356.

McLaughlin, in his "The Courts, the Constitution and Parties," traced the history of the doctrine of judicial review. He held that it arose from two theories: the theory of the separation of powers; and the ingrained belief in natural rights, which no legislature could infringe. He referred to the "prevalent and deeply cherished conviction that governments must be checked and limited, in order that individual liberty might be protected and property preserved. . . ." He added that our forefathers believed that "there was a fundamental law in all free states, and that freedom and God-given right depended on the maintenance and preservation of that law. . . ." [59]

When the argument became general as a result of the Progressive campaign of 1912, Brooks Adams, in his "The Theory of Social Revolutions," said bluntly: "I contend that no court can, because of the nature of its being, effectively check a popular majority, acting through a coordinate legislative assembly. . . ." [60] Our courts, he said, have been legislative chambers, attempting to enforce a rule of economic morality. He traced the history of the impress of the courts on the legislature from Chisholm vs. Georgia, the Dartmouth College case, and the Charles River Bridge case. [61] He declared that the courts had assumed a "supreme function which can be only compared to the Dispensing Power claimed by the Stuarts, or to the authority which, according to the Council of Constance, inheres in the Church, to grant indulgences for reasonable causes." [62]

He noted the weakening of the power of the courts through the police power doctrine which, as we have seen in the two decades following the Civil War, was held to permit most of the desired activities of the State.

Then, he said, capital gained power. He noted that in the case of Chicago, Milwaukee & St. Paul Railroad vs. Minnesota, the Supreme Court, as we have seen, finally held that the courts could decide what was a reasonable rate. He also noted the series of labor cases, which I have already referred to. "Ever since Hamilton's time," he concluded, "it has been assumed as axiomatic, by conservative Americans, that courts whose function is to ex-

---

[59] A. C. McLaughlin, *The Courts, the Constitution and Parties*, p. 106.
[60] Brooks Adams, *The Theory of Social Revolutions*, p. 75.
[61] *Chisholm* vs. *Georgia*, 2 Dall. 419 (1793); *Dartmouth College* vs. *Woodward*, 4 Wheat. 518 (1819); *Charles River Bridge* vs. *Warren Bridge*, 11 Peters 420 (1837).
[62] *Ibid.*, p. 76.

pound a written constitution, can and do act as a 'barrier to the encroachments and oppressions of the representative body.' " [63] But he said, "I apprehend that courts can perform no such office, and that, in assuming attributes beyond the limitations of their being, they, as history has abundantly proved, not only fail in their object, but shake the foundations of authority and immolate themselves." He even felt that our courts "have ceased to be true courts, and are converted into legislative chambers, thereby promising to become, if they are not already, a menace to order." [64]

He said that, supposing a President, supported by a Congressional majority, were to "formulate some policy no more subversive than that which has been formulated" by the then British cabinet, "and this policy were to be resisted, as it surely would be, by potent financial interests, the conflicting forces would converge upon the Supreme Court. . . . In this case, a dilemma would be presented. Either the judges would seek to give expression to 'preponderant' public opinion, or they would legislate." If they "legislate," a tribunal, "nominally judicial, would throw itself across the path of the national movement." [65] As Harlan had himself warned, the Court would then be in for trouble.

Professor Burgess, of Columbia, opposed the recall of judicial decisions on the basis of his theory that the three war amendments guaranteed liberty beyond the reach of the government. In his "Reconciliation of Government with Liberty," published in 1914, he carried out the theory advanced in his "Political Science and Comparative Constitutional Law," written many years before, that the great English struggle for freedom from the arbitrary power of the monarch, which was continued in this country, was not completed until constitutional restraints had been placed on the new monarch,—the controlling majority.

There he had said that a true and perfect political science requires the organization of the state, that is, the sovereignty back of the constitution; by which he meant the means of amending the constitution; the organization and tracing out of the sovereignty and the domain of civil liberty within the constitution; the guaranty of civil liberty against every power, except the sovereignty organized within the constitution; the organization of the government within the constitution; and, lastly, the security of the govern-

[63] *Ibid.*, p. 111.   [64] *Ibid.*, pp. 111, 112.   [65] *Ibid.*, pp. 130–31.

ment against all changes except by the sovereignty organized within the constitution.[66]

The essential element was the clear separation of the government bound by the constitution, from the sovereign power back of the government, which alone had the power to change the constitution.

The legislature had been considered the great weapon against executive power, but the legislative majority had proved to be "a far more consummate despot than any King or Prince has ever shown himself to be. Against such a Legislature, the Individual is in the most helpless condition possible. It has rarely any sense of justice, and is almost never influenced by considerations of mercy. It readily becomes the instrument through which brute force tyrannizes over intelligence and thrift, and seeks to bring society to an artificial dead level." Until a political system could find some protection against this power of the legislature, "the most ruthless organ of government," it would "not have solved our great problem." [67]

Burgess insisted that in England and on the Continent there was no true civil liberty, for the very reason that liberty was not guaranteed by any constitutional provisions binding on the government of the moment. It had not been understood that protection was needed from the legislature. They had established bicameral legislatures, responsibility of ministries, impeachment, and property qualifications for voters. But qualifications for voters and bicameral legislatures are being abolished, and it was more imperative than ever that some protection be found by an organization of the state back of the government.

The United States alone, he said, fulfilled these requirements. In the United States,—and in the United States alone,—the system was perfectly organized by a constitution laying down the limits of legislative action. In the United States, moreover, the rights of the individual are protected against legislative encroachment. The first ten amendments granted the individual a large measure of protection, and the work was completed by the three war amendments.

We have had several protections for the individual besides the

---

[66] John W. Burgess, *Political Science and Comparative Constitutional Law,* Vol. I, p. 263.
[67] John W. Burgess, *Reconciliation of Government with Liberty,* p. 250.

constitutional protection. We divide our powers between the Federal and State governments, we have trusted in the election of our representatives, but this protection we find to be of little avail now that we realize that "an elected body proceeds with less consideration for Individual Liberty than a King." [68] We have relied on the distribution of powers. But, chiefly, we have relied on the protection by the judiciary. The three war amendments, enforced by the judiciary, gave the United States "the most perfect system of Civil Liberty, the best protected and guaranteed against governmental power, ever attained in the civilized world." [69] We thought then that the work was completed, that we had found the necessary protection, when "suddenly, almost like a bolt out of blue sky, came the upheaval of 1912, which has changed the face of things almost beyond recognition." [70]

He traced the change in our national temper to the Spanish War, which brought us new land, with people different ethnically from us and separated from us by distance. We had governed colonies despotically, and had become used to standards not our own. He deplored the Sixteenth Amendment, which gave Congress power to tax incomes without limit. The sovereign back of the government, which should not govern, had handed over to the government unlimited power over incomes,—the power to take from one group and give to another. "It is folly for us to imagine that we have any longer a Constitution in regard to the relation between Government and the Individual, in his rights to property or even to his own physical or mental efforts." [71] There was nothing now to prevent our entering on a course of conquest and empire in the two Americas, nothing to prevent a Napoleon. The initiative and referendum would, he said, accentuate the power of the government at the expense of the individual, but most fatal of all would be the recall of judicial decisions.

In a series of articles Dean Pound, of the Harvard Law School, traced the history of the phrase "freedom of contract," which had been used to deny the legislative power in the token money cases. He traced it to Spencer's "Justice," and to the influence of the classical English economists, Smith and Mill. The fountainhead of the theory was, in his opinion, the case of Butchers' Union vs. Crescent City, where Justice Field, repeating the theory of his

[68] *Ibid.,* p. 304.   [69] *Ibid.,* p. 325.   [70] *Ibid.,* p. 302.   [71] *Ibid.,* p. 371.

dissenting opinion in the Slaughter House cases, had invoked the doctrine of freedom of contract in declaring that Louisiana could abolish the monopoly it had once granted and which had been upheld in the Slaughter House cases. The leading state case, Pound thought, was Godcharles vs. Wigeman, in Pennsylvania.[72]

Pound argued that the strength of the theory of freedom of contract was due to seven causes: our individualistic idea of justice; our mechanical jurisprudence, namely, the traditional legal habit of decision by deduction from fixed rules; our juristic notions of the state, economics, and politics; the fact that the bar had been trained in the Eighteenth Century philosophy of the law; the great vogue of the theory of natural rights, as exemplified in our Bills of Rights; the fact that our early labor legislation came before we were ready for it; and, lastly, the fact that, ordinarily, constitutional questions are not questions of fact, whereas the question of the reasonableness of a labor statute—and, indeed, of the reasonableness of any statute under the police power—is, after all, a question of fact based on an examination of the conditions sought to be remedied.[73]

Pound was severe in his criticism of the failure of the courts to take account of our modern economic and political thinking. He said that it "is still good form for the lawyer to look upon our Eighteenth Century Bills of Rights as authoritative text-books of politics, of ethics and economics." [74] Our Bills of Rights, he declared, "represent the Eighteenth Century desire to lay down philosophical and legal charts for all time, proper enough in men who believed that they had achieved finality in thought in each connection." [75]

The discussion died down. The fact that it did die down and that nothing was done of a radical nature, led some opponents of the attack on the power of the courts to say that the demand was but a temporary flare-up, due to the emotions of the moment. But the very discussion—the conflict itself—had been a potent force in broadening the conceptions of the courts and advising them of the state of public opinion. The discussion of the proposed change did much to make the change unnecessary.

[72] *Yale Law Journal*, Vol. 18, pp. 454, 470.   [73] *Ibid.*, p. 457.
[74] Roscoe Pound, "The Scope and Purpose of Sociological Jurisprudence," 25 *Harvard Law Review*, April, 1912, p. 512.
[75] Courts and Legislation, *American Political Science Rev.*, August, 1913, p. 377.

But, as we have indicated already, the question is never settled any more than any other question of our politics. In 1924, indeed, the proposal was made again by the La Follette party.[76] If the United States Supreme Court should ever make three or four important decisions on crucial political questions, which antagonized both the majority in power and public opinion, we may be certain that the contest would become acute. The situation is much like that of the House of Lords in England until the constitutional change of 1911. The House of Lords had opposed the Commons before, without fatal result, because the Commons did not have public opinion strongly back of it; but when the Lords opposed the majority in the Commons on a matter where the Commons had public support, the Lords were shorn of much of their power.

Little more need be said in summary of this great debate. But a brief general discussion may serve to clarify the issue.

To judge of the effect and desirability of the power of the Court, it is necessary to see just what it has done. In the period from 1865 to 1917, the Court held thirty-six acts of Congress unconstitutional. Of these, three were income tax cases, three were cases under the Civil Rights Acts, two were statutes under the Fifteenth Amendment.[77] Only eight were cases of what may be called, roughly, social or political legislation; namely, the legal tender case, soon reversed; a statute limiting sales of petroleum; the income tax cases; the first employers' liability act case; the Adair case, holding void a statute forbidding a railroad to require that an employee could not join a labor union; and a statute forbidding the harboring of alien women for purposes of prostitution.

The income tax case, under the act of 1894, was politically unfortunate, and many able lawyers have always felt that it was based on entirely too technical a ground. But the income tax case involved the division of powers between the State and Federal governments, and there is no question that only the Supreme Court can decide such issues. The first employers' liability act was decided on a narrow but an entirely tenable basis, and the effect of the decision was easily avoided. The Adair case was clearly decided on an economic and not a legal theory.

In his "The Supreme Court in United States History," Charles

---

[76] And, of course, in 1936 the old discussion flared up again.
[77] *West Publishing Company Docket*, Jan., 1924, pp. 2711-17.

Warren summarized the decisions holding void State statutes under the due process and equal protection clauses of the Fourteenth Amendment. Between the years 1889 and 1918 inclusive, he found that the Supreme Court had decided seven hundred and ninety cases, in which statutes were attacked under those clauses. Of these, four hundred and twenty-two involved the police power; one hundred and ninety-six, State taxing statutes; and one hundred and seventy-two, administrative or judicial procedure.

Of the four hundred and twenty-two cases under the police power, the Court held the statutes unconstitutional in fifty-three cases. Warren stated that two-thirds of these were rate cases and cases involving the regulation of public utilities; two involved municipal improvements; five, anti-trust laws; and "only fourteen involved legislation affecting the general rights and liberties of individuals." Of these fourteen, he felt that only two "aroused any widespread criticism,"—the Lochner case, later practically overruled; and Coppage vs. Kansas, decided in 1914, which (following the reasoning in Adair vs. U. S., involving a Federal statute applying to interstate carriers) held that a Kansas statute forbidding employers to coerce or influence employees not to join unions, was invalid.[78]

Of course, the influence of one decision may be very deep and lasting. The Lochner case held up legislation as to hours for six years. The Adair and Coppage cases still prevent any legislation forbidding employers to insist that their men do not join unions, though recently we have had Federal legislation forbidding employers to do that very thing.

But we may agree with Warren—however we may regret the occasional tendency of the Court to decide cases on economic and political opinions—that the record of the Court was generally "broad and liberal in the period under discussion."

Under the Commerce clause the Court has held forty-six State statutes unconstitutional, of which twenty-four were corporation regulation cases; nine, liquor and cigarette laws; and thirteen were "general progressive legislation." [79]

Of the State courts, of course, not so much can be said. The record up to 1900 showed frequently a tendency to decide complicated economic questions on a priori grounds, on the basis of

[78] Warren, Vol. II, pp. 741–42.   [79] *Ibid.*, p. 742.

the Eighteenth Century Bill of Rights. Partly, as we have seen, the fault was due to the lawyers, who did not keep the courts abreast of the stream of modern thought and experience. The record for the twenty years after 1900 was much more liberal.

It is evident that the question is many-sided. The power of the courts over legislation in the fifty years from the Civil War to the World War, has exerted a national control by the Federal government over the legislation and the governmental action of the States. It has therefore been an impressive source of nationalism. No State and no city can establish rates; no commission can fix a rate which, in case it is confiscatory, is not subject to the control, in the end, of the Supreme Court. No person can be denied a fair trial, can be denied the right to counsel; for the Supreme Court stands in the way. It is true that, in the Leo Frank case, the Court refused to interfere, although it clearly appeared that the jury was under the domination of a mob just outside the courthouse; but it is doubtful if the Court would go so far today.[80] Broadly speaking, the Court has the power to enforce a trial by the usual processes of the jurisdiction. No State can tax property outside the jurisdiction. These restraints, added to the restraints in effect when the constitution was adopted,—that no State can impair the obligations of contracts, nor burden interstate commerce,—have been powerful aids to nationalization.

In 1911, Justice Holmes, considering with some sadness the current attack on the courts, remarked: "I do not think the Union would come to an end, if we lost our power to declare an act of Congress void. I do think the Union would be imperiled, if we could not make that declaration as to the laws of the several states." [81] Those in his position knew, he said, how often "a local policy prevails with those not trained to national views." In a Federal government which leaves broad powers of legislation to the States, it can not be doubted that some national power must be able to prevent encroachment of one State upon another, of one State upon the Federal government. The whole first seventy years of our national existence showed the necessity. That period was

[80] In *Moore* vs. *Dempsey*, 261 U.S. 86 (1923), the Court held that where a mob dominated the jury, the defendant was denied due process. See *Frank* vs. *Mangaum*, 237 U.S. 309 (1915).
[81] Holmes, "Law and the Court," address of February 15, 1913, in *Collected Legal Papers*, pp. 295–96.

likewise a continual debate on the question of national supremacy; and, of course, national supremacy won.

Secondly, there is the question of the effect of the power of the courts on the rights of individuals and the power of legislatures. Of course, the power of the courts over both Federal and State legislation is involved.

Rate cases, of course, are in a class by themselves. It is a tenable and perhaps a necessary point of view, to hold that the legislature should not be allowed to deny a public utility the right to a reasonable return on its investment. Once that theory is adopted, its application is no longer a political matter; and it is well that we have turned the matter over to commissions, subject in case of alleged confiscation to review by the courts.

Justice Bradley, in the case of Chicago etc. Co. vs. Minnesota,[82] said that it was a legislative matter, and that the remedy was to get better legislatures. But we have learned since he wrote that political power goes usually to those with the biggest stake; and if we had left the legislatures as a prize for the public utilities, the public utilities would have sought and obtained the prize. The disinterested public would have been helpless before an organized force driven by an active and positive interest. It is well that the matter of the mere determination of rates has been, in general, removed from legislative control. Moreover, questions of eminent domain are susceptible of determination according to legal rules.

But the control of legislation regulating labor and business under the police power, is quite a different thing. Such cases, we have seen, are political in nature. They are questions of fact, and can not be decided by the normal deductive legal method. They involve the whole question of the limits of state action. The fiercest struggles of the seventeenth and eighteenth centuries were waged to obtain rights of the individual, free from arbitrary power. Those struggles—or at least their dogmas and slogans—carried over into the democratic regime. Much was said that Demos was a tyrant more despotic than any czar.

Lawyers reverenced customary law,—they thought of law as a science; and judges did their best to render ineffective statutory attempts to change the common law, and even the common law procedure. Scholars of other lands have envied the United States

---

[82] 134 U.S. 418.

its possession of a method of holding the legislature in check. Duguit, the dean of law at Bordeaux, envies us the exercise by our courts of the power to declare laws invalid, and hopes that France will adopt our policy.[83] Though he admits that the written law is a necessary limit for the judge, he will not admit that any declaration of the legislature is the law just because the legislature decrees it. But no one has ever suggested how legislation can be permanently controlled by courts. Law, as we shall see, is the satisfaction of the needs and desires of the people; it is not an exact science, and sooner or later, the public desires will have their way.

It is true that the United States has a problem that England and France do not have, and that is the existence of forty-eight State legislatures, which can tax and legislate on all the matters which concern property, labor, descent, and the making of contracts. England's trust in parliaments might be very much reduced if she had a parliament for every shire. It is difficult enough for us to obtain able men for our Congress; but, it is well nigh impossible for each State to do so likewise. Many of the State legislatures, moreover, meet only for sixty days every two years, and the work of legislation is crowded and hasty. In view of the impediments to ordered legislation, the legislatures have really done very well. Yet, when we talk of the danger to minorities, we must remember that most legislatures contain representatives of those minorities, and that there is an immediate protest against action of too partial a nature.

Indeed, if we glance over the list of State statutes which the courts have held invalid, the number that outrage our sense of justice is remarkably small. Many, as we have seen, which the courts have annulled, have been such as public opinion has persistently approved.

Most of us, after all, would prefer to see the power of the courts, both State and Federal, remain as it is, believing that it is a wholesome restraint on vicious legislation. A few specific restraints should certainly be maintained. The prohibition of ex post facto laws, of special legislation, of unreasonable searches and seizures; excessive

---

[83] In his *Traité de Droit Constitutionnel*, Vol. III, p. 673, he affirmed his conviction that he had formerly been in error in doubting the power, and concluded: "It appears evident to me that it is the logical and necessary consequence of the hierarchy of law." There was nothing in the positive law of France to deny the power. He added that "a country which does not recognize this power for its jurisdictions, truly does not live under a régime of a state of law." p. 674.

bail; of interference with freedom of speech, the press, and religion, should be retained. The due process clause is necessary to ensure a day in court and an orderly hearing, according to accepted forms. It is too late to restrict it merely to procedure; but certainly our experience has shown that it should never be used to prevent legislation which is opposed merely on an economic or political bias, and that only when legislation shocks the conscience of reasonable men, can it be said to lack due process.

Always, we must realize that if the power is abused, it will surely—and we must add, properly—be taken away. The power is an anomaly in a democracy, and it can persist only if it is used with great restraint and wisdom. Whenever the court oversteps, the question will become acute again. The Supreme Court is keenly aware of this limitation in all times of stress, and its willingness to act on legislation is then firmly tempered. The trend and tone of its decisions in the past year must cause some foreboding. But if our courts are discreet and liberal, there is little likelihood that their power will be seriously challenged.

REFERENCES

ADAMS, BROOKS, *The Theory of Social Revolutions.* New York: The Macmillan Co., 1913.

BOUDIN, LOUIS B., *Government by Judiciary* (2 vols.). New York: William Godwin, Jr., 1932.

BROWN, ROME G., "Judicial Recall." Senate Doc. 617, 63d Cong., 2d Sess.

———"The Judicial Recall, A Fallacy Repugnant to Constitutional Government," *Annals*, Sept., 1912. Sen. Doc. 892, 62d Cong., 2d Sess.

———"Recall of Judges." Sen. Doc. 649, 62d Cong., 2d Sess.

BRYAN, WILLIAM J., *The First Battle.* Chicago: W. B. Conkey Co., 1896.

BURGESS, JOHN W., *Political Science and Comparative Constitutional Law* (2 vols.). Boston: Ginn & Co., 1890–91.

———*The Reconciliation of Government with Liberty.* New York: Charles Scribner's Sons, 1915.

HOLMES, OLIVER WENDELL, *Collected Legal Papers.* New York: Harcourt, Brace & Howe, 1920.

KALES, ALBERT M., " 'Due Process,' the Inarticulate Major Premise and the Adamson Act." 26 Yale Law Journal 519, May, 1917.

MARTIN, EDWARD S., *The Life of Joseph Hodges Choate* (2 vols.). New York: Charles Scribner's Sons, 1920.

McCLURE, A. K., *A History of the Presidency.* New York: Harper Bros., 1909.

McLAUGHLIN, ANDREW C., *The Courts, the Constitution and Parties.* Chicago: University of Chicago Press, 1913.

POUND, ROSCOE, "Liberty of Contract." 18 *Yale Law Journal* 454, May, 1909.

———"The Scope and Purpose of Sociological Jurisprudence III." 25 *Harvard Law Review* 489, April, 1912.

———"Courts and Legislation." *American Political Science Review*, August, 1913, p. 361.

RANSOM, WILLIAM L., *Majority Rule and the Judiciary.* New York: Charles Scribner's Sons, 1912.

ROOSEVELT, THEODORE, *Progressive Principles.* New York: Progressive National Service, 1913.

ROOT, ELIHU, *Addresses on Government and Citizenship.* Cambridge: Harvard University Press, 1916.

SMITH, J. ALLEN, *The Spirit of American Government.* New York: The Macmillan Co., 1907 (Chautauqua Press Ed., 1911).

STEPHENSON, NATHANIEL W., *Nelson W. Aldrich.* New York: Charles Scribner's Sons, 1930.

THAYER, EZRA RIPLEY, "Recall of Judicial Decisions" (From *Legal Bibliography*, March, 1913). Sen. Doc. 28, 63d Cong., 1st Sess.

THAYER, JAMES BRADLEY, *Legal Essays,* Chapter II. Boston: Boston Book Co., 1908.

WARREN, CHARLES, *The Supreme Court in United States History*, Chapter II. Boston: Little, Brown & Co., 1926 (revised edition).

WEAVER, JAMES B., *A Call to Action.* Des Moines: Iowa Printing Co., 1892.

WEST PUBLISHING COMPANY DOCKET, *Unlawful Laws of Congress.* Jan., 1924, pp. 2711–17.

WISTER, OWEN, *Roosevelt: The Story of a Friendship.* New York: The Macmillan Co., 1930.

CHAPTER IV

THE NATURE OF THE UNION

THE END OF THE SECESSION ARGUMENT

THE Civil War had been fought partly over a question of authority, —the question of whether the national government or a single State government had the final word in case of dispute. That question involved the whole question of the nature of the Union,—whether it was a league or a Federal government or a nation. The war settled the question of authority, but it was inevitable that there should be some final discussion of the old question.

Naturally, the defeated South, while it might acquiesce in the result, would not concede the argument. Principles are ever and rightfully dear. An able and fine spirited defense of the Southern position was given by Alexander H. Stephens in his *Constitutional View of the Late War Between the States,* published in 1868. His argument was presented with great fairness, and with much greater force than the dry disquisitions of Calhoun. The colonies, he admitted, were not sovereign; but the Union created by them was the act, not of the governments of each colony, but of the people of each colony, respectively acting for themselves.[1] The colonies could not do a revolutionary act. A revolutionary act could be done only by the people. It was done by "the Paramount authority of the people of each colony respectively for themselves."[2] The Congress was one of States. The delegates in 1776 considered that each State was "Sovereign and Independent."[3] The power came from the people of each State, not from the people nationally.

He quoted from Marshall's argument in Ware vs. Hylton,[4] and his decision in Gibbons vs. Ogden[5] that, under the Confederation, the States were absolutely sovereign, and that the Confederation was simply a compact between sovereign States.

If, then, the States were sovereign once, when did they lose

[1] Stephens, *A Constitutional View of the Late War Between the States,* p. 67.
[2] *Ibid.,* p. 67. [3] *Ibid.,* p. 69. [4] 3 Dall. 199 (1796). [5] 9 Wheat. 1 (1824).

sovereignty? Sovereignty, he said, could not be granted away by implication.

He instanced all the limitations on the power of the Federal government under the Confederation, and said that the two great defects were the lack of power to tax and the lack of power to regulate trade. Attempts to grant greater power failed, and finally the convention was called to revise the articles merely to give additional power to tax and regulate commerce. The result was the new constitution. Was anything done, he asked, to change the sovereign character of the States?

He answered, no. The Constitution was adopted by States and for States. The traditional argument—that the preamble stated that it was the work of the people of the United States—he answered by saying that the clause first stated that, "We, the people of New Hampshire," enumerating each State in turn, and that the committee on style changed the clause into its present form.

All through the new Constitution, he found that States were acting: States had senators; States had representatives. States were restricted in powers. Only four new powers were added to those of the Federal government: the taxing power; power over aliens; copyrights and patents; and commerce.

He quoted from many contemporary leaders to the effect that they considered the Constitution a compact.

The only new restraints the Constitution placed on the States were the prohibition of bills of credit, ex post facto laws, and duties on imports. These restraints, he contended, did not limit the sovereignty of the States. The States merely wanted to be protected against unjust legislation of other States, and not against their own legislation. This was rather a naive argument; for it meant simply that no State wanted to limit its own power, but did want to limit the power of other States. This, of course, is exactly the point at issue. No one feels that any government is necessary to restrain one's own acts: it is always the others that need the restraint. But in restraining others, one, of course, submits to restraint on oneself.

Stephens went on to argue that the fact that amendments to the Constitution could be effected only by three-fourths of the States, and the fact that there could be no change in equal representation in the Senate, showed where sovereignty was.

But Stephens came, then, to the clause which made the Constitution the supreme law of the land. He declared that this meant only on judicial matters. The Supreme Court could pass only on justiciable questions. On those, its interpretation of the laws and the rights of the parties was final. But the judicial power extended only to cases in law or equity: it did not extend to political matters.

Stephens, therefore, admitted the full legal power of the Federal government. He did not believe in nullification. "Many," he said, "who believed in the perfect right of Secession, and looked upon that as the proper remedy in such cases of abuse of power as South Carolina complained of, were utterly opposed to Nullification. How a State could remain in the Union, with *Senators and Representatives* in Congress, and yet *refuse obedience to the laws of Congress not set aside by the Judiciary as unconstitutional,* was to this class utterly incomprehensible." [6]

At first thought, this seems inconsistent with his argument that, to say that the Constitution is the supreme law of the land, means only that the Supreme Court is the court of last resort in all cases at law and in equity. There are few statutes of the Federal government which may not involve at last a controversy between citizens or States, affecting property rights, and therefore justiciable questions. But Stephens would have said that the Supreme Court's word was final. He was a nationalist to that extent. But, if a State felt that the other States were not obeying the Fugitive Slave Law, for example, or that a tariff law or a law forbidding slavery in the territories was a violation of the compact, that State had a political right to withdraw. While she was in the Union, the law was law and must be obeyed. But a State could always withdraw.

Stephens himself opposed secession in 1860. But when his State left, he felt bound by her decision, and he felt that she had a right to make the decision.

By the end of the Civil War, the traditional northern opinion had become that of Webster and Lincoln. In his first inaugural, Lincoln said that the Union was perpetual. It was older than the Constitution. "It was formed, in fact, by the Articles of Association in 1774." If the Union were perpetual, if the Union formed by the Constitution were a more perfect Union, how could only part of the States destroy it? Even if it be held that the Union were formed

[6] *Ibid.,* p. 421 (Stephens' italics).

by a mere compact, he asked how the contract could be "peaceably unmade by less than all the parties who made it?"[7]

In his message to the special session in July, 1861, he declared that the States had neither less nor greater power "than that reserved to them in the Union by the Constitution, no one of them ever having been a State *out* of the Union. The original ones passed into the Union even *before* they cast off their British colonial dependence, and the new ones each came into the Union directly from a condition of dependence, excepting Texas; and even Texas, in its temporary independence, was never designated a State."[8]

He emphasized that the Union was declared to be perpetual, and that the States were declared free and independent States, not of each other, but of Great Britain. At the same time, they declared their mutual dependence on each other. "Having never been States, either in substance or in name, *outside* of the Union, whence this magical omnipotence of 'State rights,' asserting a claim of power to lawfully destroy the Union itself?" He said that much is said of the sovereignty of the States, but that the word was not even in the Federal Constitution, nor he believed, even in the State constitutions.

He asked if it would be wrong to define a sovereignty as a " 'political community without a political superior,' " and concluded that, tested by this, no one of our States, except Texas, ever was a sovereignty; and even Texas gave up the character on coming into the Union, by which act she acknowledged "the Constitution of the United States, and the laws and treaties of the United States made in pursuance of the Constitution, to be for her the supreme law of the land. . . . By conquest or purchase, the Union gave each of them whatever of independence and liberty it has. The Union is older than any of the States, and, in fact, it created them as States. . . . Not one of them ever had a State constitution independent of the Union."[9]

In his *The American Republic,* Brownson followed the same line of argument. Declaring that the question was one of fact and not to be determined by the opinion of statesmen, he followed the standard line, that, "the colonies unitedly declared their independence," and unitedly won it. "Severally," he said, "they have

[7] Richardson, *Messages and Papers of the Presidents,* Vol. VI, p. 7.
[8] *Ibid.,* p. 27.   [9] *Ibid.,* pp. 27–28.

never exercised the full powers of sovereign states; they have had no flag, symbol of sovereignty recognized by foreign powers, have made no treaties, held no foreign relations," coined no money, made no foreign treaties or alliances.[10] The Union, therefore, "was not a firm, a co-partnership, nor an artificial or conventional union, but a real, living, constitutional union, founded on the original and indissoluble unity of the American people, as one sovereign people." [11]

Pomeroy took, in general, the same view. The acts of the Continental Congress, the Declaration of Independence, the Revolutionary War, were unified acts. "There never was, in fact, a moment's interval when the several states were each independent, and sovereign." If there had been, he admitted, "I can see no escape from the extreme positions reached by Mr. Calhoun." [12]

"This nation," he said, "or in other words, the collective People of the United States, as a political unit, existed prior to the adoption of the Constitution, and was not therefore called into being as a consequence of that instrument." [13] The Constitution was not the work of the separate States, but of the collective people. The powers held by the general government were delegated to it, not by the States, but by the people. He admitted that in the Confederation, the separate State power triumphed over the national idea; but the people, he said, remained one. Yet he conceded that in the Articles of Confederation, there was no "formal recognition of, or reference to, the existence of a nation." [14] The people were not mentioned. The Federal government had no power to enforce obedience, there was no power to tax, there was no independent judiciary, and the result was failure. The new Constitution, he rightly said, was revolutionary.

But the people remained supreme through it all, and therefore the nation. The new Constitution was definitely framed by the people. Like many others, he stressed the words of the preamble. The new government was given powers that the States never possessed, and hence he said it might be inferred that these powers did not come from the States. The Constitution was made the supreme law of the land. The Federal government was given power

[10] Orestes A. Brownson, *The American Republic*, p. 109.   [11] *Ibid.*, p. 144.
[12] John N. Pomeroy, *An Introduction to the Constitutional Law of the United States* (3d ed., 1875), p. 38, 39.
[13] *Ibid.*, p. 22.   [14] *Ibid.*, p. 47.

to legislate as to aliens, to regulate commerce, to tax; and, above all, power of amendment was granted without limit. Three-fourths of the States could make an amendment of any nature without the consent of the other States, save only the provision as to equal representation in the Senate. This provision, like many others, he said, was "utterly inconsistent with any assumed sovereignty in the separate commonwealths." [15]

To be sovereign, Pomeroy concluded, a State must be an independent society among other similar nations. No other power may control its legislation or prescribe what its law shall be. On this basis, he said, the United States was sovereign, and no State was. The States were permanently subordinate.

John C. Hurd, a prominent Boston lawyer, in his book, *The Theory of Our National Existence,* gave a severely logical and rigorous examination of the theories of secession, and of the nature of the Union. He rejected all theories that sovereignty was divisible: it was indivisible. It might be divided in exercise, but not in possession. The war had settled that it was indivisible; a unit. None of the States had ever held sovereignty individually. It was contrary to the facts to suppose that the thirteen colonial governments had acquired "each for itself, within its original jurisdiction, any of the powers which the imperial government had before exercised therein, or generally, that they acquired any sovereign rights whatever." [16] No one colony had had the power to maintain war alone. "Severally, the colonies had no force adequate to sustain either local or external sovereignty or independence." [17] The people could not have existed at all save as united; therefore, no State alone could be sovereign.

On the other hand, he as vigorously rejected the theory that authority belonged to the mass of the people, to the "nation or to the people as one homogeneous political personality holding all sovereignty as a unit, in distinction from the organized people of the several States." [18] He asked when the people as a whole had ever exercised sovereignty. Sovereignty, he said, had "never been held by *the people* or by *the nation,* except as the politically organized people of the several States are *such people* or *nation. . . .*" [19] So he concluded: "Sovereignty in the American Republic was not

[15] *Ibid.,* p. 73.   [16] John C. Hurd, *The Theory of Our National Existence,* p. 123.
[17] *Ibid.,* p. 124.   [18] *Ibid.,* p. 108.   [19] *Ibid.,* p. 112.

popular sovereignty; the sovereignty of so many millions of human beings. The political people organized as the people of the States held it; and might be described as a *democratic oligarchy.*" [20]

Certainly, he said, when the Constitution was adopted, no one thought that the people as a mass held sovereignty, and if they did at the time he wrote there must have been a later revolution. He asked where and how it had occurred. He denied that there had been any "revolutionary proceeding whereby 'the people' or 'the nation,' as an aggregate of individuals, reassumed those sovereign powers which were by the Constitution invested in or entrusted to the government organized by it; while the residue of sovereign powers continued in the possession of the several States, or the people of these States." [21]

Hurd put the sovereignty rather in the States United,—united in organized communities. The States United could suppress rebellion, since they had authority over the territory of the seceded States to enforce the laws and Constitution of the United States. [22]

A prominent group still followed the theory of dual sovereignty long ago expressed by Marshall, Webster and Story. Reverdy Johnson of Maryland, in answering Garrett Davis' argument against the Thirteenth Amendment, admitted that Davis was "right in saying that in a certain sense the States are not sovereign; but if he means by that, to say that the United States in another sense are not equally sovereign, he is mistaken." The States were never disunited. As one, they declared independence. As one, they fought and conquered the independence so declared. "As one, in order to make that independence fruitful of all the blessings which they anticipated from it, they made the Constitution of the United

---

[20] *Ibid.*, p. 140.   [21] *Ibid.*, p. 104.

[22] Jameson also rejected the State Rights position. The States, he said, did not ratify the Constitution as States, but the people ratified it, acting through State units. Even if the acts of ratification were the acts of States, and even if States had been sovereign before, a nation could still have been formed, if that had been the intention. He quoted various contemporaries on the need of greater national power to the effect that there were not thirteen separate sovereignties, "but a common sovereignty of the whole in their united capacity." Jameson, *Constitutional Conventions* (4th ed., 1887), p. 52. Jameson argued that the States had never been sovereign. He quoted Madison as declaring in the Federal Convention that "The States never possessed the essential rights of sovereignty." *Ibid.*, p. 52.

So also Burgess said that from the first moment of the existence of the Continental Congress, "there was something more upon this side of the Atlantic than thirteen local governments. There was a sovereignty, a state: not in idea simply or upon paper, but in fact and in organization." John W. Burgess, *Political Science and Comparative Constitutional Law,* Vol. I, p. 100.

States. They met in conventions, they adopted the Constitution in conventions, and recommended it, not to the States in the capacity of States, not to the governments of the States as governments, but to the people of the States, for their adoption; and they could have submitted it in no other way." Any other way, he said, would have been inconsistent, for they acted as a people, and not as States. The people of each State, then, agreed with the "people of every other State, that that should be the form of Government." They consented in adopting the Constitution as a people, that the Constitution, if adopted by the people of nine States, "should be the Constitution of the people of those States in the aggregate." Therefore, the national government and the States were each invested with a portion of the sovereignty.[23]

The Supreme Court continued after the Civil War to follow this theory, that sovereignty is divided between the National and State governments. As Cooley said: "In American constitutional law, however, there is a division of sovereignty between the national and State governments by subjects; the former being possessed of supreme, absolute, and uncontrollable power over certain subjects throughout all the States and territories; while the States have the like complete power within their respective territorial limits, over other subjects." [24]

But none of these men held that, in case of dispute between the Federal and State governments over the exercise of any power, the drawing of the boundary line could be done by the States. Stephens, himself as we have seen, said that the national power must decide. Marshall, Story, Webster, and the Supreme Court itself all were strong nationalists. As between the Federal and State governments, they all held that on the question of final authority and decision, that sovereignty was in the Federal government. The United States could not only decide in case of dispute, but by amendment the people of the United States could take power away from the States, despite the opposition of any particular State. It is more accurate to say therefore, as is the modern tendency, that undivided sovereignty is in the United States, but that its exercise is divided between the State and Federal governments.

Willoughby, in his *The American Constitutional System,* pub-

[23] *Congressional Globe,* April 5, 1864, pp. 1422–23.
[24] T. M. Cooley, *Constitutional Limitations,* (1871 ed.), p. 2.

lished in 1906, gave a scholarly resume of the opposing arguments, with more sense of perspective of the historical bases of the old controversy than most of the disputants showed. He held, in the first place, that a national state could not be created by an agreement between Federal States. It could only be created by a "sentiment of unity" among the individuals of the country "sufficiently strong to lead them to surrender themselves to the control of a single political power for the sake of realizing the desires to which such a sentiment gives rise." [25] Therefore, a state can not arise by a contract.

Accordingly, he rejected the arguments of those who said that, assuming the States were severally sovereign before the adoption of the Constitution, they surrendered their separate sovereignty when they formed the Union. This, he said, assumed that the Union was created by States, although if a true Union was formed, it was done by the people.

He noted the argument that the States were never sovereign. But he answered that the "non-sovereign character of the Central Government established by these Articles, [i. e. of Confederation] is practically beyond dispute." [26] Hamilton, Webster and Madison conceded the non-sovereign character of the Confederation and the sovereignty of the several thirteen States after 1776. Let us then assume, he said, that they were sovereign until 1789. Did they create a sovereign national government in 1789? Webster, he noted, said that they did. But Willoughby asserted that the question was subjective. It depends on what the people intended, and we do not clearly know what they intended. They really intended both results. They believed that they had created a sovereign national State, and at the same time kept the sovereign character of the thirteen States. They left the matter unsettled. They "desired and thought that they were obtaining a result that we now know to have been a logical impossibility—namely, the creation of a legally indissoluble Union by an agreement between sovereign States,—one in which not simply the exercise of sovereignty, but the power itself should be divided between the national state and its member Commonwealths." [27]

No one, he concluded, knows what they wanted most. But, in

[25] W. W. Willoughby, *The American Constitutional System*, p. 6.
[26] *Ibid.*, p. 14.   [27] *Ibid.*, p. 30.

the course of time, they came to regard the Union as one of people and not of States. It was a revolutionary change. It can "properly be said," he concluded, "that there soon came into being a national feeling that was objectively realized both in explicit declarations and in fact." [28]

I can not agree with Willoughby that the Union did not, in a real sense, begin before 1789, or that the non-sovereign character of the Confederation and the sovereign character of the thirteen States are "practically beyond dispute." That the Federal government under the Confederation was tragically weak, can not be doubted. The Federal government had no power to tax, nor to regulate trade, nor to enforce its will. But the people did unite in a common government, they associated together in a war, they conducted that war to a successful end. It is true that the Articles could not be amended save by consent of all the States, and that the people of the thirteen States could establish a new government only by a revolutionary act.

On the other hand, surely the several States were not themselves sovereign, in the sense that we call a national state, sovereign. Without the consent of Congress, no State could send an ambassador to any foreign state, conclude any treaty, make any agreement with another American State, lay any duty contrary to any Federal treaty, keep any ship of war, have any army except to garrison its own forts, engage in war, or issue letters of marque.

The Congress of the United States was made the sole judge of disputes between States, and a court of arbitration was set up for such purposes.

The United States alone could regulate coinage, weights and measures; declare peace and war; make treaties; and send ambassadors. A State which could exercise none of these rights could not be considered sovereign.

The Federal Constitution not only gave far greater powers to the Federal government than it had before, but it provided that the Constitution could be amended by two-thirds of Congress and three-fourths of the States. At one stroke, every State which consented to the power of amendment, lost the right to be the sole judge of what the Constitution should provide. The Constitution and laws of the United States were made the supreme law of the

[28] *Ibid.*, p. 33.

land. It is true that the convention refused to vote that Congress could annul any law passed by the States, contravening, in its opinion, "the articles of Union, or any treaties subsisting under the authority of ye Union." [29] The vote on this proposal was seven States to three. Gouverneur Morris, opposing the suggestion, said that a law "that ought to be negatived will be set aside in the Judiciary departmt. and if that security should fail, may be repealed by a Nationl. law." [30] Sherman, of Connecticut, said that "such a power involves a wrong principle, to wit, that a law of a State contrary to the articles of the Union, would, if not negatived, be valid & operative." [31]

The proposal would, of course, have been impossible of operation. Luther Martin thought it would require that every State law be first referred to Congress. [32] Yet several who opposed the motions said that a State law in contravention to the Constitution, would be inoperative anyway. Moreover, immediately afterwards, the convention passed a resolution that "the legislative acts of the U. S., made by virtue & in pursuance of the articles of Union, and all treaties made & ratified under the authority of the U. S., shall be the supreme law of the respective States," and that the "Judiciaries of the several States shall be bound thereby in their decisions, anything in the respective laws of the individual States to the contrary notwithstanding." This was agreed to unanimously. [33]

Of course, it is incontestable, as Willoughby says, that there were conflicting views by leading men of the time as to the nature of their Union. I agree with Stephens that the wording of the preamble has been overworked by the friends of the national idea. Yet it seems fair to conclude that even when adopted, the majority believed that in case of dispute on a question of authority between the Federal government and a State government, the Federal government should decide. That is the real test of what we mean by sovereignty as between the State and Federal governments. Indeed, the opposition to the Constitution which failed was based largely on the objection that, in case of dispute, the Federal power would control.

It was not until the Kentucky and Virginia resolutions of 1798, that the theory of nullification received definite expression. Jackson

[29] Max Farrand, *The Records of the Federal Convention*, Vol. II, p. 27.
[30] *Ibid.*, p. 28.   [31] *Ibid.*, p. 28.   [32] *Ibid.*, p. 27.   [33] *Ibid.*, p. 29.

sternly repudiated it, amid general approval. Even Stephens, seventy years later, would have none of the theory that the Federal government could not decide on a conflict of authority. As long as a State was in the Union, it should submit to the supreme authority.

We may argue with Lincoln and with Story that even a compact is not dissoluble at the will of any party to it; that the Union was not a compact but a Union, formed by the people and not the States; and here, of course, the argument depends on our emotional and personal reactions. There is reason and history and emotion on both sides. As time went on, the number who believed that secession was desirable and permissible diminished, and in the end, lost. To some of us, it seems difficult to conceive that the new States which were formed after 1789 could ever have such a right, and yet they were admitted on an equality with the old States. But, in any event, the fact that the loyalties of the citizens of many of the new States were inevitably with the Union in preference to their own States, had a tremendous effect on the final decision.

It is not necessary for us to add much to the foregoing. The question is settled. Like so many questions of politics, it depends, after all, on deep emotional reactions and personal loyalties. As Willoughby remarks, the whole nature of the question changed with time. It is the fashion now to emphasize the economic aspect of the change, and to note that the influx of people into the Middle West, whose economic needs were fostered by the spread of railroads and the extension of trade between the States, destroyed the old State parochialism and generated the national idea. No one should minimize these factors.

But, after all, economic factors do not make loyalties or psychological states of mind: they rather give them an opportunity to develop and grow. The national idea was strengthened by economic factors, not made by them. The essential fact was the growth of the national idea. This was aided by railroads and trade, and the extension of territory. This sentiment was also aided by the growth of a national tradition,—by the fact that, in time, people grew up who were born after the Union had been formed, and who could not remember the time of separation. Common sufferings were undergone, and common joys were experienced.

Barrett Wendell observed that, in 1815, "the secession of an

American State would have meant only reversion to a state of affairs which everybody in the prime of life could vividly remember." By 1861, he said, "secession had come to mean reversion to a state of things which had long since passed out of living memory. It had become a palpable breach of what had grown to be an immemorial national tradition." [34] He recalled that Webster was said to have read the Constitution while he plowed. He was only seven years old when it was adopted. He was from the beginning a citizen of the United States. "He belonged, in brief, to the first generation of Americans whose memories, like our own, embraced no other form of government than that under which we live; and thus his career embodies in its earliest form the full type of character which we now call American." [35]

Many people, then, came to regard the Union with affection, and to consider it as indissoluble. Many economic and social ties, many of what Lincoln called the mystic chords of memory, made its dissolution a thing grievous to contemplate. And after four years, it was decided that it should not be disrupted. The question was settled.

The Theory of Reconstruction

Scholars, of course, as we have seen, continued the debate. Yet, even in practical affairs, the old conflict on the nature of the States continued. It permeated the whole question of reconstruction. Even those who held that secession was treason, could not avoid considering a State of the Union as something different from a mere division of territory.

The practical construction of the government in the course of the war had been contradictory, as perhaps it was bound to be. The North steadily insisted that the States were still in the Union. They could not secede. Every act of secession was null and void; as if it had never been. Yet we passed a confiscation act and confiscated property of persons within the Southern lines, whether or not they were participating in the Rebellion; we blockaded the Southern ports and confiscated ships from those ports, whether or not they were aiding the Rebellion; and we freed the slaves within the lines of the Southern armies, whether or not they were owned by men aiding the Rebellion. Finally, we counted the Southern

[34] Barrett Wendell, *Liberty, Union and Democracy*, p. 219. [35] *Ibid.*, p. 220.

States in the ratification of the war amendments, although we held that they had forfeited their rights and were not entitled to be represented in Congress.

When the war was over, the Southern representatives, taking us at our word that all their acts of rebellion were as if they had never been done, asked for representation in Congress. Then they were met by the demand that they must meet certain tests before they could be re-admitted.

Lincoln looked at the question in a very simple and practical way. Either he had little patience with the theoretical arguments which were soon to become so prominent, or else he feared to entangle the whole question in the very sort of metaphysical argument which actually developed. In his last speech, delivered on April 11, 1865 (four days before he died), he said:

"As it appears to me, that question has not been, nor yet is, a practically material one, and that any discussion of it while it thus remains practically immaterial, could have no effect other than the mischievous one of dividing our friends. As yet . . . that question is bad as the basis of a controversy, and good for nothing at all,— a merely pernicious abstraction.

"We all agree that the seceded States, so-called, are out of their proper practical relations with the Union, and that the sole object of the Government, civil and military, in regard to these States, is to again get them into that proper practical relation. I believe that it is not only possible, but in fact, easier, to do this without deciding or even considering whether those States have ever been out of the Union, than with it. Finding themselves safely at home, it would be utterly immaterial whether they had ever been abroad. Let us all join in doing the acts necessary to restore the proper practical relations between these States and the Union, and each forever after innocently indulge his own opinion whether in doing the acts he brought the States from without into the Union, or only gave them proper assistance, they never having been out of it." [36]

Here is an admirable illustration of the Anglo-Saxon dislike of formal theory. It was, of course, not widely imitated in Congress. Yet even Lincoln, while he was stating that he refused to theorize,

[36] Fleming, *Documentary History of Reconstruction*, Vol. I, p. 115.

was himself theorizing: for his policy itself was necessarily based on a theory.

He proposed to admit to Congress representatives from each seceded State, whenever ten per cent of the people who voted at the 1860 election had taken an oath of allegiance to the government of the United States, and had elected representatives to Congress. His policy was therefore avowedly based on the theory that the States were not and never had been out of the Union; that all that had happened was that certain groups had seized control of the State governments and diverted them from their lawful purposes.

All that was necessary, then, was that the State governments be placed again in the hands of loyal persons, who would elect representatives to the national Congress. Yet if something had not happened to the Southern States, he would never have asked that new governments be constituted. His theory, therefore, was that the States were still in the Union; but that they had, in effect, to be re-admitted, for they had to do certain things before they could have any part in Congress again. After all, he too, was treating them as territories applying for admission as States.

As Burgess pointed out, Lincoln's theory assumed that one-tenth of the voters constitute a State. But, as he said, "local self-government can not really exist where the part of the population holding the legal authority does not really possess the sinews of power; and where the conditions of the society are democratic, or anything like democratic, one-tenth of the population can not really possess the sinews of power." The actual power, he argued, would have to come from the outside. While such a situation could exist temporarily, or in a territory, it could not be permitted as a principle upon which to base self-government in a "State" in a Federal system. It was simply not State government. He concluded that on this point "Mr. Lincoln's reasoning was crude and erroneous, and when applied, was destined to result in mischievous error." [37]

But President Johnson proceeded on the Lincoln theory, and when Congress met in December, 1865, reconstruction by executive action had made great progress. Then the Republican leaders decided to call a halt. They proceeded to advance their own theories.

[37] Burgess, *Reconstruction and the Constitution*, p. 13.

The first was Thaddeus Stevens' famous theory that the defeated States were conquered provinces. He said that the President "assumes, what no one doubts, that the late rebel States have lost their constitutional relations to the Union, and are incapable of representation in Congress except by permission of the Government. It matters but little, with this admission, whether you call them States out of the Union, and now conquered territories, or assert that because the Constitution forbids them to do what they did do, that they are therefore only dead as to all national and political action, and will remain so until the Government shall breathe into them the breath of life anew and permit them to occupy their former position. In other words, that they are not out of the Union, but are only dead carcasses lying within the Union.

"In either case, it is very plain that it requires the action of Congress to enable them to form a State government and send representatives to Congress. Nobody, I believe, pretends that with their old Constitutions and frames of Government, they can be permitted to claim their old rights under the Constitution. They have torn their constitutional States into atoms, and built on their foundations fabrics of a totally different character. Dead men can not raise themselves. Dead States can not restore their own existence as 'it was.' " [38]

"Unless the law of nations is a dead letter, the late war between two acknowledged belligerents severed their original compacts, and broke all the ties that bound them together. The future condition of the conquered power depends on the will of the conqueror. They must come in as new States, or remain as conquered provinces."

But he added that if, "as some dreaming theorists imagine," the Southern States had "never been out of the Union, but have only destroyed their State governments," so as to be incapable of political action, "then the guaranty of republican government article applies. . . ." [39]

He declared that there had been a war,—a war waged by States on the United States. We had recognized the South as a belligerent power. "Individuals can not make war. They may commit murder, but that is no war. Communities, societies, States, make war." [40] There had been a war; there had been a blockade under which

[38] *Congressional Globe*, Dec. 18, 1865, pp. 72–73.   [39] *Ibid.*, p. 73.   [40] *Ibid.*, p. 73.

prizes were treated as legitimate prizes of war; we had treated the Confederacy as a warring power, and now, in defeat, it was simply a defeated enemy.

He found the power to impose conditions on the Southern States either under the article giving Congress the power to admit new States, or the clause providing that the United States shall guarantee to every State a republican form of government. The former was, he held, the controlling provision.

Sumner's theory was somewhat different. He agreed with Stevens that the Southern States were no longer States, but he held that they were still territories within the Union. As early as 1862, he laid down his creed in resolutions presented to the Senate. They declared that any vote of secession or other act by which any State undertook to put an end to the supremacy of the Constitution within its territory, was inoperative and void; and when sustained by force, became a practical abdication by the State of all rights under the Constitution.[41]

When the question of reconstruction first came before the Senate in December, 1865, he presented his argument fully. "The time has passed," he declared, "for phrases, which have been the chief resource in opposition to a just reconstruction. It is not enough to say, 'A State can not secede,' 'a State can not get out of the Union,' 'Louisiana is a State in the Union.' These are mere words, having no positive meaning and improper for this debate. So far as they have meaning, they confound law and fact. It is very obvious that a State may, in point of *law,* be still in the list of States; and yet, in point of *fact,* its relations to the Union may have ceased through violence, foreign or domestic. In point of law, no man can commit suicide; but, in point of fact, men do. The absurdity of denying that a man has committed suicide, because it is unlawful, is equalled by the kindred absurdity of saying that a State can not do a certain thing, because it is unlawful. Unhappily, in this world, the fact is not always in conformity with the law.

"Therefore," he said, "I put aside all fine-spun theories running into the metaphysics of Constitutional law. All such subtleties are absolutely futile. They must end in nothing. I found myself on existing facts, which are undeniable." [42]

[41] *Congressional Globe,* Feb. 11, 1862, p. 737.
[42] Sumner, *Works,* Vol. X, p. 125. Feb. 5, 1866.

In point of fact, he declared, "the Rebel States have ceased to take any part in the National government." [43] They had no officials to act for the Federal government, no senators, no representatives. They had actually been at war with the Union. The result was that necessity and duty joined that we require of the Southern States that they become republican, before they could be re-admitted again into the Union.

Like Stevens, he found the power in the guaranty clause of the Constitution. The development of that argument we have already considered in the debate on the war amendments. Here it is enough to say that he held that Article IV of the Constitution gave to Congress the sole power to determine whether or not a State had a republican form of government; and if not, to determine what the requirements of such a government were, and to demand of the Southern States that they conform to those requirements before their representatives could be admitted into Congress.

But there was a middle theory,—the theory of forfeited rights. Fundamentally, it was that the States were still States, but had forfeited their rights as States by rebellion; and that under the guaranty clause, Congress had power to impose its conditions before their representatives could be admitted into Congress.

Congressman Shellabarger well expressed this theory. In the House on January 8, 1866, he argued, "It is under our Constitution possible to, and the late rebellion did in fact so, overthrow and usurp in the insurrectionary States the loyal State governments as that, during such usurpation, such States and their people ceased to have any of their rights or powers of government, as States of this Union; and this loss of the rights and powers of government was such that the United States may and ought to assume and exercise local powers of the lost State governments, and may control the re-admission of such States to their powers of government in this Union, subject to and in accordance with the obligation to 'guarantee to each State a republican form of government.' " [44]

To constitute a State, he said, there must be, first, a fixed abode and a definite territory belonging to the people who occupy it. There must be a body of people united together for the purpose of promoting their mutual safety and advantage by their combined strength, and there must be traditional obedience of its members

[43] *Ibid.*, p. 126.　[44] *Congressional Globe*, Jan. 8, 1866, p. 142.

to those in whom the superiority is vested. These were tests of a State,—a national State,—rather than a State of the Union. Indeed, even the most vigorous advocates of national power instinctively argued, when talking of the States of the Union, as if they were national states, instead of mere subdivisions of a national state: so strong was the old State feeling among all of us. Shellabarger was, however, aware of the difference, and he used it to strengthen his position. Surely, he said, "if habitual obedience to law was 'necessary to the legal idea of a State,' even under the vague and general precepts of the international code, it will not be insisted that habitual, persistent, and universal disobedience will be tolerated by the well-defined, express, and rigorous provisions of the American Constitution in the citizens of one of its States." [45]

The citizens of a State under the Constitution owe obedience to the Constitution; the State legislators are bound by it, by oath; the State was subject to the guaranty clause, and thereby became entitled to certain rights under the Constitution. The State has duties as well as rights, and these duties and rights were conferred on the States as States. Without duties, there were no rights, and the Southern States had performed no duties.

The blockade, he argued, treated the States as States, as organized bodies which had levied war and not as mere rebellious individuals. The Prize Cases, he said, which had upheld the blockade, and treated as a lawful prize any vessel which came from a blockaded port without proof that the owner was a party to the Rebellion, strengthened his theory that the Southern States were still States, and that they had made war as States. The very cases usually urged as inconsistent with the congressional theory, on the ground that they treated the Southern States as States, acting together in rebellion, he held strengthened his position. The Southern States had not seceded; that is, the rebellion had not been successful, but they had acted as States and not as masses of persons, and they had lost their rights and powers as States. They could be restored to their rights as States not by mere cessation of the war, but only by an act of Congress prescribing "the time and manner of their return." [46]

He rejected the theory that the power could be found under the right of each House to judge the qualifications of members. To

[45] *Ibid.*, Jan. 8, 1866, p. 142.   [46] *Ibid.*, Jan. 8, 1866, p. 145.

argue that you could exclude a Representative or Senator who was qualified in every other way, was to concede the whole argument of the power of the central government, but on a false basis; since, if it were done under the power to decide the qualifications of members, there might be twenty-four States in the Union in the Senate, thirty-four in the Union in the House, and "Heaven knows how many in the Union for electing a President." [47]

The Committee on Reconstruction, in its report in June, 1866, gave the final statement of the forfeited rights theory. This report, except for a few verbal changes, was the work of Senator Fessenden, of Maine. It declared that from the time the Southern States "withdrew their representatives in Congress and levied war against the United States, the great mass of the people became and were insurgents, rebels, traitors, and all of them assumed and occupied the political, legal, and practical relation of enemies of the United States . . . their people reduced to the condition of enemies, conquered in war, entitled only by public law to such rights, privileges, and conditions as might be vouchsafed by the conqueror."

Consequently, as public enemies, they had "no right to complain of temporary exclusion from Congress; but, on the contrary, having voluntarily renounced the right to representation and disqualified themselves by crime from participating in the Government, the burden now rests upon them . . . to show that they are qualified to resume federal relations. . . . They must prove that they have established, with the consent of the people, representative forms of government in harmony with the Constitution and laws of the United States, that all hostile purposes have ceased, and should give adequate guarantees against future treason and rebellion." They could be restored to representation in Congress only by permission of that "constitutional power against which they rebelled and by which they were subdued." [48]

Summarizing, the report concluded in clear, definite sentences, breathing all the spirit of successful power, that the States lately in rebellion "were, at the close of the war, disorganized communities, without civil government, and without constitutional or other forms, by virtue of which political relations could legally exist

[47] *Ibid.*, p. 145.
[48] Fleming, *Documentary History of Reconstruction*, Vol. I, p. 125.

between them and the federal government"; that Congress could not be expected to recognize as valid the election of representatives from disorganized communities, who could not present their claims to representation under established and recognized rules; and, finally, that Congress would not be justified in admitting such communities to representation, without first providing such constitutional or other guarantees as would tend to secure "the civil rights of all citizens of the republic; a just equality of representation," protection against claims founded in rebellion and crime, and the temporary exclusion of those who had participated in the Rebellion.[49]

Like Sumner and Stevens, the Committee based its theory on the guaranty clause.

After all, there was not a great deal of difference between the forfeited rights theory and the State suicide theory of Sumner. Both held that Congress had the right under the guaranty clause to exact conditions, on the performance of which the Southern States could exercise their rights. Sumner simply held that they were no longer States, and could not act as States. The Committee held that they were still States, but could not act as States. Presumably, Sumner would have held that they could be divided into new States, as Congress might decide; while those who held the forfeited rights theory would have said that the people and territory of an old State constituted a state in the sense that we say that England is a state, and that that territory and people were free from control by Congress. But, in actual operation, there was no difference between the two theories.

The opposing theory was well expressed by Henry J. Raymond, of New York. "I can not believe," he said, "that these States have ever been out of the Union," or, "in any sense a separate Power. If they were, sir, how and when did they become so? . . . Was it by the ordinance of secession? I think we all agree that an ordinance of secession passed by any State of this Union is simply a nullity, because it encounters in its practical operation the Constitution of the United States, which is the supreme law of the land. It could have no legal, actual force or validity. It could not operate to effect any actual change in the relations of the State adopting it to the national Government; still less, to accomplish

[49] *Ibid.*, pp. 126–27.

the removal of that State from the sovereign jurisdiction of the Constitution of the United States." [50]

He declared that the "resolutions of these States, the declarations of their officials, the speeches of members of their legislatures," and the "utterances of their press," all were simply declarations of a purpose to secede. He asked if they carried their purpose into effect. He replied that they did not succeed in their attempt. They failed to maintain their "ground by force of arms; in other words, they failed to secede." He argued that the Prize cases merely held that for the purposes of war, the South should be treated as a belligerent power. The Court did not say that the South was "an independent nation,—that it had a separate existence, or had gone out of the sovereign jurisdiction of the United States."

The individuals went into rebellion and not the States, and the individual citizens alone should suffer the penalty of the act and the failure. "A State," he cried, "can not be indicted; a State can not be tried; a State can not be hung for treason." A seceded State still existed as "an organic member of the Union." [51]

He admitted that the "practical relations of the governments of those States with the government of the United States, were all wrong,—were hostile to that government. They denied our jurisdiction, and they denied that they were States of the Union; but their denial did not change the fact, and there was never any time when their organizations as States were destroyed. A dead State is a solecism, a contradiction in terms, an impossibility." [52]

Yet even Raymond demanded certain guaranties for the future. The right to impose guaranties rested, he said, "primarily and technically, on the surrender we may and must require at their hands." We must require that they give up their theory of State sovereignty, and they must repeal their ordinances of secession. [53]

Sumner would, of course, have answered that this was a strictly legal point of view. In point of fact, he argued the Southern States had broken off; they had changed their relations with the Federal government; indeed, they had had no relations with it for four years. And moreover, if there were no change in their relations, how could Raymond demand any guaranties whatever?

[50] *Congressional Globe,* Dec. 21, 1865, p. 120.
[52] *Ibid.,* pp. 121–22.
[51] *Ibid.,* Dec. 21, pp. 120, 121.
[53] *Ibid.,* pp. 122–23.

But Raymond's view was the common opposing view. Saulsbury, of Delaware, expressed the same theory. "I hold," he said, "that, when armed resistance to Federal authority ceased in the Southern States and the Federal authority was acknowledged, those States never having been out of the Union but always in it, their ordinances of secession being absolute nullities, the people of those States had a right to assemble as citizens of the United States, elect their own State legislatures, elect their own governors, and put into operation the machinery of government, without intervention of the President or Congress or anybody else." [54]

It remains to consider the theory of the United States Supreme Court. It had a tangled mass of questions to solve. The Administration, of course, contended that the acts of secession were void. There was no Confederacy. There were only people of the Southern States who were in rebellion against the Federal authority. We would not permit any foreign power to recognize the Confederacy. Yet Lincoln had immediately instituted a blockade of all Southern ports, and it was enforced against all ships coming out of those ports, whether or not their owners were engaged in the Rebellion. Later, he freed all slaves within the lines of the Southern armies, whether or not they belonged to those engaged in the Rebellion. As we shall see, the Confiscation Act, while directed against only those who were engaged in the Rebellion, was actually enforced against property of those who merely lived in the South. Apparently, we were waging war against eleven States united in the Confederacy, who were treated as if they were a nation outside of the Union.

The first cases to come before the Supreme Court were the Prize cases.[55] Certain prizes had been seized, outside of Southern ports, early in 1861, before Congress had even ratified the acts of the President, in suppressing the Rebellion, in calling for troops and establishing a blockade. The Court held that ships of persons residing within the limits of the Confederacy were subject to seizure and confiscation, whether or not the owners were aiding the Rebellion. "All persons residing within this territory whose property may be used to increase the revenues of the hostile power are, in this contest, liable to be treated as enemies, though not foreigners. They have cast off their allegiance and made war on their government, and are none the less enemies because they are traitors." The

[54] *Ibid.*, Dec. 21, 1865, p. 113.   [55] 2 Black. 635 (1862).

members of the Confederacy could be treated as both rebels and enemies. The Nation could exercise the rights of both a sovereign and a belligerent.

The principle of these cases was followed in the case of Miller vs. U. S.,[56] which held that stock of Miller in two Michigan railroads could be confiscated in an ex parte proceeding, although there was no proof that Miller was aiding the Rebellion. The statute itself called for proof that the owner of the property was giving aid and comfort to the Rebellion. The Court said, however, that the act was not to be confined to those who were enemies within the law of nations.

"Clearly, however, those must be considered such who, though subjects or citizens of the lawful government, are residents of the territory under the power or control of the party resisting that government. Thus much may be gathered from the Prize cases." [57] It was an unwarranted inference that, "whether persons were within the law or not, depended not on their being enemies, but on certain overt criminal acts described and defined by the law." [58] In other words, it was again held that property of a person living in the seceded States could be confiscated.

In several noted cases, however, the Court affirmed, in sweeping language, that the seceded States had never been out of the Union. In Texas vs. White, Texas sued to recover United States bonds which had been sold by the Confederate government. The suit was begun in 1867, before Texas had been re-admitted to Congress and when she was governed by a military governor. The suit had, however, also been approved by the new governor elected by the people, and by a third governor appointed by President Lincoln. The bonds had been sold during the Civil War to provide funds for the Confederate government.

The Supreme Court held that Texas could bring the suit: it was a State in the Union, and always had been. In famous language, it said, "The Constitution, in all its provisions, looks to an indestructible Union, composed of indestructible States. When, therefore, Texas became one of the United States, she entered into an indissoluble relation. All the obligations of perpetual union, and all the guaranties of republican government in the Union, attached at once to the State." The act, it proceeded, which brought Texas into

[56] 11 Wall. 268 (1870).   [57] *Ibid.*, p. 311.   [58] *Ibid.*, p. 313.

the Union was final. "There was no place for reconsideration or revocation, except through revolution or through 'consent of the States.'" The ordinance of secession adopted by Texas, and "all the acts of her legislature intended to give effect to that ordinance, were absolutely null. They were utterly without operation in law." And so the Court allowed Texas to sue, although at the time she was under military government. Grier dissented. He said the question, whether Texas was a State in the Union, was to "be decided as a *political fact*, and not as a *legal fiction*." As a political fact, she was not a State: she had no representatives in Congress, no senators; she was a military district.

Yet the majority of the Court held that the acts of Texas in disposing of the bonds were void, because in aid of the rebellion.[59]

In White vs. Hart, the Court asserted that Georgia was a State in 1868, when her new constitution made any note given for a slave unenforceable; and, since she was a State, she was subject to the clause of the Federal Constitution forbidding a State to impair the obligations of a contract. "For all the purposes of the national government, the people of the United States are an integral, and not a composite mass, and their unity and identity, in this view of the subject, are not affected by their segregation by State lines for the purpose of State government and local administration." Considered in this connection, the States were organized for the performance of their duties in the larger polity, the Union, and a State could no more secede from the Union than a county from a State. "Their rights under the Constitution were suspended, but not destroyed."[60]

Yet, of course, if Georgia were not a State, but a territory, no act of its legislature as a territorial legislature, repudiating a note founded on a slave consideration, would have been valid without the consent of Congress. The Court, however, insisted that Georgia was still in the Union, subject to the contract clause, although she was performing no function as a State.

In Keith vs. Clark,[61] the Court decided that Keith could recover money paid for taxes to the State of Tennessee, after he had tendered notes of the Bank of Tennessee, which had been refused. The Constitution of Tennessee in 1865 made such notes void. The

[59] 7 Wall. 700, 725, 726, 737. (1868).   [60] 13 Wall. 646, 650, 651 (1871).
[61] 7 Otto 454, 460 (1878).

Court held again that Tennessee had never been out of the Union. "The political society which in 1796 became a State of the Union, by the name of the State of Tennessee, is the same which is now represented as one of those States in the Congress of the United States. Not only is it the same body politic now, but it has always been the same. There has been perpetual succession and perpetual identity. . . . This political body has not only been all the time a State, and the same State, but it has always been one of the United States,—a State of the Union."

The State therefore could not repudiate its own obligations. And it said that the notes were not issued to aid the Rebellion; at least, there was nothing in the record to that effect. The decision quoted at length from Cicero and Vattel as to what constituted a state, showing again how ingrained was the tendency to treat a State of the Union as a state in the national sense.

Bradley, in his dissenting opinion, said it was immaterial whether Tennessee was a State all through the rebellion. The government of the State was a usurping government; and while its acts, which had no relation to the Rebellion, could and should be upheld in the interest of order, any act in aid of the Rebellion was void. The bank was the fiscal agent of the State, and its operations directly aided the Rebellion.

Bradley came close to the true theory. The seceded States, as territories, remained. The people in a seceded State were the same people who had declared for Rebellion. But, clearly, the governments were run by men who had repudiated all rights and duties towards the Federal government. The acts of their local governments which did not impair the Federal relation would be valid, just as the local legislation of any revolutionary body is upheld. But acts in aid of the Rebellion were void.

So, in Horn vs. Lockhart, the Court, while it said that an executor could not invest in Confederate bonds since the bonds were an investment in aid of the Rebellion, took occasion to add that "Order was to be preserved, police regulations maintained, crime prosecuted, property protected, contracts enforced, marriages celebrated, estates settled, and the transfer and descent of property regulated precisely as in time of peace. No one that we are aware of seriously questions the validity of judicial or legislative acts in the insurrectionary States touching these and kindred subjects, where they were not hostile in their purpose or mode of enforcement to the authority of the National government, and did not impair the rights of citizens under the Constitution." [62]

The theory of the Supreme Court, then, was that the States had always been in the Union: they had never left the Union. There was perpetual succession and perpetual identity. Any acts which they did in aid of the Rebellion were void: all others were valid.

The Constitution applied to them as States. When the Constitution said that no State could impair a contract, that meant that Georgia and Texas and Tennessee could not impair a contract at a time when they had no relations whatever with the Federal government. Texas could sue as a State when she was under a military government.

Evidently, if there is any conflict, the Prize and Confiscation cases must yield to Keith vs. Clark. The Supreme Court did not mean, therefore, in the Prize and Confiscation cases, that the States had seceded; but merely that the States, as States, were conducting the Rebellion.

Hurd found the decisions of the Supreme Court and the theories of the Republican majority equally unsatisfactory. He said that it was ridiculous to hold that, after the South seceded, the States existed all through the war, on the theory that the "Constitution requires or pre-supposes the existence of such states, somewhere, in some supposed human beings, supposed to wish to be citizens of a State of the United States and to be *loyal* towards the government of the United States in feeling, action being impossible." [63] The Confederate government, then, did not usurp the government of the State against the loyal people of the State, but it usurped the power of the Federal government over its territory. It refused to allow the Federal laws to be enforced in that territory. The States were gone. The war was waged against people who lived in these former States, by the States united.

Hurd declared that Boutwell came nearest to expressing his theory. Boutwell declared that when, by the voice of the people of Arkansas, the State organization had ceased to exist, the "jurisdiction of the general government under the Constitution over the territory of Arkansas exists unimpaired, exactly as it was before this so-called ordinance of secession was passed! What more re-

[62] 17 Wall. 570, 580. (1873).   [63] Hurd, p. 148.

mains? Jurisdiction and sovereignty over the people of the State of Arkansas, neither more nor less than it was before the act of secession was passed. What is the condition of the people? Speaking legally, and also as a matter of fact, they have just those rights which they can enjoy without a State organization. Of what are they deprived? Of those privileges under the Constitution which can be enjoyed only through a State organization." [64]

In other words, Hurd agreed with Boutwell and Sumner that there had been a State lapse or State suicide. But he wished to make it very clear that he arrived at his result by an entirely different road from that traveled by Sumner. Sumner's theory, he said, was based on *"ideas of political justice,* assumed to have the force of law independently of all connection with the known will of a visible possessor of sovereign power," [65] on the theory that it comprehended "those *ideas* of right and wrong which those who supported that conclusion approved as private individuals." [66] Rather Hurd based his argument on the strict theory that the United States was formed by the States United; that no State had ever been sovereign; that the people, as a mass, were not sovereign; and that therefore when the government of a State was seized by the secessionists, the State power as a member of the Union lapsed. The State was gone. There was no possibility that a State could be a State in the Union, when its government no longer recognized the government of the United States. It was simply territory belonging to the United States, subject to its laws and its Constitution, like any other territory. Therefore, Congress had merely to reconstruct new States out of that territory.

Hurd therefore found practically every step taken by the Federal government wrong in theory. He said that we insisted that a State could not secede, and yet in the Prize and Confiscation cases we had treated them as if they were separate national entities. "The individual private persons, whose property was to be affected by these statutes, were to be discriminated, not by their personal acts or sentiments, but by the fact of their being subjects of enemies' country." [67] We, in effect, restored the Southern States to statehood. Lincoln and Johnson tried to form new States from the loyal populations, as if the theory of a State required that there be found a part of the population loyal to the national government.

[64] Hurd, *The Theory of Our National Existence,* p. 277.   [65] *Ibid.,* p. 278.
[66] *Ibid.,* p. 278.   [67] *Ibid.,* p. 175.

But Hurd over-emphasized the Prize and Confiscation cases. To hold that for the purposes of war, persons living in the South should be treated as enemies, was not to recognize secession. It was a course sanctioned in many former rebellions. A rebel army must perforce be treated as a belligerent, and it is pressing the cases too far to say that to treat the inhabitants of Virginia as enemies, was to admit that Virginia had seceded. We had been treated as belligerents in the Revolution, although we were clearly rebels. In fact, Shellabarger, as we have seen, used the Prize and Confiscation cases to prove his theory of forfeited rights. The States, as States, had lost their rights, though they had failed to secede.

Dunning, in his "Essays on the Civil War and Reconstruction," argued that the forfeited rights theory was based on the guaranty clause, and he proceeded to show that the argument from the guaranty clause was untenable. Only "by a complete rejection of the old interpretation," he said, "could the moderates derive from the Constitution the power of Congress to organize a government for a State. To maintain themselves in their somewhat unsteady proposition that a State could not perish, they wrenched the guarantee clause wholly away from its history. Nor was their violence successful. For to the impartial reader, the act of March 23, 1867, is much more suggestive of an enabling act for a territory than of a guaranteeing act for a State." [68]

In short, the whole history of the guaranty clause was that the political government chosen by a State was a republican government; and it had never been held, either by the Supreme Court or by political students, that the Federal government could force a government on a State which the Federal government thought was republican in form, but which the State did not want.

It is evident that Dunning was right, that the guaranty clause gave no basis for the Reconstruction theory. But it was not necessary to the argument. I agree with Burgess, that the key to the whole reconstruction question is the definition of a State in a Federal government. He said that there had been persistent confusion of a state having sovereignty,—a national state with a State in a Federal union. A Federal State, he said, was a local self-government, under the supremacy of the general Constitution and possessed of residuary powers. We have territories, too, which are

[68] Dunning, *Essays on the Civil War and Reconstruction,* p. 132.

local governments as agencies of "the legislative department of the central Government." [69]

Why, then, he asked, were the States indestructible? As they came from territories, why could they not go back to territories? If a State, he said, renounces its allegiance to the United States, it is no longer a State "of the Union, nor has it become a State out of the Union. It is simply nowhere. The land is there and the people are there, but the form of local government over it and them has been changed from local self-government to a Congressional or a Presidential agency, as the case may be." The error that the State endures caused all the confusion of ideas on Reconstruction. [70]

Many of us, even in the Middle West, can not yet look on a State as merely a local self-government, with no more personality than a shire in England or a department in France. There are many loyalties and memories which make the statement cold and repellent. And this feeling is, of course, intensified in those of New England and the old South. Yet however tender may be our memories, there can be little doubt that a State could cease to be a State.

If the Rebellion had been successful, of course the Southern States would have ceased to be States of the Union. It was not successful, and so their territories remained within the Union, and they were still subject to the Constitution. But they had, indeed, acted as States when they attempted to secede; their governments had supported the Southern cause; they had broken all normal relations with the national government, and the people of the Southern States belonged to communities which had no State relationship to the national government. They had no representatives in Congress; they had paid no Federal taxes; the Federal laws had not been enforced,—they had, indeed, forfeited their rights and become territories.

REFERENCES

BROWNSON, ORESTES A., *The American Republic: 1865* (Works, Vol. XVIII). Detroit: Thorndike Nourse, 1885.

BURGESS, JOHN W., *Political Science and Comparative Constitutional Law* (2 vols.), Chapter II. Boston: Ginn & Co., 1890–91.

[69] Burgess, *Reconstruction and the Constitution*, pp. 1, 2.　　[70] *Ibid.*, pp. 3, 4.

——*Reconstruction and the Constitution.* New York: Charles Scribner's Sons, 1902.

COOLEY, THOMAS M., *Constitutional Limitations.* Boston: Little, Brown & Co., 1871 (2d ed.).

DUNNING, WILLIAM A., *Essays on the Civil War and Reconstruction.* New York: The Macmillan Co., 1898.

FARRAND, MAX, *The Records of the Federal Convention of 1787* (3 vols.). New Haven: Yale University Press, 1911.

FLEMING, WALTER L., *Documentary History of Reconstruction* (2 vols.), Chapter I. Cleveland: Arthur H. Clarke Co., 1906.

HURD, JOHN C., *The Theory of Our National Existence.* Boston: Little, Brown & Co., 1881.

JAMESON, JOHN ALEXANDER, *A Treatise on Constitutional Conventions.* Chicago: Callaghan & Co. (1887 ed.).

POMEROY, JOHN NORTON, *An Introduction to the Constitutional Law of the United States.* Cambridge: Hurd & Houghton, (3rd ed.) 1875.

RICHARDSON, JAMES D., *Messages and Papers of the Presidents,* Vol. VI. Washington: Pub. by authority of Act of Congress, 1898.

STEPHENS, ALEXANDER H., *Constitutional View of the Late War Between the States: 1868–70* (2 vols.). Philadelphia: National Pub. Co.

SUMNER, CHARLES, *Works,* Vol. X. Boston: Lee & Shepard, 1873–1883.

WENDELL, BARRETT, *Liberty, Union and Democracy.* New York: Charles Scribner's Sons, 1906.

WILLOUGHBY, WESTEL W., *The American Constitutional System.* New York: The Century Co., 1919 (Copyright 1904).

CHAPTER V

THE NATURE OF THE STATE AND OF SOVEREIGNTY

THE question of the nature of the Union has involved, incidentally, the broader question of the nature of the state and of sovereignty.[1] But since the conflict between national and State sovereignty depends particularly on the question of who has the authority to decide in case of dispute between State and Nation, and not on the nature of the state in itself or the location of sovereignty in the State, those questions have been left for separate treatment.

As Woodrow Wilson said,[2] the question of sovereignty is as vital in political science as is the question of value in economics, and I may add as perennial. Perhaps, after all, these discussions will go on as long as society goes on, developing and changing into new forms which require ever new explanations.

It was many years after the Civil War before we had a treatise of original force and scholarship on political science. Orestes Brownson published his "American Republic" in 1865. He was a prolific journalist, who wrote with clearness, force, and even brilliancy on many subjects. Born in Vermont of Protestant stock, he first joined the Presbyterian Church; but, always mystic, he became a converted Catholic, and his Catholicism deeply affected his political beliefs. His arguments were well-sustained, and seems to have had much influence. But his political views were so permeated by his religious faith that in the end he went off into abstractions, which one of a different religion simply can not follow. For his views on American nationality, he acknowledged himself chiefly indebted to Hurd. But his main theory of the state was derived from church-

---

[1] I have throughout (except sometimes in quotations) written the word "State" when it refers to one of the States of the Union, and written it "state" when I refer to a national state in the generic sense.

[2] Woodrow Wilson, Essay on "Political Sovereignty" in *An Old Master and Other Essays*, pp. 61–62.

men and philosophers: Plato, Aristotle, St. Augustine, St. Thomas, Suarez, Pierre Leroux, and Gioberti.[3]

Government, in the first place, he felt, has something more to do than to restrict our natural liberty and curb our passions. Its duty is to render "effective the solidarity of the individuals of a nation, and to render the nation an organism—not a mere organization—to combine men in one living body, and to strengthen all with the strength of each, and each with the strength of all,—to develop, strengthen, and sustain individual liberty, and to utilize and direct it to the promotion of the common weal,—to be a social providence, imitating in its order and degree the action of the divine providence itself, and, while it provides for the common good of all, to protect each, the lowest and the meanest, with the whole force and majesty of society." [4]

He derived the state from God. God has a right to govern, and there is a moral duty to submit.

The state of nature, he agreed, was an abstraction. There was no social compact. The only rights which the individual could delegate by a compact to society were his already, and those which the State itself ensured, and really granted, could not be delegated and surrendered. The rights of religion and property were held directly from God, and could not be delegated. A compact, moreover, would have bound only those who entered into it, and would die with them.[5] The compact theory could not explain the rights of minorities; nor how the children of those who made the compact, were included in the State. Nor could a compact create anything but an aggregation of individuals.[6] It could not create a living organism.[7]

He also rejected what he called the democratic theory,—that society is "a living organism, not a mere aggregation of individuals," with rights not derived from individuals and "paramount to theirs." This, he asserted, would end in despotism, and it would be only by "extinguishing in modern society the Christian faith, and obliterating all traces of Christian civilization, that state absolutism can be revived with more than a partial and temporary success." [8]

Nature, he proceeded, creates property and God religion, and

[3] Orestes A. Brownson, *The American Republic: 1865* (*Works*, Vol. XVIII), Preface, p. 3.
[4] Orestes A. Brownson, *The American Republic: 1865* (*Works*, Vol. XVIII), p. 15.
[5] *Ibid.*, p. 38. [6] *Ibid.*, p. 38. [7] *Ibid.*, pp. 38, 39. [8] *Ibid.*, pp. 41, 45.

the life "that man derives from God through religion and property, is not derived from him through society. . . ." The rights of "conscience and property, with all their necessary implications, are limitations of the right of society. . . ." Society does not confer them or take them away.[9]

He did not believe in pure individualism, "but no political system that runs to the opposite extreme and absorbs the individual in the state, stands the least chance of any general or permanent success till Christianity is extinguished." [10] The life that man derives from God "through religion and property, is not derived by him through society, and consequently so much of his life he holds independently of society, and this constitutes his rights as a man as distinguished from his rights as a citizen." So, likewise, the people are sovereign only in a secondary sense, only as derived from God.[11]

Still Brownson rejected the theory of the origin of government by divine right, for he admitted that public officers are selected only by human agency. The divine right theory does not explain how "authority comes from God to the people." [12] The divine right advocates, it may be said, can always be met by the simple call for the proof that the holders of power at the time got their power from God. The proof could only be of a dispensation from some Mt. Sinai. But Brownson merely compromised by declaring that government was derived from God through the people, although the fact that it did not come directly from God in no way changed the way in which it is actually exercised.

Brownson found that the national sovereignty inhered in the States, not in the States separately but in the States united,—one people, "existing in distinct State organizations. . . ." This sovereign people, he said, "can act only through their State organizations." [13]

It will be seen how profoundly Brownson's religion permeated his political theory. We may admit that the rights of property and religion are so precious to man that he holds that they are derived from God, and yet the state has made such profound modifications in the right of property that no one can say definitely what is the divine right of property. It is definable only in its actual exercise,

9 *Ibid.*, p. 46.   10 *Ibid.*, p. 45.   11 *Ibid.*, pp. 46, 47.
12 *Ibid.*, p. 71.   13 Brownson, pp. 115, 116.

which is profoundly different today from what it was one hundred years ago, and indeed from the time in which Brownson wrote. Moreover, Brownson would have admitted that his own definition of the right of religion would be very different from that of Americans of the Protestant faith. There are some who hold that the right of religion forbids the State to educate or to tax for public education.

In 1870 Elisha Mulford published his "The Nation." He was a native of Pennsylvania, educated at Yale. After two years at Andover, he became an Episcopal rector in New Jersey, but soon retired and devoted himself in his native county to the preparation of "The Nation." Later he taught in the Cambridge Episcopal Theological Seminary. Horace E. Scudder testifies to his personal charm and the vividness of his talk.[14] He seems to have been much read and appreciated by his contemporaries. Like Brownson, his book shows throughout a strongly religious basis. In his introduction, he acknowledged his debt to Hegel, Stahl, and Bluntschli. The book shows on every hand that it was formed on the Hegelian model.

Of course, he began by denying the social compact, which had long since been rejected by scholars, but was still, as the Reconstruction debates showed, a living force with our public men. The natural man, he said, was only an abstraction. From the earliest times, men appear in society dependent on each other. "The Nation has its foundation laid in the nature of man. It is the normal condition of human existence."[15] The nation does not arise as a reflective process or as the result of volition. It is an organism, a continuous organism with the characteristics of every organism, a product of continuity and growth.

Yet Mulford did not attempt to make forced analogies to physical organisms.

He followed Hegel by giving the State consciousness. It "knows its own object, and the purpose which is given it to fulfill."[16] The state, he declared, was also a moral organism and a moral personality. It is not a necessary evil, its substance is good, and it is the means of the realization of freedom. In every line we can see

[14] See T. T. Munger, "The Works of Elisha Mulford," *The Century*, Vol. XIII, p. 888 (April, 1888). Also Horace E. Scudder, "Elisha Mulford," *Atlantic Monthly*, Vol. LVII, p. 362, March, 1886.
[15] Elisha Mulford, *The Nation*, p. 3.   [16] *Ibid.*, p. 13.

the influence of Hegel, the idea of the determination of the state according to an inner necessity.

The nation, Mulford argued, did not have its origin in force nor the family, nor in a social compact. Nor could its origin be found in a sovereignty inherent in the people; for, of course, he answered that this theory postulated "the very object to be ascertained." [17] He interpreted sovereignty as being the power "which allows no limitation and acknowledges no responsibility beyond itself." [18] So he really gave it up and answered the question by not answering it, by declaring that the sovereignty of the nation is "from God, and of the people." [19] There is no human ground, he said, on which the nation can rest. "They who are intrusted with it, hold it as the representatives of the nation, and as the ministers of the divine purpose in the nation. The President, the Congress, as the Crown and the Parliament, rule by the grace of God." [20]

But, of course, religious faith can never be an explanation of political power: the answer can not be so subjective.

Mulford went on to say that the nation was the "Institution of Rights," for rights are "the process in which personality affirms itself and attains recognition in the nation." Rights come to man from God, but become positive as "defined in the nation," that is, as recognized by the nation. Rights are given to man to complete his personality. They are the process by which personality forms itself.[21]

Yet he admitted that there are no rights which are absolute or inalienable. Following the Hegelian method, he said that "Positive rights have in natural rights their content, and their immutable ground, and therein alone the nation is constituted in the realization, in a moral order, of that which is immanent in society": [22] by which he meant that natural rights have no force save as recognized by law, and that positive rights have their basis in natural rights. And yet he had just said that there were no natural rights. The use of the words, "natural rights," to denote the desires of men for certain objects dear to them (although he admitted that those rights have no force until sanctioned by law), is, of course, confusing.

Like Hegel, too, he said that the right of property lay in the

---

[17] *Ibid.*, p. 50.   [18] *Ibid.*, p. 51.   [19] *Ibid.*, p. 53.
[20] *Ibid.*, p. 56.   [21] *Ibid.*, pp. 73–74.   [22] *Ibid.*, p. 81.

assertion of the will of a person over the property, and that the ground of the right of property "is that it is the material for the work of man in his vocation on earth." Property was "the gift of God to man in the material world," and its "ground" is in "the vocation from God in the world, of the individual and of the nation." To us to-day, all this seems words, with little tangible meaning.[23]

Likewise, political rights are those which are instituted "in the normal process of the people as an ethical organism." Rights are based on personality. The right to personality is the one great original right, and the nation is the realization of rights; for only through the nation can rights be realized, and only through it can freedom be realized.[24]

Similarly, he said that sovereignty is the "assertion of the self-determinate will of the organic people," [25] and he repeated the standard statement that sovereignty is inalienable, indivisible, indefeasible, and irresponsible to outside authority.

As to the location of sovereignty, Mulford held that it was not in the reigning family, nor in certain abstractions such as justice and order. While becoming himself ever more abstract, he scorned abstractions in others.

Then, in whom does sovereignty of the nation inhere? The States of the Union were not sovereign. They could not enter into relations with other nations, and never had. He could not agree with Hurd and Brownson that the States were integral and organic parts of the Nation. The Nation did not require the States. He ended with the conclusion that the sovereignty "is of the organic people, constituted as a nation." [26] It has its condition "in the consciousness of the people, and it is the manifestation of the nation in its moral personality, and therefore, as subsistent in personality, it is from God,—it is from God and of the people." [27] The state, then, was of divine origin; rights were an assertion of personality, which came from God. The needs and desires of men were all explained on ideal and a priori grounds.

So, again, the question of sovereignty and the origin of the State was not answered. His answer was found in the inner and inherent necessity of man and his State.

[23] *Ibid.*, pp. 92, 94.   [24] *Ibid.*, pp. 100, 106, 107.   [25] *Ibid.*, p. 129.
[26] *Ibid.*, p. 135.   [27] *Ibid.*, p. 135.

In 1878, Theodore D. Woolsey, Professor of Political Science at Yale, published his "Political Science or the State." It was a long and elaborate study, but without any original force. There was no consideration of the actual forces at work in our political society, the economic demands, the psychological desires pressing for political action. But perhaps it is unfair to be severe in criticism of the students of another day, when they express the ideas of their day.

Woolsey began with a consideration of rights, which he said were powers of free action. There was general agreement, he said, that there are rights which are necessary to men in order for them to reach their full development. The nature of the individual human being, the purpose of his moral nature, "demand that he be invested with certain powers of free action." [28] Every one "has a right to be what he was meant to be," to "develop himself," to "maintain and carry out his true nature." [29] Conversely, he has a right to be free from the aggression of others. The state protects rights so that the individual may develop his nature unmolested. The only natural rights, therefore, were those necessary to such development as the state had agreed to protect. "We mean, then, by natural rights those which, by fair deduction from the present physical, moral, social, religious characteristics of man, he must be invested with, and which he ought to have realized for him in a jural society, in order to fulfill the ends to which his nature calls him." [30]

Woolsey admitted that rights are subject to limitation, on account of "inabilities or deficiencies of individuals," and to avoid collision of rights. [31] The state itself had rights which gave it the right to curtail individual rights. [32]

Yet there were rights which the state can not infringe. He approved the right of passive resistance to oppression, and the right of revolution. He denied natural rights, and yet his a priori religious feeling made him insist that man has natural rights that do not come from the state.

But as to the basis for such rights, he was not clear. He rejected Bentham, Austin, and the English utilitarians. In the very beginning of his book, he said that he assumed a "moral order of the world, not founded on utilities that are such, in a sense, dis-

---

[28] *Woolsey*, Vol. I, p. 10.   [29] *Ibid.*, p. 11.   [30] *Ibid.*, p. 26.
[31] *Ibid.*, pp. 34, 36.   [32] *Ibid.*, p. 35.

coverable by man that he could construct a system of laws for human actions upon them, however the divine author of the world may have arranged it on such a plan." [33] He discarded the greatest happiness theory, admitting that happiness was an end at which the individual and the State may rightfully aim, but contending that it is "subordinate to the right and to the ends contained in the perfection of human nature." [34]

He quoted Austin's dictum that law is a command, that duty grows out of the liability to suffer pain or evil if the command is not obeyed, and that, strictly speaking, there are no rights that are not the creature of law; and replied that, under this theory, there was no difference between an unjust and an inexpedient law, and that Austin's theory made power, not "right and righteous law," the ruler of the world. [35]

It is difficult to place Woolsey's theory of rights. Apparently, it was a sort of Kantian theory, a priori in nature, based on Woolsey's own ideas of what rights are essential for the realization by man of the ends for which God intended him. All a priori systems, after all, are based on the sense of right and wrong of the man who formulates the system.

In treating of particular rights, Woolsey clearly showed that he approved or disapproved particular rights on the basis of his own reactions, indeed sometimes almost on the basis of pragmatic tests. Thus, usually, apparently opposing theories in actual practice differ less than in the abstract. For example: he disapproved Herbert Spencer's theories on land ownership, admitting that the community had certain rights which were paramount to those of private owners, such as rights for railroads, bridges, and canals; but objected that Spencer's theory applied not only to thickly settled, but to sparsely settled communities, that it must apply to farms and mines and quarries, and that the problems of dividing up the land, which had been improved, were so serious that the theory became worthless on account of the difficulty of its application. [36]

Yet those who favored nationalization of land, did so frequently on the ground that each man had a natural right to the land.

Woolsey, of course, agreed that the contract theory of the origin of the state broke down. It does not explain, he said, "the obliga-

---

[33] *Ibid.*, p. 1.   [34] *Ibid.*, p. 2.   [35] *Ibid.*, p. 130.   [36] *Ibid.*, pp. 66, 67.

tion of subsequent generations to abide by the contract."[37] Despite his religious bias, he said that the theory of the divine origin of the state did not explain how the divine right exists.[38] He found the "foundation" of the state in the family,[39] adding that the wants of men, "their needs of one another, their social nature, even their fears, keep them together. . . ." They organize in a state by accepting "principles of justice, rules of convenient intercourse, and methods of self-protection."[40] Rationally, he said the answer is in the nature and destination of man. Like most of his time, he wrote from his study and not from the facts of anthropology. As we shall see, anthropologists now agree that the state existed even before the family.

As to sovereignty, Woolsey had little definite to say.

Various legal writers in works on constitutional law, dwelt briefly on the subject of the state and sovereignty. In his *A Treatise on Constitutional Conventions,* John Alexander Jameson, in 1887, quoting and approving Austin, defined the sovereign as "the person or body of persons in a state, to whom there is, politically, no superior."[41] Sovereignty, he said, "resides in the society or body politic, in the corporate unit resulting from the organization of many into one; and not in the individuals constituting such unit, nor in any number of them as such, nor even in all of them, except as organized into a body politic and acting as such."[42]

The real sovereign was, then, the body politic. Sovereignty was, in the standard phrase, "indivisible, indefeasible, inalienable."[43]

In the United States the sovereign could not be the State governments, for the Federal Constitution was the supreme law of the land. Quoting Austin's famous definition, he said that the people of other States gave no obedience to Virginia, and therefore Virginia could not be sovereign. Nor was the Federal government the sovereign, for the people established the Federal government. Moreover, the Federal government was limited in power. The people were the true sovereign. They had ordained and established the Constitution. Government was secondary and vicarious. The people always remained. They can change the Constitution and

[37] *Ibid.,* p. 191.   [38] *Ibid.,* p. 196.   [39] *Ibid.,* p. 198.   [40] *Ibid.,* p. 198.
[41] John Alexander Jameson, *A Treatise on Constitutional Conventions* (1887 ed.), p. 17.
[42] *Ibid.,* p. 19.   [43] *Ibid.,* p. 20.

their government. Yet it was not the people in general, but the people "acting on a particular way or under particular conditions, as in groups, discriminated from each other by state boundaries." [44]

He disagreed with Austin's theory, that our sovereignty inheres in the State governments as forming one aggregate body: meaning by that, the electors in all the States; and agreed with Brownson, that it was in all the people as organized in the States.[45]

So, likewise, Pomeroy found that the nation, meaning the state, was sovereign, and that the people are the true nation.[46]

Hurd insisted that the question was one of fact, and not of law; that sovereignty can be held only as a unit, though it could be divided in exercise. He said this sovereign could not be the people as a mass, in "distinction from the organized people of the several States," for he asked when the people as a mass ever exercised sovereignty.[47] Sovereignty had never been held by the people or nation, except "as the politically organized people of the several States are such people or nation." The States were not severally independent, they had never individually claimed or exercised sovereign rights; but, as one united people acting through the State organizations, they had formed the nation and fought the war. The sovereignty was, then, in the "political people organized as the people of the States. . . ." [48] The sovereignty was, therefore, in "the States in Union."

Burgess' was perhaps the first study of political science since the Civil War, which was founded on modern scholarship. He had studied in Germany, and was deeply permeated with German political philosophy. Indeed, he was almost an idolater of German institutions. The Teutons, he said, were the discoverers of the national state, which rescues "the world from the monotony of the universal empire," and "solves the problem of the relation of sovereignty to

[44] Jameson, pp. 29–30. Austin's definition of sovereignty was: "If a determinate human superior, not in the habit of obedience to a like superior, receive *habitual* obedience from the *bulk* of a given society, that determinate superior is sovereign in that society." In England, he said Parliament was sovereign, in the United States, the people who elect the State Legislatures. Lectures on Jurisprudence. Vol. I, p. 221.

[45] *Ibid.,* p. 64.

[46] John Norton Pomeroy, *An Introduction to the Constitutional Law of the United States,* 1887, 3d ed., pp. 5, 27, 29.

[47] John C. Hurd, *The Theory of Our National Existence,* pp. 108, 113.

[48] *Ibid.,* pp. 112, 140. Pomeroy and Hurd differed on the question of who constituted the state. Pomeroy held it was all the people; Hurd, the voters only.

liberty," so that while it is "the most powerful political organization that the world has ever produced, it is still the freest." He declared that the "national state is thus the most modern and the most complete solution of the whole problem of political organization which the world has yet produced; and the fact that it is the creation of Teutonic political genius, stamps the Teutonic nations as the political nations *par excellence,* and authorizes them, in the economy of the world, to assume the leadership in the establishment and administration of states." [49] He classed Germany, the Scandinavian countries, Great Britain and the United States as Teutonic countries. Yet, when he wrote, Germany had acquired no political liberty and shown no capacity for self-government, as time has since abundantly shown. France, which he classified as non-Teutonic, has, on the other hand, in the past fifty years shown much political ability.

Burgess was also firmly of the opinion that the nation was founded on ethnic unity, and that the Teutonic element must be kept in the majority in the United States. That a state requires for its ordered existence, for the finest development of its politics, its laws and even its literature, a population of homogeneous character or at least one which has lived a long time together so that it has common backgrounds and traditions and common reactions on fundamental matters, this country has since, let us hope, learned. And it is not political boasting to say that the only countries which so far have shown great and continued capacity for self-government, have been Great Britain and the United States.

But, again, the reference to the Teutonic element in the United States is confusing; for, while the British element in the United States undoubtedly has furnished us with our political ideals and institutions and most of our leaders, it is not all Teutonic, and not all of our Teutonic element, however admirable, is of British origin. From the point of view of today, Burgess' division of races is very crude. He underestimated the non-Teutonic element in Great Britain; and the term "Celtic," with which he designated the non-Teutonic element in Great Britain, is now wholly discarded.

There was merit in his point that success in political management requires a fused population which has common standards and

[49] John W. Burgess, *Political Science and Comparative Constitutional Law,* Vol. I, pp. 38–39.

traditions, but I can not follow him in basing the argument on the disputed standards of race.

The state, said Burgess, in traditional language, was all-comprehensive, exclusive, permanent, and sovereign. It has "original, absolute, unlimited, universal power over the individual subject, and over all associations of subjects." But he said that this unlimited sovereignty "is not only not inimical to individual liberty and individual rights, but it is their only solid foundation and guaranty." The state—the sovereign—lays down in the Constitution the restraints which shall control the government.[50]

The most scholarly and thorough American study of the state in the period covered by this book remains Willoughby's "The Nature and Origin of the State," published in 1896. As a preliminary definition of the state, he said that we may say "that whenever there can be discovered in any community of men a supreme authority exercising a control over the social action of individuals and groups of individuals, and itself subject to no such regulation, there we have a state."[51]

Government, he said, consists of "the organization of the state,— the machinery through which its purposes are formulated and executed."[52]

He rejected the patriarchal theory of the origin of the state. He concluded that its origin could not be definitely ascertained. Whether "by original force or by voluntary recognition and establishment, whether founded upon acknowledged supremacy of personal prowess and sagacity of the leader selected, or whether springing from patriarchal authority, the public authority becomes established, can not now be known and undoubtedly differed in different instances. *But however originated, a public authority once created, the state becomes an established fact.*"[53]

The state, he continued, was not a natural or physical organism. It has a will or volition, enabling it to "change its form to an extent to which no theoretical limit can be placed." The state "is essentially psychical rather than physical."[54]

The theory that the state originated in the force of the powerful, he said, begged the question. The theory that the origin was divine, did not help us; for, if it were, there still remained the question

[50] *Ibid.*, pp. 52, 53.   [51] W. W. Willoughby, *The Nature of the State*, p. 3.
[52] *Ibid.*, p. 8.   [53] *Ibid.*, p. 26.   [54] *Ibid.*, p. 38.

of how one group obtained the right to exercise this divine power.

Of course, he rejected the compact theory as a mere fiction. Man, after all, is himself a part of nature, and not separate from it; and how he rules himself must be found by a study of his relations with other men. Moreover, freedom can arise only when one man is protected against the aggressions of others. There was no freedom in a state of nature. Freedom, by "what may seem a paradox," exists "only because there is *restraint*." [55]

Therefore, he held that a moral justification of the state was unnecessary. "If the political government does not render the individual any less free than he would be without it, its authority does not require a moral justification." The positive base on which the state rests is utility,—the service and protection it renders to the individuals composing it. [56]

The state was not a mechanism. Citing Bluntschli and Jellinek, he affirmed that the state has "a will of its own; its actions are self-determined. There is life and volition both in itself and in its members." [57] He even said that "a common, conscious purpose pervades and unifies it." The state also is a person, because it has a "will of its own." The "law-making organs of government are the instruments through which this will be expressed." [58]

Willoughby agreed that the state is sovereign, and that its power is unlimited. "Sovereignty," he said, "as thus expressing a supreme will, is necessarily a unity and indivisible,—unity being a necessary predicate of a supreme will." The will may be expressed through a variety of organs, "but the will itself, as thus variously expressed and performed, is a unity. In every political organism, there must be one, and only one, source whence all authority ultimately springs." [59]

Willoughby admitted that the state could act only through its organs, and exists only through them. The state, he said, can change its organs, but is always completely organized in them. Willoughby did not accept Burgess' theory that the state is organized back of the government. "But to speak of a State as not being completely organized in its government," he observed, "seems as much an absurdity as to say that a man is not completely organized in his physical frame. The government," he went on, "is the State's or-

---

[55] *Ibid.*, p. 110.   [56] *Ibid.*, p. 111.   [57] *Ibid.*, p. 132.
[58] *Ibid.*, pp. 132, 134.   [59] *Ibid.*, p. 195.

ganization." He added: "The State is society politically organized, and there can be no State action or political existence outside of such organization." He agreed that there was "possibly, no logical objection" to Burgess' use of the terms, "government" and "state," but he felt that to apply the terms, "government" and "state," to "the body politic when acting in those two capacities, can not but create confusion." The state acting through a legislature and the State acting through a constitutional convention, was still the same state.[60]

Willoughby's theory of sovereignty is, of course, bound up with his theory of the nature of law. But as all such subjects overlap, it has been felt best to treat the nature of law separately. It is enough to say here that Willoughby held that the only rules that have legal validity are those which have the sanction of the state; and that "it follows as a logical deduction, that since no one can be bound by one's own will, the sovereign political power must necessarily be incapable of legal limitation." [61]

But when Willoughby came to find the seat of this sovereign will, he had great difficulty. He would not admit that it was in the people themselves. If, he said, we admit that "the power of the people ultimately conditions the actions of those who govern them, have we reached the end of our inquiry? By no means." First of all, we must define the word, "people." It was not the individuals as individuals, because they have no political power. If we mean the people as politically organized, we have made no advance; for a people politically organized is the state. Nor can we say that it is the people who vote, nor the majority, nor the representatives, because the whole people really take part in the governing from time to time and are part of the state. To say the whole people, merely comes to saying that public opinion is sovereign, but that is too vague.[62]

The trouble was, he said, that sovereignty is a political term and denotes political power, and can be exercised only by the people as politically organized, and the people as a whole can act only by revolution. He concluded that those are sovereign who exercise the power of the state, and that sovereignty is exercised whenever the organs of the state act. But those exercising the organs of the state change from time to time; and hence he concluded that it was almost correct to say that the sovereign will is the state, and that whenever one of its organs acted, sovereignty was exercised.[63]

So the state was sovereign, and the state was all the people politically organized. Yet the people were not sovereign. This was really to give up the question of the location of sovereignty in the state. The question has baffled a generation of students.

What, then, can we gather of our American political theory of the state and sovereignty from 1865 down to 1896 when Willoughby published his book?

Though judges still referred to the social compact, American political theory, as we have seen, had rejected the idea. It is not easy to place the time when it was abandoned. Burke and Bentham both rejected it, and they must have had an appreciable influence on our thought. Before the Civil War, Lieber had rejected it. Now we have seen Mulford, Brownson, Burgess and Willoughby all would have none of it.

In its theory of the nature of the state, American political thought since the Civil War had been somewhat sterile and unoriginal, much under the influence of the German school, first Hegel and then Bluntschli and Jellinek. It held that the state was a person and a unity. The state was sovereign; sovereignty was inalienable, indivisible, and indefeasible. But there had been great difficulty in locating this sovereignty. On this point the argument revolved around Austin's definition. The popular theory was that sovereignty was in the people themselves. But Hurd objected that the people as a mass had never acted politically. They had acted only through their States. He put the sovereignty in the States United. Brownson agreed. Mulford put it in the "organic people," constituted as a nation.

But I may answer that the people act through their States only as a mechanism in electing a president. The States, as States, do not elect presidents. The people merely vote in State units. A member of the House of Representatives is not elected by the people of a State. The Supreme Court is a real part of the government,— to my mind, a part of the legislative body, and it is not chosen by State lines.

Moreover, the people of a State do not constitute an organized

[63] *Ibid.*, pp. 287, 289, 293, 302.

group. The entire people of a State are citizens of that State; but the children do not vote, and until recently the women did not vote. Yet surely they have been at all times part of their States.

If the test be the body which can amend the Constitution, it is, of course, two-thirds of both houses of Congress and three-fourths of the legislatures, or the majority of the electors who choose to vote on constitutional amendments in three-fourths of the State. Yet, the electors are a varying body who act only once a year, or even less. Their political powers are so spasmodic and irregular that their possession can hardly constitute the test of sovereignty.

Is anyone who chooses to vote on an amendment one of the sovereign body, and not one who stays at home? Or are all the eligible voters the sovereign? If the people are sovereign, what is gained by saying that it is the people as discriminated into States, or that it is in the States United?

Willoughby, as we have seen, finally concluded that the state, that is, the national state, was sovereign, and that the sovereignty was exercised by its organs. He really gave up the question of the location of sovereignty.

All the writers we have considered so far have insisted that the state was a person and a unity, and that it has a will of its own. Yet it would be difficult for anyone to tell us what they mean. In the United States the organs expressing the will of the national state are the State legislatures, the State courts, Congress, and the Federal courts. It surely is a feat of the imagination to say that the will acting through all these organs is a unity; and it is impossible to find the source of that authority save in the national state itself, which acts and can only act through its organs.

A great body of our law is the common law. Some of it dates back for generations. When we come to the study of the nature of law, we shall see that it is impossible to say that any conscious will made it. Some of the rules of law were declared in England three hundred years ago. They were adopted in bulk by our legislatures. It is meaningless to say that a conscious will of the various States adopted each of these rules. The courts in various States have modified those rules and extended them from time to time. As a result, we find the law differing on many subjects in adjoining States. Thus, timber is part of the land in some States, and in some it is not. Spendthrift trusts are permitted in Massachusetts, and forbidden in Rhode Island. Virginia holds that the burden of a covenant runs with the land; Massachusetts takes the contrary position.

The fact of the matter is that one or more judges in one State simply felt that one rule of law should be followed, and in others they favored another rule of law, and the legislatures did not change the common law. But there was no conscious will of the State or of any organ of the State. Nor does a conscious will of any State, or of the United States, control legislation. Anyone who knows anything about the last days of a legislative or congressional session, knows that to impute a conscious will of the state to the bills it passes, is simply to close one's eyes to reality. The legislature or Congress often does not realize what it is passing, often only a few members know what the bill means, and often the courts declare that the true meaning is somewhat different from what the sponsors of the statute thought. The legislatures and Congress frequently pass laws which have been very carefully worked out, but are the work of small bodies which have made particular studies of the matters in hand, and no one else knows anything about it.

Woodrow Wilson, in a brilliant essay, attacked the question of sovereignty from a fresh angle.[64] He started with Austin's famous definition. Austin put the sovereign in Great Britain in Parliament; and in this country, in the people who elect the legislatures of the States. Wilson objected that the people in the States can not act as a unit, but only in State groups; and that, moreover, the electorate was not determinate. He agreed with others that Henry Maine had refuted Austin's definition of law as the command of this determinate superior, by his proof that many political societies "had no lawmaking sovereign at all." [65] So Wilson agreed that there was no sovereign in this country, in the Austinian sense. There was no unlimited power save in the sum of all powers, and no one determinate body had all power.

But Wilson said that sovereignty is not unlimited power. Sover-

---

[64] Woodrow Wilson, "Political Sovereignty," in *An Old Master and Other Essays*, p. 61. This essay was published in 1893, three years before Willoughby's book, and I am therefore considering it out of its chronological order. But the essay was so strikingly *sui generis;* it gave such a fresh outlook on the question, and had so little connection with other American theory on the question, that I have ventured to defer its consideration until this point.

[65] *Ibid.,* p. 68.

eigns have never had unlimited power. They have always been, themselves, organs of the state; but they have been sovereigns, nevertheless. They have been the chief legislative bodies of the state. So he made his own definition of the sovereign as the "daily, operative power of framing and giving efficacy to laws. It is the originative, directive, governing power. It lives; it plans; it executes." The sovereign power "is the highest originative organ of the state. It is none the less sovereign because it must be observant of the preferences of those whom it governs. The obedience of the subject has always limited the power of the sovereign." [66]

Wilson treated our Constitutions rather cavalierly. He said that they merely define the limits of obedience. "Sovereignty has, at all times and under all systems of government, been dependent upon the temper and disposition of the people." [67] But, he proceeded, "these preferences of the general body are exercised by way of approval or disapproval, acquiescence or resistance; they are not agencies of initial choice." Constitutions, he declared, are not the utterances of a sovereign. "They are the covenants of a community," formal statements of standards.[68] Sovereignty, he repeated, is "the highest political power in the state, lodged in active organs, for the purposes of governing. Sovereign power is a positive thing, control a negative thing." So he held that legislative bodies are the sovereigns: courts are merely organs for determining limitations.[69]

Surely this brilliant little essay cleared the air. There is no sovereign in the United States, in Austin's sense. There is no determinate body which has no superior and to which obedience is given. To make the sovereign the whole people in a mass, is simply to say that the state is sovereign and to confess that there is no body inside of the state which is sovereign. In the United States, Congress makes the laws for the country. The State legislatures make them for the States. Congress is limited by the Constitution. If the Supreme Court declares an act of Congress void, Congress is not given obedience by the people. Therefore, Congress can not be Austin's sovereign. Then, who can change the Constitution? The legislatures of three-fourths of the States, or the majority of the voters in three-fourths of the States who elect delegates to constitutional conven-

[66] *Ibid.*, pp. 80–81.   [67] *Ibid.*, p. 85.   [68] *Ibid.*, pp. 85, 86, 88, 89.
[69] *Ibid.*, p. 90.

tions. Austin made the electors of the States the sovereign. But this huge body is not determinate, and it is not continuous: it may shift from week to week.

We are forced, then, to conclude that there is no sovereign, in Austin's sense. But the insistent demand for a sovereign must be met. Apparently, obedience and authority rest on this instinctive psychological need for a sovereign to obey. If we must have a sovereign, in a limited sense, we can say, with Wilson, that the sovereign is the body which is the chief political force of the community.[70]

But I think that Wilson made his sovereign too narrow. Our Supreme Court can not be left out. It is true that it can not enact a statute; but by its power of holding a statute void, it can, with great effect, influence legislation and has actually done so. It can force Congress to pass a statute which will meet its requirements, and can prevent any State legislation from impairing the obligation of contracts, burdening interstate commerce, denying due process or the equal protection of the laws. Moreover, the president's right of veto, and his opportunity for executive leadership, are surely more than merely negative. If, therefore, we define the sovereign as the chief legislative power, it must certainly include the president, the Senate, the House, and the Supreme Court.

What, then, shall we do with the State legislatures? Since the Civil War, their field has been severely limited. Formerly, they were limited by the clause forbidding the impairment of contracts and ex post facto laws; and since the Civil War, they have been restricted by the due process clause and the requirement of the equal protection of the laws. But still they alone can legislate on all such questions as descent, liability for injury, the acquisition and use of property. They are really subordinate legislative bodies for administrative districts, with large powers of legislation, and yet subject to great control by Congress and the Supreme Court, and to still greater control when three-fourths of the States desire.

[70] In his *The State*, Wilson gave his ideas on the general aspects of the State. He declared that in the last analysis government is organized force, although the force is not always visible. Government is merely the "executive organ of society," the "organ through which its habit acts," its "will becomes operative" (p. 576). Sovereignty, he admitted, as ideally conceived, "nowhere actually exists!" (p. 601). The sovereignty which does exist is simply the "will of an organized independent community. . . ." Sovereignty, he concluded, resides in the "community; but its organs, whether those organs be supreme magistrates, busy legislatures, or subtle privileged classes, are as various as the conditions of historical growth" (p. 601).

Yet it is true that inherited loyalties to the States still prevent men from regarding the States as mere administrative units. No exact definitions are possible. Congress and the president and the Supreme Court clearly do not have supreme power. But they do clearly hold the chief power, and what they declare to be the law is the law for the whole country. When they have spoken, the last word has been spoken until a constitutional amendment is passed.

In his lectures on "The Nature and Source of Law" delivered at Columbia in 1908, John Chipman Gray showed a sure sense of reality. Hegel, he said, insisted that the state was a person. It was real. It had a will of its own. So, we have seen, Mulford, Brownson and Willoughby all agreed that the state had a personality. Gierke, and a prominent school that has followed him, have argued that corporations and social and economic groups have real personalities and real wills of their own. Gray disagreed. There is no such thing, he said, as a general, collective will. It was "a figment." [71] A will belongs to an individual only. The majority of the group, or its governing body, may decide on a policy, and the policy may be carried out by the group; but it does not become the will of the group. A different majority may decide on a different policy, or the policy may be continued after the majority becomes indifferent or even opposed to the policy.

So Gray denied will also to the state. The state had no will of its own, no separate personality. The state was an "idol,—a dumb idol," an "abstraction," which could speak only through its representatives of the moment. Its will was partly the will of those who held the power at the moment,—its legislators, and partly that of past legislators and past generations, whose will had been embodied in precedents and decisions. The people, as a whole, did not create the state nor rule it. "In every aggregation of men, there are some of the number who impress their wills upon the others, who are habitually obeyed by the others, and who are, in truth, the rulers of society." [72] They work through the others, but the others are not the rulers.

Gray admitted that the power of the state is unlimited, in the sense that its organs express only its will and can not contradict

[71] John Chipman Gray, *The Nature and Source of Law*, p. 53.
[72] *Ibid.*, pp. 65, 68.

it; and so it is impossible to find the sovereign body of the state. Austin, he noted, in his attempt to find the body in the United States which was the sovereign, put it in the body of people which elect the State legislatures. But Gray replied that their power is very limited.[73] They can act only to elect the State legislatures. Indeed, it may be added, once they have acted, they sink back into the mass of the people. Moreover, as we have noted above, amendments may be made by conventions elected for that sole purpose. The people who elect the delegates—vote and go away— are not a determinate body. And Gray asked if one-fourth of the States refuse to ratify the amendment, if that one-fourth is sovereign.[74]

"The truth is," he concluded, "that the ideal or fictitious entity, the state, can manifest itself only through organs, and these organs may be so limited that there are certain acts they can not perform, and therefore there may be no one sovereign in Austin's sense, with complete powers. Such is the case in the United States of America." [75]

Here was a flat and direct denial of the reality of the personality of the state. The state acted only through its instrumentalities. It could be known only through them. It was not real or distinct in itself. Apparently he felt that the people did not constitute the state. The state consisted of those who wielded the power.

James W. Garner's "Introduction to Political Science" is a thorough and scholarly review of the whole field of political science. However, it furnished little development in the theory of the state or of sovereignty. He defined the state as a community of persons permanently occupying a definite territory, "independent of external control, and possessing an organized government to which the great body of inhabitants render habitual obedience." [76] The state is a "sovereign community, politically organized for the promotion of and the satisfaction of common needs," and the government is the agency through which "the will of the state is formulated, expressed and realized. . . ." [77]

Garner distinguished between the state and the nation: the state being the people politically organized; and the nation, a portion of society "definitely separated from the rest of the world by

[73] *Ibid.*, p. 74.   [74] *Ibid.*, p. 75.   [75] *Ibid.*, p. 76.
[76] James W. Garner, *Introduction to Political Science*, p. 41.   [77] *Ibid.*, p. 44.

natural geographical boundaries, the inhabitants of which have a common racial origin, speak the same language, have a common civilization, common customs and traits of character, and a common literature and traditions." [78] He agreed that ethnic unity was not essential to the state; but he held, with truth, that it is an element of great strength, and that so "far as possible, the principle of nationality should be respected in the organization or reorganization of states. . . ." [79]

Garner added little new to the theory of the nature and origin of the state. He pointed out the dangers of the biological analogy of the state, which he said at many points "becomes mere fancy," [80] but admitted that the state is an organism in which the parts depend on each other and the whole on the parts, and that it grows and develops and is conditioned largely by its past.

Of course, he rejected the divine theory of the origin of the state, and the compact theory. The individual comes into the state just as he is born in the world. "The obligations of allegiance and obedience do not rest upon covenant or consent, but rather upon the general interests or necessities of society, or upon grounds of utility." [81]

The old standard theory, not based on any real study of ancestral society, was that the state arose out of the family. But Garner rejected both the patriarchal and matriarchal theories. The evidence, he said, was doubtful. "The family and the state are totally different in essence, organization, functions, and purpose; and there is little reason to suppose that one should have developed out of the other, or that there should have been any connection between them." [82]

He rejected the theory that force was the origin of the state, saying that force is an explanation of state authority but not of the origin of the state.

He finally concluded simply that the state is "an institution of natural growth, of historical evolution." [83]

Garner followed the classical theory on sovereignty. The fundamental mark of the state "is supremacy of will and action,—the supreme power to command and enforce obedience. . . . To this power, legally speaking, all interests are potentially subject, all

---

[78] *Ibid.,* p. 45. [79] *Ibid.,* p. 49. [80] *Ibid.,* p. 63.
[81] *Ibid.,* p. 113. [82] *Ibid.,* p. 118. [83] *Ibid.,* p. 120.

wills subordinate." He distinguished between the legal and political sovereign. The legal sovereign is that "determinate authority which is able to express in a legal formula the highest commands of the state. . . ." [84] Back of the legal sovereign is the political sovereign, a power legally unknown and incapable of expressing the will of the state itself, "but whose will must ultimately prevail in the state." [85] In a narrower sense, the electorate was the political sovereign; but in a broader sense, it is the whole mass of the people.

In England, he said Parliament was the legal sovereign; the electorate, the political sovereign. He did not attempt to locate the legal sovereign in the United States.

He took the standard view that sovereignty is absolute. All the restrictions on sovereignty—the law of nature, the law of nations, public opinion—have no legal effect, "except in so far as the state chooses to recognize them and give them force and validity." [86]

Henry Jones Ford, of Princeton University, in his *The Natural History of the State*, made a distinct contribution to a subject usually handled by merely repeating trite statements that the state arose in antiquity, that it is a natural organism arising out of the needs of man, or that it has its base in the family and the tribe. He said that his purpose was to examine "the foundations of political science from the naturalistic point of view established by the publication of Darwin's *Origin of Species* in 1859."

He drew, however, little of definiteness from biological data, save that man is very old, that "sociability" is highly developed in many branches of the mammalia, and that man was, from the first, "distinctively social." [87] He thought that probably the line of variation "upon which the human species was formed, was through the introduction of life in community," nor did this imply "the assumption of a mode of evolution peculiar to Man" as community life, "ranging from loose association to closely articulated polity, is displayed by numerous species." [88] The sole species that has "increased and multiplied and has spread to every part of the world, surmounting difficulties before which all cognate forms declined or retreated, has life in community as a universal characteristic. . . ." [89] Psychologically, he concluded, man has evolved

---

[84] *Ibid.*, p. 240.   [85] *Ibid.*, p. 240.   [86] *Ibid.*, p. 253.
[87] Henry Jones Ford, *The Natural History of the State*, p. 42.   [88] *Ibid.*, p. 47.
[89] *Ibid.*, p. 49.

faster than any other species. Ford felt that life in community was the greatest force in his mental development.

Speech also is the result of society. "If language be the distinctive character mark of the human species, and if the fact be established that language is essentially a social product, then it necessarily follows that Man is a product of social evolution." [90]

The lowest human beings, he concluded, have a moral sense. Self-sacrifice exists in them, and aesthetic sense.

So finally from an examination of the social data, Ford came to the same conclusion that many before had arrived at by a priori methods,—that Aristotle was right, that man is a political animal. The state existed before history has any record. It existed prior to the family or the individual. "The State is the permanent and universal frame of human existence. Man can no more get out of the State than a bird can fly out of the air. The State," he proceeded, "is an organic entity composed of human beings, whose nature, relations, and activities are conditioned by its own nature, relations, and activities. . . . Man did not make the State; the State made man. . . . His nature was formed by government, requires government, and seeks government." [91]

In my opinion, this little book greatly advanced the subject with which it dealt.

All the writers I have considered, accepted the idea that the state was a unit and that the state is sovereign; that is, that its power is not legally limited by any other power. None of them would have argued, however, that the state is not subject to inherent limitations. The moral ideas of the times, the sense of right, the fear of resistance to oppressive or arbitrary laws,—all practically restrict its action. Mulford and Brownson held that government was literally held in trust from God. Burgess would organize the state back of the government, in order to protect the rights of the individual. Willoughby laid stress on the moral factors restraining the agents of the state. But all agreed that the state was legally omnipotent.

Recently this theory has been strenuously attacked. Since the end of our period the attack has spread over a wide front. But as early as 1894, John Dewey (who later was to be, with James, the exponent of pragmatism) had attacked the problem of sov-

[90] *Ibid.*, p. 103.　　[91] *Ibid.*, pp. 174, 175.

ereignty, and found sovereignty only "in the whole complex of social activities." [92] In France, Leon Duguit, Dean of Law at Bordeaux, has brilliantly and indefatigably attacked the whole theory of the sovereign State. Harold J. Laski, likewise, rejects utterly the idea of what he calls the omnipotent state. He may be included in a book on American political thought; for, while he was born in Canada and now is a professor in the University of London, he was educated at the Harvard Law School, and two of his books were written while he was a resident of this country.

Laski has attacked both the unity and the omnipotence of the state. He began, in his "Studies in the Problem of Sovereignty," by saying: "Hegelianwise, we can not avoid the temptation that bids us make our State a unity. It is to be all-absorptive. All groups within itself are to be but the ministrants to its life; their reality is the outcome of its sovereignty, since without it they could have no existence. Their goodness is gained only through the overspreading power of its presence. It alone, so to speak, eternally is; while they exist but to the extent to which its being implies them. The All, America, includes, 'implicates,' in James' phrase, its constituent states." [93]

But Laski said that other associations claimed reality also. A labor union, an association, seemed to obtain personality also. He said that there were within the state "enough of these monistic entities, club, trade union, church, society, town, county, university, each with a group-life, a group-will, to enrich the imagination. Their significance assuredly we may not deny." [94]

Laski could not see that these organizations are inferior to the state. "Yet," he says, "so we are told, the State, itself, the society of which they form part, is mysteriously One above them. . . . Trade Unionists and capitalists alike must surrender the interests of their smaller and antithetic group-persons—to the larger demands of that all-embracing One, the State. Of that One it is first that you are part; only in secondary fashion do you belong to church or class or race. In the One, differences become harmonized, disappear. There are no rich or poor, Protestants or Catholics, Republicans or Democrats, but all are members of the State." [95]

---

[92] John Dewey, "Austin's Idea of Sovereignty," *Political Science Quarterly*, Vol. IX (1894), pp. 31, 51.
[93] Harold J. Laski, *Studies in the Problem of Sovereignty*, p. 1.   [94] *Ibid.*, p. 4.
[95] *Ibid.*, p. 5.

Laski compared the state to the philosopher's Absolute. As an Absolute, the state was a whole, a unit; and it must be good or bad as a whole, and it must be sovereign. It must have its way. If the state goes to war, so must we. What the state wills, has a moral pre-eminence.[96]

He noted, of course, the objection that the state is larger than any "other conceivable group," and "does, in fact, comprehend it." He replied that he was not at all certain that this was the case. While a state "may, in theory, exist to secure the highest life for its members," in actual fact, "it becomes painfully apparent that the good actually maintained is that of a certain section, not the community as a whole." [97]

So Laski rejected what he called the omnipotence and unity of the state. He argued for the pluralistic state by analogy from James' argument for the pluralistic universe. A trade union or other association was as real as the state, and apparently had equal rights. It might work with the state, "but it need not do so of necessity." [98] The state is distributive and not collective, but one of the groups to which the individual belongs. There is no necessity for unity in a man's allegiance. The demands of the state are "all important only to the State." [99] He declared that there could be no legally determined superior whose will is certain of enforcement. Sovereignty is only by consent. Law is not a command, but a rule of convenience. The state could not take its pre-eminence by force: it must win it by its worth. In effect, he said that the state is only sovereign when it is right.

The analogy from James' "Pluralistic Universe" is rather forced. James surely would have been surprised to find his belief that our universe can not be reduced to monistic simplicity because our knowledge is imperfect, used as an argument that there should be no final political authority even in a small part of our universe,— a state, however small,—which we can comprehend. His belief might be used against a world state, but not against a national state.

When Laski asserts that the state demands all, that it asserts a moral supremacy over the individual, that all groups are to be "ministrants to its life," [100] the easiest answer is that no such claim is made by responsible students of political theory. It is made by

[96] *Ibid.,* pp. 7, 8.   [97] *Ibid.,* p. 15.   [98] *Ibid.,* p. 10.   [99] *Ibid.,* p. 12.
[100] *Ibid.,* p. 1.

none of the writers we have considered in this chapter. It is denied by Esmein and Duguit. In France, England and America, it has little support. It is the fetish of the German Hegelian school.

But, broadly speaking, there is no claim that a trade union or a church is morally inferior to the state, or that it exists only for the state. There is no claim that all the life of the individual is owed to the state, save in time of war, when the life of the state is at stake. The individual and the group exist for their own ends, to develop their own personalities, and utilize their own freedom. The state, as Wilson said, is to serve them as much as they are to serve the state. Neither individuals nor groups, unless they are corporations which are granted special privileges by the state, owe their existence to the state; and the state does not care or know what they do, so long as they do not infringe on the rights of others.

Laski and all the pluralists wholly fail to see that the state is any different from any other group. Indeed, while Laski admits the reality of the state, he seems immediately to forget that admission and to insist that a religious or trade group is real and vital, while the state is artificial. The blindness is curious.[101]

The state is surely as real as any club or association. The membership in both church and trade union is constantly shifting. Each has many inactive members. Each has many unwilling members. The number who actually prefer not to live in a state is very small, —so small that to be an anarchist is really to be abnormal. But the number who prefer not to be in a labor union or a church is very large, and often very high-minded and intelligent. Many have joined the church or union before the age of maturity and without definite desire, and many remain against their will.

As a matter of fact, neither trade union, church, nor state has a will or a personality of its own. I have already suggested that those who say that the state is a person with a will of its own, would have difficulty if they tried to say where the will was. Laski, in fact, points out, as we shall see, that the state speaks only through its organs, and that its voice is the voice of the majority in control of those organs at the time, and therefore denies the state a coherent

---

[101] Esmein observes: "It is singular that M. Duguit, fully, without difficulty and without reserve, accords personality to the associations which are formed inside the State, for which he proposes absolute freedom, and at the same time, refuses this personality to the State, which is simply for him the most extended of associations." (*Eléments de Droit Constitutional*, 7th ed., Vol. I, p. 44.)

personality; but, at the same time, his argument proves that no club or private association has a coherent personality.

We all know that the policy of the union or the church is the policy of a few men in control at the time,—those who take the time to attend meetings and work on committees. That policy is modified by the traditions of the organization, its historic purposes, and the definite desires of the members on some outstanding question; but, broadly speaking, its mind is the mind of those who are in control. In the state, however, the control of the past is greater than in any private group; for the common law has come down through generations, statutes have been passed through decades, it has a Constitution, and the majority of the moment can change only a small part of the expressed will of the state.

But to deny personality to the state does not deny the beautiful strength of love of country; of devotion to its past, its traditions, to the mystic chords of memory of which Lincoln spoke. We personify the nation to stimulate our ideals, but it is a poetic fancy and not reality.

As we have seen, Laski notes the answer that the state includes all its parts, but his answer is that the state is ruled by those who wield the power. It is capitalists or trade unionists or Episcopalians that are the state, for the time being. Those who follow the economic interpretation of history say that the state is ruled by those with the greatest economic power and the greatest stake in the government, and that outsiders are really ignored or exploited by them. That this tendency exists, no one can deny.

But it should be stated that the economic urge is not the only one. There are powerful political and psychological motives which operate constantly, and which have no conscious economic basis. The whole force of the modern state has been to reduce the arbitrary or discriminative power of the group temporarily in control. Our constitutional amendments have no other basic reason. Moreover, the most powerful economic group of the moment does not remain so. In the state, today, the manufacturer may be in control; tomorrow, the bankers; the day after tomorrow, the trade unionists. There is a chance for all. Besides, in a very real sense, all are represented all the time. We speak of the eighties and nineties as capitalistic eras, and yet we know that there was much legislation in favor of labor,—some of it discriminatory,—and the farming group always had great power. It is well known that the protective tariff could not have been maintained without the farmer vote. No one group is ever in complete control. The state, after all, is an ensemble. Then too, there is always the great body of the law which came down from prior times, and which, itself, is a mosaic of the desires of many groups and generations.

But in a trade union, only trade unionists control. In a church, only the members of that church control. They have the same minorities that the state has, but the minority is never a representative of any other group, unless the dominant group is corrupt.

There must be some group which includes us all; and, above all, some group which can decide disputes between one private group and another. If one trade union collides with another, if a trade union injures or is injured by outsiders, who is to decide the quarrel? Who but the despised state? Here we have 125,000,000 people. Some of us are Protestants; some, Catholics; some, churchless. We are farmers, trade unionists, non-union men, merchants, manufacturers, professional men, bankers, and clerks. The state is larger than all of these groups, and it is greater and more precious. After all, we are all citizens. The pluralists may not understand it, but the great majority of us are citizens before we are business men, professional men, workingmen or farmers, and we have a devotion to the state,—meaning, not the state of the moment, but the whole historic state, with its associations—greater than our devotion to church or trade union or bar association.

On the question of sovereignty, Laski seems to confuse legal and political sovereignty, or what he calls moral sovereignty. He admits that the state is legally sovereign, but he denies its moral right to assert that sovereignty in all cases. He says that we must never forget that the state has no right to ask certain sacrifices of us. The law is based on consent. The state rules by consent. Then he says that, "Now I admit quite freely that I have been discussing a sovereignty far wider than that which lawyers are accustomed to recognize." [102]

It would seem that this gives the whole question away. No recognized student of political science in this country that I know of, would deny that there are individual rights which the state ought

102 Laski, *ibid.*, p. 16.

not to interfere with. The history of Magna Charta, Grand Re-
monstrance, Petition of Right, the Declaration of Independence,
and the Rights of Man, and the whole development of politics in
democratic countries in the past hundred years, are eloquent proof
that there are certain rights that the state ought not to infringe.
We know, too, that if it should infringe certain rights, there would
be serious and perhaps successful revolt. In that sense, government
and sovereignty do depend on consent.

But Laski proceeds to carry on his argument as if legal sovereignty requires consent in advance. Otherwise, there is no point
to his argument. But laws are enforced constantly on which no
prior consent is obtained. The mass of the people do not even know
what the rules of law are on most questions. One of our Federal
States may have an entirely different rule from a neighboring State
on the law of descent, or perpetuities, or the Statute of Frauds, or
liability for use of an automobile for a family purpose. There are
a host of legal questions on which our different States have dia-
metrically opposite rules. The people of a community consent to
the rules on these questions that are laid down for them. They
consent because the rules are the law. On only a few questions
where their personal habits and their prejudices are involved, is
their consent even important. In the few cases where popular
prejudices resist, the law is either repealed or becomes a dead
letter.

But the state could not function at all, if it had to have consent
in advance for every act. It acts because it knows that, save in
rare cases, it will have the consent. There is not time for it to get
the consent in advance. There are a multitude of questions arising
all the time; and the state acts because it is sovereign, because it
has the power, and not because it has consent, save the general
consent to act.

Laski speaks of certain rights quite in the tone of the believer
in natural rights, with whom, in fact, he sympathizes. He does not
tell us who is to define the actual application of those rights in
particular cases. There are those who believe, for example, that
the state has no right to educate, and no right to tax for the purposes of public education, and that this right is part of religious
freedom. Our courts are constantly deciding when liberty of the

press and speech becomes illegal, and yet freedom of speech and the press is one of the foremost rights of man.

When we say, therefore, that the state is sovereign, we do not mean that the state should do anything it pleases, that whatever it does is right, or that it is without practical limitations. Even in international affairs, no state can, with impunity, act so as to be brought into conflict with other states. Internally, it is limited by the fear of revolt, by the mere fact that an obnoxious law will be unenforceable. It is limited, too, by the sense of right and wrong of the legislative bodies which, despite all the exaggeration of those who believe that law is the automatic result of economic needs or psychological desires, is a potent force at all times. Moreover, most minorities are represented in legislative halls; and even where they are not, if their vote is more than insignificant, legislators and Congressmen are loathe to antagonize them.

But, legally, it is surely difficult to say that there is any limit. In the past twenty years, we have seen a draft law held constitutional, a constitutional amendment for prohibition, destroying great property values, severe income taxes and inheritance taxes; and all, on any theory, were the law of the land. Where, then, is the legal limit to authority?

Why, then, do we obey, and whom do we obey? Let us take a concrete example: A workmen's compensation statute is passed in 1912. It embodies a new principle. It places liability on the employer for an injury, in the course of employment, caused by the negligence of a fellow servant or by one of the inevitable risks of the business. An injured employee sues his employer. The employer attacks the constitutionality of the statute. He loses in the State court. He takes the question by certiorari to the United States Supreme Court. He loses. What, then, does he do? He either obeys and pays the judgment or he refuses to pay the judgment. If he refuses, his property—if he has any—is levied on. No one is willing to help him resist the execution officers. If he obeys, whom does he obey? He obeys the legislature and the courts.

Why does he obey? I suggest that he obeys, not because he consents to the particular law nor because the public consents to the particular law. In many communities the public was strongly opposed to the prohibition law; and yet juries regularly convicted men for violating it, and judges sentenced them. No, he obeys because it is the law, and because only in rare cases can anyone get any assistance in disobeying the law. He obeys, not because the law is the command of a sovereign, but because, in a very real sense, he and the public believe that the sovereign—the legislative body—can change the law if the majority wishes. The sovereign may not make the law, but it can change the law; and the sovereign we obey is the sovereign that has not changed the law—the sovereign which Wilson defined as the chief lawmaking body.

And so, where did our theory of the state stand at the end of our period? After much a priori discussion of the origin of the state, Ford gave us a solid basis for the belief that it is an historical development; that it is anterior to the family; and that man did not make the state, but the state made man.

We started with the German theory,—that the state is a person, that it is real, that it has a will of its own; and we came to believe that the state is simply composed of all persons born within its jurisdiction or who have been admitted to its membership. Most of us would not agree with Gray that the state is a "figment," a mere "abstraction," that it is made up only of those who wield the power. The state acts for all of its citizens, and is made up of all of them. They are all heirs of all the past of the historic state, its legends and traditions, its hopes and dreams. The past lives in them and through them. But the past is not real, the people is not organic. The state has no actual personality. It has personality only as we idealize it, as our affections give it form. It has no will of its own. Its commands are the commands carried down from the past, and the new commands laid down by the legislative bodies of the present and enforced by the courts.

And there is no absolute sovereign in this state. Its instruments are multiform. Every official, every county board, every legislator, is an agent of the state. But we have not acceded to the attack on the authority of the state. In each case, every agent of the state and every person subject to its jurisdiction, is subject to a power above. We obey, finally, when the Supreme Court has spoken. The national legislature may change the law of the States of the Union, the State the law in the counties; but when at last Congress has spoken and the Supreme Court has upheld it, the law is made, and we obey,—except in those rare cases when the law is frankly violated. These are really cases outside the law.

REFERENCES

BROWNSON, ORESTES A., *The American Republic: 1865* (Works). Detroit: Thorndike Nourse, 1885.

BURGESS, JOHN W., *Political Science and Comparative Constitutional Law* (2 vols.). Boston: Ginn & Co., 1890–91.

DEWEY, JOHN, "Austin's Idea of Sovereignty," *Political Science Quarterly*, Vol. IX, p. 31, 1894.

DUGUIT, LEON, *Traite de Droit Constitutionnel* (5 vols.). Paris: Ancienne Librairie Fontemoing, Deuxieme ed., 1921–25.

ESMEIN, A., *Elements de Droit Constitutionnel* (2 vols.). Paris: Librairie de la Societe Recueil Sirey, Septieme ed., 1921.

FORD, HENRY JONES, *The Natural History of the State*. Princeton: Princeton University Press, 1915.

GARNER, JAMES W., *Introduction to Political Science*. New York: American Book Company, 1910.

GRAY, JOHN CHIPMAN, *The Nature and Sources of the Law*. New York: Columbia University Press, 1909.

HURD, JOHN C., *The Theory of Our National Existence*. Boston: Little, Brown & Co., 1881.

JAMESON, JOHN ALEXANDER, *A Treatise on Constitutional Conventions*. Chicago: Callaghan & Co. (1887 ed.).

LASKI, HAROLD J., *Studies in the Problem of Sovereignty*. New Haven: Yale University Press, 1917.

MULFORD, ELISHA, *The Nation*. New York: Hurd & Houghton, 1870.

MUNGER, T. T., "The Works of Elisha Mulford," *Century Magazine*, Vol. XIII, p. 888.

POMEROY, JOHN NORTON, *An Introduction to the Constitutional Law of the United States*. Cambridge: Hurd & Houghton, (3rd ed.) 1875.

SCUDDER, HORACE E., "Elisha Mulford," *The Atlantic*, Vol. LVII, p. 362.

WILLOUGHBY, WESTEL WOODBURY, *The Nature of the State*. New York: The Macmillan Co., 1896.

WILSON, WOODROW, *The State*. Boston: D. C. Heath & Co., Rev. ed., 1898.

———"Political Sovereignty" in *An Old Master and Other Political Essays*. New York: Charles Scribner's Sons, 1893.

WOOLSEY, THEODORE D., *Political Science or the State* (2 vols.). New York: Charles Scribner's Sons, 1878.

CHAPTER VI

THE NATURE AND SOURCE OF LAW

WITH the question of sovereignty goes inevitably the questions of the nature of sovereignty and of law. The questions are inextricably woven together, and therefore in the foregoing discussion of our theories of sovereignty, references to the nature of law could not be avoided. But now let us see more specifically what our theories of the nature and source of law have been. The discussion has centered to a large extent around Austin's famous definition that, "Laws proper, or properly so called, are commands; laws which are not commands, are laws improper or improperly so called." [1] The matter of jurisprudence, he said, "is positive law: law simply and strictly so called; or law set by political superiors to political inferiors." [2] Again, "Every positive law, or every law simply and strictly so called, is set, directly or circuitously, by a sovereign person or body, to a member or members of the independent political society wherein that person or body is sovereign or supreme."

It follows, he said, that the sovereign "is incapable of *legal* limitation." [3]

Of course, Austin was confronted at once with customary law in England and the United States,—the common law enforced by the courts. No legislature enacted it in advance or expressly ratified it. Austin answered in effect that what the sovereign permitted, he in effect commanded. The legislature, that is, by permitting the court to announce the rule of law and by not annulling the rule by statute once it was announced, in effect commanded it. "The portion of the sovereign power," he said, "which lies at his disposition, is merely delegated. The rules which he makes, derive their legal force from authority given by the state; an authority which the state may confer expressly, but which it commonly imparts in the

---

[1] Austin, *Lectures on Jurisprudence*, (1929 ed.), Vol. I, p. 79.   [2] *Ibid.*, p. 86.
[3] *Ibid.*, pp. 220, 263.

way of acquiescence. For, since the state may reverse the rules which he makes and yet permits him to enforce them by the power of the political community, its sovereign will 'that his rules shall obtain as law' is clearly evinced by its conduct, though not by its express declaration." [4]

It will be seen how weakened the argument became. No one, in the ordinary sense of the word, is ever thought to command a thing which he permits. The permission may be through policy or discretion, because he realizes that he has no power to prevent, or because he agrees, or without any real knowledge of what he permits. The average legislature does not know the rules of law which it is permitting.

Francis Wharton, in his "Commentaries on Law," considered the analytical theory of law, which he ascribed to Bentham and Austin, as requiring that law must issue prospectively and not retrospectively, that it must issue from a sovereign, and that it must be a command. But he said that instead of law emanating from the sovereign, it is imposed on the sovereign. Law, he said, is an emanation from the people to the sovereign, and not a command imposed on the people by the sovereign. Custom, he argued, makes law, and not law custom, for custom is applied retrospectively. He instanced the changes made in the English common law by the colonial courts to fit our different conditions, and declared that these changes were not made by the sovereign. [5]

Moreover, Wharton said that the analytical school left out the moral sense. He rejected the theocratic theory of the origin of law, and the ethical theory, namely, that it represents the idea of right and wrong. In general, he followed Savigny and the historical school. He differed with Savigny's belief that a nation was a "continuous, perpetual person," but agreed with him that law is "the product of national conscience and need." Custom is the first stage, and custom is recognized by the courts when it satisfies the national conscience and need. Its source, then, is "reason combined with national conscience and need." By conscience, he did not mean an insulated moral sense, "intuitive or inspired," but "a part of a common nature," influenced by social and hereditary tendencies. [6]

The theory of utility with which he identified the analytical

---

[4] *Ibid.*, p. 102.   [5] Francis Wharton, *Commentaries on Law*, p. 5.
[6] *Ibid.*, pp. 23, 93.

school, left out of account, he objected, national traditions. Moreover, he argued, men do not differ on right and wrong, but they do on utility. Therefore, he felt the analytical school left criminal law especially on an uncertain base.

But, I may observe, men do differ in their ideas of right and wrong, as much as what is for the greatest good of the greatest number.

Wharton did not define what law was, nor how it arose, nor on what it is based, save that it springs from custom and the needs and sense of right of the people.

But, as we shall see shortly when we consider the theory of James Coolidge Carter, there is much law which can not be explained as derived from custom. It is an important factor, but the explanation can not be confined to it.

The American theory has been generally against the definition of Austin. A. Lawrence Lowell, in his "Essays on Government," pointed out (as Henry Maine had pointed out before) that the sovereign has no power to change customary law. Even in countries with theoretically omnipotent sovereigns, the sovereign can not command what the people will not obey. Lowell argued, therefore, that the limit of the sovereign power depends upon the limit of political obedience, and that no command is the law if it does not receive the obedience of the bulk of society.

I shall have more to say later of laws which do not command obedience. It may be said here, however, that a rule of law may be enforced in the courts and yet not command obedience, in the sense that the juries desire to convict or that it is largely accepted. The prohibition law did not command obedience in many places where it was actually, nevertheless, partially enforced. In Chicago, for example, it was very unpopular, and yet the Federal courts regularly sentenced men to prison for its violation.

Lowell went on to argue that Austin reasoned in a circle. He said that the argument ran as follows: The power of the sovereign has no limits. Therefore he has power to abolish customary law. Therefore all law is the command of the sovereign, and therefore his power has no limit. The reasoning in a circle, Lowell said, was too evident.[7]

David Jayne Hill made much the same criticism of Austin.

[7] Lowell, *Essays on Government*, p. 201.

Neither customary law nor judicial decisions, he said, could be fitted into Austin's system. Law, he said, is not essentially a commandment. "It may be merely a traditional usage, a tacit agreement, or a public convention." [8] He said that our statutes are not so much commands as agreements. He agreed that sovereign power was "essential to the very existence of the State; but it is not an *unlimited* sovereignty, capable of issuing arbitrary commandments." [9] He made clear that he was speaking of law philosophically, not in the technical sense: by which he meant, the strict legal sense. He admitted that, no doubt, "technically," the citizen was bound to obey "any law," whatever "it may be," but from the "higher point of view," there are "commandments which can never be made law without subverting the true conception of the State, which is not merely an embodiment of power, but an organ of human justice." [10] He had explained that he was speaking philosophically for he would have admitted that if the courts enforce a rule of law, it is surely the law, in the technical sense.

Willoughby, however, in his able and scholarly The Nature of the State, in the main, defended Austin's theory. He agreed that custom "has been the world over the earliest means of social regulation." [11] Soon men found that custom was too fragmentary and indefinite to fit all the relations between men, and they felt "the evils and injustice resulting from the uncertain and irregular sanctions supplied by public opinion and private might." [12] First, the state interprets custom; and then, by equitable procedure and legislation, it modifies it.

Willoughby argued that custom did not become the law until the state recognized it. The fact that, when it did recognize it, the custom was enforced from a time prior to the decision (in other words, that the decision related back), did not mean that custom was the law prior to the decision; but simply, as we must frankly admit, "that judicial legislation is ex post facto legislation."

Willoughby also argued that it was no answer to the assertion that the state is the sole creator of law, to say that no state can "maintain its control that does not, in general, accept as its will those principles of justice and utility that are evolved only by the

[8] David Jayne Hill, *The People's Government*, p. 98.   [9] *Ibid.*, pp. 100, 104.
[10] *Ibid.*, p. 104.   [11] *Willoughby, The Nature of the State*, p. 144.
[12] *Ibid.*, p. 146.

customary habit of its people. . . . This would only show that, as a principle of political expediency (i.e., of caution and prudence), a general acceptance of customary ethics is necessary." [13]

Willoughby differed from Austin, however, in that, as we have seen, he could not find any determinate sovereign that makes the law. Of course, there is no determinate sovereign. The courts are constantly making decisions on points on which the legislature has not acted, and it is stretching words beyond their natural meaning to say that such rules, the legislature by not repealing, is commanding.

In 1905, James Coolidge Carter, one of the acknowledged leaders of the American bar, prepared a course of lectures for Harvard, which he was never able to deliver, on Law: Its Origin and Growth. His book was a deification of custom as the explanation of all law. He regarded Savigny as the "most accomplished jurist of his time, at once profound and practical." [14] Law he defined as a "body of rules for the regulation of human conduct." The only thing sought to be affected by law is human conduct. The first restraint on conduct was custom. Custom, he admitted, did not become law until enforced by tribunals,[15] but apparently all law must arise from custom.[16] All the rules based on the conduct of a reasonable man are merely rules of custom.[17]

Carter, of course, did not ignore the great body of a modern legislation dealing with railroads, corporations, taxation, and public businesses; but he said, "when we search for any matter relating to the regulation of the ordinary conduct of men in their transactions with each other, that is, to Private Law, we find exceedingly little; and we may say that it is substantially true that the whole vast body of legislation is confined to Public Law, and that its operation on Private Law is remote and indirect and aimed only to make the unwritten law of custom more easily and certainly enforced." [18] He insisted that in this legislation, there was very little creation of new law. It has been, he said, "not inaptly styled, a mere fringe on the body of the law." [19]

The principal function of legislation, he said, "is to supplement and aid the operation of custom. . . ." We must realize "that it

---

[13] *Ibid.*, pp. 171, 175.
[14] James Coolidge Carter, *Law: Its Origin, Growth and Function*, p. 5.
[15] *Ibid.*, pp. 14, 120.   [16] *Ibid.*, p. 65.   [17] *Ibid.*, pp. 76–77.   [18] *Ibid.*, p. 117.
[19] *Ibid.*, p. 118.

can never supplant it," and that "its own efficiency is dependent upon its conforming to habit and custom." [20]

So far as he had definitely formulated a theory, it may be said that Carter's philosophy was that of the historical school of Savigny, which believes that law is the product of the civilization of which it is a part. That is the general theory of the great mass of lawyers who revere our system of the common law. The rules evolved from our past became to them sacred,—a sort of natural law which, though evolved from the past, are to be applied as fixed rules to all cases arising in the future.

Carter, in fact, made of custom an idol. "It is," he declared, "the imperishable record of the wisdom of the illimitable past, reaching back to the infancy of the race, revised, corrected, enlarged, open to all alike, and read and understood by all." [21] Therefore, he said, "that to which we give the name of Law always has been, still is, and will forever continue to be custom." [22]

Of course, he acknowledged that his theory combatted the theory that law is based on absolute right, and the Austinian theory that it is the command of a sovereign. He would have none of the law of nature or of the law of the sovereign. He declared that it was pure assumption that the common law was made by the sovereign, because the sovereign permitted it. He denied that the sovereign ratified the work of the courts. He denied that judges issue commands. He followed the orthodox theory that judges do not make the law, but merely find it. He answered that a judge could not ratify what he could not do, nor could the judge make a law to punish a man for what he did before the judge acted. [23]

He repeated Maine's observation that there was no such sovereign in many states, with power to change the law. He would not even agree with Maine, that Austin's theory became true in modern states where the legislature is potent. He insisted again that the legislature can not make the law. Its province was to regulate the political organs of the state; to maintain schools, almshouses, and public works; to regulate corporations, banks, insurance; and to conform the unwritten law to custom, when custom has outgrown precedent. [24]

Of course, his theory did not square with the multiform activities

[20] *Ibid.*, p. 120. [21] *Ibid.*, p. 127. [22] *Ibid.*, p. 120. [23] *Ibid.*, p. 186.
[24] *Ibid.*, p. 203.

of the modern state. State corporation laws regulate conduct. Laws punishing fraudulent corporate transactions regulate conduct, affect property and personal rights, and are as much law as the rules of descent and property. Indeed, the legislatures frequently change the rules of descent. There is certainly no custom that requires that descent should be one way or another. As we have seen, about 1911 there began a movement to abolish the common law defenses of contributory negligence, assumption of risk, and the fellow servant rule. These rules originally arose, to use the popular phrase, as "judge-made law." The legislatures changed these rules. These changes certainly made law. They changed the obligations between employer and employee.

Even Carter admitted, however, that custom was too slow to deal with the activities of men in modern society. He said that the "necessities of civilized, industrial society in modern times have required an extension of the province of penal law, by the positive enactment of numerous commands and prohibitions not to be found in the law of custom." [25] Custom is too slow for this activity. Legislation seizes hold of growing tendencies, and converts "growing custom into positive rules." [26]

This would seem to concede the argument. Of course, it is daily manifest that custom is too slow for many modern relationships. There is not time for it to develop. Something must be done to regulate human rights between persons long before custom can develop. Our modern age changes altogether too fast. A new law as to automobiles has sprung up in the past twenty years. In one or two jurisdictions there has been an attempt to treat the automobile as a dangerous instrument, and to impose liability whenever it causes an injury, irrespective of negligence. Some jurisdictions have adopted the family purpose doctrine, and have held that an owner of an automobile driven by a member of the family is liable for an injury due to negligence, although the automobile was driven by a minor son who was on a "frolic of his own." More courts reject the family purpose doctrine, but they are quicker than they were in the days of the old horse and buggy to find that the son is an agent of the father.

Custom did not make any of these rules. The judges' feeling of necessity and justice made them. We are rapidly making a law of

[25] *Ibid.*, p. 244. [26] *Ibid.*, p. 245.

the air, and there is not time for custom to make it. The Massachusetts Supreme Court has recently held that an aeroplane does not commit trespass when it crosses a man's land at a safe height.[27] Custom did not make that rule of law.

Nor can the custom theory explain why courts in neighboring jurisdictions have different rules of law. The people in the jurisdictions are the same, but the rules of law are different. The customs of the people are not different. But the courts in one State simply got started on one rule of the law, and the courts in the next jurisdiction got started on the opposite rule.

We can agree, of course, that custom is still a powerful source of law, and always will be; that decisions and statutes alike will be of little force if they run counter to custom, when there is a custom; but to say that all law is custom is simply to be carried away by a definition, and by a lawyer's dislike of legislatures and of all forces which upset the symmetry of his system. Indeed, Carter seemed to consider law as a science, whereas it is rather a mosaic of the rules worked out over a long period of time to reconcile conflicting desires and needs. Its safety and its strength lie in the very fact that it is not a perfect system, and not a logical deductive science.

John Chipman Gray, of the Harvard Law School, gave probably the soundest and most mature exposition of the nature of law our country has produced, in his "The Nature and Sources of Law," a series of lectures delivered in 1909.

Gray divided the schools of jurisprudence into three classes: the historical, the analytical, and the ethical. He said that he belonged to the historical school. The analytical school holds that law is the command of the sovereign; and the historical, that it is the product of the social and economic forces of the nation. Gray, as we shall see, rejected Austin's famous definition that law is the result of the command of the sovereign, and held that law consists of the rules enforced by the courts.

Pound, therefore, classifies Gray as belonging to the analytical school,—as holding that law is the command of the courts. But this seems to confuse the nature of law with the sources of law. To say that Gray believed that law is the command of the courts, is far from what he believed he was stating. He certainly did not

[27] *Smith* vs. *New England Aircraft Co.*, 170 N.E. 385; 69 A.L.R. 300 (1930).

think that the courts commanded, or had the power to command. As a matter of fact, while a court can command or make law in the sense of applying a new rule in a case not covered by an old rule, it is directly limited in any case where the legislature has spoken clearly, and indirectly limited by a long line of precedents, and the necessary and very powerful fiction which, as has been well said, saves us from judicial oligarchy,—that it is finding and not making the law.

Gray admitted that courts found the sources of law in custom, in precedents, in legal writings, in the sense of justice of the community of the best rule to fit the case. But once the court has applied the rule, it is surely the law if it is enforced by the court.

✓Gray also rejected the ethical theory of the nature of law. He expressed sympathy for the current trend of opinion, that judges should seek to "approach the Law from the side of the public welfare, and seek to adapt it to the promotion of the public good," but he said that we must use caution, because the question is, what are the needs of society? [28] He remarked wisely that there is little in the training and calling of judges to give them that knowledge. Law changes slowly; it has developed from custom, from decisions in many particular cases, according to the sense of the judges of the time of the best rule under existing conditions, and it is not wise or possible for a court to make itself a conscious reforming agency.[29]

Gray did not try to define rights, save to say that a legal right implies a corresponding duty. "The rights correlative to those duties which the society will enforce on the motion of an individual, are that individual's legal rights."

He noted Von Ihering's famous definition that rights are legally protected interests, but disagreed. The right is not the interest, he said, but the means by which the "enjoyment of the interest is secured." [30] Von Ihering's definition was the result of a desire to found legal rights on actualities. Von Ihering held that rights were not taken out of the air. They were not natural in the sense that, in all times and in all places, men all desired the same rights and were protected in the same rights; but they are the interests which society felt it desirable to protect. Nor by interests did Von Ihering mean economic interests solely. An interest was anything that men

---

[28] Gray, *The Nature and Sources of Law*, p. 3.   [29] *Ibid.*, pp. 3–4.
[30] *Ibid.*, pp. 13, 19.

desired. Gray's modification of Von Ihering's theory did not alter the main theory. Gray agreed that the right protected an interest, —a desire of men strong enough to be of social effect,—and which the state agreed should be protected.

Gray also disagreed with Hegel that rights are created to protect the freedom of the will. He answered that they were as much created to restrain the freedom of the will. Rights, he said, should be created "neither solely to protect the freedom of the will nor solely to restrain it, but to establish those relations among men which are most for the advantage of society or of its members. . . . If one chooses to say that the ideal at which an organized society should aim is creating human perfection, I do not know that there is any objection to it." [31]

So Gray came to the nature and source of law. The subject had been confused, he said, by failing to distinguish between law and the sources of law. No rule which the highest court refuses to follow is law. But this does not mean that courts are free to follow their whims. Courts derive their rules from "sources often of the most general and permanent character, to which they are directed by the organized body to which they belong, to apply themselves." [32]

First, he took up Austin's theory. He answered the assertion that law is a command by saying that the state can restrain its courts from following this or that rule, but it often leaves them free. When the judge has not received direct commands from the state, he goes by precedent, legal authority, ideas of sound morals. No state, indeed, could provide for all the contingencies that may arise in conflicts between persons. Our States which have adopted codes have found this out. The code must be supplemented by decisions. So Gray concluded that Austin could be correct only on the theory that "everything which the State does not forbid its judges to do, and which they in fact do, the State commands, although the judges are not animated by a direct desire to carry out the State's wishes, but by entirely different ones." [33]

He also rejected the theory that courts apply what has previously existed in the minds of the people.[34] He replied that the great bulk of the law is unknown to the people. They have no previous consciousness of it. Law, he added, is often directly opposed to the will of the people.

[31] *Ibid.*, p. 24.   [32] *Ibid.*, pp. 82–83.   [33] *Ibid.*, p. 85.   [34] *Ibid.*, p. 87.

Nor do judges merely discover the law. Yet what they decide, is the law. If they discover something different from what we expect, our different discovery does not help us.

And he added that on some subjects there was no prior law existing. "What," he asked, "was the Law in the time of Richard Coeur de Lion on the liability of a telegraph company to the persons to whom a message was sent?"[35] Or on stoppage in transitu in the days of William the Conqueror? Or when decisions are overruled?

If a statute is so opposed to public prejudices that juries will not convict, it is still the law, but not the whole law. The whole law is, that one who sells wine and is convicted shall be punished. If there is no conviction, there can be no punishment. But so far as the prohibition goes, it is still the law.

Gray disagreed vigorously with Carter on the force of custom. There was no custom when Pells vs. Brown was decided to the effect that an executory devise could be docked.[36] Nor was there any discovery of a pre-existing rule. There was no custom prevailing in Swift vs. Tyson,[37] when a pre-existing rule was reversed. He took up an illustration made by Carter of a case where an insurer failed to disclose a risk, and said that the decision was not based on custom, but on opinion as to the most desirable rule.

Judges, in short, he concluded, decide cases on precedents, by analogy with other rules, by custom when there is a custom; but, failing these, by a more or less intuitive sense of what is the best rule under all the circumstances. Statutes, custom, precedents, are sources of law, but not the law itself. Law, he said, is simply the rules enforced by the courts.[38]

Surely his book was a trenchant piece of work,—by far the

---

[35] *Ibid.*, pp. 88, 96.
[36] *Ibid.*, p. 224. Reported in Cro. Jac. 590. (1620) *Gray's Cases on Property*, Vol. V, p. 140.
[37] 16 Peters 1 (1842).
[38] Justice Holmes came to the same conclusion. In his brilliant "The Path of the Law," in 1897, he observed that some will tell us that law "is a system of reason, that it is a deduction from principles of ethics or admitted axioms or whatnot, which may or may not coincide with the decisions." But, he replied, "The prophecies of what the courts will do in fact, and nothing more pretentious, are what I mean by the law." Oliver Wendell Holmes, "The Path of the Law," *Collected Legal Papers*, pp. 172, 173.
A. Lawrence Lowell agreed that "In England and in the countries that have inherited the Anglo-Norman system of jurisprudence, a law may be defined as a rule that will be enforced by the courts." *Government of England* (1908 ed.), Vol. I, p. 6.

ablest study in this country of the nature and source of law. His theory that law is the rules enforced by the courts may seem an anti-climax, after elaborate discussions of the metaphysics of natural law, the deification of custom, and of the theory that law is the expression of the will of the state. But it is the only definition that is based on reality, and Gray's exposition has, I believe, never been answered.

In all this there has been little, if any, study of the reasons behind the rules of law, of the ends to be sought. Carter, as we have seen, made of the old rules of the common law a sort of sacred content, which should be unchanging. The old Bill of Rights—the rules of the common law—became with him, as with so many able lawyers of the time, and even today, a sort of natural law, from which all later law was to be deduced. They did not see that the rights protected by the law were, after all, but expressions of the desires of men, as sanctioned by law; and that those expressions must change as conditions change. The old rights were designed to protect the interests and the demands which were felt to be desirable or necessary in an individualistic society. And what was considered socially and economically desirable and necessary for such a society, is different from what is now so considered. We realize now that rights are not inherent and a priori, but are granted to satisfy our demands. The psychological emphasis has shifted, but it has not entirely changed. But even today, as we shall see, men still consider legal rights as more than interests or desires, which although we may not call them natural, are dearly prized, nevertheless.

Gray, as we have seen, was frankly sceptical of a definite philosophy of the ends of law. He felt that judges were bound by precedents, by custom, by a long line of legal tradition, by legal treatises; and for them to adopt a conscious philosophy of legal purposes, was not well. He felt that judges were not equipped by their training to handle such a philosophy. But, of course, consciously or unconsciously, judges have a legal philosophy, just as we all have a metaphysics. While judges can not make a system, there is no question that, in the modifications and extensions of legal rules, in the decisions of doubtful cases, their unconscious philosophy of social and economic ends has inevitably a profound influence.

In his "Centralization and the Law," Brooks Adams asserted boldly that there are no abstract legal principles, "any more than there is an abstract animal, apart from individual animals. . . ." The law, he said, is the envelope with which any society surrounds itself for its own protection. "The rules of law are established by the self-interest of the dominant class, so far as it can impose its will upon those who are weaker. These rules form a corpus which is more or less flexible according to circumstances, and which yields more or less readily to pressure. When the society, which is the content of the envelope which we call the law, expands or contracts, regularly and slowly, the envelope yielding gradually tends to conform without serious shock." If society breaks suddenly with its past, the law may not automatically "adapt itself to the change, but may be rent by what we call a political revolution." [39]

Like most such theories, there is some truth—indeed much truth —in the theory that law is the expression of the interests of the dominant economic group. But like the economic interpretation in politics, it has been vastly over-stated and over-applied. In the first place, men do not always ask for what is their true economic interest: they ask for many things—not from a conscious sense of economic interest, often indeed against their economic interests— because they want them; because they think they are right. They usually think of their desires in terms of rights, and generally are reluctant to ask for them as bald economic demands. Even today, while men are franker and have abandoned the belief in natural rights, they seldom ask that their interests be protected in the name of interests; but they seek to show the justice of their demands, and that it is to the interest of society to grant them. There is an immense field of action that economic motive does not touch.

Finally, no class at any time has been wholly dominant. It may be predominant but not all-powerful. The minorities, the less dominant classes have always been represented in our legislatures, Congress, and the courts. The conflicts between economic classes are not decided wholly by economic interests. When the public is called in, it will weigh the dispute not merely on an economic, but a social and political and ethical, basis as well. The decision is often a compromise. The law is a mosaic of the resultant of the desires

---

[39] Brooks Adams, *Centralization and the Law* (1906), p. 45.

of different groups, at different times. The decisions in effect at any one time, are chiefly derived from the past: they are the result of similar conflicts in the past. Even the current decisions are profoundly influenced by the decisions of the past, the sense of what is best for society in case of conflict between two groups; and, above all, the innate sense of justice which both legislators and courts apply. The workmen's compensation statutes, for example, would not have been adopted or upheld, solely on the strength of the economic power of the working classes. But employers came to look on them with favor, and the public believed them to be fair and in the public interest. The economic motive was only one of several that operated.

Whatever deficiencies there may have been in American legal philosophy, have been removed by the studies of Roscoe Pound. Since the end of our period, he has amplified his theories, but prior to that time, in his essays on "Sociological Jurisprudence" and "The Ends of Law," he had fully presented them, with a wealth of study of the literature on the subject.

He followed the traditional division of the schools of jurisprudence into the philosophical, the historical, and the analytical. But he further divided the three schools, and he showed that the modern tendency was to abandon "the exclusive use of any one method, and to bring these formerly divergent schools into something like accord." [40] It is not necessary here to go into all the divisions of the schools which he considered.

Broadly speaking, he defined the analytical school as considering chiefly developed systems of law; as regarding the law as something consciously made by lawgivers, legislative or judicial; as seeing chiefly the force and constraint behind legal rules; as considering the typical law as statute law; and as having, for its philosophical basis, usually utilitarian or teleological views. [41] Considering that law is a command, it comes to believe that law may be made, and then seeks to make it by rigid deductions from a system of fixed concepts as arbitrary as those of any natural law or the concepts of the philosophical school. The feeling, he said, that "a declaration of the sovereign will suffices to make law will give rise to a mass of arbitrary detail, which can not obtain the

[40] Roscoe Pound, "The Scope and Purpose of Sociological Jurisprudence," 24 *Harvard Law Review*, 591, 592. (1911).
[41] *Ibid.*, p. 595.

force of law in practise." [42] The analytical school forgets that law is a practical matter, arising from diverse needs and desires and their reconciliation.

The historical school, of which Savigny was the leader, holds rather that law is found and not made. It studies the origin and development of legal rules. It sees the social pressure behind the rules. Its type of law is custom.

Pound, of course, found much of value in its theories. But he said that once it found its doctrines, which had been evolved in the historical process, it treated them as valid a priori, and has "deduced from and tested existing doctrines by a fixed, arbitrary, external standard." [43] Having no philosophy of its own, it adopted the philosophy of its predecessors, and made it sacred for all time. Those who reverence our common law, like Carter, make its rules the test of all later rules, "parts of the legal order of nature." [44] But Pound answered that many rules are not the product of experience. Many rules are accidental, developed by analogy, and persisted in long after it has been demonstrated that they are undesirable. [45]

The philosophical school considers law according to its philosophical and ethical bases. It agrees with the historical school,—that law is not made but found; but when its principles have been found, it applies them a priori as revealed truth. Its first form was, of course, the law of nature. Later, as Pound observed, the philosophical school (of which there are many branches) showed that a philosophical theory could be developed which would take account of social and economic tendencies, and readjusted its philosophy accordingly.

But, in the past, the cruder school had, he said, shown a tendency to become mechanical, like all other schools, to become over-abstract, and to distort legal rules which have been evolved from either experience or chance, by explaining them on an a priori basis. The rules hold over, and are applied disastrously under utterly changed conditions. Thus, he said, "we find our courts and lawyers insisting upon views of liberty of contract, of risk of employment, and of the fellow-servant rule, which are out of all relation to actual life. Few juristic theories have been more barren than the eighteenth century natural law of American judges in the

[42] *Ibid.*, p. 597. [43] *Ibid.*, p. 600. [44] *Ibid.*, p. 602. [45] *Ibid.*, pp. 603, 604.

nineteenth century." [46] But, in my opinion, those theories have operated in the semi-political field of constitutional law, more than in law proper.

Pound then described the beginnings of the sociological method. Men first began to compare the three theories of jurisprudence. The philosophical school used the historical method, and the historical school used philosophy, to check their theories. The historical school came to realize that its method was but complementary to the analytical method; namely, that the old rules were actually subject to change. Then came the social utilitarians. Von Ihering argued that law is based on interests: meaning the satisfaction of the desires of men. Prior to Von Ihering, Pound observed, "the theory of law had been individualist." Von Ihering's theory was social. His conception "of law as a securing of interests or protection of relations, has all but universally superseded the individualist theory." [47]

The Neo-Kantians, of whom Stammler was the foremost representative, returned to the philosophical method. The historical school, by sanctifying and hardening its rules developed in the historical process, made it necessary that the reasons behind the rules be re-examined. Stammler, Pound said, rejected the idea that rules are eternally valid according to an a priori philosophy. He sought to find rules which are "just relatively and for the time being; he sought to give us a 'natural law with growing content. . . .'" [48] He held that the social ideal was "the criterion of justice through law." [49] In his ideal of justice, he broadened the Kantian conception of freedom based on the individual to one based on "the community of free-willing men."

He laid down four fundamental principles: that no will should be subject to the arbitrary will of another; that every legal demand

---

[46] *Ibid.*, p. 611.   [47] Pound, 25 *Harvard Law Review* (Dec., 1911), p. 143.
[48] *Ibid.*, p. 150.

It is obvious that a law with a changing content is itself a changing law: if the content changes, the law itself changes. The general concepts which supposedly do not change, obtain their whole meaning from the content which does change. The general concepts are merely summaries, or statements, of ideals or standards. A word, said Holmes, is "the skin of a living thought," which takes its color from the thought beneath. So a concept is but the skin of a living content. In fact, Stammler later abandoned what Professor John C. H. Wu, of the Comparative Law School of China, called "his own beautiful figure of speech: 'natural law with a changing content,' as a bit of uncritical mysticism." (Appendix II, "Stammler and His Critics," in Rudolf Stammler, *The Theory of Justice*, p. 569 [New York: The Macmillan Co., 1925]).

[49] *Ibid.*, p. 151.

can exist only in the sense that the person obliged can also exist as a fellow creature; that no one is to be excluded from the common interest arbitrarily; and that every power of control conferred by law can be justified only in the sense that the individual subject thereto can yet exist as a fellow creature. But he admitted that these rules were not "premises from which to deduce a whole code," that they are not merely principles of politics and legislation, and that "we must adapt them in such way that the actual material of a legal system will give effect to them." [50]

Then came the Neo-Hegelians, of which Kohler was the great representative. They attempted to infuse the old sterile historical theory with a new philosophy. The theory of Savigny's historical school was, in Pound's words, that "law was no more a result of conscious human will than is language." Kohler, on the other hand, held that it "was a product both of the culture of the past and of the attempt to adjust it to the culture of the present." Conscious adaptation was part of it: law is not automatic. Law is a product of Kultur, in Kohler's words, the "development of the powers residing in man to a form expressing the destiny of man." Law is a product of the time, of all its forces, the product "of the whole people, whose organ the lawmaker has become." [51]

Pound then considered the revival of the natural law school in France, whe're Stammler's idea of a natural law with a changing content was accepted and followed by Charmont and Demogue; and the idea of natural law was, in Charmont's words, "reconciled with the idea of evolution and with the idea of utility." Law, he said, loses its "absolute and immovable character"; but, in being transformed, "judicial idealism is not weakened. On the contrary, it is strengthened and broadened." [52]

So Pound concluded that the historical school and the philosophical school had come together in France, just as the historical and the analytical came together in England. "Each has had to concede something." History enables us to understand our rules, and to "perceive what we may hope to do with them." Philosophy enables us to understand what we have, and "the measure by which it should be judged." [53]

But, of course, the philosophical school has given up its main

[50] *Ibid.*, p. 152. [51] *Ibid.*, pp. 156, 157, 158. [52] *Ibid.*, p. 161.
[53] *Ibid.*, pp. 161–62.

contention of an absolute law. Once that is given up, the question becomes simply one of emphasis,—whether the philosophy back of the rule or the way the rule arose and the needs it meets, is more important.

Pound then came to the school of economic interpretation, and he brilliantly showed that it could explain only part of our law. Many times, he said, courts have enforced rules in advance of the ideas of any dominant economic group. The eternal sense of right, the desire to protect the weak, have always been forces in modifying rules of law asked for by the powerful. He added, too, that many rules have come down from the past, and are still applied. Indeed, the economic interpretation applies more to legislation than to law, to the action of the legislators than to the whole law. Moreover, he noted wisely that the human will is at all times "moved by tradition, sentiment, the exigencies of a received system, and many like factors, even against self-interest." [54]

So Pound came to the sociological school. In its first stage it treated law as if law were the mechanical resultant of the social forces of the time, although much that has force behind it, he said, fails to leave an impression on the law. Besides, the ideas of right and wrong continually work and play upon these social forces, diverting, modifying, or even forestalling them. Then the sociological school turned to the study of the biological development of man, and interpreted law as the rules which encouraged the survival of the fit. At first, it laid exaggerated emphasis on primitive law which Pound, of course, said could not be more than a clue to a whole system of law in an advanced stage. Again, law was interpreted as the resultant of group conflicts; and again, as in treating the economic interpretation of law, Pound said that no theory of group conflict could explain more than a fraction of our legal rules. [55]

Then the sociological jurists turned to psychology, particularly to group psychology, to ascertain the group forces back of rules of law which make them enforceable. Ward claimed that social rules were essentially psychic and not biological; Tarde found the base of group psychic forces in imitation. Thus he explained the similarity of legal rules from country to country, and their continuity in history. There is similarity because, after all, men think alike.

[54] *Ibid.*, p. 167.   [55] *Ibid.*, April p. 501.

Finally, the sociologists came to see that no one method would be sufficient, but that all must be used. And they realized that they must not only combine the various methods used, but must also relate the science of sociology to other social sciences.

These tendencies were at work in sociological jurisprudence.

Summarizing, Pound said that the sociological school of law looked more to the working of law than to its abstract content. Law could be changed: it was an institution which could be improved by human effort. It laid stress on the social purposes which law subserves, rather than sanctions. Legal precepts are to be regarded more as guides to results which are socially just, and less as inflexible molds. Its philosophical views were still diverse; though a pragmatic philosophy, he said, would find many adherents among sociological jurists.[56]

For himself, he definitely adopted the pragmatic test. In 1908, in an article in the "Columbia Law Review," he had declared that law is "not scientific for the sake of science. Being scientific as a means towards an end, it must be judged by the results it achieves, not by the niceties of its internal structure; it must be valued by the extent to which it meets its end, not by the beauty of its logical processes or the strictness with which it rules proceed from the dogmas it takes for its foundation." He added that the "sociological movement in jurisprudence is a movement for pragmatism as a philosophy of law; for the adjustment of principles and doctrines to the human conditions they are to govern rather than to assumed first principles; for putting the human factor in the central place and relegating logic to its true position as an instrument."[57]

Pound's work, then and later, constitutes a distinguished con-

---

[56] Roscoe Pound. "Sociological Jurisprudence," 25 *Harvard Law Review* 516. (April, 1912).

[57] Roscoe Pound, "Mechanical Jurisprudence," 8 *Columbia Law Review* 604, 605, 609 (Dec., 1908).

Later, Pound greatly amplified his theory. In his *Spirit of the Common Law*, published in 1921, he defined the change in the law as consisting "in thinking not of an abstract harmonizing of human wills, but of a concrete securing or realizing of human interests" (p. 196). As there are not enough material goods to go around to satisfy all our desires, we should satisfy "all that is possible" (p. 196). Our purpose should be to give effect "to individual claims to the extent that they coincide with or may be identified with a social interest. . . ." (p. 197). He quoted William James, that "since all demands conjointly can not be satisfied in this poor world, our aim should be 'to satisfy as many as we can with the least sacrifice of other demands,'" and concluded that, in law, we should aim to secure "as many interests or as much of interests as we may, with the least sacrifice of other interests . . ." (p. 199).

tribution to the philosophy of law. He insisted that law must change and adapt itself; that it must be filled with the breath of life, and not bound by the logic of ancient formulas; and that, at every turn, it must be tested by the results it achieves in our modern society.

In all this, however, there was nothing of the nature of law itself,—although, in my opinion, Pound sometimes mixes the question of the nature of law with that of its ends. His theory was all of the ends of law, of the philosophy back of the rules. But Pound's own analysis of the later schools of thought must indicate the limitations of his own theory. If those who derive law from the past are checking it with its philosophical bases, and those who lean to the philosophical method are checking their theories with the results of history, the sociological jurists must admit that the test of what rules will work best in our society depends, to a large extent, on the past, and on the sense of justice of the people of those very rules. In other words, what will work best depends often largely on historical and philosophical bases.

Pound's own criticisms of the economic interpretation of law and of what he called mechanical sociology apply, I think, with almost equal force to his own theory of a law based on the harmonizing of desires. "In the long run—" he had cautioned, "the quest of jurists and judges for an ideal of an absolute eternal justice, well or ill-conceived, to which they seek to make the rules enforced in tribunals approximate, and juristic tradition, that is traditional principles and traditional modes of reasoning therefrom have ever proved the chief influences in determining the bulk of the rules actually in force in legal systems." [58] But he did not emphasize these forces in advocating his own theory of the harmonizing of wills. I think he underestimated them, and over-emphasized the satisfaction of desires. It is true that he speaks of realizing human interests, and says that we should aim to secure as many interests as we can without sacrificing other interests; and yet he makes his test in the end one of satisfying as many desires as possible. But we can not satisfy desires without considering all the possible effects of satisfying them. The test is not

[58] Roscoe Pound, "Political and Economic Interpretations of Jurisprudence," *American Political Science Review*, Feb., 1913, pp. 94, 103.

so much directly the satisfaction of the desires, as the securing of social ends. In that, the question of desires is important, but it is not our direct or primary concern.

It is stretching language to say that the test is the satisfaction of desires, in cases where men think of the test as between right and wrong. The rule may work well because men think it just; but, in many cases, the emphasis is that they think it just,—not that they think it works. Any test of satisfying desires must be qualified at every turn by recognition of the influence of precedent, of custom, of the sense of right and wrong; indeed, of the desire to satisfy a social end which, after all, is something more than the satisfaction of desires.

I think Holmes was nearer the truth than is Pound. In his long and splendid career, he dropped out from time to time his legal philosophy in opinions studded with the most unusual historical allusions and brilliant legal epigrams. All too infrequently he gave us more elaborate studies in his legal addresses. He always insisted that law is not a changeless system of ideal perfection. He was a deep student of legal history, but he was never beguiled into thinking that history alone could give the answer. History, he admitted, of course, was necessary. "It is," he said, a part of the rational study, because it is the "first step toward a deliberate reconsideration of the worth" of the rules.[59] But it was only a first step.

Nor is law based on logic. Formally, it is logical. Formally, it is deductive. But law could not be "worked out like mathematics from some general axioms of conduct." [60] Behind the logical form, he warned us, "lies a judgment as to the relative worth and importance of competing legislative grounds, often an inarticulate and unconscious judgment, it is true," but the very "root and nerve of the whole proceeding." [61] That judgment was one as to the best rule for attaining a desired social end. The social end was the conscious or unconscious test, modified by the force of history and precedent.

With gentle irony, he observed that it was then (in 1915) fashionable to emphasize the criterion of social welfare as against "the individualistic eighteenth century bill of rights"; but added that

[59] Oliver Wendell Holmes, "The Path of the Law," 1897. *Collected Legal Papers,* p. 186.
[60] *Ibid.,* p. 180.   [61] *Ibid.,* p. 181.

he ventured to refer to his "The Common Law," published "thirty-four years ago, to show that it is no novelty." [62] In his "The Common Law," he had remarked that "no society had ever admitted that it could not sacrifice individual welfare to its own existence." The state, from the beginning of time, had conscripted soldiers, built highways and later railroads through old family properties, and generally always sacrificed the individual to the general good.[63]

Those whom Beale called "the social justiciars" may reply that men now conceive of their desires less as rights than as interests to be protected; but, as we have seen, even today the tendency of the individual to think of his demands in the terms of individual rights remains very strong, so strong that it may be the response to a deep laid instinct. Holmes, of course, admitted that the desires of men and women are important because cases arise only as desires conflict; and, of course, the criterion of the desirable end is profoundly influenced by what men think is desirable, and how strongly they think it. But evidently the test in Holmes' mind (and in this I think he was right) is not directly the satisfaction of desires, but the attainment of a social end, in which process, however, the nature and force of the conflicting desires is necessarily an important element.

As to what are the social ends, Holmes believed that no formal or final statement was possible. They could be ascertained only by a synthesis from the actual decisions. "With regard to the police power," he observed, "as elsewhere in the law, lines are pricked out by the gradual approach and contact of the decisions on the opposing sides." [64]

American legal thought, then, had arrived at the conclusion that law is the rules enforced by the courts. Generally, there was agreement among students that it is a developing and ever shifting thing. As to its philosophy, the reasons behind the rules, it had had a brilliant exposition by Pound of the sociological theory,— that law is the satisfaction of desires. But, personally, I feel that Pound tended to underestimate the role of history and precedent, and that his satisfaction of desires is too narrow a test. The sense of justice, the love of the precedents of the past, the desire for the best rule for the ends of society at the time, influence us too

[62] *Ibid.*, p. 307 (essay, "Ideals and Doubts" 1915).
[63] Holmes, *The Common Law* (1881), p. 43.
[64] *Noble Bank* vs. *Haskell*, 219 U.S. 104, 112 (1911).

strongly for us to admit that the mere satisfaction of desires is enough to satisfy our minds and hearts. And what men believe move them, is a large element in what does actually move them!

REFERENCES

ADAMS, BROOKS, *Centralization and the Law.* Boston: Little, Brown & Co., 1906.

AUSTIN, JOHN, *Lectures on Jurisprudence* (1929 ed.). London: J. Murray.

CARTER, JAMES COOLIDGE, *Law: Its Origin, Growth, and Function.* New York: G. P. Putnam's Sons, 1907.

GRAY, JOHN CHIPMAN, *The Nature and Sources of Law.* New York: Columbia University Press, 1909.

HILL, DAVID JAYNE, *The People's Government.* New York: D. Appleton & Co., 1915.

HOLMES, OLIVER WENDELL, *Collected Legal Papers.* New York: Harcourt, Brace & Howe, 1920.

———The Common Law. Boston: Little, Brown & Co., 1881.

LOWELL, A. LAWRENCE, Essays on Government. Boston: Houghton Mifflin & Co., 1897.

POUND, ROSCOE, "Mechanical Jurisprudence," 8 *Columbia Law Review* 605 (Dec., 1908).

———"The Scope and Purpose of Sociological Jurisprudence," 24 *Harvard Law Review* 591 (June, 1911), 25 *Harvard Law Review* 140 (Dec., 1911), 25 *Harvard Law Review* 489 (April, 1912).

———*The Spirit of the Common Law.* Boston: Marshall Jones Co., 1921.

WHARTON, FRANCIS, *Commentaries on Law.* Philadelphia: Francis Wharton, Kay & Brother, 1884.

WHEATON, HENRY, *Elements of International Law* (1878 ed.). London: Stevens & Sons.

WILLOUGHBY, W. W., *The Nature of the State.* New York: The Macmillan Co., 1896.

CHAPTER VII

THE THEORY OF POLITICAL ACTION, 1865–1896

Aid to Industry

The Granger, Greenback, Populist, and Free Silver Movements

THE generation after the close of the Civil War was a period of tremendous activity. Through the whole period, population poured into the Middle and Far West. The restless stream of the covered wagon never stopped until the frontier was closed. Even the Civil War did not stop the migration. The immense energy of the period is as astonishing as that in the period from 1800 to 1860, when the Middle West was in the making. In Iowa, for example, there were 674,913 people in 1860; in 1880, there were 1,624,615, or almost two and a half times as many. In Minnesota, there were only 170,023 in 1860; in 1880, there were 780,773, or four and a half times as many. In Kansas, the increase was from 107,206 in 1860 to 999,096 in 1880. In Nebraska, the population rose from 28,841 in 1860 to 452,402 in 1880.

During the same period, as in our entire history, there went on a steady movement from the country to the cities. In 1860, only 16 per cent of our people lived in places of 8,000 population or over; in 1920, the percentage was 43.8. There were ten cities of more than 100,000 population in 1860; in 1880, there were twenty; in 1900, thirty-eight; and in 1920, sixty-eight. In 1930, there were ninety-three.

Yet, at the same time, the amount of farm acreage steadily increased. From 407,212,538 acres in 1860, it had risen to 955,883,715 acres in 1920. The actual population on the farms increased until 1910, the acreage increased throughout, but the ratio of farm to total population steadily went down.[1]

The people that moved to the cities went largely into factories.

---

[1] Since 1910 the farm population has slightly decreased.

In 1859, the wage-earners in manufacturing establishments numbered 1,311,000; in 1879, they were 2,733,000; in 1909, they were 6,615,000. The young people who had lived the independent, individualistic life of our farming communities became, in constantly increasing proportions, wage-workers in the cities.

Meanwhile came an ever increasing immigration. We had always had immigration, but in the beginning it had been small in numbers, and it had been chiefly of British stock. In 1820, it was only 20,000, or one-fifth of one per cent of the total population; in 1880, it was 457,257, or nine-tenths of one per cent of the total population, in 1910, it was 1,041,570 or 1.1 per cent of the total population. In the ten years ending in 1914, immigration averaged over a million a year.

By 1920, only 43.5 per cent of our white population, were descended from people who were here in 1790; 34.7 per cent were foreign born, or the children of foreign born; and 21.8 per cent were descendants of those who had come since 1790. Fifteen per cent originated in Southern and Eastern Europe.[2] By 1920, only 20 per cent of New York City was native born of native parentage; only 23 per cent of Chicago; Pennsylvania was only 17.8 per cent of native parentage; and Ohio, 21.8 per cent. Wisconsin was 45 per cent of German parentage.

It is not necessary to adopt narrow prejudices about immigrants to realize that no such mass immigration resulting in such wide diversity, could fail to have a weakening effect on the coherence and ordered development both of our law and of our politics. Both law and politics are the product of long living together in a community with a basic unity of habits and general standards of life. Until there is time for a new fusion to develop, the ideas, the inherited beliefs and prejudices of the lands of origin, inevitably assert themselves, and clashes and lack of harmony result. The effect on our politics of an Irish vote, a German vote, and later an Italian vote, and other diverse alien group votes, has long diverted our politics from its normal course, and has delayed our natural development. There is reason to believe, too, that our law has been hampered by the same diversity; for, where the popu-

[2] Estimates of National Origins Committee (Sen. Doc. 259, 70th Cong. 2d Sess. 1929). The Census Bureau estimated that 49.9% were descended from the 1700 population and 15.5% from those who came here since 1790. *Increase of Population in the United States*, p. 255 (1922).

lation is diverse, there is not the same united response to infractions on the common welfare. Quarrels and disagreements arise between those of different groups. Juries are more apt to disagree when they are drawn from strands of different origin.

In a brilliant chapter in his "Literary History of America," Barrett Wendell found the key to much of our past in the fact that we had several eras developing at once. He said that as you read Herndon, you have a "curious sense that months and years are doing the work of generations and centuries. It is as if in 1809, Lincoln had been born under King Richard I; and when the man was fifty years old, he was abreast of our own time." In our western regions, he added, "this extraordinary confusion of the centuries is not yet past." Our government consequently has somehow to reconcile "the purposes and interests of societies, widely different in climatic conditions and historic origin." In our national politics, "we must reconcile differences which extend not only through widely divergent space, but also through generations and centuries of social and historic time."

So he concluded that it was no "wonder the most salient trait of our great confused West seems enthusiasm for material prosperity, as distinguished from spiritual or intellectual ideals." [3] So he called our West the "confused West," the West which was several countries and stages of civilization at the same time. The country as a whole was even more several countries. In New England and the old South was a civilization more than three hundred years old. Until the great immigration, New England had a settled and homogeneous population; it had had a common past for eight generations; it was unified by common sufferings and experiences; and it had developed in Lowell, Longfellow, Emerson, Whittier and Webster the beginnings of an attempt of self-interpretation. In Emerson it reached a high level. Then there came upon it a great mass immigration, bringing with it the cultures of vastly different countries, and introducing a clash of ideas and customs.

Meanwhile, the Middle West, just a generation from the pioneer days, had begun to settle down. It began to produce men and women who were interested in the interpretation and the enjoyment of life, now that their fathers had turned over to them a so-

[3] Barrett Wendell, *Literary History of America*, p. 504.

ciety where the first work of breaking the ground and clearing the forests had been done. And just as it began to fuse, the same mass immigration, excellent in many ways in its individual qualities, poured in, to delay the process of making a coherent whole of the slowly forming society.

At the same time, the great work of breaking new trails into the Far West was steadily on its way. The restless pioneer, always believing that the fields were richer and the opportunity freer in the State next beyond, never rested until the last acre of good land was taken up and the frontier was gone.

The diversity of the period can not be better exemplified than in its fiction. Contemporaneously, Mary E. Wilkins and Sarah Orne Jewett were interpreting New England; Riley, Indiana; Brete Harte and Owen Wister, the Far West; Hamlin Garland, Iowa and the Dakotas; Page and Cable, the South; and a little later, Willa Cather, Nebraska; Tarkington, Indiana; and Emerson Hough and Herbert Quick, Iowa. The diverse ideas of New England, of the South, rich in memories but poor in material things; the Middle West, of the second generation; and the Far West, with all its crude beginnings—all spoke at once in our politics and in our new literature.

It is no wonder that there was confusion in our politics, and that one part of the country did not understand what the other part was saying and why it said it. To the usual divisions based on class differences, on social and economic cleavages, there were added the divisions of periods of time.

But always there was the pioneer spirit to influence the tone and temper of the rest of the country. James Truslow Adams speaks frequently in his "Epic of America" of the American dream —the dream that here was something very different from anything that could be done in any of the old countries of Europe—the dream of a freer opportunity for the average man, and an independence, both political and social, without conscious class distinctions. The frontier long kept alive this democratic ideal. The frontier, said Frederick J. Turner in his famous essays on "The Frontier in American History," worked both for nationalism and for democracy. "Nothing works for nationalism like intercourse within the nation. Mobility of population is death to localism, and the western frontier worked irresistibly in unsettling population." [4] In the days before the Civil War, States like Indiana, Ohio and Illinois were settled in their northern parts from New England and New York, and in their southern parts by people from the Carolinas, Tennessee and Kentucky.

The inevitable result was that the strong State feeling, the separate State loyalty of the older communities of the seaboard, did not develop. The new States had grown up within the Union, and their peoples were made up from many States. The new States were less unified within themselves and more amenable to general influences. When, after the Civil War, the States of the Far West were settled, this process was accentuated. California was composed of people from all parts of the Union. Kansas, while chiefly New England in origin, had a large southern population. Iowa, Minnesota and the Dakotas each had large contingents from a dozen States, and from the beginning, large representations of immigrants.

Always the frontier made possible the continuance of democracy and a strong individualism. Complex society, Turner said, "is precipitated by the wilderness into a kind of primitive organization based on the family." The tendency is anti-social. It produces antipathy to control, and particularly to any direct control. It is "everyone for himself." Society is filled with the spirit of conquest over nature, the sense of individual opportunity is strong, and a consequent resentment of control and restriction by the government is manifested.

Turner says again, "That coarseness and strength combined with acuteness and inquisitiveness; that practical, inventive turn of mind, quick to find expedients; that masterful grasp of material things, lacking in the artistic but powerful to effect great ends; that restless nervous energy; that dominant individualism, working for good and for evil, and withal, that buoyancy and exuberance which comes from freedom,—these are traits of the frontier, or traits called out elsewhere because of the existence of the frontier." [5]

So long as free lands existed, "the opportunity for a competency exists, and economic power secures political power." [6] The free lands promoted "individualism, economic equality, freedom to

---

[4] Frederick J. Turner, *The Frontier in American History*, p. 30.
[5] *Ibid.*, pp. 27, 30, 37. [6] *Ibid.*, p. 32.

rise, democracy. Men would not accept inferior wages and a permanent position of social subordination when this promised land of freedom and equality was theirs for the taking. Who would rest content under oppressive legislative conditions, when, with a slight effort he might reach a land wherein to become a co-worker in the building of free cities and free States on the lines of his own ideal?" [7]

The frontier ended about 1890, as the census of that year proclaimed. But the free lands were not gone. "About half as much land," says Hibbard in "A History of the Public Land Policies," "107,000,000 acres, was taken from the public domain between 1890 and 1900 as during the preceding ten years." The increase in farm area was greater than ever before. Between 1900 and 1910, "the amount of public domain disposed of, almost doubled. Prices of farm produce had risen, and risen enormously. Land that had been altogether unattractive some years earlier, began to have a value." [8] The pressure of population brought more land into use. Yet Hibbard says that, while new land was being bought and new land was being added to the cultivated area, "Nevertheless, so far as general mixed farming is concerned, the free government land has offered little room for expansion since 1890." [9] The best land was gone then. Above all, the frontier was gone. Its magic appeal to our imaginations was no more. A new era was upon us. Men still found new opportunities, but the change in mental attitude was profound. [10]

[7] *Ibid.*, p. 259.
[8] Benjamin Horace Hibbard, *A History of Public Land Policies*, p. 542.
[9] *Ibid.*, p. 543.
[10] Godkin, in an article written as early as 1865, expressed a theory strikingly like Turner's. The great migrations to the Middle West and the conditions of the frontier had inculcated, he asserted, individualism, self-confidence, and a contempt for authority, experience, and theory. "Aristocratic Opinions of Democracy, 1865," in *Problems of Modern Democracy* (1896), pp. 39-41.
Ellen Church Semple, in her delightful *American History and Its Geographic Environment*, likewise expressed a belief that the common remoteness of the frontier induced equality, independence, and also a certain largeness of view (pp. 81, 243).
The current tendency of historians and economists is to hold that Turner overstated his case. They think that the pressure of the new industrialism explains our political demands in this period, rather than the frontier. Perhaps so. But I am inclined to think that up to 1900, the frontier psychology—if not the frontier conditions—still had great influence. Men were still living in the Far West, and even in parts of the Middle West, who had been themselves pioneers. The outlet to the land had only yesterday been definitely restricted. It is true that not all the discontented desired an outlet on the land, but the pressure on them was increased by the presence of those who did desire an outlet but were denied it. Moreover, the mental attitude engendered by the frontier held over after the frontier was gone. The progressive movement in 1912, when the frontier was still further in the past

The period immediately following the Civil War was one of great material development. While the people were pouring into the new West, the railroads were being rapidly extended. The mileage rose from 35,085 in 1865 to 165,597 in 1890, and 253,626 in 1917. There were tremendous developments in the steel industry; the oil fields of Pennsylvania were the scenes of feverish activity and an unrestrained competition. The competition wiped out many of the small and weaker competitors, and combinations eliminated others, so that there was a constant process of concentration.

In 1870, there were 2,076 establishments manufacturing agricultural implements. In 1915 there were only 601; although the number of wage-earners had increased from 25,249 to 48,459, and the capital from $34,800,000 to $338,500,000. In the iron and steel industry, the number of establishments decreased from 808 to 587 in the period between 1870 and 1915; while the number of wage-earners increased from 77,555 to 278,072, and the capital employed from $121,800,000 to $1,720,700,000. The percentage of establishments with over 1,000 employees rose from 3.5 per cent in 1882 to 8.1 per cent in 1907.

The problems which we had to consider rose, then, from a new concentration of industry, the rise of a wage-earning class such as we had never known before, the great restriction in the opportunity for an outlet on the land.

AID TO INDUSTRY

The dominant note of our political thought at the beginning of our period, was one of encouragement of the development of the country. The policy of the Homestead act of throwing open the government lands to actual settlers, was continued. "More than half the area of the country—1,048,000,000 out of 1,920,000,000 acres—still remained in the public domain in 1860." [11] The Homestead act of 1862 adopted the policy of giving away free farms, of 160 acres each, to settlers who would cultivate the land for five years. In 1870, war veterans were allowed to count their mili-

and the pressure of the new industrialism must have been the main force, is full of references to the vanished days of the frontier. Industrialism brought the demand for action, but the memory of the old days gave the demand much of its direction and appeal.

[11] E. L. Bogart, *Economic History of the American People*, p. 535.

tary service against the five years' residence. In 1878, citizens were allowed "to purchase 160 acres of lands unfit for cultivation but valuable for timber or minerals, at not less than $2.50 per acre. In 1909, the size of a homestead was doubled in arid regions where irrigation was needed." [12]

Meanwhile, the policy of extensive land grants to railroads was continued. Huge grants to the railroads had been made before and during the Civil War. Great grants were made to the Santa Fe and Southern Pacific in 1866. Large mining and lumber companies obtained large tracts by dummy entries by their employees. When Roosevelt investigated the land policy at the time he began his campaign for conservation, it was reported that the public land office had been little more than "a center for the distribution of plunder." [13]

The general attitude of the time was that every inducement should be made for the conquest of the continent, as if the great work of settling the country must be done in the lifetime of those engaged in the first work of opening the country, as if the continent would vanish if the work were not pushed with unremitting zeal to an early conclusion.

At the same time, the same encouragement of industry and the development of the country went on in the settled country of the east. It was a period of encouraging manufactures in every city of the land. The policy of exemption of manufacturing establishments from taxation, at least for a period of years, was widely adopted.

The philosophy of governmental aid can, of course, be best seen in the tariff policy, which, with the money policy, absorbed the attention of the old political parties during the whole period.

The Morrill tariff of the Civil War, passed in 1862, was continued after the Civil War. As Taussig says, the policy of protection there adopted was continued, and the duties were even raised, without the country being consciously committed to a protective policy. [14] The need of revenue, the chances of party politics, determined our policy more than a definite public opinion. But the opinion of the leaders became steadily more definite.

A coherent tariff theory was developed to meet the attacks on

[12] *Ibid.*, p. 535.   [13] *Ibid.*, p. 538.
[14] Frank W. Taussig, *Tariff History of the United States* (5th ed., 1903), pp. 173, 174, 193.

the protective tariff. For years before the war, Henry C. Carey, of Philadelphia, had been elaborating his theory of the protective tariff as an aid to diversified industry and to the development of an independent country. He continued his efforts with unflagging zeal after the war. He was the son of an emigrant from Ireland, and had an ineradicable prejudice against Great Britain. Like all the protective tariff adherents of the next generation, he argued that the result of every period of what he called free trade had been business depression, whereas abounding prosperity had followed our high tariffs.

He declared that the policy of free raw materials enabled our New England manufacturers to import from abroad, and thus destroyed the home market for our own producers. A policy of protection, stimulating manufactures, would have created a great home market, which would have enabled the American farmer to sell his grain at home at a good price; whereas, under free trade, he had to sell his surplus to Europe and pay the great "transportation tax." Free trade was the policy of Great Britain, whose manufacturers profited by our policy of free raw materials, and of discouragement of our own manufactures which should be enabled to compete with hers. Protection, by creating a home market, by creating a network of economic relations between the North and the South, would have created such mutual ties as would have prevented the Civil War.

What becomes, he asked, of the profits of an American industry? Do they go abroad? He answered that they did not, but that they were spent in this country, adding to the demands for human labor, promoting immigration, adding to the demand for farm products, and contributing to the "growth of both individual and political independence." [15]

In short, the expansion and diversification of industry was Carey's great ideal. He believed that when "mills and engines, villages and cities, increased rapidly in number and size, the men who make machinery generally profit thence; the harmony of all the real and permanent interests of the various portions of society being so perfect as to leave no room" for petty discords.

Carey's arguments had much effect on our post-war politicians.

[15] Henry C. Carey, "Review of the Report of the Hon. D. A. Wells, Special Commissioner of the Revenue, 1869," *Miscellaneous Works*, Vol. II, pp. 20, 23, (Letter Fifth).

Congressman William D. Kelley of Pennsylvania, known as "Pig Iron Kelley," dedicated his book of speeches to him as the "Great Master of Economic Science, the Profound Thinker." Kelley, too, desired diversified industry. To make a country prosperous, he said, "remunerative employment must be accessible to all its people; and to that end, industry must be so diversified that he who has not the strength for agriculture or other labor requiring muscle, may make his feeble sinews available in some gentler employment." Agriculture and commerce, he said, offer little opportunity for childhood which is wasted in idleness on the farm. It is strange today to read these words condemning our industry for its lack of opportunity for child labor. Agriculture, he went on, is seasonal. A diversified industry would offer employment for all at all seasons of the year; and, moreover, stimulate the market of the farmer. The farmer would find his readiest market at his door.[16]

William McKinley was the great exponent of the dominant theory of protection in the last twenty years of the century. He was a product of a small town, had been a country boy, had served in the Civil War, and was a regular party man all his life. His thought was always typical of the group he represented. His American system, in the words of his biographer, consisted in "placing (1) duties on competing importations high enough to foster American industries, whether of the farm or shop; (2) low duties, or none at all, on necessaries not competing with home products; (3) the lowering of duties, whenever in excess of actual requirements, but always with careful regard to existing industries"; and (4) the adjustments of all duties, with the "constant aim to place America and the interests of American citizens above those of foreign competitors. It meant briefly, favoritism for Americans against the rest of the world, but no favoritism within our own boundaries,— except for the purposes of promoting the general prosperity of the whole country."[17]

He believed that protection was the great vivifying force in our industrial life. "It encourages enterprise; it opens our mines; it erects our machine shops, our furnaces, and factories; it enlarges our cities and builds up villages." It adds, he said, "to the material wealth of the nation. It enhances the value of real estate.

[16] W. D. Kelley, *Speeches, Addresses and Letters,* p. 15 (speech of Jan. 31, 1866).
[17] Charles S. Olcott. *The Life of William McKinley,* Vol. I, p. 124.

More than that, it gives to the farmer a ready market for the products of his farm. It brings a market to his very door." He also believed in diversification. "We want," he said, "to be independent in that broad and comprehensive sense, strong within ourselves, self-supporting and self-sustaining in all things."

McKinley's theory was one of strong nationalism. Free trade was desirable in the United States, but the foreign producer "pays no taxes. He performs no civil duties; is subject to no demands for military service." Yet free trade admits him to equal privileges with our own people. It results in giving our "money, our manufactures, and our markets to other nations, to the injury of our labor, our trades-people, and our farmers. Protection keeps money, markets, and manufactures at home for the benefit of our own people." [18]

He, too, argued that the establishment of a furnace "has the effect at once to enhance the value of all property and all values for miles surrounding it." [19]

The argument at that time was strong for the home market. We had not yet developed a large export trade, and the protectionists were indifferent to it. They wanted a market near at home. In fact, McKinley declared that our wheat could not compete with that from India. He instanced the great diversified market of New England, and asked if it were not a better market than that of old England. "The home market," he said, "is the best, besides being the safest. It has got the most money to spend, and spends the most. It consumes the most; it is therefore the most profitable." [20]

The protectionist school was not concerned that we were at a disadvantage in any industry so long as that disadvantage was only the cost of production. Nelson Dingley, of Maine, made this very clear in the debate on the Wilson bill in 1894. He noted the argument of the "free trade" theorists, that we should "confine ourselves to industries in which we have advantage over other countries." He replied that if a natural advantage were meant, he would agree; but that the advantage Europe had over us in industry was simply a wage advantage, and that the "free trade" theory meant "we should not carry on any industry here in which

[18] Cong. Rec. April 15, 1878, pp. 2544, 2545. May 18, 1888, p. 4401.
[19] *Ibid.*, p. 4404. May 18, 1878.   [20] *Ibid.*, p. 4404.

higher wages of labor make the product cost more in money." [21]

Therefore, we should produce everything here for which the labor cost was our only disadvantage. The tariff should equal the difference between the cost of production here and abroad. Its purpose was to protect our wage system and our standard of living from foreign competition. "The object of the protective tariff," said Dingley, "is to enlarge the opportunities for labor, and to maintain a high standard of living for the masses." Its assumption was that that country is most prosperous "in which the standards of wages and of living are the highest"; that a high standard of living for the masses, which causes demand and "sets in motion the intricate machinery of production and distribution in modern civilized society, is dependent on the opportunities to use their labor at good wages, and that these opportunities widen and wages rise as diversified domestic industries multiply. . . ." [22]

One of the few prominent economists who defended protection was Simon N. Patten of the University of Pennsylvania, who, in his "Economic Basis of Protection," published in 1890, ably supported the protection argument for a diversified industry. Patten believed that the government should encourage the most advantageous industry, and not leave it to the determinations of unrelated individuals. He contrasted dynamic and passive states,—dynamic: those which assisted their peoples to adapt themselves to conditions, and aided them to newer and better use of their land; and passive: those which left development to the action of unguided trade.

It was not likely that the American people, he said, would change their demand for food "from those articles produced in a crude fashion, to other articles better fitted for the soil and requiring scientific production, until the present price of these articles has been greatly increased either through the action of the government, or through the effect of an increased demand on the part of a growing population." It was for the American people to decide "whether they will passively allow an unequal distribution of wealth to force the change in consumption through which they must go; or whether they will by a wise policy, hasten this period and remove those obstacles which stand in the way of change." [23]

[21] *Cong. Record*, Jan. 11, 1894, p. 731.   [22] *Ibid.*, July 19, 1897, p. 2714.
[23] Simon N. Patten, *The Economic Basis of. Protection* (1890), p. 124.

Patten would hasten the process. By government aid, he would encourage those uses of the land which were most advantageous, diversify the uses of the land, allow the people to adapt it to its best uses, and make developments which would "bring a better harmony between its social conditions and economic environment." [24]

Patten's argument was presented in no selfish spirit. But it may be remarked that, as in all economic planning, it is not safe to conclude that governmental aid will always be wisely and unselfishly directed. The actual determination of the aid to be given in order to encourage new developments, would be made by men of partial knowledge, subject to selfish considerations, and, moreover, by a group constantly shifting. There would be no continuity to their decisions. Patten, moreover, addressed himself to the diversification in the use of the land: he had little to say of industry. We have attained a widespread diversification in the use of land, but it has been aided by little tariff advantage.

As industry grew and became more powerful and efficient, the infant industries argument of Clay became less and less pertinent. The protectionists began to use more and more the vested interests argument which, after all, from the standpoint of political theory, is no argument at all. McKinley urged that men "have embarked in business under the existing law regulating the tariff; great enterprises have been projected; vast amounts of capital are invested all over the country upon the faith of the existing law, and relying upon its permanence; and today millions of dollars are invested in buildings, machine shops, and factories all over this land, built up on the fostering care of protection."

The vested interests argument was simply the excuse of those who needed some defense, now that the infant industry days had past. Of course, it is true that after industry had been built up under a protective system, which still could not survive if protection were withdrawn, it would be disastrous to remove the tariff props suddenly. But, after all, the vested interests argument was an appeal to fear and not to reason.

Finally, the protectionists argued that prices would not be increased by a protective tariff. After industry was established, competition would reduce the price to lower than the foreign price. As

[24] *Ibid.*, p. 138.

time went on, less was heard of this argument. After all, it was part of the infant industries theory. For, when prices are steadily lower than the foreign prices, there is no longer any need of a tariff. After the turn of the century, the protectionist theory was concentrated on the vested interests argument and on the theory of the wage level. By this time it was assumed that the wage level in the United States must permanently be higher than that in Europe; that protection caused it, or at least was necessary for its maintenance; and that protection must be permanently maintained for that purpose.

The economists of the country almost uniformly opposed the protectionist theory. A whole generation of young men came out of the universities, taught by Perry of Williams, Sumner of Yale, and Taussig of Harvard, and they swelled the forces opposed to the existing order. But the course of events was too much for them. The economists were really never answered; but, as has been well said, while they won all the arguments, they lost the elections. They insisted that the tariff did not cause high wages; that our high wages were caused by the general prosperity of the country; that a protected industry had to pay the rate of wages current in the community, and that it did not set the pace itself. They argued traditionally that a nation should produce what it could produce most advantageously, and should allow other countries to produce what they could produce most advantageously. They stressed the historic arguments of the advantages of reciprocal trade.

They pointed out that the protectionist argument—that the foreigner paid the tax—did not always necessarily follow; since, if the domestic production was not sufficient to satisfy the domestic demand, the price of the domestic article was increased to the foreign price of the foreign article plus the tariff, and that even where the domestic production was sufficient, there was the temptation of the domestic industry to combine and obtain the benefit of the tariff protection in furtherance of monopoly.

They stressed the fact that high protection encourages an artificial and hothouse growth, overstimulates some industries, and encourages and maintains others for which the country is is no way adapted. By diverting capital and labor to unprofitable fields, it actually tends to lower the productivity and prosperity of the country to that extent.

One of the most incisive attacks on the protection theory was made by Henry George in his "Protection or Free Trade," published in 1886. He brought to the task all his warm human feeling, his ardent love of fair play and justice for the common man; and he presented his argument with simple and homely illustrations in vivid style.

In general, as in the economic arguments of his "Progress and Poverty," he followed strictly the classical economic theory. But he centered his attacks not on the hampering effect of protection on production, but on the wage question itself. That part of the free trade case that deals with wages, had, he said, "not been adequately treated." [25] Yet it was the heart of the controversy. He differed with those who said that the rate of wages was not the concern of the state: it was a legitimate object of public policy. Trade, he said, was not war,—it was based on reciprocal advantage; and protection carried to its conclusion by all countries would stifle trade.

He doubted even the infant industry argument; for, while he admitted the desirability of initial aid, he sadly said that the protected industries never relinquished the protection once granted. Vigorously, he illustrated the handicaps that protection forces on us. To make us prosperous, he said, by keeping us from trading with others, "is as absurd as it would be to attempt to make a man prosperous by preventing him from buying from other men." [26] It is a distinct loss, if "industry is diverted from more profitable to less profitable occupations. . . ." [27]

If protection were necessary for high wages, he asked how England, with free trade, could pay higher wages than protected countries, and how our grain could undersell English grain. Low wages brought inefficient labor, and inefficient labor was not a dangerous competitor. Moreover, wages depend on the general wage scale of the country, on competition of the labor market; and he taunted the protectionists with their policy of protection for goods and free trade in immigrant labor,—a contradiction which the protectionists never have explained.

Boldly, he declared that protection has harmed our prosperity by

[25] Henry George, *Protection or Free Trade*, p. 5.   [26] *Ibid.*, p. 68.
[27] *Ibid.*, p. 71.

forcing overdevelopment of disadvantageous industry, and it had corrupted our public life.

Then he asked why, when the arguments for free trade were so overwhelming, it was still firmly established. Here, he came on to the central theory of his life,—private property in land. He said the trouble was that working-men were not convinced that they would gain, if free trade were established. They felt, he said, that the increased profits would simply go to capital, and that the condition of labor would not be improved. He agreed with them, and declared that nothing would aid the working-man until the monopoly in land were abandoned. We need not here pursue this argument. We shall consider the theory of "Progress and Poverty" later on.

George concluded, with all his native idealism, that the spirit of free trade was that "of fraternity and peace." [28] If we would extend the principle of free trade, which had aided the mighty growth of our own nation within its boundaries, to our relations with other nations, we would take the first step "to a federation of mankind." Tariffs were a violation of the natural rights of mankind. We must conform our institutions to the principle of freedom.[29]

In the early days of the eighties and nineties, the anti-protection argument was stoutly and ably pressed, and gave some indications of prevailing. In 1887, Cleveland devoted his entire presidential message to the tariff. At that time, the surplus in the treasury was a matter of concern. Cleveland said that the treasury, which should be only a conduit, had become a "hoarding place for money needlessly withdrawn from trade and the people's use," [30] and asked for a reduction in the tariff on that ground. But he also resolutely attacked the protection theory.

He called our tariff laws "vicious, inequitable, and illogical sources of unnecessary taxation." [31] He pointed out that, where we imported articles that were manufactured in this country, the price to the consumer was raised by the amount of the duty; and that, where the domestic production was sufficient, it was often notorious that our domestic competition "is too often strangled by combinations quite prevalent at this time, and frequently called trusts." [32] Whether or not there was such combination, it was evident that the

[28] *Ibid.*, p. 214.   [29] *Ibid.*, p. 215.
[30] James D. Richardson, *Messages and Papers of the Presidents*, Vol. VIII, p. 581. Message of 1887.
[31] *Ibid.*, p. 584.   [32] *Ibid.*, p. 588.

tariff was no longer necessary for protection, where the home production was sufficient to meet the demand at a price lower than the foreign cost.

He followed the traditional tariff for revenue demand for free raw materials. He denied that his proposal would injure American labor or American industry. The claims of labor must be carefully considered, but it must be remembered that labor would benefit with the rest of the people by a reduction in the cost of articles bought for its consumption.[33]

Then he ended that it would be of little purpose to go into a discussion of the free trade and protection theories. "It is a condition which confronts us, not a theory." [34]

As early as 1888, the feeling was strong that the protective tariff, in the words of James Russell Lowell, had stimulated an "unhealthy home competition, leading to overproduction and to the disasters which are its tainted offspring . . . that the principle which is its root is the root also of Rings and Syndicates and Trusts, and all other such conspiracies for the artificial raising of profits, in the interests of classes and minorities. . . . The true American system is that which produces the best men by leaving them as much as possible to their own resources." [35]

William Graham Sumner fiercely ridiculed what he called the "false and foolish pretensions" of the protection argument. It seemed to him "to deserve only contempt and scorn, satire and ridicule. It is such an arrant piece of economic quackery, and it masquerades under such an affectation of learning and philosophy, that it ought to be treated as other quackeries are treated." To a student who asked him what were the arguments for protection, he "thundered 'There are none.' " [36]

Sumner would not even allow the infant industries argument. The infant industries never ceased to be infant. He said that the protectionists had no plan, that they proposed to tax some for the benefit of others, to divert industry out of its normal channels; and the result was nothing but economic waste. Protection did not create industry, but merely set one "as a parasite to live upon another." [37]

---

[33] *Ibid.*, p. 586.   [34] *Ibid.*, p. 590.
[35] James Russell Lowell, *Works*, Vol. VI, p. 217.
[36] Harris E. Starr, *William Graham Sumner*, p. 235.
[37] William Graham Sumner, *The Forgotten Man and Other Essays*, p. 38.

It was impossible, he continued, to raise wages by the protective tariff, since if all prices went up, real wages were not increased. Wages, after all, he said, were only one element in costs, and high wages did not hamper our competition.[38] He was too sweeping in his statements. High wages in some industries, where our mass production methods did not give us a greater efficiency, were a distinct handicap in foreign competition. But in those industries, even high protection did not always enable us to compete. He was on better ground when he said that American high wages were due to better opportunity, to greater competition for labor, and wider choice of occupation, the sparser population, the greater availability of land.[39] Valid, too, was his point that the wage differential between Europe and America was greatest in unskilled labor; thus showing that the American wage level was higher from natural causes, and that this high wage level in the profitable industries set the pace which the protected industries must follow.

The campaign of 1892 against the protective tariff was brilliantly successful. The old individualistic spirit, the desire for a self-reliant industry, the opposition to a system of special favors to the protected class, were enthusiastically presented. The tariff law of 1894 was, however, a bitter disappointment. For twenty years thereafter, protectionists never ceased to blame the panic of 1893 on the tariff law which was passed a year and a half later. Indeed, the protectionist argument was more than a little addicted to the *post hoc propter hoc* fallacy. In this case, it was not even *post hoc propter hoc*: it was *ante hoc propter hoc.* S. S. Cox once satirized this protectionist argument as follows:

> *Major Premise:* England has free trade.
> *Minor Premise:* England has low wages.
> *Conclusion:* Free trade produces low wages.
> *Major Premise:* The United States has protection.
> *Minor Premise:* The United States has high wages.
> *Conclusion:* Protection produces high wages.

He said that "this sort of logic is very easy. There is no end to the propositions we might prove. Thus:

> *Major:* England has a queen.
> *Minor:* England has low wages.
> *Conclusion:* Queens make wages low.

[38] *Ibid.,* p. 73.   [39] *Ibid.,* pp. 71–72.

Major: The United States is infested with snakes.
Minor: The United States has high wages.
Conclusion: Snakes make wages high." [40]

I think that no apology need be offered for quoting this bit of pleasantry, since it well satirizes the argument of a whole generation.

Finally, many men who were distressed at the prevalence of the exorbitant protective rates of the Dingley law, felt that the best way to attack the problem was not on theory, but on the facts. The standard theory was that the protective duty should equal the difference between the cost of production here and abroad. In 1908 the Republican National platform actually added the requirement that the tariff should also cover a reasonable profit to American industry; as if the duty should insure not only fair competition with the foreign product but, more than that, a profit to the American manufacturer. This was government aid to industry, indeed.

But the opposition to the protection policy had been protesting for years that the difference in wages between our country and Europe, did not necessarily mean that the cost of production in this country was higher. The efficient mass production methods of America enabled it to produce many articles at far less than European cost. Indeed, Carnegie, in the words of his biographer, Burton J. Hendrick, for several years prior to 1900, "had been proclaiming that steel no longer needed protection," that we "could beat the world." He declared that he was a believer in the doctrine of John Stuart Mill, that "manufactures full-grown should not be guarded by such favors." [41]

We have seen that in 1890 the protectionists were indifferent to the foreign market. The home market was their chief preoccupation. But the long course of high protection, the growth of mass production methods, the cheapness of our raw materials, the improvement of our machinery, the concentration of capital, had enabled our industry to compete in foreign markets, and from 1900 onwards the export market was a great consideration. How explain that our manufacturers could compete abroad, if they could not compete with foreign goods in the home market?

The impression grew that a real examination of the facts would

---

[40] *Cong. Record,* May 3, 1882, p. 3577.
[41] Burton J. Hendrick, *The Life of Andrew Carnegie,* Vol. II, p. 107.

disclose that, in industry after industry, there was no greater cost of production at home than abroad.

Moreover, the feeling grew that the writing of schedules had been skillfully done to conceal the actual protection granted, and that there were many advantages not apparent on the face of the schedules.

A brilliant demonstration of the frauds and the discriminations that lay hidden in the schedules, was given in the debate on the Payne-Aldrich tariff bill of 1909. Dolliver, La Follette and Beveridge, in a series of thoroughly informed speeches, tore schedule after schedule to pieces, and drove the protectionists from the field.

From then on until the World War, the supporters of protection were on the defensive. It was common to say that the tariff was the mother of the trusts; and while, of course, it was not true that great combinations were wholly or even chiefly due to the tariff, it was probably fair to say that the extraordinary tariff rates, permitting great profits, had been to a large extent an encouragement to combination.

In the campaign of 1912, Woodrow Wilson attacked the protectionist theory with some of the old enthusiasm of the early nineties. He utilized the experience of the Payne-Aldrich tariff bill debate; and declared that, if you "will get some expert to go through the schedules of the present Payne-Aldrich tariff, you will find a 'nigger' concealed in almost every 'woodpile,'—some little word, some little clause, some unsuspected item, that draws thousands of dollars out of the pocket of the consumer, and yet does not seem to mean anything in particular." [42]

He directly attacked the cost of production theory. "It is not the same," he said, "in any one factory for two years together. It is not the same in one industry from one season to another. It is not the same in one country at two different epochs." [43] He might have added that it is not the same in different parts of the same country, and that it was difficult to ascertain in any event. He noted the old protection argument,—that home competition would reduce the price; but answered that combinations had been availed of to defeat the operation of free competition.

The present protection policy, Wilson declared, had swung far

[42] Woodrow Wilson, *The New Freedom*, p. 133.   [43] *Ibid.*, p. 135.

from the old infant industries argument of Webster and Clay. Even McKinley had seen that the necessities of trade required a greater liberality. But now we had a demand for a permanent policy of a tariff equal to the difference between the cost of production here and abroad, plus a reasonable profit to American manufacturers. We no longer desired merely to protect American labor, but to ensure a profit to industries which could easily compete, not only at home but abroad, with foreign goods.

American working-men, he said, "used to be able to do so much more and better work than the foreigner that that more than compensated for his higher wages and made him a good bargain at any wage," and he called attention to the low wages paid for labor in our most protected industries,—steel and the Lawrence mills.[44]

Wilson objected to "hothouse industry," which attempted to produce articles here at a natural disadvantage. The policy of freeing the country from the restrictive tariff would bring "a wider market and a greater competition for labor. . . ."[45] The tariff had robbed us of our self-reliance and resourcefulness. It had brought about a system of favoritism.

In his Tariff Message in 1913, he repeated that we had built up a "set of privileges and exemptions from competition, behind which it was easy by any, even the crudest, forms of combination to organize monopoly; until at last nothing is normal, nothing is obliged to stand the tests of efficiency and economy, in our world of big business, but everything thrives by concerted arrangement."[46]

Wilson's words (while, of course, they gave no original theory) were a welcome relief, after the long success of the crudest of protection arguments. They were a refreshing return to the old belief in a fair field and no favors, in the vivifying effects of freedom of trade on the prosperity and the energies of the people. The aftermath of the war was to see a return to an even more intense economic nationalism, but the desire for a freer and more natural economy would persist throughout all the iron post-war days.

There are those who assert that the policy of aid to industry was the dominant policy of a whole epoch. Parrington calls it "Whiggery,"—the philosophy which believed in internal improvements, canals, aid to railroads, grants to factories, and, finally, the

---

[44] *Ibid.*, pp. 145, 148.   [45] *Ibid.*, p. 150.
[46] *The Messages and Papers of Woodrow Wilson*, Vol. I, p. 7.

protective tariff for industry. Its theory was that anything which aided the entrepreneurs to develop the country would, in the end, redound indirectly to the benefit of the people as a whole. But the policy was clearly not all of a piece. The desire to develop the country, to build canals and railroads, and encourage infant industries is very different from the policy of permanent subsidy to industry. Even John Stuart Mill found much to say for the infant industry theory. There was no intention of permanent subsidy in the initial aid by way of canals, railroads, or even protective tariffs.

The trouble always came, of course, with development. The policy of those who would continue the government aid became, then, of course, a policy, and often a vicious policy of special favors. But even then, the attacks on the policy, which we have considered, show that the policy was never accepted by all the country as a permanent policy. Nor was it advocated baldly as a policy of aid to capital. It has been advocated as necessary to maintain the American wage scale, to give an equal chance to American industry.

President Eliot once called this advocacy "slimy altruism," and all too often it was. The real motive, he felt,—and many of us have felt—was special favor to the few, advocated behind the pretense of benefit to labor. The story of the protective tariff in its actual operation is, indeed, in many particulars a sorry and sordid story. But in a discussion of political thought we are forced to consider the expressed arguments, and not the secret motives. After all, no historian can be a psychoanalyst. He can not weigh the force of men's unexpressed motives. Moreover, men come to believe the reasons that they publicly give for their acts, even if they were originally insincere. Finally, the public decides to a large extent on the basis of the expressed arguments. The test from the standpoint of political thought must be on the argument presented. The public argument was not based on favor to the few. Direct subsidies have never been popular in our politics. The policy was not presented nor maintained as a subsidy. It was based on the theory that our business could not compete without the tariff aid, that labor and the public in general were benefited.

THE PHILOSOPHY OF LABOR

The attack on the other manifestations of the industrial regime was slower in developing. Until the election of 1888, said Samuel

W. McCall in his "Life of Thomas B. Reed," "the country had few other subjects for political discussion than the tariff." [47] Partisanship, the tariff, sound money, and civil service reform occupied all our attention. Even the railroad question and the trusts did not arouse great interest until late in the century. Some of our modern liberals are apt to be scornful of this indifference of the generation before us, which they call the cynical eighties and the smug nineties, to the great questions of the relation of the individual to the new industry. But, no doubt, we have our own blindnesses to the questions that are before us. The tariff, the money question, and the civil service question were argued out with great ability and courage, and no generation which met those questions bravely need apologize. Indeed, there is reason to believe that, on the money question, our record may not be as enviable as theirs.

But the questions arising from the dislocation of men and women in industry, the growth of cities, the rise of a wage-earning class, the concentration of capital, the gradual loss of free land were pressing upon us. Men who had formerly known the free life of the farms, had become factory hands. Men who had had their own businesses, either had been wiped out or had become parts of the organizations of large businesses. Railroads had extended over the entire continent. As yet they were not subject to public control.

The beginnings of our political theory of a generation later are to be found in the labor councils, the granges, the obscure meetings of small business men, farmers and lawyers in the late sixties and the seventies. The Levellers of Cromwell's army were the prophets of the Declaration of Independence. Justice Holmes warned us that new ideas frequently start in obscure places with humble persons, for what the world pays for is judgment and not ideas.

One of the most unique of these apostles of political ideas was Ira Steward, a Boston machinist. He developed a theory of wages and of limitation of the hours of labor which was to have a deep effect on the American trade union philosophy. His theory was that the way to get higher wages was through shorter hours, and that shorter hours should be decreed by law. In a pamphlet published in 1865, he fully outlined his theory.

Strange as it may seem, he declared to American workingmen "Your wages will never be permanently increased until the hours

[47] S. W. McCall, *Life of Thomas B. Reed*, p. 161.

of labor are reduced." Those who work the hardest, he said, and the longest, are paid the least; and he declared that, "You are receiving your scanty pay precisely because you work so many hours in a day." Men who labor excessively, he said, "are robbed of all ambition to ask for anything more than will satisfy their bodily necessities, while those who labor moderately have time to cultivate tastes and create wants in addition to mere physical comforts. How can men be stimulated to demand higher wages, when they have little or no time or strength to use the advantages which higher wages can buy or procure?" [48]

The average mechanic who worked fourteen hours a day had no time to read magazines or books, to cultivate flowers, to take baths, or enjoy his family. Half past seven in the evening comes, and he has strength only for food and rest. If he worked only eight hours a day, he would soon begin to use the extra leisure, not in debauchery, but in activities; his desires would increase; he would demand the things necessary to employ his new leisure. He said that his theory was that more leisure would "create motives and temptations" for the common people to ask for more wages; that where all ask for more wages, there will be no motive for refusing, since employers will all fare alike; that where all demand more wages, the demand could not be resisted, for resistance would be a strike against the "habits, customs, and opinions of the masses"; and that the change in the habits and opinions of the people through more leisure would be too "gradual to disturb or jar the commerce and enterprise of capital."

The cost of making an article depended, he argued, almost entirely upon the number manufactured. The workers, tempted by their new leisure to buy the luxuries then confined to the wealthy, and which were costly because bought only by the wealthy, would cause a reduction in the cost of those commodities, and there would be a practical increase of wages. The change in wages would be gradual. The increase in the demand for goods, and the resulting increases in production, would prevent increases in prices.

Steward elaborated on the increased demand that leisure would bring. The mechanic who quit work at four-thirty would be likely to go about with his wife and children, and would demand that

---

[48] Commons, *A Documentary History of American Industrial Society*, Vol. IX, pp. 284–85.

they have clothes and a home as "respectable as other folks's." [49]
They would attend concerts, would want books and magazines, and the demand of the whole community would be raised.

When labor is honored, he continued, idleness will be dishonored. Crime, pauperism, want, would decline; and "the vast moral and material consequences flowing from such a conference justify the legislation necessary to secure the time." [50]

A mass meeting, which met in Boston in November, 1865, declared for the organization of a National Labor Party, and for legislation by the National Congress and the several State legislatures making eight hours "a legal day's work." Candidates should be pledged to the eight hour demand. It asked for a law in Massachusetts prohibiting corporations to employ operatives more than eight hours; a law forbidding employment of minors for more than eight hours, and forbidding night work for children.

It declared that the eight hour program was the only way by which the laborer's wages could be increased without increasing the cost of the product. The increase would be at the cost of the capitalist. As the "vast fortunes of individuals must melt back into the hands which produced them, under a higher standard of intelligence, so also must the abuses, monopolies, and illegitimate burdens which the people unconsciously impose upon themselves. . . ." The result would be the "downfall of a corrupt moneyed aristocracy; and of its natural counterpart,—extreme poverty and pauperism. . . ." [51]

Wendell Phillips gave his support to the eight hour movement. He considered the slavery issue, to which he had given the best years of his life, to be but one aspect of the labor question. Charles Edward Russell asserts that Phillips alone "of the abolitionist leaders" saw the economic origins of the issue. To his mind, the slavery question was "a labor question . . . " The abolition of "African slavery was only one gained battle in a long warfare." He proposed to carry the fight on against wage slavery. Russell declares that he was a Socialist,—"neither more nor less." [52]

Phillips seems to have had no system, no formula. He simply applied democratic principles of equality of rights to economics. In a speech in Faneuil Hall on November 2, 1865, he followed the

---

[49] *Ibid.*, pp. 289, 293.   [50] *Ibid.*, p. 301.   [51] *Ibid.*, Vol. IX, pp. 303–04.
[52] Charles Edward Russell, *The Story of Wendell Phillips*, pp. 119, 120, 135.

argument laid down by Steward on the eight hour issue. In a government of the people, he said, the government is bound to give the people the leisure to study their own government. It was no answer to say that the working-man might not use his leisure well: it was his to use, just as the employer's was his. The problem of the day, he added, was to equalize opportunity between the rich boy and the poor,—"to make the chances of the two as equal as possible; and before this movement stops, every child born in America must have an equal chance in life." [53]

In 1866, the National Labor Union, in its convention at Baltimore, declared again in favor of eight hours. It complained of "the growing and alarming encroachments of capital upon the rights of the industrial classes of the United States," and resolved that "the first and grand desideratum of the hour, in order to deliver the labor of the country from this thraldom, is the adoption of a law whereby eight hours shall constitute a legal day's work in every state of the American Union . . . " [54]

The convention recommended the formation of a national labor party. It also declared for cooperative stores, declared against prison labor, declared that the condition of women labor should be ameliorated, and affirmed that the national domain "should be disposed of to actual settlers only." [55]

In an address to working-men after this convention, it declared again that the "question of all others, which at present engrosses the attention of the American working-man, and, in fact, the American people, is the proposed reduction of the hours of daily labor, and the substitution of the eight for the ten hour system, now recognized as the standard of a legal day's work." [56] It resented the charge that the workman would not use the added leisure well. The workman was ignorant because he was overworked, because he had been denied the privileges "which others, more favored, have reaped." [57]

The address spoke in praise of cooperation, of equal pay for women for equal work; it demanded that the public lands be restricted to actual settlers only, [58] declaring that our motto should be, "The tools to those that have the ability and skill to use them,

[53] Wendell Phillips, *Speeches, Lectures, and Letters,* 2d Ser., p. 139.
[54] Commons, *Documentary History,* Vol. IX, p. 136.
[55] *Ibid.,* pp. 138–39.   [56] *Ibid.,* p. 142.
[57] *Ibid.,* p. 147.   [58] *Ibid.,* p. 157.

and the lands to those who have the will and heart to cultivate them."

Finally, it declared that there was no hope of results through the old political parties. The legislation of the past had been "the legislation of capital"; the remedy must be legislative and a national labor party must be organized to carry it out.[59]

The National Labor Union platform adopted at its 1867 convention, declared in favor of Greenbacks. I shall consider this demand when I come to the Greenback Movement. The Union repeated the demand that the national domain be sold in reasonable quantities to actual settlers only, declared for cooperative stores and workshops, and again for the eight hour program.

Commons asserts that Steward's theory was "nearly as revolutionary as that of Karl Marx." It reversed, he said, the "theory of the older trade unionism, which, taking its logic from the wage fund theory, concluded that the way to increase wages was to restrict the number of laborers and the output of each." Steward, in short, held that wages do not depend "upon the amount of capital and the supply of labor, but upon the habits, customs, and wants of the working classes." [60] He rejected the wage fund theory entirely. The effect on working-class opinion was "far-reaching. Eight hour leagues sprang up almost as extensively as trade unions." In 1866, the National Labor Union declared for it. "Within two years," Commons notes, "several municipal councils, five state legislatures, and the federal government had adopted the eight hour law." [61]

Steward's philosophy, Commons felt, became the "instinctive philosophy" of American wage-workers. The eight hour day by legislation did not progress, but the belief that shorter hours would bring higher wages persisted and permeated our trade union theory.[62]

The National Labor Union dwindled and died. However, in 1869, the Labor Reform Party was organized. It declared for the overthrow of the profit-making system, the extinction of monopolies, the abolition of the privileged classes, perfect freedom of exchange, and the ten hour day for factory labor. It declared war on the wage system.

[59] *Ibid.*, p. 164. [60] Commons, *Documentary History*, Vol. IX, pp. 25, 26.
[61] *Ibid.*, p. 26. [62] *Ibid.*, p. 26.

Wendell Phillips supported all its demands. In a speech at Boston on October 31, 1871, he asserted that the labor movement in America is the last "noble protest of the American people against the power of incorporated wealth." [63] He advocated economic reform by political action. Politics, he said, was the safety valve. He scorned the charge that the result would be the equalization of property. "Horrible!" he exclaimed sarcastically. [64]

He proposed to achieve his ends by taxation. If a man owned one home, he would tax him $100; if ten homes, $2,000; if one hundred, $60,000; so that when he is worth $40,000,000, he "will not have more than $20,000 a year to live on." He declared: "We'll crumble up wealth by making it unprofitable to be rich. . . . We will save a country equal from end to end." It was in wealth,—"incorporated, combining, perpetuated wealth, that the danger of labor lies." The movement, he concluded, was "the grandest and most comprehensive movement of the age." [65]

In 1874 the Industrial Brotherhood was formed, to secure to workers "a just share of the wealth created," more leisure, cooperation, land for settlers, monthly payment of wages, anti-convict labor laws, cheap transportation, anti-contract labor on public works, equal pay for equal work, greenbacks, the eight hour day. [66] Its preamble was adopted, with some modifications, by the Knights of Labor. The Industrial Brotherhood had a short life. Like the preceding labor congresses, it was ephemeral.

In 1869, however, the Knights of Labor had been organized. It was a national union not based on the local craft. Its preamble spoke of the "recent alarming development and aggression of aggregated wealth which, unless checked, will invariably lead to the pauperization and hopeless degradation of the toiling masses. . . ." To secure to the toiling masses "a proper share of the wealth that they create," more leisure, and the privileges they felt they were entitled to, they asked for cooperation, public land for actual settlers only, safety laws, weekly pay, laws against contract and convict labor, prohibition of child labor under fourteen years, equal pay for women for equal work, the eight-hour day, and greenbacks. Since most of these measures must come through political action, education was essential. [67]

---

[63] Phillips, *Speeches, Lectures, and Letters*, p. 157.   [64] *Ibid.*, p. 163.
[65] *Ibid.*, p. 167.   [66] Commons, *History of Labor*, Vol. II, p. 164.
[67] Terence V. Powderly, *Thirty Years of Labor*, pp. 243–45.

Powderly, the leader of the Knights, became greatly influenced by Henry George. At the New York Convention in 1882, he declared that the land question is the "main, all-absorbing question of the hour." It was "high above the eight-hour law, the prohibition of child labor, and the currency question." [68] He was opposed to the individual ownership of land. The convention did not act on the land question.

Again in 1883, 1884, and 1885, Powderly pressed the land issue without success. But in 1883, the Knights included in their preamble a demand that public land "be reserved for actual settlers,— not another acre for railroads or speculators; and that all lands now held for speculative purposes be taxed to their full value." [69] In 1884, the Knights of Labor added a clause in their preamble, declaring for the government ownership of railroads and telegraph and telephone lines.[70] Powderly favored cooperation, and gradually drifted towards socialism, whose aim, he said, "is to make the World Better." [71]

Meanwhile, the Knights had engaged in several disastrous strikes, and lost prestige both with the public and with working-men.

A new organization, which became the American Federation of Labor, was growing up. It had a new philosophy, which was to dominate labor almost to the end of our period. The leaders of the labor movement up to this time had been dominated by the old individualistic American spirit. They were too new to the new industrial order to believe it permanent. They did not consider themselves as belonging to a permanent working class. The new leaders, however, preached the doctrine of wage consciousness. They did not believe in political action. As Commons says, "their foreign birth and upbringing kept them from contact with the life of the great American middle class, the farmers and the small employees, the class which kept alive the philosophy of self-employment and voluntary cooperation." [72] They believed that the working-man would stay a working-man, and their program was limited to obtaining better hours and higher wages by self-help, by organization and the strike.

In his "Organized Labor," John Mitchell declared, "The average wage-earner has made up his mind that he must remain a wage-

[68] *Ibid.*, p. 337.   [69] *Ibid.*, p. 343.
[70] *Ibid.*, p. 388.   [71] *Ibid.*, p. 537.
[72] Commons, *History of Labor*, Vol. II, p. 308.

earner. He has given up hope of a kingdom to come, where he him-self will be a capitalist, and he asks that the rewards for his work be given to him as a working-man." [73] The great ends to be attained were the living wage and shorter hours of work. He felt that, "Upon the whole, unions have been more successful in reducing the hours of labor by means of strikes or trade agreements, than by means of the law." [74] However, he admitted that legislation as to hours had the advantage that it applied to all employers, although he added that competition across State lines decreased this advantage. He favored legislation against child labor and employers liability laws.

In 1884, at its very first convention, the Federation of Trades, which became the American Federation of Labor, declared that legislation was not the remedy. It believed that it was inadvisable to ask the introduction of the eight-hour day by law; that a united demand for shorter hours, supported by a strong organization, would "be far more effective than a thousand laws, whose execution depends upon the good will of aspiring politicians or sycophantic department officials." [75] Powderly disagreed with this philosophy, which was to supplant his own. He felt that the land question and monopoly came first.

The head of the new organization was Samuel Gompers, an English-born Jew, who remained the head till his death in 1924. Always vigorously opposed to a labor party, he said that the workingman wanted to protect his rights; he wanted labor men in Congress and in the legislatures, but not as members of a labor party. The primary objects of the American Federation of Labor, he asserted in 1911, have been "the protection of the wage-worker, now; to increase his wages; to cut hours off the long work-day, which was killing him; to improve the safety and the sanitary conditions of the workshop; to free him from the tyrannies, petty or otherwise, which served to make his existence a slavery. These, in the nature of things, I repeat, were and are the primary objects of trade-unionism." [76]

Gompers asserted that the Federation had "uniformly refused to surrender this conviction, and to rush to the support of any of the numerous society-saving or society-destroying schemes which decade by decade have been sprung upon this country." The labor

---

[73] Mitchell, *Organized Labor*, Preface, p. ix.   [74] *Ibid.*, p. 128.
[75] Powderly, *op. cit.*, p. 499.
[76] Samuel Gompers, *Labor and the Common Welfare*, p. 20.

movement would have none of any Utopia, none of that "will-o-the-wisp, a new society, constructed from rainbow materials,—a system of society on which even the dreamers have never agreed." [77]

He was suspicious of eight hour legislation. If the workers, he said, "surrender control over working relations to legislative and administrative agents, they put their industrial liberty at the disposal of state agents. They strip themselves bare of means of defense; they can no longer defend themselves by the strike. To insure liberty and personal welfare, personal relations must be controlled only by those concerned." [78] Legislation might be the quickest way to get results, but he asked whether it were the best. If the eight hour day were forced on labor, labor either might not appreciate it or actually resent it. It must be fought for, to be appreciated and therefore permanent.

The workers wanted only such action by legislation as they could not get for themselves. He enumerated some of the things the workers demanded in legislation: the eight hour day on public work, an employers' liability law, limitation of child labor, sanitation laws, regulation of convict labor, restriction of immigration. [79] These, labor could not obtain for itself.

Gompers opposed government ownership because he feared bureaucracy, and because labor could not strike against the government.

Though his philosophy was, in Commons' phrase, one of wage consciousness, it was a robust philosophy, for all that. He ridiculed the tendency to ask a law to cure every evil; and called for a "strong, red-blooded, rugged independence and will power to grapple with the wrong of the world and to establish justice through the volition of those concerned." [80]

The dominant labor philosophy changed, then, from a general philosophy, which was concerned with all the political demands of the time (Greenbacks, taxation of inheritances and land increment, the attack on monopoly), to a philosophy of self-help, distrustful of legislation, interested in the ends desired by a class, but with a strong individualistic and self-reliant basis. I shall defer until the chapter on Socialistic thought in America, the treatment of the more radical philosophy of American labor.

[77] "Annual Report to A.F.L. Convention, 1911," *Ibid.*, p. 20.   [78] *Ibid.*, p. 45.
[79] *Ibid.*, pp. 46–47.   [80] *Ibid.*, p. 53.

GRANGERISM

Let us now revert to the political revolt against the new industrialism and the laissez faire of the post-war years. By the end of the sixties, a revolt against the railroads was under way. The railroads, which had been encouraged by public grant and hailed as blessings, were being attacked as monopolies and the source of most of the ills of the farmer and the small business man of the Middle and Far West. The great extensions had been pushed with feverish energy. Great bond issues had been floated.

Charles Francis Adams noted that the "insufficiency of Western capital and the pressing need of new channels of communication with the East, assumed an ever-increasing prominence; and thus railroads, more railroads, were the constant longing of the Western man and the unceasing burden of his speech. . . . Railroads could not," the Westerner thought, "be purchased at too high a price; no inducements were too large with which to tempt foreign capital." [81]

It was inevitable that discrimination in rates between persons and localities should result. At first, it was believed that competition would solve all difficulties. But consolidations and pooling developed, and the demand arose that the state regulate rates.

The anti-public attitude of many railroad men, high rates, discriminations in rates, and political interference by the railroads were given by Solon J. Buck, the historian of the Granger movement, as the chief causes of the Granger revolt.[82] Charles Francis Adams ascribed it to competition and bad manners.[83]

In 1867 the first local Order of the Patrons of Husbandry was organized, and in the same year the National Grange of the Patrons of Husbandry.[84] It was first organized for social and educational purposes, but soon began to express itself on the question of railroad rates and elevator charges. In 1869 the Illinois farmers, in convention, declared that "the present rates of taxation and transportation are unreasonable and oppressive, and ought to be reduced;" that the remedy ought to be enforced and if more legislation were needed, it should be enacted.[85]

---

[81] Charles Francis Adams, Jr. "The Granger Movement," *North American Review,* Vol. CXX, pp. 394, 397 (1875).
[82] Solon J. Buck, *The Granger Movement,* pp. 12-15.
[83] Adams, *North American Review,* Vol. CXX, p. 399.
[84] Buck, pp. 40, 42.   [85] Commons, *Documentary History,* Vol. X, p. 45.

Shelby M. Cullom, who was then governor of Illinois, in his message of 1869, observed that in our reliance on competition, we had granted railroad charters to all who "asked for them." The result had been the construction of railroads in all parts of the country, "many of them through districts of country without business, or even population, as well as between all business centers and through populous, fertile, and well-cultivated regions. Free trade in railroad building and the too liberal use of municipal credit in their aid has induced the building of some lines which are wholly unnecessary, and which crowd, duplicate, and embarrass lines previously built and which were fully adequate to the needs of the community." [86] But he said that competition had not resulted according to the public anticipation. The competing companies "worked without sufficient remuneration at competing points; and to make good the losses resulting, were often guilty of extortion at the non-competing points." The railroads, threatened with the power of the government, "indulged in the language of defiance, and attempted to control legislation to their own advantage." [87]

In 1869, the Illinois legislature declared that all railroads were public highways, free to all persons under such regulations as may be prescribed by law, and that the general assembly should from time to time establish maximum rates preventing extortion and discrimination. In 1871, it passed laws regulating passenger and freight rates and elevator charges.

One hundred and thirty-two granges were organized in 1871; 1,150 in 1872. Of these, no less than 652 were in Iowa. On May 1, 1873, there were 3,360, and by August 2 of the same year, 5,062. Then they spread with great rapidity. On September 1, 1874, they reached the peak,—21,697. By July 1, 1876, the number had fallen to 15,127.

The Springfield Convention of Illinois Farmers, in 1873, resolved that all chartered monopolies not regulated and controlled by law, "have proved in that respect detrimental to the public prosperity, corrupt in their management and dangerous to republican institutions." [88] Railroads not subject to control were, they said, "arbitrary, extortionate, and as opposed to free institutions and free commerce between states as were the feudal barons of the Middle

---

[86] Cullom, *Fifty Years of Public Service*, p. 308.   [87] *Ibid.*, pp. 308, 309.
[88] Commons, *Documentary History*, Vol. X, p. 52.

Ages." It resolved that this despotism, which "defies our laws, plunders our shippers, impoverishes our people, and corrupts our government, shall be subdued and made to subserve the public interest at whatever cost." It said that the contest should go on until "these corporations acknowledge the supremacy of law." [89] It demanded that the legislature fix rates; that railroads be declared public highways, and that they be required to make connections. It opposed free passes and watered stock.[90]

In 1873, the National Congress of Farmers struck the note which later was to become dominant. It declared that since a railroad, is "practically a monopoly, controlling the transportation of nearly all the country through which it passes, and that, as competition, except at a few points, can not be relied upon to fix rates, therefore it becomes the duty of the state to fix reasonable maximum rates, affording a fair remuneration to the transporter, and without being an onerous charge to the producer and consumer." [91]

Thus early these farmers realized that competition was not the complete answer in the case of natural monopolies. It took the public longer before it was willing to give up the attempt to force full competition between all natural monopolies, and to see that regulation must be the major resource.

Yet even these farmers, while doubting competition, declared against the consolidation of competing lines.

The question of the power of the legislature to fix railroad and elevator charges was fought out bitterly in the courts; and was settled, as we have seen, in the famous case of Munn vs. Illinois and its companion cases, decided in 1877.

The railroads fought the Granger legislation bitterly, and with such success that to this day the very word, "Granger," connotes to most of us hasty and ill-advised legislation. Yet the Illinois statute of 1873 is still on the statute books. In view of the evils that were to be met, the attitude of some railroad men, and the general ignorance of the problem at that time, it is doubtful if any better results could have been expected. And today, as we look back, we must give a tribute to the obscure men who, in the face of ridicule and bitter opposition, maintained the right of the public for control.

Buck notes the protest of one hundred and three Chicago

---

[89] *Ibid.*, p. 55.   [90] *Ibid.*, pp. 55–58.   [91] *Ibid.*, p. 65.

merchants against the Granger laws. They admitted that they had been subjected to extortion and discrimination, but answered that they had been generally able to obtain redress from the railroads. They said that the rate laws had hurt their business, increased the cost of shipment to the interior of the State, and had not lessened the cost of shipment to tide-water. They had rendered it almost impossible to borrow capital to build competing roads.[92]

A bitter fight was made to repeal the Illinois law, but it was defeated. Most of the Granger laws, however, were soon repealed. Their general effect was slight, but they were the necessary precursors of the better ordered legislation of later years.

The public mind was not clear on the subject of competition. Charles Francis Adams declared, "The simple truth is that competition, properly so-called, among railroads, except as a perturbing element, is simply impossible. It is impossible for two reasons: in the first place, to have it at all, every locality must be served by at least two independent and competing railroad routes, and it is a physical impossibility that nine points out of ten should have more than one; in the second place, it is obvious that an active competition between two or more agencies,—the number, however, being always very limited,—no one of which can withdraw from the field, must necessarily result in the complete mastery of the stronger, and the ultimate absorption of the weaker." [93]

Here we see the issue of the railroad and the trust questions of the next fifty years. On one side was the desire for the old competition, and the dread of combination. Carried to its end, it meant war to the uttermost until the strongest survived. It was combination by elimination. Holmes called it *bellum omnium contra omnes.* On the other hand was the constant pressure for combination. Carried to its conclusion, the demand for competition and the aversion from combination would prevent all combination. Carried to its extreme conclusion, the desire to combine would permit complete monopoly. But, in practise, there were few who would permit no combination, and few who would allow complete consolidation. It was impossible to have competition between two roads for every village. It was necessary that some communities be served by a single road. But we were not yet ready to say that a

[92] Buck, *Granger Movement*, p. 156.
[93] Adams, "The Granger Movement," *North American Review*, Vol. CXX, p. 399.

whole section of the country should be served by a single road. Nor have we come to that end yet. While we have permitted and even forced large railroad consolidations, we have kept the ideal of competition in service between the few remaining roads.

But, in any event, so long as complete competition is impossible, regulation must supplement competition. Our system is a combination of competition and regulation, and has been for a generation. The issue from first to last, therefore, in the case both of railroads and industry, has been how large the units shall be which we allow to combine. It is the issue between large units and small.

GREENBACKISM

The aftermath of the Civil War was a period of reaction, of severe decline in the price level. During the war, due partly to the usual extraordinary demand for goods during a great war, partly to the withdrawal of large numbers of men from productive industry, partly to the war inflation, there had been a great increase in prices. The price level rose from 93 in 1860 to 223 in January, 1865. Even in December, 1865, it was 184.[94] Some $400,000,000 of greenbacks had been issued. The amount outstanding on June 30, 1866 was $400,600,000.[95] As we shall see, some of the smaller issues of government securities (no one knows how much) passed from hand to hand as currency.

The rise in prices brought great distress and loud demands for alleviation of the condition. Moreover, the war issues of securities were in great confusion. A great mass of temporary securities had been issued, particularly in 1865. With the close of the war, Hugh McCulloch, Secretary of the Treasury, determined to fund the debt, to retire the greenbacks, and resume specie payments. In 1866, the funding bill, sometimes called the contraction bill, was passed. It provided for the funding of certain of the issues of war securities into six per cent gold bonds; for the retirement of $10,000,000 of greenbacks, and thereafter at the rate of $4,000,000 a month,—all in the direction of the resumption of specie payments.

The debt was funded. By 1867, the six-twenties and the seven-thirties were almost entirely converted into six per cent government

---

[94] George F. Warren and Frank A. Pearson, *Prices*, p. 12. 1910–14 is the base at 100.
[95] Davis R. Dewey, *Financial History of the United States*, p. 341.

bonds. The contraction of the greenbacks was carried out for some months, until about $44,000,000 were retired; but then clamor arose in Congress that the contraction was too sudden and too great, and the retirement of the greenbacks was stopped, never to be resumed. The Resumption Act of 1875 permitted further reduction but the power was not used. The remaining greenbacks were left part of the currency. As the saying went, the country grew up to the greenbacks. The expansion of business absorbed them.

Prices slowly fell. By 1870, they were at a level of 135. The rapid post-war expansion of business, with its feverish railroad building, the real estate speculation in the middle west, was followed by the panic of 1873 and a long and trying depression which lasted for years. By 1879, prices were down to a level of 90.[96]

The sequel to such a train of events is inevitably found in politics. John R. Commons points out that the resulting greenback demand in the United States had two stages: the first, he says, was that of the National Labor Union, from 1867 to 1872; and the second, that of the Greenback Party, after 1875.

The National Labor Union theory was an offshoot of the current socialist theory of value, money, and prices. It proposed to utilize the government's war debt to furnish capital to labor. It reasoned (according to Commons), that capital was solely the product of labor, that it "contained no independent power of production, and deserved no reward of abstinence." [97] The small farmer and merchant were pressed for capital, and they objected to paying interest to the banks, when they were convinced that capital was produced by labor and that capital deserved no reward.

"The Address to Working-men," issued by the National Labor Union in 1867, referred to the "false, vicious financial system," which "endows capital with powers of increase largely in excess of the development of national wealth by natural productions." [98] Labor, it said, increases wealth by three per cent yearly; whereas capital, in manufacturing and banking, accumulated at a rate three or four times as great.

The Convention of the Union in 1867 went into the matter more fully. It declared that property is the product of physical or

---

[96] Warren and Pearson, *Prices*, pp. 12, 13.
[97] Commons, *Documentary History*, Vol. IX, p. 36.   [98] *Ibid.*, p. 150.

intellectual labor; that money is the medium of distribution for non-producing capital and producing labor; that the power to make money and regulate its value is an essential attribute of sovereignty. It was subversive of the principles of justice to delegate the power to issue money to the national banks. The national banking act should be repealed, and the legal tender notes made the exclusive currency of the nation. The money monopoly was "the parent of all monopolies,—the very root and essence of slavery." [99] Money must be instituted on such a wise and just principle that, "instead of being a power to centralize the wealth in the hands of a few bankers, usurers, middlemen, and non-producers generally, it shall be a power that will distribute products to producers in accordance with the labor or service performed in their production,—the servant and not the master of labor." [100]

They therefore presented the greenback proposal,—that treasury notes be made a legal tender for all debts, public and private, and be convertible at the option of the holder into government bonds. If the rate on the government bonds were fixed slightly below the increase in the national wealth by natural production, say at three per cent, the national debt would be paid within thirty years without the imposition of a farthing of taxes.

If, in other words, a bondholder wanted currency, he would take his bonds to the government and get currency, and use it in his business or loan it at a rate in excess of the government rate. If he preferred bonds to currency, he would take his currency to the government and get three per cent bonds. The result might mean the increase of the currency by the amount of the bonds at that time. But any farmer or merchant could get all the capital he wanted at three per cent. He would only have to buy bonds paying three per cent interest, and get currency for them.

Then came the panic of 1873. The ensuing period of falling prices and unemployment brought a new Greenback agitation. This time it was a Greenbackism of inflation, of an attempt to raise prices.

The Greenback Party asserted that the whole trouble with the country was lack of money, and that the hard times and the falling prices were caused by the post-war contraction of the currency. Peter Cooper of New York, a wealthy and elderly iron manufacturer, of simple and kindly character, self-educated and

[99] *Ibid.,* p. 178. [100] *Ibid.,* p. 179.

untrained in economic thought, was tireless in behalf of the Greenback cause. He was its candidate for President in 1876. He began his agitation as early as 1867. He held the basic idea of the Greenbackers—that no private person or corporation should have the power "to make or unmake the money of the country." [101] The government, alone, should make the currency.

The volume of the currency should be equal to the volume at the end of the Civil War. That volume of currency had "lifted the American people into a state of unexampled prosperity, never before known in this or any other country." [102] We could restore that prosperity by restoring the currency to the same figure. This currency should always be convertible into government bonds. It should not be subject to sudden contractions and expansions; but should be "regulated by established law, based on scientific facts and principles of a just system of national finances." [103] It should be scientifically controlled, so that it would be always sufficient for the business of the country. Its volume should depend on exchanges and the growth of the population. [104]

To stimulate business again, Cooper argued that the currency should be restored to its volume at the close of the Civil War. He insisted that the circulation at the close of the Civil War was $2,192,395,527. In 1873, he said, it was only $631,488,676. He asserted time and again that it was this terrific contraction which was the cause of the fall in prices and of all our woes. In familiar language, he said that men had to pay, in dear money, the debts they had contracted when money was cheap.

So he would increase the supply of money to the amount in 1865. If his figures were correct, this would have been an increase of 240 per cent. Indeed, his plan would have permitted an increase up to the amount of the government debt, $2,800,000,000, and that would have meant an increase in the supply of money of 340 per cent.

As this argument—that the post-war deflation had been a billion and a half dollars—runs all through the arguments of the Populists twenty years later, and the free silver debate, it may be well to analyze it a little more particularly.

In the first place, the amount of money in circulation on June

---

[101] Peter Cooper, *Ideas for a Science of Good Government*, p. 10.
[102] *Ibid.*, p. 12.   [103] *Ibid.*, p. 10.   [104] *Ibid.*, p. 103.

30, 1873 was $751,000,000, or $120,000,000 larger than the figure Cooper gives for November, 1873. The amount of money in circulation on June 30, 1865 was $715,000,000, and on these figures there was no deflation at all. But Cooper and his friends claimed that well over a billion of the legal tender notes and the notes bearing seven and three-tenths per cent interest (issued as part of the war financing in 1864 and 1865), were actually used as money by the people in 1865; and when these notes were converted into government bonds after 1865, the money in circulation was decreased more than a billion dollars.

This was true to some extent; but the amount of such notes used as money, no one knows.[105] The most careful study is that of Wesley C. Mitchell in his "A History of the Greenbacks." He concludes that it is impossible to tell how far the legal tender notes, the certificates of indebtedness, and the seven-thirties were used as currency. The total amount of money, greenbacks, certificates of indebtedness, and seven-thirties outstanding in 1865 was $1,652,800,000. But, according to Mitchell, any estimate of how much of that amount was used as currency would be a mere guess and "positively misleading." [106] At any rate, the total could not have

[105] Hugh McCulloch, the Secretary of the Treasury in 1865, in his report in December, 1865, estimated that the money in circulation on October 31, 1865, was about $704,000,000. He thought that, in addition, about $30,000,000 of the interest bearing legal tender notes and some of the seven-thirties were in circulation. He said that it appeared that "without including the seven and three-tenths notes,—many of the small denominations of which were in circulation as money, and all of which tend in some measure to swell the inflation,—the paper money of the country amounted, on the thirty-first of October, to the sum of $734,218,038.20, which has been daily increased by the notes furnished to the national banks and is likely to be still further increased by those to which they are entitled, until the amount authorized by law ($300,000,000) shall have been reached, subject to such reduction as may be made by the withdrawal of the notes of the State Banks." *Report, Secretary of the Treasury, 1865,* p. 9.

[106] Wesley C. Mitchell, *A History of the Greenbacks,* p. 181.

"How far these notes (namely, the interest bearing legal tender notes and the seven-thirties) were employed as currency, is altogether uncertain." (*Ibid.,* p. 174) He notes that McCulloch reported in December, 1865, that "it was safe to estimate that $30,000,000 of the one and two year notes and the compound interest notes were so used." (*Ibid.,* p. 176.)

Indirectly, Mitchell said the banks used the notes as reserves for greenbacks that bore interest. Most of the six per cent certificates of indebtedness "were paid out to contractors, and by them used either as collateral for procuring bank loans or directly as currency. Much of the time, certificates of indebtedness were at a small discount, but despite this, they passed freely from hand to hand as current funds." Similar use, he adds, was made of the "seven-thirties." In the summer of 1864, Secretary Fessenden offered seven-thirty notes of the second issue in small denominations to army officers and soldiers, in payment of their wages. "Over $20,000,000 were thus paid out in place of greenbacks." (*Ibid.,* pp. 177–78.)

After listing the total amount of money, notes and greenbacks, legal tender green-

been more than $1,652,000,000; and how much less it was, no one knows. Yet Cooper claimed that $2,000,000,000 was actually in use as currency in 1865. It is evident that the contraction was much less than he claimed.

Cooper forgot, moreover, that at the end of the war prices were felt to be oppressively high. The very object of currency contraction had been to reduce prices. The feverish energy of the war had, of course, stimulated business, as all wars do, and had caused prices to rise; but the rise was, of course, unhealthy and reaction was inevitable. The post-war fall in prices caused great distress to debtors, as such a fall always does; but an inflation back to the old circulation, particularly if the greater volume had attained any velocity, would have caused a tremendous rise in prices and business turmoil.

The Greenback agitation for a currency stable in value was strikingly similar to much that we have gone through in the past few years. It has a familiar sound in these days of talk of a managed currency. But Cooper did not explain—any more than our current advocates of a managed currency explain—how political pressure is to leave the managers of a currency free to manage it. When warned of the dangers of his plan, he merely answered that we must trust the government and "free principles and democratic forms." [107] Moreover, today as then, there is serious question whether prices can be kept stable even if political interference is prevented.

But Cooper and his Greenback friends did, after all, strike at one of the great defects of our financial system,—that it was not elastic. It contracted the currency in time of panic, and it did not respond easily to the requirements of business. It was not until

backs, and certificates of indebtedness and seven-thirties, which may have been in use as money in 1865,—$1,652,800,000,—Mitchell adds that estimates of the volume of money in circulation in 1865 "are subject to a much wider margin of error than is commonly the case,—and few would be found to claim a high degree of accuracy for statements of this sort under the most favorable circumstances. To cast up the totals of the above tables would be not only useless, but positively misleading, because several of the items are mere guesses; and in the case of others, where the amounts are reasonably certain, not all of the sums set down were in use at any time as currency. Nor could any estimate be made on the basis of the totals that would command confidence. But, while the amount of currency in circulation is not known and can not be known, it is evident from the discussion that not least among the unhappy consequences of the legal tender acts was the disorder into which the circulating medium was thrown,—a disorder that caused much inconvenience to the business public." (*Ibid.*, p. 181.)

[107] Cooper, *Ideas for a Science of Good Government*, p. 107.

the Federal Reserve Act of 1913 that a currency was provided that could expand and contract as business expands and contracts. The question of the lack of a sufficient currency and its inelasticity was to be fought over for a generation by the populist and free silver advocates.

HENRY GEORGE

Two books in the decade after 1879 exerted a large influence on our thought. They were Henry George's "Progress and Poverty" and Edward Bellamy's "Looking Backward."

George was born in Philadelphia, the son of a ship captain. He read widely in history, fiction, and poetry, but his formal schooling was brief. He left school at fourteen and went to sea. He was a printer for a time, drifted to the gold fields, was a farm-hand and a tramp, tried several newspaper ventures, and returned to printing. He lived in California at the time of the great land boom. "Land," says his son, Henry George, Jr., in his biography of his father, "at even far removed points therefore rose to extravagant figures." Speculation in land "ran far in advance of its use." [108] George told how one day he asked a teamster how much land was worth. The teamster replied, "I don't know exactly, but there is a man over there who will sell some land for a thousand dollars an acre."

"Like a flash," said George, "it came upon me that there was the reason of advancing poverty with advancing wealth. With the growth of population, land grows in value, and the men who work it must pay more for the privilege. I turned back amidst quiet thought to the perception that then came to me—and has been with me ever since." [109]

George found that speculation in land had driven the price of land so high that an immigrant in 1871 was forced, as a general thing, to pay a charge to a middleman before he could use the land. Men were holding thousands and hundreds of thousands of acres for a price. "Across many of these vast estates," said George, "a strong horse can not gallop in a day, and one might travel for miles and miles over fertile ground where no plow has ever struck, but which is all owned and on which no settler can come to make

---

[108] Henry George, Jr., *Life of Henry George*, Vol. I, p. 210.   [109] *Ibid.*, p. 210.

himself a home, unless he pay such a tribute as the lord of the domain may choose to exact." [110]

Henry George was appalled at the misery of the working classes, and felt that the disuse of the land was a criminal failure to use the resources at hand for the benefit of the people. He had lived in the mining settlements when "there was a universal if unwritten law among them that 'claims' should be limited in size, and that ownership should be conditioned upon use." Squatters had "constantly asserted the principle commonly recognized through the whole frontier country, that any man was free to use land that was not already actually in use." So the son concluded of the father, "His political economy he got from nature herself." [111]

We need only sketch his economic theory. Here it is important only so far as it explains his political proposal. Broadly speaking, George was orthodox in his economic theory. But he attacked, with all his spirit, the wages fund theory,—that there was a fixed sum available for labor, which still had some support, and the Malthusian theory,—that population must ever press on the sources of production. He held that wages were not the product of wages and capital, but that they are the sole product of the wage-earner. Capital made possible the elaborate division of labor which we have in our society, but wages themselves are the direct product of the worker's own contribution. He argued that wages are always high in new countries, and low in old countries.

He concluded that wages are equal to what a man could make for himself on land where he paid no rent; for, if he could make more for himself without paying rent, he would do so. "Each productive laborer," he said, "as he works, creates his wages; and with every additional laborer," there is "an addition to the common stock of wealth, which, generally speaking, is considerably greater than the amount he draws as wages." [112]

Nor, he argued, does the situation change when population increases, for productivity increases with increased numbers. The older countries, with denser populations and advanced industry, are always the wealthiest countries. He claimed that history shows that countries grow wealthier as the population grows, and the division of labor is carried on progressively.

---

[110] *Ibid.*, p. 221.   [111] *Ibid.*, p. 232.
[112] Henry George, *Progress and Poverty*, p. 153.

The explanation can not be, he said, that "nature yields less to the increasing drafts which an increasing population makes upon her; for the increased efficiency of labor makes the progressive state a state of continually increasing production per capita, and the countries of densest population, other things being equal, are always the countries of greatest wealth." The earth, he said, could maintain a thousand billions of people as easily as a thousand millions. "Life does not use up the forces that maintain life." [113]

Likewise, George argued that interest is determined precisely as wages are determined. Interest is simply the return from capital, as wages are the return for labor; and capital and labor together could receive only such return as they could "have produced on land free to them, without the payment of rent; that is, the least productive land or point in use." [114]

Both labor and capital are limited by the iron law of rent. As rent increases, interest and wages will fall.

So George concluded that as population increases, interest and wages fall. Labor is inevitably forced to a bare subsistence, because it is forced to the wage which a man could earn on land which is without rent; and as population increases, this land becomes ever less valuable.

George proposed therefore to confiscate rent,—the unearned increment. This rent which had formerly gone to the landowner, would go to the state, and the vast amounts thus realized could be used not only to enable the state to forego all other forms of taxation, but enable it to build schools and roads and stimulate the distribution of wealth in a hundred fecund ways.

He said that he offered the "simple yet sovereign remedy, which will raise wages, increase the earnings of capital, extirpate pauperism, abolish poverty, give remunerative employment to whoever wishes it, afford free scope to human powers, lessen crime, elevate morals and taste and intelligence, purify government, and carry civilization to yet nobler heights," namely, the appropriation of rent by taxation. [115]

Our taxation, George argued, was a clog on progress and industry. All taxes upon manufactures, upon commerce, on capital and improvements checked production. The only taxes which did not check production were taxes upon monopolies, and land was

[113] *Ibid.*, p. 153.   [114] *Ibid.*, p. 171.   [115] *Ibid.*, p. 403.

the great monopoly. A tax on land would destroy speculation in land, and actually increase production. It would not add to prices, it was easy and certain of collection, and, above all, it was equal on all.

It would lift the burden of taxes from productive industry, and all would be free to produce, unhampered by taxation. It would increase wages by throwing new land into use, and the vast amounts realized would enable the state to support education and public services in a way never dreamed of before. He concluded, "Let imagination fill out the picture; its colors grow too bright for words to paint. Consider the moral elevation, the intellectual activity, the social life. Consider how, by a thousand actions and interactions, the members of every community are linked together; and how, in the present conditions of things, even the fortunate few who stand upon the apex of the social pyramid must suffer, though they know it not, from the want, ignorance, and degradation that are underneath." [116]

In the last part of his book, George argued that his plan was in accord with the great law of human progress. He rejected as a brutal and materialistic explanation what he called the current theory,—that progress was the result of the struggle for existence. He asked why the great civilizations of the East had decayed, and answered that they and all civilizations had declined because they had not followed the true law of progress, which is association in equality.[117]

Men progress as they tend to come closer together; but conflict and inequality lessen, then check, and then reverse the process. Civilization depends on Association, and it has always progressed as men learned to associate and work with each other, and it is always stopped or retarded when inequality develops. And the greatest cause of inequality is the inequality in land. Land should belong to all, and when it did not, the seeds of decay were inextricably planted. It was a "self-evident truth." [118] Land belonged to men by natural right. This was the ardent belief which animated the whole book: the natural right to the land.

George instanced the misery in our cities, the corruption of our politics, the unrest in industry, and declared that the signs of decay were on every hand in our own country.

[116] *Ibid.*, p. 469.   [117] *Ibid.*, pp. 505, 509.   [118] *Ibid.*, p. 542.

With great eloquence and a religious fervor, he asked us to turn to Liberty and Justice, and obey and follow them, and realize "the City of God on earth, with its walls of jasper and its gates of pearl." [119]

Quotation can not do justice to the emotional appeal, the deep sincerity, the ardent enthusiasm of the book. It was first published in San Francisco in 1879, by private subscription. In 1880, Appleton added it to its list. It was then published in England. For almost a year it was a dead book, and then it suddenly began to move. Millions of copies were sold in England and in the United States, and it was soon translated and sold all over Europe.

I have said that George derived his ideas from his own experience. He noted that "the French Economists of the last century, headed by Quesnay and Turgot, proposed just what I have proposed. . ." Geiger notes that he dedicated his "Protection or Free Trade" to the "memory of those illustrious Frenchmen of a century ago, Quesnay, Turgot, Mirabeau, Condorcet, Dupont and their fellows, who in the night of despotism foresaw the glories of the coming day"; but agrees with Professor Gide, that "his tribute loses its point somewhat, when we remember that he admits that he had never read them." [120]

George himself declared that it was a mistake to assume that men must draw their ideas from others, and not from life. The tendency of scholars to relate their thought to a long tradition, has been well characterized by William James. He referred to the infrequency "with which, in philosophical literature, metaphysical questions are discussed directly and on their own merits." [121] The over-professionalism of philosophers required, he said, that "you must tie your opinion to Aristotle's or Spinoza's; you must define it by its distance from Kant's; you must refute your rival's view by identifying it with Protagoras's. Thus does all spontaneity of thought, all freshness of conception get destroyed. Everything you touch is shopworn." [122] In a subject like philosophy, he added, "it is really fatal to lose connection with the open air of human nature, and to think in terms of shop-tradition only." [123] He insisted that a man's vision "is the great fact about him." [124]

---

[119] *Ibid.*, p. 549.
[120] George Raymond Geiger, *The Philosophy of Henry George*, pp. 172–73.
[121] William James, *A Pluralistic Universe*, p. 15.
[122] *Ibid.*, p. 16.   [123] *Ibid.*, p. 17.   [124] *Ibid.*, p. 20.

This was quite in the line of George's own conviction. He protested that it was a mistake "to which the critics who are themselves mere compilers are liable, to think that men must draw from one another to see the same truths or to fall into the same errors." The stars of the Dipper and the Southern Cross, he went on, "are seen by all who scan the starry heavens, though the names by which men know them are various." [125] In his case, he insisted, there was certainly no derivation from the past. He said that he well remembered how "the commonplace remark of a passing teamster to a commonplace question crystallized, as by a lightning flash, my brooding thoughts into coherency, and I there and then recognized the natural order,—one of those experiences that make those who have had them feel thereafter that they can vaguely appreciate what mystics and poets have called the 'ecstatic vision.' Yet at that time I had never heard of the Physiocrats, or even read a line of Adam Smith." [126]

Again, he asserted that he certainly neither picked up his theory "second-hand nor got it by inspiration." He declared that he came to it by "a long, laborious, and most conscientious investigation." If he had been enabled to "emancipate myself from ideas which have fettered far abler men, it is doubtless due to the fact that my study of social problems was in a country like this [California], where they have been presented with peculiar directness, and perhaps also to the fact that I was led to think a good deal before I had a chance to do much reading." [127]

However much we may sympathize with George's belief in direct sources, we may remark in passing that, after all, there is a mean between direct contact with reality and contact through the thoughts of others, for the studies of others frequently save us from mistakes and misconceptions which it took years to disclose.

We need not dwell long here on George's economic theory. It is clear that he was wrong in his theory that wages are the direct result of the contribution of labor; for capital, as Taussig showed, advances wages to labor far in advance of the realization of proceeds from the sale of the product. The product may not be sold until many months after labor has completed its work and been paid for it. Moreover, it may be doubted that wages are fixed by

[125] Henry George, Jr., *Life of Henry George*, Vol. I, pp. 228–29.
[126] *Ibid.*, Vol. I, p. 229.   [127] *Ibid.*, p. 325. Quoted in Geiger, *op. cit.*, p. 216.

the return of the man on no rent land. This is certainly not the measure of wages where the laborer has no access to no rent land. Moreover, labor, in highly productive industries and well-organized industrial societies, is paid more than it can earn on no rent land. Taussig makes the test of wages the present value of the marginal product of labor.[128]

Like others who believed that they have refuted the Malthusian theory, George did not refute it, but rather only showed the forces that check its operation. George asked if the fact that "all of the things which furnish man's subsistence have the power to multiply many fold—some of them many thousand fold, and some of them many million or even billion fold—while he is only doubling his numbers," did not show that, "let human beings increase to the full extent of their reproductive power, the increase of population can never exceed subsistence."[129] But, I may answer, while one grain of wheat may multiply itself many fold, one acre of land does not yield many fold the number of bushels which it yielded on the first cultivation.

George argued, too, that while wealth increased as population increased, wages declined. But it has often been pointed out that wages do not necessarily become lower as population increases; and, on the other hand, that wealth per capita does not necessarily increase as population grows. Wages—real wages—in highly developed countries, with well-organized divisions of labor and highly productive industries, are higher than in primitive or new countries; while, on the other hand, some populous countries, like India and China, have less wealth per capita than many less populous countries.

But we are here concerned with his political proposal. George proposed to make the tax on land the sole tax. The first question was whether the tax on land would be sufficient to equal the needs for revenue, particularly in countries where land values were stagnant. His critics asked also how he would distinguish the value of land from the improvements. George replied that it could be done

---

[128] F. W. Taussig, *Principles of Economics*, Vol. II, p. 214. Alfred Marshall adopted the same test (*Principles of Economics*, Vol. I, p. 586). John Bates Clark, in his *The Distribution of Wealth*, observed that George's "theory puts the man in the shanty into a position that is so strategic as to enable him to dominate workmen of every class, to fix the amount of their wages, and so to control the land on which they live" (p. 89).

[129] George, *Progress and Poverty*, p. 130.

precisely as it is done now under the real estate tax; and that if there were any difficulty, he would let the land owner suffer. Again, it was pointed out that no compensation for land owners was contemplated, where land values declined. They would be taxed if their values increased, and would gain nothing if they declined.

But the main point urged against him was that if the profit in land values were taken away, the extension and growth of the community would be threatened. Men would not risk the development of new portions of a city or of a country, if they had no prospect of reward. In our own country, it is well known that the lure of land profits was one of the greatest forces in the development of the Middle and Far West, and it was urged that the day of development had not passed when this lure was no longer necessary.

The essential clash was between a priori right and experimental politics. David Starr Jordan took issue on the central belief that there was a natural—a divine—right to the land. Property, he answered, is "not a divine right. It is a creation of social agreement." The only question was whether it worked—whether the results "on individual and social development are better than those obtained through other forms of land tenure and of taxation. . . . Argument from purpose, intention, or divine fitness is a mere quibble of words." [130]

Professor Seligman, of Columbia, objected that the central theory of the single tax advocates was that property arises only from labor, and that there could be no property in a gift of nature. Like Jordan, he answered that the theory of natural rights must yield to the theory of social utility; that ownership of land was the outgrowth of social forces and a long history, and had shown its adaptability to human needs.

Moreover, the land owner was not the only one who had an unearned increment. "Nothing," Seligman remarked, "is wholly the result of unaided individual labor." [131] The socialists, he said, were more logical than George; for they held that unearned gains were the basis of the entire property system.

Seligman also attacked the central theory that taxation should be in proportion to benefits received, instead of ability to pay. A

[130] David Starr Jordan, *The True Basis of Economics*, p. 6.
[131] Edwin R. A. Seligman, *Essays in Taxation* (Copyright, 1896), p. 69.

rich man, he replied, may receive less benefit from the state than a poor man, but he ought to contribute more because of his ability, and all modern philosophy in politics and taxation was based on this theory.

But, on practical grounds, Seligman said that the single tax was inelastic; it could not be increased or lowered at will; it would prevent custom duties, and excise taxes on luxuries or undesirable uses. It would be a tax which only a small class would pay, and would thus encourage irresponsibility in government.

Moreover, he argued, as we have noted, that land values do not always increase, but often decrease; and that in many communities, as in some countries of Europe, there would be a decreasing revenue.

And he asserted that land values were not the only unearned increment: social environment and speculation have a myriad of aspects.

In new communities, he continued, there would be no land tax, for there were no land values. The result would be to penalize farming districts at the expense of cities, where improvements were far greater than the land values.

He ended by declaring that the tale was as old as the hills; that our remedy was no panacea, but could come only through slow evolution.

In "The Prophet of San Francisco," Louis F. Post, long a single tax advocate, answered this argument of Professor Seligman. He took issue chiefly with Seligman's claim that the right to land was based on social utility, and that taxation should be according to ability to pay instead of benefits. He said that Seligman gave "absolute denial of human rights as matter of natural law." [132] Post sturdily insisted that the effect of the social utility theory was to give indefeasible rights to property, and to place social ethics on "a tottering foundation." [133] Men, he insisted, did contribute their labor to produce things, and that was theirs; and nature contributed certain values, and that did not belong to man but to all men. Secondly, he contended that the duty to pay taxes did not depend on ability to pay, but on benefits received. It was again a fundamental clash of ideals: it was natural rights against social utility.

[132] Louis F. Post, *The Prophet of San Francisco*, p. 235.   [133] *Ibid.*, p. 237.

The results of the Single Tax movement in this country were disappointing, even to its friends. George carried on his campaign through his magazine, "The Standard," for some years. In 1888, the Single Tax organization was formed. In 1890, a petition for the single tax with 115,503 names was presented to Congress. The Single Tax League was organized in 1890. But Post admits that its accomplishments were disappointing.[134] The National Conference in 1916 was practically the end.

In other countries, the results of the single tax agitation were much greater. But George's indirect influence was greater than in his specific proposal. John Dewey remarks that it is impossible to conceive "any scheme of permanent tax reform, which does not include at least *some* part of George's appropriation by society for social purposes of rental value of land."[135] Many of our most conservative economists are sympathetic with proposals for the taxation of the future increment of land values.

George had an immense influence on the liberal thinkers of his time. He was vigorously opposed to socialism, but he had great influence on socialists. Sidney Webb said that it was "the enormous circulation of his 'Progress and Poverty,' which gave the touch which caused all the seething influences to crystallize into a popular Socialist movement."[136] Geiger quotes Shaw as testifying that "numbers of young men,—pupils of Mill, Spencer, Comte, Darwin, —roused by Mr. Henry George's 'Progress and Poverty,' left aside revolution and free thought, took to insurrectionary economics, studied Karl Marx, and became socialists."[137]

George's real influence was the influence of the man and his personality,—his warm and human and fervent personality, —which made him twice, without organization, a formidable candidate for mayor of New York, and made his funeral a national event. Men everywhere felt the glowing force of the man, his intense love of humanity, and his burning hatred of privilege and extortion.

In accepting the New York mayoralty nomination in 1886, he said that when he first came to New York from the West, "I saw and recognized for the first time the shocking contrast between monstrous wealth and debasing want. And here I made a vow from which I have never faltered, to seek out and remedy, if I

---

[134] *Ibid.*, pp. 141–46.   [135] Geiger, *op. cit.*, Preface, p. xi.
[136] *Ibid.*, p. 235.   [137] *Ibid.*, p. 235.

could, the cause that condemned little children to lead such a life as you know them to lead in the squalid districts." [138] In his second New York mayoralty campaign in 1897, he was introduced as a friend of the workingman. He replied, amid great applause, that he had never asked for special rights or special sympathy for the workingman. "What I stand for," he said, "is the equal rights of all men." [139]

As Dewey says, George's whole emphasis was on the assertion that economic and political phenomena "can not be understood nor regulated apart from consideration of consequences upon human values, upon human good; that is, apart from moral considerations." [140] He wanted to make the "dismal science" human; to breathe it with the spirit of living men and women; to make hope and purpose part of its considerations. The economist and the political scientist were not merely to observe facts and report them, but they were to be the comrades of the people's hopes.

Edward Bellamy

The other book which caused much discussion in the decade of the eighties was Edward Bellamy's "Looking Backward," published early in 1888. Bellamy was the son of a Baptist minister in Massachusetts, trained to be a lawyer. He was a newspaper man and a novelist for a few years, and then set out to write his book, first, as he said, "as a mere literary fantasy,—a fairy tale of social felicity." He seems to have drawn no inspiration from other Utopias, or from the socialistic writings of the period. He himself declared that "previous to the publication of the work," he never had "any affiliations with any class or sect of industrial or social reformers, nor, to make my confession complete, any particular sympathy with undertakings of the sort." But while working on his "literary fantasy," the idea of a grand social plan developed in his mind. He was greatly interested in military organization, and the idea came to him that the military system could be applied to the industrial army. This led, he said, "to a complete recasting both in form and purpose of the book I was engaged upon. Instead of a mere fairy tale of social perfection, it became the vehicle of a definite scheme of industrial organization." [141]

---

[138] Henry George, Jr., *Life of Henry George*, Vol. I, p. 192.
[139] *Ibid.*, Vol. II, p. 605. [140] Geiger, Preface, p. xii.
[141] Quoted in Nicholas P. Gilman, " 'Nationalism' in the United States," *Quarterly Journal of Economics*, Vol. IV, pp. 50, 60, 61 (Oct., 1889).

The book was a delightful dream by a young man, Julian West, who fell asleep in 1887 and woke in 2000. In a flowing and pleasing style, Bellamy imagined that the young man woke to find himself in a country where there was no poverty, no misery; where no one worked for profit and no one worked for gain, but each for the joy of the working. The state ordered how much should be produced; the state fixed prices, or rather the number of dollars which would be punched on the buyer's credit card.

The share of each person was the same. West expressed his astonishment when told this by Dr. Leete, in whose house he woke after his long sleep.[142] Of each man was required the same effort, and the reward of each was the same. "Desert," said Dr. Leete, "is a moral question, and the amount of the product a material quantity. . . . All men who do their best, do the same."[143] To the standard question of the cynic doubters, if human nature did not still require some incentive to effort, Dr. Leete asked if West really thought that "man is insensible to any motives save fear of want and love of luxury. . . ."[144]

Not higher wages, however, but honor, the inspiration of duty, patriotism, were the motives which inspired the soldiers in West's time, and now inspired the soldiers of the industrial realm of the year 2000. Men were graded according to their abilities, and regraded from time to time, and badges were given for distinctive service. There was, moreover, a natural desire to be able to do the work of greatest service and honor, and to rise in the scale of distinction.

There was no charity. Those whom we would call incapable of self-support were, as Dr. Leete said, "also men," and the idea that the unfortunate and the sick were not treated as well as the strong and capable, the idea that they should be treated as subjects of charity, was abhorrent.[145] Likewise, there was then no idea of menial labor or of difference in the worth of human service. All were servants of the state, and all were equal.[146]

Yet Dr. Leete insisted that there was freedom in the ordering of individual lives and the selection of vocations. Each man determined for himself what he would do.[147] While the obligation of some kind of service was compulsory, each man could elect what

---

[142] Edward Bellamy, *Looking Backward*, p. 93.
[143] *Ibid.*, p. 94.
[144] *Ibid.*, p. 96.
[145] *Ibid.*, pp. 133–35.
[146] *Ibid.*, pp. 156–57.
[147] *Ibid.*, p. 65.

his own service should be. Each man must serve three years as a common laborer, at the end of which he entered the field of his choice. It was the business of the administration to prevent overcrowding in any field, by making it more arduous and correspondingly making more attractive the less sought after vocations. Elaborate systems of schools of training for the various occupations were provided.

In this Utopia, there was no money, but each person was given a card, which he took to the government stores and had punched for the value of the articles he withdrew. The cards were listed in dollars as a last deference to the money system which had been discarded. The credit card was for an amount equal to the person's share of the annual national credit. There was no need for a man to lay up for the future, since the Nation would always provide him with maintenance.

Yet, with all this order and management, there was less government than we had in the day West went to sleep. The State governments had long since been abolished. The Nation alone could direct the national industrial army. The Nation had no need for an army or navy, for there were no wars, no departments of state or treasury, no tax collectors. Congress met only every five years. There was practically no legislation. Ninety-nine per cent of our laws concerned property, and there was no property. All that was needed was to administer a perfect system.

The wealth of that society was far greater than ours, for it saved not only the expenses of all the burdensome services which property entailed, but it saved the wastes of competition, and the wastes from misdirected industry. The business crises of every five or ten years were no more. As a result of all these savings, their society was vastly richer than ours. A vast system of advanced education was carried on; books, music, and the drama enriched the lives of all; and all lived lives of fullness, security, and happiness.

This golden age had been brought about only after the dire suffering of the eighties. The strikes and the industrial unrest of that era had gone from bad to worse. Labor had felt that it was forced to organize, in order to cope with great combinations of business. These organizations had gradually suppressed the free play of business enterprise, until men felt that there was no outlet save in the state taking the whole vast system over.

Early in the twentieth century, the "evolution was completed by the final consolidation of the entire capital of the nation." [148] It was done without bloodshed. Within one generation, men "laid aside the social traditions and practises of barbarians, and assumed a social order worthy of rational and human beings." [149] Poverty and servility gradually vanished from the earth. For the first time, the greedy and self-seeking were at a disadvantage; and the generous, the just, and the tender-hearted had their day. Human nature at last showed its true capacity. Humanity had been like a rose-bush planted in a swamp, which had been transplanted to "sweet, warm, dry earth, where the sun bathed it, the stars wooed it, and the south wind caressed it." [150] Men lived like brethren in unity. Mankind was at last enfranchised.

But, alas! West woke from his dream to find himself still in 1887, with wars and rumors of wars, and the strikes of that uneasy period. He found trade and business as before,—poverty, selfishness, and misery; and he was filled with a profound sense, not of the hard-heartedness of men but of their folly. He tried to tell his people of the great dream, and of his conviction that if the famine-stricken nation would but assume "the function it had neglected, and regulate for the common good the course of the life-giving stream," the "earth would bloom like one garden, and none of its children lack any good thing." [151] He spoke with fervency, but no one heard him with belief. They thought he was a madman. To his relief, he found that his awakening was a dream, and that his Utopia was real.

Some years later, Bellamy wrote "Equality," in which he endeavored to amplify and explain some of the positions taken in "Looking Backward." Again, West had long talks with Edith and her father, Dr. Leete. They explained that the corner-stone of their system was economic equality. The government endeavored to translate the principles of the Declaration of Independence into the economic system. The old industrial system had been based, they argued, on the compulsory servitude of "the mass of mankind to the possessing class, enforced by the coercion of economic need." [152] The difference between what one man could produce alone and what he could produce working in concert with others, belonged

---

[148] *Ibid.*, p. 56.   [149] *Ibid.*, p. 285.   [150] *Ibid.*, p. 290.
[151] *Ibid.*, p. 329.   [152] Bellamy, *Equality*, p. 80.

to society,—to the general fund,—and all should share alike in it. Private capital is "stolen from the social fund." [153]

Like many other opponents of the capitalistic system today, they argued that it had been foredoomed to catastrophe. The profit system reduced wages while increasing production, and as a consequence, wage earners could not consume what was produced. Each manufacturer was eager that other wage earners should be well-paid so that they could buy his product, but each depressed wages in his own industry so that his profits would be greater, and the result was greater production with decreasing power of consumption. "It appears, then," they declared, "that in the profit system we have an economic method, of which the working rule only needed to be applied thoroughly enough in order to bring the system to a complete standstill and that all which kept the system going was the difficulty found in fully carrying out the working rule." [154]

Bellamy illustrated his theory with two famous parables. One is in "Looking Backward,"—the parable of the stage-coach. The other is in "Equality,"—the parable of the water tank. In the parable of the stage-coach, he likened society to a stage-coach, to which the masses of mankind were harnessed. They dragged it "toilsomely along a very hilly and sandy road. The driver was hunger, and permitted no lagging, though the pace was necessarily very slow." There were a few seats on the top, much sought after; but those on the top never got down to help pull the load. But the seats on the top were very insecure. People were constantly falling off, and were replaced by others who had been pulling the coach. It was a terrible misfortune to lose one's seat, and the danger clouded the happiness of those in the favored positions; but still they had no compassion for those toiling in the road, save in some crisis, when they would encourage those at work, but with no thought of actually helping them. It was believed that there was no other way in which the coach could be carried forward. [155]

In the parable of the water tank, he satirized the profit system. Some enterprising men in a dry land had obtained great stores of water, and built a great water tank. They paid one penny for each bucket of water brought, and sold water for two pennies. Then the

[153] *Ibid.,* p. 88.   [154] *Ibid.,* p. 163.
[155] Edward Bellamy, *Looking Backward,* pp. 10–12.

tank became full and overflowed, and the capitalists ceased to buy water. The people could earn no more because the capitalists wanted no more water. Soon the people could no longer afford to buy water for their own uses. There was a glut, and no one knew what to do. The power of consumption was gone, and an economic crisis was brought about. The rich then learned to waste their water, and more was needed; but the same glut arose again. At last, the people simply took over the water supply as part of the public property.

So West found that the inevitable result of the profit system was hungry and naked people, with storehouses full.[156]

"Looking Backward" had a remarkable sale. Published early in 1888, by December, 1889 it was in its two hundred and tenth thousand, and was selling at the rate of ten thousand copies a week.[157]

It came at a time when there was a great vogue for Utopian romances. Allyn B. Forbes points out that there were no less than forty-four published in the period from 1890 to 1900.[158] One of the most striking was William Dean Howells' "A Traveler from Altruria," in which the traveler told to a wondering audience the marvels of his Altruria, a state much like that of Bellamy's. The newness and rawness of the industrial system evidently shocked the sensibilities of many people of idealistic tendencies, and they wistfully projected a happier order.

Frances E. Willard was strongly moved by "Looking Backward." It was "inevitable," she wrote, "that the developement of monopolies should develop a movement of this kind. Classes can only be offset by masses. A Jay Gould demands an Edward Bellamy." [159]

In 1935, Edward Weeks, of the Atlantic Monthly Press, John Dewey, and Charles A. Beard, each selected "Looking Backward" as one of the most influential books published since 1885. And, indeed, it was a moving piece of idealism, and a vivid indictment of a crude and somewhat blatant individualism.[160]

Bellamy said that the change would come by a peaceable collapse. The capitalistic system simply broke down, and the people

---

[156] Edward Bellamy, *Equality*, Ch. XXIII.

[157] Allyn B. Forbes, "The Literary Quest for Utopia," *Social Forces*, Vol. VI, p. 184 (Dec., 1927).

[158] *Ibid.*, p. 180.

[159] Frances E. Willard, "An Interview with Edward Bellamy," *Our Day*, Vol. IV, p. 542 (Dec., 1889).

[160] *New York Times*, March 15, 1935.

agreed without dissent that the state must take control. Forbes says in his article on "The Literary Quest for Utopia," that all of the writers of the Utopian romances at this time believed in political, rather than direct, action.[161] Howells, in his "A Traveler from Altruria," has the conservative banker remark how preposterous the working-men were, when, with the farmers, they had the majority,—that they did not "make any law they want." [162] The remark evidently expressed Howells' own belief. But, of course, political opinion, even to become general, requires long preparation; and to become politically powerful, requires economic resources. The politics of the Utopians did not take much account of political realities. Never in history have those who held political and economic power surrendered it at once without a struggle; either there is gradual adjustment or there is violent change.

Moreover, Bellamy's belief that equilibrium would be reached in his communistic state seems rather naive. He said that there was little legislation; most of our legislation had concerned property, and there was no longer any individual property; therefore, an equilibrium had been reached. But, of course, an equilibrium never could be reached. The conflicting desires of men; the play and counterplay of ambitions and ideals, of selfish demands, will always require the action of the state. The immense organization of Bellamy's state would have constantly required adjustment and readjustment. The intricate and delicate decisions required of the administrators of his state, the arrangement of tasks, the amounts to be produced, all would have had to be made by human beings, subject to the jealousies, the partial vision, and the ignorance of human beings. When property is removed as the incentive, power and offices will be the goal.

It is difficult to say how much actual adherence to his dream he obtained. But the discussion was sufficient to call forth serious answers. Nicholas P. Gilman, in an article in 1889 in the "Quarterly Journal of Economics," declared that, as a romancer, "we read with pleasure his brilliant chapters," but when he "prophesies, he is a child." He thought the political bureaucracy of Bellamy's state, where all States of the Union were abolished, where all was ruled from Washington and there were no representative bodies,

---

[161] Forbes, *supra*, p. 188.
[162] William Dean Howells, *A Traveler from Altruria*, 1894, p. 154.

where all manual laborers were excluded from the suffrage for twenty-four years, where all the youth of the land from twenty-one to twenty-four years of age were in the industrial army, would be intolerable.[163] William T. Harris stigmatized it as a proposal to aid the unthrifty. It would, he felt, be "more repressive to individual development than any despotism of which we have any knowledge in recent times."[164]

Bellamy's dream was Utopian, but he insisted that his proposal was serious. He even began to believe that the change would come soon. He told a Boston reviewer that "Looking Backward" was a serious forecast "of the next stage in the social and industrial development of humanity, especially in this country," and that "the dawn of the new era is already near at hand, and . . . the full day will swiftly follow." He became convinced that by the year 2000, his dream would be "an exceedingly old story."[165]

He set out to make practical application of his ideas. The first step was the control by the government of public utilities, and Bellamy entered the struggle to bring the first step about. The first Nationalist Club was organized in 1888 by readers of "Looking Backward." In two years, there were one hundred and fifty such organizations. They had no central organization. The "Nationalist Monthly Magazine" was started, succeeded by the "New Nation," edited by Bellamy. Edward Everett Hale and Thomas Wentworth Higginson became members of the Boston Nationalist Club; but Higginson explained that he was an associate member only, that he joined because he believed in nationalizing a special industry only, namely, in his case, the telegraph; and Hale, that the American people would nationalize industry "just about as fast and as far as it will pay."[166]

In an article in the "North American Review" for June, 1892, Bellamy defined his program of nationalism, urging that the "principle of popular government, by the equal voice of all, for the equal benefit of all, which in advanced nations is already recognized as the law of the political organization, should be extended to the economical organization as well; and that the entire capital and

---

[163] Nicholas P. Gilman, "'Nationalism' in the United States," *Quarterly Journal of Economics,* Vol. IV, pp. 67, 68, and 69 (Oct., 1889).

[164] William T. Harris, "Edward Bellamy's Vision," *The Forum,* Vol. VIII, pp. 199, 207 (Oct., 1889).

[165] Nicholas P. Gilman, *supra,* pp. 62–63.   [166] *Ibid.,* p. 66.

labor of nations should be nationalized and administered by their people, through their chosen agents, for the equal benefit of all, under an equal law of industrial service."

He added that the national issue would have arisen much sooner but for the slavery question. The panic of 1873, he said, began the industrial unrest. He referred to the Knights of Labor, the Federation of Trades, the Grangers, the Patrons of Husbandry, the Farmers' Alliances, the Greenback movement, the Henry George movement, and declared that they were all part of the Nationalist movement. He declared that when he wrote, pulpits everywhere were preaching "social duty and the solidarity of nations. . . ."[167] "This," he asserted, "is the very soul of Nationalism." The immediate proposals of Nationalism were the nationalization of railroads and municipal business. Bellamy felt that the platform of the Populist Party in 1892, which we shall soon consider, was a triumph for Nationalist principles.[168]

POPULISM AND FREE SILVER

The eighties continued to be years of tremendous readjustment. The severe strikes of the period are bitter testimony to the unrest and dislocation of industry. The mechanic and factory worker, off the farms, were not accustomed to the wage system, and they did not acquiesce in conditions as they found them. The condition of the farming population was still grievously depressed. All through these years, new settlers poured into Iowa, Nebraska, Kansas and the Dakotas. The exodus was partly stimulated, as Hicks shows in his "The Populist Revolt," by the railroads, which for years maintained immigrant departments, and spent much money in advertising and encouraging settlers both in the old States and in Europe. Capital, he says, was freely loaned, and mortgages were had for the asking. Hamlin Garland's "Son of the Middle Border" vividly portrays the restlessness of the pioneer, his constant search for new lands, his belief always that in the next State he would find the final place of his seeking.

But the period was likewise marked for most of its course by steadily decreasing prices for grain. Moreover, there were crop failures for several years in the Middle Border. We know now that

---

[167] Edward Bellamy, "Progress of Nationalism in the United States," *North American Review*, Vol. CLIV, pp. 742, 747, June, 1892.
[168] *Ibid.*, p. 750.

perhaps there had been a too rapid expansion of the Far West. In addition, the extension of grain lands in other countries and the development of the reaper, had resulted in a production of grain far in advance of the need. Finally, there is much reason to believe that the supply of money was actually inadequate to meet the needs of rapidly expanding business. Currency could be issued by the national banks only on deposit of Federal bonds, and the supply of gold was not increasing fast enough.

The political leaders of the Populist movement had abundant material at hand. They told the farmer that the low price he received for his grain was caused by the lack of money. They denounced the railroads for excessive grain rates, and for discriminations not only between persons but between localities. The first organized attack on great corporations began. Hamlin Garland writes that on his trip west, near the end of the eighties, he "took part in meetings of rebellious farmers," and "watched protesting processions of weather-worn Nebraska Populists, as they filed through the shadeless cities of their sun-baked plain." Everywhere, he says, "I came in contact with the discontented." He asked why in "our great new land" man should fall "into this slough of discouragement." [169]

In 1880, a Farmers' Transportation Convention was held in Chicago. It denounced the railroads as a "virtual monopoly . . . defiant of all existing law . . . oppressive alike to the producer and the consumer, corrupting to our politics, a hindrance to free and impartial legislation, and a menace to the very safety of our republican institutions." [170] It asked Congress for government control of railroads.

Within a month, two or three hundred local organizations were chartered. In 1881, when the second convention was held, there were 24,500 farmers enrolled; and by 1882, one hundred thousand were claimed. Then for a few years crops were good, and the Alliance declined. In 1884–85, poor wheat prices revived it. Within the next few years, the Northern Alliance increased enormously in membership. In November, 1890, it had ten fully organized State alliances, five others in process of organization, and numerous locals in the States without State organizations. [171]

---

[169] Hamlin Garland, *Son of the Middle Border*, pp. 423, 425.
[170] John D. Hicks, *The Populist Revolt*, p. 99.   [171] *Ibid.*, pp. 101–03.

In the beginning, the organization was divided into two Farmers' Alliances: the Northern and the Southern. A meeting was called in St. Louis in 1889, to arrange for uniting the two organizations. The Knights of Labor were invited to join the convention.[172] But the union failed.

The Southern Farmers' Alliance of 1889, with which met a committee of the Knights of Labor, declared against the alien ownership of land, demanded the abolition of national banks, and the prohibition of dealing in futures. Above all, it declared that there was a need of more money; and advocated the issuance of greenbacks, in lieu of national bank notes "in sufficient volume to do the business of the country on a cash system, regulating the amount needed on a per capita basis as the business interests of the country expand; and that all money issued by the government shall be a legal tender for all debts, both public and private."

It also advocated free silver; namely, that the government coin all silver offered to it at the ratio of sixteen grains of silver to one of gold, or more than double the then market rate.[173]

It attacked the land policy, whereby railroads and other corporations were holding public lands beyond their actual use. It asked that all land then held by railroads and other corporations in excess of that actually used and needed by them, be reclaimed by the government and held for actual settlers.

It demanded government ownership of the railroads.

The Northern Alliance, which met in 1889 (save for the omission of free silver), made the same demands, and also called for a graded income tax.[174]

At Ocala, Florida, in 1890, a formal platform was presented by the Supreme Council of the Southern Alliance. At this convention, those who desired to organize a political party pressed their views. The Southern men were reluctant. As a compromise, it was decided to have a convention in 1892 to determine the question of merger.[175]

The Ocala platform added to the foregoing demands the proposal for a sub-treasury to loan money direct to the people at two per cent on non-perishable farm products and real estate, a demand for a currency of fifty dollars per capita; opposed a tariff on the necessaries of life; and asked for the direct election of United

---

[172] *Ibid.*, pp. 113, 114.
[174] *Ibid.*, pp. 428–29.
[173] *Ibid.*, pp. 427–28.
[175] *Ibid.*, p. 208.

States senators. It also wanted a graded income tax, free silver, and government regulation of all means of communication and transportation, and if that did not eliminate discrimination, then government ownership.[176]

At Omaha, in 1891, the delegates decided to organize a political party. The platform was, in general, the same as that adopted at Ocala. At Cincinnati, in May, 1891, the party was organized. A convention was held in St. Louis, in February, 1892, which adopted a platform and laid the plans for the national convention; and in Omaha, in June, 1892, the national convention was held. It declared: "That the union of the labor forces of the United States this day consummated, shall be permanent and perpetual." Wealth, it said, "belongs to him who creates it. Every dollar taken from industry without an equivalent is robbery. 'If anyone will not work, neither shall he eat.' The interests of rural and civic labor are the same; their enemies are identical." [177]

The bitter feeling and purpose of the movement were well expressed by Mary Ellen Lease, of Kansas. In ringing accents which were to become the commonplaces of a whole generation, she declared that "Wall Street owns the country. . . . The great common people of this country are slaves, and monopoly is the master. . . . Overproduction!" she cried, "when 10,000 little children, so statistics tell us, starve to death every year in the United States, . . . " The dilemma of 1890 was much the same as that of 1933,—overproduction with millions in want. Mrs. Lease demanded the abolition of the national banks, the right to make loans by the government direct to the person borrowing. She cried out that land equal to a tract thirty miles wide and ninety miles long, had been foreclosed, and bought in by loan companies. The "accursed" foreclosure system must "be wiped out." [178]

It is easy to be calm and dispassionate over such outbreaks after forty years; and, indeed, much of the east was then scornful of the Populist movement. But our recent experience, in which a greater proportion of us have experienced the evils of sudden deflation, has brought a greater public sympathy. But we shall postpone for a while our appraisal of the Populist demands.

The candidate of the Populist Party in 1892 was James B. Weaver, of Des Moines. He had been a general in the Civil War,

[176] *Ibid.*, pp. 430–31.   [177] *Ibid.*, p. 442.   [178] *Ibid.*, p. 160.

with an admirable record; the candidate for President on the Green-back ticket in 1880. In his speeches there rang all the defiance of a strange new order, which the pioneer did not not like and did not understand. He published in 1892 "A Call to Action," which he termed an "Interpretation of the Great Uprising: Its Sources and Causes."

He attacked the United States Senate, which he said had favored a long series of laws against the public interest; the fund-ing act of 1866, which he called the Contraction Act; the Credit Strengthening Act of 1869; the Act of 1873, demonetizing silver; the Specie Resumption Act of 1875. He charged that the corpora-tions controlled the Senate: thirty-two senators were corporation lawyers. He called for the direct election of senators.

We have already noted his attack on the political power of the Supreme Court. He referred to what he called the improvident dis-posal of the public lands, this "stupendous crime." [179]

The Populist Party valiantly attacked the problem of monopoly. For nearly "three hundred years," Weaver exclaimed, "the Anglo-Saxon race has been trying to arrest the encroachments of monopoly, and yet the evil has flourished and gained in strength from age to age." He referred to the growth of trusts. His remedy was simple. "The States," he said, "should pass stringent penal statutes, which will visit personal responsibility upon all agents and representatives of the trust who aid or assist in the transaction of its business within the State." Also, the government "should place a tax of from twenty-five to forty per cent on all plants, goods, or merchan-dise" owned or controlled by a monopoly. [180]

But Weaver was not the only one at that time, and for a genera-tion afterwards, who thought that the question was so simple that it could be settled by the simple prohibition of a penal statute.

The Populist Party called outright for government ownership of the railroads.

The central Populist grievance, however, was the currency. Weaver repeated at length the arguments of Peter Cooper in the Greenback campaign, that the currency had been contracted a billion dollars after the Civil War. Like Cooper, he argued that we had about two billions in currency in 1865, and that in 1892, with a money-using population one hundred and fifty per cent

---

[179] James B. Weaver, *A Call to Action*, p. 183.   [180] *Ibid.*, pp. 393–94.

greater than that of 1865, the currency had decreased twenty per cent to $1,588,781,729.

Weaver had no doubt of the cause of our financial ills: there was not enough money to go around. The conclusion, he said, was irresistible, that "the whole country has been reduced to the servitude of debt." [181]

He demanded a currency adequate to our needs,—a managed currency again. Money should be issued by the government—and only by the government. Like the Greenbackers, he insisted ('as did all the Populists), that the issuance of money was a sovereign function. He would pay the national debt with the national currency. It was beneath the dignity of a sovereign government to borrow money. When it wanted money, it should issue it.

By 1892, the free silver agitation had reached the Populist Party, and it favored free coinage. But free silver was, after all (as Hicks has pointed out), a side issue with the true Populists. Their real belief was in a managed currency, in having a currency responsive to our business needs, and free silver was only one means to an adequate currency.

The Populist Party and Weaver favored the sub-treasury plan by which, in each county selling $500,000 of farm products, a sub-treasury would be established which could issue currency to eighty per cent of the value of warehouse receipts for grain deposited in warehouses.

While, as we have said, the free silver demand was not populistic, its story is so closely related to the Populist movement that it may be treated here. Of course, the fact that, in depressed times when silver was in little international demand, the silver mine owners wanted a market for their product, had much to do with the whole campaign. But no mere selfish appeal attains any strength. The theory of any demand makes its relation to the political thought of the moment, and that theory becomes its true philosophy, even for those with the additional selfish motive. Its success, in other words, is not due solely to the material interests of a small class; and even that class becomes sincerely committed to the philosophy that is developed.

The free silver advocates were full of the generation-old belief that money was too scarce. The free coinage of silver would

[181] *Ibid.*, p. 314.

remove the scarcity. They believed—usually rather naively—in the quantity theory of money. The supply of money was inadequate, prices were low. Increase the volume, and prices would rise.

One of the most extraordinary statements of the free silver demand was Harvey's "Coin's Financial School." It was published in 1894 and had an enormous sale. Harvey wrote his book in a form of questions and answers,—a fictitious seminar, in which Harvey conducted the class and the pupils were the most prominent economists of the country. Always Harvey discomfited them by his clear and simple replies. Harvey wanted to make the whole situation simple. To him, it was simple.

He believed fully in the quantity theory of money. All writers on political economy, he said, admitted it, and "Common sense confirms it." If "the quantity of *money* is large," he said, "the total value of the property of the world will be correspondingly large as expressed in dollars or money units. If the quantity of *money* is small, the total value of the property of the world will be correspondingly reduced." [182] By increasing the quantity of money, "you increase the value of all property. . . . You make it possible for the debtor to pay his debts; business to start anew, and revivify all the industries of the country, which must remain paralyzed as long as silver, as well as all other property, is measured by a gold standard." [183]

"When," Harvey said, "you reduce the number of primary dollars, you reduce the value of property as expressed in dollars accordingly, and make it that much more difficult for debtors to pay their debts." The demonetization of silver, he declared, had reduced "the average value of silver and all other property one-half, except debts." [184]

The act of 1873, demonetizing silver, had "confiscated millions of dollars worth of property." It had made thousands of paupers and tens of thousands of tramps. He held the standard bimetallic belief,—that, as the supply of silver was limited, if an unlimited government demand were set up, the government price would be maintained. [185] But he was not worried if it could not be maintained. If gold went to a premium, we could merely reduce the gold content

[182] W. H. Harvey, *Coin's Financial School*, p. 96.   [183] *Ibid.*, p. 83.
[184] *Ibid.*, pp. 111–12.   [185] *Ibid.*, pp. 27, 112.

of the dollar. If gold left the country, we could get along without it.[186] He was blithely indifferent to consequences.

When we come in the next chapter to a consideration of the long attack on the abuses of the machine age, monopoly, and mass production, I shall treat the philosophy of William J. Bryan more at length. Here, I wish briefly to consider his contribution to the free silver argument. He added little to the argument itself. But he gave elan and spirit to the debate. Moreover, his speeches show reading in Jevons, Mill, Laveleye, and Laughlin,—more than average information,—and a real desire to arrive at a result fair to all.

Bryan had been prominent in the free silver debate in Congress, in 1894. He opposed the repeal of the silver purchase clause in the Sherman Act, for the same reasons by which he later advocated the free coinage of silver. He believed that there was a dearth of money, that that dearth was depressing the condition of the farmer and the middle-class business man, and that the remedy was to add silver to our basic supply. A single standard could not give enough money, and it was less stable than a double standard currency simply because the quantity was less.

He attacked the current assumption of some of the gold advocates, that gold had a non-fluctuating value. There had never been an honest dollar, he said, a dollar that did not fluctuate in value. In the language of the modern friends of the commodity dollar, he said that the only really honest dollar was one that did not fluctuate in value, that had a stable purchasing power. If, by legislative action, the demand for silver were destroyed and that for gold increased, the value of the dollar would be increased.[187] If the increase "amounts to one hundred per cent, the Nebraska farmer finds that the prices of his products have fallen and his land loses one-half of its value, unless the price is maintained by the increased population incident to a new country. The mortgage remains nominally the same, though the debt has actually become twice as great." [188]

He exclaimed that "We have been called cranks and lunatics and idiots, because we have warned our fellow men against the inevitable and intolerable consequences which would follow the adoption of a

[186] *Ibid.*, pp. 137–38.
[187] William J. Bryan, *Speeches*, Vol. I, pp. 83, 85 (Aug. 16, 1893).
[188] *Ibid.*, p. 85.

gold standard by all the world." [189] If the world committed itself to gold as the single standard, it must depend on the supply of gold alone; and he argued that the supply was not enough, that it was actually diminishing. The result was the inevitable depression of the condition of the people. He adopted the common belief that the antagonism to silver was a conspiracy against the human race.[190]

Bryan did not claim that, by the use of both gold and silver at a fixed ratio, "absolute stability can be secured." [191] He only contended that, as the supply of two metals was greater than that of one, the monetary unit would be more stable than under a single standard. It is true that in his speech on "Money" (never delivered, but printed in the Congressional Record of June 5, 1894), he declared: "The great thing to be desired is a stable currency; that is, a dollar whose purchasing power remains the same through long periods of time." To secure "the desired stability in the value of the monetary unit, the volume of money must increase or decrease exactly as the demand for money increases or decreases, and in the same proportion." [192] But he admitted that no human effort could bring this ideal result to pass. What he wanted was to reduce the degree of fluctuation by broadening the money base.

In his Madison Square Garden speech in 1896, he admitted frankly that neither monometallism nor bimetallism "gives an absolutely just standard of value." But he held that bimetallism was better than monometallism, "not because it gives us a perfect dollar,—that is, a dollar absolutely unvarying in its general purchasing power,—but because it makes a nearer approach to stability, to honesty, to justice, than a gold standard possibly can." [193] In other words, by increasing the quantity of money, the fall of prices due to a scarcity of money would be prevented; and variations in value lessened because with greater quantity the variations would be less than with a smaller quantity. "A river fed from two sources," he said, "is more uniform in volume than a river fed from one source. . . ." [194]

Bryan contended that if the United States government fixed the value of silver at the ratio of sixteen to one, the permanent demand for silver at that price would raise the market value to that level and hold it there. Because silver was limited in amount, legislation

---

[189] *Ibid.*, p. 87 (Aug. 16, 1893).
[191] *Ibid.*, p. 97 (Aug. 16, 1893).
[193] *Ibid.*, p. 259.

[190] *Ibid.*, p. 200 (June 5, 1894).
[192] *Ibid.*, p. 197 (June 5, 1894).
[194] *Ibid.*, p. 269.

could fix its value. "Any purchaser," he said, "who stands ready to take the entire supply of any given article at a certain price, can prevent that article from falling below that price." In short, we could use all the silver that would be presented.[195]

When it was argued that this country alone could not maintain the bimetallic standard, Bryan became rather chauvinistic. He said there was no hope of an international agreement, which was no doubt true; but he replied that we were strong enough to do what we wanted to do, and he appealed to our national pride. We could act without the cooperation of any other nation.

Whatever may be our opinion of the effect of free silver, there is no doubt that Bryan believed that it was a fair and righteous proposal. He did not believe that he was proposing the confiscation of property, or that the result would be a fifty cent dollar. Bryan believed in the inherent rights of property. He said that he did not propose "the reconstruction of society. . . . We do not propose to transfer the rewards of industry to the lap of indolence. Property is and will remain the stimulus to endeavor and the compensation for toil." [196]

His famous speech in the Chicago Convention of 1896, long prepared and presented with consummate skill, was the climax of his free silver campaign. Never again did he reach the fire and spirit of that speech. It is difficult for us now to realize the human emotion with which this currency question was charged. But the feeling of years came to a focus in that speech. It was not an argument: it was an appeal,—an appeal on behalf of the people Bryan represented; an appeal and a defiance.

He spoke for the pioneer American, the small farmer, the mechanic, the small merchant; for the men who, in his opinion and theirs, had been endangered by the new concentration of capital and the growth of wealth. He spoke for the West as against the East. He declared that, "You have made the definition of a business man too limited in its application." [197] The wage earner was as much a business man as his employer, the country-town attorney as much as the corporation counsel, the cross-roads merchant as much as the merchant of New York, the farmer as much as the broker on the Board of Trade. You come to tell us, he said, "that

---

[195] *Ibid.*, p. 275.　　[196] *Ibid.*, pp. 251–52 (Madison Square Garden speech, 1896).
[197] *Ibid.*, p. 240.

the great cities are in favor of the gold standard; we reply that the great cities rest upon our broad and fertile prairies. Burn down your cities and leave our farms, and your cities will spring up again as if by magic; but destroy your farms, and the grass will grow in the streets of every city in the country." [198]

The sound money people did their share of wild argument. There was much abuse, talk of socialism, assertions that the success of Bryan and the free silver cause meant the end of our system of government. Much of the sound money argument was based on the theory that gold was stable in value; although, of course, the value of commodities in terms of gold is subject to the ordinary play of the market. There was much talk as if nothing but dishonesty were back of the free silver demand. The talk of those who advocated a wild inflation in order to evade their debt burdens, gave some justification for this belief. The arguments of Coin Harvey were certainly not calculated to allay doubts.

Harvey's book, despite its facile arguments, or perhaps because of them, had great popular appeal. Professor J. Laurence Laughlin, of the University of Chicago, consented to engage in a debate with him in 1895. Laughlin contended, as other opponents of free silver, that there was no lack of money, and that the quantity of money was not the cause of low prices. The cause was the advance in methods of production, the extension of new agricultural land. Free silver would actually cause a reduction in the quantity of money, because it would drive out gold and leave silver as the sole medium.

"Free coinage," he concluded, "could not change prices, therefore, by increasing the amount of the medium of exchange. That is plain." [199] The only way "it would act would be by increasing the price of everything." Goods "would be reckoned in a cheaper medium than gold." [200] Laughlin was indignant at Harvey's "audacious impudence" in imputing arguments to prominent economists and financiers in his book, and he felt that his "juggling with history is simply audacious." His book, he said, "very cleverly appeals to the class feeling of the poor against the rich." [201]

William Graham Sumner, of course, struck valiant blows at free silver. There was an irreconcilable conflict, he declared, be-

[198] *Ibid.*, p. 248.   [199] J. Laurence Laughlin, *Facts About Money*, p. 231.
[200] *Ibid.*, p. 232.   [201] *Ibid.*, p. 14.

tween the silver miners and the inflationists. The silver miners would gain only to the extent that there was no rise in the price level. In other words, if the silver dollar were made standard, gold would be driven out, and enough silver could come in to replace the gold,—five hundred million silver dollars, he estimated. If that were all, the silver miners would gain; but there would be no rise in prices, no inflation, and no relief for debtors. But that would not satisfy the inflationists. If more silver were brought in, prices would rise, and the silver dollar would fall to its market value of fifty cents, and prices would be doubled. But the silver miners would gain nothing from then on.[202]

The scheme, he concluded, would never work. We were asked, he said, "to debase the coinage and lower the standard of value, now and for the future, as a free act of political choice, to be deliberately adopted in a time of profound peace," and this was to be done to "perpetuate a bankruptcy at fifty cents on the dollar for all existing debtors." The scheme was, he said, "silly and wicked at the same time," and beyond "the power of words to express." [203]

Even so careful a student as Professor Taussig minimized the effect of the introduction of silver on prices. Credit was, he said, the chief factor in influencing prices; and in the expansion or contraction of credit, "the quantity of money plays at any given time no important part." [204] He thought, too, that the currency of the country was adequate. There were no serious evils due to an insufficient supply of money. Our monetary system was satisfactory.[205] The long fall of prices had been due rather to new inventions, to machine production, to the introduction of new lands to cultivation, rather than to a dearth of money. But, eventually, he said, the bimetallic program would raise prices in some commodities. There would be a debasement of the currency, gold would be driven out, and there would follow a complicated series of results, in which prices in some lines would indeed rise; but there would be, at the outset, "debasement and depreciation, and in the end, an unstable and untrustworthy basis for the currency." [206]

[202] Sumner, "The Free Coinage Scheme Is Impracticable at Every Point," in *The Forgotten Man and Other Essays* (1896), pp. 157–60.
[203] *Ibid.*, p. 166.
[204] Frank W. Taussig, *The Silver Situation in the United States* (written in 1893), 1896 ed., p. 76.
[205] *Ibid.*, p. 125.   [206] *Ibid.* (in 1896), p. 156.

The economists, I think, did not realize at the time the full extent of the inadequacy of our currency. Their fear of bimetallism led them to assert that the supply of the currency was adequate. Later, most of them would have admitted that it was inadequate. But they were clearly right, I think, that the supply of silver was so large, that if one country had opened its mints to free coinage at the ratio of sixteen to one, the pressure would have been so great that gold—being the dearer metal—would have been driven out of the country; and we would have had one currency,—silver,—a disastrous readjustment, and a tremendous wiping out of values, before equilibrium was reached. Surely, disaster could not have been avoided.

Professor Taussig admitted later that whatever "doubt that there may have been regarding the probabilities of the case,—and there was much about 1890,—was set at rest by the new conditions which set in after that date." [207] The tremendous increase in gold production settled the fears of a steadily declining money supply. With silver added, as he well says, the total supply would "have increased at a portentous rate." The increase in the gold supply ended the debate. Even Bryan admitted that it had settled the question. He said that those on one side kept "the gold standard which they wanted," and their opponents secured "the larger volume of money for which they contended." [208]

At the time, the Populist movement was much scorned, and "Populist" was more a term of reproach than was "Red" a generation later. It connoted the wildest vagaries of political thought. Hicks notes that the Populists were referred to as "hayseed Socialists," and that their sub-treasury scheme was called by the New York Times, "one of the wildest and most fantastic projects ever seriously proposed by sober men." [209] Mr. Dooley asked, "What is their principles?" and answered, "Anny ol' thing that th' other parties has rijicted. Some iv thim is in favor iv coining money out iv bailed hay an' dhried apples, at a ratio iv sixteen to wan, an' some is in favor iv coining on'y the apples." Some wanted to divide the revenues among all "la-ads that's too sthrong to wurruk. Th' Pops is again th' banks an' again th' supreme court, an' again havin' gas that can be blowed out be th' human

[207] Taussig, *Principles of Economics* (1928 ed.), Vol. I, pp. 283–84.
[208] Bryan, *Speeches*, Vol. II, p. 75, 1906.   [209] Hicks, *Populist Revolt*, p. 196.

lungs." [210] The convention, he ended, would continue "ketch as ketch can." [211]

Yet the Populist movement left a deep impress on our political thought. The direct election of senators, the direct primary, woman's suffrage, the initiative and referendum, as well as the control of monopoly and the regulation of railroads, were all Populist demands. Even on the currency, the Populist demand for a managed currency has left its legacy in our day.

The Populist movement was, of course, essentially a protest, somewhat blind, somewhat incoherent. It struck directly at the evils it saw, and it asked for simple remedies. It disliked monopoly; it would forbid monopoly. It hated the railroads; it wanted to own the railroads. It thought that the people were denied the right to govern themselves; it asked for the direct primary, direct election of senators, and the initiative and referendum, because these, it felt, would give the people control. There was too little currency; then let us have free silver and greenbacks. For the arduous consideration of ways and means and the operation of political and economic forces, it had little patience. The contest against monopoly and the regulation of public utilities was carried on more thoroughly than by the Populists, with that steady attention to details which the later stages must require; but still the Populists gave the first impulse. One can not avoid a sense of pride in the courage and political spirit of these derided farmers who, with all their mistakes, carried on the tradition of American self-government.

The Populist revolt has been called the revolt of those who saw that they had no longer a free outlet on the land, and were determined to find again the same sort of opportunity where they were. As we have seen, this is an exaggeration. Free land was not gone in 1896. But the frontier was gone. The mental stimulus of the frontier was gone. The horizon had closed in. The pioneer was hemmed in by elements he did not understand, and he fought bitterly for his old freedom. As Turner says, the pioneer maintained the stark individualism of New England. The Populists, he says, were the spiritual descendants, in a long line, of the Levellers and sectaries of Cromwell's army, the minutemen of the Revolution, the Abolitionist, the Granger, who "saw the sharp contrast be-

[210] Finley Peter Dunne, *Mr. Dooley in Peace and War*, p. 197.   [211] *Ibid.*, p. 201.

tween their traditional idea of America as the land of opportunity, the land of the self-made man, free from class distinctions and from the power of wealth, and the existing America, so unlike the earlier ideal." [212]

REFERENCES

ADAMS, CHARLES FRANCIS, JR., "The Granger Movement," *North American Review*, Vol. CXX, p. 394 (April, 1875).

BELLAMY, EDWARD, *Equality* (2d ed., 1897). New York: D. Appleton & Co.

——*Looking Backward.* Chicago & New York: M. A. Donohue & Co., 1915 (Copyright 1887).

——"The Progress of Nationalism in the United States," *North American Review*, Vol. CLIV, p. 742 (June, 1892).

BOGART, ERNEST LUDLOW, *Economic History of the American People.* New York: Longmans, Green & Co., 1931.

BRYAN, WILLIAM J., *The First Battle.* Chicago: W. B. Conkey Co., 1896.

——*Speeches* (2 vols.). New York: Funk & Wagnalls Co., 1909.

BUCK, SOLON J., *The Granger Movement.* Cambridge: Harvard University Press, 1913.

CAREY, HENRY C., *Miscellaneous Works*, Vol. II. Philadelphia: Henry Carey Baird & Co., 1883.

CLARK, JOHN BATES, *The Distribution of Wealth.* New York: The Macmillan Co., 1902.

COMMONS, JOHN R., *A Documentary History of American Industrial Society* (Vols. IX and X). Cleveland: A. H. Clark Co., 1910–11.

COMMONS, JOHN R. et al., *History of Labor in the United States*, Vol. II. New York: The Macmillan Co., 1918.

COOPER, PETER, *Ideas for a Science of Good Government.* New York: Trow's Printing & Bookbinding Co., 1883.

——*Autobiography* (Old South Leaflets No. 147). Boston: Old South Meeting House.

CULLOM, SHELBY M., *Fifty Years of Public Service.* Chicago: A. C. McClurg & Co., 1911.

DEWEY, DAVIS R., *Financial History of the United States.* New York: Longmans, Green & Co., 1903.

DUNNE, FINLEY PETER, *Mr. Dooley's Opinions.* New York: R. H. Russell, 1901.

FORBES, ALLYN B., "The Literary Quest for Utopia," *Social Forces*, Vol. VI, p. 179 (1927).

GARLAND, HAMLIN, *A Son of the Middle Border.* New York: The Macmillan Co., 1917.

GEIGER, GEORGE RAYMOND, *The Philosophy of Henry George.* New York: The Macmillan Co., 1933.

GEORGE, HENRY, *Progress and Poverty* (25th Anniversary ed.). New York: Doubleday, Page & Co., 1905.

——*Protection or Free Trade.* New York: Henry George & Co., 1891.

[212] Frederick J. Turner, *The Frontier in American History*, p. 239.

GEORGE, HENRY, JR., *The Life of Henry George* (2 vols.). New York: Doubleday, Page & Co., 1904.

GILMAN, NICHOLAS P., "Nationalism in the United States," *Quarterly Journal of Economics,* Vol. IV, p. 50 (Oct., 1889).

GOMPERS, SAMUEL, *Labor and the Common Welfare.* New York: E. P. Dutton & Co., 1919.

HARRIS, WILLIAM T., "Edward Bellamy's Vision," *The Forum,* Vol. VIII (Oct., 1889), p. 199.

HARVEY, WILLIAM HOPE, *Coin's Financial School.* Chicago: Coin Publishing Company, 1894.

HAYNES, FRED EMORY, *James Baird Weaver.* Iowa City, Iowa: The State Historical Society of Iowa, 1919.

———*Third Party Movements Since the Civil War.* Iowa City, Iowa: The State Historical Society of Iowa, 1916.

HENDRICK, BURTON J., *The Life of Andrew Carnegie* (2 vols.). New York: Doubleday, Doran & Co., 1932.

HEPBURN, A. BARTON, *The Contest for Sound Money.* New York: The Macmillan Co., 1903.

HIBBARD, BENJAMIN HORACE, *A History of the Public Land Policies.* New York: The Macmillan Co., 1924.

HICKS, JOHN D., *The Populist Revolt.* Minneapolis: University of Minnesota Press, 1931.

HOWELLS, WILLIAM DEAN, *A Traveler from Altruria.* New York: Harper & Bros., 1908 (Copyright 1894).

JAMES, WILLIAM, *A Pluralistic Universe.* New York: Longmans, Green & Co., 1909.

JOHNSON, EDGAR H., *The Economics of Henry George's "Progress and Poverty."* Reprinted from *Journal of Political Economy,* Vol. XVIII, No. 9 (1910).

JORDAN, DAVID STARR, *The True Basis of Economics.* New York: Doubleday & McClure Co., 1899.

KELLER, A. G., *Reminiscences of William Graham Sumner.* New Haven: Yale University Press, 1933.

KELLEY, WILLIAM D., *Speeches, Addresses, and Letters on Industrial and Financial Questions.* Philadelphia: Henry Carey Baird, 1872.

LAUGHLIN, J. LAURENCE, *Facts About Money.* Chicago: E. A. Weeks & Co., 1895.

LOWELL, JAMES RUSSELL, "Tariff Reform," in *Works,* Vol. VI. Boston: Houghton, Mifflin & Co., 1888.

MARSHALL, ALFRED, *Principles of Economics,* Vol. I. London: Macmillan & Co., Ltd., 1898.

McCALL, SAMUEL W., *The Life of Thomas Brackett Reed.* Boston: Houghton Mifflin Co., 1914.

McCULLOCH, HUGH, *Report of the Secretary of the Treasury.* Washington: Government Printing Office, 1865.

McVEY, FRANK L., *The Populist Movement.* American Economic Association Studies, 1896.

MITCHELL, JOHN, *Organized Labor*. Philadelphia: American Book & Bible House, 1903.

MITCHELL, WESLEY C., *A History of the Greenbacks*. Chicago: University of Chicago Press, 1903.

OLCOTT, CHARLES S., *The Life of William McKinley* (2 vols.). Boston: Houghton Mifflin Co., 1916.

PATTEN, SIMON N., *The Economic Basis of Protection*. Philadelphia: J. B. Lippincott Co., 1890.

PHILLIPS, WENDELL, *Speeches, Lectures, and Letters*. Boston: Lee & Shepard, 1905 (2d ed.).

POST, LOUIS F., *The Prophet of San Francisco*. New York: Vanguard Press, 1930.

POWDERLY, TERENCE V., *Thirty Years of Labor: 1859–89*. Columbus, Ohio: Excelsior Pub. House, 1889.

RICHARDSON, JAMES D., *Messages and Papers of the Presidents*. Washington: Published by authority of Act of Congress, 1898.

RUSSELL, CHARLES EDWARD, *The Story of Wendell Phillips*. Chicago: Charles H. Kerr & Co., 1914.

SELIGMAN, EDWIN R. A., *Essays in Taxation*. New York: The Macmillan Co., 1905.

STANWOOD, EDWARD, *A History of the Presidency* (2 vols.). Houghton Mifflin Co., 1912.

STARR, HARRIS E., *William Graham Sumner*. New York: Henry Holt & Co., 1925.

SUMNER, WILLIAM GRAHAM, *The Forgotten Man and Other Eassays*. New Haven: Yale University Press, 1918.

TAUSSIG, FRANK W., *Principles of Economics*. New York: The Macmillan Co. (3d ed. rev. 1928).

——*Selected Readings in International Trade and Tariff Problems*. Boston: Ginn & Co., 1921.

——*The Silver Situation in the United States* (1896 ed.). New York: G. P. Putnam's Sons.

TURNER, FREDERICK J., *The Frontier in American History*. New York: Henry Holt & Co., 1919.

WARREN, GEORGE F., AND PEARSON, FRANK A., *Prices*. New York: John Wiley & Sons, Inc., 1933.

WEAVER, JAMES B., *A Call to Action*. Des Moines: Iowa Printing Co., 1892.

WENDELL, BARRETT, *A Literary History of America*. New York: Charles Scribner's Sons, 1922.

WILLARD, FRANCES E., "An Interview with Edward Bellamy." *Our Day*, Vol. IV, p. 539 (Dec., 1889).

CHAPTER VIII

THE THEORY OF POLITICAL ACTION, 1896–1917

THE PROGRESSIVE MOVEMENT

THE next stage is a long and ever-widening contest for the control and regulation of the forces of the new industrialism. We have seen the rumblings of that contest as far back as the days of Wendell Phillips and the Greenback Party. The Grangers were the spearhead of the attack. Weaver struck the note again and again. Bryan voiced it with full resonance. Now the base is widened. The forces of thought include wider elements. The campaign has a prestige in its clientele which the humbler Populist movement never had. Not only the major political parties, but economists and leaders of opinion take up the battle where the farmer left off.

I have already referred to some of the developments of the period: the spread of railroads over the country, the great increase in the concentration of capital, the decrease in the number of establishments which nevertheless handled a greatly larger business. The process of concentration and combination never stopped. The report of the Industrial Commission in 1900 noted that, down to 1870, "a few hundred miles in length constituted the maximum for efficient operation" of American railroads. Until after the Civil War, it said, "there was only one road with a length aggregating more than one thousand miles." By 1890, five thousand miles represented "about the maximum length of a single railroad in the United States."[1] By 1900, there were systems of ten thousand miles in length. Until after the Civil War, there was but one road over one thousand miles long. In 1887, there were twenty-eight railroads over 1000 miles in length, and in 1896, forty-four, constituting 56.9 per cent of the mileage. The two years from 1898 to 1900 witnessed a tremendous amount of consolidation. This con-

[1] United States Industrial Commission, *Final Report,* Vol. XIX, p. 304.

solidation was effected partly to extend the facilities for securing business, partly to eliminate competition, partly to combine the great systems in a few dominating groups.

The same process had gone on in industrial establishments. The process had been partly the normal operation of the so-called machine age. It was partly the result of the necessity for greater capital, partly the result of greater efficiency on the part of the survivors. The inevitable profit and loss of business, the defeat and death of weaker competitors, would alone have caused criticism and complaint, whether there had been any unfair tactics or not.

But along with the process of competition, fierce at best, there had gone many unfair trade practises, which it was felt had had a large share in the success of the survivors. One of them was railroad rebates. In a famous case in 1892, it was shown that the Standard Oil Company had received not only a rebate on all oil shipped by it, but had actually received the rebate which would have gone to its competitors.[2] Van Hise remarks, "Railroad discriminations in favor of Standard Oil were continuous, from the formation of the Standard Oil Company in Ohio until the railroads under the Interstate Commerce Commission were compelled to discontinue these practises."[3]

The Standard Oil Company also practised discriminations in prices between different localities, making the price prohibitively low where it had competition, and raising it as soon as the competition was suppressed. It commonly offered generous payments to competitors to sell out to it, and if the terms were not met, fought them with ruthless price wars.

Railroad rebates directly favored combination. The large shippers got the best rebates; and men combined, partly, simply to get rebates. Montague quotes S. C. T. Dodd in his "Combinations" as saying, "Undoubtedly this fact had much to do with the combination of refiners above referred to, and which came to be known as the Standard. But it was by no means the only reason. The men in control of that combination foresaw that a business which had thus far been disastrous, would require cooperation on a large scale."[4]

The American Tobacco Company, formed in 1890, absorbed

[2] *Brundred* vs. *Rice*, 49 Ohio State, 640 (1892).
[3] Charles R. Van Hise, *Concentration and Control*, p. 106.
[4] G. H. Montague, *The Standard Oil Company*, p. 40.

in the course of its growth about two hundred and fifty competitors. It also used many ruthless methods of competition. It had fighting brands, which were sold either at no profit or at a loss. It had secret subsidiaries, held out to the public as independent, which were used in the campaign of underselling. It made exclusive contracts with sellers, and practised espionage on its competitors.

The methods of restraint of competition and combination were multiform. In the beginning, there were simply loose associations. Then the trust developed, which was a method by which the stock of competing companies was placed in the hands of voting trustees. This was the device of the Standard Oil Company and was soon declared illegal in Ohio,[5] but the method had become so famous that it has given the name to monopoly to this day. There was the device of the holding company, which held the majority of the stock of the companies in the combination. Finally, there was the single corporation, which actually absorbed the competitors in a single corporation. As we shall see, the founders of the big corporations were impelled by the idea that a combination in a corporation was not a combination, but a single entity; and therefore, as Frederick J. Stimson says, the Sherman Law actually encouraged the formation of integrated businesses instead of loose associations.

In the period after the Spanish War (as in the case of the railroads), the process of combination went ahead with tremendous activity. By the time Theodore Roosevelt became President, the country was confronted with combinations of great power in many fields of enterprise, and the old individualist looked on the scene with disquiet and foreboding.

The Control of Railroads

The first national attack on the problem of the new industry was the Interstate Commerce Act of 1887. For ten years prior thereto, there had been sporadic attacks on the problem. The States had found that they were unable to cope with the situation. Indeed, in 1886 the Supreme Court held that they had no power over interstate rates. During the same year, Senator Cullom of Illinois, pressed for the adoption of his bill establishing the interstate commerce commission.

[5] *State exrel.* vs. *Standard Oil Co.*, 49 O.S. 137; 30 N.E. 279 (1892).

In his "Fifty Years of Public Service," Cullom details the history of the movement. He referred to the Granger law of Illinois of 1873, declaring railroads public highways; and noted that when the States tried to control interstate commerce, the Supreme Court held that it was without power.[6] So he began his campaign for Federal control. In presenting the matter to Congress, he said, "I believe I am justified in saying that there is no subject of a public nature that is before the country about which there is so great unanimity of sentiment, as there is upon the proposition that the national government ought to regulate interstate commerce."

The burden of his complaint was discrimination in rates,—not the excessive character of the rates themselves. "The general theory of the measure," he said, "is that as unjust discrimination in its various forms is recognized as the chief of all evils growing out of the existing methods of railroad management, it is the duty of Congress to strike at that evil, above all things else."[7] Senator Palmer felt that there were eighteen specific causes of complaint, which nearly all might be epitomized as "discrimination in one form or another."

He quoted Charles Francis Adams, then President of the Union Pacific, as declaring that discrimination was notorious, that "certain large business firms, the leviathans of modern business, can and do dictate their own terms against rival corporations, while the small concern must accept the best terms it can get. . . . There is thus neither equality nor system, law nor equity, in the matter of railroad charges." A complete change, Adams said, was necessary.

Palmer went on to say that all the people wanted was "a fair chance; no odds of the government, but its protection. . . ."; ending with the old democratic refrain: "Special privileges for none, equal rights for all."[8]

The discussion was long-drawn out. There was general agreement that discrimination in rates should be prevented. The dispute centered on the question of whether the prevention should be left solely to the courts or entrusted to a commission, and whether pooling should be permitted. Both questions, that is, the question of the method of control, and the question of the degree of combi-

[6] Shelby M. Cullom, *Fifty Years of Public Service*, p. 312.
[7] *Congressional Record*, April 14, 1886, p. 3471.   [8] *Ibid.*, p. 3478.

nation which should be permitted, dominated our politics for another generation.

The old preference for the traditional institutions of the courts over administrative commissions, fought a losing battle for thirty years with the modern demand for expert administrative control. But the larger question of the degree of combination, and with it, the question of the extent of desirable competition which should be insisted on, was more evenly contested. The old individualist would maintain competition, and would at the same time preserve the old units. The new individualist would permit a certain degree of combination short of monopoly, and regulate the large permitted combinations.

The pooling issue involved this historic clash. The public was strongly against pooling. It still believed in the efficiency of competition. Judge Reagan, of Texas, was the leading representative of this school of thought. He would prohibit pooling, namely, agreements by competing roads for division of territory. Reagan was an able and bitter foe of monopoly. A lawyer of the old school, he believed in free competition, and he would apply the old common law remedies. He instanced what he considered the evil effects of pooling as evidenced by four large pools, which he said "have each exercised vast power, and inflicted great injury on individuals, on other corporations, and on the whole country." [9]

He went on: "It will thus be seen that these corporations boldly enter into conspiracies in restraint of trade, in violation of the principles of the common law; and that, with reckless audacity, they defy constitutional provisions and statute laws, while they impudently set at naught the great fundamental principles imbedded in all our State constitutions denouncing monopolies as being contrary to the genius of liberty."

Yet, Reagan continued, these corporations "now ask that pooling be sanctioned by law, and claim that the adoption of a universal pool is the remedy for all grievances on this subject." He asked that Congress uphold the rights and interests of the people by "forbidding pooling in unmistakable terms."

And, as we have said, he dreaded the power of a commission. The attempt which the Senate bill proposed for a commission, "to attend to all the controversies growing out of railroad management

[9] *Congressional Record*, July 21, 1886, p. 7282.

in this country," would be futile. As the railroads had controlled the state commissions, so would they control the one national commission. "The American people," he went on, "have, as a rule, great respect for law and for the action of the judiciary, but they are not accustomed to the administration of the Civil law by bureau orders. This system belongs, in fact, to despotic governments; not to free republics." [10]

But, while the pioneer citizen wanted the old competition, the pioneer railroad man wanted the old freedom of activity. He did not want the government to control rate making; he wanted the right to make a lower rate for a long haul than a short haul, if he thought it good business to do so; he wanted the right to make rates as he saw the needs of business; and, above all, he wanted the right to make agreements for division of territory.

Leland Stanford, a pioneer railroad man, was then in the Senate. In language which has been used from time immemorial by friends of the established order, he appealed for vested interests. The regulation of rates, he said, would "necessarily impair the earning capacity of these roads," to the damage of individual investors. In all these "efforts at regulation," he said, "I find no protection to the railroad companies, no guaranty against impairment of income."

In effect, he said, the law denied the roads the right of competition. The result would be to discourage a necessary business. "All will admit," he said, "that no legitimate enterprises should be discouraged, particularly those that add most to the convenience and comfort of the people, and to the wealth, strength, and dignity of the nation." [11]

There was some ground for his apprehensions. The Supreme Court did not decide until October of the same year that the legislative power over rates was subject to court review. [12] We can not afford to leave the confiscation of railroad property to the decisions of legislatures or commissions. If the railroads are to be regulated, they must be protected. Whatever we may say of regulation, no community can permit unchecked monopoly. When combination comes, regulation must come. But regulation must be tempered by legal restraint.

Stanford was therefore against control, and Reagan was against

---

[10] *Ibid.*, p. 7283.   [11] *Ibid.*, April 26, 1886, p. 3827.
[12] *Wabash etc. Ry. Co.* vs. *Illinois*, 118 U.S. 557 (1886).

combination in the form of pooling. But the view that pooling should be permitted was held by many advocates of regulation. Senator Platt of Connecticut, a conservative and fair-minded senator, declared, "I want to look this bugbear of so-called free competition, which it is claimed must not be limited, in the eyes for a few minutes. I have heard the maxim that 'competition is the life of trade.' I have heard much of the so-called law of nature and economic life, 'the law of competition and the survival of the fittest.' In the sense in which they are invoked, I deny and repudiate them both. There is a competition, which is not lawful, which is not legal, which is not honest. There is a competition which degenerates from true competition, and becomes simply war and strife,—war carried on and conducted upon the old maxim that 'all is fair in love and war.' If by 'competition and the survival of the fittest' is meant competition and destruction of the weakest, I say it is anti-Christian; it is anti-republican."

Pooling, he said, did not destroy competition: it regulated it. He quoted Adams that the railroads were suffering from "excessive and unregulated railroad competition." The result of prohibiting pooling would be to cause rate wars far more injurious than any pooling contracts.[13]

In other words, the question was again how large the units must be that should compete, all units or the large units. If all must compete, there was no rest until the strong wiped out the weak or combined with them.

But the bill passed with its prohibition of pooling. The effect of the law was slight. The courts cut away its strength.[14] The question was to wait almost a score of years,—until Theodore Roosevelt became President, before it received effective handling.

THE FIRST ATTACK ON THE TRUSTS

The first attempts to cope with monopoly in the industrial field were animated by the same desire to preserve the old competition. The theory in the beginning was simple. It was the theory of

---

[13] *Congressional Record,* Jan. 5, 1887, p. 364.

[14] The Supreme Court held that the Commission could only declare a rate void, but could not itself fix a rate in its place. *I.C.C.* vs. *Cincinnati, etc., Ry. Co.,* 167 U.S. 479 (1897); *Cincinnati, etc., Ry. Co.* vs. *I.C.C.,* 162 U.S. 184 (1896).

In *I.C.C.* vs. *Alabama Midland Ry. Co.,* 168 U.S. 144 (1897), it held that competition with carriers not subject to the act, as well as with those subject to the act, justified discrimination between long and short haul shippers.

the common law,—that all combinations in restraint of trade were illegal. State after State passed laws against combinations in restraint of trade. In 1890, Congress, after a short debate, added to the Sherman Silver Purchase Bill the provision which became known as the Sherman Anti-Trust Act. Senator Sherman, who, according to Senator Hoar, gave the bill little but his name, said simply, "It aims only at unlawful combinations." The right to combine in a partnership, in a corporation, was still open; but "combinations to prevent competition, or for the restraint of trade, or to increase the profits of the producer at the cost of the consumer," were aimed at. Particularly, he said, the law aimed at the new device called the "trust," by which the voting stock of several companies was placed in the hands of trustees. The law, he claimed, did not announce a new principle, but applied "old and recognized principles of the common law to the complicated jurisdiction of our State and federal governments." [15] It aimed only to prevent combinations designed "to prevent competition or restrain trade."

The literature on the trust question and on the whole question of the relation of the government to the new industry is so vast that all that can be done is to take a few representative expressions of the political thought of the time. One of the most eloquent and at the same time well-sustained attacks on the evils of monopoly was Henry D. Lloyd's "Wealth Against Commonwealth." Lloyd was a newspaper man, full of a tender pity for the unfortunate, and a passionate determination for justice amid the turbulent and oftentimes ugly manifestations of the competition of the eighties and nineties. His book is an impressive massing of the facts. He loaded the record with evidence of unfair and ruthless practises, of bribery, rebating, secret advantages, price wars, underselling in certain communities until competition was stamped out and then raising the price. He quoted from court cases and from testimony before Congressional committees. It was, indeed, a black and damning picture. He declared at length: "Our industry is a fight of every man for himself. The prize we give the fittest is monopoly of the necessaries of life, and we leave these winners of the powers of life and death to wield them over us by the same 'self-interest' with which they took them from us." This was one "of the historic mistakes of humanity." The philosophy of industry from the time

[15] *Cong. Rec.*, March 21, 1890, pp. 2456–57.

of Adam Smith had been the "fallacy that the self-interest of the individual was a sufficient guide to the welfare of the individual and society. Heralded as a final truth of 'science,' this proves to have been nothing higher than a temporary formula for a passing problem. It was a reflection in words of the policy of the day." [16]

The man, he said, who would practise, in his private life with his fellows, the survival of the fittest theory as it is practised in business, "would be a monster, and would be speedily made extinct as we do with monsters." The true law of "business is that all must pursue the interest of all." For a hundred years or so, "our economic theory has been one of industrial government by the self-interest of the individual. Political government by the self-interest of the individual, we call anarchy." [17]

He called for a new *laissez faire*. "The true *laissez faire* is, let the individual do what the individual can do best, and let the community do what the community can do best. The *laissez faire* of social self-interest, if true, can not conflict with the individual self-interest, if true, but it must outrank it always." [18] The line of conflict between individual and society is "a progressive one"; the line must continually shift and change. Society passes always "from conflict to harmony, and on to another conflict. Civilization is the unceasing accretion of these social solutions." [19] Here was a philosophy of change, of testing by results, that is in refreshing contrast to much of the philosophy of static principles prevalent in the period.

Lloyd proceeded to argue that, "Business motived by the self-interest of the individual runs into monopoly at every point it touches the social life,—land monopoly, transportation monopoly, trade monopoly, political monopoly in all forms, from contraction of the currency to corruption in office." [20] Monopoly, he said, was "business at the end of the journey." [21] Industry and monopoly, he continued, "can not live together." Liberty "and monopoly can not live together." [22]

Lloyd called for the end of monopoly by state ownership. He came to socialism. I shall treat later of the socialistic theories of our period. Here I have desired to present only a brief summary of his moving indictment.

At the very beginning of the trust debate arose the confusion of

---

[16] Henry D. Lloyd, *Wealth Against Commonwealth*, p. 494.
[17] *Ibid.*, pp. 495–96.   [18] *Ibid.*, p. 497.   [19] *Ibid.*, p. 506.
[20] *Ibid.*, p. 512.   [21] *Ibid.*, p. 512.   [22] *Ibid.*, pp. 518–19.

terms, which persisted to the very end,—the confusion between monopolistic combinations and mere large scale combinations. The attack was chiefly on the evils of monopoly. The defense was likely to be a defense of large scale production, and an insistence on its advantages and inevitability. Of course, in the beginning, there was much outcry against combination as such, whether or not monopolistic or injurious in its methods, and this gave further ground for those who extolled the advantages of large scale production.

George Gunton was a staunch defender of the trusts in the days when the attacks on them were most virulent. He made his argument on the advantages of large scale production. He insisted that the trusts owed their position to improvements in quality and reductions in prices. They brought stability. They paid good wages. If control of the market, he said, "is obtained by furnishing better and cheaper goods, it is clearly an advantage to the consuming public." [23] Again and again he insisted that "it is the universal testimony of history that the aggregation of capital is indispensable to modern progress." [24] The economic difference between the trust and the corporation consisted "entirely in the fact that one represents a greater aggregation and concentration of capital than the other." [25] So he concluded that the question was simply, "Does the concentration of capital in productive enterprise . . . necessarily involve economic or social disadvantage to the community?" [26]

Agreeing that the popular answer was overwhelming that it did, Gunton denied that the large corporations tended to monopoly, or even that their methods were evil. At a time when the Standard Oil Company was anathema to the public and the politicians, he vigorously defended it and denied in toto the charges of its oppressive methods. He denied that it was a monopoly. Generally, he stigmatized all the opponents of Standard Oil as either defeated competitors or mere malingerers.

In his early articles, written in the late eighties and early nineties, he denied even the political activities of the trusts. He concluded that there was little to fear from their monopolistic tendencies "so long as arbitrary barriers are kept out of the way, because in

[23] George Gunton, "The Economic Errors of Trusts.", *Trusts and the Public* (1899), pp. 35-36.
[24] *Ibid.*, p. 75 ("Large Aggregations of Capital").
[25] *Ibid.*, p. 3 ("Economic and Social Aspects of the Trusts").
[26] *Ibid.*, p. 4.

the absence of legal restrictions the active influence of the potential competitor is ever present." [27] The limit of size would be fixed automatically by "the test of greatest productive economy." [28]

But after H. O. Havemeyer, of the Sugar combination, had testified that the tariff was the mother of the trusts, Gunton, in 1899, indignantly denounced "the sugar trust" as "a manipulator of Congress by doubtful means," and declared that the activities of the sugar men at Washington had been "a national scandal." [29] The reference to the tariff apparently touched a complex. The tariff and the trusts, he insisted, should be considered separately.

Gunton's indifference to the evils of business in his day and his reliance on competition, which was then grossly interfered with by many combinations, was typical of many conservatives. Miss Tarbell was soon to show, by a mass of evidence, that the Standard Oil Company had indulged in business practises which violated all sense of fair dealing, and the Standard Oil and American Tobacco cases in the Supreme Court settled that both corporations had shown a purpose to exclude others from the field, and had obtained monopolistic controls of their respective businesses.

But now the trust question and the whole relation of the government to business became the center of national politics.

Our political thought on the relation of the individual to his government, is dominated in the period from 1896 to 1917 by three men: William Jennings Bryan, Theodore Roosevelt and Woodrow Wilson. I recall a complaint by a university president, when Bryan and Roosevelt were at the height of their influence, that our politics was too personal. It was not concerned enough with principles. It was a politics of Bryan and Roosevelt. A few years ago, I noticed a complaint by the same man that we had no great leaders, no dominating personalities, to give purpose to our drifting politics. To cite two quotations twenty years apart may seem unfair, as we all have a right and a duty to change our opinions. I cite the quotations rather for the purpose of remarking that Bryan and Roosevelt, and later, Wilson, were more than engaging and magnetic personalities. Each had a philosophy, a political creed, more or less coherent, and the following of each was to a large extent a following of those who accepted the political faith of the leader.

[27] *Ibid.*, p. 25.
[28] *Ibid.*, p. 201 ("Powers and Perils of the New Trusts").
[29] *Ibid.*, pp. 207-08 ("The Tariff and the Trusts").

WILLIAM J. BRYAN

It is difficult to ascertain the bases of Bryan's power and influence on his time. Bryan did not rise to his place from poverty or after bitter struggle. He was not a great student. His father had been a lawyer and a judge in Jacksonville, Illinois, with sufficient means to own a comfortable home with several acres, and a deer park at the edge of the town. Bryan's boyhood and youth were the normal boyhood and youth of the small town of the Middle West. He liked the ordinary sports of boys, liked to make speeches and take part in oratorical contests. He was deeply religious from early boyhood. His father was a Baptist, his mother a Methodist, but of his own choice he joined the Presbyterian Church when he was eighteen. He attended Illinois College at Jacksonville, studied law and began the practise there, and then moved to Lincoln, Nebraska.

Soon he was engaged in politics, as have hundreds of young lawyers in hundreds of towns. His "Cross of Gold" speech in the Democratic convention of 1896 was made when he was only thirty-six years of age, and from then on he was a dominating figure in our politics. He was never successful in his major ambitions, and he met much bitter disappointment and much ridicule. He was distinctly not an executive; he was a lay preacher of great power and simplicity. Nor was he a scholar or a close student of economic and political conditions. Yet those who treat Bryan with contempt and hold his political influence to be due solely to a marvelous voice and the mediocrity of the masses, are guilty either of prejudice or of gross lack of perception.

In the first place, Bryan had a real moral courage, which kept him remarkably true to his own beliefs through his long political life. Few politicians have attacked Tammany and the bosses of his party more fearlessly than he did. The tenacity with which he clung to free silver was to his own loss. His principles were all wholesome, and he was not afraid to advocate them to his own apparent disadvantage. Bryan's faith was simple, and adapted to the prevailing morality and political philosophy of the people to whom he spoke. The root of the matter, I believe, is that he reflected in plain language the common political philosophy of the time: he told the people what they themselves were thinking.

While it is true that he was not a deep student, I think in his early days he was probably as well-read as most political leaders of his time. His "Autobiography" and the comments of his wife, his lectures on the "Prince of Peace" and the "Price of a Soul," show that he read Tolstoy, Emerson, John Stuart Mill, Jevons, Macauley and Carlyle. It is well known that he was well-versed in the Bible. He was a student of Jefferson all his life. His language in his speeches was simple and clear.

The speeches of Bryan on the tariff and the money question in the years from 1893 to 1896 show considerable reading and study, and those on the tariff particularly a real grasp of the subject. Even his bimetallic speeches are far from containing the wild heresies which his enemies ascribed to them. As we have seen, Bryan resolutely insisted that he did not intend to confiscate property values nor depreciate the currency. He believed that the currency was inadequate, and that the increase by the addition of silver would simply bring prices and values back where they ought to be.

Despite occasional lapses, Bryan was at heart an individualist of the old Jeffersonian school. In fact, the root of Bryan's political philosophy is Thomas Jefferson. He called Jefferson "the greatest constructive statesman whom the world has ever known." He said that Jefferson "quarried from the mountain of eternal truth the four pillars upon whose strength all popular government must rest. In the Declaration of Independence he proclaimed the principles with which there is, without which there can not be, 'a government of the people, by the people, and for the people.' When he declared that 'all men are created equal; that they are endowed by their Creator with certain inalienable Rights; that among these are Life, Liberty, and the pursuit of Happiness; and that to secure these rights Governments are instituted among Men, deriving their just powers from the consent of the governed'; he declared all that lies between the Alpha and Omega of Democracy." [30]

In his later years, Bryan was asked how he could be a fundamentalist in religion, and a progressive in politics. He replied that the truths taught by the Bible were eternal truths; while in politics, new developments of social and economic conditions required new adaptations of political doctrines. The reply, in my opinion, did not truly define his real basis of thought. He was really a fundamentalist in both religion and politics. His whole political theory

[30] William J. Bryan, *Speeches*, Vol. I, p. 236 (June 5, 1894).

was condensed in four or five political axioms, which he used to guide his conduct. Equal rights for all and special privileges for none, the right of the people to rule, a belief in the glowing phrases of the Declaration of Independence, a conviction that private monopoly is intolerable and indefensible, a distrust of the central government and an affection for the State governments,—these were to him the "Alpha and Omega" of politics.

One gets the feeling that his formulas hardened on him. In his lecture on "The Prince of Peace," he said, "But I repeat, while I do not accept the Darwinian theory, I shall not quarrel with you about it." [31] Again he declared, "I do not mean to find fault with you if you want to accept the theory." [32] But at Dayton, Tennessee, he distinctly did quarrel with those who accepted it. As age came upon him, like many others, he did not keep his mind sufficiently open, did not allow experience to modify his conclusions. The dogmas had settled upon him; and while he was always conscious of new developments, they had to fit into his system, rather than be allowed to make his system as he went along. The wealth of illustration, the evidence of study, which his speeches on the tariff and the currency showed in his thirties, are not present in his speeches in his fifties. The conclusion is unmistakable that he did not study and reflect in later years, as he had twenty years before. His arguments on evolution, it must be said, were puerile and intolerant.

Let us see, then, a little further how Bryan's philosophy worked out in practise. He consistently favored a tariff for revenue only on the strictest theory of the old-fashioned economists. He not only believed that it was disadvantageous to produce, with tariff protection, goods with which we could not compete without tariff protection, but he believed that tariff protection had encouraged the formation of monopolies, and in 1908 he favored the removal of the tariff on all goods produced by monopolistic industry.

As early as 1894, he favored a national income tax. He declared that taxes at that time bore inequitably on the poorer classes of society. The income tax, he said, was not new, nor was it based upon hostility to the rich. [33]

On his return from his world trip in 1906, Bryan stated at length

---

[31] *Ibid.,* Vol. I, p. 269 (in 1904).   [32] *Ibid.,* pp. 266–67.
[33] Bryan, *Speeches,* Vol. I, pp. 159–179.

his political creed. He declared again for an income tax. He favored the arbitration of industrial disputes, the direct election of United States senators, asserting that the election by legislatures was a prolific source of the corrupt use of money. He opposed interlocking directorates, and favored the guarantee of bank deposits. He repeated, as he did all his life, the maxim, "A private monopoly is indefensible and intolerable," and favored a law licensing all corporations engaged in interstate commerce. He would forbid the license to all corporations which controlled more than a fixed per cent of their products.[34]

In the campaign of 1908, he favored a license for any corporation controlling twenty-five to fifty per cent of its field, and would forbid the license to any corporation controlling fifty per cent or more. Hughes ridiculed this proposal, asking why a corporation with forty-nine per cent control should be exempt, while one with fifty-one per cent should be anathema.[35] Yet practically the same proposal, made by Senator La Follette, received the approval of Louis D. Brandeis. While it is true, as Justice Holmes often reminded us, that all questions of law and most questions of life are questions of degree, and the line must be drawn somewhere (and therefore Hughes' criticism was not as conclusive as it seemed) yet it remains true, after all, that the trust question is not to be settled by drawing hard and fast lines, but is to be determined by a judgment on each case as it arises.

Bryan admitted the advantages of large scale production, but denied the advantage when monopoly was reached.

Finally, he favored the government ownership of railroads,—a proposal which brought on him much ridicule. While we are probably tending to that result, we certainly were not ready for it at the time he spoke. Events since then,—while they have witnessed a steadily increasing governmental control, a steady integration, with ownership the probable result,—certainly demonstrate that a generation more of private enterprise was desirable.

In short, normally an old-fashioned individualist of the Jefferson school, born in a small town in Illinois, who lived in a small city of the Central West, Bryan was a sincere believer in the conclusions of a past age, which he valiantly tried to apply to the new

---

[34] *Ibid.*, Vol. II, p. 81.
[35] Charles Evans Hughes, *Addresses*, pp. 319–21 (speech of Sept. 5, 1908).

age. But his force was given consistently to the very movements of the new age, which the most inductive of his contemporaries also favored.

THEODORE ROOSEVELT AND THE ROOSEVELT ERA

Jefferson had as many intellectual interests as Theodore Roosevelt; Jackson had as varied a practical experience. But Roosevelt combined the intellectual many-sidedness of Jefferson and the varied experience of Jackson. His life in New York, at Harvard, on the South Dakota plains, in the Spanish war, in Washington as civil service commissioner, in New York as police commissioner, as Governor of New York, as President, as ex-President, with a universality of interests and appeal, had a contact with many forces and elements of our national life never equalled by any of our public men.

Roosevelt's political thought showed a steady progression. The times, when he came to the presidency, were teeming. His first message, in 1901, showed that he was concerned with the relation of the government to industry. "The tremendous and highly complex industrial development," he said, "which went on with ever-accelerated rapidity during the latter half of the nineteenth century, brings us face to face, at the beginning of the twentieth, with very serious social problems." [36] The old laws and the old customs, "which were once quite sufficient to regulate the accumulation and distribution of wealth," were no longer sufficient. [37]

He alluded to the growth of large cities and of large corporate fortunes. The creation of these "great corporate fortunes," he said, "has not been due to the tariff nor to any other governmental action, but to natural causes in the business world, operating in other countries as they operate in our own." [38] The process had caused much antagonism,—much of it without warrant. It was not true that the poor had grown poorer and the rich richer. The farmer and the wage earner had never been so well off. The captains of industry had, "on the whole, done great good to our people." [39] The mechanism of business was complex. It should not be thrown rashly out of gear. The popular hatred of trusts should not allow us to take injurious action.

[36] Theodore Roosevelt, *Works* (Scribner ed.), Vol. XVII, p. 100.
[37] *Ibid.*, p. 100.   [38] *Ibid.*, p. 101.   [39] *Ibid.*, p. 101.

Yet the great combinations had shown harmful tendencies. While combination of capital was essential, it should be supervised; and within reasonable limits, controlled. Publicity was the first essential.

Nathaniel Wright Stephenson, in his "Nelson W. Aldrich," says that these sentences expressed the belief of Senator Aldrich. "There can not be the slightest doubt," he says, "that these sentences, which so exactly expressed his own creed, were warmly approved by Mr. Aldrich along with all the rest of the passage." [40]

Roosevelt in this message also declared against competitive convict labor, and in traditional language for the protective tariff. He asked that night work for women and children be prohibited in government work.[41] He was slow in coming to a political program on labor questions.

A year later, in 1902, Roosevelt asserted again that "a fundamental base" is the "inviolability of property," but that, nevertheless, society has the right to regulate its artificial creations.[42] He repeated (as he was to repeat for many years) that "we draw the line against misconduct, not against wealth." [43] We must be careful not to stop legitimate enterprise, nor to strike wealth itself, nor to upset business. Combination was inevitable. But the government could not afford to remain idle when business did ill. Publicity, again he said, would do "no harm to the dishonest corporation; and we need not be over-tender about sparing the dishonest corporation." [44] Monopolies, unjust discrimination, which prevent or cripple competition, "fraudulent over-capitalization and other evils in trust organization," could be regulated under the commerce clause.[45]

Moreover, he favored an employers' liability law for the District of Columbia.

He repeated, in his Third Message in 1903, that the consistent policy of the government was "to hold in check the unscrupulous man, whether employer or employee; but to refuse to weaken initiative, or to hamper or cramp the industrial development of the country." [46]

It will be seen how slow he was to come to the broader supervision of business. So far, his program was limited to a demand

[40] N. W. Stephenson, *Nelson W. Aldrich*, p. 183.
[41] Roosevelt, *op. cit.*, Vol. XVII, p. 109.   [42] *Ibid.*, p. 163.
[43] *Ibid.*, p. 164.   [44] *Ibid.*, p. 164.   [45] *Ibid.*, p. 165.   [46] *Ibid.*, p. 199.

for publicity, for a general supervision of corporation issues of stock, and to a more or less general attack on the evils of corporate methods. For the first time, industrial corporations began to publish annual statements.

Roosevelt carried his policy into positive action. He succeeded in obtaining the organization of the Bureau of Corporations. He brought suit to enjoin the organization of the Northern Securities Company. The majority stockholders of the Northern Pacific and the Great Northern Railroads had organized the Northern Securities Company, a holding company, which acquired the majority stock of the Northern Pacific and the Great Northern railroads. The action caused great turmoil in public opinion. The Supreme Court held that the combination was in restraint of trade. Mr. Justice Harlan, who wrote the opinion, declared that the effect of the holding company was to make "one powerful consolidated corporation," and that the stockholders of the two companies would see to it that competition between the two roads was prevented. It was a direct combination in restraint of trade, and the law forbade all such restraints, whether reasonable or unreasonable.[47] He used language which would indicate that he thought that the Sherman Act was directed against any direct restraint of competition, and not merely the unreasonable restraint of trade. Yet I think that he really based his decision on the ground that the restraint was monopolistic; in other words, that the territory affected was too large. If the combination were not prevented, he pointed out that "the entire commerce of the immense territory in the northern part of the United States between the Great Lakes and the Pacific at Puget Sound, will be at the mercy of a single holding corporation, organized in a State distant from the people of that territory."[48]

Three justices sided with Harlan; four dissented. Brewer voted to uphold the majority, but he did not agree with its reasons. He wanted to make it very clear that he felt that the combination was dangerous; in short, that it was monopolistic. If the scheme were permitted, then in like manner "could the control of all the railroad companies in the country be placed in a single corporation."[49]

---

[47] *Northern Securities Co.* vs. *U.S.*, 193 U.S. 197, 326. (1904)
[48] *Ibid.*, p. 327.   [49] *Ibid.*, pp. 362–63.

Holmes, writing a minority opinion, declared that there could not be a combination in restraint of trade, since the law forbade only such combinations as interfered with strangers to the combination,—those outside the combination. If outsiders were not interfered with, there was no combination in restraint of trade. Combination in a partnership or a corporation could not be an illegal combination; it was an entity in itself, a new unity and, therefore, not a combination. Nor was the combination through a holding company a monopoly; it restrained competition, between its own members, but the restraint of competition was not prohibited by the act, nor was such restraint in itself monopolistic. Every railroad monopolized some business. Mere size was not monopoly. There was no attempt to exclude others from the field, "to exclude strangers to the combination from competing with it in some part of the business which it carries on." [50]

But, as we have seen, the case really went (certainly it has since been interpreted) as holding that the restraint was monopolistic. The territory affected was so great that the restraint on competition became a monopolistic restraint of trade. The idea that a mere holding company was illegal as a combination was finally disposed of in the Standard Oil, Tobacco, and Steel Company cases. All were holding companies, but the test was whether they monopolized business.

Roosevelt looked on the case as a great victory; for he felt that it removed the difficulty of the Knight case, which held that a combination of manufacturers was not against the Sherman law because it did not directly affect commerce. Many lawyers felt, as events have proved, that the Knight case was poorly presented on behalf of the government; and that if the government had shown that the combination of sugar manufacturers had a necessary result on commerce, the court would have held that the Sherman law applied. Roosevelt believed that by declaring that the holding company device restrained commerce, because it directly affected commerce, the obstacle of the Knight case that commerce is not involved in manufacture was removed. [51]

The case was widely looked on at the time as deciding that a holding company was, in itself, illegal if it affected interstate commerce; in short, that a holding company was merely a combination

[50] *Ibid.*, p. 409. [51] Theodore Roosevelt, *An Autobiography*, pp. 469–70.

of competing individuals, and that the danger could be avoided by organizing in a single corporation. It was one more step towards forcing the single corporation. But the later cases showed that the single corporation was not protected, if it actually monopolized business.

The other important step Roosevelt took was railroad rate legislation. In his message of 1905, he asked for legislation which would give the Interstate Commerce Commission power to stop rebates and to regulate rates on complaint of shippers, but not to initiate them, and subject to review by the courts. As usual, he insisted that the action was based on no dislike of wealth and power, as such; but that the railroads who had acted with public spirit needed to be protected from those whose attitude was anti-social. He did not wish to see the strong man penalized, but he wished to see that the "strong man shall be given no advantage over the weak man. We wish to insure as fair treatment for the small town as for the big city; for the small shipper as the big shipper." [52] Men had been forced to do what they deplored because of the system, and the system must be changed from a chaotic one to a well-ordered one.

The suggestion brought on a great debate, one of the ablest discussions that Congress had had for a generation. Much of it centered on the question of court review, to which I have already alluded. But the fundamental political issue was, after all, between two historically diverse political theories, the old and the new individualism. The proponents of change saw the vast extent of discriminations in railroad rates, and the only way they saw to prevent it was to give a commission power to fix rates. The opponents of restriction admitted the existence of discrimination, agreed that rebates should be prevented, but shrank from granting the power to fix rates.

Congressman James Breck Perkins of New York, a distinguished historian of certain periods of French history, spoke of the infinite delicacy and complexity of the rate question. Could seven men in Washington, he asked, settle all the rate questions of the entire country? He declared that "the railroad enterprises, like all the great business enterprises in this country, have become the greatest in the world, because they have had the most intelligent and enter-

<hr>

[52] Theodore Roosevelt, *Works* (Scribner ed.), Vol. XVII, p. 328.

prising men to manage them. No railroad can succeed, no railroad ever has succeeded, or ever will succeed, except by building up the interests of the people with whom it is to deal." The question for the people, he said, is "whether an intelligent self-interest brings them the best results, or the control of Government officials brings the best results." [53]

It is the issue of our generation in many fields of action, and for all we know, of many generations to come.

Congressman McCall, of Massachusetts, was a strict constructionist and an individualist of an old and honorable school. Well-read, scholarly, he poured his whole soul and energy into the opposition. He revered old institutions. He would prevent discrimination. He would give every man his right to go into the courts to protect his rights.

But he was unalterably opposed to government rate making, and he dreaded the power of a commission. McCall believed that individual initiative would be stifled by government control. He said that the States had generally refrained from railroad building, but had called on individual enterprise; and "the result has been the creation of a railroad system beyond comparison the most splendid of the railroad systems of the world, a system built up with few exceptions by private capital, extending to the most inaccessible regions of the country, and that has been the chief factor in the production of our unparalleled prosperity." [54]

A year later, he declared that if we had had a commission since 1865, it was a moral certainty that many now civilized portions of the West would be unsettled regions." [55]

The great factor in our advancement, he exclaimed, "has been the free play given for individual action." The bill was a big encroachment on liberty. He recalled the long struggle for Anglo-Saxon liberty against governmental action. The achievement of individuals, he cried, "has made America. To my mind, American freedom is individual freedom." Give men, he cried, "as much liberty as you can consistently with order, and under the stimulus of freedom and order and the right to enjoy what they accomplish and what they gain, this nation will keep magnificently on." [56]

Again, two eras were speaking at once: the pioneer era and the

[53] *Congressional Record*, Jan. 31, 1906, p. 1854.
[54] *Congressional Record*, Feb. 7, 1905, p. 2028.
[55] *Ibid.*, Feb. 2, 1906, p. 1971.   [56] *Ibid.*, pp. 1974, 1976.

modern era. It is true that the rate making power would have been unsuited for the pioneer era. Development would have been hampered or prevented by it. The free play of the bold individual is incompatible with it. Old railroad men still can not speak of commission control with restraint. But it was inevitable. The question was a balance of evils, but the lesser was clearly control. In most parts of the country, the pioneer era was gone forever. The railroads were predominantly developed. They had become vast organisms, and the abuses of discrimination could no longer be tolerated. Discrimination, the new order said, could be removed only by government control. It could not be prevented by law suits. Initiative would be lost, but order would be gained, and order was now more important than initiative. The times had changed.

Roosevelt broadened his program as his administration proceeded. In his messages of 1904 and 1905, he recommended an employers' liability law for all industries subject to the Federal power.

Near the end of the momentous session of 1906, the Federal Pure Food and the Federal Meat inspection laws were passed. The meat bill was the result of the disclosures which followed on Upton Sinclair's famous book, "The Jungle." Senator Beveridge took up the fight and poured forth a mass of evidence of conditions in the industry, and after a bitter fight both the laws were adopted.

In his message of 1906, Roosevelt asked that the employers' liability law be extended, declaring that "it is a great social injustice to compel the employee, or rather the family of the killed or disabled victim, to bear the entire burden of such an inevitable sacrifice." [57]

In the same message, he summarized the results that had been achieved. The "present Congress," he declared, "has taken long strides in the direction of securing proper supervision and control by the National Government over corporations engaged in interstate business," [58] namely, the rate bill, the meat bill, and the pure food law. Then he went on to speak in favor of a Federal license for corporations in interstate commerce. By it, he would prevent over-capitalization, and the procuring of inordinate favors by those in control of the corporations at the expense of the public and the stockholders.

[57] Theodore Roosevelt, *Works* (Scribner ed.), Vol. XVII, p. 422.
[58] *Ibid.*, p. 426.

Roosevelt rebuked those who said that these were steps towards socialism. He declared rather that the best way to avoid socialism was to correct the evils of the present system. It would be a veritable calamity "to fail to put a premium upon individual initiative, individual capacity and effort; upon the energy, character, and foresight which it is so important to encourage in the individual." He spoke of the "deadening and degrading effect of pure socialism." [59] Government should not conduct business, but it should regulate it.

In this message, he came to the subject which he was to discuss many times in the next six years, and on which he was much misunderstood. He declared that it was a misfortune that the law forbade all combinations, good or bad, "instead of sharply discriminating between those combinations which do good and those combinations which do evil." [60] He said, as many others said, that the business of the country could not be done without breaking the anti-trust law. He would draw the line between good and bad combinations,—a declaration which caused much criticism and misunderstanding.

In his message of 1907, Roosevelt returned to this theme. It was profoundly immoral, he asserted, "to put or keep on the statute books a law, nominally in the interest of public morality, that really puts a premium upon public immorality by undertaking to forbid honest men from doing what must be done under modern business conditions, so that the law itself provides that its own infraction must be the condition precedent upon business success." [61] He would keep the anti-trust law, but would amend it to permit "combinations that do no injustice to the public." [62]

Recurring to the Federal license plan for corporations, he suggested that a Federal board be created, which should be empowered to determine in advance whether a corporation were entitled to a Federal license.

He also asked that control over railroads be extended either by a national licensing law, or by a law giving the Interstate Commerce Commission authority to license railroads to engage in interstate commerce, and to pass upon the issuance of securities and agreements between railroads.

His references to good and bad trusts were interpreted by some

[59] *Ibid.*, p. 429.   [60] *Ibid.*, p. 430.   [61] *Ibid.*, p. 488.   [62] *Ibid.*, p. 493.

as meaning that he had no objection to monopoly, so long as it did not do evil; and it was even charged that "good trusts" would be merely those in the good favor of the administration. But, while his language was not so clear as it might have been, the conclusion is unmistakable that monopoly was not to be countenanced. A monopoly would always be able to do evil to the public. He was speaking in the light of the existing decisions which, in the opinion of many good lawyers, forbade all combinations, whether or not they were in unreasonable restraint of trade.

The conflict on the trust question arose partly, as we have seen from the mere differences of opinion on what constitutes monopoly, on what is oppressive control of the market. But a great deal of the conflict was verbal in origin; it arose from a confusion in the use of the word "trust" itself. It might mean either a monopolistic combination or simply a large combination. Therefore, a statement that there are good and bad trusts might be interpreted as meaning that there are good and bad monopolies, or simply that there are good and bad large combinations. Men protested hotly that there were no good trusts, meaning that there could be no good monopolies; whereas, the statement may have been meant simply as an assertion that there are large combinations that are not evil. This confusion cursed the trust debate for a generation.

Roosevelt spoke again in favor of a Federal employers' liability law, stating that business—and eventually the public—should assume the risks of injuries in interstate commerce, instead of the individual employees.

Next to his program for the regulation of business, came his work on conservation. It was dear to his heart and grew out of his own experience. It appealed to his instinct for the land and his strong sense of providing for the future.

In January, 1905, speaking to the Forest Congress, Roosevelt said (as he said many times during the rest of his life), "You are mighty poor Americans if your care for the well-being of this country is limited to hoping that well-being will last out your own generation." Our policies must be shaped for our "children and our children's children." [63] The forests must be preserved. Consequently, he opposed the sale of the public lands which contained

[63] Theodore Roosevelt, *Presidential Addresses and State Papers* (Homeward Bound ed.), Vol. III, p. 196.

national resources. The water power, the forests, should be preserved for the use of all.

Accordingly, he felt that the prime need was that the leasing system should "be established, and that from henceforth the Nation should retain its title to its fuel resources, and its right to supervise their development in the interests of the public as a whole." The same policy should be adopted for the forests, streams, and all natural resources. They "should be treated as public utilities." [64] We "should not now repeat the mistakes of the past." We had a right to the proper use "of both the forests and the fuel, during our lifetime; but we should not dispose of the birthright of our children." [65] He argued that the leasing system would require less capital than outright purchase, would enable large operations to be undertaken, and would prevent waste, monopoly, and high prices.

Roosevelt said that he had the heartiest sympathy with the desire of the people of the Rocky Mountain states "for the rapid development" of their communities, a desire so characteristic of new communities. But that development, he insisted, must take place in such a way as to leave the children "better off and not worse off than the fathers. Let us use, but not waste the national resources." [66]

It was the settled America speaking to the new America: two eras were conflicting. It was another illustration of the truth of Barrett Wendell's conclusion that several eras were developing in our country at once.

In May, 1908, he continued his campaign before the Conference on the Conservation of Natural Resources, which he called together because, he said, of the enormous consumption of our natural resources "and the threat of imminent exhaustion of some of them due to reckless and wasteful use." [67] He declared that our safety depends directly "on the energy and intelligence with which our natural resources are used." [68] Our natural resources were not unlimited. The pioneers had moved westward when their land was exhausted. That outlet was no longer possible. We must think for posterity.

In his last annual message, that of 1908, he went over the same ground. He was moving steadily to greater control over the rail-

[64] *Ibid.*, Vol. VI, p. 1147 (Special Message of Feb. 13, 1907).
[65] *Ibid.*, p. 1148.　　　　[66] *Ibid.*, p. 1152.
[67] *Ibid.*, Vol. VII, p. 1744.　　　[68] *Ibid.*, p. 1745.

roads. The railroads should be allowed to make traffic and rate agreements, subject to the Interstate Commerce Commission.

He insisted again that we should put a premium on individual initiative, but it must be controlled in the public interest. We could not go back to "the reign of an unrestricted individualism." [69] The true conservative was the man who would order these vast new forces with regard for the welfare of all.

Roosevelt, up to 1909, then, was chiefly concerned with the control of business, the control of great corporations in interstate commerce, the enforcement of the anti-trust law, and finally, the conservation of our natural resources.

But he showed the beginning of his program for a larger interest by the state in individual welfare, which was to have so large a share in the progressive movement in the years from 1910 to 1916. The activity of the government until then had been mainly devoted to the development of the resources of the country, with emphasis on aid to the leaders of business. Roosevelt would not only restrict the excesses of the leaders, but he evidenced the growing interest in the man who was not a leader,—the smaller manufacturer, the average farmer, the merchant, the professional man,—who was not identified with "big business." But back of all his program was the realization that our traditional independence of action must henceforth be subject to control. "No small part," he said, "of the trouble we have comes from carrying to an extreme the national virtue of self-reliance, of independence in initiative and action." [70]

For the first time in our politics, there enters the note of providing for the future. The politics of development of natural resources had been somewhat blind to the next generation. Roosevelt's conservation policy was permeated with concern for the future.

The times have changed and developed so profoundly that Roosevelt's words give little hint of the effect they had on his public. His abounding personality, the force with which he spoke, the vivid manner of the man, combined with the newness of his subject and the readiness of the public to hear what he said,—all made an enormous impression. He made politics exciting. In every part of the country, at directors' tables, in universities, in small political gatherings, his suggestions were discussed. He not only

---

[69] Theodore Roosevelt, *Works* (Scribner ed.), Vol. XVII, p. 581.
[70] *Ibid.*, p. 486 (Message of Dec. 3, 1907).

awakened a great public interest in public life, encouraged a great multitude of young men to enter politics, but he made the question of the relation of government to industry a topic of discussion the country over.

Tremendous antagonism was developed to proposals which, in the light of our modern extensions of power, seem mild indeed. Ida M. Tarbell, in her "The Life of Elbert H. Gary," says that "the virulence and the volume of the attack on President Roosevelt in 1907 can hardly be overestimated. I have been through the manuscript correspondence and have been amazed to find that the only man of importance in the business world who at that time wrote even one friendly letter—at least, which has been preserved —was Judge Gary." [71]

The Roosevelt program began a great national discussion. It is possible to mention only a few of the contributions of the time.

J. Allen Smith, Croly and Weyl

I have already referred to J. Allen Smith's "The Spirit of American Government." It was mainly concerned with political reforms. He thought that the framers of the Constitution "deliberately intended to dethrone the political majority." We have seen that he wanted the political power of the Supreme Court taken away. He thought that the Constitution was practically impossible of amendment, and that no step towards political regeneration could be made until amendment was made more easy. He would abolish the electoral college, elect the President by direct vote, elect senators by direct vote, establish the direct primary and initiative and referendum,—all in order to liberate the energies of the people and achieve an industrial democracy. Some of these political suggestions I shall take up in Chapter XII.

In 1909 Herbert Croly published his "The Promise of American Life." He had spent ten years on the preparation of his book, which came at the height of the Roosevelt campaign. It aroused great interest, was taken up by Roosevelt himself, and had great influence on the Progressive Party movement which was then (as we can see now) beginning.

In it, Croly sketched the development of the American ideal, of our religious faith in our country, its "ideal national promise." [72]

[71] Ida M. Tarbell, *The Life of Elbert H. Gary*, p. 192.
[72] Herbert Croly, *The Promise of American Life,* p. 2.

He asked what the promise was; and replied that if it were anything, it was a democratic ideal, a desire for economic independence and prosperity with free political institutions. Jefferson had phrased the ideal as equal rights for all; and Jackson had represented the pioneer in the new conditions of the early Middle West, who sought to maintain this opportunity by seizing the political power in opposition to the new economic classes of the East.

Now, economic conditions had vastly changed. As so many of the interpreters of the new days had noted, Croly too, noted that free lands had gone, and that the outlet to the frontier was closed. Great combinations of capital had arisen. We had sought our equal rights in the past by an individual scramble for wealth, but that recourse was no longer ours. We had sought in the past to protect our equal rights by general restraints of law, by inhibitions in the Constitution; we had distrusted government. But if we were to fulfill the ideal in the new conditions, we must make government the partner of our activities, and at every turn make it our ally in restraining the excessive acts of individuals which infringed on the common welfare.

Croly noted, too, the change in our individual training and development. The pioneer society had favored the pioneer virtues, —the virtues of the man who was not and could not be a specialist, but was ready and able to adapt himself to all the quickly changing conditions of the frontier. Therefore, we had distrusted the man with special training, the expert. Now, we had problems demanding the services of experts, and we had men trained to work with them, but much of the old national distrust still lingered to discourage their use.

The nub of the whole matter was that, until but recently, all classes had been seeking the satisfaction of individual economic purpose. They sought their safety in law, in provisions of the statutes forbidding activity inimical to the general welfare. Government by law was naturally distrusted, and therefore jealous restraints on the government were imposed.

The principle of equal rights, therefore, restrained by specific provisions of the law, was no longer a sufficient means of protection. To this extent, he said, the followers of Jefferson must admit the superior wisdom of the Hamiltonians; and concede that we must not only equalize individual rights, but must control "individuals in the exercise of those rights. The national public interest has to be affirmed by positive and aggressive action." [73]

As a means of exercising this control, Croly would have inheritance taxes. Existing inequalities in wealth should be mitigated, and a graduated inheritance tax was one means to that end. "The preservation intact of a fortune over a certain amount, is not desirable either in the public or individual interest." [74] Large inheritance was a restraint on the freedom of action of the individual. The descendants of the rich man were not able to use his wealth wisely, as elaborate trusts created by them prove.

But Croly's chief stress was on the regulation of corporations and labor unions. He would repeal the Sherman law. "The process of industrial organization," he said, "should be allowed to work itself out." If the small competitor could not survive against the large corporation, he should be allowed to drown. There "is no public interest promoted by any expensive attempt to save his life." [75] The Sherman law was such an attempt. It constituted an "announcement that the national interest of the American people demands active discrimination in favor of the small industrial and commercial agent." We should recognize large combinations, not prohibit them. We should therefore have a national incorporation act, to prevent those abuses that had given in the past unfair advantages to the large corporation over its competitors.

Apparently, he made no distinction between railroads and other utilities on the one hand, and manufacturing corporations on the other. He referred to his policy, however, as the recognition of "semi-monopolistic corporations." [76] He is not altogether clear in his statements (a characteristic which he showed later in his editorship of the "New Republic"); but, apparently, he would limit the regulation to the removal of abuses, and leave to the heads of the big corporations the major responsibilities of management. He dreaded the effect of government by commissions, in absorbing responsibility and destroying the initiative of business leaders, even in the utility field. Regulation had a tendency to go beyond the correction of abuses, to the damaging of efficiency. The regulation which was desirable was such as the national banks were subject to. The commission should not have the power to promulgate rates or order new equipment. The desire of the carrier to develop traffic

[73] *Ibid.*, p. 190.　　[74] *Ibid.*, p. 382.　　[75] *Ibid.*, p. 359.　　[76] *Ibid.*, p. 371.

should be enough to ensure reasonable service and fair rates, subject only to the power of the commission in case of abuses.

He admitted, of course, that in cities, utilities became monopolies; and that the railroads, by steady consolidations, were moving to that end. He would give them short franchises only, and retain the right of purchase. Taxation of excess values should be resorted to. He was not clear as to how far rate control should go in those cases where the monopoly is practically complete. Apparently, he still distrusted it, and thought that actual public ownership was preferable to complete control.

Likewise, Croly favored the outright recognition of unions. He would discriminate in their favor. The non-union laborer should be rejected as emphatically as a gardener rejects a weed. He did not deny that, in the existing order, the non-union worker had certain virtues and fulfilled certain needs. But the government, by recognizing the unions and working with them and controlling them, would make his function useless.[77]

Croly was a thorough-going nationalist, and his book gave Roosevelt his title for his "New Nationalism" of 1910. We shall reserve treatment of his nationalistic theories for Chapter X, when we consider the growth of the national idea.

In his "Progressive Democracy," published five years later, in 1914, Croly argued that the program of the progressives should be to make privilege widespread. Those who had been granted privileges should be allowed to keep them, for "their forcible dispossession would merely be to substitute one injustice for another." But they must be forced to earn their privileges. The victors must be "worthy of the spoils." The mistake of the Republicans consisted, not in passing privileges out, "but in failing to make sure that every class obtained its full share of these natural and artificial economic opportunities," and failing to see that society had an interest in the way they were exercised. We must therefore revise the distribution of our privileges, and grant them only on the assurance of "obtaining socially desirable fruits." [78]

The new privileges which he wished to grant were for the benefit of a wage-earning rather than a property-owning class. Accident, and other social insurance, laws for the protection of the wage-

[77] *Ibid.*, pp. 387, 388, 390.
[78] Herbert Croly, *Progressive Democracy*, pp. 115-16.

earner, were the privileges which he treated as comparable to the tariff favors accorded to manufacturers.

But it hardly need be said that laws designed to give the wage-earner security are not comparable to laws which give manufacturers a decided economic advantage. Croly proposed to give the wage-earner economic independence. But the economic aid which the government had granted to manufacturers and which Croly did not wish to take away, clearly gave them an unfair economic preponderance. It was impossible—and it would never be possible —to distribute privileges equally to all. Nor did Croly explain how privileges were to be distributed, nor what he meant by socially desirable fruits.

Chamberlain, in his "Farewell to Reform," says Croly believed in "a mystic, national America," and that he completely ignored the modern power-politics.[79] He calls Croly a follower of Comte, that is, that he believed that reason would control men in their decisions on public policies; Croly seemed to believe that economic groups would acquiesce in his program out of sheer reason and good-will. But Chamberlain objected that economic groups do not give up their rights or interests, save in accordance with their economic interests or in deference to other groups with antagonistic interests.

But, as I have remarked before, to say that power controls is only part of the story. Politics is the resultant of many forces,— political, psychological, and personal, as well as economic. The great interests of the public have been controlling selfish economic interests of powerful classes ever since law began. Moreover, Croly certainly did not ignore economic power. Both his "Promise" and his "Progressive Democracy" are based on the assumption that privilege is inevitable in a democracy, that property itself is privilege, that therefore the Democratic slogan of special privileges for none is impracticable. Croly felt therefore that the Republicans were justified in accepting economic privilege as the basis of a "democratic national economy," but their mistake was "in failing to insist that society, as a whole, had as much interest in the way in which privileges were exercised as individuals and classes had in the way in which they were distributed." [80]

---

[79] John Chamberlain, *Farewell to Reform*, pp. 224-26.
[80] *Ibid.*, Croly, *Progressive Democracy*, p. 115.

It can not be said, therefore, that he ignored economic interests. But it certainly can be said that he left his ideas extremely vague. It is difficult to tell just what he is advocating. He assumed, moreover, that people had the same feelings and reactions which moveo him. He showed little sense of the customs and emotions, the inherited affections and prejudices of people. While he thought he wrote from experience, actually he wrote too much from his own mind. For example, his plan for State commission government, with a small commission taking the place of the legislature, showed his lack of perception of the force of political habits.

"The New Republic," in the last three years of our period, made a deep impression on the younger intellectuals of the time; but it may be said of it (as of Croly, its editor) that it showed a singular lack of understanding of the old native-born American of the small towns and the country districts, and a singular lack of affection for the inherited beliefs and customs of the people.

Through all Croly's arguments runs the recognition of combination. He had little sympathy for the old individualistic America. He had no sympathy with political efforts to maintain the small producer. The emotional interest in the old pioneer America did not appeal to him. But I think he exaggerated the political sympathy for the small producer. By the time he wrote, the sentiment against combination, as such, was steadily diminishing. To be sure, the Supreme Court still held to the theory that the Sherman Law forbade all combination which directly restrained commerce, whether or not the restraint was unreasonable. But only two years later, in the Standard Oil decision (which, it is true, was far from clear), Chief Justice White, in labored language, held that this prohibition must be construed in the light of reason; and since then the tendency has been strong to allow combination, so long as it was not oppressive or monopolistic.

The trust subject, for a generation, has been confused by this very question, namely, whether only those combinations which oppressed trade were forbidden, or all those which restrained competition. The Standard Oil case, and the cases following it, settled that certainly a combination in a single corporation was not illegal, unless it oppressed trade or tended to a monopoly. An agreement which restrained competition between independent competitors was still forbidden, although recently there have been cases holding that even such restraint may be proper if not oppressive in nature.

But Croly would apparently allow combination even to the point of monopoly, subject to the regulation of abuses by a commission. He would give up the attempt to prevent even monopolistic combination. This was to be the subject of debate again in the Progressive year of 1912.

In 1912, Walter Weyl published his "The New Democracy." It was permeated with much the same philosophy. Chamberlain thinks that Weyl had a clearer conception than Croly of economic forces. For one thing, he recognized that political parties were, to a large extent, controlled by those who supplied the party finances, and he proposed that the state should contribute to campaign expenses. In general, Weyl's contribution was a well-balanced attempt to envisage the socialization of society, without insisting on any rigid system. He thought that in the decades to come we should hear less of the doctrine of the class war. There "would be wide ranging conflicts between coalitions of classes; but there will also be adjustments and unions for the attainment of common aims and for a succession of compromises, rendered possible by an enormous increase in the social product to be distributed." The state, he said wisely, will not be the representative of one class, but there would be a "relative increase of influence by certain classes through the nearer attainment of the rule of the majority." [81]

So Weyl's politics was an opportunist politics,—a politics growing out of the decisions on particular questions. He favored an inheritance tax to prevent great fortunes, and government ownership of railroads in Alaska. The democracy would attain its ends sometimes by government ownership, sometimes by regulation, sometimes by tax reform. What we wanted was the gradual socialization of industry by whatever means was appropriate in the particular case. "It is less a definite industrial program, than the animating ideal of a whole industrial policy." [82] In certain industries, socialization might mean government ownership; in others, government operation in competition with private business, or government ownership with private management, or a division of profits, or thoroughgoing regulation, or a deflection of profits through taxa-

[81] Walter Weyl, *The New Democracy,* p. 189–90.
[82] *Ibid.,* p. 279.

tion. There was no standard method. But it was certain, in any event, that we should have greatly increased regulation.

Specifically, he advocated publicity, government ownership of monopolies, and taxation of unearned increments.

ROBERT M. LA FOLLETTE

Robert M. La Follette, for a generation, was an able representative of the new progressivism. He was in politics from the day when he left the University of Wisconsin to the day of his death. Inevitably, as with all of us, his personal experience had much to do with his political thinking. He writes that, as a "boy on the farm in Primrose Township, I heard and felt this movement of the Grangers swirling about me; and I felt the indignation which it expressed in such a way that I suppose that I have never fully lost the effect of that early impression." [83]

About 1874, he says, the "railroads began to dominate politics for the first time in this country. They saw that they must either accept control by the state or control the state." [84] They asserted that the panic of 1873 was caused by the Grangers. The first Granger law in Wisconsin was declared constitutional, but was repealed. From then on, he says, "until my fight was finally successful, Wisconsin was a corrupted State governed not by the people, but by a group of private and corporate interests." He quotes Chief Justice Ryan, of the Wisconsin Supreme Court, as declaring at the University of Wisconsin Commencement in 1873: "There is looming up a new and dark power. . . . The enterprises of the country are aggregating vast corporate combinations of unexampled capital, boldly marching, not for economic conquests only, but for political power. For the first time really in our politics, money is taking the field as an organized power." [85]

La Follette began his efforts to control Wisconsin in 1896. I shall refer to his political demands in the chapter on "The Struggle for Political Control." In 1896 and 1898, he was a candidate for the Republican nomination for governor, but he claimed that each year he was defeated in the conventions by the corrupt use of money. He was successful in 1900, and began a fight for a direct primary law, for taxation of railroads, and for regulation of rail-

[83] Robert M. La Follette, *Autobiography*, p. 19.
[84] *Ibid.*, p. 20.   [85] *Ibid.*, p. 23.

road rates by a commission on the basis of a physical valuation of property. A bitter struggle ensued in the legislature. He declared he "never saw anything like" the organization and numbers of the lobbyists arrayed against him.[86] All his bills were beaten.

He was renominated after a hard fight in 1902. In the legislature, his railroad regulation bill failed, but his tax bill passed. The result, he says, was an increase in railroad tax revenue of $600,000 annually. He pressed his campaign for railroad rate regulation. He claimed that rebates to the extent of $11,100,000 annually were discovered. In 1904, after another strenuous campaign, he was successful again, and the result was the railroad rate law of Wisconsin. He asserts that it was predicted that he would drive capital from the State, but he replied that his object was not to "smash corporations, but to drive them out of politics, and then to treat them exactly the same as other people are treated."[87] As a result of his rate and tax laws, he claimed that the railroads did an increased business, and yet paid more taxes.

La Follette also obtained laws reducing child labor. Excessive hours for women were abolished, "the most carefully drawn of all workmen's compensation laws" was passed,[88] a State forest preserve was established, and insurance and banking laws were enacted.

La Follette's work in Wisconsin was of a high order. It created much bitter opposition; there was much talk of capital being driven from the State, and hot outcries against the La Follette political machine. His domination was indeed complete and somewhat arrogant. But it was honest and efficient, and it was the evidence of a new day in American State politics. During the La Follette regime, Wisconsin came to be, in the words of Theodore Roosevelt, "literally a laboratory for wise experimental legislation, aiming to secure the social and political betterment of the people as a whole."[89]

In 1912, Charles McCarthy, the legislative reference librarian, published his "The Wisconsin Idea," in which he detailed the ideals of the State. He told of the beginnings of railroad legislation, ending in the commission control which was extended to cover not only railroads but public utilities. Wisconsin adopted an income tax, an inheritance tax; an advanced code of factory laws, and a

---

[86] *Ibid.*, p. 244.   [87] *Ibid.*, p. 352.   [88] *Ibid.*, p. 310.
[89] Charles McCarthy, *The Wisconsin Idea*, Introduction, p. vii.

workmen's compensation law. Its legislative reference department, of which McCarthy was the head, furnished detailed information to legislators who had formerly groped in the dark. In all this, the influence of the university, of men like John Bascom and Professor Ely, had been potent. "Is all this socialism?" asked McCarthy. "Quite the opposite," he answered, "it strives to give the individual a better opportunity to possess property,—the very antithesis of socialism." [90]

McCarthy showed that Wisconsin had been greatly influenced by the experience of Europe and Canada. We should not be scared, he remarked, by the fetish of the cry of socialism. He asked if it were "good policy or good politics to allow the socialists to become the champions of women in industry, the defender of the child from exploitation, friend of the poor and the downtrodden, and yet expect to defeat them at the polls in a period characterized by growing humane feeling." [91] "The best there is of our sturdy individualism *must* be preserved." [92]

But La Follette never acquired a national following. In Wisconsin, for a generation, his word was law, but nationally there always seemed something a little foreign about him. On his death, the old "Outlook," in a trenchant editorial, suggested that his national failure may have been partly due to the fact that he "seemed to think of America with a European mind," that he represented the Americans without a national tradition.[93] Certainly on all questions of an international nature, La Follette showed the influences of his constituency. His prejudices were not the prejudices of a homogeneous community; they were the prejudices of his State. And in his advocacy of economic issues, one gets the impression that La Follette was speaking from an experience not common to the rest of the country.

He was a great favorite with many of the liberal thinkers of the country. Of his essential sincerity, his courageous advocacy of what he believed in, there can be no doubt. He made a distinct impression on his time. But there was a certain rigidity in his opinions; he had an unbending nature, and this, with his somewhat parochial appeal, kept him from acquiring a national following.

[90] *Ibid.*, p. 294.   [91] *Ibid.*, p. 299.   [92] *Ibid.*, p. 302.
[93] *The Outlook*, Vol. CXL, pp. 321, 322 (July 1, 1925).

1912—The Great Progressive Year

When Roosevelt returned from Africa in June, 1910, he found the public mind in a ferment. At Hughes' instance, he promised to make speeches in New York, and was soon engaged in a trip across the country. These speeches were later collected in a book called: "The New Nationalism." The title was obtained from Croly's book, to which he had given high praise. The theories he developed were broader than those he had outlined while president. He called again for the supervision of the capitalization not only of railways and public utilities, but of all corporations engaged in interstate commerce. He repeated that combination was the result "of an imperative economic law, which can not be repealed by political legislation." [94] We should not prohibit, but control, combinations. We must have complete and effective publicity. The only alternative to government ownership of railways was complete and effective supervision.

Then he turned, as he had never before, to questions of the rights of labor and of the individual man. "At every stage, and under all circumstances," he said, "the essence of the struggle is to equalize opportunity, destroy privilege, and give to the life and citizenship of every individual the highest possible value both to himself and to the commonwealth." [95] He spoke of swollen fortunes, and favored a graduated income tax and a graduated inheritance tax. He accepted the theory of organized labor,—that no man could make his best contribution to society unless he had a decent wage, and hours of labor short enough "so that after his day's work is done, he will have time and energy to bear his share in the management of the community, to help in carrying the general load." [96] He asked for workmen's compensation laws, and laws regulating the labor of women and children.

It was the beginning of the campaign of 1912. That year was the climax of a period of eager political discussion in books, magazines, newspapers, and on the platform. Indeed, I believe that the period from 1908 to 1914 was not equaled in the whole period from 1865 to 1917, in the range, intelligence, and idealistic purpose of its political discussion.

William James commented on the unusual service of the popular

[94] Theodore Roosevelt, *The New Nationalism,* p. 15.
[95] *Ibid.,* p. 10.   [96] *Ibid.,* p. 24.

magazines in the spread of new political standards. They were, he felt, acting as "a real popular university in giving a higher, healthier tone" to our democracy.[97] Ida Tarbell, Ray Stannard Baker, Lincoln Steffens, William Allen White, and many others launched a brilliant attack on the excesses of our business, the dangers of monopoly, and the corruption of our politics. The novels of Winston Churchill, Frank Norris, Robert Herrick, Ernest Poole, and William Allen White were permeated by the same social and political philosophy.

As always in politics, personal clashes and strong personal emotions colored and directed the development of political opinion in 1912. The dissatisfaction of those who called themselves progressives with the Taft administration, led to the candidacy of Theodore Roosevelt for the Republican nomination; and a bitter and somewhat tumultuous campaign ensued, ending in the nomination of Taft, the withdrawal of the Roosevelt forces, and the formation of the Progressive Party with a platform of new and inclusive political and economic proposals. Without the split in the old party, no such program could have been presented at that time. Moreover, there is little doubt that the Republican fight and the nomination of Taft made possible the nomination of Wilson by the Democrats.

The progressive year of 1912 still bulks large to those who lived through it. Looking back twenty-four years, I think that the scoffs of the cynics are unjustified. The progressive movement represented, after all, a deep and pervading feeling in the American people, an intelligent grasp of complicated questions, and above all, an idealistic and emotional impulse which must ever be a matter of pride to those who believe in democratic institutions. The war cut off its full fruition, but it made a great impress on our political life, nevertheless. After the war, except among the farmers, the unusual prosperity stifled political discontent, out of which economic programs usually arise; but now we are seeing in our debates many of the very same arguments which were so prevalent in those fruitful years.

When the Progressive Party was organized, there came together not only political leaders, but social workers and many of the

[97] William James, "The Social Value of the College Bred," in *Memories and Studies*, p. 323.

representatives of the whole new trend of thought. Roosevelt admitted later that it had a large "lunatic fringe," as is inevitable in all new movements; but the platform itself and the speeches of Roosevelt and Beveridge presented, after all, a well-ordered program, which in these times seems moderate enough. It declared for direct primaries; for the initiative, referendum, and recall; and for the so-called recall of judicial decisions. We shall treat of these matters more at length in the chapter on "The Struggle for Political Control."

But in the field of economics, it asked for legislation preventing industrial accidents and diseases; for the prohibition of child labor and night work for women; for the eight hour day and the six day week; for workmen's compensation laws, social insurance, and continuation schools.

The theory of students was fast progressing on the line that regulation of trusts by commission must at least be added to sporadic control through the courts. Even Attorney General Wickersham admitted that the courts and the Department of Justice were not equipped to handle the dissolutions of the Standard Oil and Tobacco companies.

Bruce Wyman, in his "The Control of the Market," published in 1911, argued that the Sherman law had hastened the creation of the single corporation, in the belief that the single corporation was not a combination in restraint of trade, but an entity by itself. The Standard Oil and Tobacco cases settled that even a single combination was objectionable, if it monopolized or attempted to monopolize business. Very soon, he said, the "time will come when the principal trusts will have fully reorganized as single corporations. And then the fundamental problem of legal regulation must be squarely faced." [98] The attempt to dissolve large combinations should be given up. They should be treated as subject to a public use, and the law of public service applied to them.

Yet even he did not advocate that legislation permit unreasonable combination, nor the licensing of monopolies. The subject is cursed with ambiguity. Practically no one on either side made his position clear. Apparently, Wyman favored the recognition of large combinations, subject to commission control. It is true that he said: "It should be the abuse—not the possession—of monop-

[98] Bruce Wyman, *The Control of the Market*, p. 261.

oly," which should "subject a concern to prosecution under the law in the future." [99] If monopolization by unfair practises and discriminations were prevented, "fair competition will always be possible." [100] Like most writers, he did not distinguish between large combinations and monopoly. At times he would seem to be complaisant towards monopoly, and at others to believe that monopoly was impossible if fair competition were preserved.

In the spring of 1912, President Van Hise, of Wisconsin, published his "Concentration and Control," which became a leading book in the campaign. He also was impressed by the impotence of mere court control of trusts, and strongly advocated commission control. He urged that large businesses "which restrain trade to such a degree as to control the market by that fact" should be declared affected with a public interest. [101] Monopoly should still be prohibited. Combinations of less than fifty per cent should be permitted, subject to commission control. The commission should have power to declare when a combination was a monopoly, and to "give the orders as to the modifications of the business which are necessary, so that the corporation shall cease to be a monopoly." [102]

He thought that his program would secure "freedom of competition, freedom of cooperation, destruction of monopoly, and justice to all." [103] But he went further, and advocated control of prices where there was control of the market, even though there be no monopoly. Yet he had just said that his policies would ensure free competition. Apparently he thought that large units would combine to fix prices, and that the only remedy was in the power of the state to control prices. But he wanted combinations to be subject to the anti-trust law which he would retain. Like all the others, his argument was not free from the curse of the ambiguity which pervaded the subject.

The Progressive platform finally declared that there should be a "strong national regulation of interstate corporations" by a federal administrative commission. It recognized that the "concentration of modern business, in some degree, is both inevitable and necessary for national and international business efficiency." But the power had been abused in monopoly of natural resources,

[99] *Ibid.*, pp. 264–5.   [100] *Ibid.*, pp. 264–65.
[101] Charles R. Van Hise, *Concentration and Control*, p. 249.
[102] *Ibid.*, p. 253.   [103] *Ibid.*, p. 254.

in unfair competition, unfair privileges, and in "sinister influences on the public agencies of State and Nation." A commission should be established which should "enforce complete publicity," and "attack unfair competition, false capitalization, and special privilege," and keep "open equally to all the highways of American commerce." [104]

The platform adopted the traditional Roosevelt policy with regard to the conservation of natural resources. Agricultural lands should remain open to the actual settler. Natural resources should be retained by the national government and leased to the operators. The policy of private exploitation must end, and the resources conserved for the benefit of all. This policy, it was asserted, would not "retard legitimate development."

The campaign was opened by a brilliant speech by Senator Beveridge, of Indiana, in the Progressive National Convention, and by Roosevelt in accepting the nomination. Let us pass over Roosevelt's discussion of the Republican primaries which, after all, was a discussion of the politics of the moment, and did not involve any essential element of his political theory. Nor shall we consider here his treatment of the recall of judicial decisions, which we have already considered. His political proposals likewise we shall take up in Chapter XII when we consider the struggle for political control.

Coming then to the industrial proposals of the Progressives, he asserted that, with England striving to make good the "human wreckage to which a scrap-heap scheme of industrialism has relegated her," with Germany putting the "painstaking resources of an empire at the work of developing her crafts and industrial science," and with the Far East developing its industrial resources, it behooved America "to keep abreast of the great industrial changes." The first charge on our "industrial statesmanship was to prevent human waste." [105] The disabled and crippled workers must be taken care of. Industrial accidents should be prevented so far as possible. He called for a living wage and for shorter hours, and for the prevention of child labor, night work, and exhausting work for women.

Then he came to the anti-trust law. He definitely stated that it

---

[104] *Ibid.*, Theodore Roosevelt, *Progressive Principles*, p. 318.
[105] Theodore Roosevelt, *Ibid.*, p. 130.

should be retained, but as a sole remedy he declared it had broken down. It was impossible to control great interstate corporations "merely by the Anti-Trust Law," merely by a succession of law suits.[106] The courts were not equipped, as Van Hise and Wyman had pointed out, to do administrative work. The Democratic platform, he said, would prevent all "business of any size or any efficiency."[107] It would, he argued, prevent combination, whether or not monopolistic or evil in tendency, while the Progressive plan would permit combination short of monopoly. He would keep the anti-trust law as a punishment of monopoly, and add a commission to supervise business steadily from day to day. The commission should not only prevent monopoly, but actual wrong done by the corporations, such as the artificial raising of prices, and the "elimination of competition by unfair or predatory practises."[108] No corporation coming under the commission should be prosecuted, so long as it obeyed the orders of the commission, and any corporation not coming under the commission should be subject to prosecution under the anti-trust law.

During the campaign, a great number of the social workers of the country joined in the campaign for industrial changes. The attack on the evils of the new industrial development was more widespread and determined than it has been at any time from then until the great depression.

WOODROW WILSON

A great effort was made both by Roosevelt and Wilson, and by their followers, to define the difference between the philosophies of the two parties. In essence there was little difference. William Allen White said it was the difference between tweedle-dum and tweede-dee.[109] Wilson himself, in 1916, claimed that "We have in four years come very near to carrying out the platform of the Progressive Party as well as our own, for we also are progressives."[110]

In the campaign of 1912, he declared for workmen's compensation laws. He asserted: "It is perfectly clear to every man who has any vision of the immediate future, who can forecast any part of it from the indications of the present, that we are just upon the

[106] *Ibid.*, p. 146.   [107] *Ibid.*, p. 147.   [108] *Ibid.*, p. 149.
[109] William Allen White, *Woodrow Wilson*, p. 264.
[110] Woodrow Wilson, *The New Democracy*, Vol. II, p. 280.

threshold of a time when the systematic life of this country will be sustained, or at least supplemented, at every point by governmental activity." [111]

But he made his great attack on the policy of the Progressives towards monopoly. He adopted in full the Brandeis interpretation. Brandeis declared that the Progressive Party tried to make the issue one between large scale production and small scale, on the ground that the Wilsonian policy was to throw away the advantage of large scale production and return to small units. But Brandeis objected that the issue was not between large and small business, but between large scale business and monopolistic business. He said that he was not opposed to mere size. He instanced, apparently with approval, the pending La Follette-Lenroot bill, under which he said a corporation could grow as large as it chose. The bill permitted combination up to thirty per cent of the country's business. If it were monopolistic, it would be condemned. If it controlled more than thirty per cent of the country's business, it would, in the absence of explanation, "be deemed unreasonable." [112] So he argued that the Wilson policy was not against size or combination as such. He proceeded to assert that there is a limit beyond which size is a burden and not a help. He held that no American "trust" owed its position to its efficiency, but rather to some unfair advantage that it had obtained. No "trust," he said, had been able to maintain itself against competition or keep its proportion of the business, without continuing to buy up its competitors.

Brandeis feared size and power, both economic and political. Fundamentally, he has always distrusted a world of big combinations. He has much affection for simpler days and Jeffersonian standards.

What he called monopolistic business was, therefore, in his opinion, both inefficient and dangerous. And Brandeis persisted that the Progressive Party policy was to legalize monopoly. This was the cue that Wilson took.

The issue, Wilson said, was between benevolence and justice, between a system which recognized and tolerated monopoly and sought merely to regulate it and a system which still, in traditional

[111] Woodrow Wilson, *The New Freedom*, p. 205.
[112] Louis Brandeis, "Business a Profession," *Collier's Weekly*, Sept. 12, 1912, pp. 198–99.

language, looked on monopoly as indefensible and intolerable. Again and again in the course of the campaign, he and his followers pressed this point. The opposition, he said, take the position that "trusts are inevitable." [113] They don't say, he answered, that big business is inevitable. Big business to a certain extent, he would admit was inevitable. He even admitted that big business was "probably desirable." [114] But the trusts were not the result of normal evolution. They were the result of unfair favors, of unnatural advantages. They were formed in order to obtain undue advantages. He believed that if the little fellow were given a chance, if he were given credit, if he were protected against unfair methods of competition, he could defeat the trust in any fair combat. "There must be," he said, "no squeezing out of the beginner; no crippling his credit; no discrimination against retailers who buy from a rival; no threats against concerns who sell supplies to a rival; no holding back of raw material from him; no secret arrangements against him. All the fair competition you choose, but no unfair competition of any kind." [115]

He repeated that he did not object to big business. It was unfair business and monopoly that he was against.

But, he also said that he was not against any business which grew big by what he called natural methods, by its efficiency, by making a better product and selling it at a good price.[116] This implied that he was against size by combination, even if it were not monopolistic.

He proposed then to keep the Sherman law against monopoly. But he would not admit that monopoly was inevitable. He called the opposing theory the trustee system of government, and declared that his opponents, both Taft and Roosevelt, believed in government by masters, by benevolent masters. But he would have none of it. He called for laws making certain acts of unfair competition unfair, stating that experience had shown that certain acts were of themselves undesirable and should be punished without proof of their results in the particular case.

He believed that his program would lead to the "liberation of a people's vital energies." He wished to set absolutely free "the energy and the initiative of this great people." [117] Restoring to the

[113] Wilson, *The New Freedom*, p. 155.   [114] *Ibid.*, p. 156.
[115] *Ibid.*, p. 164.   [116] *Ibid.*, p. 181.   [117] *Ibid.*, p. 276.

man of America "in very truth the control of his government, throwing wide all gates of lawful enterprise, unfettering his energies, and warming the generous impulses of his heart,—a process of release, emancipation, and inspiration," this was to him The New Freedom.[118]

When he became President, Wilson outlined his policies more particularly. In his first inaugural, he said that our industrial system had held "capital in leading strings, restricts the liberties and limits the opportunities of labor, and exploits without renewing or conserving the natural resources of the country. . . ." We had been proud of our industrial development, without counting "the human cost, the cost of lives snuffed out, of energies overtaxed and broken, the fearful physical and spiritual cost to the men and women and children upon whom the dead weight and burden of it all has fallen pitilessly the years through." [119]

Specifically, in his special message on Trusts in January, 1914, he proposed to establish a trade commission with power to prevent unfair methods of competition. He would immediately define certain acts of business as necessarily unfair competition. "The best informed men of the business world condemn the methods and processes and consequences of monopoly as we condemn them, and the instinctive judgment of the vast majority of business men everywhere goes with them." [120] So he proposed to forbid interlocking directorates and holding companies, and regulate the finances of railroads. Then he would forbid those methods of unfair competition which he said men were everywhere agreed upon, which should be prohibited per se.

Wilson felt that no campaign against monopoly would be of any avail unless the agencies of credit were freed. He subscribed to the Brandeis belief that there was a money trust. When governor of New Jersey, he had asserted: "The great monopoly in this country is the money monopoly." [121] Shortly after he became president, he addressed a special message on the currency, in which he asked what it would profit us to be quit of one kind of monopoly, namely, that created by the tariff, "if we are to remain in the grip of another and more effective kind?" He called for a currency not "rigid as now, but readily, elastically responsive to sound

[118] *Ibid.*, p. 277.   [119] Woodrow Wilson, *Messages and Papers,* Vol. I, pp. 2, 3.
[120] *Ibid.*, p. 49.   [121] Louis D. Brandeis, *Other People's Money,* p. 1.

credit," and, above all, not subject "to concentration anywhere in a few hands." [122]

Brandeis in 1913 and 1914 published a series of articles, later collected in his book, "Other People's Money," in which he impressively attacked many practises of banking in that day. He referred to interlocking directorships between banking firms and corporations and industrial corporations. He showed how investment bankers had become promoters, and passing from the role of promoters, entered the directorships of the corporations which they promoted or reorganized. He believed that bankers had levied a "heavy toll upon the whole community; upon owners of money for leave to invest it; upon railroads, public service and industrial companies, for leave to use this money of other people. . . ." [123]

But worse, he said, was the direct suppression of competition. He approved the Pujo Committee's conclusion that the acts "of this inner group . . . have nevertheless been more destructive of competition than anything accomplished by the trusts," for credit control struck at potential competition. [124]

And, lastly, the "money trust" suppressed industrial liberty.

He believed with the Pujo Committee that if "the arteries of credit now clogged well-nigh to choking . . . are opened . . . competition in large enterprises will become possible and business can be conducted on its merits, instead of being subject to the tribute and the good-will of this handful of self-constituted trustees of the national prosperity." [125]

Brandeis adverted again to what he called the "curse of bigness." He asserted again that there was a size limit to efficiency.

He proposed two chief reforms, those of the Pujo Committee, that "potentially competing corporations should not have a common director," and that a corporation should "not make a contract in which one of the management has a private interest." [126]

Whether there was actually a money trust in 1913 is still disputed. Many public-spirited bankers insist that the flow of credit was never monopolized. But that the currency was woefully inelastic, that it contracted in time of crisis, and did not respond to the needs of business, had been proved again and again. Moreover, the instinct that feared a single national bank under private con-

---

[122] Woodrow Wilson, *Messages and Papers*, pp. 12–13.
[123] Louis D. Brandeis, *Other People's Money*, p. 46.
[124] *Ibid.*, p. 2.   [125] *Ibid.*, p. 3.   [126] *Ibid.*, pp. 70–71.

trol, was wholly sound. Nor is there any doubt that many oppressive practises had been employed by powerful bankers.

The great trust debate was over for the time being. The issue, in a sense, was still unclarified. As we have seen, many had said rather loosely that the policy of dissolution of great combinations was a farce, and that the only recourse of the government was to regulate combinations and not dissolve them. But even these men did not propose to leave the government helpless in the face of a monopoly. It is true that Van Hise intimated that the government should declare a large combination a public service, and proceed to regulate its prices. But he also argued that the proposed commission should have the power to control monopolies and prevent the evils of monopolies. Wyman distinctly said that the anti-trust law should be maintained to dissolve any monopoly. While they were not altogether clear in their statements, it may be said that their policy was that when a combination was large but not a monopoly, it should be subject to the supervision of the commission, but that if it reached the monopolistic stage, the remedy under the anti-trust law was still available. At any rate, while there was some language of Roosevelt's that justified Wilson's and Brandeis' arguments, Roosevelt's policy as finally stated in 1912, was not to tolerate or recognize monopoly, but to tolerate and recognize large combinations. Large combinations should be allowed to remain, subject to regulation by the commission. But monopolies were still to be forbidden.

But there was confusion on the other side as well. Brandeis favored the old competition, the old individualism tempered by new restraints. But he distinctly favored the La Follette bill, which would permit combinations up to the thirty per cent of the country's output, even though the combination was one by combination and not by growth. Wilson said at one time that he was not afraid of any business that grew big as distinguished from one that combined big, indicating that he favored the old competition, tempered by new restraints again, a fair field and no favors, but opposed any combination of business, however small.

Roosevelt, therefore, tried to make the issue one between large units and small units; Wilson, one between monopoly and no monopoly. The issue, after all, was nearer the Rooseveltian issue than the Wilsonian. However much he might qualify, Wilson's instinct was all in favor of the old America, the America of many competing small units, and he distrusted all the vast aggregations of capital of the past generation. His heart was with the old order. He distrusted all combinations; Roosevelt did not. Each would prevent unfair methods; each would prevent the evils of monopoly. Neither, after all, would leave monopoly unfettered.

When Wilson came to carry out his program, he was more successful with the currency program than with the question of industrial monopoly.

The Federal Reserve was a great statesmanlike achievement. To prevent concentration of credit and money control, it provided for twelve regional reserve banks. Both the banks and government shared in the management. Interlocking directorships were forbidden. Federal reserve notes could be issued against eligible commercial paper discounted with the Federal Reserve Banks by the member banks. The recent crisis has proved that the Federal Reserve needs further adjustment, but it was nevertheless a great step forward. The World War financing would have been impossible without it.

But Wilson found more difficulty than he expected in defining the specific acts of unfair competition which he said all were agreed upon. The seven prohibitions which, as governor of New Jersey, he had caused to be enacted, were soon repealed. A Federal Trade Commission was established. The Clayton Act as passed named several acts as unfair, but not under all circumstances, but only when their effect was unduly to restrain competition. The administration of the act may fairly be said to have been a disappointment.

The result of the long battle was clearly to settle that mere size, as the saying went, was no offense. The public mind has largely changed. There is no longer the fear of great combinations. Our quiescence may be partly due to the general inactivity in our political thought from 1917 to 1929. It may be that we have become used to great combinations. It may be that the evil methods of business are less injurious than they were a generation ago. Certainly, while new forms of unfair competition are endless, it is fair to say that no great corporation today would adopt the ruthless methods of the eighties and nineties. Probably there is more competition now than then. The dissolutions of the Standard Oil

Company and the American Tobacco Company did eventually lead to competition between the old units, and new competition has sprung up.

Nor are we threatened by any such monopolistic combinations as those of the eighties and nineties. There is no corporation in the oil industry which controls eighty or ninety per cent of the oil business; none of eighty per cent in steel or tobacco, nor in automobiles. Nor is there the desire for overwhelming control that was manifested a generation ago. I think no well-advised great corporation today, with as much as fifty per cent control, would try to expand by combining with its competitors, as was done in the nineties and early nineteen hundreds.[127] Indeed, the United States Steel Corporation deliberately adopted a policy of keeping its control from exceeding fifty per cent of the total. Judge Gary noted that in 1906 Bryan had said that "fifty per cent was a legal limit for the size of a business," and Gary adopted Bryan's test for his own.[128]

Despite the tendency to consolidation (to which I shall refer in a moment), I think that Brandeis' argument against swollen size has had much effect. There is a widespread belief that beyond a certain point, increased size results in lessened efficiency, in a loss of the initiative and individuality which are essential to successful business.

While, then, the public has become accustomed to large units, while it is complaisant to large size, I am inclined to think that it would resent far-flung, oppressive combinations as much as before.

Yet although there are no such absorptive combinations such as we had a generation ago, while moreover, as Willard L. Thorp concludes, "The small establishment shows no tendency to disappear, despite the large concerns," [129] the growth of large concerns has gone steadily on. In the period between 1922 and 1929, the process of consolidation proceeded vigorously.[130] The result was

---

[127] Jeremiah W. Jenks and Walter E. Clark, in *The Trust Problem* (1924 ed.), p. 73, observe: "In later years the policy seems to have changed in many instances, and the 'capitalistic monopolist' has apparently found it wiser not to attempt to make his monopoly complete, but rather to remain content with market leadership and fairly steady high profits, without attempting to crush" competitors.

[128] Ida M. Tarbell, *The Life of Elbert H. Gary*, p. 257.

[129] Willard L. Thorp, "The Changing Structure of Industry," in *Recent Economic Changes in the United States*, Vol. I, p. 168.

[130] See Harry W. Laidler, *Concentration of Control in American Industry*, particularly pp. 434–48; A. A. Berle and Gardner C. Means, *The Modern Corporation and Private Property*, pp. 362–63.

that when the depression came, in a number of industries,—in oil, automobiles, tobacco, steel, rubber, and copper, for example,— the field was divided in each case by only half a dozen to a dozen big concerns. It would take an exhaustive examination in each case to determine how vigorous the competition is. Undoubtedly, it is more restrained, more subject to tacit agreement, than it would be if the field of competitors were larger.

Where the process will end, no one can say. The process of industrial adjustment is never-ending. New problems and new evils arise, and the old change their forms and pass away. But the old trust question of the nineties and the first fifteen years of this century, is surely vastly changed in our present America.

PROHIBITION

The manifestations of the progressive movement so far considered, may roughly be classified as regulatory and directive and not repressive. They did not restrict the liberty of action of the individual, save as that action restricted the opportunity of other individuals. The shortening of hours, token money laws, workmen's compensation laws, anti-trust laws, were aimed each at only a part of the population; and each was designed to make the race fairer for all concerned, to make a free and fair field for individual expression. But all through the period went on a campaign to control the habits of all the people. Though it was advocated sincerely on the ground that the rights and the activities of all were involved, it was, after all, inherently repressive in nature.

Of course, I refer to the prohibition movement. It had gone on for decades. The sorry aftermath of national prohibition has obscured much of our memory of the incessant campaign that had gone on for much of our national history. Throughout, it had been animated by a strong religious fervor. In thousands of homes of the old American stock, the use of liquor was habitually considered as immoral as financial dishonesty. The demand of a large part of the native stock for control, was met increasingly by the resistance of the immigrants whose customs were different. We had another illustration of the effects of the diversity of origins of our people.

Throughout the decades, the prohibition advocates habitually looked on the question as a simple moral issue. Liquor was evil, and its suppression was not to be argued. After the Civil War, such anti-slavery leaders as Gerritt Smith and Wendell Phillips turned to prohibition as the next step in the liberation of the individual. Gerritt Smith declared in 1869, "Slavery is gone, but drunkenness stays." The province of government, he went on, "being to protect person and property, it is clearly its duty to forbid the existence of the dram shop." [131] Wendell Phillips, in 1870, was the candidate for governor of the Prohibition Party in Massachusetts. Frances Willard, for years the head of the W.C.T.U., likewise compared prohibition to the anti-slavery struggle. "In 1863," she said, "slavery was the determining factor in American politics. In 1881, that final factor is the liquor traffic." [132]

The Prohibition Party first presented a national platform in 1872. Its campaign for State prohibition in the eighties met with general defeat. But the struggle went on, to limit hours, to require high license. A small but devoted band pressed steadily for national prohibition.

In 1893, the Anti-Saloon League was formed. It was frankly omni-partisan and not partisan; that is, it proposed to strike at the saloon in every way possible, by high license, by local option, by State prohibition. It called on all parties for help, and it distinctly weakened the force of the Prohibition Party.

By 1915, sixteen States were "dry," and the national movement became of serious moment.

Bryan had not originally been a prohibitionist. But he became an ardent "dry," and an advocate of national control. The anti-prohibitionists were wont to charge that prohibition was an attempt by part of the population to force its views on the rest, but Bryan did not accept the charge. Characteristically, he made the question a simple moral question. The use of liquor was injurious, "indefensible from the standpoint of health, safety, or business advantage." There was no good in it. All legislation recognized the injurious nature of the business.

Therefore, as liquor was all evil, the man who opposed prohibition was forcing his views on the righteous majority instead of the contrary. "The man," he said, "who opposes the sale of liquor is asking nothing for himself except relief from injury at the hands

[131] D. Leigh Colvin, *Prohibition in the United States*, pp. 75–76.
[132] *Ibid.*, p. 277.

of others, while the man who insists upon the sale of liquor is asking something for himself which can not be granted without injury to others." [133]

So, as liquor should be prohibited, the question was the size of the unit. He argued that when a city adopts prohibition, it was embarrassed by the fact that cities nearby permitted the sale; when counties prohibited, they were undercut by nearby counties; and that "prohibition states find it difficult to enforce the law because of the importation of liquor from surrounding states"; and concluded therefore that national prohibition was the best solution.[134]

President Eliot also was impressed with the necessity of national prohibition. In a letter written in 1924, which undoubtedly expressed his views at the time of the adoption of prohibition, he declared that he had been led to his opinion by the conviction that "the use of alcohol as a beverage threatens seriously the existence of the white race." But he said that until national prohibition became a factor, he could not see how the evil could be resisted. His summers in Maine had convinced him that state-wide prohibition could not succeed. But he believed that nation-wide prohibition might succeed, and he favored its trial.[135]

During the last years of our period, the opposition to prohibition was helpless. John Koren, in an able article in the "Atlantic," pointed out (as did many others) that if the "legally accessible sources of supply" were cut off, but with every facility for home production of intoxicants left, disaster would be sure to follow. We could not employ "an army vast enough to prevent illegal selling." We would have "avowed disobedience to law dominating political battles." [136] Taft warned of the disrespect for law which would follow an attempt to enforce national prohibition; that the "constant violation or neglect of any law leads to a demoralized view of all laws," and "constantly enlarges in the community the class of men with whom the sacredness of law does not exist." [137]

Senator Oscar W. Underwood, in an able speech in the Senate in December, 1914, predicted that national prohibition would encour-

---

[133] William J. Bryan, "Why I Am a Prohibitionist," *Independent,* Vol. LXXXVII, pp. 88–89, (July 17, 1916.)
[134] *Ibid.,* p. 89.
[135] Henry James, *Charles William Eliot,* Vol. II, pp. 417–419.
[136] John Koren, "Drink Reform in the United States," *Atlantic,* Vol. CXVI, pp. 588, 597, 598 (Nov., 1915).
[137] William H. Taft, *Four Aspects of Civic Duty,* p. 48.

age "blind tigers throughout the length and breadth of our country." He carefully analyzed the extravagant claim of the prohibitionists, that its advent brought great social gains; and argued that the death rate, the suicide rate, the divorce rate, were actually higher in prohibition Kansas than in most of the "wet" States. The averages of savings bank deposits and the proportion of church membership was lower in Kansas than in "wet" States.[138]

But the demand could not be stayed. The present generation has forgotten much of the pressure of facts and events which made prohibition possible. Mistaken though it was on any sound theory of political action (for the habits of a large minority can never be controlled by the majority), it will not do to say that prohibition was the work of a few fanatics, nor that the final result was due to war emotion. The campaign had been progressing for decades, and with ever-increasing momentum. In the end, it had the widespread support of employers. Bryan referred frequently to the rules of railroads and some industrial employers against drinking employees.

But the political evils of the liquor business were the main consideration. The liquor business for a generation had been predominantly lawless, and a vicious corrupter of our politics. No realistic history of American politics for the forty years before 1917, can ignore the force of the money of the liquor business in controlling the action of our political parties. Lyman Abbott was no intolerant bigot. He wrote in 1915 that he had believed in regulation and not prohibition, but that "the action of the liquor dealer has made regulation impossible." The liquor dealer defied the law, sold to minors, after closing hours, and on Sunday; and Abbott concluded that the question was, "whether the laws enacted by the community shall be obeyed." The saloon was not only "a local nuisance, but also a national calamity." Between a lawless liquor traffic and prohibition, the people would choose prohibition.[139]

The prohibition campaign ended just after the close of the period of our study, but the arguments presented here were the arguments on which it was passed. There was much war emotion involved, many claims of the millennium if it were adopted, crime would cease or become negligible; but there are such overstatements in all

---

[138] *Congressional Record,* Dec. 22, 1914, p. 520.
[139] *The Outlook,* Vol. III, pp. 401–402, (Oct. 20, 1915).

political movements. The real reason was the lawless nature of the liquor business and the sense of impotence if the control were not made national. Our relief at the end of what proved to be a mistake, must not cause us to forget the evils which led to the action.

But the results of national Prohibition vividly illustrated the limits of political action. The Prohibition advocates were wont to rely on the general principles of majority rule, to recite the decisive votes they had received. Thus Leigh Colvin, the historian of the Prohibition movement, cites the fact that the total vote for Prohibition amendments in thirty-two states was 5,568,719 for Prohibition, and only 4,218,235 against; and comments: "These figures absolutely disprove the unfounded assertion that Prohibition was put across against the wishes of the people." [140]

I would agree Prohibition was not "put across" against the will of the majority. It is idle to say that it was the result of hysterical propaganda. But that does not answer the question. The prohibitionists argue that the majority voted for Prohibition, and the minority ought to respond to the will of the majority. But politics does not respond to "oughts." Colvin's own figures show that forty-five per cent of the people in thirty-two states voted against Prohibition. But no law can be enforced if forty-five per cent of those against whom it must be enforced, do not want it. To speak bluntly: If forty-five per cent of the people thought that murder should not be prohibited, no law against murder could be enforced. If forty-five per cent of those with children able to work wanted them to work, and forty-five per cent of the employers wanted them to work, a child labor law could not be enforced. Laws affecting personal habits can not be decided by majority vote. A law affecting personal habits comes into effect only when the majority is so overwhelming, that the belief that the minority is undercutting is a generally accepted conclusion.

APPRAISAL OF THE PROGRESSIVE MOVEMENT

How, then, shall we appraise the Progressive movement, its leaders, causes, and results? It was more of a unity than it appeared to those who engaged in it. However they might differ in their approach, Bryan, La Follette, Roosevelt, and Wilson, all—after all —wanted much the same results. It was distinctly a movement to

[140] Colvin, *Prohibition in the United States,* p. 438.

restore or to retain the old individualistic America. All of the leaders were opposed to socialism; all felt that it was a deadener of individual initiative. They all instinctively dreaded great aggregations of capital, and all were temperamentally opposed to the methods of thought of the large business leaders. They all wished to control and regulate combinations of capital, and allow play to individual activity.

Their methods of thinking differed more than their proposals. Bryan was a Jeffersonian Democrat, who consistently applied a few fundamental formulas to our modern problems. His heart was with the small producer, the small merchant, and he would have been happier in a day when they were secure.

There was much that was a priori, and some that was mystical, in the mental processes of Woodrow Wilson. His opponents used to say that he was over-intellectual, severely logical in his thinking. I think, rather, that he was extremely emotional. Many of his conclusions were arrived at intuitively. He saw few people, talked to few. He said in 1915 that, "Standing alone here, I feel and know that I am in closer conscious touch with the people." There were no "walls of selfish humans" between him "and the country," and so he felt that he was in "conscious relation with all the people." [141]

His results, in short, to a large extent, came from his own inner consciousness. Consequently, he was often unstable in his opinions. He changed completely on the initiative and referendum, and on a national child labor law. Naturally a State Rights man and a believer in little legislation, he sponsored legislation for the Federal Reserve Act, the Farm Loan Act, the Rural Credits Act, the Federal Trade Commission, and the Federal Child Labor Law.

Roosevelt touched reality constantly. Antaeus-like, he renewed himself daily. He had a thousand sources of information, and was in contact with people and things on every side. The facts made his philosophy. At the height of his influence he had a keen insight into the popular desires, whereas Wilson frequently deceived himself into thinking that the people were thinking what he was thinking.

Like the Populist movement, the Progressive movement has been

[141] Samuel G. Blythe, "A Talk with the President," *Saturday Evening Post*, Jan. 9, 1915, pp. 3, 37.

called the child of the pioneer. It must be admitted that there was this element in its psychology. But, after all, the frontier had gone for three generations in the east, for one and a half in the middle west, and the east and the middle west were as strong for progressivism as the far west. The same industrial reforms advocated by the Progressives, were being proposed or had already been enacted in England and Germany, which had known no frontier for a thousand years. The Progressive demand for workmen's insurance, for factory reform, received great stimulus from the example of England and Germany. I think that the impact of the new industrialism was far stronger than the psychology of the frontier.

The Progressive movement has been called a disappointment. It is said that here we are in 1936 with immensely complicated economic problems arising out of the machine age, and the Progressive movement did not foresee them nor forestall them. The leaders of the Progressive movement, says Chamberlain in his "Farewell to Reform," did not think their program through.[142] They had no definite plan, no ideal end in view. Apparently he believes that the only way out is a socialist America, or what he prefers to call industrial democracy. The only remedy for the conflict of power between the economic groups is to destroy the economic groups. Apparently with him, for a program to be sound, one must know where it will end a generation hence. The idea that politics is a perpetual tacking, a perpetual adjustment, that no one can know where his program will be thirty years hence, because he does not know what thirty years will bring, is not for him. For one who does not believe in socialism, there can be no one system. There can be no final adjustment. The problem can not possibly be thought through. The adjustment is made constantly. It is an endless process, a constant decision and series of decisions,—that the state must handle this or drop that, that individual initiative must be checked here or relieved of a check there. Indeed, one suspects that even under socialism no equilibrium could be reached, but that constantly new adjustments must be made. Man is not static. As Justice Holmes finely said, "But certainty generally is illusion, and repose is not the destiny of man." [143]

All any program can do is to achieve an equilibrium for the

[142] John Chamberlain, *Farewell to Reform*, p. 304.
[143] Oliver Wendell Holmes, "The Path of the Law" (1897), *Collected Legal Papers*, p. 181.

moment, to adjust the conflicts of interest and desires of the time, so that there is no explosion. This, the progressive movement certainly did. Its industrial proposals have generally been adopted. The present generation is building where it left off.

It has been said that the Progressive movement was a movement of the middle classes. I distrust all such generalizations. It was predominantly so perhaps, but there were mingled with it men and women of all classes. Its industrial proposals had been favored for years by union labor. Its proposals for the control of trusts were the program of the larger business men. Wilson represented emotionally the desires of the smaller business man, but Roosevelt distinctly represented the larger business man, and even Wilson and Brandeis came in policy to that viewpoint.

In summary, it is difficult to say more than that the progressive movement was a program for a newer individualism, a mean between socialism and laissez faire, an attempt to make an adjustment of the forces then impinging on our national life. The program in the mind of its sponsors was essentially individualistic. They reiterated again and again the current distrust of socialism. They wished to create a new individualism, protected against the aggressions of the old regime which would enjoy some of the opportunity of a simpler day. Roosevelt summed up his theories in an article in the Century magazine in 1913. The old doctrine of "extreme individualism," he said and of "a purely competitive industrial system," had completely broken down. Uncontrolled competition between competitors mostly small and weak must be succeeded by cooperation and combination. Inheritance taxes must be used to prevent swollen fortunes, and workmen's compensation and social insurance to protect the working man against the hazards of industrial life. The result would be to make the individual stronger and better able to exert his powers in any way his capacity entitled him.[144]

The philosophy of the progressive era was therefore individualism, a new individualism designed to give the individual under new conditions, the same kind of advantages enjoyed in a simpler day. It wished to place controls on certain practises of business, not to restrain freedom but to conserve freedom for a greater number.

[144] Theodore Roosevelt, "The Progressive Party," *Century Magazine,* Oct. 1913, pp. 828, 833, 834.

It desired to protect those who could not protect themselves: children, women in industry, and men who were at an economic disadvantage. It still insisted on preventing monopoly, but where monopoly was inevitable or natural, it would accept it, subject to control. Through every item of the program was the instinctive thought that individualism, so modified, should continue. The individual would merely be made freer for a better regulated contest.

Most significant of all Progressive demands, I think, was that of the Progressive Party for social insurance "against the hazards of sickness, irregular employment, and old age,"—the demand for security which twenty years later was to reach such volume, as men and women realized the catastrophic vicissitudes of the machine age. In nothing was the change from the American of forty years before more striking. We have seen that Palmer, in 1886, in espousing the Interstate Commerce bill, asserted that all an American citizen asked for was a "fair chance, no odds of the Government, but its protection. . . ."[145] The old individualist insisted that each care for himself, and that he who could not was an incompetent and should be treated as such. But we were beginning to realize that there were human values which we must conserve; and that, in a complicated industrial age, the old individualism could not conserve them.

Professor Ernst Freund, of the University of Chicago, well said that the social legislation of the period showed two main tendencies: "the steady growth in the value placed upon individual human personality; and the shifting of the idea of the public good from the security of the state and established order to the welfare of the mass of the people."[146]

W. F. Willoughby argued that we recognized with Dicey that, in infringing upon the theoretical liberty of contract for the sake of the "greater practical freedom in other respects conferred upon the people affected," we realized that "a minimum of economic independence and comfort" is essential if "an individual is to be measurably free, and that this minimum can only be secured by the state assuming the obligation to see that it is in no case violated."[147] He called it a juristic paradox that "liberty is many times sacri-

---

[145] *Congressional Record*, April 14, 1886, p. 3478.
[146] Ernst Freund, *Standards of American Legislation*, p. 22.
[147] "The Philosophy of Labor Legislation," *The American Labor Leg. Review*, 1914, Vol. IV, pp. 41–42.

ficed by laws conferring freedom, and that laws establishing legal restraints have as their result the broadening of the field of liberty." [148]

A growing liberal opinion was ready to admit the need for important changes in our economic order for distributing wealth. Lyman Abbott, while firmly rejecting socialism, felt strongly that the wage system could not be permanent. It divides society into two great classes, "more or less hostile." [149] It creates a great concentration of wealth. The working-man, he added, thinks that the discrepancy is too large, and "I, personally, agree with him." [150] He believed that a radical change was necessary, although he thought it would be gradual. The wage system must go. The remedy was what he called industrial democracy: cooperative ownership of businesses, the increase of employee ownership and employee representation in control.

With the desire for protection and representation for the working-man, went a pervading feeling that great discrepancies in wealth were undesirable. In an eloquent appeal to President Taft in the "North American Review" in 1911, Wayne McVeagh, a distinguished lawyer, writing in his retirement in the "fullness of years and honor," called on the government to respond to the "crying need now confronting all civilized societies, that is, the narrowing of the too wide gulf between those who are too rich and those who are too poor." [151] He dwelt on the standard injustices of the tariff and governmental waste; but he went further, and bluntly asked that surplus wealth be taxed. Unearned income and accumulations could be taxed, without causing the "persons thus taxed the loss of a single luxury." [152] It was the only effective bulwark against the rising tide of socialism.

But he argued from more than the basis of such expediency. He called for a policy bringing men closer together in brotherhood, "making the poor daily less poor, and the rich daily less rich"; that we share with them "in fuller, and ever fuller measure, the measureless bounty of God." [153] He condemned our "pitiable cowardice in refusing to tax surplus wealth"; and ended by again

[148] *Ibid.*, p. 40.
[149] Lyman Abbott, *The Spirit of American Democracy*, p. 98.
[150] *Ibid.*, p. 100.
[151] Wayne MacVeagh, "An Appeal to President Taft," *North American Review*, Vol. CXCIII, p. 161, 163. (Feb. 1911).
[152] *Ibid.*, p. 173.   [153] *Ibid.*, p. 175.

calling on us to "stop widening, and begin narrowing, such a gulf between the rich and the poor." These inequalities, he said, "represent, as nothing else does, the tragedy of all human story," and he was convinced that "the struggle to establish a fairer and more reasonable evenness in human conditions" is the "most ancient, the most persistent, and most successful of all efforts of the human spirit towards a better life."[154]

Of one thing we may be fairly certain: in a political democracy, the effort to attain greater equality of wealth and economic power will go steadily on. No people who, as children, grow up in the public schools in the country and small towns in general equality, will be content that wholesome relationships are prevented by the changes of later life. The demand for greater equality is a demand based not only on economic need (for economic power is political power), not only on jealousy (which is a political force), but it is based also on a deeper instinct,—the desire for personal freedom of action, and the dignity of the person.

How far the protection and interference of the state should go, we can not say. The events of the past three years indicate that it must go farther than most of us thought necessary at the end of the progressive era. But at that time, clearly, the individualistic note was predominant. Protected against some of the disastrous consequences of the machine age, against the tragic results of industrial injury, given a chance against the mass forces of production, it was felt that the individual would be enabled to live with something of the freedom and to enjoy something of the opportunity of his fathers in a simpler time. Again and again, the desire was expressed that the old individualism must be preserved.

REFERENCES

ABBOTT, LYMAN, *The Spirit of Democracy*. Boston: Houghton Mifflin Co., 1910.

BERLE, A. A. and MEANS, GARDNER C., *The Modern Corporation and Private Property*. New York: The Macmillan Co., 1934.

BLYTHE, SAMUEL G., "A Talk with the President." *Saturday Evening Post.* Jan. 9, 1915, p. 3.

BOWERS, CLAUDE G., *Beveridge and the Progressive Era*. Boston: Houghton Mifflin Co., 1932.

BRANDEIS, LOUIS D., *Business a Profession*. Boston: Small, Maynard & Co., 1914.

[154] *Ibid.*, p. 178.

————*Other People's Money*. New York: Frederick A. Stokes Co., 1914.

BRYAN, WILLIAM J., *Speeches* (2 Vols.). New York: Funk & Wagnalls Co., 1909.

————"Why I Am for Prohibition." *The Independent*, Vol. LXXXIII, p. 88 (July 17, 1916).

————and BRYAN, MARY BAIRD, *The Memoirs of William J. Bryan*. Philadelphia: John C. Winston Co., 1925.

CHAMBERLAIN, JOHN, *Farewell to Reform*. New York: Liveright, Inc., 1932.

COLVIN, D. LEIGH, *Prohibition in the United States*. New York: Geo. H. Doran Co., 1926.

CROLY, HERBERT, *The Promise of American Life*. New York: The Macmillan Co., 1909.

————*Progressive Democracy*. New York: The Macmillan Co., 1914.

CULLOM, SHELBY M., *Fifty Years of Public Service*. Chicago: A. C. McClung & Co., 1911.

DEWITT, BENJAMIN P., *The Progressive Movement*. New York: The Macmillan Co., 1915.

FREUND, ERNST, *Standards of American Legislation*. Chicago: University of Chicago Press, 1917.

GUNTON, GEORGE, *Trusts and the Public*. New York: D. Appleton & Co., 1899.

JAMES, HENRY, *Charles William Eliot* (2 Vols.). Boston: Houghton Mifflin Co., 1930.

JAMES, WILLIAM, "The Social Value of the College Bred," in *Memories and Studies*, pp. 323-24. New York: Longmans, Green & Co., 1911.

JENKS, JEREMIAH W., *The Trust Problem*. New York: McClure, Phillips & Co., 1903.

————and CLARK, WALTER E., *The Trust Problem*. New York: Doubleday, Page & Co., 1924.

KALES, ALBERT M., *Unpopular Government in the United States*. Chicago: University of Chicago Press, 1914.

KOREN, JOHN, "Drink Reform in the United States." *The Atlantic Monthly*, Vol. CXVI, p. 588 (Nov. 1915).

LA FOLLETTE, ROBERT M., *Autobiography*. Madison, Wis.: Robert M. La Follette Co., 1911-13.

LAIDLER, HARRY W., *Concentration of Control in American Industry*. New York: Thomas Y. Crowell Co., 1931.

LLOYD, HENRY D., *Wealth Against Commonwealth*. New York: Harper & Bros., 1894.

LONG, J. C., *Bryan, the Great Commoner*. New York: D. Appleton & Co., 1928.

McCARTHY, CHARLES, *The Wisconsin Idea*. New York: The Macmillan Co., 1912.

McVEAGH, WAYNE, "An Appeal to President Taft." *North American Review*, Vol. CXCIII, p. 161 (Feb., 1911).

MONTAGUE, GILBERT HOLLAND, *The Rise and Progress of the Standard Oil Company.* New York: Harper & Bros., 1903.

ROOSEVELT, THEODORE, *The New Nationalism.* New York: The Outlook Co., 1910.

——"The Progressive Party." *Century Magazine,* Nov., 1913.

——*Progressive Principles.* New York: Progressive National Service, 1913.

——*Works,* Vol. XVII. New York: Charles Scribner's Sons, 1925.

——*Presidential Addresses and State Papers* (Homeward Bound ed.), Vols. III, VI, VII. New York: Review of Reviews Corp., 1908.

SMITH, J. ALLEN, *The Spirit of American Government.* New York: The Macmillan Co., 1907.

STEPHENSON, NATHANIEL W., *Nelson W. Aldrich.* New York: Charles Scribner's Sons, 1930.

TAFT, WILLIAM H., *Four Aspects of Civic Duty.* New York: Charles Scribner's Sons, 1906.

TARBELL, IDA M., *The Life of Elbert H. Gary.* New York: D. Appleton & Co., 1926.

THORP, WILLARD L., "The Changing Structure of Industry," in *Recent Economic Changes in the United States,* Vol. I. New York: McGraw-Hill Book Co., 1929.

UNITED STATES INDUSTRIAL COMMISSION, *Final Report,* Vol XIX. Washington: Government Printing Office, 1902.

VAN HISE, CHARLES R., *Concentration and Control.* New York: The Macmillan Co., 1912.

WERNER, M. R., *Bryan.* New York: Harcourt, Brace & Co., 1929.

WEYL, WALTER E., *The New Democracy.* New York: The Macmillan Co., 1912.

WHITE, WILLIAM *ALLEN, *Woodrow Wilson: The Man, His Times and His Tasks.* Boston: Houghton Mifflin Co., 1924.

WILLOUGHBY, W. F., "The Philosophy of Labor Legislation," *The American Labor Legislation Review.* 1914. Vol. IV.

WILSON, WOODROW, *The New Freedom* (Tauchnitz ed., 1912). *The Messages and Papers* (2 vols.). New York: Review of Reviews Corp., 1924.

WYMAN, BRUCE, *Control of the Market.* New York: Moffat, Yard & Co., 1911.

Chapter IX

CONSERVATISM

I HAVE deferred until now a detailed consideration of the political theory of those who opposed the political program of the Populists and the Progressives. We have seen it manifested as we have gone along in the decisions of the courts on the due process clause, in the arguments for freedom of contract and the sanctions of the Bill of Rights. Token money laws, workmen compensation laws, hours of labor laws, all have been opposed because they violated freedom of contract and the inherent freedom of the individual.

Railroad rate legislation was also opposed because it hampered the freedom of action of the individualistic railroad man. But let us now try to group together and analyze this theory of opposition.

After all, the theory of the opposition was more coherent than that of the proponents of the new political action. The attack necessarily varied with the subjects discussed. The pressure of facts in each case made the theory. But the opposition was naturally based more on general theory; in other words, on experience in the past which had become solidified in formulas.

Traditionally, that philosophy is called the theory of laissez faire. But, after all, there is, of course, no one who subscribes to complete laissez faire save the anarchist, and no one who is the complete opposite save the communist. Macauley said once that he could not conceive that anyone could be all liberal or all conservative. But naturally, all theories are theories of predominant trends, of prepossessions, and in the course of one hundred years since Adam Smith, a general theory had sprung up, to which men who held it tried to fit the new problems pressing upon them.

The ablest—and certainly the most trenchant—opponent of government regulation in the period was William Graham Sumner, of Yale. His father was a mechanic from Lancashire, self-reliant and from a self-reliant stock. For a generation, Sumner exerted an enormous influence on the young men of Yale and of the country.

The phrase, "Forgotten Man" came from his essays. He wrote that the "Forgotten Man" was his own father.[1] The forgotten man was the man who received no favors from the government, but carried on his work without help and without notice. Sumner might well have been the originator of the phrase, "rugged individualism"; for a rugged individualist he assuredly was. His philosophy was self-reliant, bold, and incisive. He had the utmost scorn of state favoritism, and a passionate belief in the free play of individual activity.

His words have a fine and resolute ring. He preached a manly independence. Man is born, he said, under a burden and a necessity. "The relation therefore between each man's needs and each man's energy, or 'individualism,' is the first fact of human life."[2] The first necessity was, then, that man should not be interfered with in his activity and civil liberty, for liberty under the law "means the guarantees of law that a man shall not be interfered with while using his own powers for his own welfare." That nation had the freest institutions in which the guarantees of peace for the laborer and security for the capitalist, were the highest. Civil liberty did not do away with the struggle for existence. It turned the competition of men from violence into an industrial competition, "under which men vie with one another for the acquisition of material goods by industry, energy, skill, frugality, prudence, temperance, and other industrial virtues."[3]

Society was bound by laws of nature precisely like those of the physical order, and our troubles were due, to a great extent, "to the dogmatism and self-interest of statesmen, philosophers, and ecclesiastics," who had burdened society with vicious institutions.[4] Again, he said that "these social and economic circumstances are subject to universal, natural laws which we can not alter seems to be a strange doctrine which people are slow to understand."[5] Political institutions which endure are those that grow and are not made, and there is only a very narrow limit in which man can act to advantage.

He protested against the notion that man can invent any institutions he pleases. He argued that our life was bound by conditions.

[1] Harris E. Starr, *William Graham Sumner,* p. 18.
[2] William Graham Sumner, *The Challenge of Facts,* p. 17.   [3] *Ibid.,* p. 26.
[4] *Ibid.,* p. 37.   [5] Starr, *Sumner,* p. 220.

The economic factors were apparently beyond our control. He seemed to assume that leadership in industry went always to the possessors of the ancestral virtues, and that restraint on their activities was sure to result in a lesser order of ability. He had no fear of great accumulations of wealth. "Where is the rich man," he exclaimed, "who is oppressing anybody? If there was one, the newspapers would ring with it. . . . To prove any harm in aggregations of wealth, it must be shown that great wealth is, as a rule, in the ordinary course of social affairs, put to a mischievous use. This can not be shown beyond the very slightest degree, if at all." [6]

Again and again, Sumner expressed the fear that state interference would destroy self-reliance, initiative, energy, and independence. He would leave man free to the operation of natural laws. Shortly, he said, translate it into "blunt English," and laissez faire "will read, 'Mind your own business.' It is nothing but the doctrine of liberty." [7]

Sumner vigorously opposed the Sherman Act and the Interstate Commerce Act of 1887, as unwarranted interferences with business freedom. All attempts, he insisted, "so far made to extend the domain of policy in social matters have resulted only in doubt and in warnings of danger; the proposition to adopt a policy of organization can never do anything but disturb the harmony of the societal system which is its greatest advantage. They will never really change the societal organization, for it is already controlled by the mighty forces of interest. For instance: if so-called trusts are now a real step in the evolution of the industrial organization, a legislative policy of sweeping and destructive opposition to them is vain, and after producing great confusion and animosity and loss, will have to be abandoned." [8]

The fears of monopoly were groundless. "There is no evil or danger in trusts," he went on, "which is nearly so menacing to society as the measures which are proposed for destroying trusts." [9] The enterprise of the business leaders should not be so hampered. The Interstate Commerce Act of 1887, like inflation and the pro-

[6] William Graham Sumner, "The Absurd Attempt to Make the World Over," in *War and Other Essays*, p. 202.
[7] A. G. Keller, *Reminiscences of William Graham Sumner*, p. 56.
[8] Sumner, "The Power and Beneficence of Capital," in *Earth Hunger and Other Essays*, p. 343 (1899).
[9] Starr, *Sumner*, p. 248.

tective tariff, would inevitably produce a distortion of the industrial system. It was an interference with the natural play of economic laws, and hampered the freedom of the business leaders.

Sumner's biographers warmly resent the belief that he was indifferent to human suffering; or, as Professor Keller says, that he adopted "an attitude of fatalistic passivity, indifference to social weal, or callousness to human suffering." Both Herbert Spencer and Sumner, he says, were fighting all their lives "for the betterment of social conditions. . . ." He challenged anyone to name a "prominent so-called advocate of laissez faire who was not active against the abuses of his time." [10] Harris E. Starr likewise asserts that "Nothing is more false or unfair than to picture Sumner as a cold, hard, crass individualist and advocate of laissez faire. . . . Nothing could be more contrary to fact than that he was against all attempts at reform, a scoffer at every effort for social betterment." [11]

Starr and Keller point out that Sumner was savage against what he felt to be injustice. Protection, inflation, imperialism, aroused all his fighting spirit. But when it came to economic legislation, Keller says that Sumner was led "to a let-alone policy by a realization of the damage done through ignorant, often well-intentioned, meddling." He "resented the light self-confidence of the voluble empty-head in setting out to make the world over." [12] One of his essays is entitled, "The Absurd Attempt to Make the World Over."

Sumner objected that the state, in the effort to make the world over, in the passion for state interference, was not affording the individual protection and security against such encroachments, for instance, as the boycott. But the demand for protection against unfair trade practises, the demand for protection of the laborer against token money and excessive hours, of the small shipper against railroad rebates, were certainly no different, in essence, from the demand for protection against the boycott. Discrimination by rebate was surely as vicious as discrimination by a protective tariff.

It is really amazing that a man of his reading and intellectual force should have asked, where was the rich man who was oppressing anybody, in the days when railroad rebates and the most vicious methods of business competition were rampant in the land. It is a striking instance of how much we all retain the evidence

---

[10] Keller, p. 55. [11] Starr, *Sumner,* p. 390. [12] Keller, *Sumner,* p. 54.

that suits our theory, and ignore that which does not! One can not avoid the conclusion that Sumner had never suffered personally from some of the encroachments on liberty by rapacious individual action, which the advocates of change in that era condemned. If he had been part of business himself, he would have known that all men who rose to leadership in industry were not endowed with the copy-book virtues. The demand for legislative action was largely a demand that men be protected against unfair advantages, that they be given a freer opportunity to be the individuals that Sumner wanted them to be.

Moreover Sumner spoke, as others of his school, of the immutable laws which the reformers ignored. We are now less confident of laws which work ever the same. Society is never static, conditions change, and the operation of human nature under different conditions can not always be predicted. Experience in the past makes us conclude that certain things will happen in the future if tried again, such as that bad money will drive out good, and that man needs some reward of profit to stimulate him to work. But to come down to concrete illustrations: there are certainly no immutable laws which told us a generation ago that railroad regulation would or would not work, that workmen's compensation laws were vicious, that the limitation of hours was impossible. Such laws depend, after all, largely on human desires and needs, and if enough people want them to work, they will work. Politics, after all, is still an empirical science, despite the fact that experience has convinced us that further experiment is useless in certain lines.

One of the most striking examples of the philosophy of those who watched the course of our politics with misgiving in the years of the great Progressive movement, is contained in the book, "Man versus the State," published in 1916, in which a number of representative conservatives contributed comments on chapters of Herbert Spencer's, "Man versus the State." Their comments showed clearly the great influence of the Spencerian theory in our country. David Jayne Hill spoke of the "gradual imposition of a new bondage in the name of freedom," of "the increasing subjection of the citizen to the growing tyranny of officialism." He said that with "deep prophetic insight" Spencer saw in " 'Over-Legislation,' the 'Coming Slavery,' and his predictions have been verified." But the end "is not yet, and this volume affords an opportunity to consider with deliberation and in the light of facts what the future is to be." [13] He declared that there are certain inherent rights which "the State should not be permitted to take away." If the state could take them away, "there is no basis for it but superior force." [14] There was no difference, he said, whether the suppression of such rights "is effected by one or a few, or a majority" of the individual's fellow beings. He complained of the growing "acceptance of the idea that the state should control the conduct and the possessions of the individual, including his personal habits, his business activities, and even his private opinions." [15]

Henry Cabot Lodge, commenting on the chapter, "The Coming Slavery," declared that no one "perhaps has pointed out the ultimate truths involved in this expansion of governmental functions better than Herbert Spencer, in the essays collectively entitled, 'The Man Versus the State.' " [16]

Elbert H. Gary highly approved the chapter on "Over-Legislation," but in his comments cited no single modern instance. He went back to the blue laws for his examples. Then he said that the "chief work of the Supreme Court is to prevent over-legislation," that it lays down the law that "excessive lawmaking is in itself a crime against law,"—statements surely opposed to our whole theory of government.

Gary said that "the best government is that which maintains order, protects the rights, and promotes the prosperity of the people, with the least possible amount of law writing, interference, and ingenious devices for control of the individual." Constructive laws, he said, which include "laws as to tariff, financial systems, road building, cooperating with farmers at public expense, etc.," aim "to promote the prosperity of the people as a whole." [17]

But he admitted that the State must protect children, workers of all kinds, from "unfair competition from abroad, harsh conditions, and unreasonable and unhealthful hours." But "do not," he added, "limit opportunity by limiting power." [18]

Nicholas Murray Butler likewise expressed a belief in natural rights. He exclaimed that "the thoroughly obscurantist and reactionary doctrine is now taught—and curiously enough it is taught

---

[13] Herbert Spencer, *Man Versus the State,* Ed. Truxton Beale, p. ix, xi.
[14] *Ibid.,* p. 220.   [15] *Ibid.,* pp. 220, 222.   [16] *Ibid.,* p. 31.
[17] *Ibid.,* pp. 71, 78.   [18] *Ibid.,* p. 79.

under the name of progress—that the individual has no rights save those which society confers upon him, and that society may, by majority vote to (sic.) do what it pleases with him." This, he held, was at variance with the fundamental principles on which the nation was founded, as expressed in the Declaration of Independence. These natural rights, he said, "are attributes of human personality." [19]

But he admitted that he thought Herbert Spencer's laissez faire theories went too far.[20]

Probably the ablest representative of the conservatives in the latter part of our period was Elihu Root. He had a fine legal mind and a strong sense of public duty. There is no doubting his intrinsic idealism, and indeed the fine emotion of his love of our traditions and of our institutions. Roosevelt declared his mind to be the ablest with which he had come in contact in his time. Time and again he showed that he could adjust his mind to new problems, and he was far from being a stubborn Tory. He favored, as we shall see, a direct primary law. He favored the second Federal employers' liability law. His speeches in the New York Constitutional convention showed that he fully comprehended the nature of the political organizations of his day. Yet his speeches on political theory show the same tendency to deal in platitudes, the outworn shibboleths of a past day, which was shown by these other commentators on Herbert Spencer. He too believed in natural rights, or rather considered the rights which were dear to him as in some sort sacred and inherent, and beyond the reach of legislatures. In an address on "The Lawyer of Today," he lamented the day of his early manhood when "underlying principles were never questioned," while "now the postulates are all denied." [21]

Again in an address on the "Responsibility of the Bar," he said, "We had then to appeal to established and unquestioned principles." But now, he added, "Fundamental principles are questioned, doubted, discussed, possibly endangered." Our country, "which seemed then so secure, so peaceful, so certain in its prospect of prosperity and peace and order, is passing in under the shadow of great responsibilities, and great dangers to its institutions." [22]

---

[19] *Ibid.*, pp. 177–78.   [20] *Ibid.*, p. 179.

[21] Elihu Root, *Addresses on Government and Citizenship*, p. 506 (address of March 13, 1915).

[22] *Ibid.*, p. 512 (address of Jan. 15, 1916).

In an address before the New York Constitutional Convention of 1914, he quoted the words of the Declaration, and declared that they were a denial of the theory held by the ancient republics, which was that the rights of the individual are "derived only as a member of the state." He asserted that with us, the rights of the individual "are not derived from the state" but are "independent of it." Government only secures these inherent rights to the individual. The rights themselves are "held by indefeasible title." The individual "can not be deprived of those rights by legislatures or executives or majorities or armies." [23] So far as "the principles of government declared in our Constitution are right," he said, "they do not change. No development of social or industrial life changes a true principle." [24]

Yet he admitted that the laws which "were entirely adequate under the conditions of a century ago to secure individual and public welfare, must be in many respects inadequate to accomplish the same results under all these new conditions." [25]

But in trying to adapt our laws to new conditions, he warned us, in the worn phrase, that we can not "abolish all the evils in this world by statute," that government must not attempt too much, and that all government is imperfect because men are imperfect.[26]

He called us to revere Magna Charta, the Bill of Rights, and the Constitution.

The conservative, like the radical and liberal, usually overstates his cases. His theory remains after he himself has abandoned it in practise. Root in action was far in advance of Root as a theorist. His argument was, after all, based on the formulas of a past age, which at best were only half truths when he wrote. You can not, it is true, change human nature by law, but human nature does change; its manifestations today are far different from what they were two or three centuries ago. Human nature, after all, reacts to its environment, and if the environment changes, its responses change.

The chief measures proposed at the time when these prefaces were written were child and women labor laws, minimum wage laws, prevention of industrial accidents, workmen's compensation

---

[23] *Ibid.*, pp. 167, 168 (April 6, 1915).   [24] *Ibid.*, p. 151 (Nov. 10, 1914).
[25] *Ibid.*, p. 82 (Stafford-Little Lectures, April 15–16, 1913).   [26] *Ibid.*, pp. 84–86.

laws, and laws permitting greater freedom of combination. In the last respect, the proposals of 1914 favored freer individual action than the generation before had thought desirable. As we look back now, it seems strange that men could have thought that laws forbidding child labor under fourteen or sixteen years of age, limitation of hours to ten or nine hours, or even minimum wage laws, unduly restrained individual activity.

All through these citations we see recurring the belief in inherent or natural rights—not natural rights as conferred by a social compact, though the courts still referred to the social compact, but natural rights inherent in the nature of man himself.

Whenever any right dear to men through long possession is threatened, they instinctively defend it as a natural right. But it would be difficult for them to say that such rights are static, that they do not change as society changes. What is property? what is liberty? are surely variable terms, changing from day to day. What infringed liberty yesterday is no infringement today, or at least an infringement that society may be willing to make. The content of our rights is always changing. The right is, after all, a general conclusion, based on needs and emotions from our past. But when challenged in any particular, the right will have to be re-examined in the light of new conditions. There are no immutable principles or immutable rights. There are only immutable ideals.

Generally speaking then, there were four main sources of the opposition to such legislation as the reduction of hours, token money, and workmen's compensation.

First, of course, was the Bill of Rights, the stubborn expressions of individual aspirations for liberty against the encroachments of an executive king ruling by prerogative, which were carried over and applied against an elective executive and an elective legislature. We have seen how powerful the Bill of Rights has been with our courts, trained in Blackstone, and revering the words of the constitutional fathers who were reared in the time when it expressed a fighting faith.

Bound up with the Bill of Rights was the natural rights philosophy. It has been often said that our fathers considered that the rights guaranteed by the Bill of Rights, which were the products of the Puritan Rebellion, the Revolution of 1689, and our own

Revolution, the practical results of long and very human conflicts, were after all nothing but the natural rights of man. Time and again in the decisions of our courts and in the speeches of Charles Sumner and able lawyers such as Elihu Root, we see arising the belief in the inherent rights of man, superior to all legislation. It has been a powerful source of our laissez faire philosophy.

Then there was the pioneer influence. Many times in this book we have seen the influence of the pioneer ideals on our political thought. The pioneer wanted the government's aid in building roads and canals, but he wanted no state interference with his liberty.

Croly in his life of Mark Hanna observed that, "In truth, Mr. Hanna did embody the most vital social and economic tradition in American history—the tradition, that is, of the pioneer. He was an incarnation of the spirit and the methods of the men who seized and cleared the public domain, developed its natural resources, started and organized an industrial and commercial system, and determined most of our political and social habits and forms." [27] The pioneer acted from the beginning "on the theory that the individual and social profits were indistinguishable." The government's duty, as the agent of social betterment, was to aid them "in attaining their personal ends." [28] The government was to aid the enterprising men in their endeavors, from which all would prosper, but it was not to restrict their activity. His famous admonitions to stand pat and keep on, standing pat, while uttered in regard to the tariff, expressed a general philosophy.

The old pioneer individualism, the desire to develop the country unhampered by government restriction, flared up in the opposition to Roosevelt's conservation policy. Governor Shafroth, of Colorado, exclaimed that formerly the government had recognized that "it was the explorers, the settlers, and developers who made the value of everything, in a wild and uninhabited country; that if the lands were not exploited and improved, they would remain as worthless as they had been for 6000 years." [29] Three years later, Governor Stewart, of Montana, expressed the same idea, declaring that the "Western idea has been, generally speaking, that the quicker the

[27] Herbert Croly, *Marcus Alonzo Hanna*, p. 465.   [28] *Ibid.*, p. 467.
[29] Transmississippi Commercial Congress, *Proceedings*, p. 137 (Nov. 15, 1911).

public lands will pass into private ownership, the sooner will that section of the country be developed and the more substantial will be the growth and the development." [30]

Thirdly, there was the influence of the classical economists. In the negro suffrage debates and in the tariff discussions, the words of Mill were often quoted, and it was inevitable that his laissez faire theories should likewise have great influence. Throughout the period the "Nation" exercised a great influence, particularly in the colleges and among college trained people. It stood consistently for sound money, for tariff reform, and for civil service reform, and was savage in its attacks on corruption in politics. But in economics it was traditionally laissez faire. Godkin, its editor, was, declared Wendell Phillips Garrison, another editor, a "utilitarian of the school of Bentham, an economist of the school of Mill." [31] Dicey said that when Godkin came to the United States, he was "a mid-Victorian who thoroughly shared and sympathized with the liberalism or radicalism, which from, say 1845 to 1880, colored the whole public life of the United Kingdom." [32] Reform he believed to be the law of progress. He had an intense hatred of injustice and special privileges; but when it came to positive economic legislation, he was apt to believe that it was an attempt to change economic law by legislative fiat. The intellectuals of the eighties had deep sympathy for those who were exploited by special legislation, but they were somewhat blind to those oppressed or burdened by our economic system. John Hay's novel, "The Breadwinners," to say the least, shows a great callousness to the immense significance of the beginning labor struggle. The opponents of Populism and free silver talked much of the evil of a cheap dollar and of repudiation; and it is well they did, but they said little of the conditions which gave rise to Populism and free silver.

An editorial in the "Nation" in 1878, entitled: "The Mind and Manners of the Silver Man," observed that "His condition is rapidly becoming as forlorn as that of the poor Granger, of whom we heard so much three or four years ago. At first, it was only by the railroads that that Godly man was afflicted; but when he got time to examine himself closely, he found that almost every

[30] Governors' Conference, *Proceedings*, 1914, p. 98.
[31] Gustav Pollak, *Fifty Years of American Idealism*, p. 60.　　[32] *Ibid.*, p. 66.

class in the community was armed against him and preying upon him." [33] The editorial spoke of the "wild look in his eye," with which the silver man spoke of the Money Power.[34] The fight for resumption of specie payments was a battle against "folly and ignorance." [35] Another "Nation" editorial declared that Bryan's famous speech in the 1896 convention was "an appeal to one of the worst instincts of the human heart,—that of getting possession of other people's property without the owners' consent." [36] Lack of social sympathy could hardly be more clearly shown.

Another major influence was the Darwinian philosophy. It is difficult to put one's finger on the expressions of belief in evolution as determining our political action, but the opponents of the liberalism of the twentieth century continually declared that the measures they opposed would deny the free play of the struggle for existence and the survival of the fittest. Stephenson, in his "Nelson W. Aldrich," says: "Never did a statesman have more unhesitating faith in natural selection. Part of his distinction, part of his significance in American history, is in this fact. . . . With him, it was not only: let talent come in; it was also, with equal firmness: let mediocrity stay out." [37]

The philosophy of the survival of the fittest was expressed again and again in the Progressive campaign of 1912. It was said that the men who had made the country were being pushed aside; that we should never prosper again unless we let the natural leaders control, and presumably let them pretty much alone.

Curiously enough, the conservatives were Darwinists in believing in the individual survival of the fittest, but they admitted no evolution in political ideas or institutions. Of course, natural selection can not be applied to the political life of men without immense qualifications. The ruthless survival of the fittest of nature can not be applied to society, without involving intolerable injustice and cruelty. Our whole system of law has been adopted to see that certain principles of fair play are enforced, so that the race or the game would be a fair one. Moreover, no laissez faire philosophy has failed to admit that the weak and helpless require protection,

[33] Gustav Pollak, *op. cit.*, p. 136 (editorial of Feb. 7, 1878).   [34] *Ibid.*, p. 137.
[35] *Ibid.*, p. 139 (editorial of Dec. 26, 1878).
[36] *Ibid.*, p. 188 (editorial of July 16, 1896).
[37] Nathaniel W. Stephenson, *Nelson W. Aldrich*, p. 270.

and that children should be protected at least until they are able to protect themselves. The theory of natural selection is subject to the same limitations.

THE LINE OF DIVISION BETWEEN CONSERVATIVES AND PROGRESSIVES IN 1917

Where, then, did the contest between the liberals and the conservatives stand at the end of our period? After all, it is an age-old contest: the contest between change and adaptation on the one hand, and the status quo on the other. The adjustment has been going on since time began, and will go on unceasingly until there is no longer social change. Each period can only sum up the tendencies of its period.

The period witnessed a steady integration of thought and method. Problems were not so simple as they were conceived in the days of the Populists. The attack had become highly organized, and the method of treatment more scientific. Long and patient study of details was recognized to be necessary.

Probably no person was liberal on all the matters at issue, and no one conservative on all. Undoubtedly, many of the men whom I have quoted in this chapter would have favored child labor laws, and anti-token money laws, and hours of labor laws. But there was formidable opposition on all, and the opposition was strikingly similar in tone and content. By the end of the period, however, it is possible to make a rough synthesis on the basis of Justice Holmes' famous suggestion,—that the line is pricked out by the decisions on the opposing sides. As in law, so in politics, the line appears where the long opposing forces dig in and settle down for a long trench warfare. After a long attack and advance, finally a temporary stalemate comes; and on the long western front of social contest a definite line appears!

On much there was agreement. Duguit, in his monumental "Traité de Droit Constitutionel," speaks often of the change in the conception of the state from a sovereignty which commands to a cooperation of services. "Those who govern," he claims, "are no longer the organs or the agents of the state, exercising the sovereign power with which they are invested. They are the managers of public services. . . ."[88]

[88] Vol. II, p. 134.

We may not agree with Duguit that the state no longer commands, in the sense that there is no final authority in the state. But that the state has become in large degree a cooperation of public services, can hardly be denied. As to much of these public services, there is no dispute. By 1917, there was little, if any, disagreement that the state must educate. The schools have become a recognized service of the state. Sanitation, streets, the removal of waste and garbage, fire protection, provisions for parks and playgrounds were then generally conceded to be desirable aspects of this public service. By that time, likewise, the prevention of accidents in industry, employers' liability laws, and workmen's compensation laws were generally conceded to be necessary. The line of the trenches had moved on beyond!

Opinion remained firm that monopoly in industry and general commerce, and unfair methods of competition, should be prevented. Monopoly was still dreaded, and rightly so; but by 1917 large combinations such as in 1890 would have been attacked as dangerous, were generally accepted. Bryan, La Follette, and Brandeis agreed that combination up to thirty per cent of the business of the country should not be molested.

Finally, there was general agreement that so-called natural monopolies—gas, water, light, railroads—should be regulated in the public interest. Then they were called affected with a public use. Now the courts would simply say that there was a sufficient public interest to demand their control.

The battle was to go on over a new terrain. The fixing of minimum wages; unemployment and old age insurance; the regulation of prices, of rents; the control of the sale of commodities like ice; the protection of the right to collective bargaining: such were some of the points which still remained hotly disputed. Liberals would contend that in one or a dozen places the judgment of the operators of business should be curtailed; conservatives, that it should be left free. In 1917, however, the sentiment was still strong that, in general, the judgment of the managers should be allowed free play. The preference was strong for private business.

REFERENCES

CROLY, HERBERT, *Marcus Alonzo Hanna*. New York: The Macmillan Co., 1919.
GOVERNORS' CONFERENCE, *Proceedings*. 1915.

KELLER, A. G., *Reminiscences of William Graham Sumner*. New Haven: Yale University Press, 1933.

POLLAK, GUSTAV, *Fifty Years of American Idealism*. Boston: Houghton Mifflin Co., 1915.

ROOT, ELIHU, *Addresses on Government and Citizenship*. Cambridge: Harvard University Press, 1916.

SPENCER, HERBERT, *Man Versus the State*, Ed. Truxton Beale. New York: Mitchell Kennerley, 1916.

STARR, HARRIS E., *William Graham Sumner*. New York: Henry Holt & Co., 1925.

STEPHENSON, NATHANIEL W., *Nelson W. Aldrich*. New York: Charles Scribner's Sons, 1930.

SUMNER, WILLIAM GRAHAM, *The Challenge of Facts and Other Essays*. New Haven: Yale University Press, 1914.

——*Earth Hunger and Other Essays*. New Haven: Yale University Press, 1913.

——*War and Other Essays*. New Haven: Yale University Press, 1911.

CHAPTER X

SOCIALISTIC THOUGHT

OF COURSE, through the whole period, there were those who desired a more or less complete reorganization of our society. In the beginning of the period, socialistic thought was distinctly outside the main sweep of our opinion; and, of course, its content has always been somewhat special. But the stirring was always there. The National Labor Union and the Knights of Labor had distinct socialistic tendencies.

William H. Sylvis, a native born moulder of Pittsburgh and a leader in the National Labor Union,—although apparently he had little knowledge of the new socialistic ideas of Europe,—had strong radical beliefs. He wrote in 1869 that it is "a war between poverty and wealth"; capital was the "same tyrant in all parts of the world." The Civil War, he felt, had resulted "in the building up of the most infamous monied aristocracy on the face of the earth," which was "fast eating up the substance of the people." The fight would be made at the ballot box, and if not successful, "then we will resort to sterner means. A little blood-letting is sometimes necessary in desperate cases." [1]

American socialists took part in the Greenback movement, in the Henry George movement, in Populism, and even in the Progressive movement. Bellamy's "Looking Backward" aroused such wide interest that it came into the main stream of our thought for a time, and then lapsed from view. [2] It was only near the end of our period that socialism attained strength enough to be a definite movement of its own, and that it acquired a native clientele. Through most of the period, it was handicapped by a foreign psychology, and was looked on as a foreign movement. Its disciples continued to use formulas derived from European experience, which

---

[1] Commons, *Documentary History*, Vol. IX, p. 340.
[2] For that reason and for the reason that Bellamy was not part of the Socialist movement, and joined the Populists, I have ventured to treat him in Chapter VII.

were ill-adapted to American conditions. It was another illustration of the confusion of our thought from the diverse origins of the people. Barrett Wendell wrote of the confused West, but he might well have written of confused America.

Of course, all socialistic thought in the period revolves around the theories of Karl Marx, the strange genius, who, despite all our early indifference and later antagonism, has profoundly modified the political and economic thought of three generations. There is no need, here, to detail at length his economic theory. It was based first on the labor theory of value, and deduced from that, the theory of surplus value. Value was based on labor cost, and surplus value was the difference between the labor cost and the price received. That difference was what capital received in rent and profits. Therefore, labor was exploited by the entire difference between the labor cost and the price received. Surplus value measured the exploitation of labor.

Marx found the explanation of economic development in the conflict between classes. Gradually the antagonism would increase, the concentration of capital would increase, the middle classes would be wiped out, the share of labor would steadily decline, until at last the structure would become top-heavy and the proletariat would take over the means of production. Marx's disciples still dispute as to whether he thought that the final revolution would be peaceful or bloody. He realized that in some countries it might be peaceful. But he devoted much of his life to preparing for violent revolution.

Back of all the theory lay the economic interpretation of history, first called the materialistic interpretation of history. The social and political system of any country is fixed by the economic forces of the time. Economic facts determine the forms of political life. And economic facts are based on the relationships of economic classes. The Communist Manifesto declared that "The history of all hitherto existing society is the history of class struggles." [3] These dogmas, as we shall see, were to undergo profound modification.

The Marxian theory did, however, bring socialism from the inchoate realm of Utopias to a definite and analyzable form.

---

[3] Karl Marx, *Capital* (Modern Library ed.), p. 321.

In 1872 the first National Convention of the International was held. It declared, in phrases which were to become clichés, that our present "society is founded on the exploitation of the property-less classes by the propertied." [4] The workers were bought body and soul. All "implements of labor,—the soil and other premises of production,—in short, capital produced by labor," should be changed into "societary property." [5] The political institutions were the agencies of the propertied classes, who would not resign their privileges willingly. The only recourse was force—force such as our ancestors had employed to overcome "political oppression" should be used to liberate ourselves from economic bondage.[6]

Therefore, they called for destruction "of the existing class rule, by all means, i.e., by energetic, relentless, revolutionary, and international action." [7] They called for a free cooperative society; for organization of education on a secular, scientific, and equal basis for both sexes; for equal rights for all without regard to race or sex. The famous battle cry of the Communist Manifesto was launched: "Workmen of all lands, unite. You have nothing to lose but your chains; you have a world to win."

Surely it was an alien voice in the America of 1872, when free lands were still available.

The organization was largely composed of German workingmen, and had little effect on American opinion.

In 1874 the Social Democratic Workingmen's Party of North America was organized in Philadelphia. Its platform declared for the abolition of class rule and class conditions, for abolition of the workingman's dependence on the capitalist by the introduction of cooperation, for political power as a solution of the labor question, for united struggle, and sympathy for the workingmen of all nations. This organization, Hillquit says, gained strength, and the International declined.[8] The International, of course, ran counter to all native instincts for political action. Its international appeal was foreign, and its slogans of class rule were still strange to us.

In 1876 the Working-man's Party of the United States was formed. In 1877 its name was changed to the Socialist Labor Party. Not more than ten per cent of its membership, Hillquit says,

---

[4] R. T. Ely, *The Labor Movement in America,* p. 359.
[5] *Ibid.,* p. 361.   [6] *Ibid.,* p. 363.   [7] *Ibid.,* p. 363.
[8] Morris Hillquit, *History of Socialism in the United States,* p. 208.

was native American.[9] The endeavor to Americanize it was constant, but unsuccessful, throughout its life. It never had much numerical strength. It had many internal disputes. It would gain in depressions, and lose all its gains with the return of prosperity. It was originally a group of students who made fetishes of their dogmas, and were reluctant to permit new members to join their numbers.

Hillquit admits that it "consisted largely of men who had formed their social views and philosophy in European countries, principally in Germany. They were but little in touch with the American population, and moved almost exclusively within their own limited circle." [10]

The Socialist Labor Party struggled on precariously for years, with a small membership. Its membership in 1879 Hillquit admits, was "certainly distressingly small." One estimate was one thousand, five hundred; another, two thousand, six hundred.[11] Hillquit observes that in 1881 the party's struggles "grew harder and harder, the social contentment and political indifference of the masses seemed impregnable, no new converts were made; while the old party members, growing disheartened, dropped out in large numbers." [12]

From 1890 on, the party was dominated by Daniel De Leon, a strange and brilliant zealot, who had a stormy career. John W. Burgess, whose student he was at Columbia, called him "remarkably well-informed." He knew "more international law and diplomatic history than any man of his age I had ever met." [13] Hillquit's verdict was that of many others: he thought him intensely personal. "Almost immediately," he observed, "upon his entry in the Socialist arena, he divided the movement into two antagonistic camps—his devoted admirers and followers, and his bitter critics and opponents." Hillquit added that "All who dissented from his views were enemies of the movement." But he admitted that he was "a keen thinker and merciless logician." [14] De Leon was a rigorous Marxist. One who did not subscribe to the full Marxian creed was literally excommunicated.

So clannish and narrow was the Socialist Labor Party, that in

---

[9] *Ibid.*, p. 213.   [10] *Ibid.*, p. 322.
[11] Morris Hillquit, *History of Socialism in the United States*, pp. 228–29.
[12] Morris Hillquit, *Ibid.*, p. 229.
[13] John W. Burgess, *Reminiscences of an American Scholar*, p. 182.
[14] Morris Hillquit, *Loose Leaves from a Busy Life*, pp. 45–46.

1897 the present Socialist Party was formed. Its appeal was much wider, and it sought to increase its strength by all the means of political propaganda and action. In some election years, it attained real popular strength, and with the growth of the humanitarian and progressive sentiment of the early years of the century, drew more and more native Americans to its ranks. As we shall see, it modified the rigid socialistic maxims in the light of American necessities.

In 1912 its platform declared for the collective ownership of railroads, telephone, telegraph, and express businesses; grain elevators; warehouses; mines; oil wells; forests; water power; and land, wherever possible.

Then it had a long series of demands, not socialistic in nature, but common to many in the progressive years. It called for a shorter day, a five and a half day week, factory inspection, child labor legislation, minimum wage laws, old age pensions; and, politically, for equal suffrage, the initiative, referendum and recall, abolition of the review of legislation by the courts, the abolition of the Senate and the Presidential veto.

It desired income and inheritance taxes.

Now, what of the progress of Socialist opinion in the period?

One of the earliest American expositions of Marxism was Laurence Gronlund's "The Cooperative Commonwealth," published in 1884. He said in his preface that it was an attempt to present the Marxian philosophy "digested by a mind, Anglo-Saxon in its dislike of all extravagances and in its freedom from any vindictive feeling against *persons* who are from circumstances what they are." [15]

It is difficult, however, to see much modification in the Marxian theory. He adopted the theory of surplus value completely. He dwelt on the evils of cut-throat competition, on the disastrous results of business crises, on the extent of business combinations. Foreign markets, cooperation, and trade unionism were alike, he said, unavailing as remedies. The state must become the cooperative commonwealth, and take over these vastly developed businesses. It would not expropriate the owners, but pay them in goods. And it would be only the "most important instruments of production," a fractional part of our national wealth, which the common-

[15] Laurence Gronlund, *The Cooperative Commonwealth*, p. 9.

wealth would take over.[16] He was not fearful of the resulting concentration of governmental machinery. It would be no worse than the political administration we then had, which he well said was irresponsible.

His cooperative commonwealth would not be communistic. Men would be paid according to their deeds, not their needs. It was not Utopian. He proposed, however, that the state should determine how much should be paid in labor value to each workman. Each branch would settle the amount of wages for itself.

He had the usual dream that "the Cooperative Commonwealth will be highly promotive of social welfare by securing to all its citizens abundance; by furnishing them leisure; by enabling them to follow their natural bent." [17]

It is the dream which has animated men from the first Utopia.

Gronlund, then, did not propose to confiscate capital. He would pay the owners of the means of production which were taken over by the state; but he would pay them in goods, and there, for them, it would end, for when those consumable goods were gone, there would be no more. He would leave much industry in private hands. Yet the organization of the state would still have been immense and far-flung, and the problem of the political administration of the state, the decisions on intricate questions of policy, remained as they remained under all theories of socialism.

A prominent addition to the ranks of American Socialism was Eugene V. Debs. Born in Terre Haute, Indiana, of Alsatian parentage, he started to work at fifteen years of age in the railroad shops, then became a railroad fireman, joined the Brotherhood of Locomotive Firemen, and became its president. He served a term in the Indiana legislature. He was the leader of the great railroad strike of 1894, and was finally sent to Woodstock jail for violation of a federal injunction.

He seems to have been widely read: he had read Gronlund and Bellamy with warm approval. He was well versed in the socialistic writing of the time. His friends and neighbors found him a man of great gentleness of spirit, and he was deeply beloved. James Whitcomb Riley wrote of " 'Gene Debs, with as warm a heart as ever beat betwixt here and the Judgment Seat." When Debs left prison after the war, he had endeared himself to the whole prison. And

[16] *Ibid.*, p. 125.   [17] *Ibid.*, p. 117.

yet so complex is human nature, this man of warm and friendly nature could lead a great sympathetic railroad strike, which avowedly sought to strangle the life of a great city and which almost openly based its program on violence, and could see nothing in the world war but a contest of the capitalistic classes for exploitation of the working classes. He was, after all, a man of bitter social prejudices and a warped mentality.

He says that Victor Berger converted him to socialism while he was in Woodstock jail. "What but meaningless phrases," he wrote in 1900, "are 'imperialism,' 'expansion,' 'free silver,' 'gold standard,' etc., to the wage worker? The large capitalists represented by Mr. McKinley, and the small capitalists represented by Mr. Bryan, are all interested in these issues, but they do not concern the working class." [18] What they are interested in, he said, was the ownership and control of the means of production. The question was "not of 'reform,' the mask of fraud, but of revolution. The capitalist system must be overthown, class rule abolished, and wage slavery supplanted by cooperative industry." [19]

He repeated the usual formulas of the current socialism, the usual arguments of the class struggle. Like others, he said that the "centralization of capital, the concentration of industry, and the cooperation of workingmen, mark the beginning of the end." [20]

He attacked John Mitchell of the Mine Workers' Union, for asserting that there is no "necessary conflict between capital and labor," and answered that there was no possible peace between them. "Every hour of truce is at the price of slavery." [21] But apparently he would permit private property in consumable goods. He said: "We are not going to destroy private property. We are going to establish private property,—all the private property necessary to house man, keep him in comfort, and satisfy his wants." [22]

Obviously, Debs made no original contribution to our socialistic thought. He was simply a popularizer of its hardened theories. But he remained such for two decades. Native born, magnetic, and likable, he did much to bring socialism to the native American workman. He was the socialist candidate for President in 1900, 1904, 1908, 1912, and 1920.

Meanwhile there was little detailed consideration of socialism

[18] Stephen Marion Reynolds, *Debs, His Life, Writings, and Speeches*, p. 89.
[19] *Ibid.*, p. 90.   [20] *Ibid.*, p. 146.   [21] *Ibid.*, pp. 174–75.   [22] *Ibid.*, p. 489.

by its opponents. The general public attitude was very ill-informed; and indiscriminately lumped anarchism, socialism, communism, and all other obnoxious theories together. Bellamy's book, of course, created much discussion. The intricate organization of his state merely overemphasized the objection which applies to every socialistic proposal, the fear of the political organization which would manage such a system, and that individual initiative would be stifled under it.

Our doubters of Socialism have steadily stressed this political danger Woolsey, in his "Communism and Socialism," felt that the state under Socialism "must become strong and uncontrollable," [23] and that there would be little "enterprise or of public spirit in the people of such a state under such conditions." [24]

William Graham Sumner, of course, had no patience with the socialistic proposals. "Can anyone imagine," he asked, "that the masterfulness, the overbearing disposition, the greed of gain, and the ruthlessness in methods, which are the fault of the master of industry at his worst, would cease when he was a functionary of the state, which had relieved him of risk and endowed him with authority? Can anyone imagine that politicians would no longer be corruptly fond of money, intriguing, and crafty, when they were charged, not only with patronage and government contracts, but also with factories, stores, ships, and railroads?" When the politician "and the master of industry were joined in one," we should have the "vices of both unchecked by the restraints of either." The governing committees would offer chances of wealth beyond the dreams of avarice.[25]

For many years, Richard T. Ely offered tempered criticism of Socialism and of the industrial order. He was fair in admitting the evils of our system, but he thought that the Socialists were too pessimistic of our conditions and too optimistic of the Socialistic future. He felt that the Socialistic organization would be a menace to individual liberty; and while he admitted that many businesses should be socialized, he desired private property to remain dominant.[26]

[23] Theodore D. Woolsey, *Communism and Socialism*, p. 231 (1880).
[24] *Ibid.*, p. 239.
[25] William Graham Sumner, "The Absurd Effort to Make the World Over" (1894), in *War and Other Essays*, p. 207.
[26] Richard T. Ely, *Socialism and Social Reform*, p. 189. Also, *Property and Contract*, p. 426 (Chap. V).

Lyman Abbott, defining Socialism following Spargo, as meaning that "the political organization is to control and administer the industries of the community," [27] declared, "this is not industrial liberty. It is industrial servitude to a new master." [28]

By 1910 Socialism had gained a considerable American clientele. It was beginning to attract, as it had long attracted in Europe, support among the intelligentsia. The stirrings of the progressive movement were causing a great ferment among people of education and leisure. Howells was an example of the vague longings and somewhat inarticulate and unformulated protest among literary men of the time. Partly perhaps because of the changed content of its membership, partly perhaps to increase the influence of Socialism among the same class, partly as the result of the play of criticism, American Socialism, as in England and on the Continent, was modifying many of the old dogmas of Marxian Socialism. The new leaders endeavored to show that Socialism would not destroy all private property, that it would not remove individual incentive, that it was not antagonistic to a well-ordered individualism.

Morris Hillquit was an Austrian Jew, who came to the United States when he was seventeen. All his mature life he was a leader of American Socialism. He became a member of the Socialist Labor Party as soon as he reached the age of eighteen. The party was then eleven years old, with a membership of from two to three thousand. About ten per cent. were native born; the rest were Germans, with a sprinkling of Jews and Scandinavians.[29] It was, he admitted, a foreign party, and actually started an English weekly. Hillquit observes: "In our zeal for the cause, we did not even appreciate the exquisite humor of a political party of the United States establishing a solitary American section in the metropolis of the country." [30]

Hillquit became one of the founders of the Socialist Party, formed because of the belief that the Socialist Labor Party, dominated by De Leon, was too narrow in its clientele and appeal.

John Spargo was an English Jew, who published several books on Socialism in the years between 1910 and 1913. A gentle idealist, he brought a tempered and fine spirit to the interpretation of the Marxian philosophy. After the war he abandoned Socialism.

[27] Lyman Abbott, *The Spirit of Democracy*, p. 112.   [28] *Ibid.*, p. 117.
[29] Morris Hillquit, *Loose Leaves From a Busy Life*, p. 41.   [30] *Ibid.*, p. 44.

Another conspicuous recruit at this time was Edmond Kelly, an American lawyer who had practised with success in Paris and decided to devote the years of his retirement to the socialist cause. He felt that there was no book which presented the socialist case in an adequate manner to the American public, and consequently he proceeded to write his "Twentieth Century Socialism."

It was an attempt to present Socialism to the American public free from the foreign bias and phraseology which Hillquit and Russell believed had delayed its progress. His book was free from the fierce partisanship which denies all value to those who do not subscribe to the strict creed of the advocate. He admitted, for example, that Theodore Roosevelt had done much to advance the progress of the relations of the individual to modern industry. He tried in the beginning to remove the current crude objections to Socialism: it was not anarchism; it was not communism; it would not destroy the home or religion.

W. J. Ghent, Charles Edward Russell, William English Walling, and James Mackaye, all of native American stock, also came to the socialist cause at this time. These men all brought scholarship and social enthusiasm to their advocacy of Socialism. They gave us some of the ablest political discussions of the time. They made serious modifications, however, in the Marxian dogmas of the economic interpretation of history, surplus value, the class struggle, the concentration of capital, the eventual collapse of the capitalistic system, and the ensuing revolution, whether violent or peaceful.

I shall consider the economic interpretation of history more at length in Chapter XIII on "The Tests of Political Action." But it is so involved with the Socialist theory that it must be mentioned briefly here. Spargo pointed out that Marx did not mean that economic interest was "the only power at work in human evolution"; that "ideals, patriotism, religion, and love have no influence at all; and that even the conduct of the individual is wholly shaped by his material interests." [31] Marx, he said, "never dreamed of asserting that economic force acts as the sole determinant of social evolution." [32] The materialistic theory, then, he went on, does not mean that "history is determined by economic forces only; but that

---

[31] John Spargo, *Sidelights on Contemporary Socialism*, p. 55.　[32] *Ibid.*, p. 124.

in human evolution the chief factors are social factors, and that these factors in turn are *mainly* moulded by economic conditions." [33] With this last sentence few of us would disagree.

The Marxian theory of labor cost—as was pointed out many times—assumed that value was merely so much labor, as Taussig said that value was "a something inherent in economic goods." [34] Marx underestimated the influence of demand, of utility of goods in exchange, and, above all, the contribution of capital and of management in making the surplus value possible. Anyone who thinks that value can be realized merely by expending labor,—to be disillusioned,—has only to observe the death of businesses where all the value created by labor is lost, through either the incompetence of the management, the vagaries of the market, or other vicissitudes of modern business.

Miss Hughan, the historian of American Socialism, asserts that American Socialists never directly repudiated the theory of surplus value, but she said that they generally ignored it. [35] But Spargo in effect approved it. He admitted that labor did not produce all value; he admitted the contribution of the managers, but he claimed that labor produced far more than it received. "It remains," he said, "the one central fact of capitalism, however, that a surplus value is created by the working class and taken by the exploiting class, from which develops the class struggle of our time." [36] Kelly likewise declared that all Socialism asks is that a man have what he earns. It merely asks, he asserted, that "the workers be assured, as exactly as possible, the product of their labor; and not share it with the idle and vicious on the one hand, or be deprived of it by the capitalist on the other." [37]

Even to such statements as those of Spargo and Kelly and many other socialists, that labor produces far more than it receives, we may reply that no one knows what is the exact product of labor; and, again, that the product of industry may be drastically reduced if the rewards of profit are removed. To put it crudely: a thousand men with a million dollars of capital well-managed,

[33] John Spargo, *Socialism*, p. 92.
[34] F. W. Taussig, *Principles of Economics* (1928 ed.), Vol. II, p. 475.
[35] Jessie Wallace Hughan, *American Socialism of the Present Day*, p. 81.
[36] John Spargo, *Socialism*, p. 276.
[37] Edmond Kelly, *Twentieth Century Socialism*, p. 36.

with profits to some, may produce far more for all than a thousand men with the same capital ill-managed, with profits to none. This is not to say that the profits to the few in our society may not have been too great and unnecessary to obtain the services rendered, and that the rewards of the many have not been disproportionately small. Indeed, the rewards have been many times crudely and grievously ill-apportioned.

American Socialists generally insisted on the class struggle. The most moderate Socialists were united with the radical on this point. American Socialists centered their attack on the evils and wastes of competition, and they agreed that the capitalistic system must break down,—not so much, Miss Hughan observes, because it exploited the worker, as because of its planlessness.[38]

Ghent spoke feelingly of the indifference, the snobbery of the prosperous classes, their contempt for the less fortunate, the sad failure to get under the skin of one's fellows, which explains much of politics and of economics. Like all the others of his way of thinking, he had much to say of the wastes of competition. Slowly, he said, had arisen a feeling of the waste of the system, and slowly a determination to be rid of it; to apportion, upon equitable terms, the common burdens; and "to distribute, in equitable shares, the common hoard." That determination, he concluded, "is the growing and expanding will of the producing classes, and its fulfilment will be the cooperative commonwealth."[39]

Kelly, too, dwelt long on the evils of the capitalistic system, the wastes of competition, the misery of the poor, the ghastly discrepancies of wealth and want. Everywhere were overproduction, unemployment, prostitution, strikes and lockouts, adulteration in goods, cheap and nasty business practises. No doubter of Socialism can deny the sombreness of the picture. The real issue, Kelly said, was whether security, liberty, and leisure can be enjoyed only by the few, or whether they can be enjoyed by all. He thought they could. He thought, as did those of his belief, that Socialism would eliminate the wastes of competition and overproduction, and would afford leisure and plenty for all.[40]

American Socialists at this time, however, were eager to allay

---

[38] Hughan, *American Socialism of the Present Day*, p. 88.
[39] W. J. Ghent, *Mass and Class*, p. 256.
[40] Kelly, *Twentieth Century Socialism*, p. 127.

the fears of liberals, who dreaded the tyranny of the socialist state and its monopoly of all production. Kelly admitted that he had feared its tyranny, but had become convinced that the fears were groundless.[41] He agreed with the current trend of socialist thought, —that Socialism would not suppress all competition. Some competition was good, like the emulation in games. It was the non-competitive spirit which society should encourage, and he instanced the characters of Father Damien, Florence Nightingale, and Rose Hawthorne in contrast with the characters of those who had succeeded in the competitive world.[42]

Hillquit, Spargo, and Kelly all emphasized that there would still remain private and cooperative industry under Socialism. Certain industries, Hillquit said, "are even today organized on a national scale, and may be best managed or controlled as state functions; others may come more appropriately within the scope of the municipal administration; others still may be most efficiently managed by voluntary cooperative associations, with or without state control; while a variety of industries of an individual nature, such as the arts and crafts, must of necessity remain purely individual pursuits." [43]

Hence he concluded that there would be no overpowering organization, and plenty of individual liberty and incentive for individual advancement.

Nor would all property be state property under their socialistic system. No sane socialist, Kelly asserted, would deny a person articles of use, personal belongings, or furniture. Socialists proposed not to destroy private property, but the capitalistic system. It would vest in the state only what it was essential for the state to own, "in order to rescue the unwealthy majority from the exploitation of the wealthy few." [44] He made clear that he would leave the farmers their land. The farmers would pay their taxes in produce, and the state would control production.

Spargo agreed that not all property would be state-owned under Socialism. Most "intelligent socialists," he said, "if called upon to choose between them, would probably prefer to live in Thibet, under a personal despotism, rather than under the hierarchies of

[41] *Ibid.*, p. 235.   [42] Kelly, *Twentieth Century Socialism*, p. 39.
[43] Hillquit, *Socialism in Theory and Practice*, p. 32.
[44] Kelly, *Twentieth Century Socialism*, p. 45.

most of the imaginary commonwealths which Utopian Socialists have depicted." [45]

All these men agreed that there would be differences in remuneration under Socialism. Profits would be eliminated, but the heads of enterprises and of the state departments would receive greater rewards than others, and there would be sufficient incentive in these differences of compensation and in the emulation for honor and advancement.

Spargo admitted too that the concentration of industry envisaged by Marx, which would be succeeded by the collapse of the capitalistic system, had not been realized. With full loyalty to Marx, he conceded that "there is the danger of stagnation and decay through a too complete reliance upon the wisdom of the Master, and particularly, failure to realize that principles of action which were sound and wise when advocated by Marx may be unsound and unwise as principles of action in the changed conditions of today. Candor compels the admission that there is hardly a country in which the Socialist movement has not suffered from this besetting evil of movements, which owe much of their success to individual genius." To name only one example, he added, the present "successful appeal of the socialists to agricultural workers was made possible only by the overthrow of Marx's exceedingly plausible generalization concerning the concentration of agricultural industry." [46]

But still American Socialists believed that the concentration in industry was proceeding to a stage where the state would have to take it over. It was stated over and over again that the trusts were the precursors of the Socialist state.

The great conflict arose on how the change would come. The movement split here, as in Europe, into the revolutionary Socialists, and the evolutionary Socialists who believed that the change would and should be gradual. Spargo, Hillquit, and Kelly belonged to the evolutionary group.

Spargo denied that Marx meant an actual revolution was necessary. He answered that Marx meant a social revolution. [47] It is true that Marx admitted that in some countries an actual revo-

[45] Spargo, *Socialism*, p. 282.
[46] Spargo, *Sidelights on Contemporary Socialism*, pp. 21–22.
[47] Spargo, *Sidelights on Contemporary Socialism*, p. 135.

lution might not be necessary, but he actively engaged in revolutionary propaganda. But Spargo's statement was representative of American Socialism of the time. Hillquit too, believed in gradual adjustment.

Kelly asserted that violence and revolution were not necessary, though they might come. He believed that the change would be gradual. The state might decide, for example, to take over the oil industry and buy stock of the owners, giving more to those who had earned it than to others, and leaving the personnel much as before. Or the state might decide not to own the oil industry, but rather merely to control it.[48] He thought that by increasing the activity and sphere of government, we would decrease corruption: the more government there is, the less corruption. There would be no excessive concentration of political power. An industrial parliament would supervise industry. All would be interested in government, for all would be concerned; but there would be no great prizes for the government to hand out to business men.

Kelly denied that Socialism reversed the natural process. The argument, that "because natural evolution proceeds upon the principle of the survival of the fittest, therefore human evolution must proceed upon the same lines," was totally false. Man can resist nature. Human nature, he well said, can be changed. Customs change.[49]

The family, he said in the end, is the model of what the State ought to be. A "government which should have equal concern for every member of the community, and not one which as at present surfeits some and starves others," should be our aim.[50] We are learning that we must and can mold our environment.[51]

Miss Hughan points out that American Socialists at this time gave little attention to the actual constitution of the socialist state.[52] Of course, they insisted it would be democratic.

A socialistic society is one, Hillquit said, based on "the system of public or collective ownership of the material instruments of production, democratic administration of the industries, and cooperative labor; and the guiding principle of such society must be the recognition of the right of existence and enjoyment inherent

[48] Kelly, *Twentieth Century Socialism*, pp. 251–52. [49] *Ibid.*, pp. 363–64.
[50] *Ibid.*, p. 406. [51] *Ibid.*, p. 373.
[52] Hughan, *American Socialism of the Present Day*, p. 119.

in every human being." [53] The state would persist: a different state,—not a class state, but still a state. The change would be gradual.[54] It was impossible to picture the form it would take.[55] But surely it would not be Utopian.

Spargo said it was absurd to attempt to give detailed specifications of the socialist state.[56]

The change going on in the Socialist movement is strikingly illustrated by Charles Edward Russell. The son of an Iowa editor in a small town, he brought to the party much native shrewdness, humor, and a sense of proportion. He was not attracted by the rigid Marxian dialectics of Socialism. Indeed, he confesses that when he joined the party, he had never read "Das Kapital," and "could not have told Karl Marx from Frederick Engels, if I had met them walking arm in arm up the street." [57] But he was a natural rebel, although not a dour or intransigeant one. Big Business, he said, viewed Socialism with alarm. He liked the members and joined the ranks. He was attracted by the Socialist dream, its "splendid significance of the universal man, and the general fraternity that was different and obliterated the recollections of human weaknesses, whatever they might be." The Socialists he came to know, he liked. They believed in the paradise to come, and "served it with a magnificent devotion, and often at great personal cost." [58]

Russell testifies vividly to the foreign psychology of the Socialist Party when he joined it about 1911. The native American stock continued, he remarked, "to view Socialists as an uncouth plant of foreign growth, unsuited to this soil and condition." [59] Socialism left the American born voter "absolutely cold." Yet, he went on, he and his American friends could somehow never make the German and "some of our Jewish members" understand that if "every foreign born voter in the United States should vote for us until doomsday, that would avail nothing without the support of the native Americans." Projects "to Americanize the movement and give it a start towards its necessary goal, if it was to be anything but a back-room debate, were many and almost invariably negatived." [60]

[53] Hillquit, *Socialism in Theory and Practice*, p. 87.　　[54] *Ibid.*, p. 100.
[55] *Ibid.*, p. 107.　　　　　　　　　　　　　　　　　　　　[56] Spargo, *Socialism*, p. 277.
[57] Charles Edward Russell, *Bare Hands and Stone Walls*, p. 193.
[58] *Ibid.*, p. 199.　　　[59] *Ibid.*, p. 200.　　　　　[60] *Ibid.*, p. 201.

Russell's experience was not triumphant. The simple fact, he said, "is that those who would reap most from it, never gave a dang for it, and I think this is something to remember and ponder." [61] In 1912 he was the Socialist candidate for governor in New York. He went about the State trying to "put over the fact of an approaching Unconsumed Surplus. I think that outside the Socialist Party, not a man, woman, or child ever gives the slightest attention." [62]

Although Hillquit, Spargo, and Kelly insisted that they were followers of Marx, it will be noticed how markedly they had modified the strict Marxian dogmas. Russell was not even a disciple of Marx. The same conflict was going on in the United States as in Europe: the conflict between the revolutionary and the reformist Socialists, which followed the publication of Bernstein's "Revolutionary Socialism."

But, of course, all were not agreed. William English Walling, protested vigorously against the reformist tendencies, and called for the maintenance of revolutionary Socialism. He wrote several books of much ability, which showed a vast amount of reading. His "Socialism As It Is," published in 1912, was thoroughgoing in its Socialist philosophy, and severely critical of the "reformist" tendency. The only way, he felt, to differentiate the Socialist from other parties in the reformist view, was by its distant ideal. But he objected: "If a goal has thus no necessary connection with immediate problems or actions, is it necessarily anything more than a sentiment or an abstraction?" [63] He quoted Debs as dreading Socialist absorption in ordinary reform movements.

Walling declared that Kelly's book "summed up his political faith in much the same way as any anti-Socialist reformer might have done." Reformism leads to "opportunism and compromise." [64] He denied that the reforms which Theodore Roosevelt was then advocating were socialistic. His program was not "socialistic in the slightest degree," but capitalistic. "He has not appropriated a single Socialist demand. He has merely taken up certain measures the Socialists took from other radicals." As to this, John Graham Brooks agreed with W. J. Ghent in the "National Socialist" that, "It is ridiculous to maintain that Roosevelt's program is in no

[61] *Ibid.*, p. 212.
[63] William English Walling, *Socialism As It Is*, p. 221.
[62] *Ibid.*, p. 215.
[64] *Ibid.*, p. 63.

degree socialistic." Ghent's editorial proceeded to assert that reform measures "are unavoidable as a means of entirely revolutionizing the mode of production." [65]

In this book, too, Walling showed sympathy with the program of the syndicalists. There is "little disagreement," he said, "among Socialists that 'Direct Industrial Organization' is likely to prove the most important means by which 'the workers can ultimately overthrow' the capitalistic system." [66] He favored the general strike, and declared that Socialism was traveling steadily in that direction. But he did not wish to abandon political action. Noting that the syndicalists distrusted political action because they felt that the government always became the tool of the leaders, he answered that this possibility inheres in all organizations,—unions, as well as government.

The syndicalist movement, he said, differed with the revolutionary socialists principally in emphasis. "It undoubtedly exaggerates the possibilities of economic action, and under-estimates those of political action." [67] Syndicalism, he felt, was a reaction against undue emphasis on political action. He thought that the anti-political element in the syndicalist movement would weaken, and that the syndicalists and the revolutionary Socialists would meet on "an identical program." [68] For himself, he firmly adhered to the necessity of political action. "From Kautsky and Bebel . . . the ballot has thus far remained the weapon of first practical importance, even for revolutionary purposes." [69]

But he fully expected that the socialist result would come through a revolution. Of course, he said, a peaceful revolution might be accomplished; but he thought that the capitalists would, in the end, oppose the change by all the violence within their power.

But in his "Progressivism and After," published in 1914 (after the great progressive year of 1912), Walling, to my mind, showed marked changes in his beliefs. He admitted that great changes had occurred in the two years since he had written "Socialism as It Is." While he had expected that reformist tendencies would lessen, the reformists had swept all before them. [70] Meanwhile, revolutionary Socialism had greatly increased in the unions.

[65] John Graham Brooks, *American Syndicalism,* p. 100.
[66] Walling, *op. cit.,* p. 372.   [67] *Ibid.,* p. 383.   [68] *Ibid.,* p. 386.   [69] *Ibid.,* p. 416.
[70] William English Walling, *Progressivism—and After,* Preface p. xii.

He noticed John Graham Brooks' criticism of his reference to political reforms, and said that he had been completely misunderstood. He replied that he believed in reforms as "an absolutely indispensable preparation" for Socialism. He was "unqualifiedly and enthusiastically in favor of these measures" as "starting out on the road that leads *finally* in the Socialist direction." But he considered Socialist reform as "infinitely more important than progressive reform, because it alone would lead at the present moment toward a better distribution of income and opportunity." [71]

Apparently, he abandoned his idea of a revolutionary change, and adopted the belief that the change would come gradually by an evolutionary process. The progressive movement was but a stage on the road to the Socialist state. All progressives, he said, are "headed towards that State Capitalism, that partnership of capital and government which is loosely called 'State Socialism,' and the aim of which is the *organization of capital and labor by government,—primarily for the benefit of the majority of the owners of capital, i.e., of the small* capitalists." [72] Roosevelt was farther on the road than Wilson to the collective management of business, but Wilson was more representative of the class struggle between small business and large business. The conflict, Walling declared, was between the small manufacturer and business man, the farmer and shopkeeper, on the one hand, and the larger capitalistic interests on the other. But both Wilson and Roosevelt left out of consideration the skilled working man; and above all, the unskilled, the last group which would be included in the governing classes.

Walling said, however, that the process of democracy would be the inclusion of one class after another in the ruling classes, until the socialist state was finally achieved. He seized on a quotation from Emerson, which he called Emerson's law, that "property will, year after year, write every statute that respects property." When, Emerson said, *"the rich are outvoted, as frequently happens, it is the joint treasury of the poor which exceeds their accumulations."* Walling phrased this law, "When the owners of the larger incomes are outvoted, it will be the total income of the lower classes that exceeds their total income." [73] The classes without incomes

[71] *Ibid.*, pp. vii–ix.   [72] *Ibid.*, p. 7.   [73] *Ibid.*, p. 32.

or property were therefore without political power, and the process would simply be that one class after another would attain capital and income, and therefore political power. We don't now, he said, allow the unskilled to vote when they are in a majority. But though the unskilled and the propertyless *"are at first used as mere pawns in this struggle, they come nearer to power in proportion as one topmost class after another is shorn of power."* [74] He said that "this is just what is taking place. The small capitalist government is already evolving into a 'labor' government—at least in one sense of the word." [75] The aristocracy of labor will be gradually taken into the governing majority, but the unskilled would remain outside.

Walling's argument was therefore directly contrary, as he pointed out, to the standard socialist theory. The standard theory held that the small capitalists, in Kautsky's words, were becoming bankrupt, were losing power, whereas Walling said they were actually coming into power by putting the large capitalists under the control of the state. Labor was being better paid, and as its economic power increased, its political power would increase likewise, and it too would join the governing class, in fact was already joining it.

There would then be three stages: state capitalism, when all monopolies and all very large corporations and large scale industries would be controlled or regulated by the state; state socialism, which would come when the classes included in the state were increased by the addition of the skilled workers; and finally, when all were included, socialism itself. Socialism would be reached, he said, by stages, one step at a time.

Walling summarized his theories by stating that a certain measure of progress would come through the self-interest of the governing classes. This, he said, is the national or industrial efficiency movement. Greater progress would come through the successive rise to power of new elements of the middle class and of the upper layers of the working class, but the greatest progress would come through the "revolt of the lower classes." [76]

In all this, there was none of the Marxian catastrophe, none of the thesis that the misery of the working classes was increasing.

[74] *Ibid.,* p. 132.   [75] *Ibid.,* p. 143.   [76] *Ibid.,* pp. 321–22.

The change would come through the increasing power and prosperity of the working classes, rather than through their increasing degradation.

James Mackaye, an engineer, the son of Steele Mackaye and the brother of Percy, advocated socialism on no Marxian theories. His basis was the rigorous basis of his economy of happiness, which we shall consider in Chapter XIII on "The Ends of Politics." His conclusion was that the end of society is the production of the greatest surplus of happiness, and that, hence, "unequal distribution must, in general, be wrong." The theory of utility, he said, "founds the doctrine of equal opportunity and equal distribution of wealth upon something more substantial than a sentiment—it founds it upon a *reason*." [77] Basing his end on happiness, he would diminish hard labor as much as possible, and provide as far as possible for sharing the burdens of production and the benefits of consumption. The utility principle of happiness proved, he contended, that prolonged labor causes fatigue and unhappiness.

Production must, therefore, be restricted and controlled by the state, and so distributed that all bore its burdens and no one bore too great a share. There should be greater intensity of production, and less duration. Consumption should be left to individual choice, but consumption and leisure should be approximately equal among all members of the state. His system would admit moderate differences in pay for managers and the directors of his state. Ability and initiative should be rewarded; but always with the admonition that the great rewards which our capitalistic society grants are not necessary, and are opposed to the whole theory of the equal distribution of happiness.

While the Socialists were modifying the Marxian dogmas, their opponents were attacking them root and branch. In 1913, Vladimir G. Simkhovitch, of Columbia University, in his "Marxism Versus Socialism," contributed an able and destructive analysis of the Marxian dogmas. We had come to realize, he said, that not economic conditions only, but "the independent power and influence of our traditions, our political and religious convictions, and our various ideologies, have been recognized," as forces in our lives.[78]

[77] James Mackaye, *The Economy of Happiness*, p. 316.
[78] Vladimir G. Simkhovitch, *Marxism Versus Socialism*, p. 33.
James E. Le Rossignol's *Orthodox Socialism* was another thoroughgoing attack on the classical Marxian case.

It was impossible, he said, for example, to interpret the abolition movement in America as a class struggle. Marx, he declared, had been proved mistaken in his theory of the increasing concentration of production, and in the disappearance of the middle class. Marx himself saw, he said, the introduction of the factory acts and the extension of social control over industry, which operated against his theory that economic life would be reduced to a mechanical entity. Wages, too, had increased, instead of decreasing.

Socialists, he continued, were abandoning socialism and becoming mere social reformers. "Whether they call themselves revisionists, reformers, laborites, or plain socialists, whether they go on respecting the old melodramatic phrases or not, the overwhelming majority of the socialists of today are tending to be reformers. Their Marxian training does not permit them to be Utopians, and the faith in socialism as an inevitable economic necessity is rapidly evaporating, the economic facts being what they are." Social reform, he said, could not "arouse the passionate ardor that is kindled by the apocalyptic vision of the social cataclysm. The road to social reform is flat and dusty; the journey along it is hard and dull." [79]

Hillquit, indeed, in a debate with Gompers in 1914 before the Commission on Industrial Relations,—when Gompers charged that Socialism was confiscatory, suppressed individual liberty, and believed in cataclysmic social change,—read the Socialist platform plank by plank, and asked if the American Federation of Labor advocated its demands. Gompers answered affirmatively as to all but the minimum wage and the maximum work-day. As to these, he preferred economic to political action.[80] Hillquit, in short, was eager to show that Socialism was truly reformist and not revolutionary.

In a debate with Hillquit in 1914, John A. Ryan (then of the Catholic St. Paul's Seminary, in St. Paul) pointed out that Hillquit had little to say of the increasing deterioration of the working classes. Ryan agreed with Simkhovitch that the wage earners were steadily increasing in prosperity, and the middle classes were not being absorbed. Then he quoted Spargo as saying that only those industries which could be more efficiently managed by the state,

[79] *Ibid.*, pp. 292, 294.
[80] Morris Hillquit, *Loose Leaves From a Busy Life*, pp. 97–101.

should be taken over. Ryan said that if this opinion were "accepted by the majority of authoritative Socialists, we should not be much concerned about the purely economic theories and projects of Socialism. We should be comforted by the conviction that, outside the field of natural monopolies, the great majority of industries would be more capably conducted by private than by collective agencies, and that all attempts to socialize them by the method of competition would inevitably fail. The average upholder of the system of private capital fears not fair competition with State industries, but forcible expropriation." [81]

If that were the case, the issue in each industry would simply be whether private ownership had failed and state ownership offered a better prospect. This was the issue, as we have seen, that Simkhovitch thought we were approaching. John Graham Brooks held the same idea. For years he had eloquently and ably presented the evils of our industrial systems. But he feared, as much as any conservative, the deadening effect on initiative of universal state socialism, and the danger of the political machine which would operate so vast a system. He believed that we should have in the future a great deal more government ownership and control than we then had. Business which became monopolistic or which private enterprise showed that it could not handle, would be taken over by the government. Secondly, he hoped that we should have a great increase in cooperative industry. But he concluded that we should have a great deal of individual business, just as we had then. It was not a single decision, therefore, between two systems which was involved: it was an endless series of decisions between two systems. By trial and error, by empirical decision, we should decide that this or that new restraint on private business is necessary. We should decide that some business should be handled by the state, and another perhaps should no longer be handled by the state. The process would be the endless testing process of a democracy which does not believe in systems, and distrusts long planning ahead.

The dread of the stifling of individual initiative and liberty under an all-inclusive socialist state, the general aversion from violent and revolutionary change, had influenced even the Socialists.

[81] Morris Hillquit and John A. Ryan, *Socialism: Promise or Menace*, p. 50.

From first to last, the main objection to Socialism had not been with its economics. Indeed, as we have seen, Socialists had largely abandoned the Marxian economics. H. G. Wells is probably right, —that Socialism would be farther advanced today if Marx had never lived.

After all, the difference—as on so many political questions—is temperamental. Some of us have faith that human nature could rise to the management of a socialist state without the incentive of individual profit, and some of us have not. The idealism of Socialists and the bitter evils of the competitive system, must be admitted by all fair-minded opponents of their proposals. Surely, too, we may have confidence that society will steadily endeavor— and with increasing success—to diminish and control the rapacity of individuals, the grievous discrepancies of wealth and poverty, and the vicious catastrophes of the capitalistic system. But the age-old doubt must remain,—whether so complicated a system would be workable under the operation of the habits, customs, and prejudices of men and women.

But as Socialism became empirical, as it abandoned its famous universal formulas, and descended into the age-old process of test-ing each proposal by itself, the radical elements and the revo-lutionary Socialists developed the philosophy of syndicalism, which was to reach strength just as our period was closing. Its organiza-tion, the Industrial Workers of the World, was formed of disil-lusionment of the political representatives of labor, of dislike and distrust of the milder methods of the American Federation of Labor, and of the growing conservatism of American Socialism. It was similar to the old Knights of Labor in that it was formed of all trades. John Graham Brooks said that if you would find its origins, you need only read the history of the Knights of Labor. Above all, it appealed to the unskilled, the outsiders. The uni-versal strike and direct action became its shibboleths.

Daniel De Leon was one of the leaders in its organization. Moyer and Haywood, of the Western Federation of Miners, and A. M. Simons, were also present at the organization meeting, which was held in Chicago in 1905. "The Manifesto," issued by the organ-izers, attacked craft unionism, which it asserted tends to "foster the idea of harmony of interests between the employing exploiter and employed slave." It called for "one great industrial union embracing all industries," to be "founded on the class struggle," and established as "the economic organization of the working class, without affiliation with any political party." It bitterly attacked the American Federation of Labor.[82]

The convention met in Chicago in June of 1905. According to St. John, who became its secretary, there were four main types in its personnel: parliamentary socialists (both Marxian and reformist), anarchists, industrial unionists, and the "labor union fakir." The anarchists were in the minority. In the beginning, moreover, the direct actionists were less prominent than they soon became.[83]

Haywood called the assembly the "Continental Congress of the Working Class." He scorned the idea that there was an identity of interest between the capitalist and the working-man. There could be only "a continuous struggle between the two classes; and this organization will be formed, based, and founded on the class struggle, having in view no compromise and no surrender."[84]

There was much argument on the preamble, which was finally adopted in the following form:

"The working class and the employing class have nothing in common. There can be no peace so long as hunger and want are found among the millions of working people, and the few, who make up the employing class, have all the good things of life.

"Between these two classes a struggle must go on until all the toilers come together on the political, as well as on the industrial, field, and take and hold that which they produce by their labor through an economic organization of the working class, without affiliation with any political party."[85]

The declaration in favor of both political and economic action was to be the cause of conflict within a few years.

The panic of 1907 nearly disrupted the party. For nearly two years thereafter, says Brissenden, the I.W.W. "had a precarious and, for the most part, uneventful existence."[86] In 1908 Haywood was expelled from the Western Federation of Miners, and was able to devote his entire energies to the I.W.W. Two factions developed: one, that of De Leon and the Socialist Labor Party; and

---

[82] Paul Frederick Brissenden, *The I.W.W.: A Study of American Syndicalism,* p. 63.
[83] *Ibid.,* pp. 77–78. [84] *Ibid.,* p. 83. [85] *Ibid.,* p. 92. [86] *Ibid.,* p. 213.

the other, an anarchistic element that scoffed at political action. In the 1908 convention, after a bitter fight, the words favoring political action were stricken out, so that the second paragraph quoted above read:

"Between these two classes a struggle must go on until the workers of the world organize as a class, take possession of the earth and the machinery of production, and abolish the wage system." [87]

It was a final declaration against political action, and in favor of revolutionary economic action. The amendment caused much intense feeling. A rump convention of the political action element was held, which called itself the Workers' International Industrial Union. The political order called the other anarchistic, declared that its mission was to "decry the ballot, which is a civilized method of settling social issues, to advocate physical force only," and that the bonafide I.W.W. "sets itself like flint against any organization that teaches such tragedy-producing tactics." [88]

Haywood, who became the dominant force in the I.W.W., was a remarkable figure. Powerful physically, fearless, he led a battered life until his death in Soviet Russia. He was a natural rebel, incapable of subordinating himself to order and discipline. Of old American stock, he drifted to Utah, and later became one of the leaders in the Western Federation of Miners. There he did his full share of the bitter and lawless work. In justice to—or perhaps in explanation of—him, it must be said that the methods of his opponents were not gentle, and that Haywood bore many scars on his mind, as well as body.

Haywood and the I.W.W. adopted in full and without qualification the formulas of Marxian Socialism. Indeed, I think that the I.W.W. may be largely explained as the result of the popularization of the Marxian dogmas. The Socialists, as time went on, had modified and amplified those dogmas, qualified their conclusions, and recognized how widely they had failed in many respects to meet the actualities of our economic development. But when dogmas are made popular, when they are made shibboleths, they are adopted without qualifications. The very attempt to sloganize them and reduce them to sharp and appealing forms, prevents the careful qualifications the facts require.

[87] *Ibid.*, p. 227.   [88] *Ibid.*, p. 252.

At any rate, Haywood repeated the old formulas in their crudest forms. "Long before the coming of the modern Socialist Movement," he said, "it was understood by the economists that all wealth is produced by labor." Then if all wealth is produced by labor, he asked why do not "the laborers receive their full product?" The answer, he said, was not known until "it came from Karl Marx." The theory of surplus value "is the beginning of all Socialist knowledge." [89]

In his testimony before the United States Industrial Relations Commission in 1914, he repeated the standard theories of the class struggle, asserting that the workers have "nothing but their labor power, and the capitalists have the control of and the influence of, all branches of government—legislative, executive, and judicial,—that they have on their side of the question all of the forces of law,—that they can hire detectives; they can have the police force for the asking or the militia, or the regular army." [90] So he would have nothing of political action. The industries should be owned by the workers and not the state. "There will be no such thing as the state, or states. The industries will take the place of what are now existing states." [91]

Although Haywood was a man of much intellectual force, it is evident that he had no ordered philosophy. His beliefs were those of a man embittered by long struggles with capitalists, with labor unionists; to whom the shibboleths of Marx had become sacred; and who was scornful alike of labor unions, reformist Socialists, and the current political state. His later adherence to Soviet Russia indicates that he did want a state, that he was not an anarchist, but that his state was the state of the workers.

The growing conservatism of unionism, the shedding of its formulas by American Socialism, did not mean, therefore, that bellum omnium contra omnes was over.

REFERENCES

Abbott, Lyman, *The Spirit of Democracy*. Boston: Houghton Mifflin Co., 1910.

Brissenden, Paul Frederick, *The I.W.W.: A Study of American Syndicalism*. New York: Columbia University Press, 1919.

Brooks, John Graham, *American Syndicalism: The I.W.W.* New York: The Macmillan Co., 1913.

[89] John Graham Brooks, *American Syndicalism*, p. 80.
[90] William D. Haywood, *Bill Haywood's Book*, p. 283.   [91] *Ibid.*, p. 287.

————*The Social Unrest.* New York: The Macmillan Co., 1904.

BURGESS, JOHN W., *Reminiscences of an American Scholar.* New York: Columbia University Press, 1934.

ELY, RICHARD T., *The Labor Movement in America.* New York: T. Y. Crowell & Co., 1896.

————*Socialism and Social Reform.* New York: T. Y. Crowell & Co., 1894.

————*Property and Contract in Their Relation to the Distribution of Wealth.* New York: The Macmillan Co., 1914.

GHENT, W. J:, *Mass and Class: A Survey of Social Divisions.* New York: The Macmillan Co., 1904.

GRONLUND, LAURENCE, *The Cooperative Commonwealth.* Boston: Lee and Shepard, 1884.

HAYWOOD, WILLIAM D., *Bill Haywood's Book.* New York: International Publishers, 1929.

HILLQUIT, MORRIS, *History of Socialism in the United States.* New York: Funk & Wagnalls Co., 1903.

————*Socialism in Theory and Practice.* New York: The Macmillan Co., 1909.

————*Loose Leaves from a Busy Life.* New York: The Macmillan Co., 1934.

HILLQUIT, MORRIS, and RYAN, JOHN A., *Socialism: Promise or Menace?* New York: The Macmillan Co., 1914.

HUGHAN, JESSIE WALLACE, *American Socialism of the Present Day.* New York: John Lane Co., 1911.

KELLY, EDMOND, *Twentieth Century Socialism.* New York: Longmans, Green & Co., 1913.

LE ROSSIGNOL, JAMES E., *Orthodox Socialism: A Criticism.* New York: The Macmillan Co., 1907.

MACKAYE, JAMES, *The Economy of Happiness.* Boston: Little, Brown & Co., 1906.

————*The Happiness of Nations.* New York: B. W. Huebsch, 1915.

MARX, KARL, *Capital, The Communist Manifesto and Other Writings.* New York: Modern Library, 1932.

REYNOLDS, STEPHEN MARION, *Debs: His Life, Writings, and Speeches.* Girard, Kansas: *Appeal to Reason,* 1908.

RUSSELL, CHARLES EDWARD, *Bare Hands and Stone Walls.* New York: Charles Scribner's Sons, 1933.

————*Why I Am a Socialist.* New York: George H. Doran Co., 1910.

SIMKHOVITCH, VLADIMIR G., *Marxism Versus Socialism.* New York: Henry Holt & Co., 1913.

SPARGO, JOHN, *Socialism.* New York: The Macmillan Co., 1909.

————*Sidelights on Contemporary Socialism.* New York: B. W. Huebsch, 1911.

————*Applied Socialism.* New York: B. W. Huebsch, 1912.

SUMNER, WILLIAM GRAHAM, *War and Other Essays.* New Haven: Yale University Press, 1911.

SYMES, LILLIAN, and CLEMENT, TRAVERS, *Rebel America.* New York: Harper & Bros., 1934.

TAUSSIG, FRANK W., *Principles of Economics.* New York: The Macmillan Co. (3rd ed. rev., 1928).

WALLING, WILLIAM ENGLISH, *Socialism As It Is.* New York: The Macmillan Co., 1912.

——*Progressivism—and After.* New York: The Macmillan Co., 1914.

——Editor and Contributor, *The Socialism of Today.* New York: Henry Holt & Co., 1916.

WOOLSEY, THEODORE D., *Communism and Socialism.* New York: Charles Scribner's Sons, 1880.

Chapter XI

NATIONALISM AND STATE RIGHTS

THE conflict between Nationalism and State Rights has recurred again and again in the course of this fifty year period. We have seen it in the struggle for the war amendments. We have seen it throughout the entire course of the decisions under those amendments. We have seen it in the Granger agitation and the Populist revolt. It rose to its height in the Progressive movement.

Steadily there had gone on an increasing nationalization of business and enterprise. Railroads extended from New York to Chicago, and from Chicago to the coast. Industrial organizations had plants in many States, and sold their products all over the Union. The mails, express, telegraph, and telephone knew no State lines. Not only had much business become national, but there was a constant interplay of activity between people of the different States.

Inevitably, there arose conflicts between Federal and State jurisdictions in the management of these multiform activities.

The first definite clash on an economic issue came with the debate on the Interstate Commerce Act of 1887. We have already seen something of the causes for control of railroad rates and the prevention of discrimination. We have seen, too, that the Supreme Court held in 1886 that a State had no power to prevent discrimination in rates in interstate commerce.[1]

But in 1886, there was not only no power in the States to control interstate rates or discriminations in interstate rates, but there was a vast mass of conflicting State laws and regulations on the conduct of interstate transportation. We had already found that particular and jealous State interests were too strong for any one but the Nation to control. Hugo Richard Meyer observes that the Hepburn Committee in 1879, "on the whole, endorsed the jealous and narrow spirit of local interests manifested by the complainants who appeared before it, but its common sense saved it from taking

[1] *Wabash Ry.* vs. *Illinois,* 118 U.S. 557 (1886).

the extreme attitude of the people of New York City." All the "different interests," he said, "insisted that it was the duty of the railways as common carriers so to adjust their rates as to keep alive an established trade or industry, at a particular place, under all circumstances and for all time." They persistently refused, in Depew's words, approved by Meyer, to face the fact "that the business of the United States had outgrown the boundaries of the separate States; that the people of the United States had become one in their business enterprise, and a unit in their business activities." [2]

Senator Cullom, of Illinois, declared that his "experience as Chief Executive of the State with the practical workings of the Railroad and Warehouse Law, clearly demonstrated to me that a State statute, no matter how drastic it might be, was utterly inadequate to meet the evils complained of, and that effective regulation must be Federal and not State, or probably Federal and State combined." [3]

Ripley, in his "Railroad Rates and Regulation," refers to the continuing conflict of interests between jealous State interests, "the various attempts of the Railroad commissions, notably Texas and Minnesota, to set up schemes of rates, which shall concentrate the distributive business of the community in localities as against the competition of jobbers at a distance. The extreme confusion introduced in matters of classification by conflicting authorities, has already reached a point where demand for the substitution of a single uniform schedule for the United States has become well-nigh irresistible." There were also conflicts over laws regulating service, illustrated by the Supreme Court decision in 1907, holding that the attempt of North Carolina to require fast mail trains to stop at small way stations was unconstitutional.[4] Ripley also referred to the "well-nigh intolerable conflict of authority of the many public service commissions and state courts now at work in this field. No fewer than six different state commissions are said to be taking a hand in the pending reorganization of the Wabash." [5]

It was just such conflicts that caused Justice Holmes to remark in 1911 that he thought "the Union would be imperiled" if the

---

[2] Hugo Richard Meyer, *Government Regulation of Railroad Rates,* pp. 229–30.
[3] Shelby M. Cullom, *Fifty Years of Public Service,* p. 312.
[4] William Z. Ripley, *Railroads: Rates and Regulation,* p. 632.
[5] William Z. Ripley, *Railroads: Finance and Organization,* p. 310.

Supreme Court could not declare unconstitutional the laws of the States, for he said those in his position knew how persistent and destructive were local and selfish interests.[6]

There has been a steady effort to resolve the conflicts of State laws and regulations over the conduct of interstate transportation by Congress, the Interstate Commerce Commission, and the Courts. In a long line of decisions, the Supreme Court has limited the power of the States over interstate commerce. No State can levy a license tax on interstate commerce, tax the privilege of engaging in interstate commerce, or burden interstate commerce.[7] The Supreme Court has laid down the rule that some matters in the conduct of interstate transportation are of such a nature that no State can regulate them, whether or not Congress has acted; and that on others, as soon as Congress has legislated, its jurisdiction becomes exclusive.[8] The power over interstate commerce is therefore potentially exclusive on all matters.

The Supreme Court held in the Minnesota and Shreveport rate cases that a State could not regulate intrastate rates, if to do so would affect the interstate business.[9]

The whole subject of interstate rates, and even of intrastate rates so far as they affect the interstate rates, the methods and appliances used, all the diversities which hamper interstate transportation, are within the power of the Federal government, and there is general agreement that the Federal government should have and use the power.

But the power over interstate commerce extends not only to the actual operation of commerce, but to all that directly affects interstate commerce. Here the question becomes more difficult. But it is clear that no State can hope to control combinations in restraint of interstate trade. In 1890 the Sherman Anti-Trust Act was passed, forbidding combinations and monopolies in restraint of interstate commerce.

In the well-known Knight case,[10] it was held that a combination of sugar refiners concerned production only, and did not restrain

---

[6] Holmes, *Collected Legal Papers*, p. 296.
[7] *Robbins* vs. *Shelby Taxing District,* 120 U.S. 489 (1887). A long line of decisions has consistently maintained this position.
[8] *Wilmington etc. Co.* vs. *California R.R. Com.*, 236 U.S. 151, 154, 155 (1915).
[9] *Minnesota Rate Cases,* 230 U.S. 352 (1913); *Houston etc. Ry. Co.* vs. *U.S.,* 234 U.S. 342 (1914).
[10] *U.S.* vs. *E. C. Knight Co.,* 156 U.S. 1 (1895).

commerce; and, for long, the case was considered as a determination that the Federal government could not control monopolistic combinations of manufacturers. But some years later, in the Swift case [11] (which was better prepared from the government's point of view), it was shown that a combination of packers necessarily resulted in a restraint on the resulting commerce between packers; and it has henceforth been admitted that a combination resulting directly in a restraint of commerce, could be punished by the Federal government.

Again, in the Standard Oil [12] and the American Tobacco Company [13] cases, the Court upheld the right of the Federal government to restrain combinations of oil refiners and tobacco manufacturers respectively, when those combinations resulted in monopolization of interstate business.

We come now to disputed territory, to the great field of matters which are not commerce itself, but which affect commerce. The diversity in State laws on hours, child labor, wages, may have serious consequences on the ability of businesses in strict States to compete with businesses in laxer States. Goods made in a State which permits child labor under fourteen, compete with goods made in a State which forbids child labor under sixteen. Goods made in a State with a ten hour day compete with goods made in a State with an eight hour day.

Nationalism, consequently, has been fostered by the undercutting of selfish or backward States, or States with merely different standards. So long as even one State maintains loose standards as to corporate charters, as to labor conditions, as to health conditions in its factories or packing houses, the efforts of the advanced communities are rendered partly or wholly nugatory. The competition of the State with loose or backward standards hampers the efforts of every State with modern standards. This undercutting was the chief motive force behind the meat inspection bill of 1906, the pure food law of 1906, the efforts to obtain national incorporation or Federal license laws, and the Federal Child Labor bill.

Again, on the prohibition question, we have seen, in the words of

---

[11] *Swift & Co.* vs. *U.S.*, 196 U.S. 375, (1905).
[12] *Standard Oil Co.* vs. *U.S.*, 221 U.S. 1 (1911).
[13] *U.S.* vs. *American Tobacco Co.*, 221 U.S. 106 (1911).

Bryan and President Eliot, the force of undercutting. Events proved that they were mistaken, not on the effects of undercutting, but on the broader question of whether there was a sufficiently unanimous opinion to make national control feasible.

But the mere diversity of State laws on a host of subjects where no conflicting competition results, but where confusion and clashes of jurisdiction result, has aided the demand for national action. The standard of one State which forbids lottery tickets is undercut by one that permits them. The confusion and the distress caused by divergent laws on marriage and divorce, has been so grievous that even so conservative a man as Taft declared that it would have been desirable to have granted the Federal government power to regulate marriage and divorce.[14]

The conflict of laws between the States on such questions as negotiable instruments, bills of lading, sales, and contracts, became so mischievous that in 1891 the American Bar Association appointed a committee on uniform State laws, which has labored ever since, with great ability and diligence, to bring about uniform legislation on such subjects.

The committee reported in 1891 that the answers to its inquiries showed that there was an "almost unanimous verdict in favor of greater uniformity on all the subjects designated, and a substantial agreement that the desired uniformity can be best secured by legislative action in the various states."[15] It declared that "Variance, dissonance, contradiction, nay, any unnecessary diversity in the fifty sub-divisions of the one American people, in the general laws affecting the whole people in their business and social relations, can not but produce perplexity, uncertainty, and damage. Such diversity, always an annoyance, is often a nuisance."[16]

Through the years, the committee indefatigably prosecuted its labors. But in 1909, Amasa M. Eaton, for years President of the Commissioners on Uniform State Laws, complained that, though by that time thirty-eight States and territories had adopted the uniform negotiable instruments law, the State judges "continue, unfortunately, to construe the provisions of the Negotiable Instruments Law strictly in favor of the pre-existing decisions in their own state; and sometimes, I regret to say we shall find, without

---

[14] William H. Taft, *Presidential and State Papers* (1910), p. 553.
[15] American Bar Association, *Report*, 1891, p. 366.   [16] *Ibid.*, p. 371.

citing or even examining the decisions in other states, in cases arising under the same sections of the same law." [17] He asked, "what is the use of a uniform law unless we have uniform decisions thereunder? . . ." [18] Moreover, it was seen that uniformity in amendments was desirable. In 1913 it was proposed that there be a committee on the unifying of decisions under uniform State laws.

Charles T. Terry, the President of the Commissioners, in 1914 declared that there were no such peculiarities in the various States, "of climate or location or racial distinction, as would require the differentiation of the principles of law, or such as would justify the application of divergent or inconsistent rules and regulations, to the citizens of different sections of the country in their life, liberty, and pursuit of happiness," in such matters as negotiable instruments and the other subjects on which uniform legislation was proposed. He added that, in matters of interstate concern, the State lines "are only imaginary lines which can not be allowed to interrupt or obstruct the working of principles which are in their very nature universal." [19]

Terry stated in 1914 that since the adoption of the Negotiable Instruments Law in Pennsylvania, "there have been forty-nine decisions on the points dealt in the Negotiable Instruments Law. Of these forty-nine decisions, twenty-four ignore the Negotiable Instruments Law entirely, whereas, the other twenty-five decisions, while they cite the act, make no reference whatever to decisions of other states under the same act." [20]

In 1915, Terry well stated much of the opinion of the time when he declared, "So long as there is one State which maintains corporate laws which are farcical in their claim of regulation, so long will the trusting investor and the credulous creditor remain the victim of the unscrupulous promoter. In this connection, it is literally true that 'the chain is no stronger than its weakest link.' " He asserted that "an economic and legal scandal has been created and is being perpetuated." [21]

By 1916 the Committee had approved twenty-eight different uniform State laws. By that time the negotiable instruments law had been passed by forty-seven jurisdictions, the warehouse receipts law by thirty-five, the bill of lading law by fourteen, sales by four-

---

[17] *Op. cit.*, 1909, p. 1033.   [18] *Ibid.*, p. 1051.   [19] *Op. cit.*, 1914, p. 1045.
[20] *Ibid.*, p. 1067.   [21] *Op. cit.*, 1915, p. 928.

teen, family desertion by eight, and divorce by only three. The rest had been adopted only by a handful of States.

Finally, much nationalism was due simply to the fact that the national government was the most powerful and the richest government, and the one most capable therefore of undertaking the work. The Federal government alone can undertake irrigation projects better than any State, both because the work may extend over several States and because of the expense.

Near the end of the period, the practise of granting Federal aid to the States, conditioned on the performance of work of a certain standard by the States, began to develop widely. In the Morrill Act of 1862, the Federal government granted land to the States, conditioned that the proceeds were to be used in agricultural and mechanical studies in State colleges. The process of setting standards for agricultural and experimental colleges, by making the grant of Federal money conditioned on the use, has been greatly extended. Since our period, the process has gone on. It is a process which, after all, stimulates State activity and efficiency, and lessens the burden on the Federal government, for the Federal government acts rather as a supervisor than an administrator. But it undeniably tends to make the States less States and more administrative districts.[22]

In all the efforts to attain greater national control, the commerce clause has been the great source of power. The rate cases were all upheld under the commerce clause. The anti-trust acts were upheld under the commerce clause. The encroachments of the States on each other and the Federal power, have been invalidated under the commerce clause. Under the commerce clause the lottery act was held valid,[23] and the exclusion of adulterated and misbranded foods.[24] The Federal government can punish the transportation of women across State lines for immoral purposes.[25] Before the prohibition amendment, it was forbidden to ship liquor into "dry" territory, and the Supreme Court upheld the action under the commerce clause.[26]

[22] In *U.S.* vs. *Butler, Rec.,* 80 Law Ed. 287, 1936, the Supreme Court held that money could not be raised by an excise tax otherwise valid to pay to farmers who contracted to reduce acreage, but even the majority opinion admitted that payments could be made conditioned on the performance of certain acts.
[23] *Lottery Case,* 188 U.S. 321 (1903).
[24] *Hippolite Egg Co.* vs. *U.S.,* 220 U.S. 45 (1911).
[25] *Hoke* vs. *U.S.,* 227 U.S. 308 (1913).
[26] *Clark Distilling Co.* vs. *Western Maryland R.R. Co.,* 242 U.S. 311 (1917).

The First Employers' Liability Law was held unconstitutional because it included employees who were not engaged in interstate business; [27] but when a new statute was enacted, confining itself to strictly interstate commerce employees, the Court upheld the action of Congress in removing the common law defenses in suits for injuries to such employees. [28]

But the Federal government has also great power through the taxing power. Congress taxed the State bank notes out of existence, and the Supreme Court upheld the action. [29] It was permitted to levy a prohibitive tax on oleomargarine colored as butter. [30]

Finally, the Supreme Court has been a powerful nationalizing factor in its decisions under the Fourteenth Amendment. On the questions of reasonable rates and taxation, on the power to enforce a day in court and prevent unequal laws, and ensure due process of law, it has exerted an enormous power over State legislation and action.

We now have some of the background of the conflict between Nationalism and State Rights when Roosevelt was President. He was a thoroughgoing nationalist. Time and again he repeated: "It is an absurdity to expect to eliminate the abuses in great corporations by State action. . . . The National Government alone can deal adequately with these great corporations." [31]

In his annual message of 1908 he declared: "The proposal to make the National Government supreme over, and therefore to give it complete control over, the railroads and other instruments of Interstate Commerce, is merely a proposal to carry out to the letter one of the prime purposes, if not the prime purpose, for which the Constitution was founded. It does not represent centralization. It represents merely the acknowledgment of the patent fact that centralization has already come in business." [32] Only the Federal government could control.

The fullest expression of his nationalism was given in his speeches in 1910, later collected in a book called: "The New Nationalism." "The New Nationalism," he said, "puts the national need before

---

[27] *Employers' Liability Cases* (First), 207 U.S. 463 (1908).
[28] *Employers' Liability Cases* (Second), 223 U.S. 1 (1912).
[29] *Veazie Bank* vs. *Fenno*, 8 Wall. 533 (1869).
[30] *McCray* vs. *U.S.*, 195 U.S. 27 (1904).
[31] Theodore Roosevelt, *Works,* (Scribner ed.) Vol. XVII, p. 257. (Fourth Message, Dec., 1904).
[32] Theodore Roosevelt, *op. cit.,* p. 583.

sectional or personal advantage. It is impatient of the utter confusion that results from local legislatures attempting to treat national issues as local issues." [33] He declared that "there has grown up a neutral land—a borderland in the spheres of action of the national and state governments—a borderland over which each government tends to claim that it has the power, and as to which the action of the courts unfortunately has usually been such as to deny to both the power." [34]

This was far too broad a statement. Whenever the Supreme Court denied the power to the States, on the ground that they could not regulate interstate commerce, by that very act it declared that the power was exclusive in the Federal government. [35]

Beveridge was perhaps the most uncompromising nationalist of his time. He was a thorough-going Hamiltonian, and had no patience with those who clung to what he regarded as the outworn fetish of State rights. He was the author of the meat inspection bill of 1906, he favored the railroad rate bill, the pure food bill, and he introduced the child labor bill, which prohibited the transportation in interstate commerce of all products made in factories where children under fourteen were employed.

In 1907 he conducted a debate with Bryan in the "Reader Magazine" on various political subjects. One of them was, "Nationalism Versus State Rights." "We are one people," he said, "speaking one language, living in one country, under one flag. What affects one of us, affects all of us. Most of the evils that develop among us, are common evils to be reached only by a common remedy. Scarcely any one evil is confined exclusively to one state." [36] Nationality, he said, merely means "the *American people acting in common* against evils which affect them in common. States rights means merely these same American people divided into forty-six 'sovereign' groups, and therefore acting not harmoniously and in common, but separately and therefore impotently." [37] Beveridge laid great stress on undercutting. "If one State," he said, "passes good laws and enforces them, and another State does not, then the business men in the former State are at a business disadvantage with the business men in the other State. The business men in the State

---

[33] Theodore Roosevelt, *The New Nationalism*, p. 28.   [34] *Ibid.*, p. 36.
[35] Of course if the denial were based on due process of law, the Court in effect held that no government could act.
[36] *Reader Magazine*, March, 1907, p. 363.   [37] *Ibid.*, p. 364.

that has good laws suffer from the very righteousness of that State's laws, and the business man in the State that has bad laws profits by the very wickedness of that State's laws." [38]

He said that the cry of "centralization" had always been raised. It had been raised against the exclusion of obscene literature from the mails, the lottery law, the quarantine law, the pure food and meat inspection laws. The meat bill, he said, "probably never would have been passed but for the storm of wrath that swept over the republic at the revelations of the iniquity of the beef trust." [39]

He poured forth all his energies in behalf of the child labor bill, which proposed to exclude from interstate commerce all products made in factories employing children under fourteen. At that time this proposal was considered very radical. Beveridge insisted that child labor had become a national problem. He amassed a great bulk of evidence on the evils of child labor. He declared, "I am more anxious to debate an inhuman evil than a governmental theory." Yet he did debate the theory, and argued that if Congress could exclude lottery tickets, diseased cattle, and obscene literature from interstate commerce, it could exclude products made by child labor.

The trend of events and of opinion, near the end of our period, was all in the direction of further national power. Croly declared, "Only by faith in an efficient national organization and by an exclusive and aggressive devotion to the national welfare, can the American ideal be made good." The democracy of our people, he continued, "is to be realized by means of an intensification of their national life, just as the ultimate moral purpose of an individual is to be realized by the affirmation and intensification of his own better individuality." [40] Our national organization was not a surrender of liberties in order to get other rights; not a compromise between liberty and efficiency: it was the proper selection of our national life.

But he explained that increased nationalism did not mean increased centralization. More centralization would come, but the main purpose should be to nationalize it as it came. Many of our

[38] Claude G. Bowers, *Beveridge and the Progressive Era*, p. 254 (speech of Jan. 23, 28, 1907).
[39] *Reader Magazine*, March, 1907, p. 361.
[40] Herbert Croly, *The Promise of American Life*, p. 270–71.

present Federal activities were not national. The tariff was not national, but special, in its scope. But we needed far more national action, and instead of it coming too easily, it came too slowly, after bitter opposition. We were then in urgent need of national control of corporations, a national recognition of labor unions, and arbitration of industrial disputes.

In his "Progressive Democracy," Croly declared that the first requisite was a change in the amending power of the Federal constitution. It was "the indispensable effective method of giving to the American democracy a chance to be nationalized." [41] By national laws, the nation must "promote the economic independence of the wage-earner," insure him "against unemployment, sickness, and old age," guarantee to him "wholesome conditions of work," and make it "impossible for a faithful worker to be paid less than a fair minimum wage." [42]

Here was a nationalism far beyond any then advocated by our political leaders.

But during the whole period, those who cherished the old State Rights dogma or were interested in its maintenance, stubbornly opposed each new extension. The tone and content of their objections are so strikingly similar as to make clear that they were applying an old concept, based on past experience and a past loyalty. This does not mean that the formula does not still contain much validity, but any short statement of a political conclusion can not contain the whole truth; it must be applied in the light of new conditions; in short, it must be reexamined constantly.

We have seen that when the Thirteenth Amendment was before Congress, S. S. Cox said that it would destroy the "perennial beauty, exquisite symmetry, and enduring perfection" of that system of government which reserved "to the local communities their local interests." [43] Senator Hendricks, of Indiana, objected that the old timbers were being removed by the Fourteenth Amendment.[44] In 1886, Judge Reagan of Texas, discussing the Interstate Commerce Act, exclaimed, "When we remember that this commission is to be composed of five persons only, that all their judgments are to be rendered in Washington city, . . . when we consider

[41] Herbert Croly, *Progressive Democracy*, p. 243.   [42] *Ibid.*, p. 380.
[43] *Cong. Globe*, Jan. 12, 1865, p. 239.   [44] *Ibid.*, June 4, 1866, p. 2938.

that it will have at least 130,000 miles of railroad to look after and to extend its supervision to, and that the roads cover the thirty-eight States and eight Territories of the Union, with their 60,000,000 of population, and transport not less than $150,000,000 worth of interstate commerce," annually it would be seen how impossible, how "futile" would be the attempts of one commission, "to attend to all the controversies growing out of railroad management in this country." [45]

Senator John T. Morgan, of Alabama, likewise dreaded the increase of Federal power. He said the bill proposed to bestow "autocratic and oligarchic power" upon the commission. He even suggested that a future President might instruct the commission to "let up" on a railroad in Indiana; and let "its competitor running North and South through Illinois, which is a dead certain Republican State, feel all the force of the law." [46] He concluded: "I dread to set in motion a doubtful and dangerous power which will soon become a factor of immense influence in the party politics of the Republic. It is urged that the railroads will absorb and corrupt the State Legislatures, if we leave to them the duty of checking their enormous powers. The thirty-eight legislatures number more than four thousand men.

"Is it easier to corrupt four thousand men scattered throughout thirty-eight States, than it is to corrupt four hundred men who are assembled in Washington? Or is it easier to corrupt these four hundred representatives than it is to corrupt five commissioners entrusted with very broad discretionary powers?" And he dwelt long on the virtues of the States.[47]

Twenty years later, the same fears were expressed of the rate bill of 1906. Samuel W. McCall exclaimed: "And then there is centralization. At the rate we are now moving, it will not be long before we regulate everything and everybody from Washington. You can not govern the whole universe from a single point and have a shred of liberty survive." [48]

Here, again, we see the fear of power in itself, not so much the loss of State rights as the increase of Federal power. We had not yet learned that power with responsibility, subject therefore to

---

[45] *Cong. Record*, July 21, 1886, p. 7280. [46] *Ibid.*, Jan. 14, 1887, p. 657.
[47] *Ibid.*, Jan. 6, 1887, p. 400. [48] *Ibid.*, Feb. 2, 1906, p. 1976.

control, does not necessarily lead to either corruption or arrogance. Whatever the defects of the Interstate Commerce Commission, they have been neither corruption nor arbitrary power.

No one was more torn by the conflict between his old dogmas and modern facts than Bryan. He was a staunch State Rights man. But he intuitively felt the pressure of modern evils, and he had a warm response to any demand for action. He saw that something must be done, but he never admitted that any action should be at the expense of the States. He saw that industry was national, that the railroads were national, and that national control was essential, but he could not endure the thought of national power over such vast forces of our life. He asked for Federal licenses for corporations in interstate commerce, a big step in advance, but he said that national control should be added to, not subtracted from, State control. He asked for Federal ownership of trunk lines, but State ownership of local lines. The local lines were negligible at the time. It was a striking demonstration of the force of an inherited dogma persisting after the man who held it must have unconsciously felt that it was no longer applicable.

In his debate with Beveridge in the "Reader Magazine" in 1907, Bryan favored the Federal meat and pure food laws, and the lottery law. His instinctive humanitarianism could not deny the need. Nor did he shrink from the fact that the Federal control was exclusive. "The power of Congress," he said, "over interstate commerce is complete. This power is not only complete, but its exercise is necessary, the various states being impotent when it comes to matters of interstate commerce." [49]

Yet still he repeated that "Federal remedies should supplement state remedies; they should not be substituted for state remedies." [50] Yet no State control over interstate rates was possible, and the States are helpless against undercutting.

Bryan went on to say that every reason for the States "which existed one hundred and eighteen years ago, exists now, and those reasons are even stronger than they formerly were, because of the increase in the area and population of the nation. . . . The states are even more needed than they formerly were for the administration of domestic affairs. As a matter of theory, that government is best which is nearest the people. If there is any soundness at all

[49] *Reader Magazine,* April, 1907, p. 465.   [50] *Ibid.,* March, 1907, p. 356.

in the doctrine of self-government, the people can act most intelligently upon matters with which they are most familiar." [51]

The essence of his position was, I think, that no power should be taken away from the States by Constitutional amendment. So long as the increase of Federal power came from the growth of interstate commerce, he acquiesced. But he opposed any withdrawal of power from the States by governmental act. It was the constitutional limits which must not be changed. Yet at the time there was little, if any, demand for increased constitutional powers, and yet he voiced again and again his opposition to increased Federal power. His inherited affection for the States was speaking, although on concrete issues he differed little with such a nationalist as Beveridge.

Beveridge's child labor bill seemed to the opponents of further centralization, a sort of challenge. The House Judiciary Committee felt that it "is not extreme or ridiculous to say that it would be just as logical and correct to say that Congress can regulate the age, color, sex, manner of dress, height, and size of employees, and fix their hours, as to contend that Congress can exercise jurisdiction over the subject of woman and child labor." [52]

Ex-President Taft said in 1913 that the bill attempted indirectly and by duress to compel the States to pass a certain kind of legislation, and that the "attempt of Congress to use its power of regulating such commerce to suppress the use of child labor in the State of shipment would be a clear usurpation of that State's rights." [53]

Woodrow Wilson declared in 1908, that if the Supreme Court should hold the bill valid, it would be guilty of "obviously absurd extravagances of interpretation." [54]

Yet so ill-based are our modern political concepts, in 1916 as President he signed a similar child labor bill, stating that he did so with "real emotion" and "genuine pride." [55]

Perhaps the best expression of the distrust of the child labor bill was that of Edgar Gardner Murphy, a minister in Montgomery, Alabama, author of perhaps the two best books on the race problem ever written. He was a member of the National Child Labor Committee, but resigned when it endorsed the national child labor bill. A high-minded and deeply sympathetic man, he was ardently de-

---

[51] *Ibid.*, p. 353.   [52] *Harper's Weekly*, Vol. LI, p. 256 (Feb. 23, 1907).
[53] William Howard Taft, *Popular Government*, p. 143.
[54] Woodrow Wilson, *Constitutional Government*, p. 179.
[55] New York Times, Sept. 1916.

voted to the cause of child labor reform. But he vigorously opposed
a national law. The States, he said, have been "neither indifferent
nor inefficient." The result of a national law would be to "shift
the center of moral obligation from the States to Washington."
Without local public opinion to support it, he said, "Federal enactments themselves are impotent." The proposed bill, in his opinion,
would "weaken local efforts and the development of this opinion
in the individual states." [56]

The strength of State Rights feeling, the dread of Federal power,
is nowhere better exemplified than in the annual reports of the
Committee on Uniform Legislation of the American Bar Association. Though it had struggled year after year for more than a
generation in its attempt to obtain uniform laws, though its progress
had been slow, and even after it obtained uniform laws it found
that amendments soon destroyed uniformity and that conflicting
decisions rendered uniform statutes of little avail, it steadily
affirmed its steadfast objection to Federal laws. In 1892, a speaker
on uniform State laws declared that the surrender of power by the
States was out of the question. It would change our form of government. "The States, the pride and glory and strength of our dual
political system, would disappear, and a centralized Federal power
would arise in their stead." [57] In 1915, Terry, the President of the
Commissioners on Uniform State Laws, observed that the old
sentiment for State rights was almost gone, but that if the States
abandoned the field, appeal would be made to the Federal government "to secure, in another form, which is not the natural form nor
the one contemplated by our system of government, that protection
which has been denied them at the natural source." [58]

In 1914 Terry declared, "More and more every day, citizens of
this country are coming to think in terms of the nation. The narrow
limits of state's rights, state's obligations, and state's interests
are being transcended in fields to which they do not truly pertain,
by the sound requirements of national unity." Yet in the same address, he said that our faith in the nice system of checks and
balances of our system of government, in our dual system, "has
grown strong in these latter days, as the assaults upon it from

---

[56] *Nation,* Jan. 31, 1907, p. 98. (The quotations are from the *Nation's* Summary
of his letter).

[57] American Bar Association, *Reports,* 1892, p. 288.   [58] *Ibid.,* 1915, p. 923.

both its friends and foes have disclosed at once their own futility and the inherent soundness of the object of their attack." [59]

To those who expressed fear of centralized power, Elihu Root made a memorable reply before the Pennsylvania Society in 1906. His speech was really directed at that legislation, which arose through the undercutting of so-called advanced States by the so-called backward States. Three influences, he said, had made the Union: the growth of a national sentiment, free trade between the States, and railroads and other economic factors binding the States together. Necessarily, he said, the people had come to the conclusion that the powers of the States are "inadequate for the due and just control of the business and activities which extend throughout all the States." The Federal government was in fields like the anti-trust law, the anti-rebate law, the railroad rate law, the pure food law, "taking up the performance of duties which under the changed conditions, the separate States are no longer capable of adequately performing." Then, without distinguishing between those matters which had grown national and which the States—no matter how vigorous and how efficient—could not handle and sometimes were not permitted to handle, and those matters where some States were lax and undercut the better States, he said that there was but one way they could maintain their power, and that was "by an awakening on the part of the States to their own duties to the country at large." If any State permitted activities which reacted on other States injuriously, the nation would act to protect itself. The intervention of the National Government "in many matters which it has recently undertaken would have been wholly unnecessary if the states themselves had been alive to their duty towards the general body of the country." [60]

Root was well aware of the extent of centralization. Three years later, before the National Civic Federation, he said: "Already the administration, already the judicial power, already the legislative branches of our government, are driven to the limit of their power to deal intelligently with the subjects that are before them. This country is too great, its population too numerous, its interests too vast and complicated already, to say nothing of the enormous increases that we can see before us, in the future, to be governed as

[59] *Ibid.*, 1914, p. 1078.
[60] Elihu Root, *Addresses on Government and Citizenship*, pp. 367, 368, 369.

to the great range of our daily affairs from one central power in Washington." [61]

As a matter of fact, the vast pressure of economic and political forces was daily pushing the old debate into new channels. While men argued and feared and deplored, new powers were steadily being granted the nation. Even Wilson—by inheritance a State Rights man—added to the national powers. His Transportation law of 1914, the Federal Reserve Act, the Farm Loan Act, the Federal Trade Commission Act, the Rural Credits Act, were all such extensions.

And yet, the increasing complexity of government, the increased demands on government arising from the concentration of population, the growth of cities, the spread of manufactures, applied both to the States and to the Nation. Government was becoming more arduous and complicated both in the States and the Nation. The new duties of the States were as exacting as the new duties of the nation. There was, after all, plenty of work for all to do. The State had constantly more exacting problems in the adjustment of labor conditions, education, care of the aged and the unfortunate, to enlist the ablest and highest qualities of statesmanship. Root himself referred to these new duties.

Wilson, in his "Constitutional Government," in 1908 said that we would be surprised to find how little the changes going on would alter the essential relations between the Nation and the States. The essential differences between the States would remain, and the diversity and extent of our country, its multitude of problems, would always give the States absorbing problems to handle.

"Not only," he said, "are the separate and independent powers of the states based upon real economic and social differences between section and section of an enormous country, differences which necessitate adaptations of law and of administrative policy such as only local authorities acting in real independence can intelligently effect, but the States are our great and permanent contribution to constitutional development."

The States had been a great force in integrating a vast continent, "an incomparable means of sensitive adjustment between popular thought and governmental method, and may yet afford the world, itself, the model of federation and liberty it may in God's provi-

[61] *Ibid.*, p. 377.

dence come to seek." [62] The great field of domestic relations, of torts and crime, the laws of descent and the control of the ordinary activities of life, would always be with the States. While the nation would steadily gain, so would the States.

In the light of the extensions of Federal power since 1917, the cries from the contest of that time between national power and State Rights seem, indeed, like those from a battle of long ago. And yet, in essence, the line of division was much the same then as today.

The conditions which have given rise to the demand for increased Federal power, all flow from the growth of business and its extension beyond State lines. Our affairs are interwoven and interdependent in countless ways unknown to three generations ago. The growth of interstate commerce; the increased interplay of activities across State lines under a clashing diversity of State laws, and sometimes undercutting of States with high standards by those with low standards; the mere fact that many problems have outgrown State lines, and no authority but the national authority is able to regulate them,—all have resulted from the increased national character of our life and business, and all have impelled the demand for increased national control.

In view of the total inability of the States to act in many fields, the criticisms of Root of the failure of the States must be taken with the modification that on many matters the States are helpless. He admitted that on the control of the operation of interstate commerce itself, the Nation alone could act. On the necessity of uniformity of such control, there was in 1917, and is today, little dispute. Even Bryan admitted that the States could not regulate the actual conduct of interstate commerce.

The great contest was then, and is now, on the large field of matters which are not commerce themselves, but which precede or go along with commerce. I may divide the field into three parts: First, questions of production, which nevertheless seriously affect the resulting commerce, such as the diversity of State laws on such matters as child labor and hours of labor, inspection of meats and foods. It is difficult to criticize severely all of the forty-eight States for the evil effects of this undercutting, when one lax State can charter corporations, and the other States are helpless; when one

[62] Wilson, *Constitutional Government*, p. 50.

State can permit lax conditions in meat packing, pure food legislation, child labor, and the other States are helpless.

After all, much legislation regulating conduct is the protection of those with the higher standards from undercutting by those with lower standards. The advanced members of the community feel the need of a better rule of law or standard of conduct; gradually the number desiring the new standard become a new standard and then a large majority, but still the standard can not be adopted unless those who adhere to it are protected against the minority. In a large field of action, there is no protection save by the Federal government. The question in each case becomes, then, whether the undercutting is evil enough to require protection.

Then, secondly, there is the diversity in State laws which does not undercut, which does not hamper the progress of advanced legislation, which does not affect interstate commerce, but which, nevertheless, results in confusion and clashes of policy. Such is the diversity in laws as to bills of lading, negotiable instruments, contracts, deeds, marriage, and divorce.

Finally, there is the extension of the Federal jurisdiction in matters where the Federal government is simply the most powerful and richest agency, such as aid of roads and education, irrigation and water power projects.

There is as yet little tendency to eradicate, by Federal law, diversity in such matters as the law of sales, contracts, negotiable instruments, bills of lading, marriage, and divorce. I think I share much of the feeling of State loyalty and the desire for the maintenance of the State rights and power; but surely only historic reasons, with little modern validity, prevent us from regulating these subjects by Federal laws. If the Constitution were to be framed today, there is no question that the Federal government would be given the power to pass uniform laws on most of the subjects on which the American Bar Association has been trying, with small success for a generation, to obtain uniformity. But even under our present Constitution there is strong reason to believe that Congress can provide that a note given by a citizen of one State to a citizen of another State should be governed by Federal law; and so for other business papers used in interstate intercourse.[63]

[63] This is under a broad construction of the Commerce Clause, as covering intercourse between people in the different States. (See pp. 434, 435).

On the other hand, there was not formerly, nor was there until the New Deal legislation, much contest over the entrance by the Federal government on enterprises which the States simply have not got the power nor the wealth to operate.[64]

The great conflict in 1917 was, and now is, on undercutting, which has an effect on commerce. Since the end of our period, the Supreme Court has seriously modified its nationalistic trend. It held unconstitutional the statute forbidding the transportation in interstate commerce of goods made in factories employing child labor.[65] Later it held a statute unconstitutional taxing businesses employing child labor,[66] on the ground that Congress could not effect by a tax what it had been forbidden to do by direct regulation. Thus it denied the exercise of the two great powers which the Federal government has in matters of interstate concern: the taxing power; and the power to regulate interstate commerce. Until these decisions, it was thought that the taxing power and the commerce power were each complete, and that the Court had nothing to say as to the motives or discretion with which they were exercised.[67] In these two cases the Court did look into the motive.

[64] The conflict on the activities of the TVA is not really a conflict between National and State action. No one disputes that the Federal government is the only government which could act. The issue there is how far any government should go in providing power for the people.

[65] *Hammer* vs. *Dagenhart*, 247 U.S. 251 (1918). This decision was contrary to the whole trend of the cases under the Commerce Clause. As Holmes said in his dissenting opinion, if the power over interstate commerce is complete and if Congress can keep out of interstate commerce lottery tickets, impure or misbranded foods, women under the so-called White Slave Act, and liquor destined for dry States, it is difficult to understand why it can not exclude goods made in factories employing child labor, or, I may add, in factories paying less than a minimum wage or with hours over a stated maximum.

[66] *Child Labor Tax Case*, 259 U.S. 20 (1922).

[67] It is difficult to state briefly the line drawn by the Court. It is not correct to say that if the main purpose of the tax is regulation, the tax will be held void. Revenue was a minor motive in the tax on State bank notes. It was a minor motive in the tax on oleomargarine, and in the tax on narcotic drugs.

The cases decided since 1917 will help us to determine the trend in 1917.

Roughly, it may be said that Congress can levy a tax which will result in regulating the production and distribution of articles in the States, but if the regulation extends beyond the necessary means of making the tax effective, the regulation will be held void.

Thus it has been held that a man can not be punished for having narcotic drugs in his possession, if he were not one of the class required to register and pay the tax. (*U.S.* vs. *Jin Fuey Moy*, 241 U.S. 394 [1916].) But if a duly registered physician sells opium contrary to the act, he can be punished. (*U.S.* vs. *Doremus*, 249 U.S. 86 [1919].)

But a physician can not be punished for dispensing opium in the course of his medical practise. (*Linder* vs. *U.S.*, 268 U.S. 5 [1925].) On the other hand, if the quantity dispensed is so great as evidently not to be for medical purposes, the physician can be punished. (*U.S.* vs. *Behrman*, 258 U.S. 280 [1922].)

The traditional reluctance to allow the commerce clause or the power of taxation to extend to those matters which are not commerce, but precede commerce, is still strong. The child labor amendment still meets strong opposition. The decisions in the NRA case and the AAA cases, and the public response to them,—though that response, of course, was colored by current political feelings, —indicate the strength of the feeling against too great national power.

The response is steadily made that the Federal government must not be allowed to encroach on the reserved power of the States. The Federal government, we are told, has no power to regulate production or manufacture, or to infringe on the police power of the States. Yet when acts in one State injure people in other States, the Federal government should have power to act.

One of the main evils confronted by the Constitutional Convention in 1787 was grievous dissension between the States. Professor Walton H. Hamilton, of the Yale Law School, has pointed out that Edmund Randolph, in presenting the Virginia resolutions at the opening of the convention, declared that it was essential to secure us against "dissentions between members of the Union, or seditions in particular States." [68] The commerce clause was intended to grant that power.

Professor Hamilton observes that in 1787 the word "commerce" had a broader meaning than we commonly give it today.[69] He notes that Marshall, in Gibbons vs. Ogden, observed that counsel for the "appellee would limit it to traffic, to buying and selling, or the interchange of commodities. . . . " But he said that while commerce was undoubtedly traffic, it was "something more,—it is intercourse." [70] The word, liberally construed in true Marshallian broadness, would extend to all relations between members of different States.

We have seen that the Federal government can keep lottery tickets out of the mails and interstate commerce. Yet lottery tickets

It is evident that no exact line can be drawn here, any more than in many branches of constitutional law. Again, we see that the line is made by the pricking out of the decisions. By intuition, prejudice, or opinion, the Court decides that a tax in one case can be called a tax, though it results in regulation of local matters; and in others, that the regulatory features are too prominent or not necessary for the collection of the tax, and therefore it is not a tax.

[68] Max Farrand, ed., *The Records of the Federal Convention of 1787*, Vol. I, p. 18.
[69] In lecture before Northwestern University Law School, March 26, 1933.
[70] *Gibbons* vs. *Ogden*, 9 Wheat. 1, 189 (1824).

are, in themselves, innocent pieces of paper. It can keep liquor out of dry territory, and permit liquor to enter other States. It can place a prohibitive tax on harmless oleomargarine, and thus control the production of oleomargarine in the States.

Broadly construed, the commerce power and the tax power are sufficient to regulate clashing relations between members of different States. Broadly construed, they are sufficient for our needs.

Despite the successful stand at present of the State Rights forces, I think the opposition is fighting a losing battle. The undercutting of States with high standards by those with low standards is too serious to be tolerated. The Lawrence strike of twenty-five years ago was caused partly by the low wages paid by Southern mills as compared with those paid by Massachusetts mills. It is most significant that, in the Guffey Coal case, no less than nine States filed briefs stating that the coal problem is a national problem, that no State can handle it, and that they welcomed Federal control of a business that concerns the whole nation and whose product inevitably enters into interstate commerce.

This is not the place to consider the unusual extensions of power enacted by the present administration. Some of them may involve exercises of power which we may not permanently desire to use. But to deny power altogether, as in the AAA case and in the Guffey Coal case,[71] is opposed to the whole intent of the commerce clause and the taxing power. I think it may safely be said that if the Supreme Court should persist in denying Congress all power to regulate prices, wages, and hours in businesses shipping goods in interstate commerce, to tax for old age pensions, or generally to regulate those matters of national concern which the States can not handle, the demand for a constitutional amendment would attain much force. A strong national government should not be denied the power. But I think a sweeping denial is unlikely. The power is there, and the Court can not long control the exercise of a power fully granted.

In conclusion, I do not believe that more can be said, than that, increasingly, matters which become national must be controlled solely by the Federal government; that undercutting in States with low standards will be met by Federal standards set to protect the advanced standards; that each case, after all, will be decided

[71] *U.S.* vs. *Butler,* 80 Law Ed. 287; *Carter* vs. *Carter Coal Co.,* 80 Law Ed. 749.

by itself, with a prejudice in favor of Federal action or against it, as our interests, emotions, or prejudices decide. For a long time to come, there will be increasing action by the Federal government; but, likewise, there will be an increase in the nature and dignity of the duties of the States.

REFERENCES

AMERICAN BAR ASSOCIATION REPORTS, 1891, pp. 366, 371; 1892, p. 288; 1909, pp. 1033, 1051; 1914, pp. 1045, 1067, 1078; 1915, pp. 923, 928.

BEVERIDGE, ALBERT J., *"Our Dual Government,"* The Reader Magazine. Vol. IX, March and April, 1907.

BOWERS, CLAUDE G., *Beveridge and the Progressive Era.*

BRYAN, WILLIAM J., "Our Dual Government," *The Reader Magazine.* Vol. IX, pp. 353, 464, March and April, 1907.

CROLY, HERBERT, *The Promise of American Life.*

——*Progressive Democracy.*

CULLOM, SHELBY M., *Fifty Years of Public Service.*

HOLMES, OLIVER WENDELL, "Law and the Court," *Collected Legal Papers.*

MEYER, HUGO RICHARD, *Government Regulation of Railway Rates.* New York: The Macmillan Co., 1905.

MURPHY, EDGAR GARDNER, *The Nation.* Jan. 31, 1907, p. 98.

RIPLEY, WILLIAM Z., *Railroads: Rates and Regulation.* New York: Longmans, Green & Co., 1912 (2nd ed. 1916).

——*Railroads; Finance and Organization.* New York: Longmans, Green & Co., 1915.

ROOSEVELT, THEODORE, *Works,* Vol. XVII. New York: Charles Scribner's Sons, 1925.

——*The New Nationalism.* New York: The Outlook Co., 1910.

ROOT, ELIHU, *Addresses on Government and Citizenship.* Cambridge: Harvard University Press, 1916.

TAFT, WILLIAM H., *Popular Government.* New Haven: Yale University Press, 1913.

——*Presidential Addresses and State Papers.* New York: Doubleday, Page & Co., 1910.

WILSON, WOODROW, *Constitutional Government.* New York: Columbia University Press, 1908.

Chapter XII

THE STRUGGLE FOR POLITICAL CONTROL

I HAVE postponed until now the treatment of the demand for new means of political control. It is part and parcel of the economic program of the period, inextricably woven in with it, and yet in a discussion of political thought, it seems advantageous to give it separate treatment so far as that is possible.

Many conservatives think of institutions as static; whereas, of course, nothing is static. Constantly change and adjustment is going on. Some change is open, such as constitutional amendments. Some is indirect, such as the virtual abolition of the electoral college. Some is by custom and political machinery, such as the action of political parties. The standard theory, of course, has been that the system of government set up in the Constitution, embodied final and eternal truth. It was based on the separation of powers into three separate departments, the system of checks and balances, and the protection of the rights of individuals by the prohibitions of the Bill of Rights.

The industrial and political developments of fifty years, have challenged these fundamental bases of our system at many points.

The great extensions of railroads and public utilities, the concentration of capital in great manufacturing establishments, must necessarily have challenged the political machinery of any government. The greatest political discovery of the period was that economic power, if it does not lead to political power, at least leads to the struggle for political power. Those who have the greatest stake in the government, will spend the most to control the government. Wealth can not only adopt the cruder forms of buying voters and even legislatures, but it has many more delicate and devious means. The same men who want legislation may own newspapers, control credit and, above all, contribute to campaign funds. They have powerful means of making the community believe that certain opinions are unsafe, and of controlling and influencing political action.

The great trunk railroads, the great industrial corporations, wanted favors from the governments, both of the States and the nation, and at the same time they were constantly subject to attack. It is impossible to say whether the "special interests" first went into politics to protect themselves against "strike" legislation, and then proceeded to control political action for their own benefit, or whether they went into politics to control political action for their own benefit, and the attacks on them merely gave them the excuse for maintaining the political control they already had. Probably the two tendencies were simultaneous.

There is a famous quotation of Jay Gould's at the time he was in control of the Erie Railroad, which well epitomizes the practises of the times: "In a Republican district, I was Republican; in a Democratic district, I was a Democrat; and in a doubtful district, I was doubtful; but I was always Erie." [1]

Henry Jones Ford quoted a president of the American Sugar Refining Company, as testifying before a Senate Committee: "It is my impression that wherever there is a dominant party, wherever the majority is large, that is the party that gets the contribution, because that is the party which controls the local matters." His company, he said, had large interests to protect, and he added: "Every individual and corporation, and firm, trust, or whatever you call it, does these things, and we do them." [2] There was a ruthless struggle for the control of the government by the railroads, the public utilities, and the liquor interests.

But only a political orator would say that the "special interests" ruled or controlled the government. The successful political organization ruled for the time it was in power, and the political organization was controlled by a variety of forces. It was influenced by political contributions, by the patronage, by the necessity of electing a long party ticket. It was, after all, even in the darkest days, subject to the force of public opinion, of the press, to the fear of the other political party.

The source of the party system, as it developed in our country, was the separation of powers and the long ballot. I shall let the

---

[1] *Report* of Special (Hepburn) Committee on Railroads (New York, 1879), p. 51.
[2] *North American Review*, Vol. CXC, p. 8 (July, 1909).

men whose theories we are to consider describe the operation of the long ballot and the separation of powers. But it may be well to observe in advance that through our custom of electing a host of township, city, county, and State officials at the same time, and as a result of the separation of powers, the political organization was forced to become an instrument of unification. It was the only body which undertook the task of bringing some sort of order and coherence into our system. Only the political party could maintain any sort of connection between the governor and both branches of the legislature, between the president and both houses of Congress. A long party ticket must be elected. A large number of candidates are eager for nomination and election. In order to get any order out of the government, all must be elected, as confusion results if the majority in the legislative branch is of a different party complexion from the executive. Therefore, the candidate for governor or president became one in his fortunes, with the lowly candidates for township and county offices. There is one ticket, and all candidates are in a real sense equal. The leaders therefore pay great deference to the party candidates. They dare not offend them. The result has been that the standard of ideas, of courage and intelligence, has been set by the candidate on the margin of development in courage, ideas, and intelligence. The leaders of the organization do not want to offend a single element.

The party system as it developed, had many unlovely aspects and caused deep discouragement and pessimism. The eighties and nineties were pervaded by a deep pessimism as to our city government, our legislatures, and our Congress. Moorfield Storey, a leader of the American bar, declared before the American Bar Association in 1894: "When a State legislature meets, every great corporation within its reach prepares for self-defense, knowing by bitter experience how hospitably attacks upon its property are received in committees and on the floor." He added that in Massachusetts, "during each successive session for years, I have heard on every hand: 'This is the worst legislature we have ever had.' " [3]

Governor O'Neal of Alabama, at the Conference of Governors in 1913, declared, "This distrust (of the Legislature) has in many States grown into open contempt for our law-making bodies." [4]

[3] American Bar Association *Reports*, 1894, pp. 249–50.
[4] Governors' Conference, *Proceedings*, 1913, p. 216.

The States, through distrust of the legislatures, limited their duration. In many States they meet only for a sixty day session every
two years. In Alabama it is limited to one session of fifty days
every four years. O'Neal said—and rightly, of course—that no
legislature could perform creditably under such conditions. He
added that, in our eagerness to restrict the powers of legislative
bodies, we regulated their methods of procedure; we limited the
subject matter on which they could act; we made codes of our
State constitutions.

"Feverish and unseemly haste," said O'Neal, of his State's legislative sessions prior to his administration, "was the order of the
day. Every consideration was subservient to the paramount question of the enactment of the law before adjournment. There were
few debates, and although every bill was necessarily referred to a
committee, they received scant consideration at their hands. The
necessary result was that a greater assortment of crude, ill-con-
sidered, and vicious legislation was enacted than at any previous
period in the history of the State." [5]

The period we are considering saw a great series of attacks on
our political system, commonly called attempts to restore the government to the people out of the grasp of the "special interests."

Many of them showed a complete failure to grasp the secret of
our trouble. But still the attacks were courageous and desperately
maintained, though often ill-directed and spasmodic.

CIVIL SERVICE REFORM

About the time of Garfield's death, the fight for civil service
reform became national. It was led and carried on for a generation
by such men as George William Curtis, Carl Schurz, Richard
Henry Dana, Dorman B. Eaton, William Dudley Foulke, and
Lucius B. Swift.

Swift, a sturdy and fearless fighter, called the spoils system the
modern feudalism, and likened the political boss to the feudal lord
of the Middle Ages, and his henchmen to feudal henchmen. The
Civil Service Reformers showed the waste and cruelty of the
spoils system, the tragic effect on penal and benevolent institutions.
Swift showed dramatically how each Congressman became a sort
of feudal overlord of his district, and each Senator of his State.

[5] *Ibid.,* p. 225.

Civil service reform was never a popular reform. The politicians, of course, realized that it struck at their power, for the power of appointment enabled them to maintain the party organizations. They asserted, moreover, that the spoils system was American, truly democratic. George William Curtis, in a speech in 1878, noted this belief that our system is "in the best sense, American; that it is demanded and justified by the genius of American institutions; that to appoint to the minor offices upon proved fitness is to introduce monarchical practises; and to retain upon proved efficiency is to establish a bureaucratic aristocracy." [6]

He answered that we then had a "despotic oligarchy," which maintained party organizations by the use of public money. In a country where government by party is inevitable, it "gives the initiative of party action to the paid stipendiaries of the State." [7] The system was not necessary to maintain parties. Party policies had nothing to do with the minor offices, though of course he admitted that party affiliations were pertinent considerations in the choice of Senators, Congressmen, and legislators.

Curtis said that the civil service reformers wanted to give the government back to all the people. The political machine had usurped power, so that the people were impotent to control their own political machinery. The public indifference to politics was due to the sense of hopelessness. The people felt that they could not beat the machine. He alluded, as many were to allude, to the evils of the English public service under Chatham as comparable to ours.

A small but determined and able group kept up the fight for civil service reform year after year and decade after decade. With the typical and necessary enthusiasm of reformers, they seemed to think that with its accomplishment all other desired results would follow. President Eliot himself, who after his retirement as president of Harvard became president of the National Civil Service Reform League, used "to say that the 'abolition of the spoils system is the reform of reforms.' " [8] And indeed its importance can hardly be over-estimated. We owe a great debt of thankfulness to the small and devoted band that never relaxed the fight on the spoils system.

[6] George William Curtis, *Orations and Addresses*, Vol. II, p. 131.   [7] *Ibid.*, p. 131.
[8] Henry James, *Charles William Eliot*, Vol. II, p. 189.

As a result of this valiant and intelligent struggle, a vast number of offices were removed from Congressional appointment and placed under competitive examination. But the party organizations went on. They clung with tenacity to the offices which remained, and they were sustained, moreover, by all the local offices which were not under the Civil Service, by public contracts, and by the power afforded by the long ballot to place men in the elective offices.

The movement had purified the parties measurably, but the parties were still not subject to public control.

THE DIRECT ELECTION OF SENATORS

Early in the nineties, a determined effort was made to gain a more popular control of the United States Senate. The Committee on Resolutions of the Populist Party, subsequent to the convention in 1892, declared that it was the desire of the party that United States Senators should be elected by direct vote of the people. Its Presidential candidate, James B. Weaver, in his book, "A Call to Action," gave much space to the Senate and vigorously favored this proposal. He charged that for a generation the Senate had favored the rights of what later orators would have called the "special interests," at the expense of the people. He instanced the Contraction Act of 1866, which authorized the funding of the Civil War debt, the Credit Strenghtening Act of 1869, the Act demonetizing silver in 1873, the Specie Resumption Act of 1875. He charged that there were thirty-two corporation attorneys in the Senate, and that the corporations controlled the Senate. The remedy, he said, was the popular election of Senators.[9]

A resolution for the amendment of the Constitution providing for the direct election of Senators, came before Congress in 1893, again in 1894, and again in 1896. Senator John M. Palmer, of Illinois, a high-minded Senator, who had fought in the Civil War and later was to be the candidate for president of the Gold Democratic Party in 1896, took its part in the Senate. He reminded the Senate that the framers of the Consitution were filled with a strong distrust of democracy, that they were the inheritors of aristocratic ideas, and desired to set up a second chamber which should have some of the prestige of the English House of Lords. But he said that the success of our democracy in its one hundred years "has

[9] Weaver, *A Call to Action*, p. 47.

demonstrated that whenever any portion of the American people have been entrusted with political power, they have been equal to its responsibility." He felt that the Constitutional fathers had underestimated the capacity of the people, but added that even if they had been right, "we can not be blind to the changes produced by a century of progress." Education was now far more widespread; newspapers, railroads, and the telephone had brought the country close together and given it means of information; and none of the reasons which led the framers of the Constitution "to deprive the people of the direct control of the executive department and of the Senate now exist."

The legislatures were not fit to exercise electoral functions, he declared, and the gerrymander of legislative districts, in order to control senatorial elections, had become a distinct abuse. Property had now nothing to fear from the people. Indeed, and here was the pervading sentiment of the time: the people had more to fear from the encroachments of organized property.[10]

Four years later, in speaking for the same measure, Palmer asserted that it was the party caucus that governed now; that it exercised so powerful a control over the legislators and the party representatives that the penalty of disobedience was the loss of a political career. By such means, he said, are legislatures made. If direct elections of senators were permitted, at least the choice of the caucus and the convention would be submitted to the approval of the people.

He followed the standard Jeffersonian tradition. "Every agency" he said, "which interposes between the direct expression of the popular will is of necessity the subject of abuse." [11]

Senator Hoar, of Massachusetts, with all his love of tradition and the precedents of a hundred years, opposed the amendment in several able speeches charged with strong emotion. He felt that the amendment would transfer the power from the legislature, which was a representative body responsible for its choice, to the electorate, which was irresponsible. Above all, he argued that since the elections were by popular vote, the larger voting centers would control, the cities would predominate over the rural districts; and soon the populous States would come to feel, since the voting was by the people, that their number of Senators should be increased

[10] *Cong. Record,* Feb. 18, 1892, pp. 1269–70.   [11] *Ibid.,* June 5, 1896, p. 6159.

to accord with population. The old equality of the States in the Senate was threatened. The amendment, his resolution stated, would result "in the overthrow of the whole scheme of the Senate, and in the end, of the whole scheme of the national Constitution as designed and established by the framers of the Constitution and the people who adopted it." [12]

After evidencing his reverence for the Constitution, he affirmed that its most admirable feature was "that part of its mechanism which secures the deliberate and indirect action of the popular will, instead of its immediate, rapid, inconsiderate, and indirect action." The rule of government was that we must not "trust any great power of government to their direct or inconsiderate control."

He quoted, as many were to quote in the debate on direct primaries and the initiative and referendum, the words of Madison, that "Although every Athenian citizen might be a Socrates, every Athenian assembly would still be a mob." [13] I shall consider the implications of this quotation a little later on.

The Senate, he said, represented deliberation. It was chosen by the legislatures which, represented, were the depositaries of the sovereignty of the States. He praised the Senate and the legislatures. Admitting that legislatures had occasionally proved unworthy, he asked if nominating conventions were not as apt to be corrupt. He went so far, in another speech in 1902, as to assert that it was proposed to "strike down one of the two great glories of our Republic, and let it perish from the face of the earth." [14]

The feeling that the legislatures had failed as elective bodies, the impression of the evils of legislative deadlocks and consequent loss of State representation, the sense of a lack of public control, grew in strength. Godkin, in an article on "The Decline of Legislatures" in 1898, asserted flatly that the legislatures had failed as elective bodies for the Senate. The legislatures had not continued to be the bodies De Toqueville had relied on, and they were not governed by the motives he looked for. "There is no longer such a thing as deliberation by the legislatures, over the selection of the Senators." [15] The candidate was selected by others who did not sit in the legislatures. The legislators were selected with a

---

[12] *Ibid.*, April 3, 1893, p. 67.   [13] *Ibid.*, April 7, 1893, pp. 102, 103.
[14] *Ibid.*, March 11, 1902, p. 2616.
[15] Edwin Lawrence Godkin, *Unforeseen Tendencies of Democracy*, p. 131.

view solely to their action on the senatorship. The people had struck down the intermediate body for the election of president, the electoral college; they had always been against the delegate theory; and they would not permit the legislature to intervene between them and the choice of Senators.[16]

The demand proceeded with ever increasing power. Such episodes as the Addicks case in Delaware gave increased momentum to the demand. Addicks said brutally as to the Delaware Senatorship: "I've bought it; I've paid for it; I am going to have it. It has cost me $140,000."[17] Twice for different two-year periods Delaware was represented by only one Senator, and for another two-year period, from 1901 to 1903, was wholly unrepresented in the Senate because the minority steadfastly refused to vote for Addicks.

Bryan, on his return from his world trip in 1906, made a general declaration of his political faith. "In all the countries which I have visited," he affirmed, "there is a demand that the government be brought nearer to the people; . . ."[18] Consequently, he found no difficulty in favoring the direct election of Senators. As usual, he based his belief on fundamental political concepts. The Senate, he added, had been the "bulwark of predatory wealth."[19]

It is interesting to see how little his opinions had changed in the years. In 1894, when in Congress, he had favored the same proposal on the ground that "If the people of a state have enough intelligence to choose their representatives,"—legislative, executive officers, "and judicial, county and state, . . . they have enough intelligence to choose the men who shall represent them in the United States Senate." To oppose "the popular election of Senators is to question the wisdom of our form of government."[20] Thus he decided the question by reference to a democratic dogma, without regard to the practical results of this addition to the duties of the people. At that time also, he added that great corporations were then "able to compass the election of their tools and their agents through the instrumentality of Legislatures, as they could not if Senators were elected directly by the people." Men "have been

---

[16] *Ibid.*, p. 135–36.
[17] George Kennan, "Holding Up a State," *Outlook*, Vol. LXXIII, p. 429 (Feb. 21, 1903).
[18] Bryan, *Speeches*, Vol. II, p. 69.   [19] *Ibid.*, p. 70.
[20] *Cong. Record*, July 20, 1894, p. 7775.

elected to the Senate whom no party convention would have dared to nominate." [21]

The demand drew ever new recruits. Roosevelt declared for it in the campaign of 1912. The Progressive and Democratic Parties favored it. Woodrow Wilson bluntly said that the first "thing necessary to reverence for the United States Senate is respect for United States Senators." A little group of Senators had "again and again been able to defeat programs of reform upon which the whole country had set its heart," and the power behind the Senators was some "private influence, hardly to be discerned by superficial scrutiny, that had put those men there to do that thing." [22] The direct election of Senators would touch nothing except "the private control of seats in the Senate." [23] The men elected by the legislatures were not the men who would be elected if the people did the choosing, the very reason which Root gave for opposing the change. There had been many "shameful instances of practises, which we can absolutely remove by the direct election of Senators by the people themselves." [24] He emphatically said that seats had been bought in the Senate.

The question was finally decided in 1912. In 1911, when it came before the Senate, Borah observed that, while the framers of the Constitution wanted time for sober reflection on the processes of their government, they did not want and could not foresee that some "sinister influence" would "interpose between the people's deliberate judgment and its achievement and realization." [25] He could not see the danger that Hoar feared, that the larger States would feel under direct election that population, and not States, should be represented. States would still be States, and Senators would still represent States. The long term would still conduce to deliberate judgment. Then he said that the removal of the election duty from the legislatures, would be the removal of "an exceptional and unnatural and incongruous duty." It had "demoralized State legislatures more than any one single matter with which they have had to deal." [26] The legislatures should be left free for their normal duties, which were constantly growing more important. He was a great believer in the preservation of the States, and did not want

[21] *Cong. Record, loc. cit.*   [22] Woodrow Wilson, *The New Freedom*, pp. 219–20.
[23] *Ibid.*, p. 220.   [24] *Ibid.*, p. 221.
[25] *Cong. Record*, Jan. 19, 1911, p. 1103.   [26] *Ibid.*, p. 1104.

them shorn of their power. But he said that one legislature had spent an entire session in the election of a Senator, "to the exclusion of everything else for which they were called together." [27] Fourteen States had gone without full representation because of deadlocks. Patronage and trading in bills had been used to encompass the election of Senators. He instanced the notorious Lorimer case in Illinois, which had great effect on the campaign for the amendment. The force of combination, intrigue, and even bribery, had destroyed the operation of the sober choice which the framers of the Constitution had intended, and it was well that we get back to the people. "Immediate, direct, constant contact will not hurt us." [28]

Elihu Root opposed the amendment to the last. The main difficulty, he said, was in legislative deadlocks, and that could be remedied by a simple statutory change, namely, making elections dependent on a plurality vote instead of a majority vote. He believed that the amendment was the first step in breaking down the dignity and the power of the States. Asserting that he was a "convinced and uncompromising nationalist of the school of Alexander Hamilton," he yet desired to maintain the States with all their Constitutional powers and rights. Only within the constitutional limits was he a nationalist. Curiously enough, this was apparently Bryan's position. Root went on to say that we could not keep the States without maintaining their powers and duties. The loss of their power to elect Senators might be but the beginning of the loss by other amendments encroaching on the States. Nor could anyone tell what would be the result of a constitutional amendment, as the history of the Fourteenth Amendment abundantly showed.

He feared, too, that the result would be a deterioration in the personnel of the Senate.

He said that the amendment was based on the theory that the people can not "elect legislatures whom they trust." The remedy, he said, was to "elect a legislature that they can trust." [29]

Here is an illustration of what Sedgwick called the "democratic mistake," the belief that in the ballot is the answer to our troubles.

[27] *Ibid.*, p. 1105.   [28] *Cong. Record, loc. cit.*
[29] *Ibid.*, p. 253. See his whole speech on "Acceptance of the Senatorship" (Jan. 28, 1909), in *Addresses on Government and Citizenship*, pp. 247–255. Also his speeches on "The Direct Election of Senators" (Feb. 10, 1911) and "Election of Senators by Direct Vote" (May 23, 1911), *Ibid.*, pp. 258–83, 285–89.

Usually this "mistake" is made by those who favor popular reforms. But surely to say that the people ought to do something, or can do something if they only will,—which for many years they have not done or done badly,—is an illustration of the democratic mistake, and is hardly practical statesmanship. It was induced by Root's strong love of established things and tradition. His innate conservatism rang through every sentence. He lamented the tendency of democracies to change.

The amendment was adopted by an overwhelming vote, and was soon ratified by the States. Seldom has any debate shown more strikingly the innate conflict of temperaments, and how deeply our intrinsic nature controls our arguments.

THE DIRECT PRIMARY

The campaign for direct election of Senators can not be separated from that for the direct primary, which went on largely at the same time and deeply affected the election of Senators. For soon Senators were not only elected: they were nominated by direct vote.

The movement for the direct primary was the product of the same feeling of frustration, of impotence, on the part of people who had a disturbed sense that they were no longer a part of their own government. It arose as a result of violent, and at times corrupt, manipulation of party primaries by what came to be called the "machines."

The sentiment pervaded all classes. Like the feeling for the direct election of Senators, it was far from being confined to political reformers. The sense of helplessness was so profound that a whole generation of men, who normally would have taken a part in politics, came to look on it with indifference or positive distaste. Godkin, in an essay in 1898 on "The Nominating System," said that the nominating machinery had fallen into the hands of a professional class; the control "of all entrance to public life by the boss and the machine, is the chief reason why we are cut off from political instruction by people actually engaged in the work of government." The better sort of men were out of it. "The boss and the machine hold the keys to all our leading offices." [30]

[30] E. L. Godkin, *Unforeseen Tendencies of Democracy,* pp. 79–80 (Chap. "The Nominating System").

Senator La Follette asserts in his Autobiography that he came to the Wisconsin Republican Convention in 1896 with enough delegates to nominate him for Governor on the first ballot, but that they were bought away from him the night before the balloting. "At that time," he said, "I had never heard of the direct primary." [31] There was none then in any State. In February, 1897, he advocated the direct primary in an address at the University of Chicago. "Abolish the caucus and the convention," he said. "Go back to the first principles of democracy; go back to the people. . . . Intelligent, well-considered judgment will be substituted for unthinking enthusiasm; the lamp of reason for the torchlight." [32]

Again in 1898 he came to the convention with what he asserts was a majority, and again he lost his majority the night before the vote. In 1900 he won, and he caused a direct primary bill to be introduced. The attempt, he asserts, was met by bribery. His bill was defeated. In 1904 he was successful.

One of the early advocates of the direct primary was Professor Ernest C. Meyer, of the University of Wisconsin. In 1902 he published: "Nominating Systems." His chapters on "The Corrupt Caucus of Today" and "The Modern Corrupt Convention," and the operation of "The Machine and the Corporation in Politics," should be read today by anyone who would understand the feelings of a past generation.

"It stands to reason," he said, "that to improve our government —where it has fallen into the hands of a few, we must once more place it in the hands of the many. Every voter must be given not only a nominal, but a real voice in the government. The idea, therefore, of the advocates of primary reform is sound and reasonable. They desire to place the people in power where combinations of men have ousted them. They hope to restore to every voter an effective vote, and *effective voting by all voters lies at the basis of good government.*" [33]

Although Meyer was arguing before the event and perforce had no experience to guide him, he did not follow the usual path of the advocates of political change that the reform would of its own weight follow the desired course. He argued with force that the direct primary would accomplish its purpose. He felt that the

[31] Robert M. La Follette, *Autobiography*, p. 196.   [32] *Ibid.*, p. 197.
[33] Ernest C. Meyer, *The Nominating System*, p. 263.

machine would be seriously handicapped, and doubted if it could maintain control under the direct primary. He fully realized the need of party organization, and argued that true party organization would be aided by the direct primary. The party convention, he believed, stimulated party quarrels.

The direct primary idea spread like wild-fire to other States. It was advocated as a panacea in the fight on the machine. B. O. Flower, in "The Arena," fought for it year after year as one of the essentials of the campaign for democratic control and freedom from bossism. In 1906 a typical article by Ira Cross asserted: "To-day we find that the caucus and convention no longer express the popular will. Delegates have become the mainspring of political machines. Corporate wealth and influence dictate the policies of the dominant parties, while candidates and office-holders, instead of being responsible to the voters, are responsible to the boss and the ring which nominate them." All attempts at reforming the caucus and the convention, he said, "have resulted in dismal failures." And so he concluded: "There can be but one remedy,—the government must be brought back to the people."

Here is another admirable illustration of the "democratic mistake," the belief that responsibility to popular vote will cure all our ills. The question, as we shall see, is more complicated. It depends on the extent of the burden which is laid on the people. Someone has to do the work of nominating, and we soon found that the political parties were the only organized bodies to manage the direct primaries. They did not manage themselves. There is no occult force which enables the people to act and decide.

Henry Jones Ford, whose admirable description of the operation of the long ballot and the separation of powers we shall consider later, attacked the direct primary savagely. He declared that its "pretense of giving power to the people is a mockery." [34] The direct primary would make politics still more "confused, irresponsible, and costly." [35] It added another election to our burdens; and he well said that the more burdens are laid on the people, the more power is given to the politicians who alone have a selfish interest in handling the system. The direct primary struck down party

---

[34] Ira Cross, "Direct Primaries," p. 587, *The Arena*, Vol. XXXV (1906); Henry Jones Ford, "The Direct Primary," *North American Review*, July, 1909, p. 3.
[35] *Ibid.*, p. 4.

responsibility, and it would "substitute for existing boss rule a far more corrupt, degraded, and impervious sort of boss rule." [36] This was the view of party organization men who bitterly opposed the direct primary.

President Taft also expressed doubts of the direct primary. If all delegates to party conventions were honest, he remarked rather naively, conventions would be better than the primary system.[37] He said the direct primary puts a premium on "self-seeking of an office." [38] But he sympathized with the desire for the direct primary in local elections. Local conventions, he admitted, are easily manipulated. A State convention draws a better type of delegates, and affords an opportunity for consultation.[39]

As is so often the case in our politics, the opponents of the direct primary ignored the evils which it was designed to meet. Clinton Rogers Woodruff, Secretary of the National Municipal League, replied that the convention had become, "first in the more populous centers and then practically everywhere, what we now know it to be, the automaton of skillful manipulators." [40] The great burden laid on the party by the long ballot was as onerous without the direct primary as with it. Practically all the objections against the direct primary are objections, he said, "which can, with equal force and effect, be urged against the convention system." [41] Under the convention system there were two elections, for the delegates were elected at one election, just as under a direct primary system the candidates are nominated at an extra election. The expense for any man who tried to defeat the organization under the convention system, would be perhaps greater than under the direct primary.

As for the standard argument that the direct primary was the action of the mob, he answered quite properly that the argument would find "little favor in American ears." [42]

Woodruff realized the impossible burden of the long ballot. He favored the short ballot. Nevertheless he favored the direct primary, without the short ballot. The whole trend of our "government from the beginning" he said, "has been to strike off the fetters

---

[36] *Ibid.*, p. 9.   [37] W. H. Taft, *Popular Government*, p. 111.
[38] *Ibid.*, p. 114.   [39] *Ibid.*, p. 117.
[40] Clinton Rogers Woodruff, "Nomination Reform in America," *Forum*, Vol. XLII, pp. 493, 495 (Dec., 1909).
[41] *Ibid.*, p. 497.   [42] *Ibid.*, p. 504.

which have bound the people; and direct nominations are a step in advance because they enable the people directly to express their wishes." The people must be educated to use it, but already, he said, it had increased the public interest in politics.[43]

Whatever the evils of the direct primary, there is no doubt that every man who came at grips with the party organization felt that he was dealing with a force which was not amenable to influence by public opinion, and that if he would attain any results he must have at hand an instrument of popular control. Hughes, as governor of New York, found that the most serious evil of the convention system was the consequence to the people at large. "To the extent that party machinery can be dominated by the few, the opportunity for special interests which desire to control the administration of government, to shape the laws, to prevent the passage of laws, or to break the laws with impunity, is increased." All that is "worst in our public life finds its readiest means of access to power through the control of the nominating machinery of parties." He said that in practise the delegates to conventions "are generally mere pieces on the political chess-board, and most of them might as well be inanimate so far as their effective participation in the choice of candidates is concerned. Party candidates are in effect generally appointed, and by those who have not been invested with any such appointing power." [44]

Hughes therefore favored the direct primary. But he realized the necessity of party leadership and responsibility, and the confusion that would result if the people tried to nominate men for two score of offices. He wanted to promote "true party leadership," to make the "elective officer more independent of those who would control his action for their selfish advantage, and enable him to appeal more directly to his constituency upon the basis of faithful service." [45] Yet he wanted to give the party leaders a chance to maintain a true leadership. Therefore he proposed that the voters elect the members of their party committees, and that the committees meet to nominate candidates. Within three weeks thereafter, a primary would be held for all offices for which candidates had filed nominating petitions. That is, if there were any candidate nominated by the party committees who was undesirable, or if there were any

---

[43] *Ibid.*, p. 505.   [44] *Outlook,* Vol. XCI, p. 91 (Jan. 16, 1909).
[45] *Ibid.*, pp. 91–92.

person not nominated who was very popular or who had a program of public interest, nominations could be made by petition and a primary held on the choice of men for those offices, and those alone. If there were twenty or thirty places on the ticket, the direct primary might involve only two or three offices. For the rest the convention nominations would stand.

The year 1912 was full of the democratic ideal. The direct primary and the initiative, referendum and recall, seemed destined to sweep all before them. The events in the Republican nomination campaign gave, of course, a great impetus to the popular demand. Roosevelt, in speaking before the Ohio Constitutional Convention in February, 1912, declared in favor of "direct nominations by the people" for all offices, including delegates to national party conventions. The convention system, he said, is "often used by adroit politicians as a method of thwarting the popular will." The "existing machinery for nominations" he went on, "is cumbrous, and is not designed to secure the real expression of the popular desire." We are willing, "to acquiesce cheerfully in a nomination secured by the expression of a majority of the people, but we do not like to acquiesce in a nomination secured by adroit political management in defeating the wish of the majority of the people." [46] In his Carnegie Hall speech, in March, 1912, he declared for the direct primary again, as "a check on the special interests." The party system requires that the leaders carry out the wishes of the party, but he said that the facts showing how far "that theory is from the facts," how the boss was intrenched, and how "hard he is to overthrow," need not be rehearsed. The direct primary, he concluded, "will give the voters a method ever ready to use, by which the party leaders shall be made to obey their command. The direct primary, if accompanied by a stringent corrupt practises act, will help break up the corrupt partnership of corporations and politicians." [47]

The theory was simple. The party organization controlled the nominations, and the direct primary would give the people the power to control. Yet it should be noted that Roosevelt also favored the short ballot. And when we are overcritical of these simple remedies, we must realize that a candidate antagonistic to the organization at that time stood little chance of nomination at

---

[46] Theodore Roosevelt, *Progressive Principles*, p. 64.   [47] *Ibid.*, p. 22.

a convention. The difference in the results between direct primaries and conventions was too striking to be an accident.

Woodrow Wilson declared for the direct primary in language as vigorous and as sweeping. Back of all reform, he said, lies the method of getting it. We had to break up the "inside and selfish determination of the question who shall be elected to conduct the government and make the laws of our commonwealths and our nation." Everywhere, he said, the impression was growing that we could only get control by "taking this process of the original selection of nominees into our own hands." It was the "most simple and natural thing in the world." To the objection that the plan would not work, that the people were too busy, he replied merely that he was willing to grant the power to be exercised by the people when it chose.[48]

But of course the process was there for use at all times, and with the long ballot only the politicians would use it regularly. Yet so strong was the opinion at that time that even Elihu Root favored the direct primary with, however, the distinct caution that the short ballot should go with it.

Hughes's plan was a statesmanlike proposal. It aimed to keep the party responsibility, but gave the public a right of control. It would reduce to a minimum the evils of the long ballot, by providing that the convention nominations should stand unless a petition were filed for any office. But it was never given a chance. The direct primary was adopted in full for all offices.

We are now in a position to appraise the campaign for the direct primary and the direct election of senators. Our experience with the direct primary has not been happy. The party organizations, with their accustomed skill and supple adaptability, soon began to learn to control the direct primary. The organization prepared slates of the candidates it favored, and used all the force of the organization to put the slates through. In general, the party organizations are still in control, subject to the power of the people in an emergency to defeat a bad candidate or to nominate a particularly desired candidate.

In a thoughtful essay in 1912, Evans Woollen, an Indianapolis banker, gave his opinion, after a wide survey of the country, that

[48] Woodrow Wilson, *The New Freedom,* pp. 217–18.

the direct primary had not worked well.[49] He quoted Ernest C. Meyer, of the University of Wisconsin, and Charles E. Merriam, of the University of Chicago, two earnest advocates of the direct primary, as in agreement that the direct primary had been a disappointment. Merriam admitted, "Some bosses are wondering why they feared the law; and some reformers why they favored it." [50] The primary suffered, said Woollen, because what is everybody's business is nobody's business, because deliberation is impossible as in a convention. The primary failed to select candidates so as to make a well-ordered ticket.

Most of us have forgotten the evils of the convention system, which called the direct primary into being. Those who talk of the deliberation and the sober thought of conventions and the passions of the mob in direct primaries, are perhaps as much ideologues as those who talk of restoring power to the people. A county convention which nominates thirty candidates for a party ticket in one session, is no place for deliberation; and it is more subject to the passions of the crowd, to intrigue, than the direct primary. Trading and combinations of groups are inevitable under it, and the system works only when there is a strong organization which determines matters for itself. The long party ticket is an insuperable obstacle for an "unbossed" convention.

On the other hand, the "democratic mistake" has been to think that if the people were given power to do a task, that they would do it, and continue to do it over the years. As a matter of practise, only a few will continue to take any active continued interest, and those few are generally the heads of the organization who have a special interest.

And yet it is doubtful if the American people, with their tradition of political power, with their long habit of direct influence on their political affairs, would in most States permit a return to the old system. The direct primary, with all its faults, does permit a direct action on the nominating machinery, does enable the voter to feel that he is still a part of his government. It has aroused more popular interest than the system it displaced. Indeed, if we had the Hughes system with the short ballot, probably there would be little

---

[49] Evans Woollen, "The Direct Primary Experiment," *Atlantic Monthly,* Vol. CX, p. 41 (July, 1912).
[50] *Ibid.,* p. 43.

opposition to the direct primary. If there were only a half a dozen candidates to be nominated, and the convention nominated them subject to a primary on any office when a petition was filed, we would have the system in a workable form.

I think this indicates the answer on the question of the direct election of senators. The people surely should have the opportunity to nominate the men for their chief offices; and if the senators were nominated by the party convention subject to a primary, and then elected by direct vote of the people, we should have a system which would give responsibility with popular control, and would create more public interest than the old system of choice by the legislatures.

Despite the grumblings of friends of the old order,I think that the direct election of senators has attained its purpose. The old scandals of bribery in legislatures; the prolonged legislative deadlocks, which caused the loss of representation in the Senate of the State affected; the waste of legislative time during the period of the deadlocks; the injurious concentration of the legislatures on the question of the United States Senatorship (since often legislators were elected solely on their pledges to vote for a certain candidate for senator),—all have been done away with.

The States have not been destroyed. There is no desire to take away the equal representation in the Senate. And I think there is no reason to believe that the Senate has deteriorated. In Borah, Norris and Carter Glass, the Senate has men who will rank favorably with any in our history. The Senate debate on the Versailles treaty was an able debate; and its discussions of economic measures, the World Court, the war debts, have been, I think, fairly representative of American opinion and political thinking.

On these questions, as on all questions of democratic government, of course, mere efficiency is not the sole criterion. Or to put the matter in another way: the efficiency of any democratic device is to be tested over a long period of time. It is an axiom that for a short period democracy itself may be less efficient than the traditional benevolent despotism. The sense of satisfaction of the people is itself an important element in this long time efficiency. The fact that the people have a feeling of power; that they actually believe that it is in their power to defeat a candidate at a direct primary, whereas they had no such feeling of comparable power under the convention system; the fact that the system therefore creates a certain public contentment; is a powerful consideration not to be ignored. The sense of impotence that prevailed twenty years ago is not a healthy thing in any democracy. That sense of impotence, at least, is largely gone under the direct primary.

THE INITIATIVE, REFERENDUM AND RECALL

Finally, the progressive forces attempted to gain control of the political machinery through the initiative, referendum and recall. This attempt was the product of the same deep dissatisfaction which caused the demand for the direct election of senators and the direct primary. The dissatisfaction with our legislatures, the feeling that they were subject to a hidden control, that they were under the influence of "special interests," was deep and widespread. Godkin, although it must be admitted he was acridly pessimistic, declared, "If I said, for instance, that the legislature at Albany was a school of vice, a fountain of political debauchery, and that few of the younger men came back from it without having learned to mock at political purity and public spirit, I should seem to be using unduly strong language, and yet I could fill nearly a volume with illustrations in support of my charges." [51] In this essay, written in 1898, he suggested that the referendum might be the remedy.

We had long had the referendum on constitutional proposals. But near the end of our period, the referendum began to be used in legislative matters and the initiative came into use. In 1892 the Populist Party declared for them.

Oregon was the great testing field. The protagonist in Oregon of the initiative and referendum was William S. U'Ren, a pioneer who had wandered over a number of States before settling in Oregon. He says that he first heard of direct legislation in 1893. He read "Progress and Poverty," and like so many of his generation, was deeply moved by its warm democratic appeal and its sympathy for equality of rights. In 1893 he read a book by J. W. Sullivan entitled: "Direct Legislation by the Citizenship through the Initiative, Referendum and Recall," and notes that he forgot for the time "all about Henry George and the Single Tax." All these, he adds, "I now saw to be details. The one important

---

[51] E. L. Godkin, *Unforeseen Tendencies in Democracy,* p. 140 (chap. "The Decline of Legislatures").

thing was to restore the law-making power where it belonged—into the hands of the people. Once give us that, we could get anything we wanted—single tax, anything." [52]

The initiative and referendum were adopted in Oregon in 1902. The enthusiasm of her people steadily grew. In 1910 no less than 32 direct legislation measures were voted on, eleven constitutional amendments and 21 statutes. In 1912 37 were voted on, 14 constitutional amendments and 23 statutes.

Oregon became the example for other states. U'Ren and Senator Bourne were apostles of the movement. It was ardently believed that it augured a new day in American politics, and that the reign of the boss was over. The people would rule.

Bryan argued for the initiative and referendum on the basis of the strict democratic dogma. "The doctrines of Jefferson," he said, "are marching on. Anything that makes the government more democratic, more popular in form, anything that gives the people more control over the government, will win. . . . You may help it, you may defeat it, but one of the things that is coming, that is Jeffersonian, that is democratic, is the initiative and referendum, for the control of the government. No man will make an argument against the initiative and referendum, who is not prepared to deny the capacity of the people for self-government." [53]

The question was simple. There was no need to consider how the system would actually work under the warping influences of our democracy.

In a debate on "The Initiative and Referendum" in 1912 under the auspices of the National Economic League, Robert L. Owen, Senator from Oklahoma, William Allen White, Frederick C. Howe, and Professor Lewis J. Johnson of Harvard, declared that legislative power today is largely controlled "by the greedy and highly organized few." [54] They did not ask the initiative and referendum in order to do away with representative government. They believed that direct legislation would be a desirable supplement to representative government. "Relieved of the unnatural excess of power under which they now stagger and sometimes fall," they believed

[52] Burton J. Hendrick, "The Initiative and Referendum and How Oregon Got Them," *McClure's Magazine*, Vol. XXXVII, pp. 234, 239 (July, 1911).
[53] Quoted by Edward R. Lewis, in "Political Formulas," *Unpopular Review*, Vol. VIII, p. 148 (July-September, 1917).
[54] National Economic League, *The Initiative and Referendum*, p. 8.

that under the initiative and referendum, "legislative bodies will cease to be attractive objects for bribery and secret influence. Log-rolling will greatly diminish. The power of bosses and rings will be undermined. Seats in the legislatures will then begin to be unattractive to grafters. At the same time, they will become more attractive to high-minded, public spirited citizens." [55]

It would not be necessary, they thought, to defeat a capable legislator who had voted against a measure the voters wanted. The people could vote themselves on the measure. It would give dignity to the voter. And they contended that it would work well in practise. There was no mob action in referendum votes. They answered— and with force—that there was more opportunity for mob action in conventions.

Charles A. Beard emphasized too that the initiative and referendum were not destructive of representative government. They were merely additional to it; and in most States, when in effect, were scarcely applied at all.[56] He asserted that there was no more probability of ill-drawn legislation under the initiative and referendum than in legislative bills. It did not seem important to him that the percentage of voters voting on direct legislation measures, was less than the votes for candidates. The questions, he said, were often not important; and there were strenuous efforts by party organizations to get out the vote on candidates, and no similar effort to get out the vote on measures. There was no magic, he observed, in large votes or percentages.[57]

When it came to the recall of judges, Beard pointed out that the question was deeper than the mere performance of judicial duties. As long as the judiciary retains the veto power over legislation, "it can hardly expect to escape that movement which is everywhere steadily and irresistibly making for direct popular control over all policy-determining instrumentalities of government." [58]

As for the recall of administrative officials, Beard admitted that it imposed the burden of an additional election on the people. But he felt that the recall with the short ballot "may commend itself not only to believers in direct democratic government, but also to

---

[55] National Economic League, *The Initiative and Referendum*, p. 14.

[56] Charles A. Beard and Birl E. Schultz, *Documents on the State-Wide Initiative, Referendum, and Recall*, p. 23.

[57] *Ibid.*, pp. 34, 39, 40.   [58] *Ibid.*, p. 68.

many who at first thought are unutterably opposed to the so-called 'progressive movement.' " [59]

In the years from 1910 to 1914, the movement for the initiative, referendum, and recall appeared irresistible. Roosevelt declared for them in 1911. He said that the movement for the referendum was "largely due to the failure of the representative bodies really to represent the people." [60] Yet he made distinct reservations. To subject elective officers to elections, in the middle of their terms, to a contest for re-election on a sudden dissatisfaction, under the recall, had, he admitted, certain "undoubted possibilities for mischief." [61] We should not, therefore, make the initiative, referendum and recall too easy. They were means, not ends, and the question, after all, was in each case one of fact.

The Progressive Party in 1912 declared for the initiative, referendum and recall. Yet even then Roosevelt qualified his support. He supported the program because "in actual practise, it has been found in many States that legislative bodies have not been responsive to the popular will." [62] But he, too, did not want to abolish legislatures. Action by the initiative and referendum should not be the normal method. And he said that there was no need for the recall for short term elective officers. The recall of judges should be used only as a last resort. [63]

In his "Constitutional Government," Woodrow Wilson had spoken of the benefits to be derived in legislation from common counsel, which was not possible under the initiative and referendum. The failure to realize that common counsel "lies at the very heart of our whole practise of government," causes us, he said, to assume that the initiative and referendum "are a more thorough means of getting at public opinion than the processes of our representative assemblies." [64] In his "The State," he had expressed the opinion that in Switzerland the referendum "by no means creates that quick interest in affairs which its originators had hoped to see it excite. It has dulled the sense of responsibility among legislators without, in fact, quickening the people to the exercise of any real control

[59] *Ibid.*, p. 68.
[60] William B. Munro, ed., *The Initiative, Referendum, and Recall*, p. 62 (from *The Outlook*, Jan. 26, 1911).
[61] *Ibid.*, p. 56.   [62] Theodore Roosevelt, *Progressive Principles*, p. 65.
[63] *Ibid.*, p. 70.
[64] Woodrow Wilson, *Constitutional Government in the United States*, p. 104.

in affairs." [65] Likewise, he objected to the practise of making numerous constitutional amendments of a statutory nature by the referendum, thus confusing the distinction between constitutional and other provisions, and concluded that, "The objections to the Referendum are that it assumes a discriminating judgment and a fulness of information on the part of the people touching questions of public policy which they do not often possess, and that it lowers the sense of responsibility on the part of legislators." [66]

Yet in an essay in 1910 in the North American Review, he declared that the initiative and referendum did not have the purpose of destroying representative government. "Their intention is to restore, not to destroy, representative government." We did not have genuine representative government. If we had, he said, no one would propose the initiative and referendum.

He also favored the recall for administrative officials. It was a means, he said, "of restoring to administrative officials what the initiative and referendum restore to legislators, namely, a sense of direct responsibility to the people who chose them."

But he definitely opposed the recall of judges.[67]

About the same time, Wilson declared that for twenty years "I preached to the students at Princeton that the Referendum and the Recall was bosh. I have since investigated and I want to apologize to those students. It is the safeguard of politics. It takes power from the boss, and places it in the hands of the people. I want to say with all my power that I favor it." [68]

In the campaign of 1912, he followed the same new line. In some States, he said, the initiative and referendum were not needed. But in other States there had been a feeling that they did not have representative government, a "growing consciousness that something intervenes between the people and the government, and that there must be some arm direct enough and strong enough to thrust aside the something that came in the way." [69] There was no desire, he insisted again, to supersede representative government. Direct legislation needed only be used when legislators defied public

---

[65] Woodrow Wilson, *The State*, p. 313.   [66] *Ibid.*, p. 476.
[67] Woodrow Wilson, "The Issues of Reform," *North American Review* (May, 1910); also in *The Initiative, Referendum and Recall*, ed. William B. Munro, pp. 87–88.
[68] Quoted by Burton J. Hendrick, "The Initiative and Referendum and How Oregon Got Them," *McClure's Magazine*, Vol. XXXVII, p. 235 (July, 1911).
[69] Woodrow Wilson, *The New Freedom*, p. 222.

opinion. The very threat of their use might prevent the need of their use.

He repeated approval of the recall for administrative officials, and opposition to the recall of judges. But he did not place his opposition to the recall of judges on the sanctity of the judiciary, but rather on the ground that it would do no good to recall a judge if a judge of the same character were elected in his place. The thing to do was to get at the nominating machinery. But this argument could have been used against the recall of administrative officials as well.

Delos F. Wilcox, in 1912 published the most extended treatise on the subject, which he called: "Government by all the People." It was dedicated to "William S. U'Ren and John R. Haynes, annunciators and provers on the other edge of the continent of the resurrection of the body politic; to William J. Bryan, Robert M. La Follette, Woodrow Wilson and Theodore Roosevelt, the great apostles to the gentiles; and last but not least to Joseph G. Cannon, James R. Day, Joseph W. Bailey, William Barnes, Jr. and Nicholas Murray Butler, intrepid rearguards of retreating paganism." [70]

He said that an "irrepressible conflict of politics is going on in the United States today," between those who thought the government was a "private industry" and those who thought it a "public enterprise." [71] He had a deep trust in democracy, and he did not fear the tyranny of the majority. Like many others, he felt that we were then subject to the tyranny of minorities. A people contented with its power and able to use it, would be conservative.

But his book was marred by its apriori nature. When he wrote, there had already been much experience which he could have utilized to support his conclusions, but almost without exception, his arguments were based on his own beliefs in democratic institutions, and what he thought people would do in given circumstances.

In general, the initiative and referendum debate, like the direct primary debate, represented a clash of temperaments. A. Lawrence Lowell had discussed the question as early as 1894. After explaining the Swiss system, he expressed doubt that it would work in this country. He felt that it would destroy the separation of powers. If the people passed laws, they would not long permit courts to

[70] Delos F. Wilcox, *Government by All the People*, Preface, p. viii.   [71] *Ibid.*, p. v.

upset their work. He was considering a system where every law would be subject to a referendum, and he ended by observing that "while a people may vote intelligently on five or ten laws a year, it is absurd to suppose that they could vote intelligently on four hundred." [72]

However, in his "Public Opinion and Popular Government," published in 1913, he was reserved and undecided in his comments. He doubted, as would most of us, whether there could be a real public opinion in Oregon on the thirty-two measures voted on in 1910, or the thirty-seven in 1912. He reminded us that the initiative gave no opportunity for debate or amendment. He warned us that if we try to do too much, we simply give power to the boss. But he made clear that he believed that the initiative and referendum might be valuable "when wisely and scientifically applied," but that they would not "usher in the millennium"; and that all theories "based on the assumption that the multitude is omniscient, are fallacious." [73] Representative government, universal suffrage, checks and balances—all had been considered panaceas, and none had been. This was a moderate statement enough, with which few could disagree.

But others were less cautious. A fundamental clash between innate distrust of democracy and innate trust in it, was sharply illustrated in man after man. Ellis Paxson Oberholtzer, in his "The Referendum in America," was bitter in his criticism. He admitted the evils of the boss system, but answered that a new machine had been established,—"the Grange, the Federation of Labor, the People's Power League." [74]

He said that the retort was always that "You do not trust the people";—the people who had "brought on three of the wars in which the nation can feel the least pride; who have repeatedly attacked proper money systems; who, in ignorance and on impulse, have wrecked and ruined, praised, canonized, and created measures and men;—a series of mistakes as long as history itself";—the people, he said, "who acclaim a captain who sinks a hulk in a Cuban harbor to block the way of an enemy's war-ships, a commodore

---

[72] A. L. Lowell, "The Referendum in Switzerland and in America," *Atlantic Monthly*, Vol. LXXIII, pp. 517, 523 (April, 1894).

[73] A. L. Lowell, *Public Opinion and Popular Government*, pp. 231–34 (quotations on p. 233).

[74] Ellis Paxson Oberholtzer, *The Referendum in America*, p. 502.

who sweeps a decrepit fleet from the China seas, an explorer who returns to tell of his achievements at the north pole; after a while we tire of their heroes."

What "they would do on one day, they will often repent of the next," for which reason we had a government of checks and balances. The process was not meant to be simple. There was virtue in the very complexity of our system. It was better to err through too much caution than through too much haste, "to do too little than too much." He was much irritated at the cry that such as he were afraid of the people, who can do no wrong, whose "voice is the voice of God." [75]

Distrust of democracy could hardly be more clearly shown.

In general, the opponents of direct legislation stressed their belief in representative government. Representative government became a sort of idol with them. They laid much stress on the excessive use of the initiative and referendum in Oregon; and declared that the voters of Oregon could have known little of the mass of thirty to forty laws they voted on, comprising two hundred printed pages, in 1910.[76] Governor McCall, of Massachusetts, remarked: "Of course, one must be cautious about expressing a doubt that the people in their collective capacity can accomplish impossibilities." [77]

The opponents of direct legislation repeated again and again that we were in too much of a hurry, that institutions were of slow growth, and that we expected too much of human nature. The people were not equipped to pass on details. The referendum took responsibility from legislatures. There was a mania for too much legislation.

Taft felt that the representative system could accomplish practically all the reforms the progressives called for. If the people were not intelligent enough, he added, to elect competent representatives, how then could they be intelligent enough to vote on three hundred pages of referendum measures? [78]

Elihu Root was apparently not settled in his own mind. All his

[75] *Ibid.*, p. 511–13.
[76] See article by Frederick P. Fish, F. F. A. Currier, and Governor O'Neal of Alabama, in *The Initiative and Referendum* (National Economic League, 1912).
[77] William B. Munro, ed., *The Initiative, Referendum and Recall*, p. 172 (article by S. W. McCall "Representative as Against Direct Legislation," reprinted from *Atlantic Monthly*, Oct., 1911).
[78] W. H. Taft, *Popular Government*, p. 52.

instincts were against the initiative and referendum. In the New York Constitutional Convention of 1914, he noted that other States had had recourse to the initiative and referendum, the recall of officers, and the recall of decisions. "In this convention we have offered the most irrefutable, concrete argument against those nostrums and patent medicines in government, and in favor of the preservation of that representative government which is the chief gift of our race to freedom, by undertaking to reform representative government instead of abandoning it, and to make it worthy of its great function for the preservation of liberty." [79]

In accepting the senatorship in 1909, he said that there was no reason to believe "that the citizens would perform their duty in the direct election of senators, or in voting upon the initiative or the referendum, any better than they perform it in the election of members of the senates and the assemblies of the states." He was opposed to all steps "that proceed upon the theory that the people of our states are to abandon the duty of making their states legislatures able and honored bodies, competent to perform the great duty of legislation for those great commonwealths." [80]

Again in speaking on the resolution to amend the Constitution to provide for the direct election of senators, he said: "The 'initiative' is an expression of distrust in representative government. The 'referendum' is an expression of distrust in representative government." [81]

But in his Stafford-Little lectures at Princeton in 1913, he was moderate in his expressions. He declared that the characteristics of our system were that it was representative, that it protected individual liberty by specific limitations, that it provided for the separation of powers, that it was Federal, and that it provided for court review. The initiative and referendum were attempts to cure the admitted evils of our system by reverting to "the old, unsuccessful and discarded method of direct legislation, and by rehabilitating one of the most impracticable of Rousseau's theories." He admitted that the motive behind them was commendable, but he did not think that they would prove to be "wise or successful ways of curing" our evils. But he did not think that "their trial will be

[79] Elihu Root, *Addresses on Government and Citizenship*, p. 211 (speech on Closing the Convention, Sept. 10, 1915).
[80] *Ibid.*, pp. 253–54.   [81] *Ibid.*, p. 269.

destructive of our system of government." They did not aim to destroy representative government, "but to modify and control it," and if they did not work, would be abandoned.[82]

He conceded that there were certain questions where a yes or no vote of the people was possible and desirable, such as bond issues, the location of a county seat, and prohibition; but the initiative and referendum were not suited to those complicated questions where debate is important, where amendments may be advantageously made. They permitted legislation which did not fit into prior legislation, and tended, like the direct election of senators, to the weakening of the legislatures.

Nicholas Murray Butler asked, "Why Should we Change our Form of Government?" He was deeply aroused by what he thought was an attempt "to change our representative republic into a socialistic democracy." The question, he said, "transcends all possible differences between the historic parties; it takes precedence of all problems of a business, a financial, or an economic character, however pressing: for it strikes at the very root of the government of the United States and at the principles upon which that government rests."[83]

We are told, he said, that representative government has failed. Like most of those who feared the spread of the new ideas, he dwelt on the wisdom of the Constitutional fathers, and it must be said, seemed to imply that political thought was finished with them. While he admitted that the principles of the Constitution must be adapted to new conditions, still, like Root, he felt that there were fundamental principles stated in our Constitution, and that the new States were placing a mass of statutory matter in their constitutions. So we had confused fundamental principles with changing statutory expressions.

Moreover, we had reduced our representatives to the status of delegates, and now we were proposing to end with the initiative and referendum. He instanced the standard objection that the initiative did not permit of amendment and debate, that the result would be many elections at which we should be forced to vote on matters initiated by a small number of voters, and that it would lessen the

[82] Elihu Root, *Addresses on Government and Citizenship*, p. 93.
[83] Nicholas Murray Butler, *Why Should We Change Our Form of Government?*, pp. 4–5.

dignity of legislators. "All that can possibly be accomplished by the initiative," he said, "is to strike the heaviest possible blow at representative institutions, and to remove the last inducement to bring able, reflective and intelligent men to accept service in a legislative body." [84]

Like all the other opponents of the initiative and referendum, he feared the tyranny of the majority. Like them also, he objected that votes on initiative and referendum measures were considerably less than for candidates. A minority was deciding our public measures.

The recall, he of course opposed as helping to "keep high-minded and independent men from accepting nomination and election to public office." [85] And the recall of judges was more than "stupid folly"; it was "an outrage of the first magnitude." [86] Cleveland would have been recalled in 1893; Lincoln in 1862. But so also might they have been recalled under a parliamentary system.

He wanted fewer elections instead of more, fewer elective offices, less instead of more popular interference with representative bodies. And he would not change our form of government.

The initiative, referendum, and recall were widely adopted, but, outside of the western States where they had their first considerable employment, have been little used. But some States still make considerable use of them, although not in the wholesale fashion of a generation ago.[87] But the discerning advocates of direct legislation

---

[84] *Ibid.*, p. 26. [85] *Ibid.*, p. 39. [86] *Ibid.*, p. 40.
[87] An examination of the session laws of all the States in 1933, 1934, and 1935 shows the following direct legislation activity:

Arizona. 1932 general election: 5 constitutional amendments voted on—2 adopted, 3 defeated; 4 initiative and referendum measures voted on—all defeated. 1933 general election: 6 constitutional amendments voted on—1 adopted, 5 defeated; 2 referendum measures voted on—both adopted.

California. 1932 special election: 2 referendum measures voted on—both adopted. 1932 general election: 17 constitutional amendments voted on—10 adopted, 7 defeated; 2 initiative measures voted on—both adopted. 1933 special election: 8 constitutional amendments voted on—6 adopted, 2 defeated; 2 referendum measures voted on—both defeated.

North Dakota. 1932 Presidential primary election: 1 initiative measure voted on—adopted; 1 referendum measure voted on—adopted; 3 constitutional amendments voted on—adopted. 1932 primary election: 7 initiative measures voted on—all adopted. 1932 general election: 1 constitutional amendment—adopted; 8 initiative measures—adopted. 1933 special election: 2 constitutional amendments—adopted; 2 initiative measures—adopted; 3 referendum measures—adopted. 1934 primary election: 3 initiative measures—adopted. 1934 general election: 1 initiative measure—adopted.

Oregon. 1932 general election: 5 constitutional amendments voted on—4 adopted, 1 defeated; 8 referendum measures voted on—1 adopted, 7 defeated. 1933 special election: 4 constitutional amendments voted on—2 adopted, 2 defeated; 5 referendum measures voted on—1 adopted, 4 defeated. 1934 special election: 2 constitutional amendments voted on—1 adopted, 1 defeated; 3 referendum measures voted on—

never intended or asked that it supplant the legislatures. They asked only for the right to use it as an occasional additional expedient, as an outlet for popular expression when the desire was felt; and that purpose direct legislation has fulfilled.

What, then, shall we say in conclusion? As usual, each side overstated its case. There was less difference than appeared on the surface between the reasonable men on each side. After all, those who thought it desirable for thirty or forty direct legislation measures to be voted on at one election, were an insignificant minority. No political body will take the time to study so many measures. President Lowell had declared that the people could intelligently vote on five or ten measures a year. Few advocates of the initiative and referendum would have suggested that more than five measures be voted on at one election. But in the situation we were then in, it seems difficult to say that the people should not have had the right to vote on two or three measures a year. The timidity of legislative assemblies, the control of "special interests," were too notorious to be disputed, and it was not unstatesmanlike to provide an outlet for popular expression. Some such considerations, I think, must have been in President Eliot's mind when he wrote in 1914 to Charles Francis Adams, "I do not agree with you in classing together as nostrums the Initiative, the Referendum and the Recall. The Referendum seems to me in most cases harmless, and in some, positively useful. The Initiative is so little used that it is unimportant; and the Recall, particularly the recall of judges, seems to me positively mischievous." [88]

The referendum did allow for debate, for consultation. All the benefits of the representative system could be retained under it. Nor do I think that a moderate use of the referendum lessens the dignity of legislatures. Legislators are subject to re-election at short intervals, in any event, and a specific vote on two or three questions does not tend to destroy their influence any more than a contest for re-election.

The initiative would seem to have been unnecessary and unde-

---

1 adopted, 2 defeated. 1934 general election: 2 constitutional amendments voted on —both defeated; 1 referendum measure voted on—defeated.

Washington. 1932 general election: 1 constitutional amendment voted on—adopted; 5 initiative measures voted on—adopted. 1934 general election: 2 initiative measures voted on—adopted.

[88] Henry James, *Charles William Eliot*, Vol. II, p. 239.

sirable. It allowed no debate and no chance of amendment. There are few legislatures which, if public opinion is strong enough, would not allow a referendum on an important measure.

As for the recall, it would seem that both sides lost their sense of proportion. The recall of judges by popular vote is a vicious thing, but so is their election. The remedy in the case of judges, of course, is to make them appointive, and to provide for removal for cause by a regular tribunal. As for administrative officials, our long ballot and frequent elections give us the right to recall any officer by not re-electing him, and the terms are so short that it seems a useless burden to have an extra election to recall him in the middle of his term. On the other hand, when in effect we had the recall already, it seems strange that anyone could have been greatly disturbed at a slight extension of the recall principle.

But the opponents of the initiative, referendum and recall did not deal with reality. They argued from fixed conceptions, and generally from the dogmas of a hundred years ago. They admitted the weaknesses of our legislatures. For years our business and professional men have expressed great contempt of our Congress and legislatures. Their criticism has been most unjust in its severity and indiscriminateness. As a matter of fact, our Congress has, on the whole, functioned with marked ability; and even our legislatures, considering the handicaps under which they have worked, the short sessions, the poor pay, have done surprisingly well. But for men who have had nothing good to say of actual legislatures, who talk of ill-written and foolish legislation, to turn from actual legislatures to an abstraction like representative government and worship it as a shining thing of excellence, was not to deal with actualities.

Time and again, moreover, as we have seen, the opponents of direct legislation, the direct primary, and the direct election of senators, spoke of the passions of the mob, and the necessity of protecting minorities from the temporary whims of majorities. We have noted that Taft quoted the Federalist as declaring that if every Athenian were a Socrates, still the Athenian assembly would be a mob. As the Revolutionary fathers relied largely on the experience of Greece and Rome, the opponents of the political proposals of the progressive era, who relied on the Revolutionary fathers for most of their arguments, likewise rested largely on the experience of Greece and Rome. Their arguments were chiefly derived from the experience of the past, although there was a mass of current evidence in our own country and in other democratic countries which they could have drawn on. Politics with them was a closed book, based on eternal laws of conduct.

But in the first place, the Athenian assembly was an assembly where all the citizens, about twelve thousand in number, met together. A referendum vote, a vote for United States senator, bore no slightest resemblance to a vote in a large assembly. Indeed, if any comparison with the experience of Greece and Rome were possible, it was against legislatures and conventions, for there a large number of men meet and act together, while in an election the voters vote singly and not in a mass. If the people who vote for senators and in direct primaries and in referendum elections are a mob, then the people that elect candidates are also a mob. Whether or not it is desirable for us to have the initiative and referendum, it is clear that formulas based on mob psychology have no point in Australian ballot elections. The psychology is utterly different.

Moreover, naturally, the experience of Greece and Rome in their popular assemblies, can have little bearing on the behavior of a different people three thousand years later under utterly different conditions. Our people have shown, for example, none of the volatile and cruel character which made Athens kill or ostracize unsuccessful generals.

A classical politics, which knew not the Australian ballot, nor newspapers, nor books, nor telegraph, can not answer our modern politics.

Executive Leadership and the Short Ballot

In all these attempts at political control—the direct election of senators, the direct primary, and the initiative, referendum and recall—the advocates of reform had not sensed the central defect of our system. We have seen that the initiative and referendum had been opposed because they struck at the separation of powers. Our system, we were told, had been made complex and difficult for the very purpose of protecting minorities and preventing hasty legislation. Slowly we came to see that the complexity was so successful that the system would not work at all, unless outside forces were brought into play.

For a century we had been brought up to believe that the separation of powers was "the bulwark of our liberties." If the system did not work, we laid the failure to the depravity of human nature. The public belief was implicit and unquestioning. In a typical statement of the standard belief, George W. Wickersham said in 1911 that the framers of the Federal Constitution devised a "scheme of representative republican government, framed in the light of the experience of the ages, with the powers of government carefully distributed between three equal and coordinate branches, limited and defined in no niggardly spirit, and yet with a restraining hand; each one designed to be a check upon the other, and each one confined to its separate sphere, contributing to that harmonious result about which the hopes and aspirations of the framers so fondly and so confidently clung." [89]

Elihu Root, as late as 1913 declared that the essential qualities of our system were that it was representative, that it protected individual liberty, that it provided for the separation of powers, that it was Federal, and that it provided for judicial review.[90]

At the Conference of Governors in 1913, Governor Ammons, of Colorado, said that he was "still in favor of the old principle that the people shall rule through all three departments. . . and that none of these departments shall infringe upon the other." [91] Governor Hatfield, of West Virginia, declared that he was satisfied with the "principles of Madison, Jay, Hamilton and Jefferson, . . . and I believe that as long as we adhere to the three branches of government, the judicial, the executive, and the legislative, just so long will the Stars and Stripes float over the homes of a free and prosperous nation. . . ." [92] Governor Haines, of Maine, put the idea in a common form: "My idea is that governors do not govern. They should not govern: they should execute the laws. . . ." The laws should provide in detail every step that should be taken, and if so, "you will have no trouble." [93] This was just what our legislatures had tried to do, and yet we had had trouble.

One of the most conspicuous trends of thought of the period was the demonstration that the very balance of our system, the cum-

---

[89] George W. Wickersham, "Concerning Certain Essentials of Representative Government," *New York State Bar Assoc., Proceedings*, 1911, p. 185.
[90] Elihu Root, *Addresses on Citizenship and Government*, p. 91.
[91] Governors' Conference, 1913, p. 281. [92] *Ibid.*, p. 324. [93] *Ibid.*, p. 134.

brousness on which we prided ourselves, was one of the main difficulties with which we had to contend.

Woodrow Wilson, in his brilliant "Congressional Government," struck at the core of the issue. He described our traditional theory of the separation of powers and checks and balances. Fearing power above all things, dreading irresponsible authority, the authors of our Constitution, he said, had created, first, a nice balance between the State and the Federal governments. The Federal government they had constituted on the famous dictum of Montesquieu, —that ordered liberty requires the separation of powers. They did not realize that they did not, and could not, make a complete separation of powers. The executive could veto acts of the legislature. The legislature could pass laws over the veto. The legislative body approved appointments of judges and foreign ambassadors. The judiciary had the power to pass on legislation. But the dogma of the separation of powers was dear to our courts, our legislators, and became an axiom of our government.

Yet, although vast changes had occurred in a hundred years in the practice of our government, we continued to treat our system as if it were static. We continued, Wilson said, to think "according to long-accepted constitutional formulae, and it is still politically unorthodox to depart from old time phraseology in grave discussions of affairs." Yet he said that it was plain "to those who look about them that most of the commonly received opinions concerning federal constitutional balances and administrative arrangements are many years behind the actual practises of the government at Washington; and that we are farther than most of us realize from the times and the policy of the framers of the Constitution." [94]

Constantly, he went on, change in practise was going on. The Constitution had balanced the State and Federal governments. But there had been a great growth of Federal authority and sentiment. The great extension of the national territory, the Louisiana purchase, had greatly aided the Federal power. The power of the courts over legislation had been a powerful source of Federal power. Internal improvements, and the commerce clause giving control over railroads and navigable waters, had from the beginning been a magnet for Federal power.

[94] Woodrow Wilson, *Congressional Government*, p. 6.

With the growth of the nation had gone a vast increase in national sentiment. The new settlers of the Middle West had a loyalty to the nation before that to the States.

Likewise, Wilson said that there had been a profound change in the relations of the Federal branches to each other.

The Senate and House, he charged, were run by their standing committees. But there was no concert between the chairmen of the various committees. The individual member was helpless under the principle "never disallowed or abrogated" that "the committees shall rule without let or hindrance." [95] The House had ceased to be a deliberative body. A few years later, Speaker Reed thanked God that it was not a deliberative body.

Party discipline was slight. There were few measures which were party measures. The Speaker had great power through the appointment of committees, and our government was a government "by the chairmen of the standing committees of Congress." [96]

He said that Congress did not "come into direct contact with the financial officers of the government," in devising the budget. "Executive and legislature are separated by a hard and fast line, which sets them apart in what was meant to be independence, but has come to amount to isolation." [97] The budget prepared by the House went to the Senate, which generally "renders worthless the painstaking action of the House." [98]

Congress, he concluded, "evades judgment by avoiding all coherency of plan in its action." The voter has lost interest in Congress, he said, "because he can't control it." [99]

The Senate too had declined. There were no great issues before the Senate, and no great place was a prize, such as the Premiership in England or France. The highest prize was the chairmanship of some committee. Yet the Senate still had free and open debate.

Time and again he noted the decline in the prestige of the Presidency. The President had little power over his own cabinet. His contact with Congress was limited to his executive messages, and his contact with department heads to private consultations and written correspondence. The Senate had encroached on his treaty-making power.

In a word, there was no unity or responsibility anywhere. We

[95] *Ibid.*, p. 74.   [96] *Ibid.*, p. 102.   [97] *Ibid.*, pp. 146–47.
[98] *Ibid.*, p. 155.   [99] *Ibid.*, pp. 188–89.

were afraid of power, afraid of the executive, as we had been afraid of the king.

But Wilson said that the rule ought to be that "somebody must be trusted." [100] We should grant power with "strict accountability for its use." [101] Our central defect was that we had parcelled out power and confused responsibility.

He felt that we were in just the position that England was in before she achieved the reform "for which we are striving." [102] Congress was startlingly like Parliament in England before 1689. It was a conclusion which many were to reach in the next thirty years.

Wilson concluded that as at "present constituted, the Federal government lacks strength because its powers are divided, lacks promptness because its authorities are multiplied, lacks wieldiness because its processes are roundabout, lacks efficiency because its responsibility is indistinct and its action without competent direction." Nobody, he concluded in ringing sentences, stands sponsor for the policy of the government. "A dozen men originate it; a dozen compromises twist and alter it; a dozen officers whose names are scarcely known outside Washington, put it into execution." He repeated that this was the central defect to which "I recur again and again; because every examination of the system, at whatsoever point begun, leads inevitably to it as to a central secret." [103]

Wilson did not outline his remedy. He did not say that he wanted a parliamentary system for the United States. He was deeply read in Burke and Bagehot, and was an ardent admirer of the English parliamentary system. But, undoubtedly, his sense of tradition and historical development was too strong for him not to realize that the parliamentary system could not be adopted fullgrown in America. He knew that institutions develop and can not be forced. Yet he spoke of the reform "for which we are striving" in America. And his whole book had no point, unless he desired some adaptation of the parliamentary system for this country.

President Lowell, then a young lawyer in Boston, seized the challenge. He said that his object was not to discuss the relative merits of the English and American systems of government, but simply to show that a responsible ministry "can not be grafted into our institutions without entirely changing their nature and

[100] *Ibid.*, p. 283.   [101] *Ibid.*, p. 284.   [102] *Ibid.*, p. 283.   [103] *Ibid.*, p. 318.

destroying those features of our government which we have been in the habit of contemplating with greatest pride." [104]

If the parliamentary system were adopted, the President, if he were given a seat in one of the Houses, might become a leader, but few Presidents were capable of leading Congress. If the opposite party came into control of the House, the President would have to resign. But he said that the advocates of a parliamentary system in this country go no farther than to suggest that the "advisers of the President shall sit in Congress, and that they alone shall be responsible to it for their actions." [105] If so, he said, the President would remain for four years, but his cabinet would change when the party control changed. The President would become a mere figurehead.

Moreover, he argued that one legislative body, probably the Senate, would lose power, as under the parliamentary system one body always shrank in power in comparison with the other.

Likewise, the States would lose and the Federal power would gain. Moreover, he felt that the power of the courts over legislation would decline, since they could not continue to oppose the legislative will when the power of the legislature was greatly increased.

Indeed, Lowell seemed to fear a responsive system. He spoke of the influence of the courts in preventing hasty legislation. He said that in the United States the first object of government was "to protect the individual; to prevent the majority from oppressing the minority and, except within certain definite limits, to give effect to the wishes of the people only after such solemn formalities have been complied with as to make it clear that the popular feeling is not caused by temporary excitement, but is the result of a mature and lasting opinion." [106]

This, I think, is a principle that can not long work in any democracy. With affairs changing as fast as they do in America, to ask for a proof of mature and lasting opinion before passing a labor law, or a railroad rate law, or a workmen's compensation statute, is simply to invite explosion. By attempting to prevent hasty legislation, we also prevent or delay well-ordered legislation, if there is any appreciable opposition to it. In fact, we do not prevent hasty legislation. Anyone who has seen the last days of a

---

[104] A. L. Lowell, *Essays on Government*, p. 23.   [105] *Ibid.*, p. 27.
[106] *Ibid.*, p. 22.

legislative session and has watched the speed with which a hundred bills are passed, knows that hasty legislation is typical of legislatures. But the separation of powers greatly increases the difficulty of passing any legislation to which there is opposition.

Moreover, I think, we over-emphasize the evil effects from legislation. There are many corrective forces in any democracy which minimize the effects of even vicious legislation, and the opposition to evil legislation in most legislatures is usually potent. A democracy must have the right to experiment, and it will usually be found that it is wiser to allow it to experiment and to drop the experiment if it prove unwise, than to prevent action altogether or unreasonably to delay it. After all, we must in the end trust our legislatures. We can prevent action of an arbitrary nature, and special legislation, but mere mistakes, mere hasty legislation, we can not under any sound theory of politics prevent, save by normal legislative processes, nor should we delay legislation save by the processes of public opinion.

Lowell concluded his essay by a specific consideration of Wilson's argument. He expressed doubt of Wilson's conclusions as to the current distribution of power. He doubted Wilson's dictum of the loss of power by the Senate and by the courts. He thought, too, that the President still had great power.

That the adoption outright of the parliamentary system would radically change our system of government, was of course true. Nor could the system have been adopted by any legislative fiat. Any modification in that direction would, of course, have to have been a gradual development. But that our system called for a new executive leadership in legislation, for some workable method of cooperation between the executive and legislative branches, could not be denied.

In his "The Rise and Growth of American Politics," Henry Jones Ford presented a masterly analysis of the unfortunate results of the separation of powers in our government. As many others were to emphasize in the next twenty years, he declared that "it is due solely to the extra-constitutional means supplied by the party organization that the presidential office is able to perform the function imposed upon it of executing the will of the nation. Party organization acts as a connective tissue, enfolding the separate organs of government and tending to establish a unity of control, which shall adapt the government to the uses of popular sovereignty." [107] In other words, with a President elected by the people, a House elected by the people once every four years, at a different time, with a Senate then elected at staggered intervals by State legislatures, the only possible unity was through the party organization. The occasion for the party was, he said, "the need of means of concentration so as to establish a control over the divided powers of government." [108]

Like Wilson, Ford noted that there was little "change in political ideas." The public and public men still believed implicitly in the separation of powers, still considered that it was operating. Although, as he said, "the working of the Constitution has undergone profound change, the theory has remained almost intact." [109] If the system did not work well in practise, it was not the fault of the system. "The constitutional ideal is noble; but the politicians are vile." So we demanded more checks and balances, instead of responsibility with power. The situation, he said, as Wilson had said, was startlingly like that in England at the time of Walpole, before the parliamentary system introduced a unity between the executive and the legislature.

We were subject then to an oligarchy intrenched in the Senate. He quoted Senator Hoar as saying that, "Thus no change in the popular opinion can compel a change of policy during the four years of the President's term, nor can it compel a change of policy in a body where great and small States meet as equals, unless a majority of the States agree to the change. But the purpose and desire of the numerical majority of the American people may be baffled twenty years by the local interests and feeling of a majority of the States, and those, perhaps, the smallest in population." [110] This, Ford concluded, was usurpation. The system of checks and balances inevitably leads to usurpation.

Ford's own proposal was for a combination of the parliamentary system and our own. He would work through the House and not the Senate which he distrusted. He proposed that the cabinet officers be given seats in the House. They would thus become subject to the majority in the House, and the House would come to be the contfolling legislative body. The President would remain out-

[107] Henry Jones Ford, *The Rise and Growth of American Politics*, p. 215 (1898).
[108] *Ibid.*, p. 297. [109] *Ibid.*, p. 334. [110] *Ibid.*, p. 361.

side. He would still be responsible for administration, but the Congress would be responsible for policies. "The limitations," he said, "of the Constitution, and the direction taken by constitutional development, provide an exclusively executive structure for the administration, and it will be independent of parliamentary vicissitudes." Congress, he said, would "retain the power to inhibit altogether any determination of the government requiring legislative assent, but will have no power to prevent the government from shaping its proposals, defining exactly its position, and confronting the opposition with an explicit responsibility for which it must answer to the people." [111] Having reached such a position, he said, administration would have nothing to ask "of party but the cultivation of public sentiment, and the propagation of opinion. Party organization will therefore tend to revert to more simple structure, and to become dependent upon spontaneous effort, while its present violence will disappear." [112] This reform, Ford thought, would give all of the value there is in the parliamentary system, while "avoiding its defects."

It is difficult for us now to realize the extent of Congressional domination, and of the lack of influence of the executive on legislation, in the eighties and the early nineties. However, we must be careful to avoid sweeping generalizations. We know that Cleveland exerted all his influence for the repeal of the Sherman Silver purchase bill and for the passage of the Wilson tariff. But Gamaliel Bradford notes that when Cleveland "wrote a letter to Mr. Wilson, Chairman of Ways and Means, as to the details of the tariff, it was regarded in Congress, and to a considerable extent by the press, as an unwarranted departure from his proper functions." [113] Bradford, writing in 1899, observed that if the President, "the nominal head of the nation and the only man chosen by the votes of the whole, should address the people, he would be obliged to have a positive policy, to tell what he intends to do, and how and why he proposes to do it. But he can not have a policy, because he has no means of enforcing it." [114] He could only request and recommend, and had no power save the veto, a purely negative power.

The Spanish War, the pressure of new problems, and the dynamic

[111] *Ibid.*, pp. 369, 370.   [112] *Ibid.*, pp. 370–71.
[113] Gamaliel Bradford, *The Lesson of Popular Government*, Vol. I, p. 357.
[114] *Ibid.*, Vol. I, p. 361.

personality of Theodore Roosevelt were to work a vast change in our practise and ideas.

Bradford manfully and ably set himself to the task of advocating the entrance of the cabinet officers into Congress. Much in the vein of Wilson's "Congressional Government," he declared that anarchy had resulted from government by the legislature; that there was no team work between the committees; that individuality was suppressed in the House; and that only party power, with log-rolling and lobbying, worked the system. He considered briefly proportional representation and the rhapsodic arguments of Commons in its behalf; and answered that, if successful, it would merely strengthen the power of groups.

Woman's suffrage, the referendum, compulsory and plural voting, —all he rejected as remedies, because he said, and rightly, that they did not reach the central defect, the absorption of power by the legislature and the impotence of the executive.[115] He noted then, as I may say now, that we wear ourselves out with denunciations of our politicians or of the lethargy of the people, although our politicians have really done an excellent job with the materials at hand, and the people have unusual political ability. The central defect was lack of coordination between executive and legislature.

He adverted, as had Ford, to the report of the Senate Committee of 1881 (a remarkable document now almost forgotten), which recommended that the cabinet officers have the right to sit in the House and Senate and take part in the debates, and that on two days of each week they should be under the duty of appearing in the Senate and on two days in the House to answer questions.[116] He had no elaborate theories of the evolution of the process. The first thing, he said, "is to get them in, and then trust to a process of evolution to achieve the rest." [117] But he added the conflict of powers would begin at once and could hardly fail to work a revolution.

He insisted that the cabinet would not become subject to the will of Congress, since the cabinet officers would be appointed by the President and subject to removal by him only.

---

[115] *Ibid.*, Vol. II, p. 175.
[116] *Sen. Rep.* 837. 46th. Cong., 3rd. Sess. 1881. (The report was signed by George H. Pendleton, John J. Ingalls, O. H. Platt, J. G. Blaine, J. T. Farley, D. W. Voorhees, W. B. Allison, and M. C. Butler.)
[117] *Ibid.*, Vol. II, p. 329.

The President should not be submitted to this process. Bradford declared that to submit him to the "promiscuous conflict of debate was not to be thought of." [118] But the introduction of the cabinet into the legislature would give new prestige to the executive and curtail the absorption of legislative power, and it would bring a coordination between executive and legislature.

The attack on the working of our theory of the separation of powers continued. Goodnow pointed out that there had been, in fact, no complete separation, as all three departments take part in each function. There were, he said, two functions of government: politics, or the framing of policies; and administration, or the execution of policies. Either the executing authority had to be subordinate to the expressing authority, or the expressing authority had to be subordinate to the executing authority; and he argued that "popular government requires that it is the executing authority which shall be subordinated to the expressing authority, since the latter, in the nature of things, can be made much more representative of the people than can the executing authority." [119] This control, he too agreed, had developed in the party system. So parties must be made responsible. The boss was a necessary result of our system, but the boss was irresponsible. We could limit the power of the local party by administrative centralization, by the referendum and the short ballot. He concluded that, "Not only must our system of government be subjected to a reasonable degree of centralization from the administrative point of view, but the party must receive pretty full legal recognition." [120]

Hadley likewise declared that the separation of powers and the long ballot had made of our politicians too often, brokers, not of opinion but of offices. [121] He too noted that "the English government in the eighteenth century had this characteristic in common with the American government in the nineteenth; that the executive and legislative branches of the government were so far separated that no means of harmonizing their action was provided or allowed by the Constitution." In England at the beginning of the eighteenth, and America at the end of the nineteenth centuries, parties were principally occupied in keeping men in office. The separation of

---

[118] *Ibid.*, p. 355.   [119] Frank J. Goodnow, *Politics and Administration*, p. 24.
[120] *Ibid.*, p. 258.
[121] Arthur T. Hadley, *Undercurrents in American Politics*. p. 101.

powers had the almost necessary result, in order to prevent dead-locks, of the "dominion of the party manager. . . ." Walpole and Tweed, he said, "were but different specimens of the same genus," and "their power, however widely different in its methods of exercise, was an outgrowth of the same cause." [122]

McLaughlin, also recognized that only parties made our system workable. At present, he said, we had a "despotism tempered by assassination." Sometime, he concluded, we shall "democratize and constitutionalize parties." [123]

Meanwhile, there had been striking changes in the actual flow and distribution of power. If Wilson's analysis of the actual distribution of power was correct in 1889 when he wrote his "Congressional Government," it is clear that it was not correct in 1900, and even less so in 1910. It is probably fair to say that he over-emphasized the domination of the Senate and the decline of the Presidency. But he did not err in his searching analysis of the grievous disunion caused by the separation of powers.

Yet so fluid is our politics, so quickly does it shift in its development, so much does it depend on the personal element, that in a few years we were talking of executive usurpation and of the decline of the Senate.

Wilson himself, in the preface to the 1900 edition of his "Congressional Government," noted "the greatly increased power and opportunity for constructive statesmanship" in the Presidency. He laid the increase of the executive power to the Spanish War, which greatly increased the executive prestige. The President, he admitted, is "now, of course, at the front of affairs as no President except Lincoln" had been since the first quarter of the nineteenth century. He thought that a new executive leadership of the executive might be arising, which might give "the heads of the executive departments a new influence upon the action of Congress." [124] It may bring about, "as a consequence, an integration which will substitute statesmanship for government by mass meeting. It may put this whole volume hopelessly out of date." [125]

Broadly speaking, there are only two methods by which the

---

[122] Arthur T. Hadley, *Standards of Public Morality*, p. 127.
[123] Andrew C. McLaughlin, *The Courts, the Constitution and Parties*, pp. 147–48.
[124] Woodrow Wilson, *Congressional Government*, Preface to 1900 (15th) ed., pp. xi–xii.
[125] Woodrow Wilson, *Ibid.*, pp. xx, xxi.

President may exercise an influence on Congress: one is executive leadership; one is the patronage. Cleveland had used patronage unblushingly to obtain the repeal of the Sherman Silver Purchase Bill. Cleveland was not a party leader, but his fighting integrity, his courage and character, had given the Presidency a new prestige in time of national crisis. McKinley, although not a man of strong character, was a skillful politician, and he was an adept in the employment of patronage. Mr. Dooley well said that the Congressmen would get the real Presidential message when they went to see the President about the fourth class postmasterships. But Roosevelt used both methods. Beginning with his swing around New England in the fall of 1902, when he discussed the control of corporations, he developed an amazing ability to talk to the people and obtain their support for his policies. The railroad rate law was an example of the power of public opinion to secure action from Congress, which never could have been obtained by the old methods. Roosevelt was enabled time and again to obtain action from Congress which it was reluctant to grant, because the strength of public opinion was too much for it to resist.

When Hughes became Governor of New York, he followed the Roosevelt lead. He went to the people of his State on the race-track gambling bill, the direct primary bill, and the public utilities bill.

Wilson, as Governor and later as President, also assumed the role of a political leader. But he added the practise of appearing in person to address Congress, instead of sending it written messages.

Roosevelt, Hughes and Wilson were the most outstanding examples of the realization, on the part of executives, that our system of balanced and separated powers required that the executive assume the responsibility for leadership in legislation. These executive leaders were not chosen by the normal process of parliamentary winnowing, but became leaders by virtue of their position and ability. Roosevelt called the executive power "the steward of the public welfare." [126] Hughes declared that "Against the scattered exponents of local interests," the State executive represented "in the public mind not simply the administrative power, but legislative

[126] Theodore Roosevelt, *The New Nationalism*, p. 28.

initiative." The executive represented "the people at large." [127] Wilson, then Governor of New Jersey, likewise testified that the people wanted "their governors to be leaders on matters of legislation." [128]

This was far from parliamentary government. It was far from the combination system suggested by Ford. The executive did not sit in the legislature. The cabinet officers did not sit there. The leader was not chosen from the legislative body. He had the advantage of the prestige of his office, but men without the gift of leadership would not be able to exert this power of executive leadership.

But it was the natural way for our system to develop. The outright adoption of the parliamentary system is, of course, impossible. Moreover, it is to be doubted if it is adapted to our needs. Lowell was correct that under it one of the two houses would surely decline. Moreover, the people are not used to it, and would not understand it. We should start with allowing cabinet officers and, I think, also, the President to sit in Congress, and see what would happen by natural development.

Nor can I visualize the Ford system. It does not seem desirable that the President should remain for four years at a time, with power over administration and the veto, and with the opportunity to influence legislation, in a system where the cabinet officers are subject to a legislative house. A strong President could defeat or hamper a legislature under the Ford system. And our system has tended to develop leadership in the executive, rather than in the houses of Congress. The popular psychology is favorable to development of leadership in the elected executive.

The movement for executive leadership in legislation caused bitter opposition. Roosevelt's statement that the executive was the steward of the public welfare, was called an advocacy of executive usurpation. Men still made an idol of the separation of powers. They still called it an evidence of the profound wisdom of the Constitutional fathers, although it was shown abundantly that it was based on a misconception of the British system, and that it was responsible for the American boss system.

A striking illustration of the conflict of ideas on the changing role of the Presidency was furnished by the third term controversy.

[127] Governors' Conference, *Proceedings*, 1910, p. 15.   [128] *Ibid.*, 1911, p. 49.

Since the foundation of the government, no President, elected to succeed himself, has ever been elected to succeed himself again. Nor has any President, after he had filled two elective terms, ever been a candidate again.

The dogma has broadened into a declaration that no President should hold three terms. The tradition is deemed to be essential to the preservation of our institutions, to the prevention of a dictatorship.

In 1880, Grant was a candidate for the Republican nomination, after he had been elected President in 1868 and 1872. His opponents raised the third term tradition against him. The fear of executive power was potent, and whether or not the third term dogma was the decisive factor, at least it was not repudiated.

Again, in 1912, Theodore Roosevelt was a candidate for the Republican nomination for President, and later became the candidate of the Progressive Party. The third term tradition was constantly and bitterly employed against him. He was referred to as the "third term candidate." One Middle Western newspaper never spoke of him save as the "third-termer." Taft even said that if Roosevelt were elected, he would never leave the White House again until his death. The fear of a dictatorship was expressed again and again.

Roosevelt replied that a President in office could, indeed, use the power of the patronage to encompass his re-nomination and re-election, but that "every shred of power which a President exercises while in office vanishes absolutely when he has once left office." A President out office, has no more power than any other citizen,—perhaps less. The tradition, he continued, had "no application whatever to anything except consecutive terms." Otherwise applied, it was a mere formula, a source "of mischievous confusion." A democracy, he went on, should be free to use the services of any man it desired.[129]

The antagonism of 1912 extended to any attempt of the President to succeed himself. The Democratic platform pledged the party to a constitutional amendment for a single presidential term. After the election, a resolution providing for a single term of six years and forbidding the President to serve a second term, was introduced

[129] Theodore Roosevelt, *An Autobiography*, p. 423.

in Congress. The debate on it was largely one between the old and the new idea of the executive.

Senator Works of California, who introduced it, clung to the idea that the President should be a mere executive. The idea that he was a political leader shocked him. It was "degrading" that the President should be a seeker for office; a "vicious system," that he should appoint men to office with a view to aiding his candidacy for re-election. He objected bitterly to a President going on the stump. "Candidates for that great office," he complained, "have gone on the stump and canvassed for their own election. That was shame enough." But one was the present President and one was a former President. That increased the shame. It was "undignified and beneath the office of any man fit to be President." [130]

The fear of dictatorship was strong; but I think that equally strong was antagonism to the strange new idea that the President was an executive leader. Works called it a "most pernicious doctrine." He predicted that if the amendment were adopted, the President as a political leader "would be useless. He would have no motive or desire other than to do his duty as President, and make for himself an honorable record as a public official." [131] Hitchcock declared that "the President of the United States ought to be removed from political struggles." [132]

But the new conception was that the President must be a political leader, must take part in political struggles, if he would fulfil his function. Borah was refreshing in his reply. "There was no possible way," he asserted, "to remove the President of the United States from political struggles if he is at all fit to be in the Presidential chair." If he were fit to be a President, "he will be a political leader and will direct the political forces of his party." All our great Presidents had been political leaders. [133]

Lodge pointed out that the patronage was often a hindrance rather than a help. The cry of Caesarism did not disturb him. Our safeguard against dictatorship lay in ourselves. "When the people are ready to fall into the hands of an imperial despot, or a perpetual dictator or President, paper barriers will not prevent the calamity." [134]

---

[130] *Congressional Record*, Dec. 9, 1912, pp. 295–98. [131] *Ibid.*, p. 295.
[132] *Ibid.*, Jan. 30, 1913, p. 2269. [133] *Ibid.*, Jan. 30, 1913. p. 2269.
[134] *Ibid.*, Jan. 30, 1913. p. 2259.

Then he added that lengthening the Presidential term would actually increase the defects of our system, since it would increase the chance that the President in power would be of the party opposite to the majority of one of the Houses of Congress.

The ablest reply came from Wilson, just elected President. He stressed the changing conception of the Presidency, the conception that the President was a political leader. Four years was too long for a President who did not have the country with him. It was too short for one who had a program to achieve. The crux of the demand for a single term was that a President might elect himself through the use of the patronage. Then nominate by preferential primaries, where the patronage would be of no avail. But to take away the chance of a second term, would deprive the President of much of his opportunity to influence the country to adopt his policies. It would not only weaken his hold on his party, but it would deprive the country of the opportunity to hold him to responsibility. He exclaimed that the governors of New Jersey could testify to the weakening effect of the single term. The politicians banded against an executive who had no election to hold over them as a threat.

And Wilson concluded that we would belie our principles if we denied the people the power to elect a man whom they desired.[135]

The amendment died in the House. To a large extent it was a product of the campaign, and lost its force as the campaign receded from mind. But, moreover, it was opposed to the whole trend of the times. Its advocates had no conception of the true role of a Presidential campaign. Like many business and professional critics of politics, they seemed to feel that a political campaign is a mere nuisance, a waste of time; whereas, from a true political standpoint, it is a great educator of the people in the work and problems of the government, and a vital part of the process of government. The fear of a dictator was unworthy of a self-reliant and capable democracy. Great Britain does not feel in danger because a prime minister can be elected time after time. A democracy should have the right to elect the President it desires. Lodge was right. If our liberties are in danger simply because we elect a President for a third or second term, no paper barrier can save us.

[135] Woodrow Wilson, *The Public Papers of Woodrow Wilson, The New Democracy,* Vol. I, pp. 21–26 (Letter of Feb. 5, 1913).

Much of the talk was surely strange to hear in a country with democratic traditions. There seems to persist a feeling that the President is like a King, and that it is undignified for him to take part in the ordinary occupations of men and women. It is difficult to understand the declamations against the degradation of a President on the stump and the waste of time from his official duties. For what could be more important than talking to the people on the issues of the campaign? Surely, it is as important for the President to talk to the people on railroad rates, meat inspection bills, conservation, and monopoly, as to sign routine appointments of second lieutenants and ensigns and postmasters. It would be undignified, and a breach of political duty as well, for the King of England to speak on the stump; but Salisbury, Gladstone, Balfour, Campbell-Bannerman, Asquith, Lloyd George, MacDonald, and Baldwin never conceived it against their official dignity to speak on the stump at the same time they were prime ministers. It is a poor dignity which is so easily injured.

But, above all, we had found that our political system would not work at all unless the executive undertook the role of leadership. He must be a political leader, or our system would return to the ineffectual impasse which Wilson had described years ago as the rule of the Congressional committees without let, hindrance, or responsibility. The amendment would not destroy the leadership of the President. He could still, of course, try to encompass the nomination and election of his successor. But if the President with a great program to achieve could not be a candidate to succeed himself, could not bring his policies up for approval or disapproval, his leadership would, of course, as was intended, be greatly weakened. The candidacy of a President to succeed himself, and so for approval of his policies, is the nearest thing we have to the going to the country in the Parliamentary system.

Meanwhile we had been examining the whole system of the long ballot and the choice of candidates. As early as 1879, Albert Stickney had examined them in his "The True Republic." Gamaliel Bradford had supported the short ballot in 1899, in "The Lesson of Popular Government." Stickney presented his ideas again in "Organized Democracy," published in 1906. He said that it was not possible for us to "get wise and efficient administration," [136]

[136] Albert Stickney, *Organized Democracy*, p. 3.

that we did not get the men of our choice, but simply had to choose between the tickets selected by two rival organizations. The reason was that we had turned "government into an election machine. Our political life is a never-ending series of popular elections so called." [137] The cause of the difficulty was the individual ballot combined with short terms. Only the organization heads could take the time to manipulate the system, and in practise "the professionals have the entire control of the selection of candidates." [138] The long party ticket and frequent elections entailed great expense, and the party therefore came under the domination of those who provided the campaign funds. We have achieved, therefore, he said, "not democracy, but plutocracy," [139] and the candidates were the "slaves of the election machines." [140]

His analysis was keen, but his remedy seems fanciful and impracticable. He was sound in desiring to make the administration single-headed; to have department heads select their subordinates; to have only a few of the chief officials elected. But he proposed to establish a representative body in each community, which would select the candidates, both the few executive candidates and the legislative, and then the officers once elected would serve during good behavior. He seemed naively to assume that the popular assemblies would automatically select the best candidates. The citizens in their primary meetings, he said, "will be able to oppose combinations made beforehand by the politicians, with combinations made on the spot by themselves." [141] A completer lack of knowledge of practical politics could hardly be evidenced. Of course, the slates of the politicians would succeed in ninety-nine cases out of a hundred. After a year or so, the citizens would become tired.

Stickney dwelt long on the waste of money in our presidential elections. "Once in four years," he said, "we have a national revolution," [142] and he quoted a railroad president to the effect that the cost was "incalculable." [143]

He would have one national legislative house, would abolish terms, and give to two-thirds of the House power to remove the President.

Yet he said in conclusion that the "political life of a community"

---

[137] *Ibid.*, p. 5.   [138] *Ibid.*, p. 10.   [139] *Ibid.*, p. 19.   [140] *Ibid.*, p. 21.
[141] *Ibid.*, p. 107.   [142] *Ibid.*, p. 209.   [143] *Ibid.*, p. 210.

must be "one of steady, continuous growth. It should not be a series of revolutions." [144]

His own proposal involved a drastic revolution. Moreover, it would have eliminated elections not only for administrative officials but for legislative candidates, and the enormously valuable educative influence of the Presidential campaign. A democracy is not a business, and business efficiency is not its test. Nothing could be more necessary in a democracy than that the people should pass on legislative candidates periodically, and consider the policies of these candidates. The root of our trouble is not in legislative or Congressional elections. It is in loading the people with the impossible task of electing fifty or more administrative officers, —county, state, and even township. Necessarily, the party organization was the only body which would or could assume the burden of selecting and electing the long party ticket. The result has been to create vast, intricate organizations, which hamper every man who seeks political office. He is bound hand and foot by the party organization. He has to conform his ideas to that of the party organization. The candidate for the highest office has to take into account the prejudices of the lowliest candidate on the same party ticket. The organization fills up the slate with the candidates who are regular party workers and whom it desires to reward.

In 1911, Richard S. Childs, who was Secretary of the short ballot organization, published an incisive little book which he called: "Short Ballot Principles." He declared that it "is *lese majeste* to allege that there are any limitations to the people in either morals or learning." [145] He put forward as essential principles that the office to be voted for must be important, the district must be wieldy, the office must be visible, and the government must be strong and unhampered.

In his Godkin lectures at Harvard in 1909, published in 1912, Arthur George Sedgwick continued the argument in "The Democratic Mistake." He said that it was natural that when the sovereignty became popular, that the right of control over the appointment of officers should have been given to the new sovereign, as it had been held by the personal sovereign. The only means, it was thought, of "preventing the abuses of power and securing the welfare of the community, was through responsibility

[144] *Ibid.*, p. 252.   [145] Richard S. Childs, *Short Ballot Principles*, p. 6.

to the community; the corollary, that the most effective way of enforcing this responsibility was through sending representatives to prevent and do away with abuses, and keeping those representatives responsible through elections, seemed to follow naturally." [146] We widened the base by making suffrage universal. We believed that where annual elections end, tyranny begins, and we adopted short terms. We established, in short, an elective responsibility by short terms and by providing that a great number of small administrative offices should be filled by direct vote of the people.

This democratic mistake, he said, was "predestined to promote the development of the machine." [147] It was the machine which filled the tickets and saw that they were elected. The merit system was a great aid in reducing the power of the old machine, but it merely increased the power of the elective machine, for men who could not get appointments swarmed after the elective offices. So he concluded that the only way to "get rid of the machine," was to give up "the delusion that the multiplication of offices and elections is the way to enforce responsibility to the people or that they can do anything but intensify the evil." [148] The way out was in the simplification of political machinery. We are not to be saved by the ballot alone. The fundamental difficulty, he said, was that no one but the "professional politicians and their henchmen, the 'workers,' have time to devote to picking out candidates and organizing the forces of the party." [149] In an able book, "Unpopular Government in the United States," Albert M. Kales, a Chicago lawyer, presented the same argument.

In the later years of our period, these theories began to be tested. The commission form of city government, of course, operated under the short ballot. The most striking proposal, however, was for the short ballot for State governments. In the years from 1912 to 1915, a number of States began to realize that their governments had become overgrown and unmanageable. The expenses of State government had increased far out of proportion to the increases in population. Partly, no doubt, this was due to the increasing complexity of government, the growth of cities, the increase of manufactures, and the consequent need of sanitation, factory inspection, paving, schools, parks, police and fire pro-

---

[146] Albert George Sedgwick, *The Democratic Mistake*, p. 92.
[147] *Ibid.*, p. 125.   [148] *Ibid.*, p. 147.   [149] *Ibid.*, p. 151.

tection. It has been shown that even under the best administration, government expense increases faster than the population.

But a vast deal of the expense was due to the cumbrousness of our system. As new functions were called for, we had added new bureaus without prevision, until in most States we had a great mass of overlapping state agencies. We elected a dozen State administrative officers. The appointive Federal cabinet was unknown in the States.

In 1913, Governor Lowden, of Illinois, proposed a sweeping consolidation of State bureaus and departments. An Iowa commission published an able report on the reorganization of State government. The New York Constitutional Convention of 1914 attacked the problem with great thoroughness and ability. John H. Delaney, former Commissioner of the New York State Department of Efficiency and Economy, stated before the committee that there were "one hundred and sixty-nine departments, boards, commissions, officers, and other official bodies exercising some kind of governmental activity. Of those, one hundred and eight are boards and commissions." [150] He described the overlapping nature of their functions. The Governor had practically no control over these multitudinous boards and commissions. The system was too unwieldy for control, even if he had the power. Moreover, the people elected not only the governor, but the judges, the legislature, the lieutenant governor, the state engineer and surveyor, the secretary of state, the state treasurer, the comptroller, and the attorney general.

The convention proposed that all the one hundred and sixty-nine bureaus be consolidated into eleven departments, the heads of which were to be appointed by the governor. For political reasons, it left the comptroller and the attorney general still to be elected by the people.

It was an intelligent attempt to make government responsible by reducing its task to reasonable proportions. The governor was to be given power, with responsibility. The political organization was to be deprived of its power to deal with the elective offices, except the attorney general and the comptroller.

The proposal met strong disapproval. Senator Brackett, a veteran legislator from Syracuse, protested that the short State ballot

[150] Bureau of Municipal Research, *State Administration*, July, 1915, p. 544.

"came from a heart that in its inmost core hates self-government, and that seeks for an opportunity to limit and curtail it." It was conceived "in the malignancy of one who despises the control of the people of their own affairs. . . ." [151] This was quite in line with the protest of a Kentucky delegate, whom Charles A. Beard quoted as declaring in a convention "a quarter of a century ago, in protest against permitting the governor to appoint the state treasurer," that he loved our form of government; but that he loathed, "in the deepest recess of my heart, any effort whatever that will go in the direction of taking from the people of Kentucky the right to choose their own officers." [152]

Another delegate in the New York Convention exclaimed, "Why not go forth and tell the people of the State that they are degenerate, that you take away their power of self-government, and the right to select their officials?" [153] Another called on the convention to defeat "this un-American plan of centralization of power in those who hope to rule, not by popular will but by Divine Right." [154] Another declared that when the number of officials for whom the people vote is lessened, "I think we have marked the beginning of the end of our scheme of government." [155]

Against this inherited democratic complex, the leaders of the convention were helpless. Frederick A. Cleveland, then one of the Directors of the New York Bureau of Municipal Research, explained the advantages not only from a consolidation of the departments and bureaus, but from the elimination of the election of the governor's cabinet. He explained the advantage of the budget system by which the governor would propose a budget to the legislature, and no amendment could be made to an appropriation bill of the governor save to reduce an item. The governor and the heads of departments were to be allowed to appear before the legislative committees.

What "we have had in mind," he said, "is make the governor a responsible agent for getting things done, and to provide him with the machinery for becoming effective." [156] We must, he went on, "locate responsibility somewhere in the government, and we believe

---

[151] New York Constitutional Convention, *Rev. Record* 1915, Vol. IV, p. 3422.
[152] Bureau of Municipal Research, *State Administration,* July, 1915, p. v.
[153] New York Constitutional Convention, *Rev. Record,* 1915, Vol. IV, p. 3493.
[154] *Ibid.,* p. 3549.   [155] *Ibid.,* p. 3363.
[156] Bureau of Municipal Research, *op. cit.,* July, 1915, p. 515.

that it should be vested in the governor." [157] The Constitution should provide a means whereby the state could "bring the performance of its officers to the test of retaining the support of public opinion. . . ." [158] This was, he said, a fundamental democratic idea,—responsibility with power.

Elihu Root brought to the proposals all the force of his personality and ability. Of course, he said that "One hundred and fifty-two outlying agencies, big and little, lying around loose, accountable to nobody, spending· all the money they could get, violate every principle of economy, of efficiency, of the proper transaction of business." [159] But, after all, the consolidation of departments did not involve any difference of opinion on the theory of government. The political issue was in the short ballot proposal. Root spoke of the "invisible government,"—the striking phrase originated, I believe, by Senator Beveridge. The boss behind the scenes was the supreme ruler of the State; not the constitutional and statutory officers of the State. "For I don't remember how many years Mr. Conkling was the supreme ruler in this state." The governor did not count, comptrollers, and secretaries of state, and what-not did not count. "Then," he said, "Mr. Platt ruled the state; for nigh upon twenty years he ruled it." [160] How is it done? he asked; and he answered that it was done by the use of the patronage. The boss appointed men who would maintain the power of the organization. If we refused, he said, to make the governor elected by the people the "real chief executive, we make inevitable the setting up of a chief executive not selected by the people, not acting for the people's interest, but for the selfish interest of the few who control the party, whichever party it may be." He said that the system ought to be changed. He would not admit that it could not be changed. If the system under which Walpole ruled England could be changed, so could ours. We could take this step "toward robbing an irresponsible autocracy of its indefensible and unjust and undemocratic control of government, and restoring it to the people, to be exercised by the men of their choice and their control." [161]

The attempt failed. Yet progress is being made in executive leadership. We now have a national budget, and a number of

[157] *Ibid.*, p. 515.   [158] *Ibid.*, p. 515.   [159] *Ibid.*, p. 625.
[160] *Ibid.*, p. 627.   [161] *Ibid.*, pp. 629–30.

States have budgetary control. The process of consolidating government departments and of making the governor the responsible appointing head, is steadily gaining.

REGULATION BY COMMISSIONS

As we have gone along in this study, we have seen the progress of another tendency in political machinery, which has had a deep effect on the old theory of the separation of powers and on our judicial system: that is the growth of commission control of corporations, railroads, and labor and health conditions. We have seen how Reagan and Morgan feared commission control in 1887, when the Interstate Commerce Act was passed. They would prohibit by law, and leave the injured party to his action in the good old Anglo-Saxon way. McCall, in 1905 and 1906, expressed the same fear and the same affection for the historic processes of the courts.

And yet the process was inevitable, and has gone steadily on. Van Hise felt that the result of the belief, "that the wrongs to individuals perpetrated by the great public utilities corporations were to be redressed through the courts and that competition was to regulate prices," was that "millions of wrongs went unredressed; and competition led to unnecessary duplication, great loss to the public, destruction to the weak, and finally, complete dominance of the great public utilities and especially the railroads." [162]

This administrative control through commissions was rendered necessary both because sporadic suits by individuals were not an adequate protection of the public's rights in the case of railroads and other utilities, and because no statute could lay down all the rules and regulations to govern complicated questions of rates, service, and other aspects of business. The commissions, therefore, were both executive bodies for the enforcement of the law, and administrative bodies with power to make rules and regulations interpreting the law.

As S. O. Dunn, editor of the "Railway Age Gazette," observed, many people seemed to believe that regulation by commission was "a great discovery in political science." [163] Dunn believed in commission regulation, but he insisted that the commissions limit them-

---

[162] Charles R. Van Hise, *Concentration and Control,* pp. 233–34.
[163] S. O. Dunn, "Regulation by Commission," *North American Review,* Vol. CXCIX, p. 206 (Feb., 1914).

selves to regulation, and that the management of business be left in the hands of the managers.[164]

Roscoe Pound pointed out in 1914 some particulars in which the tendency had gone too far. He recalled that formerly we had resorted to the courts for all purposes, and there was no administration at all.[165] But now we were threatened from all sides. In California and Vermont, the findings of commissions were deemed conclusive. Even the United States Supreme Court had held that the decision of an administrative officer on the citizenship of an applicant for admission to the country, was final.

We were in danger of reverting to executive justice, instead of justice according to law. He noted the claim that executive justice is direct, expedite, free from technical forms and rules of evidence; and replied that rules make for justice, that no one can "be trusted to dispense with rules but one who knows the rules thoroughly, and knows how to apply them on occasion." [166] It was not wholly a defect that judicial justice changed its principles slowly, for stability makes for justice.

Judicial justice gave, he asserted, more certainty and flexibility than any administrative justice. The judge is subject to checks, to criticism, that no administrative officer is subject to. Judges will uphold the law against clamor.[167]

These warnings were well taken. The courts, however, were even then exerting steady and persistent pressure to bring order and established custom to administrative rulings. They have insisted that the administrative officers or boards must give a hearing, and that their action must not be arbitrary.

Justice Lamar, in one case, declared that the orders of the Interstate Commerce Commission were final unless beyond its constitutional power, unless beyond its statutory power, if based on mistake of law, and in addition, if the rates fixed were confiscatory, or if the commission had acted so arbitrarily and unjustly as to fix rates contrary to the evidence or without evidence to support them.[168]

[164] *Ibid.*, p. 211.

[165] Roscoe Pound, "Justice According to Law," II, 14 Columbia Law Review, pp. 1, 13 (Jan., 1914).

[166] *Ibid.*, p. 25.   [167] *Ibid.*, iii, pp. 103, 107–09 (Feb., 1914).

[168] *Interstate Commerce Commission* vs. *Union Pacific R.R.*, 222 U.S. 541, 547 (1912).

Although in the case referred to by Dean Pound, the court held that the decision of the administrative officers as to the citizenship of an applicant for admission to the United States was final, in later cases it has made clear that the decision of the Department is final as Holmes remarked, only on the "presupposition that the decision was after a hearing in good faith, however summary the form." [169] Or, as stated in another case, if it were shown that the "proceedings were manifestly unfair, that the action of the executive officers was such as to prevent a fair investigation or that there was a manifest abuse of the discretion committed to them by the statute," [170] the administrative action could not stand.

Secondly, the courts have insisted that the statute must lay down some general standards to be followed. As Bruce Wyman said, we would not be "content to have our rights determined by administrative fiat." We "must have some objective standards to go upon, or we have no security from subjective differences," no security from "benevolent despotism subject to all the corresponding risks of arbitrary power." [171]

From the beginning of our Government, Justice Lamar reminded us, "various acts have been passed conferring on executive officers the power to make rules and regulations." Congress, in Marshall's words, could delegate "power to fill up the details" by the establishment of administrative rules and regulations.[172] But the legislature must lay down the standards: the commissions could not legislate.

Moreover, the commissions themselves have been becoming more like courts, and conforming their decisions to settled legal forms. Dean Pound noted, at the time of his criticism, that the reports of the Wisconsin Commission read much like those of a court.

The subject of administration through boards and commissions is one of vast and growing importance, as our life becomes steadily more complicated. It is clear that the courts alone can not alone enforce many of our laws, and that our legislature can not foresee all the situations that must arise; and therefore there must be commissions and boards to enforce, and, as Marshall and Lamar said, "to fill up the details," in many legislative acts.

[169] *Chin Yow* vs. *U.S.,* 208 U.S. 8, 12 (1908).
[170] *Low Wah Suey* vs. *Backus,* 225 U.S. 460, 468 (1912).
[171] Bruce Wyman, "Jurisdictional Limitations upon Commission Action," 27 *Harvard Law Review* 545, 569 (April, 1914).
[172] *U.S.* vs. *Grimaud,* 220 U.S. 506, 517 (1911).

Woman's Suffrage

We must now consider one more attempt to obtain political control; this time an attempt not by the whole electorate, but by the women for woman's suffrage. We could have taken it up in the course of our study and continued it through the period, but it seems more desirable to treat it as a unit. The struggle went on, of course, for generations. But when the Civil War ended, the woman suffragists felt, of course, that their time had come. With all the fervor of the moment, with the current insistence on natural rights and equal rights for all, they felt that it would be impossible for the leaders of the Republican Party to refuse women their demand.

In May, 1865, Susan B. Anthony asserted that "Woman must now assume her God-given responsibilities, and make herself what she was clearly designed to be, the educator of the race." [173] She called for a Constitutional amendment granting suffrage to all.

In an address to Lincoln, she and Elizabeth Cady Stanton asked him to "finish the work by declaring that nowhere under our national flag, shall the motherhood of any race plead in vain for justice and protection." [174]

But she was soon to have a bitter shock. At the Women's Rights Convention in Boston, on May 10, 1865, Beecher and Wendell Phillips spoke, and she thought that they evaded the issue. She was soon to find that Charles Sumner believed that woman's suffrage was "most inopportune." [175] It was the negro's hour. He and the dominant leaders were set on negro suffrage, but they did not wish to cloud the issue with woman's suffrage. No doubt this was good practical politics, but Charles Sumner, as we have seen, had declared in glowing words his belief in natural rights, in equal rights for all. The ballot was a protector, a shield; the ballot was necessary to freedom, and now he was irritated at the demand of the women for the same shield and protector. Those who state their ideas in terms of the absolute usually are soon embarrassed.

But the suffrage leaders did not relax their efforts. In 1866 the First Woman's Rights Convention issued an address to Congress written by Miss Anthony. In the tenor of the day, she based the demand on natural rights. "Men and parties," she said, "must

[173] Rheta Childe Dorr, *Susan B. Anthony*, p. 159.   [174] *Ibid.*, p. 161.
[175] Susan B. Anthony *et al.*, *History of Woman Suffrage*, Vol. II, pp. 96–97.

pass away, but justice is eternal; and they only who work in harmony with its laws are immortal." The only tenable ground of representation, she declared, "is universal suffrage, as it is only through universal suffrage that the principle of 'Equal Rights to All' can be realized." Almost in the words of Sumner, she cried, "Our demand must ever be: No compromise of human rights. No admission in the Constitution of inequality of rights or disfranchisement on account of color or sex." [176]

At the same convention Beecher demanded in a similar vein that "you take expediency out of the way, and that you put a principle that is more enduring than expediency in the place of it,—manhood and womanhood suffrage for all." [177]

The woman suffragists obtained support in Congress. Senator Henderson, of Missouri, and Senator Cowan, of Pennsylvania, supported woman's suffrage in language that was to be repeated many times over in the next fifty years.

But the effort failed. Miss Anthony wrote, with insight into the future and with grief at the defeat, that the negro would be the "victim for generations to come of the prejudice engendered by making this a white man's government." She evidently believed that the discrimination against women would encourage discrimination against the negro. It would be hard to say that a constitutional discrimination encouraged an illegal discrimination, but of course she was right that there would be illegal discrimination. But she deeply felt that while "the enfranchisement of all men hastens the day for justice for her, it makes her degradation more complete in the transition state." She even spoke of the added "tyranny, persecution, insults, and horrors, which will surely be visited upon her in the establishment of an aristocracy of sex in this Republic. . . ." [178]

Despite bitter disappointments, the campaign never relaxed. The suffragists presented their case before the New York Constitutional Convention of 1867–8. Again Miss Anthony asserted that the suffrage is not the gift of society, but a natural right. The principle of inequality in government, she said, had been thoroughly tried, and it was always fatal. [179]

[176] Carrie Chapman Catt and Nellie Rogers Shuler, *Woman's Suffrage and Politics*, p. 39.
[177] *Ibid.*, p. 40.   [178] Rheta Childe Dorr, *Susan B. Anthony*, p. 214.
[179] Susan B. Anthony, *et al., History of Woman Suffrage*, Vol. II, pp. 185–86.

George William Curtis supported it, not in the terms of historic natural rights, but in terms of personal rights, which were so essential as to take on the ideal aspect of rights natural to man from his intrinsic nature. "Despite the brilliant and vehement eloquence of Mr. Choate," he said, the framers of the Declaration of Independence "did not deal in glittering generalities. . . ." The rights, he said, "which they declared to be inalienable, are indeed what are usually called natural as distinguished from political rights, but they are not limited by sex." If, he said, "I have a natural right to my life and liberty, I have the same right to everything that protects that life and liberty which any other man enjoys." [180]

The woman suffragists tested their rights under the Federal constitution. Miss Anthony claimed the right to vote, and was tried for an attempt at illegal voting. In the case of Minor vs. Happersett,[181] the Supreme Court finally decided that the Fourteenth Amendment did not grant the right to vote. Only the States could grant the right to vote, and they were free to restrict it so long as they did not discriminate on the ground of race.

All through the long debate, it is noticeable that the suffragists were influenced by a feeling of an affront to personal dignity in allowing males, of however ignorant and debased character, to vote, while the privilege was denied to all women, however intelligent and public-spirited. As we shall see, the economic motive was influential, but it is evident that the demand from the beginning was animated by an assertion of personality. At the suffrage convention in 1869, Elizabeth Cady Stanton asked if the freest government on earth would be the first to establish "an aristocracy based on sex alone," if it would exalt "ignorance above education, vice above virtue, brutality and barbarism above refinement and religion." In the Southern States, she said, "women were not humiliated in seeing their coachmen, gardeners, and waiters go to the polls to legislate for them; but in this boasted Northern civilization women of wealth and education, who pay taxes and obey the laws, who in morals and intelligence are the peers of their proudest rulers, are thrust outside the pale of political consideration with minors, paupers, lunatics, traitors, and idiots, with those guilty of bribery, larceny, and infamous crimes." [182]

---

[180] *Ibid.*, pp. 290–91.   [181] 21 Wall. 162 (1874).
[182] Catt and Shuler, *op. cit.*, pp. 68–69.

In the New York Constitutional Convention of 1894, the question came up again. An eloquent statement of the suffrage case was presented by Mary Putnam Jacobi, a sister of George Haven Putnam, the publisher. She, too, placed the demand on the basis of right; again, not the right of any social compact, but the right necessary to realize the fullest expression of human personality. "Today," she said, "a fine and certainly widely diffused scorn prevails for doctrines of Abstract Rights, and of claims based on them." Yet she asked how a demand for rights could be formulated except abstractly. The gist of every conflict is "the question: On which side does the Right lie? which both sides claim?" [183] It is evident that she was speaking of those demands for personal expression, which are held to be so precious that people conceive of them instinctively as rights. The philosophy of results, of economic interpretation, can never remove this native desire of men and women to think of their desires, not as expressions of economic interests or as mere demands, but as native and intrinsic rights.

But by 1894 the day of women in the professions and industry had come, and Dr. Jacobi argued, as many were to argue in the ensuing years, that women in industry, who had no men to act for them, needed the protection of the ballot. Women were legally free, they were achieving economic independence, but like the negro, they would not attain "to a condition of full personality in the social estimate," in the absence of political right.[184]

Like Miss Anthony, Dr. Jacobi was indignant that the illiterate negro could vote; the immigrant could vote; but the "white woman of purest blood, and who, in her own person or that of mother or grandmother, has helped to sustain the courage of the Revolutionary War, to fight the heroic battle of abolition, and to dress the wounds of the Rebellion,—this woman must keep silence." All the women "remain excluded from the franchise, desired behind this dense cloud of often besotted ignorance." [185]

She adverted to the stereotyped arguments that the suffrage is based on force, and that only those who could defend the State by arms should have the right to vote, and replied that force was the servant of intelligence. Goldwin Smith, she said, who had objected that the suffrage was an attempt to change the rela-

---

[183] Mary Putnam Jacobi, *Common Sense Applied to Woman Suffrage*, pp. 10–11.
[184] *Ibid.*, p. 28.   [185] *Ibid.*, p. 74.

tion betwen the sexes, and to break up the family which was a unit, was apparently unaware of the domestic revolution which had brought women into business. She denied the antagonism between the sexes, and answered that women are "not homogeneous with each other, but are so with the men among whom they live." [186]

She concluded that the "most important effect of the suffrage is psychological." [187] It would give a consciousness of power, of personal worth and effectiveness. The consciousness of power and personal dignity would bring a great release of energies, a development of the capacities of women. The state, she said, suffers "when energies, which might be usefully applied, are repressed, crippled, or allowed to rust; . . . interests suffer when entrusted for their defense to anyone but those directly concerned in them. . . ." [188]

For a decade and a half little progress was apparent. But beginning about 1910, suffrage began to gather great momentum. The influence of the English movement was potent. The great democratic surge of the first ten years of the century had its effect on the suffrage cause, too. In 1912 the Progressive Party declared for woman's suffrage. Jane Addams, in the National Convention, spoke briefly in its behalf, emphasizing, as she always did, the demands of women in industry, and the special interests of women and their special capacities in those matters which had been transferred from the home to the shop and the factory.

Crothers, with his habitual whimsicality and gentleness, quietly explained that feminism was not the driving power of suffrage, but rather democracy. Women and men were not two diverse races. Man, he said, is born of woman, and woman has the same inheritance as man. To say that women are inexperienced in politics, was no more true than to say that men were inexperienced until they had had the chance to vote. To the objection that the ballot would break up the home, he reminded us that people do not vote all the time, and that voting is not so arduous as vote getting.

He realized too that the demand, after all, was based on an assertion of the normal rights of personality. The women wanted the vote, or at least a large number of them did, and they would not be satisfied until they got it. It did not matter whether the suffrage paid them or not. "Of course," he said, "it is a question whether people should be high-spirited, and whether they do not

[186] *Ibid.,* p. 176.　　[187] *Ibid.,* p. 180.　　[188] *Ibid.,* p. 191.

lose money by it; but as practical persons, we must take them as they are." He concluded that the "mistake of the ruling classes has always been that they have reversed the order of precedence. They have considered expediency first, and have postponed questions of rights to a more convenient season." [189]

Only as it was incidental to the arguments of the exponents of suffrage, have we noted the arguments of the opposition. As in the case of the exponents of laissez faire, the arguments of the opponents of woman suffrage changed little through the years.

Reverdy Johnson, in December, 1866, in opposing the demand for suffrage for women after the Civil War, used the argument that the women did not want it, and he used the argument of the fighting test. As to the need for protection, he asked if the women "govern those who govern, is not that protection enough?" [190]

Elihu Root, in the New York Constitutional Convention of 1894, felt that the suffrage would be a loss to women. It would involve woman in the strife of political factions; she would become "harsh, hard, unlovable, repulsive; as far removed from that gentle creature to whom we all owe allegiance and to whom we confess submission, as the Heaven is removed from earth." [191]

Molly Elliot Seawell, a popular writer of children's tales, was a spirited representative of the women who did not want the suffrage. She asserted that less than three per cent of the women desired the vote. The anti-suffragists, she insisted, "are in an enormous majority." [192] Woman's suffrage, she declared, was opposed to two basic principles; and a basic principle, she said, "works with the merciless mechanism of a natural law like gravitation, and is indeed a natural law." [193] The first basic principle was that an electorate must enforce its own laws. The women could not enforce their own laws. The second was that no voter ever can claim maintenance from another voter. Voting, she concluded, was neither a moral nor a legal right. She seized on the extravagant claims that woman suffrage would bring equal pay for equal work, and asked how the vote could affect the rate of pay.

Lyman Abbott, valiant and life-long liberal as he was, yet op-

---

[189] Samuel McChord Crothers, *Meditations on Votes for Women*, p. 41.
[190] *History of Woman Suffrage*, supra, Vol. II, p. 132.
[191] Elihu Root, "*Speech of August 15, 1894*" (Pamphlet issued by New York Association Opposed to Woman Suffrage), New York City.
[192] Molly Elliot Seawell, *The Ladies' Battle*, p. 11. [193] *Ibid.*, p. 17.

posed woman suffrage. Suffrage, he felt, was not a natural right: it was not a right at all. He believed still that woman has a separate and precious function. Shall she, he asks, take man's tasks in addition to hers, and become "not only the mother, the nurse, the teacher, but also the magistrate, the policeman, the tiller of the soil, the sailor of the ship, the worker of the town?" [194] He begged men not to lay the burden on women unless they wanted it, and he added that the evidence was all that they did not want it. Finally, he urged women not to turn from their "great vocation, the ministry to life," in order to take up this "lower and lesser vocation." [195]

The opposition generally was based on a settled philosophy or prejudice. The antagonism of some men to the suffrage for women was partly, as the women charged, due to a desire to maintain sex domination. It was partly due to the fear of such interests as the liquor business, that woman suffrage would be inimical to them. The old belief that suffrage was founded on physical force and that only those who could fight should vote, was widely held. There was much sincere feeling that women would lose something fine in politics.

The conservative had a nostalgia for simpler days. A great proportion of the men—perhaps a majority of the women—were in opposition until the very end. The suffragists answered the argument that the women, themselves, did not want the vote, by saying that that argument had never been used against the men. In truth, the whole point was whether a sufficient number wanted it. If the number were large enough, the demand must be satisfied; and those who did not want it, would go along with the rest, as in all other political changes. Mr. Dooley had predicted that intelligence would not "give ye the vote," but "enough iv ye at one time wantin' it enough." [196]

As the contest became more heated, the arguments on both sides became more extravagant. The fears of the breaking up of the American home with the advent of suffrage, were matched on the other side by extravagant claims of a political millennium when the women could vote. Suffrage would destroy bossism, would purify politics, would eliminate the saloon. Despite Crothers'

---

[194] Lyman Abbott, *The Spirit of Democracy*, p. 187.
[195] *Ibid.*, p. 188. [196] Finley Peter Dunne, *Mr. Dooley Says*, p. 32.

affirmation, there was much of sex antagonism in the claims of some of the suffragists. They assumed that men and women were of two different species, and the male was distinctly inferior and less moral.

The result has shown how mistaken both sides were. Woman's suffrage has not greatly changed our politics. Political manners, indeed, I believe are better, and the presence of the women may be partly responsible. The polling places are certainly better conducted and more attractive, and the presence of the women undoubtedly must be given most of the credit. The women voters' leagues in many localities have done hard and intelligent service. But it is fair, I think, to say that their activities have been directed more towards candidates than issues. Women vote much as men do. They are no more irritated than men at the manifestations of political corruption.

On the other hand, suffrage has not broken up the home. It has not debased or hardened women. The true political answer has already been indicated. The vote was an assertion of human personality. The very slogan of the suffragists: "Women are people," asserted it. The women wanted to be counted. They felt—or at least a large number felt—a personal slight in the denial of the suffrage. They wanted to express themselves directly, and the demand could not be denied.

Resume of the Struggle for Political Control

It is difficult to arrive at any clear resume of this struggle for political control in the period from 1865 to 1917. On the one hand, we have such efforts as the demand for woman's suffrage; the direct primary; the direct election of senators; the initiative, referendum, and recall,—all efforts for greater direct democratic control. On the other hand, we have civil service reform; the short ballot; executive leadership; and regulation by commissions,—all looking for greater efficiency.

Civil service reform, the short ballot, and executive leadership were bitterly attacked because they were opposed to the democratic principle. It might be thought that the contest was between efficiency and the democratic dogma. But I think it is fairer to say that, in a real sense, all were aspects of the same movement, all were attempts to obtain control of the political organization and make it responsive to the desires of those advocating the various remedies.

The period was a constant struggle against the political machine. For long it was not perceived that the political machine was the necessary result of our political system itself. At first it was thought that civil service reform would destroy the power of the organization. Civil service reform was achieved in reasonable measure, but the organization remained. However, it is far less arrogant and much more intelligent than it was forty years ago.

Then came the various attempts to capture control directly: the direct election of senators; the direct primary; the initiative, referendum, and recall; and finally, on the part of the women, woman's suffrage. Woman's suffrage was, in the main, as I have said, a demand for the means of self-expression, animated by the same instinctive urge that has animated the demand for universal male suffrage in Europe, England, and in this country. The direct election of senators; the direct primary; the initiative, referendum, and recall, were all advocated on the simple ground that the people should rule. To give them the opportunity to vote for senators, to vote for their own candidates, for legislation directly was all that was necessary. Of course, the results have been less than the expectations. The direct primary has brought greater public interest, but it is a clumsy and unwieldy instrument when used with the long ballot. The initiative and referendum have been little used, but undoubtedly have done little harm and probably considerable good. The short ballot gains ground slowly; and executive leadership is still only personal, aided by no political machinery.

On the whole, it must be confessed that the great democratic ideals of the progressive years have met with disappointment. The general political activity of the people has been at a low ebb ever since 1917. Until the somewhat feverish discussions of the "New Deal," there was nothing comparable to the eager activity of the campaign of 1884; the intense interest shown in the gold-silver campaign of 1896, when every street corner held a knot of excited arguers; the vivid and intelligent discussion of the years between 1904 and 1916, when books and magazines were filled with talk of the new nationalism and the Roosevelt and Wilson policies. It is not only in the direct primary and direct legislation, then, that there has been a slump: the slump has been general.

But 1912 was the climax of a political impulse of unusual force and strong emotions. A relapse from that high tide was inevitable. Nor could the high hopes of such a time be fully realized. When, indeed, in politics are high hopes ever realized? Moreover, until Franklin Roosevelt, we had no political leaders with an appeal, comparable to the influence of Bryan, Theodore Roosevelt, and Wilson.

Then, too, the war was followed by a period of unusual prosperity, except for the farming classes; and except for them, political quiescence followed on economic satisfaction. And the war may have its share of responsibility. I do not think it is to fall into the easy quackery of blaming the war for all our ills, to say that the relapse in emotions after the war partly explains our temporary political indifference.

Significant changes have been going on in our habits and in the makeup of our people. It was inevitable that the great masses of immigration should begin to have an influence on our political action. In many cities and States, one-half to two-thirds of the population are foreign born or the children of foreign born. The finest political activity is the product of a people that has lived a long time together, that has common backgrounds, that understands each other. In many places our population is unfused,—new and unused to our political tradition. The heterogeneity dulls the impulses of even those of the native stock, who, in a homogeneous community, would be politically active.

Forty years ago, in many communities in the Middle and Far West, and no doubt in New England and the older States as well, the activities of the people were generally limited to the church, the lodge, and politics. In rural districts and small towns, the church social, the revival, the political rally, and the lodge meeting were almost the sole forms of amusement and activity. Now, there are golf, tennis, the automobile, the movie, the radio, which have greatly widened the interests and range of amusement of the people, and undoubtedly lessened the attraction of politics.

Finally, I am inclined to believe that the growth of large corporations, absorbing the activities of men who formerly would have been more independent in their business and political expressions, has had much to do with our political silence.

REFERENCES

ABBOTT, LYMAN, *The Spirit of Democracy*. Boston: Houghton Mifflin Co., 1910.

BEARD, CHARLES A., AND SCHULTZ, BIRL E., *Documents on the State-Wide Initiative Referendum and Recall*. New York: The Macmillan Co., 1912.

BRADFORD, GAMALIEL, *The Lesson of Popular Government* (2 vols.). New York: The Macmillan Co., 1899.

BRYAN, WILLIAM J., *Speeches* (2 vols.). New York: Funk & Wagnall Co., 1909.

BUREAU OF MUNICIPAL RESEARCH, *State Administration*, July, 1915.

BUTLER, NICHOLAS MURRAY, *Why Should We Change Our Form of Government?* New York: Charles Scribner's Sons, 1912.

CATT, CARRIE CHAPMAN, AND SHULER, NETTIE ROGERS, *Woman's Suffrage and Politics*. New York: Charles Scribner's Sons, 1923.

CHILDS, RICHARD S., *Short Ballot Principles*. Boston: Houghton Mifflin Co., 1911.

CROSS, IRA, Direct Primaries, *The Arena*, Vol. XXXV (1906), p. 587.

CROTHERS, SAMUEL MCCHORD, *Meditations on Votes for Women*. Boston: Houghton Mifflin Co., 1914.

CURTIS, GEORGE WILLIAM, *Orations and Addresses* Vol. II. New York: Harper & Bros., 1894.

DORR, RHETA CHILDE, *Susan B. Anthony*. New York: Frederick A. Stokes Co., 1928.

DUNN, S. O., "Regulation by Commission," *North American Review*, Vol. CXCIX, p. 206 (Feb., 1914).

DUNNE, FINLEY PETER, *Mr. Dooley Says*. New York: Charles Scribner's Sons, 1910.

EATON, ALLEN H., *The Oregon System*. Chicago: A. C. McClurg & Co., 1910.

FORD, HENRY JONES, "The Direct Primary," *North American Review*, Vol. CXC, p. 1 (July, 1909).

——*The Rise and Growth of American Politics*. New York: The Macmillan Co., 1898.

GODKIN, EDWIN LAURENCE, *Problems of Modern Democracy*. New York: Charles Scribner's Sons, 1907.

——*Unforeseen Tendencies in American Democracy*. Boston: Houghton Mifflin Co., 1898.

GOODNOW, FRANK J., *Politics and Administration*. New York: The Macmillan Co., 1900.

GOVERNORS' CONFERENCE, *Proceedings*. 1910, p. 15; 1911, p. 49; 1913, pp. 134, 216, 225, 281, 324.

HADLEY, ARTHUR T., *Standards of Public Morality*. New York: The Macmillan Co., 1907.

——*Undercurrents in American Politics*. New Haven: Yale University Press, 1915.

HAYNES, GEORGE H., *The Election of Senators*. New York: Henry Holt & Co., 1906.

HENDRICK, BURTON J., "The Initiative and Referendum and How Oregon Got Them," *McClure's Magazine*. Vol. XXXVII, p. 234 (July, 1911).

HUGHES, CHARLES EVANS, "Governor's Message of 1909," *The Outlook*. Vol. XCI, p. 91 (Jan. 16, 1909).

JACOBI, MARY PUTNAM, *Common Sense Applied to Woman's Suffrage*. New York: G. P. Putnam's Sons, 1915.

JAMES, HENRY, *Charles William Eliot*.

LA FOLLETTE, ROBERT M., *Autobiography*.

LOWELL, A. LAWRENCE, *Essays on Government*.

——*Public Opinion and Popular Government*. New York: Longmans, Green & Co., 1913.

——"The Referendum in Switzerland and in America," *Atlantic Monthly*, Vol. LXXIII, p. 517 (April, 1894).

McLAUGHLIN, ANDREW C., *The Courts, the Constitution, and Parties*. Chicago: University of Chicago Press, 1913.

MEYER, ERNEST CHRISTOPHER, *Nominating Systems*. Madison, Wis.: E. C. Meyer, 1902.

MUNRO, WILLIAM BENNETT, *The Initiative, Referendum, and Recall*. New York: D. Appleton & Co., 1912.

NATIONAL ECONOMIC LEAGUE, *Debate on Initiative and Referendum*, 1912. Articles by Frederick P. Fish, Charles F. A. Currier, Emmet O'Neal, Robert L. Owen, William Allen White, Frederic C. Howe, and Lewis J. Johnson.

NEW YORK CONSTITUTIONAL CONVENTION, *Rev. Record*, Vol. IV (1915).

OBERHOLTZER, ELLIS PAXSON, *The Referendum in America*. New York: Charles Scribner's Sons, 1911.

OUTLOOK, THE, articles in Vol. LXXIII, p. 429 (Feb. 21, 1903), and Vol. XCI, p. 91 (Jan. 16, 1909).

POUND, ROSCOE, "Justice According to Law," 13 *Columbia Law Review* 696 (Dec., 1913), 14 *Columbia Law Review* 3, 103 (Jan., Feb., 1914).

ROOSEVELT, THEODORE, *Progressive Principles*. New York: Progressive National Service, 1913, *Autobiography*.

ROOT, ELIHU, *Addresses on Government and Citizenship*. Cambridge: Harvard University Press, 1916.

SEAWELL, MOLLY ELLIOT, *The Ladies' Battle*. New York: The Macmillan Co., 1911.

SEDGWICK, ARTHUR GEORGE, *The Democratic Mistake*. New York: Charles Scribner's Sons, 1912.

STANTON, ELIZABETH CADY, ANTHONY, SUSAN B., AND GAGE, MATILDA JOSLYN, *History of Woman's Suffrage Vols. II to VI*. Published by Susan B. Anthony and National American Woman's Suffrage Assoc., 1881–1922.

STICKNEY, ALBERT, *The True Republic*. New York: Harper & Bros., 1879.
——*Organized Democracy*. Boston: Houghton Mifflin Co., 1906.

STOREY, MOORFIELD, *American Bar Association Reports*, 1894.

TAFT, WILLIAM H., *Popular Government*. New Haven: Yale University Press, 1913.

——*Presidential Addresses and State Papers*. New York: Doubleday, Page & Co., 1910.

VAN HISE, CHARLES R., *Concentration and Control*. New York: The Macmillan Co., 1912.

WEAVER, JAMES B., *A Call to Action*. Des Moines: Iowa Printing Co., 1892.

WICKERSHAM, GEORGE W., "Concerning Certain Essentials of Republican Government," *New York State Bar Association Proceedings*, 1911.

WILCOX, DELOS F., *Government by All the People*. New York: The Macmillan Co., 1912.

WILSON, WOODROW, *Constitutional Government*. New York: Columbia University Press, 1908.

———*Congressional Government* (copyright 1885). Boston: Houghton Mifflin Co. (1925 ed.).

———*The New Freedom* (Tauchnitz ed., 1912).

———*The New Democracy, The Public Papers of Woodrow Wilson* (Vols. I, II). New York: Harper & Bros., 1926.

———*The State*. Boston: D. C. Heath & Co., (rev. ed., 1898).

WOODRUFF, CLINTON ROGERS, "Nominating Reform in America," *The Forum*. Vol. XLII, p. 493 (Dec., 1909).

WOOLLEN, EVANS, "The Direct Primary Experiment," *Atlantic Monthly*. Vol. CX, p. 4 (July, 1912).

WYMAN, BRUCE, "Jurisdictional Limits upon Commission Control," 27 *Harvard Law Review* 545 (April, 1914).

Chapter XIII

THE TESTS OF POLITICAL ACTION

WHAT shall we say of the philosophy of our political action in this period, the tests by which we decided, and the ends we sought?

We have seen how persistent has been the habit of arguing on the basis of formulas, by deduction from abstract principles. Natural rights have been evoked time and again. The belief in natural rights appeared in the debates on the war amendments. Sumner and Julian held it implicitly. It appeared in the woman suffrage debate. Henry George espoused it. Root expressed it in his opposition to the recall of judicial decisions and the initiative, referendum and recall. The courts, in their decisions under the due process clause, have based their opinions again and again on natural rights. Without examining the facts, they have decided that token money statutes, and the limitation of hours, violate the liberty of contract, which is a natural right of man.

There are references in the decisions of the courts to the social compact as the basis for our natural rights. But it is doubtful if many actually believe at this late day in the social compact. By natural rights they mean, as we have seen, rather those rights so dear and precious through long possession, so necessary to the full enjoyment of life, that they are natural to mankind and must not be infringed. It has frequently been noted that the rights guaranteed by our Bills of Right, which were the definite results of a long struggle in England, were commonly regarded as natural rights.

In any event, the statements of these rights were treated as valid concepts to be applied without examination of the facts in the particular cases.

Likewise the theories of laissez faire, which are statements of the experience or expressions of the desires of a class of a different time, are applied as final truth in the settlement of our economic and political conditions today.

Finally, the dogmas of popular sovereignty, embodied in the

Declaration of Independence and promulgated early in our history by Jefferson, have been rigidly applied as revealed truth to settle all the questions of the political machinery of the Twentieth Century. "Only those who are false to the principles of the Declaration of Independence, will seek to prevent actual, as well as theoretical, rule of the people, by the people, and for the people," a strenuous magazine editorial in favor of the initiative, referendum and recall, declared. A prominent political reformer, quoting a statement that "no man could oppose direct legislation unless he is at heart opposed to popular government," went on to say: "This is bed-rock. To deny the initiative and referendum is to deny self-government and democracy, and to affirm self-government and democracy is to affirm the initiative and referendum, and the whole literature of the subject focusses upon this fundamental fact." We have seen that Bryan declared that no one will make an argument "against the referendum who is not prepared to deny the capacity of the people for self-government."[1]

On the other side, we have seen formulas rigidly applied that direct legislation violates the separation of powers, that it is government by the mob, that it is opposed to representative government.

Not only popular argument, but the arguments of the courts, of leading public men, of party leaders, were largely formulistic in method. The political slogans of the past, the idealizations of the contests of the past, the summaries of the experience of the past, useful in their place, have been used as final tests of our political and economic action. One Middle Western politician reduced the whole political world to five great formulas "growing out of and based upon the fundamentals of human nature and the essentials of human conduct." To President Wilson's charge that the Republican Party had not had a new idea in thirty years, he replied, "In one sense, new ideas are not necessary to progress, for the constant application of well-defined principles that are as old as the race, will enable this country to solve all of its problems."[2]

It is little exaggeration to say that in the period under discussion, the advocates of change relied on but two or three maxims for the determination of every question before us, such as, "Equal

[1] Quoted by Edward R. Lewis in "Political Formulas," *Unpopular Review*, Vol. VII, pp. 147–48 (July, 1917).

[2] *Ibid.*, p. 153.

Rights for all and special privileges for none," and "Let the people rule." The advocates of the established order relied commonly on the separation of powers, the aphorisms of individual liberty and laissez faire, and the old formulas of distrust of democratic government. There was a common effort, as Walter Lippmann said in his "Preface to Politics," to "harness mankind to abstract principles —liberty, justice, or equality—and to deduce institutions from these high-sounding words." [3]

We must not too greatly discount the value of political concepts. They serve a necessary purpose. "Causes, as anti-slavery, democracy, etc.," said Josiah Royce, "dwindle when realized in their sordid particulars. Abstractions will touch us when we are callous to the concrete instances in which they are imbedded." The concepts of freedom and of the Union in the North, the concept of State sovereignty in the South, animated millions to heroic sacrifices. The concepts drawn from our experience, the expressions of the ideals and desires of past generations, become enshrined in stubborn and affectionate memories, and truly constitute, in the trite phrase, one of the "bulwarks of our liberty." Political concepts, in short, fulfil one of the great purposes which William James admitted for concepts in philosophy: They act as inspirers of multitudes, "they reanimate our wills." [4]

But they are also valuable as summaries of experience. They fulfil the second purpose which James admitted for concepts in philosophy: They make our world orderly and usable. They are great time-savers in the rapid decisions of life. They "provide an immense map of relations among the elements of things. . . ." [5]

But change and development were going steadily on. Not only were things changing; but ideas—the method of thought—were changing. The Darwinian philosophy was permeating every avenue of thought. Though men clung to the belief in a politics of fixed conceptions, the facts were rapidly becoming too much for them. We were beginning to realize that ideas are not static; that evolution was going on in political institutions, as well as in physical organisms.

Our political formulas, which were the statements of the desires or the condensations of the experience of other times, were not

[3] Walter Lippmann, *Preface to Politics,* p. 84.
[4] William James, *Some Problems of Philosophy,* p. 73.
[5] *Ibid.,* p. 73.

complete statements of the experience even of the time in which they were formulated. No short statement of the results of our experience can state the whole truth of that experience, much less that of a later time when the facts are altogether different. And the facts were in 1917, and are now, vastly different. The facts have burst the confines of our old statements of political wisdom, and we repeat our old formulas while acting in response to modern facts.

Actually, we have seen that both the advocates and opponents of change in our political and economic machinery,—while, no doubt, animated by certain deep-set desires,—have expressly argued on the basis that the results of the measures advocated would be good or bad. In the end, their opinion was based on a belief that the measures in question would achieve some end which was desirable or undesirable. The formulas merely gave some of the reasons, based on a past generalization, for the ends desired.

But, owing to the condensed form of our formulas and the fact that the experience from which they were derived was so different from that to which they are applied, their use inevitably has led to great inconsistencies. Again and again in the course of this book, we have seen the inconsistencies of formula users. Thus Root opposed the initiative and referendum because they were not representative government; and favored the direct primary, which was not representative government. Wilson repeated the maxims of State Rights, and yet actually favored great extensions of Federal power. Men have repeated the maxims of laissez faire and liberty of contract, and yet admitted the necessity of important restrictions on the activity of individuals.

When a new question arises, if there is slight demand for it and we are in a hurry, we can reject it by the application of a principle drawn from the past. But if the demand continues, we can not satisfy those who press it by a mere formula. The facts must soon cause us to make exceptions to and qualifications of our formulas. Thus those who still believe in the general theory of laissez faire have been forced to make many exceptions and qualifications. So likewise those in this country who believe in the dogma of State Rights.

We are constantly forced to make our formulas so general that they are merely expressions of ideals, or so to load them with exceptions and qualifications that they become meaningless as guides to decisions. Even in law, the conceptual method of decision must continually be broken up by modifications and exceptions. But we have no Supreme Court in politics to do this for us; no arbiter to sift and winnow our concepts, and determine when they apply.

Finally, we saw that many questions do not lend themselves yet even to modest generalization. They can not be treated even by a tentative deductive method. The political decisions made by the Supreme Court, as we have seen, can not be based on deduction from an articulate major premise. They are questions of fact to be decided by the experience before us. The facts, the rapid changes of our economic, social and business world had greatly altered our old world, and all the "king's horses" could not put it together again. What was politically desirable a hundred years ago, could not decide what was politically desirable in 1917. We came to realize that political ideas are not static, that our political concepts are mere conveniences and not final arbiters, and that to apply them rigidly meant to subject ourselves to grievous mistakes. We came to realize that in some cases immediately, in all cases ultimately, our test must be in the facts, in actual results, in the way things work or may be expected to work in our democracy. As with Pound in the law, so in politics, we came to a politics of results.

Despite our long adherence to the doctrine of natural rights, in spite of our idealization of the statements of our Bills of Right, our whole national tradition, after all, was against an a priori political philosophy and in favor of one based on results. Like the English, our tradition is empirical. Locke, who believed that all ideas came from experience; Burke, who refused "to enter into these metaphysical distinctions of rights," who hated "the very sound of them,"[6]—both had much influence on our leaders of political thought. Though we did not adopt the utilitarian philosophy of Bentham and Mill, the philosophy of results which underlay their utilitarianism necessarily helped to undermine belief in a static politics.[7]

[6] Edmund Burke, *Works* (Oxford World's Classics ed.), Vol. II, p. 147 (speech on American Taxation, April 19, 1774).

[7] In an address before the Indiana State Bar Association in 1906, Jesse E. Reeves expressed the opinion that, though the direct influence of Bentham in the United States, save through his disciple, Livingston, was perhaps small, "The spirit of his utilitarianism, harmonizing as it did with the principles of American democracy, had far-reaching effect" (*report* of Indiana State Bar Association, 1906, pp. 212, 236).

In philosophy, the pragmatism of William James and John Dewey was a brilliant expression of this conviction that the world was too diverse, too complex, too changing, to be comprised any longer within fixed concepts. Dewey defined it as the "rule of referring all thinking, all reflective considerations to consequences for final meaning and test." [8] The truth would "coincide with their tested consequences effected by intelligent action." [9] James declared that the truth is that which works; that " 'The true,' to put it very briefly, is only the expedient in the way of our thinking, just as 'the right' is only the expedient in the way of our behaving." [10] Pragmatism became the philosophy of most of the apostles of change, more so after the end of our period than before.

We have seen that Pound cited James' test in his argument for a law based on the harmonizing of wills. Pragmatism was considered by some who adopted it, and by most of those who opposed it, as a philosophy of cheap and transient standards, satisfied with materialistic and immediate rewards. But James emphasized that when he said the test was expediency, he meant "expedient in the long run and on the whole, of course." [11] Dewey retorted that those who argued that the pragmatic test was only the immediate and transient consequences, merely showed their inability to think "concretely in empirical terms." The more liberal and generous the consequences, the better. [12] Nor would Dewey limit the consequences to those already realized. He adopted an instrumental pragmatism, and in this he differed with James. The consequences by which he tested, included those we could effect by intelligent action. [13]

Clearly, pragmatism—certainly a philosophy of results—did not mean merely present or material results.

If, then, our test is in results, what are the results by which we judge? What are the tests of our political action?

Willoughby found the basis in the Kantian formula,—that one should act on a principle "which thou canst will to be a universal law." [14] But, as we shall see, he did not make his test purely a priori, as Kant did. Kant, of course, had scorned the test of conse-

---

[8] John Dewey, *Essays in Experimental Logic*, p. 330 (1916 ed.).
[9] *Ibid.*, p. 347.   [10] William James, *Pragmatism*, p. 222.
[11] *Ibid.*, p. 222.   [12] John Dewey, *Creative Intelligence*, p. 62.
[13] *Ibid.*, p. 64.   [14] Westel W. Willoughby, *Social Justice*, p. 19.

quences. There is, he declared, "no genuine supreme principle of morality, which is not independent of all experience, and based entirely upon pure reason." [15] Willoughby made clear that, in his opinion, there are no absolute rights; a man has only those rights necessary "for a realization of his highest ethical self," [16] and which are open to others on the same terms. Rights can not be absolute, because whether they should be granted or not will depend on the particular circumstances. He quoted T. H. Green to the effect that every right "must in some way be relative to circumstances." [17] Therefore, what is right and wrong for us as members of a society, can be determined only after we have ascertained all the circumstances which have led to a state of affairs, as well as the conditions by which a given line of conduct is to be influenced in the future." [18]

The above is taken from his chapter on "Justice," in his "Social Justice." In his chapter on "The Right of Coercion," he endeavored to find the basis of the right of the state to control the individual, and the ends it should seek. Since, if the state did not interfere between the conflicting desires of men, no freedom could exist, the issue was not "between coercion and freedom, but between coercion by law and coercion by individual force." [19] Freedom has "no meaning apart from restraint." [20]

Willoughby denied the utilitarian justification for social control, which he defined as self-interest. He noted that Mill admitted that infants and backward peoples could be coerced under the principles of utilitarianism, and agreed with Fitz-James Stephen that Mill there yielded the whole question. [21] All coercion, he continued, is

[15] Benjamin Rand, ed., *The Classical Moralists*, p. 539 (Kant's "The Metaphysic of Morality," translated by John Watson).

Kant's test was based on what would be good from the idea of right reason. The actual results were too real and earthy to be worthy of notice. A man's will, he said, "is good, not because the consequences which flow from it are good, nor because it is capable of attaining the ends which it seeks, but it is good in itself, or because it wills the good" (*Ibid.*, p. 539).

"From what has been said it is evident that all moral conceptions have their seat and origin in reason entirely *a priori*, and are apprehended by the ordinary reason of men as well as by reason in its purely speculative activity." (*Ibid.*, p. 546.)

Dewey observes: "Kant, moreover, insists, as he is in logic bound to do, that the motive which measures duty is wholly inner; it is purely a matter of inner consciousness. To admit that consequences can be taken into account in deciding what duty is in a particular case, would be to make concessions to the empirical and sensible world which are fatal to the scheme." John Dewey, *German Philosophy and Politics*, p. 51.

[16] Willoughby, *Social Justice*, p. 24.   [17] *Ibid.*, p. 23.
[18] *Ibid.*, p. 26.   [19] *Ibid.*, p. 222.   [20] *Ibid.*, p. 233.   [21] *Ibid.*, p. 240.

based on the ground that the wielder of force is wiser than the one coerced, and that the result will be for the greatest good of the greatest number. But above all, utilitarianism, he argued, would justify the most arbitrary interference with the rights of the individual, if it increased "the happiness of those not coerced."[22] No coercion, therefore, was justified save on the ground that not mere happiness, but the moral responsibility of man was the end to be sought for. The test was not the material self-interest of the critic, but the eternal transcendental test, the subjective test of subordination to the universal rule of the realization of the moral personality of man.

But however transcendental Willoughby's principle was, its application was necessarily dependent on the facts and circumstances of each individual case, as he himself stated in his chapter on "Justice." The more general the test, the less it helps in any individual case. In brief, his test is: What will aid to develop the moral personality of man? But that question depends, after all, on the wants and customs of men, on the harmonizing of the conflict of wills in our society. Decisions which depend on the intensity of the desires of men, can not be decided with Olympian calmness of judgment.

It would be difficult for any of us to say that political questions, the initiative and referendum, woman's suffrage, and even many economic questions such as the eight hour day, the regulation of rates, the minimum wage, can be determined by what aids the moral personality of men. The question of what will aid the moral personality of men, depends partly on how much some men want the change and how much others resist it. The question in each case is particular, and can only be answered by an examination of the facts in each case. A new synthesis can be arrived at only from decisions on numerous new questions pressing upon us.[23]

Then, as we have seen all through this book, there have been

---

[22] *Ibid.,* p. 242.

[23] In his address "The Individual and the State" (*American Political Science Review,* Vol. VIII, p. 1, Feb., 1914), Willoughby clearly showed that his test was the pragmatic one of results. He declared that "no a priori limits may be placed upon the State's sphere of control. Each and every exercise of political control is to be justified by the results reached, or reasonably expected to be reached, by it; and the worth of these results is to be measured by the degree to which they contribute to that highest social goal which, is but a statement, in social terms, of the several goals of the individual members of the group" (p. 8). In such an examination of results, his transcendental test could hardly be more than a general ideal.

those who found the test in the economic factor. Professor Seligman, in his "The Economic Interpretation of History," defines the theory as holding that the ability of man to sustain himself, and therefore the economic life, is the fundamental condition of all life. "To economic causes, therefore, must be traced in last instance, those transformations in the structure of society which themselves condition the relation of social classes and the various manifestations of social life." [24] Seligman traced its development in the Marxian theory. In an article in 1845 on "Wage Labor and Capital," Marx asserted that the relations of production "collectively form those social relations which we call society, and a society with definite degrees of historical development. . . . Ancient society, feudal society, bourgeois society, are simply instances of this collective result of the complexes of relations of production, each of which marks an important step in the historical development of mankind." [25] We have seen that the Manifesto declared that the history of peoples is the history of the class struggle.

In 1859, in his "Contributions to the Criticism of Political Economy," Marx wrote that "legal relations, like the form of government, can be understood neither of and in themselves nor as the result" of the human mind, but "they are rooted in the material conditions of life." The "totality of these relations of production" constitute the real basis "on which is erected the legal and political edifice. . . . The methods of production in material existence condition social, political, and mental evolution in general." [26] By methods of production, Marx did not mean technological methods only. He included all the factors of production: soil, climate, and geographical elements all played their part.

Engels was aware that there was great possibility of over-statement of the theory. He confessed that Marx and he were "partly responsible for the fact that the younger men have sometimes laid more stress on the economic side than it deserves." He pointed out that "the actual form of the social organization is often determined by political, legal, philosophical, and religious theories and conceptions." [27]

Seligman therefore concluded that the economic interpretation of history meant not that "all history is to be explained in economic

[24] E. R. A. Seligman, *The Economic Interpretation of History*, p. 3.
[25] *Ibid.*, p. 39.   [26] *Ibid.*, p. 43.   [27] *Ibid.*, p. 63.

terms alone, but that the chief considerations in human progress are the social considerations, and that the important factor in social change is the economic factor." The economic factors do not exert an exclusive influence, but the preponderating influence "in shaping the progress of society." [28]

Seligman instanced the change from feudal to modern society; the political changes of the nineteenth century as greatly influenced by economic forces. He emphasized the economic causes of slavery, of the Crusades, and of the Reformation.

He noted the objections to the doctrine: that it was fatalistic; that it assumes historical laws, the very existence of which is open to question; that it is socialistic; that it ignores ethical and spiritual forces; and that it leads to absurd exaggerations. He denied that it was fatalistic. He quoted Huxley's question, that granting that we are free to do what we like, what determines what we like? There are certain causes, Seligman said, which are responsible for our decisions. Every man is what he is because of the influence of his environment. Moreover, he said, that because we are unable to discover the laws of our society, does not mean that such laws do not exist. "To deny the existence of historical laws," he replied, "is to maintain that there is to be found in human life no such thing as cause and effect." Naturally, he considered the socialistic objection as "utterly immaterial." [29]

As for the objection that the economic theory ignored the spiritual forces of society, he answered that "all individual ethics is the outgrowth of social forces." [30] Quite properly he reminded us that social and economic forces constantly change and modify our ethical ideas. He did not deny the existence of the higher ideals. But he reminded us that what we have generally forgotten, and it is necessary to "emphasize again and again, is not only that the content of the conception of morality is a social product, but also that amid the complex social influences that cooperated to produce it, the economic factors have often been of chief significance, that pure ethical or religious idealism has made itself felt only within the limits of existing economic conditions." [31]

Material conditions, he went on, precede the ethical, and material conditions continually modify the ethical conception. So he concluded that the economic interpretation did not deny the ethical

[28] *Ibid.*, p. 67.   [29] *Ibid.*, p. 104, 105.   [30] *Ibid.*, p. 113.   [31] *Ibid.*, p. 126.

or spiritual factors, or minimize them, but only emphasized the sphere in which they can operate. Unless the social and economic forces are ripe, the ethical ideas will have no chance. But he insisted that the economic interpretation did not "for a moment subordinate the ethical life to the economic life." [32] And he admitted the absurdity of many of the applications of the doctrine by its enthusiastic disciples. It was plainly inadmissible to ascribe everything to economic changes. "The strands of human life are manifold and complex." [33] But after all, he concluded, we are still subject to the inexorable law of nature, with its struggle for existence through natural selection. Only when we have complete mastery, will economic conditions fall into the background.

With his general conclusions few could disagree. Yet, although he made all the above quoted scholarly qualifications, he declared that "it is no longer open to doubt that the democracy of the nineteenth century is largely the result of the industrial revolution; that the entire history of the United States to the Civil War was, at bottom, a struggle between two economic principles; that the Cuban insurrection against Spain, and thus indirectly the Spanish-American War, was the outcome of the sugar situation; or, finally, that the condition of international politics at present is dominated by economic considerations. Wherever we turn in the maze of recent historical investigation, we are confronted by the overwhelming importance attached by the younger and abler scholars to the economic factor in social and political progress." [34]

Surely, in these words, he forgot all about his own carefully stated qualifications.

As early as 1907, as we have seen, J. Allen Smith had asserted that, while the Constitution "was in form a political document," its "significance was mainly economic." It was intended to insure the ascendancy of the property-owning class. Democracy would mean the abolition of all private monopoly; and by the system of checks and balances, by giving power to the Senate, by giving the courts the veto power, the framers of the Constitution hoped to prevent the free play of the democratic impulse. His was, I think, the first economic interpretation of the Constitution.

Charles A. Beard, a few years later, carried on the argument more elaborately. He has been a leader in the American school

[32] *Ibid.*, p. 133. [33] *Ibid.*, p. 151. [34] *Ibid.*, p. 86.

which ascribes all importance to the economic factors. He explains the Constitution and the spread of Jeffersonian democracy largely on the economic basis. In his "An Economic Interpretation of the Constitution of the United States," he observed that, next to the repression of physical violence, "the making of the rules which determine the property relations of members of society," was the primary object of government; and that therefore the dominant classes "whose rights are thus to be determined must perforce obtain from the government such rules as are consonant with the larger interests necessary to the continuance of their economic processes, or they must themselves control the organs of government." The Constitution was merely a secondary derivative, determined by the nature of the "economic groups seeking positive action and negative restraint." [35] The property-owning class sought the political action desired by that class; class and group divisions based on property lie at the base of modern government; "and politics and constitutional law are inevitably a reflex of these contending interests." [36]

So he proceeded to undertake a study of the clash of property interests in the Revolution and succeeding years. He made an elaborate examination of the property interests of the members of the Convention, and concluded that the "movement for the Constitution of the United States was originated and carried through principally by four groups of personalty interests, which had been adversely affected under the Articles of Confederation: money, public securities, manufactures, and trade and shipping." He ended with the conviction that the Constitution was essentially "an economic document based upon the concept that the fundamental private rights of property are anterior to government and morally beyond the reach of popular majorities." [37]

In his "Economic Origins of Jeffersonian Democracy," he continued the study for the period in which Jefferson was building up his new party. In the beginning he re-affirmed his belief in the predominantly economic basis of the new Constitution, and asserted that the contest over the Constitution "was not primarily a war over abstract political ideals, such as state rights and centralization, but over concrete economic issues, and the political

[35] Charles A. Beard, *An Economic Interpretation of the Constitution of the United States*, p. 13.
[36] *Ibid.*, p. 16.   [37] *Ibid.*, p. 324.

division which accompanied it was substantially along the lines of the interests affected. . . ." [38] The conflict was "chiefly between the capitalistic and agrarian classes." [39] He scorned the theory that Jeffersonian democracy was founded "upon some general principles of American liberty," and replied bluntly that Jeffersonian democracy "simply meant the possession of the federal government by the agrarian masses led by an aristocracy of slave-owning planters; and the theoretical repudiation of the right to use the Government for the benefit of any capitalistic groups, fiscal, banking or manufacturing." [40]

We have already indicated the answers to this interpretation. The extravagances of its claimants must not beguile us into denying its partial validity. Seligman has stated admirably its strength and limitations. He was himself, however, as we have seen, not free from the blandishments of the theory. Beard vastly overstates the case. Shailer Mathews, in his "Spiritual Interpretation of History," fervently attacks the exaggerations of the economic interpreters. He adds to the objections which Seligman listed, one more objection: that the economic interpretation is too simple. "Every monistic interpretation of human life is too simple," he added.[41] Eloquently, he said that the economic interpreters ignored the creative factor in human personality, the element of racial pride, the ideals in social customs. He emphasized the force of emotions, such as parental love, adventure, honor, glory, social loyalty. He dwelt on the part which moral and religious ideals have played. As society develops, he said, an altruism appears, in which men look on the interests of others, as well as their own, and come to "see in social solidarity something more than an opportunity for economic advantage." [42] In custom, he said, we see the social origin of conscience, and law seeks for a moral sanction. The antagonism to slavery was not essentially economic; the protection of women and children in industry, the protection of old age, the humanizing of industrial relationships, were all based on personal values, as well as economic bases. In the transformation of rights into justice, many non-economic advantages are recognized. The Bill of Rights, he asserted, was not essentially economic, but religious in its basis. He referred to Beard's interpretation of the Jeffersonian democ-

[38] Charles A. Beard, *Economic Origins of Jeffersonian Democracy*, p. 3.
[39] *Ibid.*, p. 4.   [40] *Ibid.*, p. 467.
[41] Shailer Mathews, *Spiritual Interpretation of History*, p. 22.   [42] *Ibid.*, p. 45.

racy, and asserted that Beard ignored the whole immense significance of "the personal values" in the demand for political rights by the new democracy of the Middle West.[43]

The same answers which Roscoe Pound made to the economic interpretation of law, will apply to politics. We have seen that the socialists themselves have realized that the materialistic interpretation is only partial. The economic interpretation does not explain the whole picture. It does not explain which group will prevail. It is simply not true that it is the most powerful economic group which always prevails. Society has been controlling the most powerful economic group ever since law began. The emotional side of man, his idealism, his sense of justice, may not be ignored. The economic factors may condition man's emotions, but they do not express them. The very fact that men base their reasons on ethical or moral grounds preferably to economic grounds, is most significant. Men are reluctant to make their demands on the basis of their economic group desires. They seek to show that they are for the general good. Nor is this mere hypocrisy. They genuinely convince themselves that their proposal is for the good of all, and in any event the public decision is made largely on that ground.

Smith and Beard made the explanation of our Constitution far too simple. Charles Warren points out that, in addition to the economic motives, "many other factors were actually determining the course of events"[44] on the question of the ratification of the Constitution. No communities or States were divided on economic lines. The "same class of people in different States took divergent positions as to the Constitution," and "within the same class of people in each State, there were circumstances and motives pulling in opposite directions."[45] Many of the differences were purely sectional; some were racial.

Some of the bitterest opponents of the Constitution also favored the clause forbidding the impairment of contracts; and were opposed to stay and tender laws and paper money. He adds that it was significant that not a single amendment was proposed to change any of the clauses which the economic historians "allege were inserted to favor the propertied and creditor class," such as those forbidding paper money, stay and tender laws, and the impairment of contracts.[46] Men, in short, differed on the Constitution largely

[43] *Ibid.*, p. 203. [44] Charles Warren, *The Making of the Constitution*, p. 746.
[45] *Ibid.*, p. 747. [46] *Ibid.*, p. 775.

on the basis of their temperaments, for reasons that they believed to be—and which largely were—sincere and public-spirited.

One of the most persistent exaggerations of the economic interpretation is the current popular explanation of wars as the mere result of economic clashes. Again we must not be misled in our disagreement into denying the force of economic disputes. But, if business men are actuated by economic interests, it is strange that they are so fatuous as to seek them by wars. It is only when popular passions, desire for aggrandizement or for glory, racial prides and passions, the desire for power, are added to economic motives, that economic motives play a part in bringing on wars.

Halévy, in his "Histoire du Peuple Anglais au XIXᵉ Siecle," remarks that the conflict between the Boers and the English in South Africa was "not a conflict of interests: between rival interests, compromises are always possible. It was a conflict between two nationalisms, two beliefs, two passions, two absolutes. Between these absolutes, there was no arbiter but the arbiter of force." [47] Again he noted that in 1901 England had more cause for industrial alarm from America than Germany; and yet she pursued towards America a policy of extreme conciliation, whereas her feeling towards Germany became ever more tense. He concluded wisely, "One must take care before attributing an excessive importance to the economic motive in the explanation of historic phenomenons." [48]

Surely, economic motives can be only a partial explanation of our Civil War. Economic pressure, indeed, brought on the demand for new slave territory; but the resistance to that demand, like the resistance to many acts of economic aggression, was not itself predominantly economic in motive. The free labor of the North was everywhere more prosperous than free labor in the South. The class which suffered most, in an economic sense, from slavery was the "poor white class" of the South, but the "poor whites" did not lead the anti-slavery cause. While in the border States the "poor whites" were generally for the Union, in the South they formed the backbone of the Southern armies. The farmers of southern Indiana and Ohio, who had come from the South and who certainly had not benefited from slavery, showed throughout much sympathy for slavery and the Southern cause.

In his "The Anti-Slavery Impulse," Gilbert Hobbs Barnes, after

[47] Vol. I, p. 69 (Epilogue). [48] *Ibid.*, p. 120.

a long study of the anti-slavery propaganda, concludes that from "first to last, throughout the anti-slavery host, the cause continued to be a moral issue and not an economic one. Neither in their propaganda nor in their sentiments was the economic issue dominant." The areas of anti-slavery strength "coordinated with no single Northern interest." They were near to the South and far from it, where trade with the South was important and where it was not. Predominantly, the anti-slavery cause was "a religious cause,—a moral crusade." [49]

Again, I must insist that the reasons men give for their actions, the motives which they deeply believe actuate them, are important. To a large extent, the motives which men sincerely believe actuate them, do actuate them. In any event, the man who ignores the enormous pressure of moral ideas in the anti-slavery cause and in our Civil War, is simply obtuse.

It is an anomalous thing that, in a period when economists were admitting that the "economic man" was a myth and that economics must take into account the political, personal, social, and non-rational motives of men, the economic motive was vastly over-emphasized in political matters.

The economic motive is not, then, the philosopher's stone.

Professor Carver, in his "Social Justice," gave a variant of the economic interpretation. He found the test for social morality in that which enables the group to survive. The ultimate problem of any variety of life, he said, "including the human race, is that of adjustment to the material universe." Anything, therefore, "which facilitates the adjustment of man to the universe is, for man, good. Anything which hinders that process of adjustment is, for him, bad." [50] Nature, he went on, is "the final authority on morality, and our opinions, likes and dislikes, approvals and disapprovals, must be modified to suit that final authority." If we once perceive, he continued, "that morality is merely social hygiene, and that anything is moral which works well for society in the long run, which prolongs its life and enables it to grow and flourish and hold its own in competition with other societies, and beat out all those which are organized on immoral bases, we should no more think of questioning the moral order of the universe than we now

---

[49] Gilbert Hobbs Barnes, *The Anti-Slavery Impulse*, p. 197.
[50] Thomas Nixon Carver, *Essays on Social Justice*, p. 24.

do of questioning the hygienic order. We should then frankly say that whatever the order of the universe is, that per se, is the moral order; likes and dislikes, approvals and disapprovals, to the contrary notwithstanding." We should then say "that whatever social customs and conventions are found to fit into the order of the universe, and whatever private conduct is found to permanently strengthen the social group, that is per se morality." [51]

That anything is moral for society which works well for society in the long run, I should agree. But that nature is the final arbiter on every decision of what works well, does not follow, unless we broaden the term nature to include all the emotions and ideas of men. For only a part of our decisions are on questions which involve the permanence of the group. Of course, it is necessary that the group survive, and on a large class of questions the issue of survival will determine the matter. We can do nothing which endangers the food supply or the production of goods.

But there is a whole realm of values which this interpretation, like the economic interpretation, does not answer. There is a whole group of questions above the scarcity limit. The satisfaction of political demands; the demand for the suffrage, for the initiative and referendum, for freedom of speech and the press, for religious freedom; indeed, most of the demands contained in the Bill of Rights; even, I believe, for many economic results, such as a shorter work day and for a minimum wage, are not primarily determined by the test of the survival of the group.

Such demands must be refused if they would endanger the survival of the group, but once that question is resolved, the decision has still to be made on other and deeper grounds. It will depend largely on the desires of men. If men do not want them, the group will not be concerned. If they want them badly enough, the group must grant them or suffer.

Arthur F. Bentley's "The Process of Government" based all political action on the satisfaction of group demands. It was a searching analysis of the process of political action rather than of the tests of political action. But his argument practically claimed that there were no tests. Political tests and standards, he asserted, are merely the reflex of the activities of groups. He insisted that there are no political ideas in the abstract. The tests of conduct

[51] *Ibid.,* p. 25.

which Lester Ward, Albion W. Small, Spencer, Giddings, Dicey and even Von Ihering had proposed, became entangled, he said, in inevitable contradictions, because "There is no idea which is not a reflection of social activity. There is no feeling which the individual can fix upon except in a social form." [52] Ideas by themselves, "soul-stuff" as he called them, have no meaning, he claimed, save in their social content. The ends which Von Ihering posited, he declared, were all abstractions. They obtained their meaning from the activities of the men employing them.

So far I would agree. To quote Holmes' pregnant phrase again: "A word is the skin of a living thought, and may vary greatly in color and content according to the circumstances and the time in which it is used." The abstract idea is meaningless outside of its particular use. There are no Platonic ideas in politics existing by themselves.

But after Bentley had resolved ideas into mere reflections of social activity, he proceeded to resolve social activity into the conflict of groups. "What a man states to himself as his arguments or reasoning or thinking about a national issue, is, from the more exact point of view, just the conflict of the crossed groups to which he belongs." [53] All social activities, he held, are evolved from the group conflicts of men, groups that embody an interest. He did not mean mere economic interests, he warned. The interest was "nothing other than the group activity itself." [54] Reasoning was simply the "technical agency of the transaction." [55] Law was always the expression of a group interest; politics, the resolution of group conflicts.

While I have admitted that ideas by themselves are barren and meaningless, it is quite another thing to assert that ideas, argument, and reasoning arising from the concrete facts of the problem, are merely the reflexes of group conflicts. It does not follow that it is the strongest group that always prevails. In a conflict between two groups of nearly even size, disinterested outsiders acting as a compromising and umpiring force may hold the balance of power. You may call them a group, but they do not act as a group or think as a group, and they may be inferior in numbers to each of the militant groups, and yet they may control.

[52] Arthur F. Bentley, *The Process of Government,* 1908, p. 177.
[53] *Ibid.,* p. 204.   [54] *Ibid.,* p. 271.   [55] *Ibid.,* p. 372.

Again, why is the strongest group the strongest? Why do people adhere to the strongest group? The activity of groups is not automatic: it is the result of conflicting desires, of differing ideas of right and wrong, of differing conceptions of the evil and of the remedies proposed. Feelings of economic interest, of desire for power, of right and wrong, of the evil consequences of a policy, work constantly to attract or repel people to or from one program or another.

The reasoning is part of the activity. Ideas are not merely the weapons by which we obtain what we desire: there is a constant interaction. Desires are influenced by our ideas, and our ideas are influenced by our desires. But it is, surely, grossly to minimize ideas to say that they are the utter slaves of our wills. The ideas arise from the activity, but they also make the activity. The groups, in short, form after the program is started as well as before. The groups are made by the ideas as much as the ideas by the groups. Theodore Roosevelt was an expression of his time, and yet there is no doubt that his great vitality, his engaging personality, the force and energy of his thought, brought many to adhere to his proposals who would not otherwise have done so. They were brought into his group, if we must call it that, as he went along.

James Mackaye, in two able and rigorously analytical books, made another attempt to found political action on the greatest happiness principle. Undeterred by the failure of Bentham and Mill to bring agreement on their attempts to spread the gospel of utilitarianism, he boldly set out to establish "a science of political engineering, not upon vague 'moral ideals,' alleged 'natural rights,' mythical 'social compacts,' or other arbitrary foundations, but upon the simple and unassailable assumption that the goal of nations or of society is to do right and to avoid doing wrong." [56] There are, he said, only four kinds of perceptions: approbation, disapprobation, happiness, and unhappiness. All intuitional codes, were based on the first two; all hedonistic on the second two. But the test of approval or disapproval is variable. It depends on the conscience of the man who decides. There is no unanimity among the consciences of men. What is approved by some, is disapproved by others. Unconsciously many intuitionists adopt a code of utility, that is, their decisions of what is right or wrong are based on a more or less

[56] James Mackaye, *The Happiness of Nations*, p. 14.

conscious judgment as to how the proposal will work out in practise. The Golden Rule, Mackaye argued, was a test of utility. But he argued that we should use the utilitarian test consciously. We should base our decisions consciously on the test of happiness.

A right act was simply that one "among those available at any given movement which presumably yields the maximum excess of happiness over unhappiness for mankind as a whole." [57]

Mackaye noted that it might be objected that "to have too much fun is a bore, that pleasure too long continued becomes tiresome." He replied that it is not pleasure that becomes tiresome, but one kind of pleasure. We could never get too much of happiness. We might get a surfeit of one kind of happiness.[58]

He insisted that all systems of ethics unconsciously aim at happiness as an end. Political economy aims at wealth as an end, but it is really only a means, a means to the end of utility. The real end was happiness, and human conduct should be directed to the end of the greatest happiness. Our economic system aims at the greatest amount of production and the minimum of consumption, whereas utility would aim at the maximum of consumption and the minimum of production. All the economists were on the wrong track. We must harness intelligence and self-interest to the end of utility. Self-interest should impel and intelligence direct us on that course.

Quantity of pleasure and quantity of pain he proceeded, "are the most important magnitudes known to sentient beings." [59] Men have always desired happiness and to avoid unhappiness.

Mackaye admitted that men were not always guided by his philosophy of utility. But he answered that to show that men do not always follow utility, does not refute it. It merely showed that there was a difference between what is and what ought to be; between correct and incorrect reasoning.

Mackaye's books are closely reasoned. He relies much on the most elaborate mathematical charts for determining the surplus of hedon hours, namely, hours of pleasure, over pathon hours, namely, hours of pain. But it need hardly be said that pleasure and pain are alike incommensurables. No one could ever measure pleasure and pain so as to arrive at any of his painstaking curves. The hap-

[57] *Ibid.*, p. 53.   [58] *Ibid.*, p. 78.
[59] James Mackaye, *The Economy of Happiness*, p. 114.

piness of a man or of a community is not susceptible of reduction to logarithmic curves.

Moreover, the question has never been answered what happiness is, nor do men know what will produce it. Time and again men voluntarily act in ways which do not produce immediate happiness, and with full knowledge of the fact. And the decision we deeply feel is right. They ought not to consider happiness in certain cases. The decision for war is seldom made on the happiness principle. The heroic king of the Belgians did not make his fateful decision in July, 1914 on the happiness principle, nor England hers on the fourth of August. The sacrifices for religious and political freedom are not made in response to the desire for happiness under any normal definition, but to the desire for something higher and finer. It does not answer to say that men act in such cases for a distant happiness. They can not envisage the distant happiness. They act in response to a deeper impulse, often an uncontrollable and unconscious response to some deep yearning. To say that they act on the happiness principle, is simply to broaden the definition of happiness until it becomes meaningless.

Nor can I see that Mackaye has avoided the pitfalls that beset all the utilitarians. It is true that he includes everybody, indeed every sentient thing, in his system. If, he says, an act produced in a plank (assuming it could feel) one hedon minute, and another act produced in the most worthy being on earth nine-tenths of one hedon minute, the first act would be right and the second wrong.

It is true, also, that he believes in the widest diffusion of happiness. Thus he remarks that there "is the best of justification for the all but universal conviction that happiness should be equally distributed, since its unequal distribution means, in general, the unequal distribution of its causes, and this in turn involves bad efficiency and a consequent diminished return of happiness." [60] As we have seen, he opposed unequal distribution of wealth as inimical to the equal distribution of happiness.

But when it came to deciding between an equal amount of pleasure for one as an alternative to an equal amount for many, he said there was no answer save in individual choice. It was the dilemma of distribution; the same dilemma that appears, he insisted, in all systems. But he did not consider the question of an amount of

[60] James Mackaye, *The Economy of Happiness*, p. 316.

pleasure for one, as contrasted with a lesser quantity of pleasure to be divided among several. On his theory, the greater amount of pleasure for one is to be preferred to the lesser quantity divided among several.

Nor do I find that he answers the old question of the choice between a pleasure for A, which causes a lesser quantity of pain to B. Nor the case where a few receive pleasure, and the many either no pleasure or a lesser quantity of pain. Let us consider the case of an aristocracy served by slaves. The actual number of slaves may be less than the number of those they serve, and the pleasure of the masters may be greater than the pain of the slaves, measured by graphs and charts, and yet society will not tolerate the slavery. It will not approve an act causing misery to one person, no matter if it causes pleasure to a hundred.

William James, in his essay, "The Moral Philosopher and the Moral Life," considered briefly the various tests for our action. None of them, he said, has given general satisfaction. "Some are obviously not universally present in all cases,—e. g., the character of harming no one, or that of following a universal law; for the best course is often cruel; and many acts are reckoned good on the sole condition that they be exceptions, and serve not as examples of a universal law." The survival test, he went on, is quite indeterminate in its consequences, and leaves us in the lurch when we most need its help. A philosopher of the Sioux Nation, for example, he pointed out, "will be certain to use the survival criterion in a very different way from ourselves." The best answer, he thought, was the happiness principle, but he added that in order not to "break down fatally, this test must be taken to cover innumerable acts and impulses that never *aim* at happiness; so that, after all, in seeking for a universal principle, we inevitably are carried forward to the *most* universal principle, that the *essence of good is simply to satisfy demand*. The demand may be for anything under the sun. There is really no more ground for supposing that all our demands can be accounted for by one universal underlying kind of motive than there is ground for supposing that all physical phenomena are cases of a single law." [61] No single abstract principle could be used. A demand might be selfish and desired only by a small group. It would then be re-

[61] William James, *The Will to Believe*, pp. 200-01.

sisted and not granted. If one group collides with another, the answer is in the satisfaction of both so far as is consistent with the demands of other groups.

As we have seen, Roscoe Pound adopted James's test as his test for law in his theory of sociological jurisprudence. Law, he said, is the satisfaction of the demands of the various groups in a society. Lippmann phrased the principle, that "if we think in terms of men, seek to supply what they really want, hold their experience sacred, we shall find our sanction obvious and unchallenged." [62] The real "question always turns on what an idea is worth in the satisfaction of human desire." [63] Men's desires, he said again, "are what move and govern." [64]

Mackaye objected that the whole question is what desires should be gratified. When different desires conflict, what is to be done? Why ought desires to be satisfied, anyway? [65] But the answer would be that they should be satisfied because men will have them satisfied, because they are unhappy if they are not satisfied, because men need the things they desire, because they must act and express themselves.

And how choose between desires, but to permit play to those which do not conflict with others or conflict only in a minor way, and restrict those which conflict with the desires of others or cause resentment? Aggression, greed, violence, exploitation, cause opposition. They can not be satisfied, without causing a clash with the desires of those who are outraged or who have a higher ideal. But the desires, for example, for literature, for art, for sport, do not cause opposition, do not clash with the desires of others. If they do, the question is as to the preponderance of the intensity and force of the desires on each side.

After all, politics—like law—must take people as they are. It can not create desires. No rulers or judges could resolve desires in favor of a happy and harmonious state, if those desires are cheap, or selfish, or ephemeral. But the satisfaction of desires does not mean the satisfaction only of materialistic and selfish desires. The nobler aspirations are there: the desires that satisfy the sense of right, for the attainment of a social end, for benefit to society.

Many elements will continually influence our desires,—tradition,

[62] Walter Lippmann, *A Preface to Politics*, p. 202.
[63] Walter Lippmann, *Drift and Mastery*, p. 260.
[64] *Ibid.*, p. 316.   [65] James Mackaye, *The Happiness of Nations*, p. 94.

custom, the love of the past will continually modify or determine what we want. The ignoble or selfish desires will meet opposition from those on whom they infringe. Law and politics can see that the finer desires have a chance, and are not suppressed by the lesser demands. In any event, the government alone can resolve the conflict in desires; and, in the end,—in a large sense,—the government must meet the demands of its people. If it does not, it will perish; and in that case, it ought to perish!

The satisfaction of desires, therefore, is no ignoble business.

Yet, when all is said, I can not feel that the test of the satisfaction of desires meets all our needs in politics any more than in law. James, of course, proposed it for the determination of the good in private conduct. The test for political action does not always involve questions of the good. Whether we should adopt the direct primary, the initiative and referendum, the short ballot; whether we should have workmen's compensation laws, or antitrust laws, are not questions of good and evil, of right and wrong. They depend on the nature and extent of the conditions to be remedied, the efficiency of the proposed remedies, the desires to be satisfied, the customs and habits and psychology of the people.

The real question, in short, is whether they will work,—whether the results will be good or ill. The question of desires enters into all such decisions, as in questions of law; for, how much and how strongly men want things, is an important element in deciding whether they should be adopted, and whether they will work if they are adopted.

But some plans will not work however much some people want them to work. Inflation may be desired by the great majority, but a minority will still insist that it will end in great distress. The English poor law worked badly, and it took a long time to show how badly. Desires could not prevent that failure. Nor is it correct to say that the desire for inflation is met with antagonistic desires. It is met with desires and habits which lead to disaster; but the mere antagonism may be negligible, or too weak for effective action.

Many political proposals, however, do involve the idea of good, the sense of right and wrong. While a permanent dole, free silver, greenbacks, and the protective tariff have been advocated by highminded and sincere persons, they arouse in others feelings of deep injustice. These persons will not be satisfied with the answer that such proposals satisfy the greatest demand. They will insist that if, in the end, they work badly, they are undesirable; and that the test is the weighing of all the results, including the result on desires, and not the weighing of the desires alone.

Again, we see that what men think actuate them, is at least an important element in what does actuate them. Men do not think it is enough to say that they want things. They seek to show that, to give them what they want, will aid or at least not hurt society. The test of considering desires is strange to us. It is not consciously adopted. The test of considering all the results of an act is commonly employed. It was implicit at least in every argument on the political and economic proposals I have considered in this book: initiative and referendum, direct primary, direct election of senators, limitation of the work-day, token money, workmen's compensation, free silver, trusts. Happiness was not the sole determining factor, nor economic conditions, nor the mere satisfaction of desires, nor the resolution of group conflicts, nor survival; but in most cases all were in a real sense involved, and a consideration of all the results, after all, had a part in the decisions.

Survival, then, is necessary; but once that question is resolved, the choice between two or three proposals, none of which threatens survival, must be made on other grounds. Geographical conditions, the economic elements, the psychological nature of man, the mere test of the efficiency of the proposed plan,—all are important, but no one alone is sufficient. In a given case, happiness may be the test; and in others, reliance on happiness alone may lead to disaster. Desires are important; but desires which will not work or which work injustice, ought not to be given free play. Not one test alone, but all together are our tests. We need them all. The answer, I think, is that there is no monistic answer.[66]

REFERENCES

BARNES, GILBERT HOBBS, *The Anti-Slavery Impulse.* New York: D. Appleton-Century Co., 1933.

BEARD, CHARLES A., *An Economic Interpretation of the Constitution of the United States.* New York: The Macmillan Co., 1913.

[66] In this chapter I have been much indebted to G. E. Moore's *Ethics* (Home University Library). He rejects the happiness principle and all other monistic tests, and bases conduct on the test of *all* the consequences.

————*Economic Origins of Jeffersonian Democracy*. New York: The Macmillan Co., 1915.

BENTLEY, ARTHUR F., *The Process of Government*. Chicago: University of Chicago Press, 1908.

BURKE, EDMUND, Speech on American Taxation. *Works*. (Oxford World Classics ed.), Vol. II, p. 91.

CARVER, THOMAS NIXON, *Essays in Social Justice*. Cambridge: Harvard University Press.

DEWEY, JOHN, *Essays in Experimental Logic*. Chicago: University of Chicago Press, 1916.

————*Creative Intelligence*. New York: Henry Holt & Co., 1917.

JAMES, WILLIAM, *Some Problems of Philosophy*. New York: Longmans, Green & Co., 1911.

————"The Moral Philosopher and the Moral Life," in *The Will to Believe* (Copyright 1896). New York: Longmans, Green & Co., 1905.

————*Pragmatism*. New York: Longmans, Green & Co., 1907.

LEWIS, EDWARD R., "Political Formulas," *Unpopular Review*, Vol. VII, p. 145 (July-Sept., 1917).

LIPPMANN, WALTER, *A Preface to Politics*. New York: Henry Holt & Co., 1917, Copyright 1913.

————*Drift and Mastery*. New York: Mitchell Kennerley, 1914.

MACKAYE, JAMES, *The Economy of Happiness*. Boston: Little, Brown & Co., 1906.

————*The Happiness of Nations*. New York: B. W. Huebsch, 1915.

MATHEWS, SHAILER, *The Spiritual Interpretation of History*. Cambridge: Harvard University Press, 1916.

MOORE, G. E., *Ethics*. New York: Henry Holt & Co., 1912.

RAND, BENJAMIN, ED., *The Classical Moralists* (Kant's "The Metaphysics of Morality," trans. John Watson). Cambridge: Houghton Mifflin Co., 1909.

REEVES, JESSE E., "Jeremy Bentham and American Jurisprudence," *Report of Indiana State Bar Association*, 1906, p. 212.

SELIGMAN, EDWIN R. A., *The Economic Interpretation of History*. New York: Columbia University Press (2nd. ed. Rev., 1912).

SEMPLE, ELLEN CHURCH, *American History and Its Geographic Conditions*. Boston: Houghton Mifflin Co., 1903.

WARREN, CHARLES, *The Making of the Constitution*. Boston: Little, Brown & Co., 1928.

WILLOUGHBY, WESTEL W., *Social Justice*. New York: The Macmillan Co., 1900.

————"The Individual and the State," *American Political Science Review*, Vol. VIII, p. 1 (Feb., 1914).

TABLE OF CASES

INDEX

Abbott, Lyman, on lawless character of the liquor traffic, 360; favors industrial democracy, 366; distrusts socialism, 393; holds woman's suffrage a burden on women and not a right, 502, 503

Adams, Brooks, on power of courts, 133, 134; follows economic interpretation of law, 221, 222

Adams, Charles Francis, on railroad expansion, 263; causes of Grangerism, 263; limitations of competition for railroads, 266; on railroad rebates, 311, 314

Adams, James Truslow, his "The Epic of America" referred to, 235

Addams, Jane, for woman's suffrage, 501

Addicks, Edward, 445

Aldrich, Nelson W., his opinion of Roosevelt's message of 1907, 324; on natural selection, 381

American Bar Association Reports, on diversity in State laws, 418–420; on fear of national power, 428–429

American Federation of Labor, organized, 260; Commons on mental characteristics of leaders of, 260; Mitchell's philosophy, 260–261; its first platform, 261; Gompers and his self-reliant philosophy, 261–262

American Tobacco Company, 309, 310

Ammons, Elias M., on separation of powers, 471

Analytical school of law, 222

Anthony, Susan B., presses for woman's suffrage in 1866, 497; appeal to Lincoln, 497; to Congress, 497; disappointment at failure, 498; in New York Convention of 1868, 498

Anti-Saloon League, 338

Articles of Confederation, Union not sovereign under, 153, 154

Assessment statutes, under Fourteenth Amendment, 90, 91

Assumption of risk, defined, 98; abolished by employers' liability and workmen's compensation statutes, 99; constitutionality of, 99–100, 105, 124, 125

Augustine, St., 177

Austin, John, Woolsey on, 182, 183; Jameson on, 184, 185; Wilson on, 192; theory of sovereignty, 185 fn., 190, 191, 192; his definition of law, 208–211;

Austin, John—*Continued*
Lowell on his theory, 211; Willoughby on, 211, 212; Maine on, 192; Gray on, 196, 216, 218

Baker, Ray Stannard, 345

Ballot, See Long ballot, Short ballot

Barnes, Gilbert Hobbs, holds anti-slavery movement moral, not economic, in motive, 524, 525

Bayard, Thomas F., on Civil Rights Acts, 53, 54

Beale, Joseph H., 230

Beale, Truxton, editor of "The Man Versus the State," 375 fn.

Beard, Charles A., on influence of "Looking Backward," 288; on initiative and referendum, 459; on short ballot, 492; quoted from one economic interpretation of Constitution, 520, 521; on Jeffersonian democracy, 521

Beecher, Henry Ward, found cold to woman's suffrage, 497; on woman's suffrage, 498

Bellamy, Edward, 273, 283; origin of "Looking Backward," 283; outline of "Looking Backward," 284–8; "Equality," 286–288; other Utopian romances, 288; Howells on, 288; Frances Willard's approval of, 288; estimates of, by Dewey, Weeks and Beard, 288; his theory of a peaceable collapse chimerical, 288, 289; Gilman's criticism, 289, 290; Harris on, 290; his belief in actual possibilities of his state, 290; organizes Nationalists' Clubs, 290; Higginson and Hale join, 290; joins the Populists, 291

Bentham, Jeremy, 182, 190, 514

Bentley, Arthur F., on ideas as barren save in context, 526, 527; on ideas as reflexes of group conflicts, 527; criticism of, 527, 528

Berle and Means, their "The Modern Corporation and Private Property" cited, 356 fn.

Beveridge, Albert J., his Progressive Party speeches, 346, 348; a strong Nationalist, 422, 423; his child labor bill, 423; debate with Bryan on Nationalism, 422, 423

Bill of Rights, influence on Conservatives, 378

Mob, assertion that people are, 129, 130, 451, 469, 470

Money Trust, Brandeis on, 353; Wilson on, 352, 353

Montague, Gilbert Holland, on railroad rebates, 309

Morgan, John T., his fear of national power, 425

Mott, Rodney L., on source and development of due process of law, 69

Mulford, Elisha, his theory of the state, 179; on social compact, 179; holds state a person, 179; holds state a unit and legally omnipotent, 181; on sovereignty, 190

Munger, T. T., on Mulford, 179 fn.

Nation, The, its editorial on "The Mind and Manners of the Silver Man," 380, 381; editorial on Bryan in 1896, 381

National Congress of Farmers, resolutions of 1873, 265

National Labor Union, on eight-hour day, 257; convention of 1866, 257, 258; of 1867, 258; end of, 258; its Greenback theory, 268, 269; its socialistic tendencies, 385

Nationalism, persistence of conflict with State Rights, 414; Interstate Commerce Act of 1887, 414; H. R. Meyer quoted, 414, 415; Cullom quoted, 415; inadequacy of State regulation, 415; Ripley on diversity in State laws, 415; Supreme Court on clashes between Federal and State power, 415–417, 420, 421; national power and taxation, 421; undercutting, 417, 429, 432; Taft on divorce, 418; Eliot and Bryan on need for national prohibition, 417, 418; diversity in State laws, 418; American Bar Association's efforts for uniform laws, 418; Amasa Eaton on, 418, 419; Terry on, 419, 428, 429; Federal government as largest and most competent force, 420; commerce clauses, 420; Roosevelt and his "New Nationalism," 421, 422; Beveridge and his national child labor bill, 422; debate of Beveridge with Bryan, 422, 423; Croly's national power theory, 423, 424; opposition to national power of Cox, 424; of Morgan and McCall, 425; Bryan's dilemma, 426, 427; national child labor bill, opposed by House Committee, Taft, Wilson, Murphy, 427, 428; American Bar Association on distrust of national power, 428; Root's Philadelphia speech, on State failure as cause of demand for national action, 429, 430; influence of undercutting and national needs, 430; Wilson's national extensions, 430; and on persistence of States, 430, 431; States remain important, 430;

Nationalism—*Continued*
summary of causes for national demands, 431–436. *See also* Thirteenth, Fourteenth, and Fifteenth Amendments; Civil Rights Acts (particularly pp. 51–4, 57, 58, 60–62, 74, 75)

Nationalist Magazine, 290

Natural law, Stammler's theory of, with changing content, 254; abandons his theory, 254 fn.; Demogue and Charmont follow him, 255

Natural rights, to suffrage, Sumner on, 16, 35, 36, Godkin on, 32, Julian on, 37–39; to the land, George and Jordan on, 276, 280; Root and, 376, 377; conservatives and, 378, 379, 510; and tests of political action, 514

Nature, state of, Brownson on, 179

Negro suffrage, Stevens, 14, 22, 41; Henderson favors, 38, 41; Garfield, 38, 39; James Russell Lowell favors, 31–33; Charles Sumner, 16, 35, 36, 44; Godkin, 32; Julian, 37–39, 44; Garfield, 38, 39, 44; Henderson, 38, 41; Blaine, 43, 44; causes of adoption of Fifteenth Amendment, 43–45; wisdom of, 45; cases under Fifteenth Amendment, 57–59; grandfather clauses, 59, 60; Federal Election Law of 1894, 60; Tillman on, 60; Hoar, 60, 61; Root, 61; results of, 61, 62. *See also* Fifteenth Amendment

Neo-Hegelians, 225

Neo-Kantians, 224, 225

New Republic, 336, 339

New York Times, on McCardle case, 118

Norris, Frank, 456

Norris, George, 456

Northern Securities case, 452; Harlan in, 325; Brewer, 325; Holmes, 326; Roosevelt, 325, 326

Nullification, Kentucky and Virginia resolutions, 155, 156; Jackson and, 155, 156

Ocala platform, 293, 294

Omaha Populist platform, 294

O'Neal, Emmet, on State legislatures, 439, 440; on initiative and referendum, 464 fn.

Oregon, its experience with initiative and referendum, 457, 467 fn.

Otis, James, on limitations on legislative power, 65

Outlook, The, on La Follette, 343

Owen, Robert Dale, on Fourteenth Amendment, 18–20

Owen, Robert L., favors initiative and referendum, 458

Page, Thomas Nelson, 235

Palmer, John M., on Interstate Com-